THE
STORY OF
AMERICAN GOLF

HERBERT WARREN WIND

THE STORY OF AMERICAN GOLF

Its Champions and Its Championships

THIRD EDITION, REVISED

 ALFRED A. KNOPF   NEW YORK 1975

THIS IS A BORZOI BOOK
PUBLISHED BY ALFRED A. KNOPF, INC.

Copyright © 1948, 1956, 1975 by Herbert Warren Wind
All rights reserved under International and Pan-American Copyright Conventions.
Published in the United States by Alfred A. Knopf, Inc., New York,
and simultaneously in Canada by Random House of Canada Limited, Toronto.
Distributed by Random House, Inc., New York.

Library of Congress Cataloging in Publication Data

Wind, Herbert Warren, (Date)   The story of American golf.
Bibliography: p.   Includes index.
1. Golf—United States—History. I. Title.
GV981.W5 1975   796.352'0973   75-8244
ISBN 0-394-49020-7

Manufactured in the United States of America
Third Edition, Revised

For Mother and Dad

CONTENTS

ACKNOWLEDGMENTS

No book is ever completely a labor of love, no matter how dear the subject may be to the heart of the writer. The preparation of this book, however, was made appreciably more pleasant because of the genuine cooperation of the many golfers and critics on whom any golf historian is necessarily dependent. I should particularly like to acknowledge my gratitude to the following persons: Mr. Henry O. Tallmadge, the sole surviving charter member of the St. Andrew's Golf Club; Mr. Joseph C. Dey, Jr., of the U.S.G.A.; Mr. Fred Corcoran of the P.G.A.; Mr. Archibald M. Reid, son of John Reid, "the father of American golf"; Mr. John G. Jackson; Mr. William Shields; Mr. Robert Trent Jones; Mr. Leonard J. Stacey; Mr. Linde Fowler; Mr. Harold W. Pierce, who "discovered" the identity of the formerly nameless "young lady from Pau" and who, with Mr. Herbert Jaques, made possible the stroke-by-stroke re-creation of the Ouimet–Vardon–Ray playoff. Of the hundreds of books, pamphlets, magazines, and newspapers consulted, three books and one magazine deserve mention as being especially helpful in my research: *The St. Andrew's Golf Club*, 1888–1938, by Harry B. Martin and Alexander B. Halliday, the official history of the first American golf club; *Fifty Years of American Golf*, by Harry B. Martin, which is the most complete work on the game's early years in this country; *Down the Fairway*, by Robert T. Jones, Jr., and O. B. Keeler, as well as Keeler's other definitive studies of Bobby and his triumphs; and the *American Golfer*, first edited by

Walter J. Travis and later by Grantland Rice. I am agreeably indebted for their down-the-stretch aid to Mr. Lloyd C. Ahlgren, the enduring listener; Miss Mary Borg, the typist; Mr. John W. Filoon, the first reader; and my brother, John Wind, the syntax pro.

HERBERT WARREN WIND

New York, August 1948

There seems to be no need to add anything to the preceding acknowledgment except to note the passing of three extremely fine men who were very helpful in the preparation of the first edition—Mr. Herbert Jaques, Mr. O. B. Keeler, and Mr. Henry O. Tallmadge, each of whom enriched American golf considerably by his presence and activity.

H. W. W.

August 1956

It has been almost a score of years since the last edition of this book appeared. So much has changed in American golf (and world golf) in the interval that it has taken far more work and words than I had anticipated to bring things up to date. Acknowledging all the people who have assisted my continuing education would be an impossibility, but I would particularly like to mention the following: Mrs. Robert T. Jones III; Al Laney; Richard S. Tufts; Gerald H. Micklem; Ben Hogan; Joseph Schwendeman, an original cornerstone of the P.G.A.'s Tournament Players Division; Sam McKinlay; Laurie Auchterlonie; Mrs. Barbara Nicklaus; H. Richard Isaacson; Dudley Sutphen; Jack Ryan; Bud Harvey of the P.G.A.; Mrs. Henri Prunaret; Carol McCue; Joseph Walsh; George and Brenda Blumberg; Donald "Doc" Giffin; Michael Aronstein; Don Rossi of the National Golf Foundation; P. G. Wodehouse; Tom Peterson; and Robert Sommers, John S. Ward, and the indefatigable Janet Seagle; and, finally, Frank Hannigan, assistant director of the U.S.G.A. and a friend indeed, who found time to read the galley proofs and who assisted in many other valuable ways.

H. W. W.

March 1975

PART ONE

SOWING THE SEEDS

1888–1913

THE
APPLE TREE
GANG

Today, just about wherever you travel, golf courses with their green fairways, greener greens, and pristine white bunkers have become an intrinsic part of the face of America. The game has also penetrated deep into the American consciousness. Nearly fourteen million people, from every class of society, now play at least a couple of rounds a year. Most Saturdays and Sundays, from January to October, one or another of our national television networks carries that week's professional tournament, a segment of the series of tournaments that fills up almost the entire year and is currently close to the ten-million-dollar mark in total prize money. Attendance at the big, well-established events has reached the point where tickets for the Masters, which takes place in April, are completely sold out months before, and where the United States Open, which takes place in June, must annually set a limitation on attendance, depending on the maximum number of daily spectators that each particular course can comfortably accommodate. Presently there are over seven thousand registered professionals in our country—and about sixty thousand unregistered pros, the fellows you run into at every club who, if you will just ripple through a few swings for them, will be delighted to tell you what you are doing wrong, gratis.

This rampant golf-consciousness is rather remarkable, considering that the game has been played in our country for less than a hundred years. While the first permanent Canadian golf club celebrated its centennial in 1973, the first permanent American club, St. Andrew's, in Ardsley, New York, will not reach that milestone until 1988, which is still quite a few years away. In 1888 the United States was, generally speaking, a sports-minded nation, but not to the extent it was to become later. The big game was baseball, which, in mid-century, had evolved from a number of regional variations into a standardized national pastime. The first professional league, the National League, was established in 1876, and all America followed it with tremendous interest. It would be decades before there would be another professional team sport to challenge baseball's monopoly of the public's devotion. There was professional horse racing, of course—the Travers Stakes at Saratoga was first run in 1864 and the Kentucky Derby in 1875—but that was not the same thing. Neither was professional boxing, though it should be noted that when one of the big heavyweight fights was looming, people talked of little else for weeks and weeks. The adoption of the Marquis of Queensberry rules, which supplanted bare-knuckles fisticuffs in 1885, had something to do with boxing's increased popularity, as did the arrival of John L. Sullivan of North Abington, Massachusetts, as world heavyweight champion (and last of the bare-knuckles champions) in 1882.

What else was there? Well, among the amateur sports, college football was at the top. It had been since 1869, when it was introduced in rudimentary form by Princeton and Rutgers. There was some sailing, but the America's Cup involved a comparatively small section of the country. There was some tennis, the national championships having been instituted at the Newport Casino in 1881. Basketball wasn't invented until 1891, when Dr. James Naismith had the janitor nail up that historic pair of peach baskets in the gymnasium at Springfield College. Some running and jumping competitions existed, but enthusiasm for track and field sports was laggard until the first modern Olympic Games were organized in 1896 by Baron Pierre de Coubertin. If golf caught on rapidly in America, it was partially because there was room for another new game and partially because it was such a good game.

Golf started off with a great advantage over many other sports: you did not have to be a young, fast, beautifully coordinated athlete to play it acceptably. As a result, it found ready converts among the two sexes and people of all ages. They soon discovered that once golf gets you in its grip, it never lets you go. On the one hand, there was Andrew Carnegie declaring thoughtfully that golf was "an indispensable adjunct of high civilization," and, on the other, there was the story of the Scotsman who threw his clubs into the ocean after a bad round and nearly drowned trying to rescue them. Both statements added up to about the same thing.

In 1888 there was no Ouimet, Hagen, Sarazen, Jones, Nelson, Snead, Hogan, Palmer, Nicklaus, or Trevino, but the game had been played in Scotland for many centuries and had from the beginning produced many attractive and skillful players. Looking back from today's perspective, perhaps the greatest of the early golfers was Young Tom Morris, the son of Old Tom, who had won the second, third, fifth, and eighth British Opens in 1861, 1862, 1864, and 1867. Young Tom also won the British Open four times—in 1868, 1869, 1870, and then, after a one-year hiatus in which no championship was held, again in 1872. He would have undoubtedly gone on to win it many more times, but he died in 1875 of heartbreak soon after the death of his wife and their newborn child. He was only twenty-four at the time.

Young Tom's finest achievement took place in the 1870 Open, which was held at Prestwick, on the west coast of Scotland, as were all the early Opens. Prestwick was then a twelve-hole course, and each entrant played three rounds. Young Tom's total for the thirty-six holes was 149, the equivalent of a 74 and a 75. An idea of how amazing a performance this was can be gained from the fact that no one had previously scored below 160 in the championship. Young Tom's 149, for that matter, was never beaten or even approached through 1891, after which the championship was changed to a 72-hole event. Undoubtedly the most effective way to bring out the quality of Young Tom's golf in the 1870 Open is to chart his progress hole by hole:

HOLE	LENGTH	1ST ROUND	2ND ROUND	3RD ROUND
1	578 yards, 1 foot, 9 inches	3	5	5
2	385 yards	5	5	5
3	167 yards, 7 inches	3	2	3
4	448 yards, 2 feet, 5 inches	5	5	7
5	440 yards, 1 foot, 4 inches	6	6	4
6	314 yards, 1 foot, 9 inches	3	5	5
7	144 yards, 1 foot, 7 inches	3	3	3
8	166 yards, 4 inches	3	4	3
9	395 yards, 1 foot	4	5	5
10	213 yards, 1 foot, 2 inches	3	3	3
11	132 yards	4	4	3
12	417 yards, 2 feet, 1 inch	5	4	4
		47	51	51

It is not going too far to say that Young Tom Morris' three rounds in the 1870 British Open, made with the old gutta-percha ball, were the first glimmer of modern golf, the game we know today. (Imagine a 35 for the first nine way back then!) Young Tom's scoring in an important competition certainly bears comparison with the celebrated 36-hole bursts of later years, such as Bobby Jones' 66-68—134 at Sunningdale in 1926, Gene Sarazen's 70-66—136 at Fresh Meadow in 1932, Ben Hogan's 71-67—138 at Oakland Hills in 1951, Cary Middlecoff's 68-68—136 at Inverness in 1957 (which didn't win for him), Mickey Wright's 69-72—141 at Baltusrol in 1961, Arnold Palmer's 67-69—136 at Troon in 1962, and Jack Nicklaus' 66-68—134 at St. Andrews in 1964 (which didn't win for him either).

Over the last hundred years, golf has changed in many ways. It is difficult to picture Bernard Darwin careening down a fairway at the wheel of a golf cart, or Walter Travis fluffing out the sleeves of an alpaca sweater, or Harry Vardon in the press tent patiently running down his round hole by hole ("On the fifth, driver, brassie, two putts. On the sixth, drive, brassie to four feet, one putt for the birdie . . ."), but, essentially, golf has remained the same strange, elusive, maddening, beckoning, wonderful game it has always been.

Considering that it has been a part of the American scene for less than ninety years, golf's expansion has been incredible. In 1888 there were less than a dozen golfers in this country. Today, as we noted, there are over fourteen million. To take care of this multitude, there are more than eleven thousand courses, a major part of a capital investment that now surpasses $3,500,000,000. Each year, by the way, American golfers spend close to half a billion dollars for golf balls, clubs, shoes, gloves, bags, tees, hats, and what have you. The number of American golfers expert enough to play in the national tournaments is rather astounding too. In 1971, a record-breaking year, 2,329 golfers entered the United States Amateur Championship, 4,174 entered the United States Public Links Championship, and 4,279 entered the United States Open Championship—quite a jump from the combined total of 43 who entered the first official Amateur and Open. The course laid out by John Reid, "the father of American golf," consisted of three abbreviated holes in a cow pasture. American golfers today miss their first shots cold and hit their practice shots unerringly on courses where the turf has been scientifically bred for the 3-wood and the putter, the holes designed and redesigned to punish the weekend golfer and the professional in correct proportion. Some of our modern golf courses have been blasted from the wild forest and pushed through swamplands and, occasionally, dredged from the sea. There are courses that stretch to 7,400 yards and courses where each par 3 is built in duplicate to alleviate the Sunday driving. The clubhouses at these layouts are a far cry from the tent that served John Reid and his cronies as their headquarters. A good number of the contemporary clubhouses have cost over half a million dollars, and they offer all the accommodations of a metropolitan hotel, and sometimes the unreal stare of a European castle transported half-timber by half-timber across the Atlantic.

Every year more and more young Americans set their sights on making golf their profession. It is easy to understand. Today a successful tournament golfer can make over $300,000 a year in prize money alone. If a pro who wins a major title is moderately photogenic and articulate, he can scoop up, additionally, several hundred thousand dollars in advertising sorties and related ventures. He can retire to a spreading ranch in Texas, like Byron Nelson, with periodic returns to the outside world to serve as an announcer on national telecasts; he can, like those two other Texans, Jimmy Demaret and Jack Burke, Jr., establish the Champions Golf Club outside Houston and develop it into one of the region's finest golf plants; or like still another Texan, Ben Hogan, he can manufacture his own line of golf clubs and golf balls. It is impossible, of course, to keep up with Arnold Palmer's and Jack Nicklaus' myriad global activities, they are so far-flung and diverse.

American attitudes toward golf have changed as America has changed, but the game itself has remained fundamentally the same frappé of pleasure and pain it was for Reid and his Apple Tree Gang, and for the Scots and the English before them. There is a fascination in golf that every player at one time or another has tried to define, but no one as yet has been able to put his finger on. He and the fourteen million other American golfers, all of whom have given up the game at one time or another, will be

John Reid, "the father of American golf." A transplanted Scot from Dunfermline, Reid was the driving force in the founding of St. Andrew's, the first permanent golf club in the United States, established at Yonkers in 1888.

out on the fairways the next sunny afternoon, cheerfully enslaved again. There is apparently no release. Of course, someday, shortly after everyone knows what the Mona Lisa and Sphinx are thinking about, golf's secret will out and the Man-on-the-Tee will understand perfectly why golf has become the most successful game in the world.

John Reid, the father of American golf, was a transplanted Scot who lived in Yonkers, New York. As a young man, Reid had emigrated from Dunfermline at about the same time as his fellow-townsman, Andrew Carnegie. While Reid had carved no empire for himself in America, he had risen to a top executive position with the J. L. Mott Iron Works in Mott Haven and by 1880 had attained that degree of prosperity which allows a man to devote a good share of his energy to his recreation.

At first John Reid was content to pass his weekends away from the plant hunting and shooting. In a nation of good shots he stood out as a very good shot, and yet field sports left Reid curiously dissatisfied. As a boy in Scotland he had observed the first big boom of the cult of games, and though he had not then had the time to take up golf, rackets, or cricket, Reid was a games-player at heart. In Yonkers he first tried his hand at tennis, converting a part of his front lawn into a court where his friends could gather on weekends and on which he could unleash some of that tremendous vitality exclusive to self-made men. A few years after this, Reid and his friends decided there was everything to be gained in importing the equipment for golf, a game that was winning an amazing number of converts in England and was, as Reid reminded himself, certain to be a remarkable sport since it was a Scottish sport. Robert Lockhart, another lad from Dunfermline who had made good in the new country, was returning to Britain in 1887 on a business trip, and Reid asked him to purchase a good set of golf clubs and some golf balls for him.

Lockhart did not spare himself in executing his commission properly. To make sure he got the best, he went to St. Andrews, the old gray town by the North Sea revered as the cradle of the game. There, in the shop of Old Tom Morris, the most celebrated professional of the day, Lockhart purchased two dozen gutta-percha balls and a set of clubs: three woods—driver, brassie, and spoon; three irons—cleek, sand-iron, and putter. He arranged for the box to be shipped to his home in New York and went on his way, quite unmindful that his morning had been in the least historic or that the box from St. Andrews, in the minds of millions of Americans in later years, would be esteemed the surest antitoxin ever devised by man to combat the evils set loose from an earlier box, Pandora's.

When the clubs and balls arrived in New York, Lockhart tried them out on an open stretch near Seventy-second Street and the Hudson and, finding nothing amiss, turned them over to his friend Reid.

Washington's Birthday, 1888, was a wondrously mild day. Reid had originally planned to wait until late March or April before trying the clubs himself, but that twenty-second of February was the kind of a day that makes a man want to hurry the spring, and John Reid could wait no longer. He got in touch with his old sports crowd, and buoyed with the sense of adventure, they crossed to the field that Reid used as his cow pasture. Three short holes each about a hundred yards long were laid out over the hilly ground, and "cups" were scooped out of the earth with the head of a cleek. There weren't enough clubs for everyone to play, so John B. Upham was selected to oppose Reid in this, the

Golf at St. Andrew's in 1888. The golf bag had not as yet made its appearance here.

first game of golf to be played by the men who later formed the St. Andrew's Golf Club, the first permanent golf club in the United States. No scores were kept that morning, fortunately, and the two players and the spectators were in full agreement that golf was great fun, a game with a very bright future. Scotland could well be proud of itself.

Immediately following this first exhibition, other sets of clubs were ordered by the members of Reid's circle. Future rounds, however, had to be delayed for a while, for winter returned in earnest: on the twelfth of March the most severe blizzard in the history of New York paralyzed the entire area. When warm weather finally came, the men, dressed in old derbies or slouch hats and their loosest-fitting jackets, drove the cows off their three holes and played their rude version of golf. In April they decided they needed a larger course and moved to a cow pasture at the northeast corner of Broadway and Shonnard Place, an expanse of some thirty acres owned by the local butcher. Here they proceeded to lay out six rough holes.

This new course, apart from the increased length of the holes, was hardly closer to the standards of the Scottish links than the original three-hole field. The greens were circles about twelve feet in diameter, slightly less bumpy than the rest of the turf, and responded with equal infidelity to the putter or the midiron. But Reid, Upham, and the other regulars—Harry Holbrook, Kingman H. Putnam, and haberdashing young Henry Tallmadge—were entirely pleased with their new home. The pioneers played through the heat of summer, supported by the first 19th hole, an improvised table presided over by a servant of Reid's who handled the ice and water.

The St. Andrew's Golf Club was officially founded at a dinner at John Reid's house on November 14, 1888, sort of an informal celebration of the golf group's successful first year. With dinner out of the way, the ebullient Reid, with little coaxing, rose and cut loose with his renowned rendition of *Scots Wa Hae* and other Scottish ballads. Then he got down to business. The real purpose of this dinner, he reminded his friends, was to devise the best ways and means for continuing their enjoyable outings on the golf

Five of the country's cracks who answered the call to compete in the first Amateur Championship at match play at St. Andrew's in 1894. Reading from left to right: James Park of the Richmond Country Club, Laurence Curtis of The Country Club, C. B. Macdonald of the Chicago Golf Club, George Armstrong of St. Andrew's, and Louis Biddle of the Philadelphia Country Club. In those days a golf jacket was *de rigeur*.

course. Reid felt that it was time now to set up some form of organization—not that there was anything wrong with the informal way they had gone about things in 1888, but there were undeniable advantages to an organization. For one thing, expenses were bound to be higher the coming year, and a club could handle financial matters much more effectively than men acting as individuals. For another thing, it probably would not be long before other members of the community would want to join them, and there again they needed the machinery of a club. The four regulars present—Messrs. Upham, Holbrook, Putnam, and Tallmadge—did not have to be sold. They were all for founding a club, and moved to get on with the election of officers. Reid was unanimously elected president, Upham was elected secretary-treasurer, and the other three original members were to make up the board of governors of the St. Andrew's Golf Club. That was the name they all wanted. St. Andrews in Scotland had been the cradle of golf, and who knew, perhaps this new St. Andrew's would assume the same role on the American continent? Robert Lockhart, the man who had made all this possible, was named the first active member of the St. Andrew's Golf Club. A few toasts in that other great importation from Scotland, and the first meeting of the St. Andrew's Golf Club was adjourned. The men walked to their homes with the good glow that they had accomplished a lot that evening—and they had.

The next few seasons of the first American golf club were relatively uneventful. In March 1889, in the first mixed-foursome played on the six-hole course, John Reid and Miss Carrie Low defeated the team of Mrs. Reid and Henry Upham in a very close match. The membership rose to thirteen. Occasionally one of the group would suggest that the six-hole course was becoming too confining and that the club should find a larger piece of land. No action, however, was taken in this direction, and the expansion might have been delayed a few more years had the City of Yonkers not decided to extend Palisade Avenue farther north, right through the heart of the course. So once again, in April 1892, the players gathered their clubs and the tent that served as a clubhouse and headed north. This time they settled on an apple orchard on the Weston estate, about a quarter of a mile up the road from their old course. They spent a happy day exploring the thirty-four acres of their new home and laying out six holes amidst the apple trees. The tent was pitched beside the land marked for the first tee, and the superb apple tree bending low behind the home green became the new 19th hole. During shirtsleeve weather, the players tossed their coats into the crotch of the tree, and a basket of sandwiches and a wicker decanter were hung on a low bough. Life was pleasant in the shade of the old apple tree.

The Apple Tree Gang, as the golfers of Yonkers were now called, and much to their delight, were more than willing to overlook the fact that the orchard's unique hazards were developing a breed of golfers who played two-thirds of their shots with the niblick or the lofter. When seven new members were admitted, however, the first serious rift within the club was precipitated. Now, when a simple majority of the members were out playing, the six holes were acutely overcrowded. A number of the younger men, such as Harry Tallmadge, were all for moving to a larger tract. The conservatives, older members like Reid, were staunchly in opposition. As they saw it, the primary purpose of the club was to promote good fellowship and there was the danger of losing this if St. Andrew's expanded. The younger members argued that the apple orchard was hardly a golf course in comparison with the nine holes Newport had built or the fine seaside course that Willie Dunn had laid out for the Shinnecock Hills Golf Club on Long Island. Shinnecock had seventy-five members and a wonderful clubhouse designed by Stanford White—they were doing things right down there. St. Andrew's had been started well before those clubs, the expansionists continued, and their club should have been *the* leader in the growth of golf rather than an also-ran. Now take Chicago—way out there in the West. Already there were two eighteen-hole courses on the outskirts of that city, and judging from the number of prominent Chicagoans who were joining the clubs, good golf and good fellowship hadn't proved to be incompatible.

It took time but gradually the sincerity of the younger element wore down all opposition to their campaign for an up-to-date course. St. Andrew's was on the move again, for the third time in six years. A committee selected to study possible sites for a new course reported that an ideal one had been found in the Odell Farm at Grey Oaks, three miles north on the Sawmill River Road. Nine holes, of respectable length, were laid out over the sharply rising ground. It took two or three days before this layout was completed, but, as Harry Tallmadge commented, it was worth all the trouble. On May 11, 1894, the St. Andrew's Club, twenty strong, the conservatives as jubilant as the youngsters, moved to their new course at Grey Oaks and went to work transforming the Odell farmhouse into their first real clubhouse and locker room.

The cradle of American golf had proved to be a very portable one. Some three years later, in August 1897, the St. Andrew's Golf Club moved again, this time to its present location at Mt. Hope, where there was room for eighteen good holes. However, it was during the years the club was situated at Grey Oaks that St. Andrew's found itself. The membership began to climb rapidly. The new course was nicely accessible by train from New York, and up from the city came the tired businessmen seeking relaxation along with gentlemen-sportsmen eager for a new merit badge. Andrew Carnegie joined the club and Sir Arthur Conan Doyle was a frequent visitor. St. Andrew's guarded itself against becoming too social by barring ladies from membership, but it did succumb to the fad for fancy clothes promoted by Shinnecock Hills and Newport. In addition to the required red coat with brass buttons, the well-dressed St. Andrew's man wore a blue checked cap, a winged collar, a blue checked waistcoat, gray knickers, plaid stockings, and gray gaiters.

What is more to the credit of its members, the club became a forerunner in the spread of golf. The first United States Amateur Championship at match play was held at Grey Oaks in 1894, and St. Andrew's players participated in the first team match between American golf clubs. St. Andrew's was instrumental in the formation of the United States Golf Association, and in arranging the American tour of Willie Park, Jr., the famous British Open Champion, who incidentally took the Grey Oaks course apart with a brilliant 81, although handicapped by a giant boil on his neck.

John Reid stepped down from the presidency after nine years, but he remained the leader of the descendants of the Apple Tree Gang and a vigorous force for many years in American golf. He was extremely pleased when his son John, a student at Yale, won the Intercollegiate Golf Championship in 1898. He was not so pleased when another son, Archie, was defeated one year in the United States Amateur. Reid read about this in the morning paper at breakfast, and said gruffly to his wife, "I see where your son has lost a golf match."

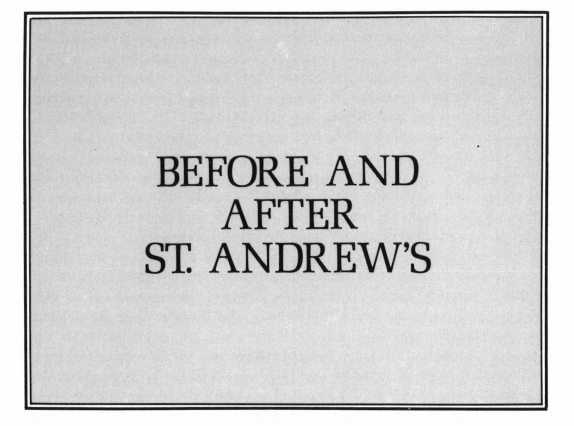

BEFORE AND AFTER ST. ANDREW'S

Some four-hundred-odd years before John Reid's gang invaded their first cow pasture, golf was a flourishing game in Scotland, and in the minds of not a few historians, most of them of Dutch extraction, a flourishing game in The Netherlands as well. The age-old controversy as to who originated the game of golf, the Scots or the Dutch, has never been settled to the complete satisfaction of the contending parties, and there are some antiquarians who propose that both nations climbed aboard a bandwagon that had been rolling for centuries. The difficulty in establishing once and for all the birthplace of golf arises from the fact that striking a ball with a stick toward a certain object is a very natural movement, notwithstanding the impression to the contrary one receives on Saturday afternoons watching his brethren coiling and uncoiling off the first tee. No one has ever tried to pin down the person who first writhed to a drumbeat and became the world's first dancer, and yet striking a ball with a club is an action hardly more involved than moving one's body to a certain rhythm.

If you follow the theories of the romantic historians, then the first golfer was a shepherd—place him on a hillside in Greece, Palestine, or Scotland, as suits your taste—who was bored with his work. He started to swing his crook at stones, just to give himself something to do, and then, purely by accident, one of the stones disappeared into a hole and a strange tingling sensation raced up and down the shepherd's spine. He tried hitting a few more stones as close to the hole as he could, and when he had mastered the shot, called over to a colleague and invited him to match his skill at the sport. They became the first twosome and had the right-of-way all over the hillside.

Even when we step from legend into recorded history, it is difficult to fix upon the first emergence of the sport because of the number of ancient games that bear some resemblance to golf. The Romans at the time of Caesar, for example, went in for the game of *paganica,* in which the opposing teams, armed with club-shaped branches, tried to bat a feather-stuffed ball against their rival's goal, a post planted several hundred yards down the street from the one they were defending. A few centuries later the French *seigneurs* were going in strong for a less shinny-like game called *jeu de mail.* The courses this time were the old national highways with their borders of heavy hedges, and the players swung at peach-sized spheres carved from boxwood with clubs shaped like croquet mallets. The goal was a raised pole down the highway. Bypassing such other stick-and-ball games as *chole* and *cambuco,* the trail then leads to Holland, and it is here that the mystery of the origins of the game begins in earnest.

The scholars who favor Holland as the home of golf can make out a fairly provocative case. They can point out that in the middle of the fifteenth century the town of Naarden issued an ordinance forbidding the playing of a game called *het kolven* within the sacred precincts of the church. For pictorial proof that Dutchmen played a game called *kolf* on their frozen canals, they can refer to the illustrations in the *Book of Hours* (1500–1520) and to later Delft tiles depicting children and men preoccupied with a sport that looks very much like the real thing. These scholars find it harder to explain away *kolf's* development into an indoor game played on a hard floor sixty feet long and twenty-five in width and bounded by walls two feet high which the player could employ as he saw fit in his efforts to hit wooden posts placed at each end of the court. John Tunis, one of the most recent writers to enter the fray, sides with the pro-Holland set. According to Tunis, there was no golf in Scotland until shortly after a Scottish vessel, the *Good Hope,* ran aground off the Zuider Zee. A number of the crew, who had been shaken up in the accident, spent the last days of convalescence playing *kolf* and were sufficiently intrigued to take home with them some clubs and balls. The iron egg-shaped ball used on the frozen canals could not be adapted to Scottish links, and a more suitable ball was arrived at by plucking a handful of feathers from the breast of a fowl and encasing them in leather. This is, very probably, a good explanation of the origin of the first feather golf ball, but is the earlier part of the story a bit too convenient? It's hard to know.

One thing is certain, though: the Scots were the first to play a game in which the player used an assortment of clubs to strike a ball into a hole dug in the earth. This is the essence of the game we know as golf. Impartial historians don't go as far as the Scot who laughed off the claims of the Dutch with the crack that *kolf* was no more golf than cricket was poker, but it is generally accepted that golf is the product of Scotland.

By 1457, when we meet the first recorded evidence of golf in Scotland, it is apparent that the game had already attracted a sizable following. In that year the Scottish Parliament decreed that *wapinschawingis be holden by the Lordis and Baronis spirituale and temporale, foure times in the yeir, and that the Fute-ball and Golfe be utterly cryit doune, and nocht usit.* This ban on golf was understandable, for the small highland kingdom had to maintain a stout defense against her enemies, and golf was luring the potential defenders away from their archery practice. Despite this ban and similar and stronger acts by Parliament in 1471 and 1491, the game had such a grip on the Scots that they continued to play it on their seaside linksland. Then, in the sixteenth century, the Church as well as the State began to make it rough for the addicts who played the game on the Sabbath. It was a very fortunate thing for golf and golfers that James VI of Scotland, who later became James I of England, appeared on the scene at that time. James had the golf bug very bad, and shortly after he mounted the throne, he let it be known that he was all for allowing golfers to play on Sundays as long as they had previously attended church. To take care of his own golfing needs, James appointed a Royal Clubmaker and, fifteen years later, to combat the high prices Dutch manufacturers were asking, he set up an official ballmaker and a ceiling of four shillings on balls.

While James I was the most actively sympathetic of the Stuarts, several other members of the house, probably because of their Scottish fiber, had a majestic weakness for the game. Mary Queen of Scots is supposed to have played golf a few days after Darnley's murder to exhibit her indifference to his fate; Charles I was in the middle of a round on the links of Leith when word came to him of the Irish Revolution; in 1681 the Duke of York, who later became James II, partnered himself with John Patersone, a poor shoemaker, in a big money match against two English noblemen at Blackheath, and Patersone won enough that day to build himself a new house. A wonderful family, the Stuarts! They made the game royal as well as ancient.

The focus of Scottish golf was St. Andrews. As early as Queen Elizabeth's day— indeed, as early as the twelfth century, according to some historians—there was a course on the stretch of duneland alongside St. Andrews Bay, although the Royal and Ancient Club was not officially inaugurated until 1754. A century or so later—in 1848 to be exact—the old town was a scene of the controversy that resulted in the first "foreign" expansion of the game. That was the year a few revolutionary sportsmen decided to introduce balls made of the juice of the gutta-percha tree. Allan Robertson, the fine golfer who owned St. Andrews' leading golf shop, declared himself dead set against this new ball. Golf had always been played with a feather ball, he maintained, and, besides, if this gutta-percha ball was adopted, it would ruin the men who owned golf shops. It took a measure of skill to pack and stitch a "feathery" and the ball was worth the half crown for which it sold, but no shopkeeper could charge that much for a ball he molded from a glob of gum. Robertson personally bought and burned every "guttie" he could lay his hands on, and in his fight he had the cooperation of all the other golf craftsmen except one, Old Tom Morris, his own assistant. Tom was of the opinion that the guttie would give the game a big boost, not only because of the reduction it was bound to bring in the players' expenses but because it could be hit farther than the feathery and golfers would revel in the added distance. There was no patching up the feud that arose between Robertson and Morris; Old Tom went in business for himself and in time became the game's high priest. It wasn't long before the guttie established its marked superiority over the feather ball, and a new age of golf was ushered in. It was the new ball that swept the game triumphantly into England and started the boom that finally swept around the world.

Though St. Andrew's was without question the first golf club organized in the United States that really meant business, golf was played in America before its introduction in Yonkers. It might be well to touch all the bases, however lightly.

Once again the Dutch are on hand to complicate the picture. The first reference to what might have been golf appears in the minutes of the Court of Fort Orange and Beverwyck, a settlement of the New Netherlands that eventually became Albany. This court, in Ordinary Sessions in 1657, reprimanded and fined three Dutchmen who presumed to play *kolven* on ice one Sunday. Two years later the magistrates of Fort Orange and the village of Beverwyck issued a warning to all sportsmen that in the future anyone caught playing *kolven* in the streets would be subject to a fine of twenty-five florins. Both documents were written in Dutch, leaving ample room for argument as to the correct translation of *kolven*. Was it ice hockey or field hockey, was it golf or was it *kolven?* There are no further details to help us.

The next allusion to golf in America turns up in the issue of *Rivington's Royal Gazette* dated April 21, 1779, and this time the game referred to is golf, unmistakably. Rivington, the King's Printer in New York City, was a shopkeeper on the side who stocked sporting goods. On that day he ran an advertisement in his paper to inform the public that he had a supply of the "veritable Caledonian balls." No one knows the response he received, but a few nostalgic Scots may have thought about it, anyway.

Two serious claimants to the honor of being the birthplace of golf in America are Savannah and Charleston. At the close of the eighteenth century a species of the game may or may not have been played in these prospering Southern ports, but in both communities golf clubs definitely existed. From 1788 on, the *Charleston City Gazette* carried the notices of the South Carolina Golf Club—in the main, reminders to the members of club anniversaries. Some anniversary meetings were held on Charleston Green, where a putting green may have been maintained, but there is not so much as a word to indicate that golf was played, and none of the implements has been discovered. The purpose of the South Carolina Golf Club would appear to have been purely social, and the same would appear to have been true of the Savannah Golf Club. In addition to the notices of meetings that appeared in the *Georgia Gazette*, through the vigilance of the Johnston family, which has preserved the invitation, we know that in December 1811, "the honor of Miss Eliza Johnston's Company" was requested "to a Ball to be given by the Golf Club of this city." The outbreak of the War of 1812 may have put a damper on social activities, and, in any event, after this date, newspaper references to the Savannah and South Carolina Golf Clubs slowly began to die out.

In 1873 the Royal Montreal Golf Club, the first on this side of the Atlantic, was formed, and at about this time followthroughs began to ripple south of the border. These were the gyrations of Scottish settlers who had brought their baffies and gutties to the new world with them, the way Italians carried their violins and Frenchwomen their needles. In 1883, for example, Colonel J. Hamilton Gillespie, investigating the possibilities of a lumber business in Florida, used to relax after a hard day's work by hitting shots up and down what is now the main street of Sarasota. American boys who had learned the game while studying at English and Scottish universities occasionally carried their clubs back to the States with them, but like Gillespie and other would-be missionaries, none of them was successful in transmitting his enthusiasm for very long. The immune, then as now, ridiculed the idea of "hitting a ball with a stick and chasing after it," and after their supply of balls ran out, the young men's mashies became little more than souvenirs, like that photograph of the Tower of London and the old school blazer.

The Meadow Brook Hunt Club of Long Island had the opportunity of becoming the first American golf club presented to it on a silver platter, and muffed it. In 1887 Horace Hutchinson, the British Amateur Champion, was invited to give the members of Meadow Brook a demonstration of the game. They were bored by his shot-making, and even Hutchinson's great personal charm and eloquence cut no grass. There was for a period a vibrant golf colony at Foxburg, in western Pennsylvania, but it remained for Russell W. Montague, a New Englander, to come closest to setting up a permanent golf club that would have antedated St. Andrew's. Montague owned a summer place in Oakhurst, West Virginia, a few miles from the fashionable spa at White Sulphur Springs. In the summer of 1884, one of Montague's Scottish neighbors had as his guest a young man who had been an ardent golfer in the old country. Montague was not at all indifferent when the suggestion was made that they lay out a course on his property and see what the game had to offer. The group formed the Oakhurst Club and went as far as to hold tournaments on Christmas. Then, after a few seasons, the men lost interest. The course was allowed to grow over and Oakhurst became just another Roanoke colony of golf—like Sarasota and the unknown meadows farther inland where other transplanted Scots had practiced the game but had not continued it. St. Andrew's was different. The club endured.

Within a year after the founding of St. Andrew's, the exclusive colony of Tuxedo Park had built itself a course, and the pros and cons of organizing a club were being discussed at the pleasure patches of the wealthy along the eastern coast. (Across the Alleghenies, entirely isolated from this movement, what may have been the country's first nine-hole course was built about this time in Middlesborough, Kentucky, by English settlers pioneering the iron industry in that region.) The completion of what is generally regarded as the country's first nine-holer at Brenton's Point near Newport in 1890 stemmed from the enthusiasm of Theodore A. Havemeyer, better known to the readers of rotogravure sections as "The Sugar King." Havemeyer had been introduced to the game while wintering at the French resort of Pau, and a violent love affair was underway. From the beginning, Havemeyer was positive golf would be much more than a passing fad. Upon his return to America he talked the game incessantly, built the course at Brenton's Point, fanned the flickers of interest among the members of

The first clubhouse built in America stands at Shinnecock Hills in Southampton.

America's richest summer colony, and became the president of the Newport Golf Club and later of the Newport Country Club, capitalized for $150,000 by Havemeyer, Cornelius Vanderbilt, John Jacob Astor, Oliver Belmont, and other old Newport hands. In time golf almost completely replaced Havemeyer's earlier loves—his horses, his polo, his yachting.

In 1891 the United States for the first time had a golf course that looked like a golf course—Shinnecock Hills. This course was the work of Willie Dunn, a young Scottish professional who doubled as an architect. In 1889 Dunn was designing eighteen holes at Biarritz in France when he was approached by three gentlemen from Long Island, W. K. Vanderbilt, Edward S. Mead, and Duncan Cryder. They had heard a lot about this new game and wanted to see how a real professional played it. Dunn led them to the famous chasm hole, a pitch over a deep ravine to a green about 125 yards away. There he hit several crisp shots, all of them onto the green, some quite close to the hole. It was an impressive demonstration. Vanderbilt immediately remarked that this was, to his way of thinking, the kind of a game that would go in America, and arrangements were made whereby Dunn would come to Southampton and lay out a course for them, once his commitments in France were fulfilled. Dunn finally arrived in America in March 1891, and set to work almost at once transforming four thousand acres along Great Peconic Bay into a twelve-hole golf course. With a crew of 150 Indians from the nearby Shinnecock reservation and a few horse-drawn roadscrapers, Dunn cleared the fairways, removed the blueberry bushes from the rough, utilized the Indian burial mounds as obstacles before the greens or made them into sandtraps, cropped and manicured the sandy turf. By June, in spite of his unskilled help and crude implements, Willie Dunn had finished his job, and Southampton had a seaside links of which it could be proud.

Vanderbilt was right. The Southampton set was fascinated by the game, and Shinnecock Hills, as the course was called, was given the full Long Island treatment. By September, forty-four men and women had purchased from one to ten shares in the club at $100 a share, and the club was formally incorporated. Stanford White, the renowned architect of the firm of McKim, Mead, and White, was given a free hand in designing a clubhouse. By the time White's clubhouse was opened the following summer, Shinnecock Hills' membership had burgeoned to seventy. The twelve-hole course was unable to accommodate all the players, and a nine-hole course for the women members was undertaken. Scarcely eighteen months after Willie Dunn had first surveyed the treeless stretch by the bay, the inner sanctum of Shinnecock Hills, the prosperity of its project assured, decided to limit membership to persons in the Southampton area whose social status was agreeable. Shinnecock Hills, in addition to being the first golf club on Long Island, the first in America to be incorporated, and the first to have a clubhouse, assured itself one further distinction: it was the first golf club to establish a waiting list. Perhaps, in the long run, Shinnecock lost out by emphasizing the social side of golf-club life, but in the Nineties, it was *the* course. Pilgrims came from far and wide to study the links, to admire the women hacking away with gusto on their own preserve, and to envy the men, restrained and resplendent in their bright red coats with monogrammed brass buttons.

Boston golf had a godmother. Until 1948, she was anonymous, identified only by the limerickish tag of "the young lady from Pau." Now we know that she was an American girl, Florence Boit, who returned to the States after a spell on the continent to spend the summer of 1892 with her aunt and uncle, the Arthur Hunnewells of Wellesley. Florence had picked up the game at Pau and, assuming that there would be several courses around Boston, brought her clubs with her. Her description of the game and front-lawn exhibitions aroused the curiosity of her uncle. Hunnewell's neighbors were his brother-in-law and his nephew, and by pooling their lawns, enough room was found for seven pitch-and-putt holes. Florence added the woman's touch by improvising flowerpots for the cups.

Again it is the same old story: the novices were quickly and entirely won over to the new sport. Laurence Curtis, one of the young men who had been invited to play at the Hunnewells', was so captivated by the game that he wrote a letter to the executive committee of The Country Club, in Brookline, recommending that golf be given a trial. Curtis estimated that a course could be built for no more than fifty dollars, and the executive committee promptly gave Curtis' suggestion the green light. The following March a six-hole course was constructed and formally opened by an exhibition by Curtis, Hunnewell, and G. E. Cabot. Hunnewell, the first to tee off, amazed himself by stroking his first shot smack into the cup some ninety yards away. The gallery of archery, shooting, and riding enthusiasts were not at all impressed. As they saw it, Mr. Hunnewell had done no more than he had set out to do. As a matter of fact, the archers, riders, and marksmen were rather let down when Hunnewell and the other golfers failed to supply further holes-in-one and went away very skeptical about the future of so imperfect a game.

But golf boomed at The Country Club and at the other early courses—Chevy Chase, Philadelphia, Richmond County, Essex County (Massachusetts), Essex County (New Jersey), Baltusrol, Apawamis, Montclair, Dyker Meadow, Baltimore, and many others. The "firsts" were nicely distributed. The Lake Champlain Hotel built the first hotel course. George Wright of Boston first played the game in a public park, and Van Cortlandt Park in New York was the first authentic public course. The Philadelphia Country Club, with characteristic gentility, was the first to use French-pea cans for holes. Tuxedo was host at the first match between teams representing different clubs, and a side from The Country Club played in the first international team match against Royal Montreal.

As for the first American to gain renown as a phenomenally long hitter, there was no challenging the record drive unleashed one winter's day by "Uncle Samuel" Parrish, the first secretary of Shinnecock Hills. As Parrish tells the story, "We were at the north end of Lake Agawam, Southampton, New York, looking south toward the ocean. There was a strong north wind blowing down the lake at the time, and, as I was able to steady myself on a patch of snow, the drive was a fair success, so that the ball went sailing down the lake until it struck the ice, and then kept on with but little diminution in its velocity. Had the ice and the wind held out, the ball would doubtless still be going, but it finally struck a snow bank on the shore of the lake and stopped. Morton then solemnly paced off the drive and reported its length to have been four hundred eighty-nine and a half yards, being very particular about the extra half yard. He then posted up in the clubhouse a statement to the effect that I, 'under favorable conditions' (no particulars being given) had made a drive of four hundred eighty-nine and a half yards. The result was that for a short time, until the facts became known, I enjoyed a tremendous reputation as a driver, my fame having penetrated to Boston, and I was the recipient of many congratulations."

C. B. MACDONALD AWAKENS THE WEST

While the oases of wealth in the East were still thinking in terms of six-, nine-, and twelve-hole courses in 1893, Chicago charged straight ahead and built the nation's first eighteen-hole course. The leaders of the new sport in the East were well aware that St. Andrews in Scotland, the game's recognized law-making body, had designated eighteen holes as comprising a round of golf, but certain doubts that the game had come to stay bothered the trustees of these golf clubs and made them wary of rapid expansion. The men in Chicago did not hesitate. Less than twelve months after the game was introduced in that eager metropolis of the Middle West, the members of the Chicago Golf Club, in Belmont, were playing over a full eighteen-hole layout, mighty pleased with themselves, too, at having outdistanced for once their smug cousins along the Atlantic who thought they did everything quicker, better, and on a larger scale than the boys in the backwoods.

Early golf in Chicago is the story of one man, Charles Blair Macdonald, who was recognized by all who knew him, and by Charles Blair Macdonald, as a most remarkable personality. There were only two ways to take Macdonald. Either you liked him intensely or you disliked him intensely. There was no middle ground. Endowed with a massive build and great strength, his natural self-reliance bolstered by a sizable personal fortune, stubborn, loyal, humorless, and intelligent, C. B. Macdonald swung his weight into every controversy American golf experienced until his death in 1928. To his admirers, "Old Charlie" was a genius whose mind never entertained error. In the eyes of his detractors, Macdonald's contributions were far outweighed by his marauding ego.

One reason why Charles Blair Macdonald made staunch enemies was the impression he forced on other men, used to leadership themselves and anxious to have a hand in the growth of golf, that he and he alone had been divinely appointed to supervise the spread of the game in America. They had to admit that the big man with the big mustache played the game very well, probably better than any other amateur in the country, but his attitude toward other people's golf upset them. Why did he insist on being such a stickler for the rules, and why did he hawk his adversaries to detect the slightest infraction of the St. Andrews code? This was America, not Scotland. Golf should be allowed to develop naturally in America, they believed, and if the personality of the game underwent moderate revisions in the new locale, it was a healthy sign. Macdonald's blind allegiance to the way he had been taught the game at St. Andrews was not going to help the sport to find roots in America.

Charlie Macdonald was an extremely articulate man, and through the years his words as well as his acts provided ample data for those who branded him the arch-reactionary. Whenever the growth of the game bred new regulations, Macdonald let it be known that golf had been far better off in the old days when the original thirteen rules and no others governed the play. Subsequent national, sectional, and local rules only made for unnecessary confusion and were superfluous if "the spirit of the game prevailed." He was against all moves for allowing balls to be wiped on muddy greens, against "preferred lies" under any conditions. Touching the ball with the hand was anathema to him. When the campaign to abolish the stymie was the topic of the day, Macdonald declared himself vigorously against a change that would "distinctly lower the morale of the game." He frowned upon four-ball matches as "a degradation" when this form of match threatened to displace the foursome, the type of competition in which partners on two-man teams play alternate shots and drive from alternate tees. "The best people in England and Scotland," he rebuked the upstarts, "adored the foursome." He was saddened when the old red coat, the badge of the golfer, was replaced by the odd-jacket and eventually by the sweater. Toward the end of his life, when golfers carried as many as twenty-five clubs in their bags, he played with only six, as a protest against the excess.

In locker-room arguments throughout the country over the evils and advantages of Charles Blair Macdonald, there were many golfers who sided with his efforts to keep a noble game noble, and there were some who contended that Macdonald was actually a great liberal. They would remind his critics that the Chicago Golf Club was the first to adopt the out-of-bounds rule, that Macdonald quickly endorsed the new rubber-cored ball, and that the National Golf Links he designed in Southampton revolutionized golf-course architecture in America. Old Charlie had merely stepped out of character on these occasions, his critics would rejoin. In each instance he had a purely selfish motive. The out-of-bounds at Chicago penalized only the hookers, and since Charlie sliced, the new rule simply afforded him a safer means of winning his matches. And his favoring the rubber-cored ball—why, Charlie was beginning to slow up then and needed the extra twenty yards the Haskell ball gave him over the gutta-percha. They could not

Old Tom Morris. It was in Old Tom's shop at St. Andrews that the young Charles Macdonald—and scores of American pilgrims after him—savored the essence of the old Scottish game. Old Tom was a champion in the gutta-percha era.

attack the importance to American golf of the great course at Southampton, but they could insinuate that a reactionary motive had engineered this revolutionary construction. In building the National, Charlie Macdonald was out to show Americans what a first-rate British course looked like.

Macdonald's fans and foes could agree on one thing: the mold of the future hero, or villain, was determined during his years as an impressionable college student in St. Andrews.

In July 1872, when Charles Macdonald was sixteen years old, his father, a prosperous Chicagoan, arranged for him to be educated at the United Colleges of St. Salvador and St. Leonard's in St. Andrews. The unhurried charm of the old town offered a sharp contrast to the Chicago the young man had left behind, a city still sagging from the Civil War and devastated by the great fire only nine months before his departure. The moment Charles saw St. Andrews he knew he would be happy there. The morning after his arrival, Charles was taken by his grandfather, a resident of the town and a member of the Royal and Ancient Golf Club, to the famous shop run by Old Tom Morris, where the boy was properly outfitted. Charles' grandfather also arranged for him to have a locker in Old Tom's shop, since juniors were not allowed inside the clubhouse of the Royal and Ancient. The first few times he played, Charles was not especially keen about the game, and then, suddenly, it got him. He could not stay off the links. On Sundays, when the course was supposedly closed, Charles and his friends would sneak onto some out-of-the-way hole where they had hidden their putters the evening before, and, safe from observation behind high bushy whins, they would putt back and forth all afternoon.

Charlie Macdonald developed into a fine golfer. He was good enough to play with Young Tom Morris, who had shattered the course record with a 77, and with Davy Strath, who fathered the famous bunker on the eleventh hole that in later years would cause the downfall of hundreds of ambitious invaders. During the long days of June and July, when the light holds until ten thirty or eleven in the evening, Charlie was able to get in several rounds a day and still have the time to practice and to talk golf with Old Tom in the shop. In Charlie's mind nothing in the world could compare to golf on St. Andrews. It wasn't just the links themselves, though they were peerless. It was the whole pervading flavor—the larks floating over the whins, the sailing boats in the Bay that you could see from the High Hole, the old red-brown and gray buildings brooding behind and alongside the eighteenth, the golfers of every class, tailors and authors, grocers and lords, all playing with "the spirit of the game prevailing." Charlie Macdonald could never forget his boyhood in St. Andrews.

Macdonald had planned, to be sure, to continue playing the game he loved when he returned to Chicago. As it turned out, he played only one summer, in 1875, when one of his classmates visited him. They went out to the wide clearing that had been Camp Douglas during the Civil War, and played their approaches to holes they had made from old ration cans that were still lying about. But outside of this one summer, Macdonald was forced to give up playing golf in America. These were the "root, hog, or die" days in Chicago and no one had time for outdoor sports. The gloom of this golfless life, which Macdonald called the Dark Ages, was relieved by his business trips to England. Between 1878 and 1888, Macdonald took at least five trips across and kept his long St. Andrews swing in shape by playing at Coldham Common, Wimbledon, and Royal Liverpool.

Living in Chicago, Macdonald was left out of the first experiments by the Eastern clubs. His chance came in 1892. Sir Henry Wood, England's Commissioner-General to the World's Fair in Chicago, had brought with him a staff of young men who had played golf in their college days and who talked it at all the parties they attended. Macdonald's earlier monologues on the merits of golf had never stirred his friends in Chicago to take any action. The constant golf talk of Sir Henry's young men did. Hobart Chatfield-Taylor decided to lay out a course on the estate of his father-in-law, Senator John B. Farwell, at Lake Forest. He asked his friend Macdonald to act as architect.

The limited plot at Lake Forest afforded Charlie Macdonald little room for self-expression. He had to be content with devising seven midget holes, none of them over 250 yards in length and most of them less than 100 yards. It was a beginning, nevertheless. Macdonald found his friends at the Chicago Club, his downtown hangout, much more willing now to go along with him on a golf venture on a larger scale. Twenty or thirty members of the club agreed to contribute ten dollars to enable him to build a nine-hole course on a stock farm at Belmont, twenty-four miles west of the city. In the spring of 1893, Macdonald added nine more holes to the Belmont course. A year later he was able to sell the members of the Chicago Golf Club an even more ambitious program. For $28,000—which was money in 1893—the club purchased the two-hundred-acre Patrick farm in the town of Wheaton, twenty-five miles out of Chicago. Macdonald set out to turn the lush rolling meadows into eighteen holes that would approach the standard of the finest inland courses of Great Britain. He did a splendid job. The Chicago Golf Club was an outstanding layout, and in the formative days of American golf many important championships were staged on it.

The only members who had reservations about the excellence of the new course in Wheaton were the hookers. Macdonald had laid out the holes clockwise around the perimeter of the property, so the golfer who unleashed a fair-sized hook found himself off the course and playing his recovery from a farmer's cornfield. To appease the hookers, the Chicago Golf Club adopted the out-of-bounds rule. This permitted the golfer who hooked his tee shot, for example, to play "two" off the tee rather than thrash the cornfield until he succeeded in hitting his ball back onto the fairway. Charlie Macdonald, to be sure, was never out-of-bounds. The clockwise layout was made for his slice as perfectly as the short rightfield fence at Yankee Stadium was made for Babe Ruth. When Charlie sliced, the severest penalty he suffered was the rough between holes, and when he was really wild, well, he would be on the adjoining fairway.

After 1895, Chicago went crazy over golf. By the turn of the century twenty-six clubs were operating, among them Hinsdale, Riverside, Onwentsia, Washington Park,

Charles Blair Macdonald, from the painting by Geri Melchers which hangs in the Links Club in New York. A man of unusual vigor and stubbornness, Macdonald was resented by some, venerated by others, but no man could deny his exceptional gifts both as a player and as a designer of superlative championship courses.

Elmhurst, Exmoor, LaGrange, Homewood, Midlothian, Glen View, and Westward Ho. Onwentsia, perhaps, had the most interesting genesis. It was founded by a group of young men, friends of Hobart Chatfield-Taylor, who preferred baseball or tennis to golf. One Sunday Chatfield-Taylor persuaded them to come out to his father-in-law's place in Lake Forest and try the game on the seven holes Macdonald had rigged up on the estate. Four of the holes were under 75 yards in length and only a few were over 200—"not real golf" at all, as Macdonald commented—but Chatfield-Taylor's friends were sufficiently impressed by the sample to band together and build a nine-holer on the McCormick farm. Five years later, in 1899, the Onwentsia Club, the beaming possessor of a new eighteen-hole course, was host to the United States Amateur.

Charles Blair Macdonald in later years left Chicago and made New York his headquarters. He did not mellow with age. If anything, his ideas became more fixed, his oaths more explosive, his loyalty to St. Andrews stronger than ever. Whether he was fighting the United States Golf Association or designing his wonderful courses or "replaying" old championship matches on the leather chairs at the Links Club, he remained a law unto himself. Now and then he asked the advice of people he respected, but ninety-nine times out of a hundred, he followed his own judgment. (On the odd occasion he probably listened to Jim Whigham, his son-in-law and an early amateur champion.) The younger men who later came to the leadership in golf found Macdonald a very charming person when he wanted to be. They could also congratulate themselves on a cable they sent him one summer when he went to Britain for a visit: *We hope you are enjoying your holiday. We are.*

Charles Blair Macdonald was not "Mr. American Golf," though this was undoubtedly his life's ambition. He did, however, contribute more to the advancement of golf in America than any other person of his generation.

THE U.S.G.A.
AND
THE FIRST
CHAMPIONSHIPS

Today a golf club would no more think of permitting stone walls to traverse its fairways than Ohio State would lobby to de-emphasize football. In some ways 1894 does not seem so far away, and it is not easy to understand how, pioneer days or no pioneer days, stone walls were esteemed fine golf hazards and a club was considered lucky to have them. When the Newport Golf Club, to keep up with the times, opened a new nine at Rocky Farm, the members appraised the rambling stone walls as one of the chief merits of the new course. Willie Davis from Montreal, whom the club had taken on as pro, further tightened up the layout with a liberal sprinkling of mounds and pot bunkers. These were the accepted "artificial hazards" of the day, easy to build and maintain, hard for a player to avoid. The mixture made for a stiff course rather than a good test of skill, but then few of the golfers in the mid-Nineties appreciated the difference. The Rocky Farm course kindled a new enthusiasm among the members of the Newport club in the summer of 1894, and with one notable result: they voted to invite golfers from all clubs to come to Newport in September and meet in competitions that would decide the champion amateur and professional players in the country.

All the stars accepted. Down from Boston came Herbert Leeds. Laurence Stoddart trained over from St. Andrew's. And out of the West, with a retinue of well-heeled backers, came Charlie Macdonald, supremely confident that he would leave the field of dilettante-sportsmen far behind. Twenty players in all teed off in the tourney, but the toughness of the course and the physical wear and tear of eighteen holes of medal play on two consecutive days killed off all but eight. Macdonald had been established as a heavy favorite from the beginning, and his play on the first day justified that tribute. His 89 gave him a four-stroke lead over his closest competitor, W. G. Lawrence, a member of the Newport club who had put in some time at Pau, in France. On the second day calamity struck the Chicagoan and his supporters. Macdonald blew to 100, and Lawrence's 95 gave him a total of 188, a stroke lower than Macdonald's. A topped shot had cost Charlie the championship. It had rolled into one of the stone walls and died there, and Macdonald had been forced to take a two-stroke penalty.

Charlie Macdonald took the defeat hard. He refused to recognize Lawrence as the champion, claiming that a stone wall was not a legitimate golf hazard and, accordingly, the two-stroke penalty was not a legitimate penalty. He also beefed loud and long that medal play was no proper method of determining an amateur champion. Amateur championships in Great Britain, as any true student of the game could tell you, were invariably match-play tournaments. He suggested that the Newport tournament be ruled "no contest" and that they start all over again, at match play. Macdonald did succeed in stirring up a hot controversy and gained a chance to redeem his reputation when the St. Andrew's club announced that it would be host to a *match-play* tournament in October to settle once and for all who was the American amateur champion. Invitations were sent to twenty clubs, and twenty-seven golfers from eight clubs came to the course at Grey Oaks to stop Macdonald. There was plenty of Eastern money to encourage them.

As at Newport, Charlie Macdonald started out like a house on fire. Fidgeting as always before the ball, champing impatiently while he waited for his opponents to play, he won his first match by the lopsided score of 8 and 6 and his second 4 and 3. The next morning, in the semi-final round, he got sweet revenge by defeating Lawrence, his conqueror at Newport, 2 and 1. Now all Macdonald had to do to prove his point that he was the true master of the amateur field was to win his final match that afternoon from Laurence Stoddart. No one doubted that he would. Stoddart, who had been a member of Hoylake (or Royal Liverpool), gave the long-hitting Chicagoan a good fight. Stoddart refused to crack under pressure, as he was supposed to, and they finished the eighteen holes all square. On the first extra hole Macdonald sliced his tee shot into a ploughed field—this was a counter-clockwise course—and when he took three to get back onto the fairway, he had lost another championship.

Once more Macdonald had an alibi. He had been ill. The night before his semi-final and final matches, he explained, Stanford White had thrown a party for him at the Waldorf. It was five in the morning before Macdonald remembered that he had arranged to meet his semi-final opponent, Willie Lawrence, for breakfast at seven o'clock. At White's advice he had taken some strychnine pills after a nap, and thus stimulated was not only able to make his breakfast date but to go out and defeat Lawrence 2 up and 1 to play. At lunch he had confessed to White that he wasn't feeling at all himself and had asked White's opinion as to how he should doctor himself. White had prescribed a good steak and a bottle of champagne. It was this foolhardy lunch, Macdonald insisted, which had caused his downfall.

Macdonald refused to recognize Stoddart as the national champion. As he saw it, Stoddart had won a tournament, an invitation tournament sponsored by one club. One club could not presume to speak for a nation. Before a tournament could be designated a national championship, it would have to have the approval of all the clubs in the country, and those clubs would have to be joined in an official organization. He was sorry, but under the circumstances he could not recognize either Stoddart or Lawrence as the national amateur champion.

Macdonald's elaborate post-mortems brought about, quite accidentally, the birth of the United States Golf Association. Theodore Havemeyer of Newport, Laurence Curtis of The Country Club, and Henry Tallmadge of St. Andrew's were disturbed by the thought that this war of words between Macdonald's partisans and the gloating East would be only the first of a series of crippling controversies unless some recognized authority was set up to settle points of difference and lay down laws all golfers were bound to follow. Tallmadge wrote to the five clubs the three men had checked as most prominent in their sections of the country—Shinnecock Hills and the Chicago Golf Club as well as Newport, The Country Club, and St. Andrew's—inviting each club to send two delegates to a dinner he was planning in New York for the purpose of establishing a governing body for American golf.

On December 22, 1894, the delegates met at the Calumet Club—John Reid and Tallmadge from St. Andrew's, Theodore Havemeyer and Winthrop Rutherford from Newport, Laurence Curtis and Samuel Sears from The Country Club, Charles Macdonald and Arthur Ryerson from Chicago, and Samuel Parrish from Shinnecock Hills. (General T. H. Barber, the other delegate from Shinnecock, was unable to attend.) Through these representatives, the five clubs agreed to unite and invited other clubs to join them in the Amateur Golf Association of the United States, whose aims would be "to promote the interests of the game of golf, to promulgate a code of rules for the game, to hold annual meetings at which competitions shall be conducted for the amateur and open championships in the United States." The honor of being the organization's first president narrowed down to two candidates, John Reid and Theodore Havemeyer. Havemeyer won out, largely through the campaigning of Laurence Curtis, who felt that an infant organization could well use the prestige and financial support a man like the Sugar King would provide. Tallmadge was selected secretary; Parrish, treasurer; Curtis, first vice-president; and Macdonald, second vice-president. In this way each of the five original clubs was honored with an office, and the A.G.A.U.S. got off to a harmonious start.

The association was very fortunate in the selection of its key officers, Havemeyer and Tallmadge. Havemeyer was a man of exceptional tact and unusual charm, three hundred and sixty-five days a year. Where other men might have failed, he was able to placate the members of Meadow Brook, Tuxedo, Essex County, and other clubs who had felt slighted by not being invited to attend the original meeting, and to persuade them to join the association. In more material ways, as Curtis had foreseen, Havemeyer was a tremendous help. One of his first acts was to donate a handsome thousand-dollar

Henry O. Tallmadge,
the U.S.G.A.'s first secretary
and a man of charm and ability.

trophy for the Amateur Championship. Whenever there was a bill that ready funds could not cover, Havemeyer paid it. Tallmadge was a hard-working secretary with the valuable gift of knowing how to handle the rambunctious Macdonald, who from time to time mistook the national organization for the Chicago Golf Club.

The United States Golf Association was the third name the body adopted. The original name, the Amateur Golf Association, was not suitable since the A.G.A.U.S. also dealt with professional golf. The American Golf Association, the second try, was incorrect, too, since the A.G.A. had no jurisdiction over Canadian golf. By any name, the U.S.G.A. through the years has been a competent organization. It has had its moments of weakness—like its ridiculous disbarment of Francis Ouimet from amateur golf, its wavering policy as to whether or not a golf architect was a professional or an amateur golfer, its tardiness in stopping jackrabbit balls from running away with the courses. On the other hand, the U.S.G.A., when still a stripling, stood firm in the face of the R. & A. when that august body barred the Schenectady putter following Travis' incredible exploits in the 1904 British Amateur. It has tried to make rules for American golf that have suited the changing game, agreeing with the R. & A. whenever it was possible but not afraid to break with tradition when it had good reason. The U.S.G.A. has done a very satisfactory job in working with the R. & A. to create a universal set of rules, an excellent job in staging the national tournaments, a superior job in improving turf conditions and aiding the hard-pressed greenkeeper, and a superb job in keeping golf the one major sport in which an amateur must adhere to the rules of amateur status. Some of the past presidents of the U.S.G.A. would still be voting for Calvin Coolidge or Rutherford B. Hayes if they could, but a far greater number of the organization's officials have not been brass hats and have fought to make the management of the game as democratic as the game itself. The U.S.G.A. looks very good when you compare its record with that of an organization with quite similar functions, the United States Lawn Tennis Association, or, for that matter, with most national bodies governing sports.

The first official United States Amateur Championship, or the first one sponsored by the U.S.G.A., was held at Newport the first three days of October 1895. There was no qualifying round, the players immediately tackling each other in eighteen-hole matches with the final set for thirty-six. Theodore Havemeyer went out of his way to make the U.S.G.A.'s maiden championship an unqualified success. He arranged the parties and personally paid the expenses of the thirty-two entrants. In the main they were gentle-men-golfers (who were more gentleman than golfer), but among the entries there were a few characters, such as the golfing minister, the Reverend William Rainsford, and clubman Richard Peters, who used a billiard cue on the greens, not because he wanted to clown around but because he was convinced he could putt better that way. Society turned out for the tournament, the ladies in their gayest silks and the men in their red jackets. The officials of the U.S.G.A., pleased as schoolboys over their new red-white-and-blue badges, dashed around energetically in circles trying to help out.

Yet, in the minds of the Easterners, a dark cloud hung over the championship—Charlie Macdonald. Macdonald had been playing even better than usual that season, and as the "golfing reporter" of the New York *Herald* stated in between descriptions of what the ladies were wearing, the man from the West was regarded as the "probable champion." None of the Eastern players, as their backers glumly perceived, had scored nearly as low in their practice rounds as Macdonald. Furthermore, Macdonald was avoiding any chance of a repetition of his fiasco at St. Andrew's by going into what for him amounted to training. At no time was he seriously pressed as he marched through his half of the draw. To make matters worse for the East, Laurence Stoddart, the one man who might have stopped Macdonald—Willie Lawrence was not entered—was eliminated by a much poorer player than himself. Stoddart's conqueror was in turn eliminated in the semi-final round by Macdonald. The other finalist was Charles Sands, a very green golfer from the home club. On the eve of the final between Sands and Macdonald, the East was praying for a miracle, and nothing less than a miracle was needed if the haughty Macdonald was going to be defeated. Young Sands was a fine tennis player, but unfortunately this was a golf championship. He had played his first golf only three months before and had entered the tournament just for the fun of it. No miracle was forthcoming. This time Macdonald would not be denied. Five up at luncheon in the 36-hole final, he won every hole in the afternoon and closed out the match 12 and 11. On his third try Macdonald had made it, and he became the first official Amateur Champion. "I entered this championship in excellent form," he later wrote, "and was well taken care of, stopping with Mr. and Mrs. Henry Clews."

As Macdonald played out the bye holes, rightfully rejoicing in his long-sought triumph, he may have toyed with the thought that winning the Amateur could well become an annual habit for him, one he would not find the least bit objectionable.

The first Amateur Champion
of the United States,
C. B. Macdonald,
follows through.

Macdonald played in the Amateur, without fail, during the ensuing years, and though he was always a dangerous contender until 1900, he never won again. It wasn't that his game deteriorated; if anything, he played a shade better. It was simply that the standard of everybody's golf was improving, and Macdonald was no match for the American college boys and the young men from the British Isles who had come to the States. When the Amateur was held in 1896 at Shinnecock Hills, H. J. Whigham was easily the class of the field. An Oxford man who was doing newspaper work in this country, Jim Whigham wrapped up the qualifying-round honors with an 86 and a great 77, and rolled on until he won his final match 8 and 7. Whigham successfully defended his title at the Chicago Golf Club the next year. His short game was outstanding. He used his wooden putter not only on the greens but also ran up some of his chip-length approaches with this limber-faced club. Whigham married Charlie Macdonald's daughter, so Macdonald at least had the satisfaction of knowing that the championship remained in the family.

In 1898, when the Amateur was played at the Morris County Golf Club, in New Jersey, Whigham failed to qualify. He had recently returned from Cuba, where he had covered the Spanish-American War as a special correspondent, and had not fully recovered from a siege of malaria. (At one time Whigham was rumored captured by the Spanish, and clubmen debated an absorbing question: Should a nation ransom its Amateur Golf Champion?) With Whigham out of the running, the crown went to Findlay Douglas, a twenty-three-year-old Scot who had captained the University of St. Andrews' golf team. Douglas found the 5,960-yard course at Morris County made to order for his aggressive, long-hitting game. More than once he drove into the bunker in front of the green on the 234-yard fourth hole, and since a few of the other contestants also encountered this unusual penalty, it began to look as if the players were getting ahead of the courses. Douglas was favored to repeat in 1899 at Onwentsia. He had little difficulty with any of his opponents until he reached the final, but there he succumbed, quite unexpectedly, to Herbert Harriman by the score of 3 and 2. Harriman was a short, awkward swinger who was never a threat in subsequent championships. However, he was very good on the day it was important for him to play his best game, and his victory at Onwentsia marked the close of American golf's period of infancy: For the first time a foreign-born star had not won the Amateur Championship. For the first time the champ was a "homebred."

TURN
OF THE
CENTURY

Golf did not graduate into a truly popular sport in America until the Open Champion-ship of 1913, when Francis Ouimet, an unknown ex-caddie, stunned the nation into acceptance by defeating the celebrated British professionals, Harry Vardon and Ted Ray. However, as early as 1900, the year that Vardon made his first American tour, the game had established itself as more than the coddled crush of the gilded set—something more than hard rackets or court tennis, to use a modern analogy. Only twelve years after its introduction in Yonkers, golf had come to be regarded by Americans of that day more or less as skiing was by mid-century Americans: an outdoor recreation, open to both sexes and a wide range of ages, whose environment was as attractive, if not more attractive, than the exercise itself; a sport whose first professionals came from overseas and whose leading missionaries were the college crowd, and which offered its followers an occasion for dashing outfits, endowed them with the bright aura of being fashionable, and demanded from them a good slice of their incomes.

Findlay Douglas may have been a trifle exuberant in estimating that by the turn of the century 250,000 Americans had seen the light and were spending over $20,000,000 annually on golf, but there was no denying that the game was growing and growing fast. The length and breadth of the United States were dotted with golf courses, over a thousand of them. There was at least one course in every state. The Atlantic seaboard states New York and Massachusetts led with 165 and 157 respectively, but there were 57 courses in Illinois, 43 in California, 17 in Florida, and already 5 in Texas. Cincinnati, Philadelphia, Boston, and Providence were some of the cities that supported courses that were open to the public. Chicago had created its municipal course by filling in Jackson Park with the bricks, concrete pillars, and other debris from the World's Fair buildings. Van Cortlandt Park in New York, the original public course, sported a 700-yard finishing hole, and after hitting his four or five brassies on that hole, a player *was* finished.

In the other direction, men who could afford it—like Theodore Havemeyer, John Jacob Astor, and A. G. Spalding—built private courses on their estates. In the beginning, Spalding and the other manufacturers of sporting goods had been afraid to touch the game, but now they were setting up plants especially tooled for turning out gutta-perchas as well as the baffy spoons, cleeks, iron and wooden niblicks, mashies, and the other weapons demanded by the increasing number of players.

America looked more and more like the promised land to Scottish professionals, and the Mackies and the Nicholls and the Rosses and the Smiths headed West *en famille* to make their fortunes. Alex started the wholesale migration of the Smiths from Carnoustie in 1898. His brother Willie followed him a year later. George came over and then Jimmy. Shortly afterwards, Mr. and Mrs. John Smith, the boys' parents, joined them in the greener pastures, bringing with them the baby of the family, Macdonald, who developed into the greatest golfer who never won a major championship.

The Scottish professionals—and the other British and Irish emigrant professionals—found themselves playing and teaching on layouts remarkably different from the true links back home—that belt of sandy soil deposited by the receding ocean along the coast of the British Isles. Lacking this linksland, with its natural bunkers and dunes, Americans had used their native genius, often excessively, in providing themselves with comparable hazards for their inland courses. Stone quarries, pigeon traps, ploughed fields, railroad tracks, and wooden pavilions were accepted as obstacles that added interest to the game, and self-appointed architects remedied Nature's absent-mindedness by digging cross-bunkers the width of their fairways and scooping circular pits—pot bunkers—around their greens. To many Americans, these devices were not a substitution for the natural hazards of a seaside links; they were an improvement on them.

The men who banded together to finance golf courses in their communities discovered it was an expensive proposition. By the time a syndicate had purchased its two hundred acres, built its course, and added an adequate clubhouse, the costs had already soared to $200,000—a figure to be respected in 1900. The syndicates were always faced with the possibility that the game might not catch on in their particular community, and to protect their investment they usually purchased wooded land. Then, if the venture collapsed, the land could be cut up and sold to prospective builders, who were always partial to leafy lots. Apart from the considerable initial outlay, it took money to operate a golf club; the artificial hazards, greens, and watering systems had to be maintained, and there was always the clubhouse to think about.

After Stanford White had showed the way at Shinnecock Hills, every self-respecting club had to have a clubhouse. The social advantages of a good clubhouse were inextricably bound up with definite economic factors. Wealthy men would join a golf club that possessed a well-appointed clubhouse, even if they were not attracted to the game itself. Many of these men would, sooner or later, be converted to golf and grow to love their eighteen holes as much as their drinks and their dinner; yet, however they reacted to life in the rough, wealthy members were essential if a club was to remain solvent. And unless it could point to a handsome clubhouse, no golf club could hope to attract the women of the community, without whose presence the project would not click socially. For these reasons, golf clubs were forced, or thought they were forced, to charge high initiation fees and healthy annual dues, and golf grew up in America as a rich man's game, viewed with a certain antagonism by the average workingman, who distrusted any diversion pursued almost exclusively by the wealthy. The man who didn't play golf glibly shrugged it off as an effeminate sport for old fogies with one foot in the grave.

The adoption of golf by the college boys helped to spotlight the sport as one that could be enjoyed by vigorous young men. Outside of the contestants, few Americans cared who won the Intercollegiate title, but many Americans, consciously or unconsciously, had to revise their opinions of the game when the Amateur Championship of 1904 was won by a strapping, clean-cut young man named Chandler Egan who was still an undergraduate at Harvard. On the other hand, the endorsement by the college crowd did not make the game any more democratic, immediately. Harvard, Yale, and Princeton men took turns in winning the Intercollegiate Championship, and the golf teams at these universities were the especial preserves of the very social set.

Egan the collegian thrilled the galleries with his recoveries from the rough, a type of shot he had mastered through practice, since, like most young golfers, he was extremely long and extremely erratic off the tees. At Chicago, where he successfully defended his title in 1905, there were three degrees of rough: a width of five yards cut fairly close; then a really formidable growth; and finally a hayfield that looked much tougher than it actually was. Egan fortunately was wild enough to reach the hayfield quite consistently.

The early golfers liked to find pretty women lounging on the verandas of their clubhouses, but they were not in favor of women playing the game. To keep them off the course, the men invoked stringent club rules, argued the fantasy that golf developed unbecoming muscles, and talked loud and laboriously about the dangers lurking on the wild frontier bordering the holes farthest away from the clubhouse. A favorite story at every course was the close call George had had the other day when that wild bull in the adjoining pasture caught sight of his red coat and charged through the fence and would have gored poor George if he hadn't had the quick wits to dive into the water hazard. The hardier girls refused to be intimidated by these frock-and-bull stories and investigated life on the frontier for themselves. Others played golf for the very sufficient reason that they wanted to. In 1893 an enterprising group of New Jersey ladies got back at the men by organizing a course "for women only" in Morris County. Two years later they held their first national championship at Meadow Brook, Long Island, with Mrs. C. S.

The golfing fashions of the time make it difficult to comment upon the pivots of these Wellesley College golfers, but in any event they are diligently at work polishing their skills at a game that was a definite social asset. The outstanding woman golfer at the turn of the century was Beatrix Hoyt of Shinnecock.

Brown carrying the day with a sporty 132. By the turn of the century the women had won their fight. In Beatrix Hoyt they had a champion who could play in the eighties, on a calm day, and Peggy Curtis could bang a brassie farther than most strong men.

To accomplish these wonders the women had shortened their skirts—they now reached to the *top* of the ankle—and defrilled their blouses. "For once," said H. L. Fitzpatrick, writing in *Outing*, "comfort and fashion united in the attire of the sex." Down through the years as the demands of sports, more than any other single factor, encouraged abbreviation in feminine styles and brought the age of the sweater and sensible skirt a little nearer, man was always on hand with an appreciative word.

Golf's popularity among the "best people," of both sexes, was not overlooked by the established summer resorts nor by the men transforming the South into a winter playground. By 1900, Poland Spring, Saratoga, Manchester in Vermont, Shennecossett near New London, and the Lake Placid Club had added golf courses to attract the couples who wanted to play the game during their vacations. Henry M. Flagler, who opened up the east coast of Florida, and Henry B. Plant, who concentrated on the west coast, talked up the game as a year-round sport: there was no need any longer for golfers to stow away their clubs during the winter months, now that Palm Beach and Ormond Beach and Tampa and Belleair were waiting for them. The Belleview Biltmore at Belleair assured them of grass greens, built from topsoil imported by the carload from Indiana. Pinehurst, the colony founded by James W. Tufts in the sandhills of North Carolina, had a good eighteen-hole course, and Donald Ross, just over from Scotland, was starting work on the famous Pinehurst #2. There were courses at Aiken, South Carolina, Jekyll's Island in Georgia, Hot Springs, Virginia, Del Monte in California, and the resorts without a few holes were writing interesting letters to the best Scottish pros.

Realizing that golf had come to stay, newspaper editors allotted increased space to accounts of the tournaments, and golf reporters learned the names of a few of the sticks. W. G. Van Tassel Sutphen wrote *The Golficide* and other tales, and led the way in publishing periodicals in which an addict could read about the game in those rare moments he wasn't talking about it. Golf acquired a literature, or at least many books on golf were published. Charles Stedman Hanks, who gloried in the pseudonym of "Niblic," was one of the first to write an "instruction book." In *Hints to Golfers*, Niblic advised "keeping the eye on the ball and not on the ground behind it" and generally explained his credo that "no other game requires such a variety of physical and mental adjustments." William Garrott Brown, who had written biographies of Andrew Jackson and Stephen Arnold Douglas, was one of the "minds" who tried to get down in black and white the overpowering fascination the game had for him. Was it the delicate adjustments and self-control the game demanded of its players? Brown wasn't sure. But he knew that the red-coated hordes issuing from the city each weekend to play golf were in for a *moral* outing. H. W. Boynton's tribute, *The Golfer's Rubaiyat*, contained such hedonistic sentiments as—

> A Bag of Clubs, a Silvertown or two,
> A Flask of Scotch, a Pipe of Shag—and Thou
> Beside me, caddying in the Wilderness—
> Ah, Wilderness were paradise enow.

The humor of golf and golfers began to get around, and insinuated itself into the he-she jokes magazines used as fillers.

There was the joke about the specialized language golfers used—

Sphinx-like Magistrate: "What are these prisoners charged with?"
Policeman: "I arrested them for fighting, your honor. They are a couple of golf
    players, and—"
Magistrate: "Send for the court interpreter."

And the one about the suitor—

"Hasn't Willoughby Perkins proposed yet?"
"No, Mamma. His approach is all right, but then he gets nervous and foozles."

And a switch called "Cruel Treatment"—

"I proposed to her in a smooth, well-modulated tone."
"Well?"
"She rejected me in her golf voice."

The year 1900 brought into the focus of American golfers three men whose talents were
to prove invaluable in promoting the growth of golf in this country: Walter J. Travis,
Harry Vardon, and Coburn Haskell.

Walter J. Travis was Australian-born, but learned his golf in the States, and was
regarded as an American golfer. Travis had taken the game up in his middle-thirties, at
an age when few men are able to master a sport they have never played before because
their muscles are "set" and their reflexes slowed. Travis, a man with a mind of his own,
entered the United States Amateur less than two years after he had started the game,
and made his way into the semi-final round before being ousted by Findlay Douglas.
That was in 1898, and the next year the "Old Man" was back for more. Again he
reached the semi-finals and again it was Douglas who put him out, but the score was
closer this time and Travis was encouraged. He met Douglas for the third time in the
final of the Amateur at Garden City, Long Island, in 1900, and this time Travis turned
the tables on the long-hitting Scot, defeating him 2 up.

 After the tournament, newspaper men approached the new champion and asked
him how he had managed to add 25 yards to his drives, to hit them 200 yards now where
he had averaged 175 yards in previous years. Guarding his elation over his victory,
Travis remarked indirectly, "I am only just learning this game."

 "Do you think you will work your game up to a greater degree of proficiency?"

 "I should say so," Travis answered. "Why, I am now just scratching on the outside,
and if I don't improve my game by at least another three strokes by another year, I shall
be very much surprised."

 Walter Travis went on to win the Amateur twice more and to do things in the
British Amateur of 1904 that left Americans gasping, particularly those Americans who
wanted to believe that golf could begin at forty and could see from Travis' example that
it could.

America's first glimpse of the master: Vardon at Pinehurst on his tour in 1900.

Harry Vardon, who is regarded as one of the four greatest golfers of all time—a distinction he shares with Bobby Jones, Ben Hogan, and Jack Nicklaus—made his first trip to America in 1900. The impeccable swinger from the Isle of Jersey had already won three of the six British Open titles he would amass. He had grooved his rather upright swing so perfectly that his opponents declared that when he played his second nine on a nine-hole course, his drives ended up in the divot marks he had cut from the fairways his first time round. Americans had heard about his deeds, and had a chance to see the peerless one himself when the Spalding company arranged for him to tour the country to promote their new guttie, the Vardon Flyer. The tour came on the eve of the emergence of the new rubber-cored ball, and from this point of view it was not successful. But the tour sold golf.

In a long series of exhibitions, Vardon played against our best homebreds and the outstanding Anglo-American pros, and dropped only one match. He took time off to compete in the U.S. Open and finished nine strokes ahead of the field. Most important, he showed Americans, much more convincingly than the transplanted pros who had won the earlier championships, how the game could be played. With his brassie he could pick the ball cleanly from any lie and propel it high and floating to the green, where it sat down abruptly. With his irons he merely brushed across the turf with the clubhead instead of taking a large divot, and faded his shots into the pin from left to right. He hit the ball with an utter absence of visible effort, and yet his timing was so fine that he sent his shots yards farther down the fairways than his straining opponents. After they had seen Harry, American golfers knew that the game, in the hands of a master, could be an art.

Coburn Haskell was a fair golfer who lived in Cleveland. Not unlike many other golfers of his day, Haskell was not at all satisfied with the performance of the gutta-percha ball and had frequently thought about substances from which a superior ball could be developed. One day in 1898 he called in at the Goodrich Rubber Company to pick up a friend, an official of that company. Haskell's friend found himself unable to get away immediately and suggested that Haskell take a turn around the plant and look things over. On his walk Haskell's attention was caught by a pile of thin rubber stripping, and he was struck by the idea that an improved ball might be built by wrapping these strippings tightly around a rubber core and covering them with a sheath of gutta-percha. With the assistance of his friend at the Goodrich Company, Haskell worked out the new rubber-cored ball, which revolutionized the game as thoroughly at the turn of the century as the guttie had done fifty years earlier. The tendency of the first rubber-cored balls to "duck" in flight was corrected by impressing a bramble marking on their smooth covers. Later the gutta-percha for the covers was replaced by balata.

The "Bounding Billies," as the new balls were called, were harder to control around the green than the old gutties, but a golfer did not have to strike them perfectly to get a reasonably straight shot, and, far more important, the average golfer found his drive a full twenty yards farther down the fairway. Now the game was really enjoyable for the weekend player. Now it took only one long whistling drive with the rubber-cored ball to convert an infidel.

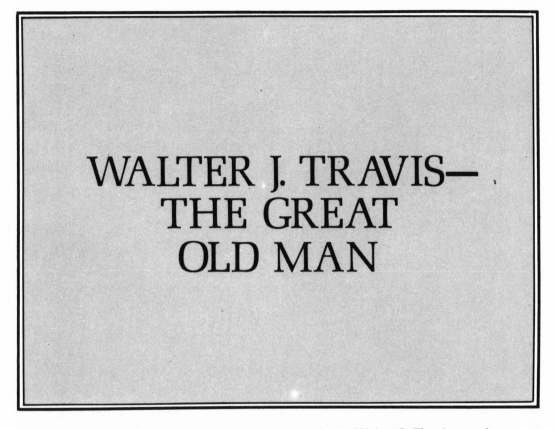

WALTER J. TRAVIS—
THE GREAT
OLD MAN

Golf fans in Great Britain have a far clearer idea of who Walter J. Travis was than most Americans do. Should a Briton's picture of Travis begin to blur, a torrid round by some American in a British championship is all that is necessary to evoke golf writers' references to 1904 and that unforgettable first invader, Travis. In America today, however, the name of Travis rings few bells, and those who claim to remember him well too often have his doings confused with those of his homonymous contemporary, Jerome Travers. And Walter J. Travis is worth the knowing.

The thing about Travis that first startled the golfers of his day was the thoroughgoing way he blasted the current idea that a man had to play golf from the cradle on if he nurtured any ambitions to score in the seventies, let alone become a champion. Born in the state of Victoria in Australia, Travis had come to America when still a small boy. He was athletically inclined, but golf seemed a waste of time to him, and he spent the leisure hours of his young manhood playing tennis or cycling. On a visit to England he took a house in Streatham, close by the course at Tooting Bec, and on his daily strolls stopped to watch the players. This closer inspection only confirmed his previous opinion: golf wasn't a game for him. While in England, however, he did purchase a set of sticks but only because his friends at the Niantic Club in Flushing, Long Island, had written him that they were thinking of starting a golf course, and Travis thought he should support such a venture. He started to play the game with these friends at the Oakland course on Long Island when he got back in the fall of 1896. Travis was then thirty-five.

Walter J. Travis pauses at the top of his compact swing. Travis was not a long driver, but he seldom strayed from the center of the fairway. From there he could go to work with his fine iron shots and his remarkable short game. In 1900 he won the Amateur Championship in what was only his fourth year of golf.

Walter J. Travis—The Great Old Man

Walter Travis was one of those men who saw no sense in doing a thing at all unless he did it well. Since circumstances had led him to take up golf, he made up his mind to become something more than a dub. During the winter he gathered around him the best books on the game he could acquire. He realized that learning from books could be dangerous unless the reader had great powers of concentration and an extraordinary diligence in investigation, but he knew that he had those abilities and kept on reading, setting aside Horace Hutchinson's theories in the Badminton Library series as worthy of more detailed study, marking Willie Park, Jr.'s, manual as material that should be helpful, tossing aside the books by other authorities who advocated methods he felt were not in harmony with his slight physique and limited brawn. Travis recognized the fact that a good golfer plays half of his shots on the putting green, and slowly, scientifically, arrived at what he approved of as a sound putting method for himself. This was to use a short-shafted putter and grip it well down the shaft, the palms working in direct opposition to each other to produce a pendulum stroke, the body held absolutely motionless. The next spring he played three or four rounds but chose to spend the bulk of his time practicing his self-taught swing. A few months more and he terminated this trial-and-error period, satisfied with the product of his disciplined search. It wasn't the prettiest swing in the world and it may have had a homemade quality, but it was Travis' and he knew and controlled every inch of it. He did not hit the ball far but he hit it straight, and from the beginning he was far too good for the other players at Oakland. In his second year he was ready to test his skill against the country's best in the United States Amateur, and got to the semi-finals. Two years after that, less than four years after he had started golf, Travis led the fast field in the Metropolitan Championship and topped off his season (as noted previously) by winning the Amateur, no less.

When he won his first national championship, Travis wore a heavy dark beard that, along with the Rough Rider type of hat he then favored, gave him the aspect of a junior-sized Stonewall Jackson. His opponents found him a tough customer. He was always perfectly polite, but he had little to say and preferred the company of his long black cigar. Even when he shaved off his beard, his opponents could not read his emotions. They knew only that the Old Man was out to win and did not want to risk disturbing his concentration by any social bantering. His accuracy nullified the greater length of his rivals, and on the greens he putted them to death, dropping the 20-footers as smoothly and as confidently as the 7-footers. Then, with just the slightest flicker of pleasure in his menacing dark eyes, he was off to the next tee, taking a careful practice swing, stroking his drive down the middle and walking slowly after the ball, his neck stuck out like a turtle's, the smoke of his cigar curling over the rim of his rolled-up twill hat.

During the winter of 1901, Travis' health was poor and he went to Scotland for a rest. By summertime he was back on the fairways stalking his foes not one whit more leniently and proving beyond a doubt that he was no flash in the pan. He finished third in the United States Open. Playing the rubber-cored ball for the first time, he won the qualifying medal in the national Amateur at Atlantic City by three strokes. In the semi-finals of that tournament, though putting less devastatingly than usual because of the more resilient ball, he eliminated his most dangerous challenger, Findlay Douglas. In the final he won as he pleased from Walter Egan.

Travis' hopes of making it three in a row the following year were smashed when he came up against young Eben Byers in the third round at Glen View. Travis shot a fair enough 78 but Byers came up with a 77 and won 1 up. In 1903, Byers and Travis again met in the Amateur, this time in the final round. Playing almost errorless golf, Travis went around the Nassau Country Club course in 73 on his morning round and coasted to a convincing 5 and 4 victory. The Old Man was not to be trifled with.

During his holiday in Britain in 1901, Travis had played several matches against the ranking Scottish and English players. He had lost most of these matches, and his experience had pointed out to him the deficiencies in his game. By 1904, when he had won three of the last four United States Amateur crowns and had clearly established himself as the nation's leading amateur golfer, he was filled with the desire to return to Britain and prove to himself that he was now just as good if not better than the men who had licked him three years before. He decided to enter the British Amateur Championship in 1904, to be held at Royal St. George's in Sandwich, Kent. Deep down in his heart, the Old Man believed his game was good enough to win despite his shortness off the tees and the length of the links at Sandwich—6,135 yards of harsh duneland whipped by the winds off the North Sea. With the same detached calculation that had marked his efforts to learn the game without a teacher, this man who loved a fight mapped his conquest of the British Amateur: He would arrive in London three weeks before the start of the tourney; he would tune up for a week and a half at St. Andrews and North Berwick; then he would go down to Sandwich and spend the last ten or twelve days before the tournament getting to know the championship course and practicing his shots in the wind and rain.

When he found himself playing very badly at St. Andrews, Travis had to scrap this plan. He stayed on in Scotland, trying to discover why he wasn't hitting the ball. He played worse and worse. He bought himself some new clubs, hoping these would give him a psychological lift, and found they were no help at all. He was still in this slump, the worst of his career, when he arrived at Sandwich seven days before the start of the tournament. He wanted to get in as many practice rounds as possible, and at the same time he was loath to make his first round at Sandwich a bad one and become antagonistic toward the course. He debated the dilemma a full morning and decided to go out with only one club, the new putting cleek he had bought at North Berwick, and simply beat the ball for a few holes. With the first shot he hit, he felt his old timing returning. The next day he went out with his full set, and gradually his game came back during his practice rounds and his frame of mind began to improve. Only one thing about his golf was bothering him now. He couldn't hole a putt. He tried putting off his left foot, off his right foot. He opened his stance, closed it, opened it again. He shortened and then lengthened his stroke, tried new grips, varied the arc of the club, and still could not sink a putt of over three feet. In desperation he borrowed a friend's Schenectady putter the

Travis with two of his faithful companions, his putter and his cigar. His keen competitive spirit still intact, the Old Man could, at fifty, step with the young stars for two or three rounds, and sometimes more. At fifty-three he outplayed a strong field to win the Metropolitan Amateur Championship.

day before the tournament began. This was a putter with the shaft inserted in the *center* of a mallet-shaped head. It was called the Schenectady, since it was a resident of that city, Mr. A. W. Knight, who had introduced this unconventional model. Finding he could putt a little better with the Schenectady, Travis decided to sink or swim with it during the tournament.

In addition to his purely golf worries, the Old Man's spirits were weighed down by several extracurricular irritations during that week preceding the start of the tournament. He and the Englishmen in charge of the Royal St. George's Golf Club did not hit it off, at all. The English thought him cold and impolite, and he felt the same way about them. There are, of course, two sides to the story. From the viewpoint of the Englishmen running Sandwich, Travis had responded uncivilly to their attempts at friendliness. When they had asked him to join them for a dinner party or an after-dinner drink, Travis had firmly rejected their invitations. This went against all their ideas of the guest's role in the English code of hospitality; in the eyes of his hosts, it was about the same as if Travis had entered a house without wiping off his muddy shoes. They concluded that he wanted to be left alone, and in the future they left him alone.

Travis, for his part, believed he had suffered a series of consciously wrought insults. He was not able to obtain quarters in the buildings usually reserved for guests of the Royal St. George's, and he and his American friends were obliged to take rooms at the Bell Hotel. He had asked to play his practice rounds with some of the star British golfers, but this was not arranged. He was assigned a cross-eyed caddie whom he believed to be a congenital idiot, and was not able to get him replaced. He and his American friends, he claimed, were cut dead by the same Oxford and Cambridge golfers whom they had entertained royally when the combined team had visited the States the year before. Travis felt like a pariah. As he saw it, he had done nothing wrong but his hosts had gone out of their way to frustrate his every simple request and render him ill at ease. Under the smart of these real and/or imagined discourtesies, Travis pressed his thin lips even tighter and made up his mind to get even the only way he could: he would carry that precious championship home with him. He talked himself into the state of mind where he asserted he was damn glad the English had treated him so poorly. Now he would never relax for a moment in his efforts to win. "A reasonable number of fleas is good for a dog," he told his American friends gathered sympathetically around him at the Bell. "It keeps the dog from forgetting that he is a dog."

Travis' opponent in the first round—all the matches in the British Amateur except the final were eighteen holes—was a Mr. Holden of the Royal Liverpool Golf Club. Travis started out well by rolling in a couple of good-sized putts with the Schenectady, and went on to win 4 and 3. On the seventh hole Travis "called" Holden for soling his club in a bunker, and the remainder of the match was played in a very disagreeable atmosphere.

It had rained and rained hard that morning, and when Travis came off the course at ten minutes before two, he was soaked from head to foot. He asked the officials to allow him time to change into dry clothes, but he was informed that he was due on the first tee for his second-round match at twenty-eight minutes past two, unless he wished to default. Travis toweled himself in the hallway—he had not been given a locker—and went out in the same wet clothes to play his second-round opponent, James Robb. Robb was as fresh as a daisy. His morning-round opponent had defaulted, so he had avoided the downpour. On the out-nine, Travis hung on, and then, encouraged by a few long putts that found the cup, worked himself up to a two-hole lead with three to play. Robb halved the sixteenth and won the seventeenth, but the Old Man lasted out a half on the eighteenth for a tight 1-up victory.

Again the match had been marred by an unpleasant incident. On the eleventh hole Travis' idiot caddie, who had been making his usual quota of mistakes, had flagged the hole improperly for Robb. Robb was momentarily upset, but he was a sportsman and made no protest. When the match was over, Travis asked Robb if he could have his caddie, now that Robb had no further need for his services. Robb was perfectly willing, but the caddie-master, while not definitely turning down Travis' request for a change in caddies, managed to find some reason for inaction. Travis was stuck with the cross-eyed idiot for at least another day, if he remained in the tournament that long.

In the third round Travis defeated A. M. Murray 3 and 1. In the fourth round he came up against H. E. Reade, a golfer with a good all-round game. When Reade reached the fifteenth tee 2 up with only four holes to play, it looked as if the foreign invasion had been quelled. Travis chewed hard on his cigar and gave no outward sign of his distress. On the long fifteenth, he knocked in a fine 4. That made him one down with three to play. He followed with a birdie 2 on the 180-yard sixteenth, dropping his putt after sticking his tee shot twelve feet from the pin. Now Travis had drawn even with Reade. On the seventeenth, a 350-yard par 4, Reade just missed his putt for a 4 and Travis holed his. One up now with one to play, Travis held on with a halving 4 on the eighteenth, and that was the match—1 up.

Many Britishers who had not conceded Travis a chance of winning even one match against first-class golfers found themselves forced to revise their first estimates now that the dour, set-jawed, imperturbable man from America had knocked out four good opponents and won four good matches. Those who had scoffed at his mechanical swing and his lack of distance off the tees now admitted, quite openly, that he was a sound golfer. However, they believed he had gone as far as he was going to go. On the next day he would face Harold Hilton in the fifth round. Hilton had won two British Opens as well as two British Amateurs and stood forth as the greatest amateur in the world. He had trounced Travis when they had played in 1901. Against a master of Hilton's class, Travis was bound to fold. Sooner or later his drives would catch the high dunes down the fairways that they had been clearing by a scant matter of feet. Sooner or later those 40-footers and 20-footers he had been sinking with that center-shafted putter would begin to slide off.

In the enemy camp—and that term is not too strong, for Travis had urged his pugnacity upon his seconds—the Old Man's friends did everything in their power to steady and stimulate their hero. To take his mind off the championship, they played cribbage with him and fed him large portions of stout. To keep him on his toes, they extolled the abilities of Hilton and his other possible opponents. The British Amateur was now more than a golf tournament in their minds; it was an international feud.

On the next morning Walter Travis went out and defeated Hilton in their "return match." Travis won the first three holes and protected that lead by going out in 34.

Hilton cut the margin to two by winning the eleventh, but the Old Man snapped back hard, won the next three holes in a row and the match 5 and 4. Hilton had not played up to form, and Travis had not cracked.

For the first time now, the men who had been waiting for the invader to be ousted were confronted by the black thought that he could win, could very definitely win. In the sixth round—the semi-final—he would face Horace Hutchinson, and that was not too good. Hutchinson was now an old man, well past his peak. It would have been better if Hutchinson had lost to Robert Maxwell, as he had been expected to. By defeating Maxwell, Hutchinson had eliminated a man who could have probably stopped the foreign threat more robustly than himself. These forebodings proved correct. Against Hutchinson, Travis went out in 34 to go 3 up, but coming in he played his worst nine holes of the tournament. He took two 6s. Maxwell might have seized this opening and marched to victory. Hutchinson didn't. Where Travis faltered, he faltered. Instead of picking up holes, Hutchinson actually lost one. Travis closed out the match on the sixteenth green, 4 and 2. He had reached the final.

The one man who now stood between Travis and victory, or between Great Britain and calamity, was Edward "Ted" Blackwell. A tall, strong man, with heavy eyebrows, Blackwell could drive a golf ball farther than any man, pro or amateur, on the island. Once he had banged a guttie 358 yards on the straightaway, and another time he had driven the eighteenth green at St. Andrews, an even more colossal wallop. On the eve of the final Travis was nervous but confident. He had overcome his complex about his caddie. Now he regarded his chronic irritant as a being designed by Fortune to remind him at every glance of the full importance of his conquest.

Both Travis and Blackwell started out shakily. Neither had a 4 on the 366-yard first hole, but Travis' 5 was better than Blackwell's 6. Both men were on the second green in two, and then Travis, to the great consternation of the gallery, sent his 36-foot putt into the bottom of the cup for a winning 3. Neither of the players had spoken a word to each other on the first two holes. On the third tee, Travis ventured to break the ice with a complimentary remark on Blackwell's driving. Possibly because he was 2 down at the time and in no mood for conversation, Blackwell's answer was a sort of monosyllabic grunt and nothing more. Travis never again addressed Blackwell during their match nor did Blackwell at any time say so much as a word to Travis.

The men halved the third in 5s, and then Travis played an excellent 4 and a perfect 3 to win both the fourth and fifth and increase his lead to four holes. He lost the sixth, the treacherous Maiden, when he missed his first putt of the round. The gallery was so on edge that they applauded the miss. At the turn Blackwell was still 3 down. He won the tenth to cut his deficit to two holes, halved the eleventh, and the twelfth, and looked to be in position to pare away another hole on the thirteenth. Two good woods into the teeth of the wind left Blackwell with an easy pitch, while Travis, 100 yards farther back, had a long, difficult iron to play. Travis hit a low, boring shot well onto the green, and when Blackwell hooked his pitch badly, he lost the hole and went 3 down where he had stood the chance of being only 1 down. The next hole, the 505-yard Suez Canal, was a repetition of the thirteenth. Both hit good drives, with Blackwell some 35 yards in front. Travis played his brassie second about 25 yards short of the Suez Canal, the deep ditch running the width of the fairway. Blackwell also elected to play safe. He took out his cleek, and hitting the shot too cleanly, sent it into the ditch. Travis pitched on . . . and down went another long putt. The way he did it was what hurt. After he stroked a putt, he would stand absolutely still and eye the ball like Svengali as it dipped off the rolls and found its way into the cup. He acted as if there were no other possible outcome for the stroke.

Travis made no mistakes on the last four holes, and went to lunch with a comfortable 4-up lead.

When Travis started the afternoon round with a 7, the English gallery, which had been looking for any sign that the Old Man was cracking, thought that this moment had at last arrived. Travis killed off this hope by winning the second. He lost the third, and then roared back to take the next three holes with a 4 and two 3s and go 6 up with twelve holes to play. Blackwell managed to shave this down to 4 up at the turn, but coming in he was unable to do any better than halve five consecutive holes and carry the match to the fifteenth. When he failed to beat Travis' 5 on the long fifteenth, Blackwell had lost the match, 4 and 3, and Walter J. Travis had become the first "foreigner" ever to win the British Amateur Championship.

Travis' winning putt was greeted by a loud silence. Though the inevitability of his victory had been impressing itself upon the spectators hole by hole, the end of the match had left them stunned and still unbelieving. Then gradually, as the shock began to wear off, the gallery for the first time began to see Travis as he really was: a great golfer with a great heart. One man, who had been rooting against Travis all the way, turned to his fellows in the gallery and shouted, "Well, I'm damned glad. I'm damned glad." Another galleryite shook his head in admiration and soliloquized, "Travis could *write* with his putter if you put a nib on it." Some of the spectators still argued that Travis' win, much as they respected the man, was a fluke. He had putted his way to victory, won the championship solely because of the wizardry of his weird Schenectady. The men who really appreciated the game knew better. Inspired as Travis' putting had been at Sandwich, he had played excellent golf the entire week. In the rough cross-winds on his final rounds, when the least flaw in shot-making was exaggerated into a punishing error, he had stroked the ball cleanly down the fairways with his compact, controlled swing.

Exultant as he was over his victory, Travis was hurt by some of the remarks made by Lord Northbourne during the cup presentation. Northbourne's family had lived for centuries in the old castle on the hill close by the course. From time to time Northbourne came down from the hill to lend a hand in the ceremonies at Sandwich, regarding this as a genial display of interest in the affairs of his tenantry. His speeches were invariably long and maladroit. On this occasion Lord Northbourne spoke for almost an hour—dwelling at length on the early history of the county of Kent under the Romans, rehearsing the glories of British golf and British golfers, and then, very briefly, congratulating Mr. Travis on his triumph and piously hoping that such a disaster would

When the Old Man grew old, his beard became as white as the bunkers at Sandwich.

never again befall British sport. Travis hid his annoyance and made a short, graceful acceptance speech. The conquest was over.

Several years later, under a ruling by the R. & A., the Schenectady putter—and its cousins—was barred from British tournaments.

The Old Man grew older, but he got a few more licks in before he closed his tournament career. In the United States Amateur of 1904, it took three 2s by George Ormiston to knock him out. Ormiston played an orthodox 2 on the tenth, holed a full mashie for a 2 on the twelfth, and clinched the match by rolling in an approach shot from 125 yards out for a 2 on the seventeenth. (One of Travis' sympathizers sought to console him with the obvious remark that Ormiston had been extremely lucky. "You seem to forget," Travis answered him calmly, "that luck is a part of the game, and a good golfer must be good at all parts of the game.") Three times after this the Old Man won the medal in the Amateur, and in 1909 he led all the other amateur entries in the national Open. He never won the Amateur again, though. He could play superb golf for two or three rounds—rather similarly to the way Bill Tilden, after he reached fifty, could still hold his own with any tennis player for one set. But the Old Man's stamina was failing, and toward the end of the tournament week the youngsters could take him. He devoted more and more time to his other golf interests: the Old Guards clique at Palm Beach; the *American Golfer*, which he inaugurated and edited with a clear, bold hand; the designing and remodeling of golf courses. As a golf architect he was not noted for his inventiveness. Rather, he was a tightener-up of courses, a follower of the penal rather than the strategic school of design.

One day when he was remodeling some holes at the Essex County course in Massachusetts, Travis inadvertently disclosed the secret of his success as a golfer and, particularly, as a putter. He and the consulting parties were discussing the probabilities of turning a stretch of land into a new short hole. Asked how far he thought it was to a certain tree, Travis estimated the distance to be between 155 and 157 yards. "Why not say between a hundred and fifty-five and a hundred sixty yards, Walter?" one of the group asked. "It isn't," Travis answered. "It's between one fifty-five and one fifty-seven." He hadn't meant to be dogmatic, but he had seemed so sure of his estimate that the group decided to measure the distance and see how close the Old Man actually was. He was a little off. The tree was 157½ yards away. This incident impressed upon those to whom it was related a fact about Travis that they had always sensed but had never quite known: he was an infallible judge of distance, probably the greatest in this respect of all American golfers.

The Old Man finally gave up tournament golf in 1915 when he was well into his fifties. He finished like a true champion. He won the Metropolitan Amateur. On his route to victory he defeated five capable young men, including Jerry Travers. In his final match against John G. Anderson he sealed his victory on the home green with a gesture so completely fitting that it has the ring of high fiction: He lined up a 30-foot putt, and with the palms of his hands in direct opposition to each other to produce a pendulum stroke, tapped the ball and watched it meander off the roll and make its way confidently into the center of the cup.

JEROME D. TRAVERS— THE GREAT YOUNG MAN

From Jerry Travers down through Bill Campbell, a very high percentage of the ranking American amateur golfers have been the sons of well-to-do families, who were able to start the game young, develop under the guidance of the best teachers, play and practice whenever they chose. These factors, and particularly the last, afforded young men like Bob Gardner, Max Marston, Bobby Jones, Jess Sweetser, George Dunlap, Charlie Yates, Dick Chapman, and Frank Stranahan—to name a few of the many blessed with the advantages of life—a much easier avenue to championship golf than amateurs who had to work five days a week for a living, or, more precisely, to work when they would have liked to have been out on the course perfecting the intimate timing required of the topflight golfer. The amateur without a provided income could solve his problem of work versus golf by combining the warring elements and becoming a professional golfer—as did George Von Elm, Lawson Little, and, more recently, Cary Middlecoff, Gene Littler, Ken Venturi, and Johnny Miller, to name some of those who come first to mind. Failing this, he could ride on the prestige of a series of good showings into a job where a sympathetic boss, almost a sponsor, allowed him to take off for the fairways and get in the practice he needed in the weeks preceding an important tourney—as Chick Evans did, for instance, or Johnny Goodman or Harvie Ward. The amateur confined to weekend golf by the necessity of earning a living cannot hope to stand up to the rigors of championship play, no matter how talented he may be.

The story of Jerome D. Travers is more than the story of a rich man's son who made good in golf. It is the story of a pertinacious student and a gifted match-player. But it is still the story of a young man who had every assistance in his quest for championship honors, and as such it is nicely typical of the pattern that through the years has produced some of our finest shot-makers.

Jerome Dunstan Travers' adventures in golf began on the lawns of his father's estate at Oyster Bay on Long Island. When he was nine years old, Jerry tried out the game by hitting midiron shots from the windmill on the back lawn toward the house, 100 yards away. The next year, home from school, he teed a ball at the windmill and drove it through a window in the house. At his father's suggestion, Jerry then shifted the area of his industry to the larger front lawn. Here he improvised three shatter-proof holes. The first ran from the flagpole to an old oak 150 yards away; the second, from the oak to a narrow tree in the right-hand corner of the lawn 180 yards off; and the third stretched from the small tree back to the flagpole. Jerry set to work mastering his triangle. The first time he hit the tree on the first hole in one shot, he became highly excited and went to pieces; it took him seven blows to hit the narrow second "hole."

When he was thirteen Jerry began to play regularly at the Oyster Bay course. Matches with the three Mahon boys—two of them were caddies and one gave lessons—brought the youngster's game along in the right channels. Two years later Jerry's father joined the Nassau Country Club at Glen Cove and Jerry became a junior member. One day after he had lost a match to a boy his own age, Jerry was approached by Alex Smith, the pro at Nassau.

"Do you want to become a real golfer, kid," Alex asked, "or are you just going to dub around at the game?"

The fifteen-year-older said he wanted to become a real golfer.

"All right," said Alex. "Now that we understand each other, let's see what you can do."

Smith watched the youngster hit out a batch of balls and gave him his first lesson. He pointed out three distinct faults. The youngster was overswinging. He held his arms too stiff. His right hand was too much on top of the shaft.

Two years later, after constant practice and regular lessons with Smith, Jerry Travers won the Interscholastic Championship. That same summer—1904—he attracted national attention by defeating Walter Travis in the final of the Nassau Invitation tournament. Two holes down with five to play, Travers squared the match by the eighteenth and won it with a birdie on the 21st. His father was so jubilant over his boy's triumph that when Jerry asked him for two dollars to pay his caddie, he handed him a twenty-dollar bill by mistake.

This was the first of a long series of duels between Travers and Travis. It was a serious rivalry. The young man and the Old Man were of the same basic temperament: they always went out to win, not just to play well. It was also a friendly rivalry. After his defeat in the Nassau tournament, for example, Travis had remarked, "There is no aftermath of bitterness in such a defeat. It is a match I shall always recall with pleasure." For his part, Jerry Travers never forgot that the Old Man was a remarkable golfer and a

Always a dedicated
practicer, Jerry Travers,
the Young Man,
works on hopping stymies.

fine sportsman. At the time Jerry may have regarded their rivalry as one hard match after another from which he derived intense pain or pleasure, depending on the outcome. In retrospect, however, his duels with Travis formed the crucible in which a talented young golfer was made into the greatest match player of his decade.

In 1905 Jerry, who was then all of eighteen, defeated Travis 7 and 6 in the Metropolitan Amateur Championship. At Westbrook, Travis retaliated measure for measure. He overwhelmed Jerry 8 and 7 and thought that after that thrashing the boy would never be able to beat him again. He looked to be right when they met next at Shinnecock, for he pulled out the match on the 21st green when it was Jerry who had had the openings in the extra holes. But at Nassau, Jerry came back to win 4 and 2. For ten more years after this, the two bulldogs went after each other, and sometimes the young bulldog beat the old bulldog and sometimes he didn't. It was a rivalry from which both, really, emerged victorious.

The following year Jerry Travers captured his first big championship, the Metropolitan. The "Kid Champion" caught the fancy of the Eastern golf fans, and one New York reporter pulled out all the stops. "The feature of the winner's game," he wrote, "was the length of his full shots and their perfect direction. W. J. Travis in his palmiest days was never truer on line. Then again the youngster had a versatility in playing various iron and approach shots which few veterans could surpass, and what slight weakness there might have been in his game was an occasional lack of strength in his approach putts."

Jerome D. Travers—The Great Young Man

Travers was knocked out of the United States Amateur that year by Travis, with an assist going to the young man's loss of temper after a camera clicked as he was about to hit a shot. The next season, 1907, a more mature Travers climaxed his steady improvement by winning the Amateur at the Euclid Golf Club in Cleveland. Travers was then just twenty-one, a medium-sized young man of wiry build and the deceptive strength that usually accompanies it. Alex Smith had not been able to shorten his swing appreciably. The new champion's backswing was overly fast as well, but his hands were good and he brought the clubhead beautifully into the ball. He had corrected his tendency to lapse on the putting green. In the final of the Amateur against Archie Graham, he putted like a Travis, and came to the thirteenth green in the afternoon needing only to hole a simple 4-footer to close out the match. Then, under the unnerving realization that he would win if he sank the putt, Travers froze. He found he had no feel of his hands or the putter. Walking away from the ball, he explained to Graham that he just couldn't begin to go through the motions of the shot. "Oh, drop it anyway and end the agony," Graham told him shortly. "You couldn't miss it with your eyes shut." He dropped it.

Travers successfully defended his title in 1908 when the Amateur was played at the Garden City Golf Club. Stern-faced and uncommunicative, the twenty-two-year-old veteran of twelve golfing seasons marched relentlessly through one match after another and defeated Max Behr 8 and 7 in the final. His only moment of danger came in his semi-final match with Travis. All even coming to the seventeenth in an eighteen-hole match, the young man fired a magnificent second, a 240-yard brassie that hooked into the opening to the green and left him with a short putt for his birdie. To keep the match alive, Travis now had to win the eighteenth. The eighteenth at Garden City, Travis' home course, is a devilish short hole over water to a green surrounded flamboyantly by bunkers that Travis himself had designed and had refused to eradicate or make shallower in spite of the vigorous objections of the members. One bunker in particular struck the members as unfair—a pit six feet deep with perpendicular walls, to the left of the green. It was this bunker that Travis found with his tee shot. Travers put his tee shot on the green and stood by his ball as the Old Man lowered himself into the pit and passed out of sight. From the pit came the sound of a heavy thump, and then a spray of sand flew up, but no ball came into sight. Then another thump, another spray, but still no ball. The Old Man then pulled himself out of the bunker, walked over and congratulated Travers. One member of the gallery could not resist commenting in a stentorian stage whisper, "I guess the Old Man dug his own grave that time." Travis accepted the humor, nodded and smiled.

Travis was extremely pleased with the triumphs of Jerry Travers. He devoted the key pages in the first issues of the *American Golfer* to a pictorial analysis of the champion's game. Travis' editorial comments left no doubt that he believed that any young man learning the game would do well to adopt the basic features of Travers' style, if not his slightly open stance, very full pivot, and effortful followthrough. For this series of photographs the champion wore his favorite golf attire: a small cap, a regular white shirt buttoned at the neck but without a tie, cardigan sweater, white duck trousers, and white low-cut sneakers. He also wore his favorite expression: a bland poker face.

Jerry Travers made a disappointing showing in 1909 when he attempted to repeat the triumph of Walter Travis in the British Amateur. He was knocked out in the first round. He did not choose to defend his American Amateur crown that year—Bob Gardner, the Yale pole vaulter, won it—nor did he enter the event in 1910, when it went to Bill Fownes of Oakmont. The following spring Jerry returned to tournament play in earnest, having learned during his two lean years that a young man cannot be both a professional playboy and an amateur golf champion. He won the Metropolitan and the New Jersey Amateurs—he was now playing out of the Upper Montclair Country Club—but Harold Hilton beat him in the third round of the national Amateur. Travers put up a stout fight against Hilton after a poor morning round, but looked up on a 2-foot putt when he had the Englishman worried.

The Amateur of 1912 was called "the Blazing Championship." Only a few days before the tournament, the clubhouse of the Chicago Golf Club burned down; the weather was torrid; and in the final Jerry Travers cut loose with some of the hottest stretches of golf ever played in the championship. His opponent in the final was Chick Evans, a young Chicagoan who looked as awkward as a farm boy until he took his stance before a golf ball and released the prettiest one-piece swing on the continent. Three times before, he had reached the semi-final round of the Amateur. Now that Evans had chased his semi-final jinx and, moreover, was playing on home ground, his supporters could not see how the local star could be beaten. Travers had been playing much less convincing golf than Evans, but the Easterners who had come out to watch the championship were confident that their man would rise to the occasion and produce his best golf when he had to. On the eve of the final, sectional feeling ran high and the wagering was heavy.

Travers was lucky to finish the morning round only 1 down. Where Evans was stroking the ball from tee to green with his lyrical accuracy, Travers was all over the course. Jerry could not correct the hook he was getting with his woods off the tee, and was forced to drive with an iron most of the time. He hung on by some courageous scrambling, playing deft pitch-and-run shots on the sun-baked course and canning three putts of over twenty feet. The last of these was a 35-footer on the eighteenth green that cut Evans' margin to 1 up and, simultaneously, pared away some of Chick's confidence. Chick had been "inside" of Travers and had visions of going to lunch 3 up, and certainly not lower than 2.

The fourth hole of the afternoon round decided the match. Evans had now lost his lead, and the partisan gallery was beginning to feel uneasy as they saw his usually smiling face grow long and fretful. Maybe Chick could pull himself together if Travers would do something wrong. On the fourth tee Travers made a mistake, a bad one. His drive was a wide, sweeping hook that flew over the edge of the fairway and headed for

Jerry Travers at the Euclid Country Club in 1907, the scene of his first victory in the National Amateur. All in all, Jerry took the Amateur four times, a record surpassed only by Bobby Jones. Travers was not a great medal scorer, but he had the ideal temperament for match play—dogged when behind, ruthless when ahead.

the high, tough rough that would cost him one or possibly two recovery strokes. The ball, however, slapped into a mound and rebounded back onto the fairway. This break shattered whatever fight was left in Evans. Travers won the hole and saw to it that his opponent had no further openings. He raced to the turn in 34 strokes to win six of the nine holes and go 5 up. He won the tenth as Chick plodded down the fairway in a daze. Two holes later he ended the slaughter, 7 and 6. On the walk-in Jerry allowed himself to relax for the first time. During the match he had spoken to only one person, Freddy Herreshoff, a golf crony of many years' standing who caddied for him in the final.

In 1913 the national Amateur was played once again over the tight, multi-trapped course of the Garden City Golf Club. Never noted for his medal scores, Travers this time barely qualified. On the famous last hole, the short one over the pond, Jerry took a 7. One more shot and he would have been out. As it was, he gained the chance to defend his title by winning a place in the most amazing playoff of all times. Twelve players fighting for eleven places teed up on the first hole to determine which one of them would not qualify. This distinction fell to Heinie Schmidt, the man who had the best drive of the lot. Instead of making sure that he hit his second shot well over the bunker protecting the green, Heinie elected to go for the pin with a niblick, caught the far edge of the bunker, and that was that. There was a further note of irony in Schmidt's elimination. Had he used his head and played in the clothes the steaming weather demanded, Heinie would have been among the lowest scorers. Instead, Heinie wore the heavy tweed golf suit he had just purchased in England—cap, jacket, and knickers in a large hound's-tooth check. Any sensible man would have discarded this English-winter outfit, but Heinie—he had added red socks and a matching bow tie—was going to show the boys how the well-accoutered Britisher dressed, and he balked at peeling off his new suit even when the men in shirtsleeves were feeling the heat.

Once assured of a place in the match-play rounds, Jerry Travers got down to business. Bellwood, the pro at Garden City, showed him what he was doing wrong: his left wrist was breaking in toward his body as he started the club down. After this correction, Jerry was able to squeak by in his early matches although he was far from his top form. He shanked his irons periodically, and was getting that perniciously sharp hook with his driver. He practiced between rounds, and when his woods still gave him trouble, decided to use his black driving-iron off the tee in his semi-final match should his opponent, an unheralded youngster from Boston named Francis Ouimet, put up a battle. Ouimet put up such a battle that Travers used his driver only twice during the morning round—he hit one fair and one very poor shot with it—and on the second eighteen Travers did not use his driver at all.

Against Ouimet, Travers went to lunch with a 1-up margin produced by a 20-foot putt on the home green. In the afternoon Jerry won the first hole, but then the cool young man from Boston came fighting back to take the second and the third and square the match. Ouimet went 1 up when he took the seventh, and appeared to be on his way to add to his lead on the eighth when he planted his second shot, a 180-yard iron to an uphill green, eight feet from the cup. Travers took a little more time than usual before hitting his second. It would be a crucial stroke and he wanted to think it out fully. A mild practice swing and finally he was ready to play. He came through with a shot that covered the flag all the way, sat down smartly on the green, and ended up ten inches from the hole. Ouimet missed his try for a birdie, and knew then that he was licked.

In the final Jerry had a comparatively easy time with John G. Anderson, 5 and 4. At the ripe old age of twenty-six the erstwhile Kid Champion had won his fourth, and what proved to be his last, Amateur Championship. No player before had won the crown four times, and the best golf heads, with reason, could not see any later golfer equaling this record. With the exception of Jones, no one ever has.

Off the course Jerry Travers was an amiable person, but during a match he was as cold as a halibut, and as expressionless. He was aware that his manner distracted many of his opponents, but this was secondary and somewhat accidental. What was important was that alone with his game, keen but not tense, Jerry could play winning golf. Along with Hagen, although Hagen's temperament was quite different, he stands out as a golfer who could somehow win matches when he was far off his game. He had the ability to hit an iron ten inches from the cup, like that crusher against Ouimet, at the critical moment. He developed into a remarkable putter, one to be ranked in the same category with Travis, and in this department again his forte was the unexpected ones—which means the putts his opponent did not expect him to drop and which broke hearts and hopes when they did. Like most rich men's sons who have played a sport well, Travers could afford to play the game as if his next meal depended on winning.

CHILDE HAROLD'S PILGRIMAGE

In the interim between Jerry Travers' two-year reigns in 1907–8 and 1912–13, the United States Amateur Championship acquired an international flavor when Harold Horsfall Hilton crossed the Atlantic to play in the event in 1911. Hilton held a position among British amateurs akin to Harry Vardon's unquestioned supremacy among the pros. In 1900, 1901, and 1911, Hilton had triumphed in the British Amateur, and before that, in 1892 and 1897, he had done the unthinkable for an amateur and won the British Open. In the spring of 1911, just when it looked as if he would carry off his third Open title, he had stumbled. On the short sixteenth at Sandwich, the 70th hole of the grind, Hilton had caught a trap with his iron off the tee. A 3 on that short hole would have won for him; his 5 left him one stroke behind Vardon and Arnaud Massy, who tied for first. Had Hilton won, the thought of coming to America might never have entered his mind. He lost, and set out to drown his sorrows in the wine of victory, in our Amateur.

As Harold Hilton sailed for America, the press came up with a bright tag for his purposeful visit—"Childe Harold's Pilgrimage." It was a good phrase and deserved to stick, although, as the literal-minded pointed out, Hilton was a middle-aged man and not a child and rather devoid of the other qualities that made a Byronic hero. He was medium-sized, suave, contained, and worldly—the kind of chap you would expect to take plenty of time choosing the colors in his hose and who would have H. H. H. neatly engraved on his cigarette case. He smoked fifty cigarettes on the days he played golf—another record that Jones beat—and in the evenings exhibited a continuous concern for the King's health and the health of the American president. He appreciated the nuances of the English language and expressed himself with practiced delicacy. He was sensible about his golf. He knew precisely how well he could play, and experience had taught him that few amateurs could keep up with him, so he played his own game and let nature take its course.

Hilton's challenge in 1911 altered the attitudes of the Americans assembled at the Apawamis Club in Rye, New York. For the first time since Harriman's victory in 1899, the dominance of the native-born players was endangered. The customary rivalry between the Eastern stars and the Western stars was momentarily shelved, and the homebreds united their energies to throttle the foreign threat. (In many ways Hilton's invasion was Travis' in reverse.) Chicagoans would have preferred one of their own boys—say, Chick Evans or Albert Seckel or Paul Hunter—to gain the glory of stopping Hilton, but if Jerry Travers or Oswald Kirkby or some other Easterner could turn the trick, well, the honor of America came ahead of that of Chicago. Every loyal American prayed for a week of sunshine to sere the turf and harden the ground. On a wet, slow course, they confided to one another, Hilton would be a much tougher man to beat.

It rained. As everyone feared, Hilton found the soggy turf to his liking. But even on the dryer days, he played crisp, steady golf. There was nothing poetic about his swing. Before playing each shot, he planted his feet with deliberation, waggled his club for a moment, and then, with a little jump forward onto his toes, took the club back quickly and brought it down into the ball with a rapid hitting action. It was a deceptive style, for beneath this fast smash of a swing the studied art of controlling the ball lay concealed. Hilton thought out each shot well in advance. Whenever the wind or the topography advised it, he played intentional slices or hooks—or perhaps it is more accurate to say that he played the shot for drift or draw. This is an easier thing to do with irons than with woods, but in his wood play Hilton had a phenomenal skill at bending the shot to order. Unlike Joe Kirkwood, the trick-shot artist of later days, Hilton could also hit the ball straight when he wanted to. Sometimes he played his approaches in the pitch-and-run style and at other times he lofted the ball to the green with a dancing backspin. When he appeared at Apawamis, Hilton was a shot or two past his peak but he showed the record galleries some subtleties of the game the native sons had not yet mastered.

Hilton started off by taking the qualifying medal with 76-74—150, two strokes better than Bob Gardner and Albert Seckel. In the first round, playing well within himself, he disposed of Samuel Graham of Greenwich 3 and 2. Next he took care of Robert C. Watson, the secretary of the U.S.G.A., by the score of 11 and 10, carding a nice 73 on the first eighteen. Moving into the third round, he met Jerry Travers. On the first eighteen Hilton did not play his best game, but Travers was very erratic and stood 4 down to the Englishman at lunch. Travers shook some great golf shots out of his bag in the afternoon, and by the 27th had reduced the Englishman's margin to one hole. Calm and assured, Hilton stalled him off with four halves in a row, won the 32nd and 33rd, and shut the door on Jerry, 3 and 2, with a half on the 34th. C. W. Inslee of Wykagyl fell an easy victim to Hilton's steadiness in the semi-final round; Hilton led by one hole at the ninth and slowly drew away to be 4 up at the eighteenth, 6 up at the 27th, and 8 up with six holes to play. In making his way to the final, Hilton had had to exert himself only during his match with Travers.

Hilton's opponent in the final was Fred Herreshoff. Herreshoff had been there before—in 1904, when he was a boy of seventeen and not good enough to stay with Chandler Egan. This nephew of Nat Herreshoff, the famous boat designer, had grown up into a broad, easygoing giant who could paste his tee shots ten or fifteen yards beyond the best efforts of men who prided themselves on their long-hitting. Herreshoff took an understandable delight in his slugging prowess, and perhaps the other departments of his game suffered from lack of attention. In any event, his irons were inconsistent and his putting was weak. When his driving was on, it took inspired golf to beat Herreshoff. When it was off, he was just another golfer. Freddy drank a good deal, but he apparently played as well after a big night as he did after an evening by the fireside. At Apawamis he fell into a hot putting streak that helped him through a much harder bracket than Hilton faced. In the semi-finals he had been expected to lose to Chick Evans but had stormed back after being 3 down at the halfway mark and put Chick out on the 34th green.

Hilton started off to make short work of Herreshoff. Actually, he did nothing exceptional himself but kept his shots on-line and let Herreshoff hand him three holes on the first nine through spotty driving and multiple putting. On the in-nine Hilton ran into errors himself and made no further headway until the eighteenth green, where he got down a 12-footer to give himself a comfortable four-hole lead to work on. When the match was resumed in the afternoon, Herreshoff presented Hilton with another hole when he pulled his drive on the first. Freddy topped his drive on the second but a fine chip enabled him to halve in 4s. Still 5 down. On the 310-yard third, Freddy tried to win the hole with his tee shot, lost his timing by pressing, and hooked his drive into an almost unplayable lie. It took him three strokes to reach the green and, of course, this cost him the hole. He was now 6 down. It looked like a rout. Freddy managed to halve the fourth, and the fifth as well when Hilton, with a chance to become 7 up, three-putted. Encouraged by this reprieve, on the 330-yard sixth he played three fine shots, the last a sizable putt for a winning three. This was Herreshoff's first birdie of the day, and it gave him a terrific mental lift. He went on to halve the seventh and win both the short eighth and the 612-yard ninth. He reached the turn only 3 down.

Herreshoff had played himself back into the match. On the fourth (or 22nd) tee, all that the three thousand spectators had hoped for was some sort of a comeback by the American that would prolong the match a respectful number of holes and prevent Hilton's winning by too humiliating a margin. Now that Herreshoff had taken three of the last four holes, the spectators discovered that they would be satisfied with nothing less than an American victory. They realized that it would take very hot golf for a man to pick up three holes down the stretch from a campaigner of Hilton's caliber, but then, Herreshoff was now playing very hot golf. He was beginning to hit the ball fairly straight as well as for distance off the tees, and he had regained his putting touch.

Herreshoff did not let up, now that he had Hilton on the run. He pulled his drive on the tenth, but a chip shot stone-dead to the pin enabled him to halve in par 4s. He won the eleventh, to become only 2 down, when Hilton sent his tee shot out-of-bounds. Now, Herreshoff and his excited gallery knew that the Englishman, for all his studied composure, was feeling the pressure. On the twelfth, a 241-yard par 3, Freddy boomed his drive onto the green, won the hole, and was now only 1 down. He was moving but the holes were running out and one error might ruin the stirring rally that had won for him five out of the last seven holes. On the thirteenth Herreshoff left himself a hard 15-foot putt for a half in 4—and made it, when he knew he had to. He played the long fourteenth in a poor 6, but Hilton also messed up his fairway shots and could do no better than a 6 himself. With four holes to go, the Englishman still retained his narrow one-hole lead and was playing wisely if not too well. He appeared almost as debonair as when he had stood 6 up, and he hit his shots with the same cool urbanity, and yet it was obvious that he was not striking the ball at all well for him and was trying to avoid errors rather than gambling on bold winning shots. He was going to force Herreshoff to do the gambling.

On the fifteenth, the 33rd hole of the match, Herreshoff smashed out a long drive, and a lofted approach left him a birdie putt of some fifteen feet. He pushed the putt off-line. Still 1 down. On the 217-yard sixteenth (or 34th) he socked his tee shot hole-high but was off in the rough. Then he played a beautiful recovery to within four feet of the cup. Again he had the putt for the hole, and this time he made it. The match was now all square. Herreshoff's courageous comeback had won six holes for him, and he had not lost a hole since the 21st. Freddy was now in the driver's seat. When a player rallies down the stretch and catches his opponent, in golf, like in all sports, nine times out of ten his momentum, and his opponent's loss of confidence, will carry him on to victory.

Freddy had a chance to win the 35th but he rimmed the cup from five feet in his try for a birdie. He had a 7-footer for the hole and the match on the 36th, and again he failed to get it down. The gallery groaned, and then was off for the first hole, where Hilton and Herreshoff would begin their sudden-death struggle now that they had finished all even after thirty-six holes of grueling attack and counter-attack.

The first hole at Apawamis is a testing par 4, slightly uphill after the drive. In 1911 it measured 377 yards and called for two good shots. There was trouble on the right—rough, rocks, and woods. To the right of the green the ground sloped up moderately, and players might have used it as a bank for their approaches had the incline not been studded with rocks. There was less trouble on the left, and practically none whatsoever as Herreshoff and Hilton mounted the tee, for a wall of spectators lined that edge of the fairway all the way from tee to green.

It was Herreshoff's honor. He hit a good one, long and down the middle. Hilton faded his tee shot a bit but the ball sat down before it reached the rough. As usual, he was shorter off the tee than Herreshoff and prepared to play the odd. He looked the shot over, and asked for a spoon. He set his feet heavily in place, made that little spring onto his toes, and brought the club down fast. If Hilton had been playing for drift, he had overdone it. The ball streaked off to the right, heading straight for the rocky slope—and trouble. It was a poorly hit shot and deserved whatever harsh ricochet befell it; it would probably end up deep in the woods. The ball struck the incline hard—and dribbled easily down the slope and onto the green, well onto the green. For Hilton it was the luckiest of breaks. For Herreshoff it was the kiss of death. He half topped his approach short of the green. He was still twenty feet short of the pin with his chip. Hilton would almost surely get down in two for a 4, and to keep the match alive, Herreshoff had to sink his 20-footer. It was never in. Hilton, 1 up, thirty-seven holes.

Hilton's spoon to the 37th green became the most-discussed single shot ever played in an American tournament. Eyewitnesses could not agree as to what actually had happened when Hilton's ball struck the incline. Some men who were in a perfect position to see the shot were positive that the ball had evaded the rocks and taken a normal carom off the turf. Others who were in an equally good position were equally certain that the ball had struck a rock—and they could point out the exact culprit. In time, golf fans throughout the country, undoubtedly because the rock story made Hilton's victory seem less deserved, adopted this explanation. Golfers who visited Apawamis for the first time were let down when they found out that they had heard wrong and that there was no Hilton Rock nearby the first green duly inscribed with the grim facts of the extra hole.

Hilton had no comment to make on the winning break or on his campaign in general. However, his traveling companion, a Mr. Philip Samson, got some things off his chest when the London reporters interviewed him. Samson explained that he had never seen a gallery as unruly as the three thousand who had dogged the players at Apawamis. They didn't know the first thing about golf or golf deportment. Whenever Herreshoff won a hole they hollered and shook rattles. The officials, Samson opined, were just as bad. They were continually yelling at the crowd through megaphones, often when the players were hitting. Now the reporters could understand why Hilton had not been his usual impregnable self during the latter stages of the match.

Hilton's victory proved to be a blessing in disguise for American golfers. In the cool of reflection, the ranking amateurs came to understand how faulty they had been in presuming that they had already caught up with the best standards of play in Britain. Bizarre ending or no bizarre ending, the middle-aged Britisher had played better golf during the week at Apawamis than any of the homegrown hopefuls. Now they knew that they would have to work harder if they wanted to be the best golfers this side of the Nizhni Novgorod Country Club.

The effect of Hilton's victory on Americans who did not play golf was even more significant. Travis' overseas heroics in 1904 had never been circulated beyond the clubhouses, but the Hilton–Herreshoff match, because of its native setting, became a topic of the day for thousands of Americans. They were not at all pleased that a foreigner had carried one of our championship cups out of the country, and men who had never cared a straw about golf before now wanted to know the real inside story. The press was a good touchstone. A New York newspaper that had referred to the Englishman as "Horace H. Hilton" on his arrival got the name right when he left.

If it was solace American golf fans were seeking, they could find it in the fact that in the same year Hilton carried off the U.S. Amateur trophy, a homebred for the first time won the U.S. Open. Not that Johnny McDermott's victory could balance Hilton's. In the first place, McDermott had not beaten any "real foreigners," just the Scottish- and English-born professionals who had become as permanent a part of the American scene as Swedish masseurs and Chinese laundrymen. And, in the second place, in 1911 the Open was not as important a championship as the Amateur, for the very ample reason that no native son had ever won it. From its unofficial inception in 1894—when Willie Dunn beat Willie Davis and Willie Campbell, and many Americans had deduced that every golf pro had to be named Willie—the Open had been a gathering of the clans. The Smiths and the Nichollses and the Rosses and the McLeods exchanged news from home, chatted about the courses they were designing and the wealthy duffers they were stuck with, and topped off their annual convention with seventy-two holes of medal play to see which one of the old familiar faces was playing the best golf that week. The winner received $300 and became even more godlike in the eyes of his pupils.

The two outstanding champions in the early days of the Open were Willie Anderson and Alex Smith. Anderson picked up his first title in 1901 when he defeated Alex in the playoff at Myopia, north of Boston, after they had tied at 331. Before he succumbed to a lingering illness, Anderson won the Open three more times, in '03, '04, and '05. Along with Jones and Hogan, the dour, flat-swinging Scot stands as the only four-time winner of the event. Alex Smith won it twice. (His brother Willie had crashed through before him in 1899.) After many seasons as a top contender, Alex finally made the grade in 1906. In winning, he totaled 295 for his four rounds, the first time anyone had broken 300 in the championship. (At the time, this performance was viewed as nothing short of miraculous, and experts doubted if Smith's record would ever be broken. Only three years later, George Sargent returned a total of 290 in winning the Open over the moderately easy Englewood Golf Club, in New Jersey. Then the experts were just as positive that no one would ever again come close to Sargent's mark.) Alex Smith was a hearty man with a grand sense of humor and a temperament that is often the crucial difference between a splendid player and a champion. He never took his golf too seriously, never dawdled before a shot. His motto for putting was "Miss 'em quick." Alex won his second championship in 1910 when a person of less equable temperament might have groaned himself groggy. On the 72nd green he missed a simple 3-foot putt that would have given him the championship outright then and there. He grinned it off—and meant it—and the next day went out and won the playoff hands down from his kid brother Macdonald and Johnny McDermott.

The victory by a homebred, when it finally came in 1911, was a surprise and a shock, and yet it should not have been. The American pros had been gradually closing the gap between themselves and the foreign-born professionals. In the 1909 Open, Tommy McNamara of Boston had scored a remarkable 69—to become the first man to break 70 in major competition in America—and had gone down the homestretch neck and neck with the winner, Sargent. The next year, McDermott, the chesty little pro from Atlantic City, had reached the playoff only to lose to Alex Smith. Sooner or later a homebred was bound to snap the monopoly of the transplanted, and McDermott did it in 1911 at the Chicago Golf Club, when he again tied for first and this time won the play-off. The following year McDermott demonstrated that he was a worthy champion by successfully defending his title at the Country Club of Buffalo before a happy gallery that included a young assistant pro from Rochester, Walter Hagen.

McDermott had expected to win at Chicago and Buffalo. He expected to win every tournament he entered. As shy as Mark Spitz and as reserved as Howard Cosell, McDermott feared no man. He was willing to wager on his ability to outplay any golfer in the world—Vardon not excepted—any time, any place, and for any amount of money. For two or three seasons, while his nerve held high, the 130-pound bantam-cock was almost as good as he thought he was. In the Shawnee Open of 1913 he did defeat Vardon. And then, almost as quickly as he had appeared, McDermott vanished. The nerves on which he had relied so heavily to carry him to the top suddenly snapped. By 1915 he was forced to retire from active tournament competition. Four scant years after Johnny McDermott had won at Chicago, golfers had to pause a moment and ponder before they could remember the name of the little firecracker who was the first American to win the United States Open.

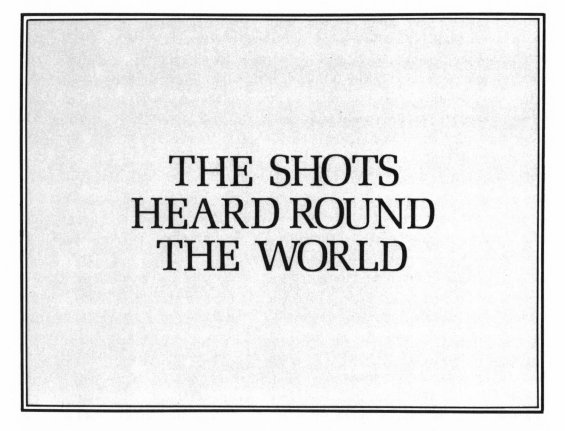

THE SHOTS
HEARD ROUND
THE WORLD

Whenever the peerless Harry Vardon came to America, something of great consequence invariably happened. Vardon made his second tour of this country in 1913, with the backing of Lord Northcliffe, the owner of the *Times* of London. For his series of exhibition matches, Vardon had in Edward "Ted" Ray the ideal partner, a perfect Pythias for their four-ball matches and a dramatically long hitter born to attract galleries. Whereas Vardon's swing was a flawless fusion of grace and power, Ray was all power. A bulky, slope-shouldered man standing an inch over six feet and weighing about two hundred pounds, Ted Ray threw all of his weight and strength into his strokes. He broke the rules of correct body movement right and left. He swayed on his backswing and came into the ball with a lurch, but he could get away with it because of the fundamental rhythm of his swing and the grooved arc of his clubhead. He could be wild, all right, but he had won the British Open at Muirfield in 1912 and had done this by clearly outplaying Vardon, James Braid, J. H. Taylor, Sandy Herd, and the other formidable British professionals. A large laissez-faire mustache gave Ray's otherwise mild face a rather fearsome aspect. He played in a long, loose tweed jacket and a crushed felt hat, and was never seen on or off a golf course minus a pipe, usually a big Sherlock Holmes model.

The Vardon–Ray tour of 1913 was an unprecedented success. Wherever they played, record or near-record crowds turned out to learn from watching Vardon how easy the game became in the hands of the master and to gasp at Ray's Brobdingnagian tee shots and his surprisingly delicate touch on the greens. Bobby Jones, a boy of eleven, saw the Englishmen when they played an exhibition in Atlanta after the national Open, and he always remembered one recovery played by Ray as the greatest golf shot he ever saw. After a long but wild drive, Ray found his line to the green directly stymied by a spreading tree more than forty feet high. Since his ball lay about thirty feet from the base of the tree, lofting over it was out of the question, and the spectators speculated as to whether he would try to slice or hook it around the obstacle. Ray took a look at the green 170 yards away and pulled out his mashie-niblick. Then, as Jones tells it, "he hit the ball harder, I believe, than I have ever seen a ball hit since, knocking it down as if he would drive it through to China. Up flew a divot the size of Ted's ample foot. Up also came the ball, buzzing like a partridge from the prodigious spin imparted by that tremendous wallop—almost straight up it got, cleared the tree by several yards, and sailed on at the height of an office building, to drop on the green not far from the hole."

Another stop on the Vardon–Ray tour was Chicago, where one of their opponents was a left-hander. He played way over his head during the match and, bent on doing a little fishing afterwards, approached Vardon and asked him whom he considered to be the best left-handed golfer he had ever seen during his lifetime on the links. "Never saw one who was worth a damn," grunted Vardon.

Ray and Vardon interrupted their tour in mid-September to play in the national Open, held at The Country Club in Brookline, outside Boston. Two other European professionals were in the field assembling there—Wilfred Reid from Banstead Downs, in England, and the diminutive French star Louis Tellier. Johnny McDermott was primed to defend his title, and Mike Brady, Tommy McNamara, and Jerry Travers, among the homebreds, and Macdonald Smith and Jim Barnes, among the transplanted Britons, were on hand for what loomed as the most turbulent tournament ever staged in this country.

The 1913 Open was the big leagues, the big test for American golf—no question about it. The United States had demonstrated that it could hold its own in international sports competition by defeating teams representing Great Britain in tennis, yachting, and polo, but was it still too early to hope for a declaration of independence on the golf course? It could be done, of course. McDermott had confessed to his countrymen that he was just as good as Vardon, and Brady and McNamara knew The Country Club course by heart. Yet when Americans weighed the mild talents of the native-born players against the furious talent of Ray and the genius of Vardon, they reluctantly concluded that it might probably take another few years.

Because of the large number of entries, the qualifying round of thirty-six holes was divided into three sections, with some of the players assigned to the first day of play and the rest finishing up on the second. Vardon led the first-day qualifiers with a total of 151, a stroke ahead of twenty-year-old Francis Ouimet, a local boy who held the Massachusetts State Amateur title and had given Jerry Travers quite a tussle in the semi-finals of the national Amateur. Mac Smith had played two steady 77s and would bear watching. On the second day, Ted Ray paced the qualifiers with 148, three strokes better than his countryman Reid. McDermott and Brady played poorly, though they managed to qualify. A kid named Hagen playing his first national tournament hit the ball impressively in posting a total of 157.

With the formality of the qualifying round out of the way, and no casualties among the favorites, the players started the championship test—seventy-two holes of medal play (thirty-six on both days) over a hard par-71 layout. At the halfway mark Reid and Vardon were tied for the lead with 147, two strokes ahead of Ray and three ahead of Mac Smith and Barnes. The youngsters, Ouimet and Hagen, were still in the running with 151, as was Tellier with 152, but McDermott and Brady were still having trouble. Travers was too far behind at 156, and McNamara had blasted his chances by adding a wretched 86 to his opening 73.

At the end of 54 holes, Vardon, Ray, and Ouimet were tied for the lead at 225. Ouimet had caught the two favorites with a round of 74, but no man in his right mind could expect the inexperienced amateur to stand up to the enormous pressure of the last round of a major tournament. Reid had blown sky-high. Tellier had not made up enough ground. Hagen, Smith, Barnes, and McDermott would have to play sub-par golf to catch the leaders, and the sodden condition of the course definitely argued against the realization of any such hopes.

Ray was the first one of the leaders to finish his fourth round. He had taken a 79 on the rain-soaked course and would have to stand by at 304 and see how his rivals fared. One by one they faded. Vardon straggled home with a 79, which was only good enough for a tie with Ray. Harry's putting, his old Achilles' heel, had let him down. Back to the clubhouse over the grapevine came the news that Barnes' rally had petered out. Hagen and Smith were done too. Tellier had a fighting chance until he reached the twelfth, and then he had cracked wide open. Simultaneously the report came in that Ouimet, the one man left who could catch Vardon and Ray, had gone to the turn in 43 and had killed off what slim chance remained for him by taking a 5 on the short tenth. To get his 304 now, Francis would have to play the last eight holes in one stroke under even 4s, and under the circumstances that was asking for the impossible. The young man deserved enormous credit for sticking with the Englishmen as long as he had.

Ouimet did not think he was finished. Even when he had taken a 5 on the par-4 twelfth after getting his par on the eleventh, he did not give up the fight. On the thirteenth tee he figured out that he would now have to play the last six holes in twenty-two strokes, 2 under par, to gain a tie. He went over the six holes in his mind and selected the thirteenth and the sixteenth as the ones on which he had the best chance to pick up the two birdies he needed. He had been putting for 3s regularly on the thirteenth, a short par 4; the sixteenth was a relatively easy par 3, but Francis had not gotten a deuce there all week and had a hunch that this could be the time.

Francis got his birdie on the thirteenth, but had to hole a chip from the edge of the green to do it. On the fourteenth, he got his par 5 comfortably enough. He hit a nice drive on the fifteenth, a testing par 4, and then completely mis-hit his approach. To stay in the hunt, Francis had to get down in 2 from a snug lie in the rough, and did this by playing a superb chip shot less than a yard from the pin. He came to the short sixteenth, the hole he had a hunch he might birdie. His hunch was wrong. Francis had to sink a 9-foot putt to get his par.

To tie now, Ouimet was faced with bagging that all-important birdie on either the seventeenth, a dogleg to the left, or on the eighteenth, a somewhat lengthier par 4. The gallery appreciated as clearly as the boy himself the full size of that task. There was an almost tangible tension in the air as Francis followed his drive down the seventeenth with a jigger shot some twenty feet from the pin. On the green the young man did not fidget or pose. He looked over the sliding downhill, sidehill putt, and concentrating so intensely that he did not hear the blare of automobile horns that unnerved the gallery, stroked the ball boldly for the cup. The ball took the roll nicely, slipped rapidly down the slope, struck the back of the cup hard, and stayed in. The keyed-up spectators crammed around the seventeenth green could not contain themselves. They yelled, pummeled each other joyously, swatted their friends with umbrellas, and shouted delirious phrases they had not thought of since boyhood. Jerry Travers, the icicle himself, jumped three feet in the air. The stirring battle of the hometown David against the two Goliaths had cut deeper into their emotions than the gallery had been aware.

Francis Ouimet was the calmest man on the course as he walked to the eighteenth tee. He needed a par 4 now to tie Ray and Vardon. He forgot about everything else but getting that 4. His drive was satisfactory, straight and long enough. He hit his second shot accurately and saw it kick up the mud at the top of the soft bank in front of the green. His chip shot left him five feet short of the cup. Then, with a complete disregard for the feelings of the spectators, he stepped up to his putt as if he had not the vaguest idea that history was riding on that shot. He placed his putter in front of the ball once, took a look at the hole, and hit the ball firmly into the back of the cup.

The moment the ball entered the hole, the rarefied air of The Country Club was filled with a mass cheer and individual outbursts the like of which for pure spontaneity and heartfelt joy may have never been equaled on any golf course. The impossible and the historic had happened, and the spectators felt it in the pits of their stomachs. In what was a positive ecstasy, they mobbed their hero and hoisted him on their shoulders and might have done him physical damage with their demonstrations of affection and congratulation had some cool head not reminded them that Francis Ouimet had to play off the next morning with Harry Vardon and Ted Ray.

Americans turned to their newspapers the following morning and read about the incredible accomplishment of Francis Ouimet. Outside of Massachusetts, no one had ever heard of him. Who was this Ouimet? What had he done before? How was that name pronounced—*Oymet* or *Umet* or *Weemay* or what?

The name was pronounced *Weemet*. In time the country received the answers to the other questions and learned that its hero was ten-tenths a hero, compounded from the very best parts of Charles Dickens and Booth Tarkington with a touch of Horatio Alger.

When Francis Ouimet was starting grade school, his father moved the family from a thinly populated section of Brookline to a modest house he had bought across the street from The Country Club. Mr. Ouimet was a workingman with no interest in golf, and had it not been for the proximity of the course his sons might have emptied their childhood enthusiasm in other channels. Francis first walked the fairways as a trespasser, on his way to and from the Putterham School. On these walks he found a few gutta-perchas now and then—Silvertowns, Ocobos, Vardon Flyers, Henleys, and the other popular brands of 1900. No one ever seemed to lose a club on the course, though, so Francis' golf for several years consisted of hoarding his collection of balls. One afternoon in 1902, while kicking his way home through the rough, he uncovered his first rubber-cored ball. He recognized that it was different from his other balls, but had no idea why it was different. It was a beat-up arc, so Francis painted the ball and put it in the oven to dry, beside the bread his mother was baking. Shortly afterwards a terrific stench came from the oven. The heat had melted away the gutta-percha cover and left a smoking glob of elastic bands. Mrs. Ouimet had to throw out the batch of bread, which was the least of her worries since she had first thought that the house was on fire. This incident may have been at the bottom of her distrust of golf. Mrs. Ouimet was sure the game would be the ruination of her boy.

Shortly after Francis' older brother Wilfred had become a caddie at The Country Club, a member had given him one of his old sticks. While Wilfred was off caddying, Francis practiced swinging with the club. He watched the tournaments across the street, and whenever he saw someone play an exceptionally good shot, he photographed the golfer's form in his mind's eye and then rushed home to try out the swing himself. Wilfred was as crazy about the game as Francis. It was his idea that they convert the land behind their house into three golf holes—slightly more primitive than Jerry Travers' triangle, since they took in a gravel pit, a swamp, a brook, and patches of long rough grass. The first hole was 150 yards long, with a brook crossing the "fairway" about 100 yards from the tee. The second was a 50-yard pitch, and the third was a combination of the first and second played backwards. The boys built themselves some greens and sank tomato cans for their cups.

On one of his trips into downtown Boston, Wilfred learned that the Wright and Ditson Company would trade a good golf club for three dozen balls. The boys exchanged thirty-six balls from their collection for a mashie and, via a similar transaction, later added a brassie. Francis was still too young to caddy, so he spent all of his time practicing in the backyard. It paid dividends, as practice always does. One Saturday morning he drove across the brook on the fly with the brassie. He had never been able to do this before, and he couldn't wait until he could unveil the new Francis Ouimet, the long-hitting Ouimet, before his brother. His first exhibition was a failure, but the next morning after the boys had returned from Sunday school, Francis drove over the brook on two of his three attempts. After that he was never worried about that tee shot.

When Francis was eleven, he followed Wilfred to The Country Club as a caddie. During the big tournaments he saw his heroes at close range—Chandler Egan, Jerry

Travers, Fred Herreshoff, Walter J. Travis, Alex Smith, Willie Anderson. He loved the atmosphere of the golf course, and the members were fond of the bright, clean-cut boy. One day after Francis had caddied for Samuel Carr, Mr. Carr gave him four old clubs from his locker—a driver with a leather face, a lofter, a midiron, and a putter. Nothing could stop him now. He got up at four thirty or five in the morning and practiced on the big course until the greenkeeper shooed him off. These early-morning sessions didn't satisfy the boy's hunger for golf, and occasionally on Saturdays Francis and a school friend would spend the whole day on the nine-hole public course at Franklin Park. One Saturday the boys played fifty-four holes and would have gone on indefinitely had the light permitted.

The first red-letter day in Francis Ouimet's life was the afternoon he first played the eighteen holes at The Country Club. Francis was assigned to caddy for Theodore Hastings, who usually played by himself. Before they set out, Hastings asked Francis if he played golf. Francis said he did. He asked him where he lived. Francis told him across the street. Hastings then told him to run home and get his clubs and they would play a round together. It was against the rules for caddies to play at the club, but Francis was so excited that the rules completely slipped his mind. He tore home and got his bag and joined Hastings at the first tee. He played the first nine in thirty-nine strokes. He was doing nicely coming in until he came to the fifteenth hole, which passed by the caddie-shed. As Francis came over the hill to play his second, he saw the caddie-master taking it all in. Francis became so nervous that he topped his second, missed his third, put his fourth in a bunker, and ended up with a 10. Even with this figure, he finished the round in eighty-four shots. Hastings straightened things out with the caddie-master.

In the summer of 1908, when Francis was fourteen and about to enter Brookline High, he turned up for the Greater Boston Interscholastic Championship. The officials told him he was not eligible to play since he was not attending high school, but the boy argued that he didn't see why he couldn't represent the school he was going to enter in the fall, and won his point. He qualified with an 85, but was eliminated in the first round by J. H. Sullivan. He later married Sullivan's sister.

While a freshman, Francis was the driving force in organizing a golf team at Brookline High. The team, with Francis in the number-one position, played twice a week against Fessenden, Worcester Classical, Newton High, Roxbury Latin, and other schools where a handful of boys played golf and had formed a team. Francis and his teammates brought their clubs to school on the days matches were scheduled and came in for a lot of good-natured kidding—such as the notices chalked on the blackboard to the effect that the marbles or tiddlywinks team would meet at Woodland at 1:00 p.m. The golfers at Brookline High put their riders in their place by winning the high school team championship held at Commonwealth. Francis, who was only fifteen, won the Greater Boston Interscholastic Championship, overwhelming his final-round opponent 10 and 9.

In 1910 the United States Amateur was scheduled to be played at The Country Club and Francis decided to enter. To be eligible for the Amateur, a golfer had to be a

Francis Ouimet, on the historic day he defeated Harry Vardon and Ted Ray in the playoff of the 1913 U.S. Open at The Country Club. The twenty-year-old ex-caddie nearly beat the best-ball of the two English masters, though no one had conceded him a chance. Throughout the round, Francis was the calmest man in Brookline.

member of a recognized golf club. Francis applied for a junior membership at the Woodland Golf Club. He prevailed on his mother to advance him the twenty-five dollars it cost to join, and paid her back with the money he earned while working that summer for four dollars a week in a Boston drygoods store. Francis failed to qualify by one stroke in the Amateur that year, and was dogged by that same one-stroke margin when he tried the Amateur again in 1911 and 1912. Around Boston, though, he soon established himself as one of the up-and-coming young golfers. In 1912 he reached the final of the Massachusetts State Amateur, where Heinie Schmidt, the well-dressed man, defeated him. In 1913, when the State Amateur was played at Wollaston, Francis won it. In his semi-final match against John G. Anderson, he went completely berserk on the last six holes, playing them 2-3-3-3-3-3, 6 under par. In addition to his astonishing natural ability, Francis had a quality even rarer among young athletes: he used his head. He learned something from every match he lost, and from some matches he won. He did not copy the mannerisms of other players and allowed his admirable competitive temperament to develop unforced. He knew himself.

In 1913, in his fourth try, he succeeded in qualifying for the Amateur and gave Jerry Travers a good match in the semis before bowing on the 34th green. The Open was scheduled for The Country Club, but Francis did not plan to play. He had to be talked into entering by Robert Watson, the president of the U.S.G.A. Once entered, the boy achieved the impossible, tied the untieables, Vardon and Ray.

The circumstances of the playoff and its outcome made it the most momentous round in the history of golf. Embellishment would only obscure the drama. The full impact of the historic match comes through if the story is told simply, stroke by stroke, hole by hole—the way it happened.

After tying with Harry Vardon and Ted Ray, Francis Ouimet went home and took a bath. He went to bed at nine thirty and slept until eight. He ate a light breakfast, and then walked to The Country Club and hit some practice shots out to his ten-year-old caddie, Eddie Lowery. The shots felt fine. Johnny McDermott, who had watched Francis practice, took him by the arm and said, "You are hitting the ball well. Now go out and pay no attention whatsoever to Vardon and Ray. Play your own game." Francis promised Johnny he would do his best. A few minutes before ten he joined the Englishmen on the first tee for eighteen holes of medal play.

In the tent beside the first tee, the three contestants drew straws to determine who would have the honor of hitting first. Francis drew the longest straw, and teed up. He was nervous but got off well. Vardon and Ray also hit good drives. As the players walked down the first fairway, they were followed by a gallery that swelled to 3,500 as the match progressed. Thirty hours of continuous rain had turned the low stretches of the course into a quagmire, and a drizzle was still coming down, but this was a match that even the old and the gouty had to see for themselves.

The first hole at The Country Club was a lengthy 430-yard par 4, and under the sopping conditions only Ray had a chance of reaching in two. Ray, however, pushed his second into the mounds off to the right of the green, and had to be satisfied with a 5 when the wet grass held up his chip. Vardon took a 5, and Francis got his when he holed a 3-footer. That putt was very important. The instant it dropped, Francis lost all sense of "awe and excitement."

Ouimet was down the middle with his tee shot on the second. So was Vardon. Ray's timing was still off, and he again pushed his drive, into the rough just off the fairway. All three played orthodox pitches to the green, and all got their par 4s.

On the third, a testing two-shotter measuring 435 yards, Ouimet and Vardon were again nicely down the fairway, Francis ten yards in front. Ray once more was off to the right. Vardon was on with his second. Francis followed him on with a well-played midiron. Ray's line to the pin was blocked by a big oak tree, and he elected to play an intentional fade into the green. The shot did not quite come off as Ted had planned it, but it kicked off the slope on the left and onto the corner of the green about forty feet above the cup. Ray was left with a difficult downhill putt, which he stroked five feet short of the hole. He missed that putt and went one stroke down to Ouimet and Vardon, who made their 4s.

To make certain he got his ball up quickly enough to clear the abrupt rise in front of the fourth tee, Ouimet used a wooden cleek with a small head and narrow face. He got the results he wanted. Vardon, as usual, was down the fairway. Ray pulled his drive off to the left, overcorrecting his errors off the first three tees. None of the players was attracted to the cross-bunker cutting across the fairway thirty yards short of the long, low green. All three played tidy pitches to the green and got down in two putts for their 4s.

The fifth proved to be a very interesting hole. On this long par 4, a player drove from an elevated tee and tried to keep well away from the woods hugging the right-hand side of the fairway. On his second shot, which on wet turf was a brassie or spoon for even the good golfer, he avoided the pot bunker to the right of the green, if he could. He worried about the green slanting from right to left, when he got there. All in all, a very tough par 4—420 yards long. Ouimet, still up, continued his steady driving. Vardon was a little behind the amateur but down the middle too. Ray was off to the left again in the high grass. His second was short of the green. Vardon cut his brassie a shade too much and was off to the right. Ouimet also elected to play a brassie. The ball streaked crazily off to the right and crashed into the overhanging branches of the trees—out-of-bounds. It was the first error the young amateur had made. Had the shot been just a little awry, Francis might have started to worry about what he had done wrong. Fortunately, it was such a totally bad shot that Francis was able to dismiss it immediately. He didn't alibi to himself that his hands had slipped on the wet shaft, nor did he change his club. While the gallery was speculating on the effect his loose shot would have on Ouimet, he dropped another ball quickly over his shoulder and played his third without the briefest hesitation. It was a ringing brassie that ended up on the edge of the green. Ouimet got down in 2 from there, and came out of the hole with a 5. When

Harry Vardon: the flawless swinger set the standard for all others.

Ted Ray: one of the first long-hitters who also had a beautiful putting touch.

Vardon and Ray both needed a chip and two putts, Ouimet had gained a half and a valuable psychological boost. His opponents had failed to capitalize on the opening, and this reinforced Ouimet's confidence in his ability to keep pace with them. Vardon and Ray were not infallible. Then, too, he felt that he had been lucky when that second shot had ended up out-of-bounds, for if he had been forced to play it out of the brush, he might have dropped several strokes to par instead of just the one.

The sixth was a shortish 4 uphill, the sort of hole on which a player might well pick up a birdie. All three were down the middle, with Ray, straight for the first time, the longest. Vardon played first and sent an elegant little pitch close to the cup. Ouimet and Ray could not match it. They two-putted for their 4s, and when Vardon sank his putt for a birdie 3, he went into the lead, one stroke in front of Ouimet, two in front of Ray.

It was Ray's turn at the seventh. None of the three was on the green on this stern one-shotter. Ray and Ouimet were both short—Francis had played his midiron—and Vardon, though nearer the pin, was in the high grass fringing the left side of the green. Francis went twelve feet by with his chip and Vardon was even stronger. They missed their putts for 3s and lost a stroke to Ray, who had played a brilliant run-up. Ray had now drawn back on even terms with the American and was only one stroke behind Vardon.

There was not much to choose among the drives on the eighth. The players were left with approaches of about 160 yards from the valley at the foot of the incline on which the large green was perched. Ouimet played a mashie, and the wild shout of the spectators gathered around the green told him that the shot was near the cup. Absolutely stone-dead, Eddie Lowery, his caddie, thought. Francis wanted to think so too, but as they walked up the hill, he guarded against disappointment by reminding himself that approaches that looked stony from a distance often turned out to be ten or fifteen feet away. But it was dead, eighteen inches from the hole. Francis got his birdie, but Ray matched him by rolling in a curving 35-footer. Vardon got his 4. Now, after eight holes of play, Vardon, Ray, and Ouimet were tied at 33 strokes apiece.

Ray was feeling better now. He had picked up two strokes on Vardon and one on Ouimet on the last two holes, and his length gave him the best chance of snagging a birdie on the ninth, a 520-yard par 5, which dropped from an elevated tee into a flatland crossed by a brook 350 yards out and then broke sharply up to a well-trapped green. Ray played his tee shot down the right-hand side of the fairway, which gave him the shortest line to the green if he was going to try to get home in two. Francis declined to press and was comfortably down the middle. After Vardon had hit, Ray commented, "Nice shot, Harry," the only words that passed between the Englishmen during the round, as Ouimet remembered it. Actually, Vardon's drive was not a nice shot. It was off-line, remarkably off-line for Vardon, and his lie in the rough made it necessary for him to play his second safe, short of the brook. Ray had to forgo any ideas he might have had about putting everything into his second in an attempt to reach the green when he found that his drive had ended up in a close lie on sloping ground. He played a regulation 5, on in three and down in two, as did Ouimet. Vardon had to work harder for his 5, but he got it by hitting his midiron third close to the green and chipping up for one putt.

Everything had happened and yet on the scorecard nothing had happened. All three were out in 38.

They started in. Ray, Ouimet, and Vardon, in that order, put their iron shots onto the Redan-type green of the 140-yard tenth. Ouimet was nearest the pin. The Englishmen were about thirty-five feet away, with Vardon's line to the cup stymied by the hole his ball had dug when it landed on the soft green. Harry three-putted. Ray also three-putted. Francis got his 3 and for the first time in the match he was out in front.

Vardon and Ray both had chances to get that stroke back on the eleventh, a 390-yarder, but they missed holeable putts for their 3s and halved with Ouimet in 4.

Ouimet had been outdriving Vardon regularly, and on the twelfth he outdrove Ray as well. The approach to the twelfth green was not blind, but the green lay at the bottom of a contoured slope, and this made for a certain difficulty in judging the distance to the pin. Ouimet was the only one to get home in two; he hit a superb mashie ten feet from the cup. Vardon was short, halfway down the slope, and Ray was down the embankment to the left. The Englishmen could do no better than 5s. Ouimet was timid on his try for his birdie, but his comfortable par increased his lead to two strokes.

On the thirteenth, the short par 4 on which Ouimet had picked up a birdie the day before, all three were on in two—Ray on the edge, Vardon about nine feet away, and Ouimet just inside Vardon. Ray made a fine bid for a 3 with his long putt. Vardon holed his 9-footer. Ouimet missed his. Vardon was now only one stroke behind Ouimet, the perfect position for the experienced campaigner with five hard holes left. On the long fourteenth, however, Vardon played poorly although he got his par 5. He hooked his drive into the rough, and after an adequate recovery, hooked his mashie third. This was not like Harry. If he didn't hit his irons perfectly straight, he faded them. Linde Fowler, the pioneer golf reporter, had not been looking for indications that Vardon was feeling the pressure, but Harry had hit that hooked approach so uncharacteristically that Linde could only deduce that Vardon was becoming worried. Ouimet apparently was not. He topped his brassie second on the fourteenth—his first poor shot since the fifth—but he put his third confidently onto the green as if he had already forgotten his second. The young man's poise was amazing. On one hole, when a member of the gallery had stupidly buttonholed him between shots and asked for some advice on his own golf troubles, Ouimet had patiently answered the intruder's questions. Ray seemed to be getting restless about his inability to do the things he wanted to do. He also played the fourteenth badly, pushing his second far to the right, but he took advantage of a lucky opening to the green and also got his 5. Three pars on the scorecard.

Ray finally went on the fifteenth, the par 4 over the hill and across the driveway. Ted's tee shot was headed for the rough on the right when it hit a spectator's derby and rebounded onto the fairway. (The spectator was incensed and left the playoff then and there.) Ray, however, did not take advantage of this break. He underclubbed himself on his second, and his soaring mashie thudded into a trap. He took two to get out, and only a good putt prevented him from taking a 7. But Ray's 6 put him four strokes behind Ouimet and three behind Vardon—who had taken 4s—and with only three holes remaining, Ted was out of it. On this hole Vardon, who never smoked on a golf course, lit a cigarette.

On the short sixteenth, Vardon and Ouimet got their 3s. Ray three-putted carelessly for a 4. He had given up the fight.

They came to the seventeenth, the 360-yard dogleg to the left, with Ouimet still protecting his one-stroke lead over Vardon. It was still Vardon's honor. Harry elected to play his drive close to if not over the corner—a risky shot, but he had decided that the time had come to gamble and he wanted to be in a position after his drive to stick his approach very close to the pin. That drive proved to be Vardon's undoing. His right hand got into the shot too much, and he hooked it into the bunker in the angle of the dogleg. From his lie in the bunker, Vardon could not go for the green and was forced to play out to the fairway. He put his third on, but not stone-dead. He had to take a 5. Francis had driven straight down the fairway to about the same spot from which he had played his jigger approach the day before. This time he selected his mashie—and hit a lovely shot eighteen feet from the hole. His long-shafted, narrow-blade putter had not let him down all morning, and now he called on it to get him down safely in two putts for the 4 that would give him that valuable insurance stroke over Vardon. He tapped the ball over the slippery grade . . . and holed it.

Francis now held a three-stroke lead on Vardon as they came to the home hole. He did not let up. His drive was down the middle, his second on. His approach putt, however, left him with a good 4-footer for his 4. As Francis lined up his putt, he realized for the first time that he was going to win, and with that awareness the astounding

The United States Open Champion
of 1913, twenty-year-old
Francis Ouimet.

calmness that had sheathed him from the first hole on instantly disappeared. The boy
felt himself shivering all over. He steadied himself as best he could, and made the putt.
It was quite irrelevant that Vardon had taken a 6 and Ray a birdie 3.

The crowd who had slogged around the course in the drizzle, worn out from
playing every shot with Ouimet, still staggered by the boy's nerveless poise and his
brilliant golf, reeled around the eighteenth green and the clubhouse in the gayest stupor
many of them ever experienced in their lives. They recalled the great shots the new
champion had played—that brassie to the fifth green after he had knocked his first out-
of-bounds, that mashie to the eighth and that equally fine mashie to the twelfth, that
conclusive putt on the skiddy seventeenth, which perhaps more than any other single
shot was the one heard round the world. In the visitors' party there was no rancor.
Bernard Darwin, the Englishman who became the greatest of all golf writers, had been
scoring for Ouimet during the playoff. Naturally, Darwin had been hoping that one of
his countrymen would win, if he played the better game. By the seventeenth hole, when
it looked as if Ouimet would do it, Darwin had stopped hoping for a comeback by
Vardon. The slim, mild-faced youngster had played the better game, and Darwin
rooted Ouimet home with his whole heart. Vardon and Ray, though disappointed, could

have nothing but praise for the boy who had not only beaten them but had nearly beaten their best-ball.

The cards of the match:

	OUT			IN		
Par	444	444	345—36	344	454	344—35—71
Ouimet	544	454	435—38	344	454	334—34—72
Vardon	544	453	445—38	445	354	356—39—77
Ray	545	454	335—38	445	456	453—40—78

And what about the new champion? After the battle he was the same exceptional young man—exhilarated but modest, still unbelieving and still unbelievable. "I am as much surprised and as pleased as anyone here," he said in accepting the trophy from the U.S.G.A. secretary, John Reid, Jr. "Naturally it always was my hope to win out. I simply tried my best to keep this cup from going to our friends across the water. I am very glad to have been the agency for keeping the cup in America."

The next day, when The Country Club was the scene of an all-out celebration, Francis Ouimet walked over from his house across the street and joined in the merriment by tossing down, one after another, a drink called a Horse's Neck, a compound of lemon juice and ginger ale.

AFTER OUIMET

American golf has always been fortunate in the men who have been its champions. Macdonald, Travis, and Travers were sharp personalities. Jones, Hagen, and Sarazen were mature and four-square men with the power to communicate with their idolators. Though less articulate individually, Hogan, Nelson, and Snead produced excitement through the clean, metallic perfection of their golf. Palmer, Nicklaus, and Trevino, each in his own way, have exerted a tremendous influence on galleries here and abroad. The luckiest thing, however, that happened to American golf was that its first great hero was a person like Francis Ouimet.

Had a pleasant young man from a good Fifth Avenue family or some stiff and staid professional defeated Vardon and Ray, it is really very doubtful if his victory would have been the wholesale therapeutic for American golf that was Ouimet's. Here was a person all of America, not just golfing America, could understand—the boy from "the wrong side" of the street, the ex-caddie, the kid who worked during his summer vacations from high school—America's idea of the American hero. Overnight the non-wealthy American lost his antagonism toward golf. He had been wrong, he felt, in tagging it a society sport. After all, the Open Champion was a fine, clean-cut American boy from the same walk of life as himself.

The hundreds of thousands of Americans who had been inspired by Francis Ouimet's victory to take up golf found that their hero was an even greater person than most heroes: he was a fine man. He never allowed his successes to swell his head. He remained free from affectation. He was an instinctive gentleman. He was the great boy who became a great man. If the hero-worshipping American boy accidentally learned of some of the "real details" about his heroes in baseball and football, his ideals were frequently shattered. The more Americans learned about Francis Ouimet, the more they admired him. American golf was lucky, very, very lucky, that it was Francis who won at Brookline.

Under the impetus of Ouimet's victory, within a decade golf became an all-Americans' game. Less than 350,000 played golf in 1913. Ten years later there were 2,000,000 golfers in the country. The man who took the trolley to his club, wearing his knickers and carrying his sticks, still attracted comment, but fewer and fewer people snickered out loud and referred to him as Reginald or Little Lord Fauntleroy in tones he was supposed to overhear. During this decade, and largely because of the game's increasingly democratic base, the quality of American players improved. Slowly but surely they caught up with the best British amateurs and professionals—and then passed them. By 1923 golf was a game Americans played better than any other people in the world.

Following Ouimet's epic victory in the Open, the members of the Woodland Golf Club tendered their favorite son a whopping banquet at which high-flying poems were recited and his deeds commemorated in song—such as this one, in which the words were sung to the tune of "Marching Through Georgia":

> Hurrah! Hurrah! There's Ouimet on the tee!
> Hurrah! Hurrah! The smallest of the three.
> The boy who trimmed the British when they came across the sea.
> When he goes playing to victory.

The members of the Woodland Club also presented Ouimet with a trip to England so that the boy could play in the British Amateur of 1914. Francis met with no more success than the other Americans, the Old Man excepted, who had tried to beard the lion in his own den. Francis was ousted in the second round by a golfer of little reputation. In that same championship, Jerry Travers was whipped by an elderly gentleman suffering from lumbago who barely broke 90. Chick Evans, in his second try overseas, played well but had the misfortune to run into a man named MacFarlane, who went completely mad and played the first nine at Sandwich in thirty-one strokes. That was the way it went with American professionals, too, when they tried for honors on foreign soil. For some reason or other, four out of every five rounds American pros played overseas were three or four strokes higher than the scores they made on American courses of almost comparable difficulty. On the rare occasions when they played well, some Britisher always played better. The best showing an American pro had ever made in Great Britain was Johnny McDermott's tie for fifth in the 1913 Open. Even in France, where the going should have been easier, our pros could not win. An American team composed of McDermott, Brady, Alex Smith, and McNamara lost all four matches in a team competition in 1913 with the best French professionals.

After Ouimet

In Ouimet, America was backing a thoroughbred. After his wobbly performances in Great Britain, Francis showed the European skeptics the golf he was capable of when he won the French Amateur Championship. He had profited from his experiences in England, too, which was more than his less conscientious compatriots could claim: he had changed his style of iron-play to the punch method advocated by Hilton, and so bolstered what had been the weakest department of his game. In the U.S. Open played at Midlothian, near Chicago, that summer, he fired a first round of 69 and finished in a tie for fourth place, a more than creditable performance. (That young pro from Rochester, Walter Hagen, won the Open, defeating Chick Evans by a stroke.) When the amateurs gathered at Ekwanok, in Manchester, Vermont, for their tournament, young Ouimet proved that he was just as good at match play as he was at medal by winning that championship. On his way to the final he defeated two former champions, Bob Gardner and Bill Fownes, and in the final against Jerry Travers, *the* match player, Francis took seven straight holes and beat him soundly, 6 up with five to play. Against Travers, Francis was off-line only once in thirty-one holes; on his morning round he hit his approach a few yards to the right of the fifteenth green. Curiously enough, winning the Amateur thrilled Ouimet more than his victory in the Open. He had never given much thought to the Open, but as a boy he had dreamed of winning the Amateur—and now he had.

The next season, 1915, Francis was eliminated in the second round when he attempted to defend his Amateur crown at Detroit. The winner, and a most deserving one, was Bob Gardner. When he had taken the Amateur for the first time in 1909, Gardner was an undergraduate at Yale who could play all the golf he wanted. When he repeated six years later, he was an executive in a coal company in Chicago who took time off from business only for the major tournaments. Bob always played well, once he had the chance to warm up. Pole-vaulting (over thirteen feet) had developed his arms and shoulders, and he was long off the tees. He coupled this with a great flair for competition. For example, in an early-round match in the Amateur against Tom Sherman, he watched Sherman put his tee shot twelve inches from the hole . . . and then holed his. He was 2 down with five to go against Max Marston in the semi-finals, won back those two holes with 15-foot putts, and beat Max on the 37th green. In the final he defeated John G. Anderson 5 and 4.

Considering the little competitive golf he played, Gardner compiled a truly remarkable record in the major tournaments. In 1916, despite an infected finger, this handsome collar-ad man stopped the challenge of the youthful phenomenon from Atlanta, Bobby Jones, and went all the way to the final before surrendering his title. Though he never won another national championship, Gardner went to the final of the British Amateur in 1920, the best showing an American had made in sixteen years, and in 1921 he was a finalist against Jesse Guilford in our Amateur. Bob Gardner never beat himself. It took fine golf to beat him.

Jerry Travers' loss of his Amateur crown in 1914 and his failure to recapture it in 1915 did not get him down, for in 1915 he became the second amateur to win the United States Open. No one could argue Jerry's ability in match play. As a medal player, however, he was looked on as just one of the boys, and his victory in the 72-hole test at Baltusrol came as a decided surprise.

Jerry's first two rounds left him in fourth place. A 73 on his third round gave him a one-stroke lead on the field. He was one of the last starters on the nerve-racking last round, and knew all the way the exact number of strokes he could take and still come in a winner. Knowing what they have to do is, for most golfers, an invitation to crack. They fight against cracking, they overfight, they outthink themselves, they play too safely, they worry, they weave, and they lose. The easy way to win a medal tournament is to come in early and coolly smoke your panatela as the reports filter in that, one after another, your rivals have blown up trying too hard to catch you. When Jerry came to the tenth tee on his final round to play the 64th hole of the Open, he learned that he would have to play the last nine holes in one stroke under par in order to beat Tom McNamara's total of 298. To make certain he hit his tee shot down the middle on the tenth, a drive-and-pitch par 4, Jerry used his driving-iron. He sliced the ball far out-of-bounds. Then he wrapped himself around his second tee shot and hooked it into the wheat drifts. For all intents and purposes, Travers had cooked his goose through these two loose shots. The green on the tenth was completely encircled by a water hazard, and Jerry would be lucky to get out of the hole with anything less than a 6, and could take even more if he went for the green. Jerry hunched over his ball, and rapped a magnificent biting iron over the water and onto the green two feet from the pin. He holed for his 4.

He got his par on the eleventh when a player of less courage would have again thrown in the sponge. He took a chance on his always-treacherous wooden driver and topped his tee shot barely forty yards down the rough. Two mashies got him to the green, and there he dropped a 35-footer for his par 4. He played his pars on the next three holes without having to call upon himself for further true-tempered evidence of his resourcefulness. On the fifteenth he nailed the birdie he was looking for, in typical Travers fashion. On this par 5, he gambled on carrying a deep cross-bunker with an iron on his second shot, and won this gamble by four yards. Then he got down in 2 from off the green. Pars on the last three holes would do it now, and concentrating with frigid fervor, this spiritual ancestor of Ben Hogan reeled off his par on the 70th, his par on the 71st, his par on the 72nd. Perhaps he had won because he had known what he had to do, just as in match play.

This was Jerry Travers' last championship victory and he made it a good one. Soon afterwards he retired from competitive golf save for some Red Cross exhibition matches during World War I. When he tried to come back after the war, this great putter could no longer putt. In other ways, too, he was not the same Jerry Travers who had won four Amateur titles and the 1915 Open.

Now that Ouimet had once and for all taken the curse off golf as a diversion for the rich and the elderly, each warm summer weekend saw the ranks of the converts swelled by the thousands—men who had "made their pile" and had the time for relaxation; men who were making their piles and saw the advantages of good contacts afforded by the friendliness of the locker room; college and high school athletes no longer in shape for body-contact sports but keen for some competitive outlet; women who had been sold on the game by the prowess of their new champion, Dorothy Campbell Hurd. At the strongholds of society in the East and at many strata-conscious golf clubs throughout the country, the cost of joining and playing remained prohibitively high, but, as the game spread, an ever-increasing number of clubs—golf clubs as distinct from country clubs—supplied the demand for golf at popular prices. That helped. Jerry Travers, in the cool of retirement, estimated that it now cost the average golfer less than $200 a year to play the game. Travers broke it down this way:

Initiation fee	$50.00	
Annual dues	50.00	
Balls	20.00	(1 ball to every 36 holes)
Clubs	17.50	($2.50 apiece for 7)
Carfare	20.00	
Caddies' fees	25.00	(40 cents a round)
	$182.50	

If, as Travers suggests, a golfer could average two full rounds with one ball, the caddies in those days must have been a distinctly different breed from the present-day crop—what remains of it. In some ways they were. For many ambitious boys in junior high and high school, the golf course was the land of opportunity—the place where they could earn more money than by mowing lawns, learn to play a game they could carry with them through life, and meet men who often became their valuable friends off the course. Many clubs, following the example set by Alexander H. Revell of the Chicago Country Club, fixed up "caddie shacks" for the boys, with lockers for their clothes and lunches, and cleared adjacent fields for baseball diamonds and putting greens. The atmosphere of the golf course was a salutary change from tenement life, as were the "caddie camps" organized at summer resorts where underprivileged kids from the city "paid" for two months of sunlight and air by toting the bags of the vacationers. For quite a number of youngsters about to be swallowed up by the necessity of going to work to support their parents, the summer at Bretton Woods or Poland Spring was the bright spot in their childhood, and sometimes in their lives.

Throughout the country the expansion of the game produced many local heroes, golfers who never cut much of a swath in national tourneys but who were practically invincible in their own sections. Sam Reynolds won the Nebraska Amateur seven times, and Larry Bromfield hung up a similar record in Colorado. Harry Legg in Minnesota and E. J. Barker in Montana won their state Amateurs nine times. George V. Rotan took the Texas title five times and shared the rule in that realm with that strange and wonderful character, Commodore Bryan Heard of the Houston Country Club. The Commodore stumbled into golf at the age of forty-five only because he was unable to get up a poker game one afternoon. His golf grew better as he grew older, and at sixty-five he was "shooting his age." At seventy-five, he played a 74. It looked as if he would keep going forever, when an automobile accident and cataracts in both eyes finally forced the doughty Commodore to give up competitive golf. Bobby Jones was only one of the infant prodigies the Commodore helped up the ladder by giving him a sound trimming.

Happily, as the game began to make considerable headway in the various sections of the United States, the aberrations of the first golf architects were corrected and Americans began to play on bona-fide golf courses. Gone were the days of the "Sunday architects," the snowy-haired Scots who six days a week "proed" at their respective clubs and on the seventh hustled around the countryside "designing" at least one and sometimes as many as three courses for communities newly golf-conscious. These oldtimers forgot about Prestwick and Leven, for speed was of the essence and so were the desires of their clients. Few of the Sunday architects went so far as to suggest a sporty little railroad track before the green—though some American golfers still regarded tracks as a legitimate and enviable hazard, better even than a quarry or a stone wall—but their layouts had been littered, prodigally and unimaginatively, with chocolate-drop mounds and pot bunkers and tantalizing combinations of these fashionable, now-obsolescent hazards. One obvious deficiency of this all-I-need-is-an-afternoon school of designers was their necessary addiction to formula. For some, a good course and a billygoat course were synonymous—the more blind shots, the better; for others, no hole except a dogleg was a worthwhile challenge, regardless of the natural contours of the terrain.

More than any one other architect, it was Charles Blair Macdonald who opened the eyes of American golfers to the shortcomings of the pioneer trends in this country. Near Southampton on Long Island, old Charlie built the National Golf Links, America's first heroic course. The character and beauty of the National became the subject of prose poems by the leading British and domestic authorities. A walk around the course, and syndicates preparing to build in New Mexico, Tennessee, and Idaho tore up their first blueprints and adopted the National as their criterion. It influenced the members of the Olympia Fields club drawing up plans for four courses (on 627 acres twenty-seven miles south of Chicago's Loop) and, to a lesser extent, the budget-bound designers of the nation's public courses. The National Golf Links dramatized for Americans what a real golf course looked like.

The inspiration for the National had come to Macdonald as early as 1901, when he read an opinion poll conducted by the English periodical *Golf Illustrated*. Called "The Best Hole Discussion," this consensus disclosed that the best one-shot holes on the island, in the minds of the British golfers, were the Eden (the eleventh) at St. Andrews and the Redan (the fifteenth) at North Berwick; similarly, the most-favored two-shotter was the Alps (the seventeenth) at Prestwick, with the fourteenth (the Long) and seventeenth (the Road) at St. Andrews awarded the distinction among the long holes. It was Macdonald's idea to build in America a seaside links in which the holes would be duplicates of the most famous British holes. Charlie made several trips to Britain to research his project, and came home loaded with sketches and surveyors' maps of the holes he had in mind. Always a shrewd salesman and organizer, he persuaded seventy men to put up $1,000 apiece to back his venture, and found the natural links he wanted in an undulating, untouched stretch of duneland along Sebonac Bay, three miles from Shinnecock. The development of the land was begun in the spring of 1907, and four years later the course—ultimately 6,650 yards of great golf—was opened.

The National had many features altogether new to American layouts. It was a lengthy course, several hundred yards longer than many that had been adjudged to be of championship caliber. This added length was important, because golf balls were becoming more and more lively as manufacturers vied for the patronage of the golfers who wanted more distance, which meant all golfers. The course was also a blessed departure from the penal type of architecture that had become epidemic from coast to coast. Macdonald did not traffic with the artificial. Cross-bunkers and pot bunkers and symmetrical mounds had no place at the National. His hazards conformed to the contours of the ground. His bunkers were the sides of slopes that cried out to be made into bunkers. Starting from the land and not from a blueprint, Macdonald "found" one natural hole after another, his Redan and his Alps, his Road and his Eden. He was wise enough to let his copies modify their originals as the topography suggested. He implanted the strategic spirit of these fine Scottish holes in the original holes he designed, or, more in the spirit of his approach, which he "discovered" as he walked his acres tirelessly looking for golf holes.

Whereas a *penal* hole is designed to punish the player who strays from the straight and narrow, a *strategic* hole places the emphasis on initiative. The player is given a choice of several routes to the green. On a one-shotter like the Redan, for example, he can generally get a 4 by steering away from the one serious hazard, a large, harsh bunker cut into the bank just below the front edge of a raised green built on a traverse. The player who goes for the small unbunkered opening to the corner of the green can get his 3, but he leaves himself a long putt and just about forfeits his chance for a possible 2. The player who goes for the pin and gambles on carrying the bunker, suffering the consequences if he plays his stroke inadequately, is rewarded for hitting the required shot with an easy 3 and a good chance for his 2. In other words, on a strategic course boldness is repaid. The man who carries a fairway trap with his tee shot has a shorter and easier route to the green on his second than the man who has elected to play short of the trap or to one side or the other of it. The man who goes for the pin on his approach is the man who has the chance to get down in 1 on the contoured green. While making low scoring harder for the good players with its banked plateau greens slanted behind hungry hazards, Macdonald's National was not unfair to the average golfer. In truth, his off-line shots were dealt with more leniently than on penal courses. By using his head

William Howard Taft,
the first American president
to be converted
to the new religion.

and taking the discreet routes, the golfer who could play a 95 at Thorny Lea could play a 95 at the National. If he tried to play the pros' game, then the average golfer invited disaster. Macdonald's hazards carried out his dictum that "the object of a bunker or trap is not only to punish a physical mistake, to punish lack of control, but also to punish pride and egotism."

Charlie Macdonald's revolutionary achievement at Southampton led to many offers from wealthy Eastern groups to construct comparable courses for them. Macdonald was happy to oblige. Working with his engineer, Seth Raynor, he built such Churrigue-resque courses as Lido, Mid-Ocean (in Bermuda), Piping Rock, and Yale, spending hundreds of thousands of dollars in his pursuit of perfection. They were all interesting layouts, and yet they lacked something the National had: the true breath of the game. On the dunes off Sebonac Bay, old Charlie had built himself a majestic monument.

Teddy Roosevelt, as was to be expected, found golf too mild a sport for his tastes, but, with each passing month, the leading men in the country were becoming increasingly golf-conscious and rabid to spread the gospel. Ex-President Taft, his ardor intact although his figure in profile now resembled Fujiyama standing on end, proclaimed that "golf is in the interest of good health and good manners. It promotes self-restraint and, as one of its devotees has well said, affords the chance to play the man and act the gentleman." Where else could you find a game that made you a better man for having a good time? A prominent churchman gave golfers his blessing: "They walk with saints and poets whose souls have been lifted by contact with the lowly violet and the snow-crowned mountain peak."

And yet, in candor, there was something to be said *against* the game. Good men, who could take liquor or leave it alone, who smiled at pretty women but kept on walking, who remembered their wife's birthday and their children's names, went to the dogs once they became golfers. Under the spell of the game, they lived on the golf course, trying to break a hundred or ninety, pitifully oblivious that back home in those little white cottages or hulking Gothic showplaces sat the "golf widows" of America. Many reformers spoke of the inroads that golf, with all its insinuating sinuosity, had made on American family life, but it remained for Russell W. Hobson to immortalize in verse the new menace to our mores.

"Who's the stranger, Mother Dear?
Look! He knows us! Ain't he queer?"

"Hush, My Own! Don't talk so wild;
That's your father, dearest child."

"That's my father? No such thing!
Father died, you know, last spring."

"Father didn't die, you dub!
Father joined a golfing club.

"But they closed the club, so he
Had no place to go, you see—

"No place left for him to roam
That's why now he's coming home . . .

"Kiss him, he won't bite you, Child!
All those golfing guys look wild."

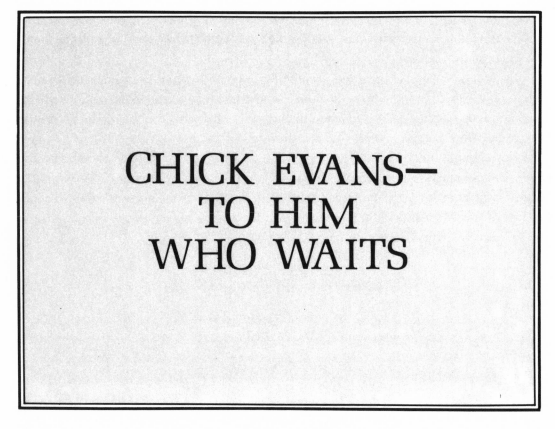

CHICK EVANS—
TO HIM
WHO WAITS

The January 1912 issue of the *American Golfer* carried a rather provocative verse. Charles (Chick) Evans, Jr., the author, had entitled it "A Chronic Semi-Finalist":

> I've a semi-final hoodoo, I'm afraid.
> I can never do as you do, Jimmy Braid.
> I've a genius not to do it,
> I excel at almost to it,
> But I never can go through it, I'm afraid.

Chick Evans was not one to keep his joys and his sorrows to himself. He had to get them out of his system verbally or in writing, and this verse was only one of his many attempts to shoo his hoodoo by looking it squarely in the eye. Everyone who had watched Evans in action recognized that he owned a champion's game. No amateur could match him as an iron-player. As a matter of fact, from tee to green he was the superior of the best American professionals. He could be a shaky putter in crises, it is true, but it wasn't his putting alone that kept him a bridesmaid whenever he entered the national Amateur. It was something deeper, and deepening—a complex that gained a tighter grip on him the harder he tried to free himself.

By the winter of 1912, when he tried to exorcise his complex with poetry, Chick had played in three Amateurs and been ousted in the semi-finals each time by opponents whom he had definitely outplayed. In 1909 he had lost 1 down to Chandler Egan. (He balmed the wound by winning the playoff for the medal from the new champion, Bob

Gardner.) In 1910 he allowed Bill Fownes to beat him when he had stood 2 up with only three holes to play. (He rationalized that it was his putting that had licked him.) In 1911 he had again reached the semis and had again wilted like a morning glory, losing to Fred Herreshoff after he had built up a commanding lead over the first eighteen. By this time Chick was no longer amused by his inability to win the Amateur. Blaming his putting, blaspheming his opponents' luck, and other such intellectualizations now failed to assuage the sting of losing. He would have been hurt had his friends not consoled him with the bromide that he was the uncrowned champion, and he was hurt when they did. What good did it do to be the best amateur golfer in America when some other guy always won the title?

It looked as if Chick, perhaps with the help of his poem, had finally chased his jinx in 1912. For the first time he got safely through the semi-final round of the Amateur. In the final, surrounded by his host of fanatic Chicago admirers who had come out to watch him finally win the big one, he had played himself into a three-hole lead over Jerry Travers on the morning round. Then, with the crown he dreamed about at his fingertips, Chick had petered out like an exhausted skyrocket. Travers captured one hole after another in the afternoon, and Chick had not been able to fight back. The score was 7 and 6, and Chick was inconsolable. Depressed and bewildered, he dodged the parties at the clubhouse and wandered aimlessly down a country road, trying to forget what had happened. He walked for several hours and was well into the country when he heard the sound of music and merriment coming from a barn across a field. At the door of the barn he stood watching the squaredancers for a heavy moment, and then joined in. By morning he had danced himself healthy.

Chick's tribulations (and the dramatized versions concocted by emotion) were far from over. In 1913 at Garden City his semi-final hoodoo caught up with him again. None of his previous disappointments had been so hard to bear. All year long he had played irresistible golf. On a spring tour through the Northwest he had broken course record after course record, and the fans in Tacoma, Portland, Salt Lake City, Kansas City, and Omaha had reiterated the superlatives of his earlier worshippers. He had won the qualifying medal in the Amateur for the third time, and had won it sensationally by playing the in-nine on his second round in 32 strokes. He had continued to hit the ball beautifully as the tournament moved into match play, and then, once again, his putting touch had evaporated, just as it always seemed to do under the pressure of championship match play. Against Eben Byers, Chick had put on an exhibition on the greens that was both tragic and comic. On hole after hole, bee-line approaches had left him with "gimme" putts for wins, and on hole after hole, switching desperately from one to another of his four putters, he foozled these short putts. He teetered through to the semis, where John G. Anderson put him out of his misery.

Well, maybe 1914 would be the year. Chick went over for another shot at the British Amateur. In 1911, in his first try, he had been ousted in an extra-hole match by a left-handed Tasmanian. This time an outgoing nine of 31 by a man named Macfarlane was too much even for the good golf Chick was playing. Back home, he took the

Chick Evans putts on the sixth green at Sandwich during the 1914 British Amateur. Chick did better than any of the other Americans who had crossed the Atlantic in an attempt to duplicate Travis' triumph of 1904. Evans lasted until the fourth round, when his opponent, C. B. MacFarlane, shattered his dream with an incredible 31 on the front nine. Evans' great season was to come two years later, in 1916.

Western for the third time—those sectional tournaments, match play or medal, never bothered him. His putting appeared steadier than it had been for years. In the Open at Midlothian, near Chicago, he amazed even his most adoring supporters by flashing two out-of-this-world finishing rounds that brought him to the last hole needing an eagle 2 to tie with Hagen. And Chick had almost done it—his chip had ended up nine inches from the cup. But in the Amateur at Ekwanok that year, for the first time he was eliminated before he had reached the semi-finals. He lost to Eben Byers, who had taken ten putts on the first nine holes while Chick was helping himself to twenty.

1915 made it worse. With the exception of Jerry Travers, the winner, Chick did better than any other amateur in the Open. In the weeks before the convocation for the Amateur, he was unbeatable around Chicago, and then he was whipped and whipped badly in the first round of the big event by Ned Sawyer, a fellow-Chicagoan whom Evans had trampled on all summer.

Nothing insucceeds like insuccess. By 1916 one searing disappointment after another had made Chick Evans a far more complicated person than he was intended to be. He had been born, the son of a librarian, in 1890 in Indianapolis, in a brown shingled house four minutes away from President Benjamin Harrison's home. When Chick was three, the Evanses had moved to Chicago. At eight, he had started to caddy at the old Edgewater Golf Club, earning his ten cents for nine holes, his fifteen cents on the weekends. A friendly, freckled boy, Chick became the most popular caddie at Edge-water because of his sunny disposition and his record for rescuing lost balls. When a ball was buried in high grass and no amount of poking could uncover it, Chick would stretch out full length in the rough and keep rolling until his body struck something round and hard. He quit the caddie ranks the day before he reached his sixteenth birthday so as not to jeopardize his amateur standing. By that time he had developed the smooth, flowing, thrillingly simple swing that had made him a champion among boys and would, Chicagoans were positive, earn him many national titles. At the age of sixteen he qualified for the Western Amateur and started on the golf career that brought him both glory and grief.

Golf galleries liked Chick Evans. He talked to everyone, he remembered faces and names, he laughed and he joked, and he could really hit the ball. Chick Evans liked golf galleries. Something of an extrovert—in the East they called him a "Western" type—he opened himself to their affection and plaudits with a readiness the super-concentrators like Travers could not understand. Some contemporaries of Chick's always maintained that he loved to play in front of crowds so much that he purposely lost holes when he was ahead in some matches in order to prolong his sessions before the galleries.

Whenever he was playing well and a gallery was whooping it up at his heels, Chick was a happy young man—a slim, sandy-haired kid with something attractively rural about him even after he had joined a brokerage firm. On the other hand, during or just after the heat of defeat, he was prey to a streak of bitterness. Without being fully aware of it, he resented Francis Ouimet. It wasn't so much Ouimet the person as Ouimet the young man who had done what Chick had wanted to do—captured the Open and the Amateur and gained center stage as America's darling. Chick felt that he was a better golfer than Ouimet and did not hesitate to discuss in public their comparative records in national events, especially in the qualifying rounds of the Amateur and other medal affairs in which he knew his record was incomparable. He prided himself on the judgment expressed by Harry Vardon, who everyone knew had lost to Ouimet, that Chick Evans was the best amateur he had played with in America. And, quite understandably, he loved to hear statements that supported his frustrated ego, like the one by Jerry Travers that "if Evans could putt like Walter J. Travis, it would be foolish to stage an Amateur tourney in this country." He didn't know whether to be insulted or pleased when the gag went around Chicago that, in his search for a remedy for his woes on the green, Chick had raced toward a store with the window inscription "New Way of Putting," only to discover that the words "On Soles" followed below in smaller type.

And then, in 1916, it came. Just like that.

A siege of illness had forced Chick to forgo the junket to Del Monte for the Western, but he was back in shape by the time the national Open was scheduled to get underway at Minikahda, outside Minneapolis. He brought to Minikahda his own caddie from Chicago, a good-luck Billiken a friend had purchased in Hawaii, and, for the nth time, a new method of putting. The night before the Open began, the parched course came to life under a heavy downpour. The turf was fine and gripping, and Chick raced to the turn in 32 before he knew what had happened. He got a little frightened of his score coming in, but a 38 gave him a 70. He went out in good spirits in the afternoon, and repeating the word *Relax* to himself before each shot, added a 36-33—69 for a total of 139 and a three-stroke lead over the nearest man, Wilfred Reid. The next day was a blazer. Reid crumpled under the heat, and Evans, playing streaky golf, was lucky to go no higher than 74 in the morning round. He missed his shots at the right time. He still retained a three-stroke lead over the man in second place, lanky Jim Barnes, the Cornish-born professional who had dug in with a 71. Now if he could only hang on.

On the fourth hole of his tense last round, Evans buried himself in a bunker, three-putted for a 7. For once Chick did not interpret the 7 as a sign from the gods that he was not supposed to win. He accepted the 7 and kept on going. Information reached him at the turn that Barnes, playing three holes behind, had caught him. He kept on swinging. As he prepared to play the 540-yard twelfth hole, he was told that Barnes had hooked his drive badly on the ninth. That would give him a one-stroke lead, Evans reflected on the tee, but he would lose that advantage unless he went for his birdie 4 on the twelfth, as Barnes was sure to do. Chick split the fairway with his drive, and after checking his lie, made up his mind to go for the pin on his second rather than play short of the creek that crossed the fairway twenty yards before the green. He came through with one of the finest fairway woods he ever hit, an arrow-straight whizzer that cleared the creek and pulled up on the green. The birdie was easy. Chick stayed in there, dropping those troublesome 3- and 4-foot putts, and it mattered little that he three-putted the home green for a 73. His total of 286—an average of $71\frac{1}{2}$ per round and a new record for the Open—gave Evans a margin of four strokes over Barnes and two over Jock Hutchison, who had come flying home in 68. Chick Evans, the chronic disappointment, had not come close this time. He had *won* a major championship.

The Amateur in 1916 was held at the Merion Cricket Club, outside Philadelphia. Chick was the man to beat, and no one could beat him. He played his way to the final through Nelson Whitney, the New Orleans crack (3 and 1), John G. Anderson (9 and 8), Clarke Corkran (3 and 2), and in the final against Bob Gardner defeated the defending champion with an exhibition of the new staying power he had acquired by winning the Open. Between seven and eight thousand spectators parked over two thousand cars and

Bob Gardner (left) and Chick Evans, just prior to their meeting in the final of the 1916 Amateur Championship at Merion. Chick was, in a way, the Snead of his day—flawless from tee to green, but as shaky as an aspen on the greens. In his match with Gardner, however, Chick holed the putts that mattered.

followed the two Chicagoans over the sunbaked course. They witnessed a vibrant battle. Evans started with a birdie 3 and fought off Gardner's challenges to lead by three holes at the halfway mark. Curiously enough, Evans had gained his advantage by outplaying Gardner, the great clutch putter, on Merion's difficult greens. In the afternoon Gardner rallied to be only 1 down at the turn and seemed to be on his way to squaring the match on the tenth, but Evans staved him off by sinking a sweeping 40-footer. That putt was the Gettysburg of the match. Chick had halved a hole he should have lost, using the same weapon so many others had used against him. He won three of the next five holes, playing with confidence and forcing Gardner into errors. On the 33rd green the match was over—Chick, 4 and 3. Chick Evans had become the first American to win the Amateur and the Open in the same year.

Chick's erratic public relations added a needless wrangling footnote to his great double victory. Instead of ignoring the taunts of die-hard Easterners that the absence of Ouimet and Travers had made his triumph at Merion much easier than it might have been, Chick popped off. Francis and Jerry, he declared, would not have won had they entered. "There is a certain provincialism about the East," Chick continued, "a sort of ostrichlike spirit that believes that when its own eyes are hidden no other eyes can see. . . . In the West it is generally understood that when a leading player fails to enter an event, he knows he has little chance to win it." Once again he recalled Vardon's opinion that Chick Evans was the best amateur in the country. The Eastern critics, rushing to the defense of Ouimet, asked Chick if he remembered his tussle with Francis in the East–West matches just before the 1915 Amateur in which Francis, 3 down with three to play, won out on the first extra hole.

Quite a batch of bitterness was brewed and it did neither of the disputing parties any good, especially Chick. He should have been satisfied that at the end of his rainbow he had found two pots of gold. It had been a long and arduous journey, but Chick had stuck with it, and no golfer in the country, whether he was irritated by the vagaries of Chick's personality or hailed them as further halos, could debate the record: From 1909 on Chick Evans had been one of the country's best golfers; in 1916 he had proved himself the best.

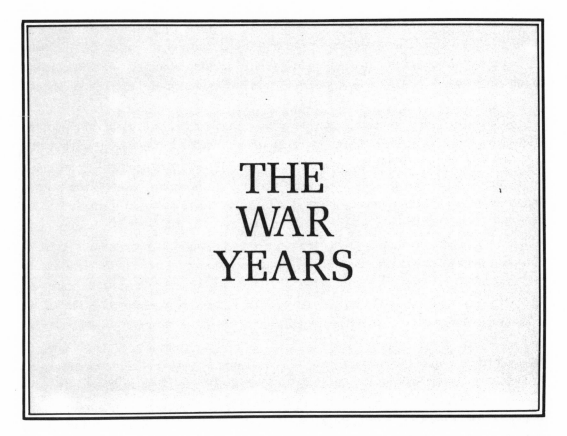

THE
WAR
YEARS

In April 1917 the United States entered World War I. Under the first sobering realization of how serious life could be, the nation abandoned all that was trivial. Then, just as during World War II, Americans tempered their attitudes to the task of winning a long struggle and gradually came to endorse a duration species of sports as a necessary balance for the increasing strain thrown on the home front. A man worked better if he could get out and exercise now and then, and cast off that heavy-hearted mood.

Americans filed back to their golf courses, occasionally to contracted courses in which three or four or nine holes had been given over to growing food. Some golfers ridiculed these miniature grain gardens as a bogus ascetic gesture—rather like wearing a hairshirt with matching plus-fours. A person either played golf or he didn't, and there was no sense kidding ourselves about the tremendous good sacrificing the ninth and tenth holes was going to do for our boys Over There. The bulk of American golfers knew that fact supported the cynics, but it made them feel less guilty about indulging their pleasures when they saw the wheat tossing on the old tenth. Some clubs spared their holes and satisfied their consciences by turning other tracts they owned into farms.

As 1917 wore on, the issue of "to golf or not to golf" gave way to measures for manipulating the Saturday and special tournaments so that they were in some way integrated with the war effort. On Independence Day, Liberty Tournaments, held concurrently at 485 golf clubs in forty-four states, grossed a total of $72,000 in war bond subscriptions; the members of the Allegheny Country Club showed the way by subscribing over $4,000 worth. Many clubs voted to divert 50 percent of their tournament fees into a fund for buying an ambulance. Nearly all clubs substituted War Savings Stamps and Liberty Bonds for the traditional tournament prizes. In a favorite type of war tourney, each entrant bought a bond, ranging from $50 to $5,000, before teeing off; the prizes for the winners were checks for one-tenth of the purchase price of their bonds.

Shortly after the nation's declaration of war, the U.S.G.A. canceled the national championships. No official Open or Amateur was held during the war, but the U.S.G.A. answered the public demand for a meeting of the "name golfers" by staging a tournament called the Patriotic Open and distributing the receipts among war-service organizations. The Professional Golfers Association, which had been formed in 1916, took the cue and encouraged its stars to offer their services gratis for all exhibitions in which the proceeds went to war charities. However, it was the Western Golf Association that, more clearly than any other golf organization, perceived the role exhibition golf could play in raising funds and carried out the most ambitious wartime program.

The scope and progressiveness of the W.G.A.'s activities made the U.S.G.A. look moribund in comparison, and this was all right with the large majority of American golfers. In the winter of 1916 the U.S.G.A. had made itself highly unpopular by barring Francis Ouimet from amateur golf. Technically, the association had a good case. At that time the U.S.G.A. definition of a professional was, in a nutshell, a person engaged in any business connected with the game of golf. Ouimet had been warned that he would forfeit his amateur standing if he went through with his announced intention to open a sporting goods store with his friend Jack Sullivan. Francis had persisted in his plan, and the U.S.G.A. had no other alternative than to consider him a professional—at least in the opinion of President Frank L. Woodward. Over the agonizing months in which Ouimet's status hung fire, his conduct, as always, was above reproach. He thought the action grossly unfair, but kept his thoughts discreetly to himself. He obeyed the U.S.G.A.'s order to refrain from amateur competitions until the summer of 1917, when his patience was exhausted and he entered (and won) the Western Amateur. If ever a golfer possessed the true spirit of the amateur, it was Ouimet. Close upon his epochal victory in 1913, he had been besieged with many attractive offers, including contracts for vaudeville and movie appearances that would have netted him $15,000. He had turned them all down flatly. He had worked in sporting goods stores before deciding to go into partnership with Sullivan. If the new ruling of the U.S.G.A. made him a professional—okay, it made him a professional. He had given Sullivan his word and intended to keep it. As Ouimet's friends pointed out, had Francis wanted to be cute, he could have accepted any number of jobs offered him by wealthy admirers that would have assured him a handsome income and would not have endangered his amateur status, technically. Obviously what was wrong was the definition of what constituted a professional, but this was lost on President Woodward, who went gunning for his man, won his legal case, saved face, and lost the day.

No one attacked Woodward and the U.S.G.A. with more vituperation than Walter J. Travis. The Old Man had a personal grievance to settle: under the new definition,

Travis, like all architects, was judged a professional. In his column in the *American Golfer* Travis lambasted the U.S.G.A. for its failure to be a body truly representative of the country's golfers, for the "intense conservatism" of its self-perpetuating clique, its archaic constitution, and, to be sure, its highhandedness in L'Affaire Ouimet. The most penetrating remarks on the controversy were made by W. O. McGeehan. "Some of the men who compose the U.S.G.A.," commented that outstanding sports writer, "seemed to believe that there was some intensified stigma attached to the word *professional*. Personally I prefer the professional writers from the late Mr. Shakespeare down to George Ade to talented amateur authors. I would rather hear Caruso sing one aria than I would a gifted amateur tenor sing a dozen—much rather. . . . And I would rather see Nazimova on the stage than the most talented amateur actress-lady in all the Middle West."

For its jampacked schedule of exhibition matches, the Western Golf Association had a willing workhorse in Chick Evans. While he was sweating out acceptance into the Aviation Service, the double champion gave up every weekend during the golfing seasons to play exhibitions for the Red Cross and other charities. In 1918 he traveled twenty-six thousand miles in the course of performing in forty-one different cities, and assisted in raising $300,000. Some Sundays he teamed up with his amateur colleague, Warren Wood, and fought it out in four-ball matches with the ranking professionals, Walter Hagen, the Western Open Champion, Jim Barnes, the P.G.A. Champion, and Jock Hutchison, who had bounded to fame by winning the Patriotic Open by seven strokes. At other times Evans filled out a foursome in which the other players were pros, and, as often as not, was low man for the round. When Warren Wood fell ill, Bobby Jones stepped into his shoes, and Jones and Evans made a very successful swing through the East.

Previous to teaming up with Evans, fifteen-year-old Bobby Jones had played the full exhibition circuit with three other youngsters—Perry Adair, Alexa Stirling, and Elaine Rosenthal. Elaine was the best woman golfer in the Middle West, and Alexa, when she was only nineteen, had carried off the United States Women's Championship in 1916. Perry was the Atlanta neighbor and boyhood rival of Bobby Jones and a youthful prodigy in his own right. The troupe usually played mixed four-ball matches. One day Bobby would team up with Elaine, the next with Alexa. Now and then the girls would sit out a date and watch the Dixie Kids, Jones and Adair, fire away against players twice their age. No one who saw the kids ever forgot Alexa and Elaine clouting their mashies as naturally as most girls took to dancing, or Bobby and Perry wearing their red Swiss Guard berets and having the time of their lives making the hard game of golf look as easy as hopscotch.

While he was awaiting induction into the army, Francis Ouimet participated in many Red Cross exhibitions in New England. Francis' regular partner was Jesse Guilford, a big bruising fellow from New Hampshire who had earned the sobriquet of "The Siege Gun" when he appeared at Ekwanok in the 1914 Amateur and had

Woodrow Wilson, another of the many American presidents who have been devoted to golf.

walloped tee shots that had to be seen to be believed. Jesse's drive on the first hole, for instance, had *carried* a bunker 280 yards from the tee. Francis and Jesse made a formidable combination, and their matches against Mike Brady and Louis Tellier were packed with good and exciting golf. (Brady, incidentally, had tied a record on Labor Day 1917 by scoring holes-in-one on the sixth and thirteenth holes during the course of a round at Siasconset on Nantucket.) In the winter of 1918 when Ouimet was inducted at Camp Devens, he was reinstated as an amateur by the U.S.G.A. There was no strict legal logic behind the reinstatement. The *good* reason given by Howard W. Perrin, the new U.S.G.A. president, was that things were different now that Francis had severed his connections with his sporting goods firm upon entering the service. The *real* reason was that the Perrin administration was anxious to right the wrongs that had brought down upon the head of the U.S.G.A. such deserved unpopularity. An opportunity to make amends to Ouimet had presented itself when he was inducted, and Perrin's alacrity in seizing it met with the approval of every golfer in the country.

Because of its record in raising millions of dollars during World War I, golf achieved a new dignity in the eyes of Americans. They came to know the star players as respectable citizens, and to re-evaluate the professionals in particular. The non-golfers were startled and agape at the generosity of the fairway fraternity—men who shelled out hundreds of dollars for the privilege of acting as caddie or fore-caddie for Evans and Barnes, who paid thousands of dollars for the balls used by Jones and Hagen or for the favorite clubs of Travers and Hutchison. The two hundred members of the Lake Shore Country Club in Chicago set the record high when they contributed $35,000 to the Red Cross the day Evans played their course and Julius Rosenwald came out from Washington to act as auctioneer.

The afternoon before the Armistice, Findlay Douglas and Walter Travis, those two arch-rivals of turn-of-the-century golf, pulled themselves together and played a bang-up exhibition match. Travis was the winner, 1 up. In the auction following the match, the Schenectady putter the Old Man had used in winning the British Amateur went for $1,700. At that price, it was a steal.

SAM'S BOYS
AND
JOHN'S BOYS

World War I ended in the autumn of 1918. Compared with the suffering of nations nearer to the battlefields, the United States had got off lightly, but there had been strain and sorrow and sacrifice, and the Armistice found Americans in a furious hurry to enjoy themselves. The post-war neurosis led to many excesses, and perhaps the national mania for sports that erupted was excessive too, but it seemed so healthy and innocent, so prophylactic, almost, in contrast with some of our other enthusiasms that it struck most Americans as the perfect fusion of the good old days and the brave new world. The nation played sports and watched sports with a wild-eyed seriousness it has never abandoned and modified only slightly in times of depression and war. The nation asked for champions, and got them aplenty in the "Golden Age of Sport" that followed—Jack Dempsey, Babe Ruth, Bobby Jones, Charlie Paddock, Bill Tilden, Red Grange, Helen Wills, Johnny Weismuller, the Four Horsemen, Glenna Collett, Gene Tunney, Aileen Riggin, and hordes of satellites who, in less abundant heavens, would have been stars of the first magnitude.

Golf rode forward on the crest of the wave. Golf courses cut their grainfields and resurrected the plans for enlargement that the war years had postponed. The men newly rich from the war became the most ardent of the ardent recruits, the country-clubbers made architecture a paying profession, the golf ball manufacturers started their search once again for balls that would go ten yards farther and possibly develop an allergy to sand traps and rough. This fever for doing things bigger and better communicated itself to our leading players, amateur and professional. The war had, of course, prevented our amateurs from taking a crack at the British Amateur, and now they were burning to make up for lost time and show the world that they had outgrown their ineptitude at playing good golf in Britain. The American pros, spurred on by the unexpected esteem they had earned during the war, set their sights on the British Open. Winning this championship would be the quick way to rid themselves of the inferiority complex acquired through their previous humiliations on foreign courses. A period of high-pitched international rivalry was in the making, for on the other side of the Atlantic the British had returned to their links after five years of war with a similar eagerness for the game and great expectations for their new stars and renascent champions.

The year 1919 was one of preparation for both sides. Though no national championships were conducted in Britain, the British golfing fans studied the form and the competitive spirit of their golfers, and marked down the men on whom they could rely to uphold the nation's supremacy. Among the pros, George Duncan and Abe Mitchell looked to be the logical successors to the now superannuated Great Triumvirate of Harry Vardon, James Braid, and J. H. Taylor. Duncan was playing perceptibly better than before the war, and if he would only stop his interminable theorizing, there was no knowing what heights George could reach with his sound, stylish swing and those not in-frequent "mad rounds" in which he could do no wrong. Mitchell wasn't in a class with Duncan for style—his followthrough was the shortest ever sported by a first-rate golfer—but he could score and he could do wonderful things in match play. Behind these two standouts in the professional ranks came golfers like Charles and Ernest Whitcombe and young Arthur Havers, who apparently had the stuff from which champions are made. Ted Ray was now in his forties, and while Britishers recognized that their stars had a miraculous longevity that enabled them to continue in competition at an age when their American contemporaries were content to give lessons—well, anything that Ted won would be so much velvet. And that went double, naturally, for Sandy Herd, the color-ful Scot who had made nineteen holes-in-one during his long career on the links and now, approaching his fifties, was beginning to show signs of slowing down.

And how about the British amateurs? Two of the best bets were those youngsters up at Oxford, Tolley and Wethered. Cyril Tolley was a rugged fellow with a leonine head who had spent thirteen months in a German prison camp. Roger Wethered was a big chap, too, rangier in build than Tolley, long off the tees though inclined to be wild, and with an understanding of shot values as instinctive as his sister Joyce's. Willie Hunter, the son of the professional at Deal, Tommy Armour from the Braid Hills of Edinburgh, Robert Harris, Sir Ernest Holderness—they were all good and getting better, though it was a pity Holderness spent so much valuable time working at the Home Office. All in all, both the amateur and professional contingents were strong, and Britons were not worried about the assaults being mapped in America.

After the wartime hiatus, the United States Open and Amateur were restored in 1919. No Britishers had come over to play in them, and Americans were able to scan the new and old faces of our native golfers with the impersonal objectivity of a football coach watching his squad work out on the Wednesday before the big Saturday game. Davy

Herron, who won the Amateur at Oakmont, was a competent golfer—anyone who won the Amateur had to be—but it was questionable if Davy had a game that, day in and day out, was in a class with those of the other rising amateur stars, such as Jesse Guilford, Max Marston, Fred Wright, and especially the youthful veteran whom Herron had whipped in the final of the Amateur, Bobby Jones. From all sections of the country reports were coming in on the dazzling scoring feats of kids barely out of high school. Let them get a little more experience under their belts and they would be playing low-seventy rounds in big-league competition as well as on their home courses. And to steady these youngsters, we had Francis and Chick and Bob Gardner, who seemed old only because they had come upon the scene at such tender ages. They were still young men and topnotch golfers.

American golf fans also liked the looks of our pros. At the head of the heap there was Walter Hagen—he took the Open again in 1919—and close behind "The Haig" were Jock Hutchison and Jim Barnes. Both Barnes and Hutchison had been born overseas, Jim in Cornwall and Jock in St. Andrews, but they had developed their games in the States and were looked upon as American golfers. Barnes was six foot three, as lean as Chile, with a thatch of undisciplined light-brown hair swirling above his studious face. There was a bit of a loop at the top of Barnes' crouching swing but even the loop was grooved and Jim had very few off-days, as his sweep in 1919 of the North and South, the Western, the Shawnee, the Southern, and the P.G.A. Championships well corroborated. On and off the course, he was serious-minded but relaxed, and Americans came to associate him with the cloverleaf he liked to chew in the corner of his mouth. Hutchison's temperament was the antithesis of Barnes'. In a friendly round or off the links, Jock was talkative, high-spirited, and a contagious chuckler. In competition, he was dourness itself and as nervous as a mosquito. He walked around restlessly between shots. He sweated lavishly and took to waving his arms in the air to dry them. He literally twiddled his thumbs. Jock, who had the map of Scotland written all over his face, was in some ways our George Duncan. He had a theory for everything. He had his moods. When he shifted into a brilliant streak, Jock could play one plus-perfect hole after another, each shot, like mountain views in Switzerland, seemingly more breathtaking than the one that went before. Along with the swaggering Hagen, "Hutch" and "Long Jim" comprised our Triumvirate. Their supporting cast consisted of seasoned players like Mike Brady and young pros like Leo Diegel working their way to the top step by step—caddie, caddie-master, assistant pro, pro at a small club, pro at a large club, with the last jump more often than not depending on their degree of success in sectional and national tournaments.

In 1920 the Americans were ready for light attacks on the British citadels, the Open and the Amateur.

The assault force on the British Amateur at Muirfield, east of Edinburgh, consisted of gentleman golfers like Nelson Whitney and Bob Gardner (who was in Britain as the representative of the U.S.G.A. to discuss rules and regulations with the Royal and Ancient). Gardner started slowly. M. M. Burrell of Troon carried him to the eighteenth green, and Ted Blackwell, the man Travis had defeated away back in the final in 1904, held on until the sixteenth. As had often happened in the past, Gardner's stamina made him an increasingly dangerous opponent as the tournament progressed and players less bountifully endowed physically began to fold under the strain of playing two matches a day. Bob moved safely through the fourth round (where Whitney was ousted), and his 36 on the out-nine sewed up his fifth-round match. In the sixth, he shook off the challenge of Gordon Lockhart by birdieing the eighteenth for a 2-up victory, and he won his semi-final match with Michael Scott by once again playing the home hole superbly. In the other half of the draw, Cyril Tolley, the burly Oxfordian, had played his way into the final. On his march Tolley had never given his opponents a look-in, and Britishers, now that Gardner had worked his way into a position where he could repeat Travis' triumph, were prepared to cheer Tolley on to still greater heights in the final.

The Tolley–Gardner match was a hectic battle between two stalwart athletes. It was a hard match to lose and a great match to win. With thirty-two holes behind him and only four to play, Tolley stood 3 up. Gardner cut it to 2 up by winning the 33rd when Tolley overpitched the green. He cut it to 1 when he took the 34th. Both players holed missable putts to halve the 35th, and this brought Tolley to the home hole dormie 1. Gardner followed his drive on the 36th by fading a cleek beautifully into the pin, won the hole, and sent the match into sudden death.

The first hole at Muirfield in those days was a one-shotter. Gardner, up first, found the green with his iron. Tolley hit an even better shot, about fourteen feet from the pin. Gardner put his putt up close and stood by helplessly as Tolley rolled his bid for a deuce straight into the back of the cup and was immediately engulfed by his ecstatic countrymen. It had been touch-and-go but Britain had held.

Gardner's performance at Muirfield had given British golfers the jitters. The mediocre play of Barnes and Hagen's ignominious debut in the British Open restored their aplomb. Hagen had come to Deal, on the coast of Kent, ballyhooed as the greatest golfer ever produced in America, a dashing competitor who time after time cut loose with a finishing kick as irresistible as Snapper Garrison's. At Deal, Hagen failed to break 80 on any of his four rounds. His finishing kick was a hot 84, and he ended up in 55th place, twenty-six strokes behind the winner, George Duncan. Duncan had made up a deficit of thirteen strokes on Mitchell on the third round, a comeback and a crash that were debated in the pubs for many weeks afterwards but scarcely interested Americans. Barnes had finished sixth at Deal, but that was cold comfort.

To make matters worse, Ted Ray topped off a British counter-offensive by taking *our* Open in 1920. Ray and Vardon, grayer now and shaggier at the mustache, had come over that summer for a second tour, another financial and artistic success. But when it came to the Open, much as Americans respected the evergreen prowess of the two Jerseymen, we were less awed by their reputations than we had been in 1913, when we had practically conceded them the title. In 1920 we looked to Hagen and Barnes to make up for their fiasco in the British Open, and Hutchison, Evans, and Jones could be counted on as a second tide.

All the Opens from 1909 on had been rich in excitement, but the 1920 championship at Inverness, in Toledo, topped every one except the classic Open of 1913 in the tumultuous, nerve-tingling drama that unfolded on the afternoon of the final round. Old Harry Vardon, the master himself, led the field at the three-quarter mark. Vardon's 218 gave him a one-stroke lead over Hutchison and inexperienced Leo Diegel, two over Ray. (Hagen and Barnes were not far back but they never looked like winning.) Harry was playing the same immaculate golf he had exhibited a quarter of a century earlier in winning his first British Open, and all transatlantic rivalry was momentarily forgotten as the gallery spilled over the course to pay homage to Vardon and watch the great man win what would probably be his last championship. At the 64th tee it looked as if Harry would do it. He had gone out in 36 with no trouble. He could take as many as forty-one strokes coming in and still top the best total so far posted, a 296 by Jack Burke, a young homebred who had turned in a last-round 72. Harry began the long voyage home with a par on the tenth and a birdie on the eleventh. As he stood on the twelfth tee preparing to play that 522-yard hole, the sky suddenly grew indigo and a vicious gale blew off Lake Erie and ripped across the fairways. Playing into the teeth of the gale, Vardon needed four shots to get home on the twelfth, and took a 6. He stood firm against the smashing wind on the thirteenth until he set himself to sink a 2-footer for his par, and jabbed it wide. The fifty-year-older was utterly weary now. He three-putted the fourteenth, and try as he did to summon one last measure of skill, he three-putted the fifteenth and the sixteenth. On the seventeenth, he failed to carry the brook before the green with his second shot and limped home, spent and forlorn. Vardon had gone 7 over par on the last seven holes, and his 78 was good enough only for a tie with Burke. The storm had been too much for his years.

The crowd raced back from the clubhouse to find Ray, Diegel, and Hutchison.

Ray had swept out in 35. His putter had compensated for his early lapses. On the first four holes he had gotten down putts of thirty, twenty-five, forty, and fifteen feet. He really couldn't kick when he missed comparatively short ones on the eighth and ninth. Like Vardon he wobbled badly coming home, but his 40 gave him a 75 and a total of 295, a stroke better than Vardon's and Burke's.

Diegel, from Lake Shore, had gone out in 37. The young man was becoming more and more nervous as he moved into the in-nine, yet he was still hitting the ball handsomely. He had putts for birdies from four feet and seven feet on the tenth and twelfth, and although he had missed them both, pars would see him through. Chick Evans had taken over Diegel's bag from his caddie in an effort to lend the youngster the benefit of his years of tournament experience, and by the thirteenth hole an ever-swelling gallery had clustered around the neophyte to pray him home. The fourteenth finished Diegel. He half-topped his drive when a spectator coughed. His tenseness mounted. As he was lining up his brassie, about to play his second, a homebred pro, trying to be helpful, broke through the front line of the gallery to report a high score by Ray. Understandably upset by this interruption, Diegel threw his brassie to the ground. "I don't care what Ray took," he said in disgust. "I'm playing my own game." When he finally hit that brassie, Leo hooked it into trouble and could do no better than a 6, two over par. He came to the seventeenth faced with birdieing either that hole or the eighteenth to tie with Ray, but missed a 10-footer and a 25-footer and had blown the first of his many chances to win the Open.

Like Diegel, Jock Hutchison needed a birdie and a par on the last two holes to tie Ray, and couldn't get the birdie. On the 69th green Jock had commented after choking on a 3-foot putt, "That shot cost me the championship." It had at least cost him a crack at a playoff.

Ray won the championship on the dogleg seventh. On each of his four rounds, he had thrown all of the power in his rough, sloping shoulders into his tee shot and carried the trees in the V of the dogleg 275 yards out. Twice he had driven the green, and on all four rounds he had snared his birdie 3. Ray was forty-three years old at Inverness, the oldest golfer ever to win our Open.

A fragment of our national honor was salvaged in the Amateur of 1920, played at the Engineers' Country Club on Long Island. Tolley, Tommy Armour, Lord Charles Hope, and Roger Wethered had come over for the event, but Armour was the only one to get by the qualifying round and he went out early in the match play. Chick Evans, who won the tourney, almost came a cropper in the second round when he had to sink a wicked 14-foot sidehiller on the last hole to tie Reggie Lewis and then had to last out five extra holes before the ordeal was over. In the final Evans faced Ouimet, who had eliminated Jones. This was only the second time Evans and Ouimet had met in a national championship. The year before Francis had taken Chick 1 up. This time it was Chick's turn. In winning 7 and 6, Chick covered a stretch of nineteen holes in 71 strokes, was trapped only twice all day, and didn't miss a putt he should have holed. Chick was rightfully pleased with all this.

American golfers did better in 1921. In the two of the four major championships played in the United States, the British entries were held in check. Neither Duncan nor Mitchell, who came over for the Open at the Columbia Country Club, in Chevy Chase, Maryland, could keep up with the torrid pace set by Long Jim Barnes—and for that matter, none of the homebreds could. Jim finished with a margin of nine strokes over Hagen and Freddy McLeod, who tied for second. In the Amateur at the St. Louis Country Club, Willie Hunter, the British postal clerk who had won the British Amateur earlier in the year, looked dangerous when he upset Bobby Jones in the third round, but Bob Gardner stopped Willie in the semis. In the final, played over a waterlogged course, Jesse Guilford put on an astounding exhibition of slugging and golfing—in one spurt he tied four birds together—and gave Gardner a bad beating. (Jesse was as shy as they came and, for laconic honesty, his acceptance speech has yet to be equaled: "If I am expected to give a speech," Jesse drawled, "I am sorry I won the title.")

In the spring of 1921, well before these domestic championships had taken place, a half dozen or so American pros and a larger group of amateurs had sailed to England on their first full-scale invasion. Because of their disappointing records in both the Opens of 1920, we were not overly sanguine about the chances of our pros. Gardner's success, on the other hand, had hoisted our hopes that the British Amateur crown might be carried off by one of the young men in the party Bill Fownes was taking across. It turned out just the other way.

In what was more or less a warmup for the British Amateur, Fownes' boys met a team of British amateurs at Hoylake in an informal match that set the pattern for the Walker Cup competition officially inaugurated the next season. At Hoylake the American team—Francis, Chick, Fownes, Jones, Guilford, Paul Hunter, Woody Platt, and Fred Wright—won all four of the foursomes and five of the eight singles matches. This convincing 9–3 victory, coming on the eve of the Amateur, reinforced our faith in the chances of the American players and spread a corresponding gloom through Britain. The fans in Scotland and England steeled themselves to accept an American champion. Sooner or later a foreigner was bound to break through again, they rationalized, and if this was destined to be the year, there was nothing to do except to get it over with.

In the Amateur our players failed to hold the form they had displayed in the team match. One by one they fell by the wayside, and often at the hands of "unknowns" who had entered the tournament principally because it gave them a more intimate view of the proceedings. Jones' showing was typical. In the second round against a nobody by the name of Hamlet, who clocked an 87, Bobby had all he could do to win 1 up. He was more like himself in winning his third match, but in the next round Allan Graham, an old gentleman with a brass putter, went out after Jones from the first tee and nailed his man 6 and 5. By the fifth round, Paul Hunter and Freddy Wright were the only two Americans still surviving. In that round Hunter was defeated by Bernard Darwin, and it was Darwin who also accounted for Wright in the sixth. The evening after he had ousted Wright, the last American threat, Darwin, the famed golf correspondent of the *Times* of London, walked into a marvelous incident. He was shuffling in a happy mood down a village street when he found himself the object of an inquisitive stare from a man advancing up the sidewalk from the opposite direction. Darwin didn't place the face, and, concluding that the stare was just an idiosyncrasy of the stranger's, made up his mind to keep on walking. As Darwin was about to pass him, the stranger suddenly shifted over, intentionally it seemed, and blocked Bernard's path. "Sir," said the stranger solemnly as he looked Bernard in the eye, "I would like to thank you for the way in which you have saved your country."

The British Open in '21 was scheduled for St. Andrews, Jock Hutchison's hometown, and the local boy who had made good in America decided to combine a long-delayed visit with a try for the title. He arrived in St. Andrews in the winter, long

Long Jim Barnes. The angular Cornishman spread his major conquests over a period of nine years. In 1916 he won the first P.G.A. Championship, in 1921 the U.S. Open, and in 1925 the British Open. A fine student of the game, Barnes was one of the first of the name pros to cash in by writing an instruction book.

before the other contenders. In the months before the Open, Hutchison gave his admiring townsmen something to look at—the most consistent low scoring on the Old Course since the days of Young Tom Morris. If he continued to play golf of that caliber, Jock would be a hard man to beat, but his supporters were afraid that he might go stale before the championship got underway. Jock had done that before. At Brae Burn in 1919 and Inverness in 1920, he had spent his brilliance during the qualifying rounds and was relatively played out when the championship proper began.

In the qualifying round for the Open, Jock was up to his old habits. Two effortless rounds gave him a total of 146, and if he could stay in that groove, he would take some beating. Jock's first round in the championship was a 1-under-par 72 in which the popular native son just missed scoring holes-in-one on two consecutive holes. He got an ace on the 135-yard eighth, and on the ninth, then 278 yards long, Hutchison smacked a drive that ran onto the green and, trickling up to the hole as softly as if it had been putted, caught a corner of the cup, twisted out, and just stayed out. Jock's second round, a 75, kept him up with the leaders but at the same time worried his backers. He did look over-golfed. Then in the crucial third round—all rounds of an Open are crucial but the third is often the real killer—Hutchison fell apart. A 79 gave him 226 at the three-quarter mark and left him four strokes behind Barnes, who had played three 74s, and Sandy Herd, the 1902 Open Champion, who refused to act his age. Jock was also a stroke behind Roger Wethered, whose 225 included an unlucky penalty stroke; Roger had accidentally kicked his ball on the third round as he backed up to play an approach after sighting the terrain ahead. Hutch was one of the last to go out on the final round, teeing off at about the same time that his father, caddying for another entry, came down the eighteenth. Hutch's work was cut out for him. Herd and Barnes had soared to 80s but Wethered had added a final 71, and to tie, Jock had to play a 70, 3 under par. His 36 out looked to be a little too much, but Jock sent his home-town gallery into raptures by turning on his maddest golf just when he had to and played the difficult last nine in 34. He came within a hair of holing his putt on the home green for an outright win. In the 36-hole playoff against Wethered, Jock caught the amateur on one of his more erratic days, and playing a heady 74 and 76, won the title with nine strokes to spare.

That was something, Hutchison's victory in the Open. For the first time since Arnaud Massy of France had won at Hoylake in 1907, the cup had gone to a foreigner, and this time to a foreigner from a distant country. Some Britishers persisted in viewing Hutchison as one of their own, but Jock was an American citizen when he won, and indeed an American golfer, and back in the States his spectacular triumph was acclaimed the first twist in the lion's tail by "one of our boys." Subsidiary praise was in order for Barnes, Hagen, and Tom Kerrigan of Siwanoy. Kerrigan finished with a pair of 72s to come within two strokes of the winning total. Though he had played indifferently for him, Hagen had tied for sixth, and this was at least an improvement over his performance the year before at Deal.

The climactic victory came in 1922. Hagen won at Royal St. George's, in Sandwich. This time there was no escape from the facts for the British, as there had been the year before in Hutchison's dual nationality. Hagen was a homebred, as American as apple pie—or perhaps a mint julep would be a more appropriate symbol. Walter's break-through at Sandwich, in the minds of both the American and British publics, signalized success-at-last for the American invasions of the island where golf was born.

Hagen was himself at Sandwich. He led off with a mediocre 76, but a 73 in the

Jock Hutchison, along with Barnes and Hagen, formed the triumvirate that dominated American golf during and just after World War I. As fidgety as the second hand of a watch, Jock could on occasion cut loose with rounds of absolutely inspired golf. The deeply punched faces on Jock's irons imparted great spin to the ball.

wind put him in the lead by one stroke at the halfway mark. His bad round, a 78, could have been much higher had he not come through with sensational recoveries several times when it looked as if he had again played himself out of the championship. At the end of fifty-four holes, even with the 78, he was bracketed with Jim Barnes and Charles Whitcombe just one stroke off of the pace set by Jock Hutchison. On the last round, all of the leaders stood up fairly well. Barnes played a 73, Whitcombe a 75, Hutchison a 76. Hagen won because, for the first time in Britain, he uncorked his tremendous finishing kick, what we in American termed a "Hagen finish." His 72 put him one stroke ahead of Barnes, and all he had to do now was sweat out George Duncan. George, well behind the leaders all the way, was off on one of his dream rounds, putting for birdies from twelve feet or less on every other hole as he snubbed the elements and the gathering darkness. Duncan came to the 72nd needing a par 4 to tie Hagen. All his valor went for nought when he tightened up on his chip and had to take a 5. Hagen was in.

The British Open was the only one of the four major championships in 1922 with a robust international flavor. In winning our Open at Skokie, Gene Sarazen, a new name, had surprised a field that included only two British entrants—Duncan and Mitchell. None of our ranking amateurs went over to try for the British Amateur (which Ernest Holderness won), for they were too busy preparing for the first official Walker Cup Match, to be played at Macdonald's National. While the British title still eluded them, U.S. amateurs demonstrated that on American soil, at any rate, they were now more skillful than the men from the British Isles. The American team took the Walker Cup competition 8 points to 4, and in the national Amateur, which followed shortly afterwards at The Country Club, in Brookline, our golfers quickly converted the foreign threats into innocent spectators. As it turned out, Jess Sweetser, the strong boy from Siwanoy who won our Amateur that year, became some four years later the first American-born golfer to win the British Amateur.

In the four years that had elapsed since the end of the war, American players had completely altered the complexion of international golf. Our amateurs had won one unofficial and one official team match against their British rivals, and while they had been repulsed in their efforts to take the British Amateur, it was clear that it would be only a matter of time before that enemy citadel would fall. Our pros, led by a homebred and a naturalized American, had captured the British Open two years in a row and were on their way to creating what would be, for over a decade, virtually an American championship. There would be times when British golfers, pro and amateur, would rise and demonstrate with authority that America did not have a monopoly on the first-class shot-makers, but these British triumphs were few and far between, sporadic protests rather than the clarions of a national resurgence.

By 1923, the leadership in golf had passed from Great Britain to the United States. Here at home our first successes ignited the ambitions of a younger generation to become the builders of a golfing empire of more grandiose proportions. In Great Britain, the golf fans began their long wait for an emancipator, yet there was no mourning. Harold Hilton, the old victor at Apawamis, voiced the feelings of the nation when he said in his most delicate phraseology: "There can be no doubt that the American player of the game has somewhat rudely annexed that presumptive hereditary right of ours. Recent events have proved beyond dispute that the standard of the game as played in the United States is at least of a more consistent and accurate description than that which we are in the habit of witnessing on courses in the British Isles. To put the matter in the very plainest of language, American players of the present day are better golfers than their British cousins."

SIR WALTER

Unlike many of the golfers who went before and after him, the long career of Walter Hagen does not present one great year, one great tournament, or even one great round towering high and as incontrovertible as an Everest over the ridges of his other accomplishments. If charted on a graph, Hagen's two decades and more as a top tournament golfer would show a series of peaks, many of similar altitude, with the tallest peaks invariably following a sizable depression. The reader of the graph, as a result, is able to make out a fairly good case for whatever peak in the zagging line strikes him as the man's finest hour—winning the U.S. Open in 1914, the U.S. Open in 1919, the British Open in 1922, the British Open again in 1924, 1928, and 1929, or taking the P.G.A. title four years in a row, overwhelming Jones in their one "private" match, leading our Ryder Cuppers, or urging his ancient bones in a last brave challenge in the Open at Oakmont in 1935. They were all great moments, and it can be argued that the sum of the man's deeds is more readily appreciated because of the absence of any one overriding climax.

Hagen's essentially dramatic personality made him acutely conscious that there was something unfinished, something incomplete, about his career. In one tight spot after another, he had demonstrated to his own satisfaction and to the delighted astonishment of the public that he, like no other golfer, could call upon himself for the one shot he needed and come up with it. In the latter stages of his career, believing that in his bag one last parade of winning shots lay unplayed, he continued to appear in tournaments hoping that under the stress of competition he would be able to summon these shots and win that crowning championship. Hagen never quite got them out, and so he never went into an abrupt retirement, but continued to make one farewell appearance after another, very much in the tradition of Sarah Bernhardt.

Somehow it is difficult to picture Hagen having a childhood or a period in which he put his game together by stern, unglamorous practice. He etched his personality so deeply on the minds of sports followers that the mere mention of his name still evokes the full image of the man—hair brilliantined, face tanned and smiling with an almost Oriental inscrutability, clothes that would have looked showy on anyone else, the haughty stride back onto the fairway after punching a recovery shot through the brambles and onto the carpet. This man, you felt, had always been that way. Like Athena, he had undoubtedly emerged full-blown from the forehead of some twentieth-century Zeus.

Walter Hagen, who was of Dutch extraction, was quite a boy. Like the other kids in his neighborhood in Rochester, Walter was crazy about golf and baseball. He had far more talent for both games than any of the fellows he grew up with. In baseball he pitched, naturally. He had no brothers so he taught his sister how to catch in order that he would have someone to hold his stuff in the backyard. He threw with either hand. In time Walter became the best pitcher in the district, and for many years could not make up his mind as to which sport he would make his profession, golf or baseball. A few weeks before he won his first national Open, he finally decided on golf. He had just been offered a contract by the Philadelphia club of the National League, but the way he looked at it, in baseball there were eight other men who could lose a game for you. In golf, there was only yourself. Even so, baseball never lost its fascination for Walter. As late as 1934, when he resembled a third-base coach in portliness, he climbed into the flannels and spikes and worked out with the Detroit Tigers in spring training. There is no knowing how far Walter would have gone in organized baseball or how it would have shaped his personality, but there are many folks who believe he would have attained the same eminence he did in golf. They believe that Walter Hagen was one of those rare ones who would have been an unqualified success in whatever profession or business he chose as his lifework.

Walter caddied at the Country Club of Rochester. Noticing how adept the boy was at fielding any sort of a ball, Andy Christie, the pro, picked out Walter to shag balls for him whenever he gave lessons. Walter graduated to the pro shop and helped with the caddies. On the slow mornings he played nine holes with Christie, and worked in the shop until six. He practiced then until it was dark, took a dip in the creek, and walked home to eat the supper that his folks had left in the oven.

When the Open was played at Buffalo in 1912, Hagen asked Christie for a week's leave of absence from his duties as assistant pro to play in the tournament. Christie couldn't see it. The kid was only twenty years old, too inexperienced for that sort of competition. If Walter wanted to take a couple of days off to watch the tournament, all right, but there was no sense letting the kid make a fool of himself trying to keep up with the gang who played in the Open. Walter went to Buffalo and watched Johnny McDermott win the championship. He picked up a few pointers from studying the stars, but by and large he was not impressed by what he saw. The big boys weren't as good as he thought they would be.

The next season, 1913, Hagen tested his belief that he could stick with the best professionals by playing in the Shawnee Open and the national Open. He didn't set any worlds on fire at Shawnee, but he didn't disgrace himself, and in the Open he finished in a tie for fourth. That was the year Vardon and Ray were expected to take the title out of the country. None of the leading pros gathered at The Country Club knew the black-haired assistant from Rochester and they got quite a boot when the kid introduced himself to Johnny McDermott in the locker room and explained that he'd "come down to help you fellows stop Vardon and Ray." Ouimet did the stopping, but Walter outscored every American pro except McDermott and brought in the same total as the ex-champion. He was in the running until the last nine, when the pressure told on him. He took a 7 on the fourteenth and sprayed his way home.

Having decided not to be a ballplayer, the kid was on the firing line for the Open in 1914. He turned up at Midlothian wearing what he thought was the last word in rakish straw hats. He liked clothes and had a horror of looking like a hick. When he had made his Open debut at Brookline, he had worn a checked Scottish cap, a fancy bandanna, a striped silk shirt, gray flannels, and shoes with the tongue stylishly doubled back over the instep. He'd show them that he knew how to dress! At Midlothian, a long course for those days, measuring 6,355 yards, Walter jumped into the lead by shooting a 68, a new competitive record for the course. A 74 and a 75 kept him up front, four strokes ahead of Chick Evans as the field entered the last round. All Chicago, it seemed, was following Evans. Playing about three holes ahead of Chick, with no gallery to speak of, Hagen heard one mighty roar after another come from Evans' mob. That could only mean that Chick was hot. He was. He took 35 for the out-nine and had shaved Hagen's lead to one stroke. All the way in, Hagen heard the bursts of applause from Evans' gallery telling him that Chick was still coming. To make it the more menacing, these shattering salvos often split the air just when Walter was engaged in digging himself out of trouble. Walter tried to erase Evans from his mind and to concentrate on his own score. He made up for a hooked midiron on the thirteenth by sinking a 12-footer for his par. On the sixteenth he pulled his brassie and stubbed his chip, but coolly got down a long putt for his birdie. He missed from seven feet on the seventeenth, but on the last green he sank an 8-footer. This last putt constituted Walter's margin of victory.

Hagen had won the Open the right way; he had got out in front and stayed there. He had displayed unusual control of his nerves and seemed to have the physical equipment necessary for a topflight golfer—good hands, good wrists, good forearms. His swing, though, had too much body in it, a good deal of sway. The kid didn't swing, really. He brought the club into position and then *hit* the ball. Walter was a cocky, unapologetic young man, but at the same time he was neither boastful nor disrespectful,

Golf's greatest showman, Walter Hagen, when he was first gaining prominence in 1914. Only two years out of the pro shop in Rochester, Walter captured the Open title at Midlothian in his second shot at the championship. He did it convincingly, jumping into the lead with a 68 on the first round, then outrunning the pack.

and when the older pros commented that the new champion might be only a flash in the pan, their judgments were based on no personal antipathy (apart from a natural touch of jealousy) but on a distrust of Hagen's somewhat unorthodox style.

The new champion was not champion long. He made a poor showing defending his title at Baltusrol, and in 1916 he was not a contender. The experts who had criticized his form could point to these and other disappointing performances as bearing out their prediction that Hagen was not a fundamentally sound golfer . . . and yet some weeks they weren't quite as sure as they would have liked to have been. Walter never went very long without winning some kind of tournament. In 1915 he had to be content with the Massachusetts Open, but in 1916 he took the Metropolitan Open, a big championship in those days, the Shawnee, and the prestigious Western; in winning the Western he had played five holes in thirteen strokes, two 2s and three 3s, terrific golf whether you swayed or you pivoted. Walter always made it a practice never to be without a title during his long career. He preferred it to be a United States or British Open, but during the years he missed out on the big ones, he always had the P.G.A. or the Western or the Metropolitan or the North and South to put under his name. Even when he was supposed to be slipping—and Hagen was supposed to be slipping from 1914 on—he would shift into high long enough to garner a Canadian or some other tournament of distinction, which was a lot more than most of his detractors could say for themselves.

Whether you liked his style or not, by 1917 Walter Hagen had left all the other native-born professionals far behind and was the unanimous choice to captain the team of Homebred Pros when they faced the English Pros, Scottish Pros, and Amateurs in a four-cornered exhibition for war charities. By the close of the war he had joined Jim Barnes and Jock Hutchison as the triumvirate dominating the money-golfers and had earned a reputation as the most colorful shot-maker in the country. He was an amazing finisher. In an exhibition four-ball match in Rochester, for instance, with his side 3 down with five to play, Walter pulled out the match by playing the last five holes in birdies. He could take a course apart in medal play with the best of them, but there was something about match play, the chances it offered for dealing with one crisis after another, that seemed to bring out the sharpest shots in his repertoire. Above all, Hagen was interesting to watch. The other star golfers made the game look easy: all you had to do was knock the ball down the fairway, pitch it on the green, and get down in two putts. Hagen made the game look hard. Once or twice a round he hooked or sliced a drive as savagely as a 90s-golfer, leaving himself a shot that looked absolutely unplayable until he executed a fantastic recovery. These violent errors by a champion had the same effect on the spectators as if they had watched a supposedly flawless tight-rope walker suddenly lose his balance and go hurtling through space into the net below. Then when the performer went back to his perch and this time successfully waltzed on the wire, the spectators realized how hard it really was to walk a tightrope, or play par golf.

A born showman, Hagen could feel the grip he gained on galleries. He discovered that they liked him best when he gave full rein to his developing personality—his unruffled poise in the face of disaster, an unmalicious condescension toward his opponents and toward the galleries themselves, a touch of bravura at those very moments when he could have been forgiven for quailing. But he built his performance on good golf. He was the best putter of his day. His mashie-niblick and spade-mashie play, from 70 to 165 yards, was without peer. This made him especially destructive on a short course. His fairway woods were either very good or very bad, and in important tournaments he preferred to play a long iron to the green if the shot resolved itself into a choice between an iron and a wood. The drive, which for most professional golfers is the easiest shot in the game, always gave Hagen difficulty. He would hit seven or eight straight and long, and on the next tee, with no advance intimation, he would lose the rhythm of his sway the faintest fraction and whack the shot on a vicious curve to either the left or the right—he was impartial. He threw his right side into a drive with such force that on his followthrough his right shoulder was the part of his body nearest the green.

Until the twilight of his career, when whisky fingers destroyed his putting touch and nullified his tardy straightness from tee to green, Hagen was seldom able to play eighteen holes without hitting at least one or two weirdly loose shots. Nine hundred and ninety-nine golfers out of a thousand would have been ruined by this affliction, would have worn themselves out worrying about when that wild shot was coming and fretted themselves helpless when it eventually raised its ugly arc. Hagen didn't let these errors upset him. He was a philosopher, an honest one. He accepted the fact that three times or so a round he would hit a very poor shot—and what was so calamitous about that? No golfer could expect to hit every shot perfectly. As a result, Walter was able to forget about a bad shot almost instantly. Other golfers, knowing that the index of the ideal golfing temperament is the ability to ignore a costly error and keep hitting the ball, asserted that they, too, never let a mistake eat into their confidence, but most of the time they were simply saying words. Hagen was genuinely able to forget his lapses. Equally unique and invaluable was his penchant for remaining relaxed at all times. He regarded this gift as the key to whatever success he enjoyed, and it is significant that he devoted the first chapter of an instruction book he never finished to the importance of relaxation.

In the Open at Brae Burn in 1919, worldly at twenty-seven, as fearless on the golf course as Cobb was on the diamond, Walter won the crown from Mike Brady. It was a triumph of temperament. Walter came to the last nine holes knowing that he had to match par to equal Brady's total. On the 65th hole, he hooked out-of-bounds and lost what could have been a critical stroke. "I'll get a birdie and make up for that little error," Hagen told his fretful friend Harry Martin. He got that bird on the 67th. He stayed with par from then on and arrived at the 72nd tee needing a par 4 on that demanding hole to tie with Brady. Hagen's drive left him with a long iron to the green, a two-level dipper with the pin positioned on the upper deck. Most golfers would have played for a safe 4, aimed for the middle of the green and allowed themselves two putts to get down for a tie. Hagen wasn't built that way. A stone wall fringed the back of the green, ready to punish the bold golfer who overshot the upper level, but Hagen eschewed all cautious tactics and hit a screaming midiron straight for the pin. The ball faded slightly, landed on the dangerous top terrace, and spun itself out eight feet to the right of the hole—a really wonderful shot. Before attempting the putt that could give him an outright win over Brady, Hagen brashly had Mike summoned from the clubhouse so that he would be on hand to watch his own funeral. Mike obliged and shivered in his spikes as Walter tapped his sidehiller into the corner of the cup, only to have it twist out again and linger on the lip.

In the playoff the following day, Hagen defeated Brady by a single stroke. A golfer of less spontaneous shrewdness than Hagen might have lost. On the seventeenth hole of a nip-and-tuck battle, Hagen hit one of his typical loose drives, slicing the ball into the spongy rough. After a lengthy search, the ball was found deeply imbedded in the earth. It looked to Hagen as if some spectator might have inadvertently stepped on his ball, and he requested a free lift. The officials ruled against this: they were not sure the ball had been stepped on. Hagen then asked the officials for permission to identify the ball as his own, a request they were bound to grant. Before the identification was completed, the ball was loosened and some of the mud uncaked. Hagen was able then to play one of his most awesome recoveries.

Such tactics as these time and time again upset the concentration of his adversaries and, just as often, made them so grimly determined to outthink the resourceful Haig that they ended up outthinking themselves. It was this psychological aptitude of Walter's, supplementing his versatile shot-making, which made Americans confident that if any American could bag the British Open Championship, it would be Hagen. There was, as always, a clique of old-school golfers who did not share the general optimism concerning Hagen's chances of beating the British. By 1920 they were willing to admit that on American courses under American conditions Walter was our best tournament scorer but they didn't think he had the shots for the winds that would be swirling over the seaside links at Deal, where the 1920 British Open would be played. Walter, they advanced, hit his shots too high. They would get caught in the wind and blown all over the course. Walter replied to his belittlers that "there are no bunkers in the air." He intended to hit the ball at Deal the way he always did, and he expected to win.

At Deal there were no bunkers in the air but there were plenty on the ground, and Hagen visited a good many of them. The critics of his game had been absolutely right. While shots of low trajectory could bore into the wind and hold their line, Hagen's arching woods and irons were scattered as ruthlessly as the Spanish Armada. He was far behind the leaders after his first round, and with each ensuing round he fell farther and farther back, finishing a dismal 55th. On his four rounds he had averaged over 82 strokes—undoubtedly the most painful comeuppance a national champion ever received. Hagen did not alibi. He never alibied. "I tried too hard, just like any duffer might play," he said, and added with as much audacity as he could collect, "Guess I figured these boys were tougher than they were."

Walter managed to win the French Open at La Boulie on that trip across, and back home he licked Jim Barnes in the playoff for the Metropolitan, but in the U.S. Open, in

The Haig in a not uncharacteristic pose. Two or three times during every round, Walter would come up with fantastically loose strokes, hooking or slicing into a spot previously untrodden by man. He would inspect his lie leisurely, register several shades of disgust, then play a superb recovery to the shadow of the flag.

which he had a chance to redeem himself by stopping Vardon and Ray, he finished with two disappointing 77s. 1921 was a duplication of 1920. He won his first P.G.A. crown and gobbled up his share of minor affairs, but in the pay-off tournaments Walter didn't have it. In the British Open at St. Andrews, though he finished a respectable sixth, he played unimpressively. In the U.S. Open at the Columbia Country Club, he was nine strokes behind the winner, Jim Barnes. These failures in major events reduced the public's faith in Hagen. In 1919 they had sincerely believed that no one could stop him. Now, ever since that awful beating at Deal, American golf fans no longer felt that Hagen would come tearing down the stretch in one of his famous finishes and drive all other scores off the board. Perhaps they had oversold themselves on him back in 1919. Or maybe he was simply past his peak. Whatever the reason for Hagen's decline, they had been wrong in considering him in a class by himself. Obviously, he was just another good pro.

Hagen changed all this by winning the British Open of 1922, at Sandwich. One stroke behind the leader as he set off on his last round, Walter came through with a 72 that gave him a total one stroke below Barnes'. He sat placidly on a mound by the first tee smoking a big cigar as he waited for the last man to come in. The last man was George Duncan, and Hagen went over and watched Duncan blow himself to a bogey 5 on the final hole when he needed a 4 to tie. From fifty-fifth to sixth to first! That was more like it. Hagen went home with the title and made a fortune.

When he defended his title at Troon the next year, Walter failed to catch the winner, Arthur Havers, but was glorious in defeat. When Havers added a 76 to his three 73s, Hagen was left with a 74 to tie. (A 74 may seem like tall shooting today, accustomed as we are to fancy figures in the sixties in *tour tournaments;* a review of the scoring in the major championships will readjust a too glib condescension toward the scores of the Twenties.) After a tough battle in a wild wind, Hagen reached the home hole confronted with the necessity of playing a birdie 3 for that 74. A good drive left him an iron of some 160 yards to the green. He hit a firm spade-mashie but it faded off as it came up to the pin and overran the green into a bunker. Unperturbed, Hagen marched into the bunker and lined up his shot as carefully as if it were a putt and not an explosion shot he had to hole. He studied the texture of the sand, the distance between the bunker and the pin, the rolls of the green . . . and then he played an absolutely beautiful stroke that almost did find the hole. He nonchalantly rolled in the putt that didn't count.

Walter Hagen had a sterling contempt for second place. He believed that the public only remembered the winner, that a man might as well be tenth as second when the shooting was over. At Troon as at Brae Burn before and in many crises still to be faced, Walter went all-out for victory, disdaining a sure second place and several times finishing farther back than second when a one-in-a-million shot for first failed to come off. When the Open was held at the Worcester Country Club in 1925, Walter was informed on the 72nd tee that a par 4 would gain him a tie with the lowest man in. Hagen decided to gamble on a 3, although this meant shaving an approach inches over a brutal bunker backing right up to the pin on the extreme front edge of the terraced green. Walter cut that shot a shade too fine, caught the bunker, and ultimately finished in a tie for third. In the 1926 British Open at Lytham and St. Annes, Walter had a probable second place all wrapped up, but that wasn't good enough. If he could somehow get an eagle 2 on the 72nd hole, he could tie with Bobby Jones for first, and then he would have a chance to win the title in the playoff. Hagen put everything he had into his drive on this last hole, and then all he had to do was to sink a full iron approach.

Before playing that shot, Walter strolled down the fairway to the green, the better to study the terrain. He than ordered his caddie to stand close by the hole so that he could remove the flagstick if his approach, after landing on the front of the green, was headed for it. He then walked back to his ball and played an heroic shot which came extremely close to entering the cup on the fly . . . and Walter was not the least bit regretful when he holed out in 6 after playing back from the hazard into which the approach had rolled.

Hagen's order to his caddie to, in effect, flag the hole on the home green in the Open would have been absurd had any other golfer ordered it. Coming from Hagen, it was wonderfully in character. On and off a golf course, the ex-caddie and sandlot hurler comported himself in a manner as imperial as a king or a Hollywood star. He loved the high life. He drank what would have been for other people excessive quantities of liquor. While it was not exactly habitual, it was not uncommon for him to drive directly from an all-night party to the first tee of the tournament in which he was involved. Some of the other pros who tried to live like Hagen were back mowing greens in Keokuk in a very short time; Walter broke eleven of the Ten Commandments and kept on going. He knew how to take care of himself. He had the right words and the right tie for every occasion. Loving clothes as he did, whenever he had the time he changed into a new outfit between his morning and afternoon rounds. His favorite diversions during the off-season were fishing, shooting, and big-game hunting, and he indulged these tastes with the same lack of restraint that made him so attractive a playmate for those who could afford to play. He liked the big gesture—ordering the pin to be tended or keeping the Prince of Wales waiting or giving his prize money for winning the British Open to his caddie. He refused to enter British clubhouses by the back door, the traditional entrance for professionals; if he was good enough to enter at all, he would use the front door with the other gentlemen, and there was nothing contradictory about being a professional golfer and a gentleman. Sir Walter, as he came to be called, was proud of his profession. More than any other golfer, he brought it a new stature. However, for all his sophistication and velour, Hagen never lost his love of battle or that brash badinage he cultivated on the way up. Sir Walter was only half kidding when he quipped as he teed up on the first hole, "Well, who's going to be second?"

Hagen's never-say-die spirit made him a terror in medal competition. The low man could never relax until Hagen was in, regardless of how poorly Walter seemed to be playing, for it was common knowledge that though Walter hit more rank bad shots in a single round than most pros hit during an entire tournament, somehow he could always score. In match play, when he confronted his opponents in person, not indirectly over the grapevine but solid and satanic in the flesh, Hagen was even more to be feared. His personality was completely dominating. If you tried to kid along with him between shots you could never get down to business when the strokes had to be played, but Walter could. If you tried to shut him out of your mind, the harder you fought to ignore him the more strongly his presence enveloped you. You were attacked by the uneasy feeling that he knew everything you were going to do well in advance, and though you laughed when people attributed sinister powers to him, there were times when you privately agreed with this explanation. There you were, beating your brains out and playing far from your best golf when you wanted more than ever to play your best. And there he was, so damned casual, polite as hell, but with that indelible smirk of superiority playing over those bland features. You could understand from your own experience how a seasoned big-timer like Leo Diegel could lose to Hagen even when he stood 5 up with six holes to play.

Hagen won the P.G.A. Championship, a match-play tourney, five times in all and four years in a row. He had won twenty-two consecutive matches when Diegel finally stopped him in 1928. Only Gene Sarazen, who was as intrinsically cocky as Hagen and could fight fire with fire, was able to stand up against him in man-to-man combat. In 1926, when Bobby Jones was playing some of his finest golf, he and Hagen hooked up in a 72-hole match in Florida, and Walter crushed Bobby 12 and 11.

There are many tricks to match-play psychology and none escaped Hagen's attention. Against pertinacious foes, Hagen occasionally resorted to playing his approaches purposely short of the green to lure his opponent into unconsciously letting up on his shot. Hagen knew he could get down in a chip and a putt, and that the percentage would be working against his opponent. In one P.G.A. tourney he picked up a hole he had to win by an involved yet rather simple piece of chicanery. He and his opponent were about even after their drives, with Hagen a little in front. Hagen drew a long iron from his bag, as if he meant to use that club on his second shot. Observing Hagen's selection, his opponent asked his caddie for a similar iron. His shot ended up yards short of the green. Hagen then replaced his iron, took out the wood he intended to play all along, banged it home, and won the hole. Against players who were weakest on the greens, Hagen was generous in conceding putts in the early stages of a match; then, more likely than not, his opponents would miss the 2-footers that Hagen did not concede at crucial junctures. In later years, when his rivals were on the alert for his wiles, Hagen always gave a truthful answer to the questions they asked. This policy paid off for Hagen as richly as it had for Bismarck in diplomacy; the other fellow persisted in thinking he was being misled. Hagen's reputation as a match player reached such proportions that each error he made was interpreted as a deliberate move to set up some stratagem. In one P.G.A. final, for example, he sliced his drive into a cluster of trees. He frowned as he studied the possible avenues of exit, and shaking his head as if he would be forced to play a sacrifice shot, glumly surveyed the lateral line to the fairway. He returned to his ball and lo! why, he could play it to the green through that small aperture he hadn't seen before. Hagen got the ball on, nicely. His opponent, who thought he had the hole in his pocket, received such a jolt that he mishit his approach and handed Hagen the hole and the match. The gallery was convinced that Walter had sliced into the rough on purpose.

In the Twenties, Hagen established a record in the P.G.A. Championship no one has ever approached. Season after season his average per round for the winter tournaments in the South surpassed the averages of 90 percent of the campaigners. From 1920

Sir Walter at his peak, addressing his British admirers after winning the third of his four British crowns, at Sandwich in 1928. Hagen first tried the British Open in 1920, with disastrous results. He failed to break 80 in any one of his four rounds, and finished 26 shots behind the winner. The next year Walter was a fair-enough sixth, and then in 1922 he broke through at Sandwich.

through 1930, with the exception of Jones, he had the best record in the Open. That was the title he wanted to win the most, just one more time, yet try as he would, Walter was never quite able to do it. His very best golf seemed to come out in England and Scotland.

Hagen won his second British Open in 1924 at Hoylake with one of his most arresting last-ditch spurts. As they set out on the final round, Hagen and Ernest

Whitcombe were locked at 224 in what was virtually a two-man duel. Whitcombe started out ninety minutes before Hagen. Ernest dropped four strokes to par on the first five holes and didn't really get hold of himself until he had reached the turn in 43. However, he fought his way home in 35 strokes over one of the toughest finishing stretches in golf, and his 78 began to look like more than a courageous effort when Hagen, in an erratic mood, ran into three 6s and used up 41 strokes going out. Hagen had been built up by the press as a man who reveled in a chase, and no doubt he did like to set out behind his man and chew up the distance between them, but to beat Whitcombe Hagen had to play home in 36 strokes, and on Hoylake that is a very tall order indeed. He seemed licked at the par-4 tenth when he lay twenty feet from the pin after playing his third. He took what was, even for Hagen, an exceedingly long time before he was satisfied with his line on the putt. Then he rapped it in. On the eleventh, Walter was on the ropes again when he steered an iron into a bunker, but a fine out and a fine putt saved him. On the twelfth he was in another trap, and again pinched the ball perfectly with his niblick. He lined up his 11-footer for his par off his left toe and stroked it into the middle of the hole. How long could he keep this up, this desperate scrambling? He missed his iron on the short thirteenth, and yet once again he managed to get down in 2 from a trap when he followed a delicate cut shot with another nerveless putt. Then he settled down, and where he had been holding on by sheer strength of will, now he began to hit his shots right on the nose, and his pars came easily. At the seventeenth he rifled a 2-iron through the narrow opening to the green and eight feet from the cup, but he failed to drop the birdie putt that would have put him one stroke under even 4s coming in and given him some leeway for error on the last hole, a short par 4. He still needed that par for victory. There was nothing wrong with his drive, but his second shot was too strong and his chip back left him a 9-footer for that 4. The man who could sink the crucial ones sank this putt, and did it so coolly that many spectators wondered if he had realized its importance. "Sure, I knew I had to make it to win," Hagen explained with characteristic bravado, "but no man ever beat *me* in a playoff."

One week before the British Open in 1928, Walter walked into the most humiliating defeat of his long career. Just off the boat after a session before the cameras in Hollywood, badly out of practice, Walter met Archie Compston in a special 72-hole match at Moor Park when that rawboned giant was playing nothing but sub-par figures. Compston clipped off a 67, 66, and a 70, and the fourth round had hardly begun when the match was over—Compston 18 and 17, the most ignominious drubbing ever inflicted in a match between ranking professionals. While the London press was joyfully building up Compston as the native son who would restore British prestige in the Open, Hagen took himself down to the seaside and went into intensive practice. His lacing at Moor Park had fired his old will to win, and he meant to show the world that at thirty-seven, with fifteen years of competition behind him, he was far from finished.

Walter later admitted that he never started a tournament feeling shakier than when he teed up at Sandwich in 1928. He got himself a fair enough 75 to start with, and his confidence returned as he hit the ball more convincingly on each succeeding round. A 73, a 72, and another staunch 72 gave him an aggregate of 292, two strokes lower than Sarazen's and three lower than Compston's. Hagen's margin over Sarazen actually depended on a great recovery he played on his final round. Hagen, out first, was moving along in good style until he slapped his second on the fifteenth into a bunker just before the green with a full Chevalier lip. An explosion shot was not an easy stroke, but under the circumstances it was the safest shot to play, certainly less risky than attempting to pick the ball clean off the sand and hazarding quick and absolute ruin if the blade caught the ball a fraction of an inch too high or contacted a grain too much of sand. So Hagen cut the ball out as cleanly as if it had been the top of the dandelion, got down in one putt; he was safely past his crisis.

The British never learned to leave Hagen alone. Having won the Open three times, Walter had no ardent designs on the 1929 championship. However, in the Ryder Cup matches played at Moortown previous to the Open, George Duncan made the mistake of mauling Hagen 10 and 8, a defeat as personal and as humiliating as the one at the hands of Compston, since Duncan had rubbed it in over the 36-hole route. There was no other course open to Walter but to take the Open at Muirfield and restore his prestige.

This was a championship that showed Hagen at his best. His opening salute was a 75 that might have been an 82 in the hands of a less dauntless golfer. Hagen went four strokes over par on the first four holes. He had to play through a punishing rainstorm the early starters escaped. Again he showed his unapproached courage for staying with a bad round, fighting it out by will power alone until he had made it, from the standpoint of figures, a fairly decent round. He went out the next day and broke the British Open mark for a single round with a 67, and Muirfield is a course that resists a 70. He topped off this sacrilegious performance when his mashie second to the eighteenth, overhit, caught the flapping flag of the flagstick and ended up in the middle of the green. This 67 brought Walter from a tie for eighteenth to second place. On the last day, when the third and fourth rounds were played, a furious storm blew over Muirfield. It sent Diegel and Sarazen reeling into the 80s, and none of the top five finishers broke 75. Walter collected two 75s for 292. No Britisher was under 300. To keep his shots low in the storm, Hagen had switched to a deep-faced driver and, according to Henry Longhurst, hit no drive more than twenty feet off the ground. This was the fellow who nine years before had been blown to fifty-fifth at Deal.

As a young man, a highly realistic young man, Walter Hagen had eyed the world and concluded that the golfer who didn't win was forgotten overnight. Hagen's triumph at Muirfield proved to be his last victory in a major championship, but Walter was never forgotten. Great as he was as a golfer, he was even greater as a personality—an artist with a sense of timing so infallible that he could make tying his shoelaces seem more dramatic than the other guy's hole-in-one. Whenever he entered a tournament, buoyant

Hagen leans into a tee shot at Muirfield en route to a fourth British Open title.

crowds ran out to find him, passing up the pacemakers so that they could watch Sir Walter. On his tours back and forth across the country, Hagen would step, shining and unconcerned, from the limousine his chauffeur had moored near the first tee, always a little late for his matches, since he had no idea of time and had once kept the Prince of Wales waiting; he would have disappointed the crowds if he had arrived on time. With hardly so much as a practice swing, the ex-caddie from Rochester, the closest thing to a "noble" many Americans had ever seen, would take a disdainful look at the first hole and rock himself into his drive. He would stride erect down the fairway, his black hair gleaming above his weather-beaten face, and not until he had holed out on the last green did he relinquish, even for a moment, the attention of every person in the gallery.

JONES
BREAKS
THROUGH

The last hole at Inwood, on the southern shore of Long Island, is a terror. Four hundred and twenty-five yards long, its narrow fairway fringed with clumpy rough and shut in by trees along the length of the drive, it would be a stern enough par 4 without the additional menace of a water hazard. But just before the green a deceptively mild lagoon stands guard, and this makes the eighteenth at Inwood, along with the eighteenth at Pebble Beach and Carnoustie, one of the most frightening finishing holes in golf.

One golfer who apparently knew how to play the eighteenth at Inwood was Bobby Jones. On his first three rounds in the national Open in 1923, Bobby had picked up two birdies and a kick-in par on this hole by the simple expedient of hitting two brilliant shots on each round. From the day he first strode onto the championship stage back in 1916 as the fourteen-year-old wonder from Dixie, no one argued Bobby Jones' genius for hitting golf shots. There was no room for argument. The chubby youngster had everything—a graceful full swing, perfect hand action, a nice feel in his fingers, and a pretty fair competitive temperament for a child prodigy. The puzzling thing was that Jones, head and shoulders above the other amateurs and as good as the best professionals, had won none of the ten national championships in which he had appeared.

Walter Hagen had predicted that Jones would win the Open before he won the Amateur, and Walter looked to be right when the young man from Atlanta placed his ball on a high peg on the eighteenth tee at Inwood for the fourth time during the championship and set himself to play the 72nd hole. Rounds of 71, 73, and 76 had given Bobby a three-stroke lead on the field when he began his final spin around the difficult

Long Island layout. He had gone out in 39, better golf than it appears to be at first glance, since the par on that nine was 37. Starting with the tenth, his putting and his niblick recoveries had made up for his minor lapses, and his start back of 3-4-3-4-4-3 had given him just the cushion he wanted for the bogey 5s he ran into on the 70th and 71st holes. Bobby had probably made all the 3s he was going to get on that last hole, but a 4 would give him a 74 and 294 for his four rounds. That total would be too good for the one man who still stood a chance of catching Jones, wee Bobby Cruickshank.

Jones cracked another fine drive up the eighteenth. The wind was blowing slightly against him, so he took a spoon for his second rather than press a long iron over the lagoon. The ball came off the clubhead fast, heading for the front left-hand corner of the green, and then it began to hook and it kept on hooking until it finally came down in the rough near the twelfth tee. Not a shot to be proud of but nothing to worry about. Bobby had a simple little pitch left over a pot bunker, so he could still get his 4, and, anyway, his 5, and that would probably be good enough. The officials removed the chain around the twelfth tee. Bobby took a comfortable stance and pitched the ball smack into the pot bunker. When it took him three to get down from the bunker, Bobby had taken an inglorious 6, and his 294 had become 296.

Playing well behind Jones, Bobby Cruickshank, one of the strongest hearts the game has ever known, was meanwhile banging away at the three-stoke lead Jones had held going into the last round. When he was all over the course on the first five holes, it looked as if Cruickshank could never do it. When he followed his 2 on the sixth with a 3 and a 3 and a 4 and then another 3 and a 4 and still another 3—an incredible burst of one over 3s for seven tough holes—Cruickshank had forged ahead of Jones' figures. He could do it now, very definitely. Cruickshank slipped to 5-5-4, three strokes over par, from the thirteenth through the fifteenth, but he could still win now that Jones had stumbled so pathetically with two 5s and that miserable 6 on the last three holes. Three pars, three 4s, would give Cruickshank a winning total of 295.

And then the picture suddenly changed once more. Cruickshank pushed his approach to the sixteenth into the rough. He played a weak recovery, and going too hard for one putt, took three—6 costly strokes. Winning was out of the question now. To draw even with Jones, Cruickshank would have to shoot a par and a birdie. He hooked his drive on the seventeenth but fought back and got his par. Now he needed a birdie 3 to tie.

Cruickshank bisected the fairway with his drive on the eighteenth. With everything depending on his second shot, the courageous little Scot rose to the occasion and played one of the finest clutch shots of all time, a slashing midiron that cleared the lagoon, braked itself on the green, and ended up six feet from the hole. Cruickshank looked his putt over carefully, and holed it. He had caught Jones.

That evening Bobby Jones was way down in the dumps. It wasn't Cruickshank's valiant finish that hurt. If there was a silver lining in Bobby's clouds, it was the opportunity he would have the next day to go out in the playoff, now that Cruickshank had tied him, and prove that he could *win* a championship, not back into one. He couldn't get over the way he had butchered the last hole. When his great friend and biographer, O. B. Keeler, had met him as he dragged himself in disgust off the eighteenth green, Jones had refused to be cheered up. "Well, I didn't finish like a champion," Bobby had said, shaking his head. "I finished like a yellow dog." He brooded over his collapse all through dinner at the Engineers' Club and was still thinking about it when he turned in for a night's rest back at Inwood in the room he shared with Francis Ouimet.

The 6 on the final hole of the 1923 Open epitomized for Bobby his failures to produce at the critical junctures the golf he knew he had in his system. There was always something wrong. At one time it had been inexperience. He had outgrown it. Later it had been a wicked temper. He had conquered it. Sometimes it had been just plain bad luck. It seemed that all a golfer needed to play the hottest golf of his life was to find himself matched with Bobby. Frequently it was Jones' own lack of intelligence. It took Bobby many seasons and many heartaches before he learned to stop worrying about what the other fellow was doing and to pit his skill against the proper opponent, Old Man Par. When he finally learned this lesson, there was no one who could stay any place close to Bobby Jones.

In a country so overflowing with infant prodigies that the child who couldn't break off a curve sharper than Christy Mathewson's, dash off a song hit, or exhibit some other startling precocity appeared to be an out-and-out case of arrested development, Bobby Jones was *the* infant prodigy. He had taken up golf at five. His mother and his father, a well-to-do Atlanta lawyer, had joined the Atlanta Athletic Club's East Lake golf course that summer, and while they were learning their fundamentals from Jimmy Maiden, the new pro, Bobby knocked a ball up and down a road bordering the course. A digestive ailment had prevented him from eating any substantial food until he was five, and Bobby was a frail, thin little fellow. The next summer the Joneses took a cottage on the East Lake property near the old thirteenth green. Bobby used to follow his parents around the course, batting the ball with a cut-down cleek, worried more about keeping up with the grownups' pace than hitting the ball correctly. He liked to follow Stewart Maiden, who had succeeded his brother as the pro at East Lake, but Stewart paid no attention to the little fellow with the oversized head, and after being ignored for five or six holes, Bobby would wander home. He didn't dislike golf, but then, he liked all sports. He inherited his father's passion for baseball; Jones, Sr., had been such an outstanding ballplayer at the University of Georgia that the Brooklyn club had tried to sign him. At one period in his childhood Bobby had the tennis bug, at another the fishing bug. An old dodge of his was to tread in all the puddles he could find on his way to school so that he would be sent home; then he would pick up his rod and go fishing.

When he was nine, Bobby won the junior golf championship of the Atlanta Athletic Club, trouncing a boy seven years older than himself in the final. Young Bobby had a talent for imitation. One of the standard entertainments the Joneses provided for their guests was to call on Bobby to give his impressions of the odd addresses and the patented followthroughs of the East Lake characters. Bobby could also imitate the flat

Carnoustie swing of Stewart Maiden's, which was a very good thing. A few years later when he had grown to Stewart's height and had added some poundage, he was often mistaken for Stewart by golfers who had watched him swing from a distance. Bobby's attitude toward golf, however, was always a little patronizing until he read about the 1913 Open and later saw Vardon and Ray play when they visited Atlanta. The exciting aspects of Ouimet's triumph and the first-hand thrills he felt when Ray uncorked one of his leviathan shots and Vardon nursed the ball so neatly persuaded Bobby for the first time that golf was a game that deserved a young man's full attention and respect. Later that same autumn—Bob was eleven then—he shot his first 80. Two years later he carried off the club championships at East Lake and Druid Hills, scoring a 73 in the final of the latter tournament. Bob never took formal lessons from Stewart Maiden but would search him out whenever he felt he was doing something wrong or had struck a sour streak. Stewart could straighten him out in three minutes.

Bobby's father was rightfully proud of the progress his son was making. In 1916, when Bobby was fourteen, Robert Tyre Jones, Sr., sent him around to the various tourneys sponsored by the principal Southern clubs. George Adair, an old friend of the Joneses and a leading figure in Southern golf, looked after the youngster and reported enthusiastically on his improvement, and sometimes this must not have been the pleasantest thing in the world for Mr. Adair, since young Jones was eclipsing the brilliance of his own boy, Perry, a lad a little older than Bobby who had the infant phenomenon field to himself before Bobby came along. That summer Bobby won the invitation tournaments at the Cherokee Club in Knoxville and the Birmingham Country Club (with a 69), defeated Perry Adair to win the East Lake tournament, and defeated Perry again in the final of the Georgia State Amateur Championship. Bobby's father rewarded him by sending him to Philadelphia with the Adairs for the United States Amateur.

When Bobby appeared at the Merion Cricket Club, in Ardmore, about ten miles from downtown Philadelphia, he was fourteen and a half, a chunky boy five-feet-four and weighing 165 pounds. Cocky as they came, too, not the least bit impressed by any of the names assembled for the meeting, and rather temperamental, to put it mildly. After a poor shot, the youngster threw clubs and recited some of the more fragrant cusswords he had learned on the back steps of the Jones house on Willow Street from the cook's brother. Bobby managed to qualify, and in the first round he was paired with Eben Byers, who threw a nice club himself. Bobby won a battle of tempers 3 and 1; Byers, Bobby used to explain in later years, ran out of clubs first. He moved along by defeating Frank Dyer 4 and 2 and came up against the defending champion, Bob Gardner, in the third round. Taking advantage of Jones' wildness and putting splendidly himself in the afternoon, Gardner stopped the kid on the 31st green, but not before he had been called on to play every bit of golf he knew. Jones was the sensation of the tournament. Everyone went home raving about the boy from Atlanta who hit the ball so naturally and hit it so perfectly in the bargain that, even at fourteen, he was one of the longest drivers in the field. Old Walter Travis, a tough man to please, was bowled over by the shots he had seen the youngster play. "Improvement?" snorted the Old Man when someone asked him about Jones' potential. "He can never improve his shots, if that's what you mean. But he will learn a good deal more about playing them."

Bobby did learn more about putting his shots together as he toured the country playing Red Cross exhibitions during the war, but it took him a good while longer to learn how to control his temper. Young Jones knew he was a crackerjack golfer, but Bobby was not a prima donna in the sense that he demanded special attention and kid-glove handling. On the contrary, he was an exemplary sportsman in all his dealings *with other people,* so much so, as he grew older, that more than one of his rivals remarked that a chief reason why Bobby had never won a championship was that he went out of his way too much to comfort and cheer his opponents when they hit a bad streak. But *with himself* Bobby was rough. The target of Jones' tantrums was always Bobby Jones, the dope who was continually making some inexcusable error, missing some silly shot through carelessness and lack of concentration. Bobby would storm around getting more and more worked up with himself, playing with decreasing effectiveness, of course, in his petulance. On one round, according to Glenna Collett, Bobby blew up so fast when an errant shot of his ended up in an old shoe that he could not see the humor in the situation and grimly gave the shoe a terrific belt.

Though he had stopped throwing clubs at helpless elms by 1919, rub-of-the-green incidents continued to upset Bobby more than a tournament golfer could afford. In the final of the 1919 Amateur against Herron, Bobby was 3 down with seven holes to play yet still very much in the fight as he prepared to hit his wood second on the long twelfth at Oakmont. Jones was already into his swing when some megaphone-happy official started to shriek directions to the gallery. Jones not only mis-hit his shot but allowed himself to become so irritated by the official's stupidity that he never got back in the match. Francis Ouimet was playing grand golf the day he opposed Bobby in the semis of the 1920 Amateur and would have undoubtedly defeated the young star anyway, but Jones made it easier for him by chasing a pesky bee that had alighted on his ball clear off the 25th green, and eventually three-putting. Fortunately for Bobby, in the 1921 British Open he was guilty of an impetuous gesture of which he was so ashamed after he cooled down that, once and for all, he graduated from adolescence. On his third round in that tournament, it had taken him 46 strokes to reach the turn. He was burning up. On the tenth, Bobby ran into a double-bogey 6, and when he had played five strokes on the short eleventh and was still not in the cup, he picked his ball up—the equivalent in golf of throwing in the towel. Bobby Jones had quit in competition. This, as he saw it, was an unforgivable breach of the sportsman's code, and the ever-rankling memory of what he had done on the eleventh at St. Andrews, as much as any single factor, was responsible for the magnificent standard of deportment Bobby Jones created in later years.

In 1922, after he had failed to overhaul Gene Sarazen in the Open at Skokie, the maturing Jones eliminated another bad habit. He had steadily improved his position in the Open, moving from eighth in 1920 to fifth to second. Second was not bad, but it was still a long ways from first, and as Bobby and his friend O. B. Keeler reviewed the week and analyzed the various elements that might have contributed to Bobby's chronic inability to get really hot in a big championship, they came to the matter of Bobby's diet. O. B. had often mentioned to his young friend that stuffing himself at luncheon between rounds wasn't likely to be conducive to playing sharp golf in the afternoon, but Bobby had continued to go in for heavy luncheons topped off with apple pie à la mode or, when there was no ice cream, with something on the order of loganberry sherbet. O. B. was able to convince Jones that these gustatory adventures could quite possibly have accounted for the stroke difference between tying Sarazen and being second. From that time on, the reforming Jones was a tea-and-toast man between rounds.

All that Bobby needed to win a championship, now that he was emerging from the cocoon of adolescence, was a little more patience and a little more luck. Someday the law of averages would come out of hiding and Jones' opponents would not take a quick look at Bobby and then shoot one of the dizziest rounds of their lives. Jones' experience at the hands of Jess Sweetser in the 1922 Amateur was typical of this curious bad fortune that dogged him. Jess played crushing golf at Brookline before and after beating Bobby, but against Jones, the favorite, he put on his most devastating exhibition. Over the first nine holes Jess piled up a six-hole lead. Bobby hadn't played his best golf, but he had hit a number of fine shots—at precisely the wrong times. On the second hole, for example, he had stuck his second, a full mashie-niblick, six inches from the pin, and yet this birdie merely boiled down to a brave but futile try for a half since Jess had already put his spade-mashie approach right into the cup for an eagle 2. From the tenth through the eighteenth, Bobby used only 34 strokes, and for all his pyrotechnics won back only one hole from Jess. In the afternoon Jess kept pumping his irons next to the pins, and Bobby, not playing badly at all, could make no headway whatsoever against the Yale undergraduate and went down 8 and 7, the most humbling defeat he had ever encountered in tournament competition.

While Bobby had never won a major title, the consistent excellence of his golf stamped him as the nation's leading amateur. The press and the public agreed that he was fulfilling the promise of his earlier youth and was bound to break through to a glorious triumph sooner or later. Bobby could not share these sanguine feelings. His game had never really caught fire during a championship, yet year in and year out he had played good enough golf to win and hadn't. He resigned himself to the probability that something would always pop up to prevent him from winning—that is, if he continued to play in tournaments. On more than one occasion Bobby was on the verge of retiring from competitive golf, a game so grueling for him that he lost as many as eighteen pounds during a championship with no victory to compensate for the punishment. He had entered the Open at Inwood in an I'll-give-it-one-more-try frame of mind. He had hoped he would win, and yet by this time he had reached the point where he genuinely believed that winning and losing were out of his hands. Where competitive golf was concerned, Bobby had become a fatalist. He would go out on the course and play his heart out, but his efforts didn't really matter unless some larger destiny had

H. Chandler Egan (left)
shares a light moment
with Bobby Jones,
the young veteran.

marked him down as the man who would win. All golf tournaments, Jones was firmly convinced, had been settled before the players stepped on the course, and the shots that they made and the scores they turned in had been ordained by Fate well in advance.

If Fate was looking for a deserving fellow to tap for the 1923 Open, Bobby Cruickshank's credentials were in order. Long before he had come to the 72nd hole at Inwood, Bobby had shown the stuff he was made of in some of the most severe tests of life. As a foot-soldier in the British army in World War I, Cruickshank had been in the thick of the fighting. He had seen his brother blown to bits two yards from him. He had been captured and assigned to the same prison camp as Sandy Armour, Tommy's brother. Sandy was weak with dysentery and Cruickshank had deprived himself of most of his scanty rations so that Sandy might have them. Then Bobby had escaped and rejoined his outfit. This tiny thoroughbred had gone back to golf when the shooting was over, turned professional in 1921, and come to the States to make his living. Bobby Cruickshank was a very good man.

Because of the psychological advantage he would draw from his marvelous finish, Cruickshank went to the first tee in the eighteen-hole medal playoff a 10 to 7 favorite over Jones, the chap who had taken a 6 on the last hole. Both men went out to win on their own shots, not on the other fellow's errors. Only three of the eighteen holes were tied. By the fifth, Cruickshank had snared three birdies and Jones had got one. Jones rode back into the fight, rubbed out his deficit, and built up a two-stroke lead by the thirteenth. Then back came Cruickshank to pick up one of these strokes on the fourteenth and the other on the fifteenth. Jones attacked again and went out ahead by a shot on the sixteenth, but the determined Scot dug himself out of the trap by the seventeenth green and went down in one putt to retrieve that stroke and square the playoff.

And so the two battlers, Bobby Jones and Bobby Cruickshank, came to the eighteenth at Inwood all even. Cruickshank, with the honor, tried to keep his ball low in the face of the stiff breeze and hit a half-topped drive that hooked into the rough. Jones laced a long tee shot down the right side of the fairway; at the last moment, the ball bobbled into the loose dirt at the edge of the rough. Jones stood by his ball and watched Cruickshank play the only shot he could from the rough—a safety short of the lagoon. It was now squarely up to Jones. Should he play safe from his extremely poor lie and gamble on wearing down his pertinacious adversary in extra holes? Or should he go for it? If he decided to try for the green and found the lagoon, he would be playing 4 where Cruickshank was playing 3 and . . . Jones eyed his ball in the loose dirt and glanced at the flag rippling on the green over the lagoon 190 yards away. Without hesitation, he took his midiron, one of the most difficult clubs to play even from the most perfect of lies. Back came the club and down it went, and *swick!* the ball came up like a rifle shot and, white against the gathering storm clouds, drilled itself directly for the flag. Over the lagoon it went and onto the green and up, up, up to within six feet of the cup.

That was the match. And the championship. And if anyone had ever won it like a true champion, it was Bobby Jones. With that gallant shot, the young veteran had finally broken through. An era had ended and the Age of Bobby Jones had begun.

PART THREE

THE AGE OF BOBBY JONES

1923–1930

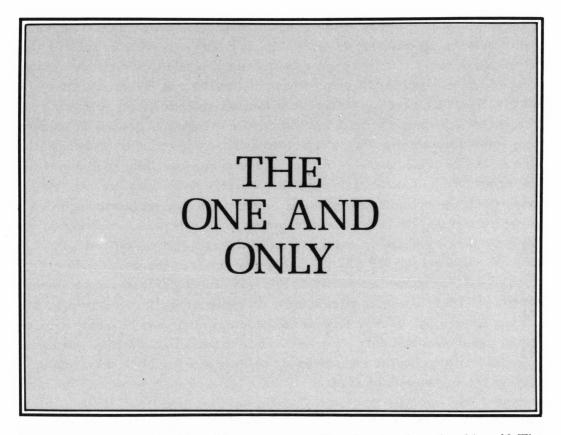

THE
ONE AND
ONLY

There are three types of golf—golf, tournament golf, and major championship golf. The difference between the three is one-tenth physiological and nine-tenths psychological. It is hard enough for a man to play a good round of *golf*, the informal game most of us play with a putt conceded here or there and double-or-nothing on the eighteenth. It is three or four strokes harder to play a round of *tournament golf*, although the rules are just the same and a player merely has to hole those insignificant putts he was conceded only because he was a cinch to make them. These are the very putts he misses when he plays in competition; along with this, he half-hits those explosion shots he plays so confidently on his friendly rounds, is short on his approaches although he keeps reminding himself to be up, slices on the dogleg to the left that he always plays with a slight intentional hook—and all for no apparent reason. There is a reason, of course, and it is readily apparent. The knowledge that he is playing for keeps and for glory makes the tournament golfer a worrying golfer, forces him to be ever-mindful that a 2-foot putt may be the barrier between him and victory, drives him to adopt half-unwittingly a negative attitude whereby he concentrates on avoiding error, playing safe, taking the conservative route. When victory is beyond his reach, only then does the average tournament golfer throw caution to the winds and release the shots that have been stifling inside him.

It takes time and experience and some intelligence for the talented professional or amateur to digest the rigors of tournament play so that he can feel almost normal as he goes about the business of winning the Greensboro Open or the Colonial or the Crosby. After a while the professional professional or the professional amateur becomes adapted to his environment. If he can shoot a 68 in a practice round, you can count on him to approximate that figure during the tournament, and often to improve it. The men who are used to playing under fire have long ago learned how to harness their nervousness. They seldom lose because of a jumpy feeling in their stomach, and contradictory as it seems at first, they worry about not being worried, about becoming phlegmatic and missing that little tingle that keeps a player sharp and dangerous. But put the seasoned campaigner of *tournament golf* into a *major championship*—say the United States or British Opens—and he begins to sweat like a novice, that welcome little tingle becomes a nauseating thump, and the golfer finds himself playing his shots by some cloudy memory of his formula and praying that his trained reflexes will see him through. There are some exceptions, but for most big-time golfers the jump between *tournament golf* and *major championship golf* is as wearing and as real as the jump between *golf* and *tournament golf* is for the less cultivated players. The results are about the same—three or four strokes more. The reasons are about the same—the greater glory and material rewards for winning, the consequent greater strain. Occasionally a golfer can hold himself together long enough to carry off one major championship, and he merits enduring respect regardless of how fluky his victory seemed or the quick oblivion his subsequent flops cast over him. But the men who have won more than one major championship—they are the true champions. They are a select body. Since 1919, among American amateurs, only Jones, Lawson Little, Johnny Goodman, Bud Ward, Willie Turnesa, Frank Stranahan, Harvie Ward, Dick Chapman, Jack Nicklaus, Deane Beman, Bob Dickson, and Steve Melnyk have won two national titles. (Across the water, Joe Carr has won three British Amateurs and the amazing Michael Bonallack five.) The only repeaters among the pros in the two big Open Championships have been Hagen, Sarazen, Barnes, Armour, Ralph Guldahl, Henry Cotton (of England), Bobby Locke (of South Africa), Ben Hogan, Peter Thomson (of Australia), Cary Middlecoff, Arnold Palmer, Jack Nicklaus, Gary Player (of South Africa), Julius Boros, Billy Casper, Tony Jacklin (of England), and Lee Trevino.

Only Harry Vardon, Ben Hogan, and Jack Nicklaus merit comparison with Jones as *major championship golfers*. Over a period of eight years, Bobby won the U.S. Amateur five times, the U.S. Open four times, the British Open three times, and the British Amateur once. Approach this record from any angle, and its mold looms more and more heroic. In eight cracks at the U.S. Amateur between 1923 and 1930, Jones was defeated once in the first round, once in the second, and once in the final; he was victorious the five other times. In the U.S. Open over the eight years between his first victory in 1923 and his last in 1930, Jones once finished in a tie for eleventh but on no other occasion was he worse than second; he won twice without a playoff, won twice after a playoff, lost twice after a playoff, and the other time was an untied second. In other words, in six years out of the eight, Bobby either won the Open outright or finished in a tie for first, necessitating a playoff. He won the British Open in three of his four attempts—he picked up at St. Andrews on his maiden effort and then was successful in his last three starts. The most difficult championship for Bobby, and perhaps the most difficult championship for anyone to win, was the British Amateur, with its seven rounds of 18-hole matches before the 36-hole final. It took Bobby three cracks before he finally won it. No one except Jones, of course, has ever won the two big national Amateurs and Opens in one golfing season. And while history has demonstrated how foolhardy it is to predict that certain sports records will never be equaled or broken, it does seem reasonably safe to predict that men will be pole-vaulting twenty-two feet and women will be running the four-minute mile before another golfer comes along to match Jones' Grand Slam of 1930.

There are some elderly fans who contend that Harry Vardon, peerless in his own age, was the equal of Jones. Those who would rank Vardon with Jones have a fairly good case, since he was as outstanding in his age as Jones was in his. In Vardon's period there was really only one major championship, the British Open, and he won it six times—in 1896, 1898, 1899, 1903, 1911, and 1914. (The other two members of the illustrious Triumvirate, J. H. Taylor and James Braid, each won the British Open five times.) In addition, Vardon won the U.S. Open in 1900, lost it in the historic playoff with Ouimet and Ray in 1913, and again lost it by a whisker in 1920 at Inverness when he was unlucky enough to catch the full force of the gale off the lake as he was coming down the last nine holding the lead. To maintain one's form for a quarter of a century—from 1896 through 1920—was something in those days, particularly when your golf possessed Vardon's picture-book quality. Old Harry's left arm may have been bent as he took the club back, and he may have taken it back in a very upright arc in the eyes of his contemporaries, but that was, in a way, the plane of the future, just as his overlapping grip was the grip of the future and his elegant left-to-right fade was, possibly, the flight of the future. Old Harry was something, but was he really as good as Jones? In the long run, that is a matter of opinion, as is, for instance, one's reaction to the inescapable argument waged during World War II as to whether Byron Nelson's achievements matched, if not exceeded, Jones'.

The indecent precision with which Nelson clicked off one tournament after another in 1944 and 1945 gave his supporters sturdy grounds indeed for pressing their argument: What other golfer had ever finished in the money in over a hundred consecutive tournaments, won eleven consecutive P.G.A.-endorsed tournaments, or averaged 69.67 for 85 rounds as Lord Byron did in 1944, or his even more stunning 68.33 for 120 rounds in 1945? It was this last feat, in particular, which convinced Nelson's supporters of his superiority over Jones, for, as they shrewdly noted, the old Emperor had never approached a sub-70 average. All very well and good, all very wonderful, rebutted defenders of Jones' pre-eminence, but . . . Nelson had rung up his records in relatively minor tournaments held on courses far easier to score on than the arduous championship layouts, and he had worked his wonders against a field depleted by the exigencies of war.

Back and forth it went, and the controversy soon bristled with rhetoric about Nelson's failure to win more than one national Open, what Jones would have done if he had gone in for the minor tourneys, how Nelson would have swept every major championship in sight had the war not canceled these meetings, why Nelson had played such high scores in all but one Open, what Jones might have done in the line of scoring if the hypoed balls, the foolproof blasters, the steel shafts and other refinements of the Forties had been available to the stars of the Twenties. The controversy was filled with speculative *ifs* that couldn't be settled in combat, to be sure, and so it ran its course, a forum between two generations.

Quite similarly, especially after Ben Hogan's banner year in 1953, when he swept the Masters, the U.S. Open, and the British, many admirers of the fabulous Texan asserted that he had demonstrated a skill not only equal to Jones's but of an even higher order. The Hoganites pointed to Ben's superior scoring. Marvelous, but under vastly different conditions, replied the partisans of Jones, who felt that this argument suffered from a lack of objectivity. Moreover, continued the Jonesmen, all that talk about Bobby's compiling his record against a weaker group of adversaries than Hogan faced was way off the mark; his contemporaries, in fact, may have been finer players than the modern gypsy band who were so accustomed to driver-wedge-putter courses that they were all at sea when they came to a championship course that made them play the full bag. Not at all, answered the Hoganites, who felt that this argument suffered from a lack of objectivity. And so it went. No one, of course, will ever know for certain how the Hogan of 1953 and the Jones of 1930 would have come out had they met in a prolonged series of tournaments. And, actually, the comparison is unfair to both, since neither could have accomplished more than he did. They belong in a class by themselves along with Vardon and the phenomenal Jack Nicklaus, whom many today rate the best golfer of all time. In some ways, each was incomparable. Bobby Jones certainly was.

From 1924 until Jones' retirement, major championship golf is the chronicle of Jones versus the field. The amateurs were a so-so lot, but the professional troupe was filled with colorful and capable golfers—Walter Hagen, Gene Sarazen, the brilliant but unfortunate Leo Diegel, the equally brilliant and more unfortunate Macdonald Smith, Tommy Armour of the whistling irons, Johnny Farrell the immaculate, Joe Turnesa, Bobby Cruickshank, Wild Bill Mehlhorn, the young Harry Cooper, Denny Shute, the young Horton Smith, Craig Wood, George Duncan, Abe Mitchell, Archie Compston, and the usual collection of in-and-out tournament golfers like the Espinosas, Abe and Al, Willie Klein, and Wiffy Cox. Any one of these men could get red-hot, yet 50 percent of the time Jones defeated them *en masse*. Perhaps the full devastation of the Georgian's march through golf can be best appreciated if one reviews his annual campaigns during the seven great years that followed his seven lean years. Such a retabulation, year by year, tournament by tournament, runs the risk of sameness, but, then, there was a sameness to golf in the Twenties: Jones nearly always won.

After his victory at Inwood in 1923, Bobby was an odds-on favorite to win the Amateur when the "gentlemen" gathered at Flossmoor, near Chicago. Max Marston eliminated him in the second round. From the seventeenth hole in the morning through the seventeenth in the afternoon, Max was 5 under par, and this was too good for Bobby. This early-round defeat at Flossmoor had beneficial repercussions. As he was going through his usual post-tournament analysis, Bobby decided that the time had come to examine the causes for his continual unsuccessful play in match competition. He concluded that he was chucking strokes away by playing his opponent when he should have been battling Old Man Par, as he did on his better medal rounds. This was not a victory-proof formula, Bobby realized. If his opponent made more headway against par than Bobby, as Marston had, then his opponent would win, and this would be perfectly agreeable with Bobby. What he did want to eradicate was his tendency to toss away matches in which he had not been outplayed. After Flossmoor, Bobby adhered to a policy of dueling exclusively with par, and from that time on he was defeated only three times in championship match play, on each occasion by a foe who had given Old Man Par a thorough going-over.

The 1924 Amateur was all Jones. The steep margins by which he routed his adversaries—6 and 5 (W. J. Thompson), 3 and 2 (Clarke Corkran, the medalist), 6 and 4 (Rudy Knepper), 11 and 10 (Francis Ouimet), 9 and 8 (George Von Elm)—testified to the effectiveness of his new philosophy of match play. For the sixty-one holes on his afternoon rounds at Merion, Bobby's card added up to one stroke under par: forty pars, ten holes in a stroke above par, and eleven birdies, and this over a layout heavily scarred with hazards. Early in the tournament week, the rains had made the fairways heavy with moisture, and in a rather interesting move, Jones allowed his clubs to grow rusty rather than have the faces regularly buffed after a round; he deduced that on the soaked turf the ball was likely to skid off polished faces and could be gripped more effectively by the rougher blade; in any event, Bobby got remarkably good results. Everything went well. Never an exceptional putter before, Bobby was so consistently expert on the big greens at Merion that Jerry Travers, who knew a good putter when he saw one, exclaimed that he had never observed a better stroke than Jones' during the championship. Hard work and intelligent experimentation lay behind this reformation. In the winter Walter Travis had looked over Jones' putting style and had recommended that the young man strive to have his wrists work more in opposition to each other. He also suggested that Jones concentrate on taking the club back with the left hand, and pounded home in his emphatic fashion the other theories that had served him so well during his long career. Jones also changed his putting grip, overlapping the index finger of the *left* hand—the reverse overlapping grip. As a final alteration, to check the nervousness that sporadically visited him on the greens, he adopted a breath-control tempo that was slow and easy—what Bobby called "tranquillized breathing." His new dietary discipline justified itself. In addition to watching his noonday snack, Bobby ate sensible breakfasts of a sliced orange, cornflakes, and coffee. In the evenings he let himself go and stowed away whatever he wanted, yet his over-all menu was one that would have received the approval of Bunny Austin, the fragile English Davis Cupper of later years and one of the most accomplished dieticians sport has ever known. All in all, the week at Merion was a joy. All of Bobby's investments paid dividends, and one accurate shot after another poured from his clubheads.

This triumph in the Amateur followed a respectable if not wholly satisfying showing in the 1924 Open—not wholly satisfying because Jones did not win, respectable since he finished second to Cyril Walker, although he skied to a last round of 78 in one of those gales off the Great Lakes. (Any time you want to amaze your friends with your powers of prophecy, one of the surest bets, it would seem, would be to predict a gale on the last day of the Open.) By losing, Bobby inadvertently wrote a happy ending to a short-short story. A month before the Open, Cyril Walker, the little 118-pound pro at Englewood, confided to his wife Elizabeth that he was absolutely certain he was going to win the Open that year. Walker had never been close in his previous shots at the title. Furthermore, he had not fully recovered from the ravages of insomnia, which had made his slight frame a bundle of nerves. Cyril seemed so sincere about his chances that Elizabeth, or "Tet" as he called her, told him that by all means he should go to Oakland Hills if he felt that way. Tet went along too, for moral support and protection against Cyril's staying up all night with the boys. Walker began with a pair of 74s that put him up with the leaders for once, since the high winds militated against any fancy scoring. On the last day, when the winds really roamed the course, Walker, another one of that army of good golfers trained on the links at Hoylake, found that his seaside education served him in good stead. The gale that blew over fellows almost twice his size did not bother Cyril. He kept his shots low, and his last two rounds, a 74 and a 75, gave him the only sub-300 total among the eighty-five players. Walker never again came close. His victory was labeled a freak. But as Tet never let him forget, he had played like a champion in winning, and no one could ever take away from him that wonderful week at Oakland Hills.

Jones formed the habit of carrying off either the Amateur or the Open each year. In 1925 it was not the Open, although Bobby played himself from thirty-sixth to tenth to fourth and into a tie for first with Willie Macfarlane. The double playoff between Jones and Macfarlane was a fitting climax to a tournament that will hold its own with any when it comes to thrilling finishes. *Eight* men came down the stretch at the Worcester Country Club, each of them with the championship in his grasp if he could fashion a 70. All eight were golfers accustomed to playing 70s—Hagen, Diegel, Farrell, Jones, Ouimet, Macfarlane, Sarazen, and old Mike Brady. That afternoon none of these stars could get his hands on the figure he wanted. As the afternoon wore on and one by one they came to the 72nd hole, *seven* of them, all but Brady, were still in the hunt. Diegel was the first to try the 335-yard eighteenth, a drive and a pitch—but a wickedly touchy pitch—to a sloping, raised green surrounded by a bodyguard of deep bunkers. Leo proceeded to break his heart with an awful 8. Next came Johnny Farrell, and he nailed his 4. This gave Johnny an aggregate of 292 and the lead at this point. Francis Ouimet, looking for all the world like a Chinese mandarin in his straw tropical helmet, calmly played himself into a tie with Farrell when he got his 4. Sarazen needed a birdie 3 for his 292. He had to be satisfied with a 4. A 4 would have given Hagen his 292, but Walter had his eye on 291 and, passing up a certain par, went all out for his birdie by trying to drop his approach inches behind the front bunker so that he would be close to the pin on the very front edge of the green. This time The Haig just couldn't pull it off. He caught the back wall of the bunker, and got a 5 for his daring. Then Jones came along needing a 4 for 291, which would make Farrell and Ouimet also-rans. Bobby made no mistakes: on in 2, down in 2. One man, Willie Macfarlane, could catch Jones by getting his 4 on the eighteenth, and Willie did it by getting down in 2 after he had placed his approach on the high back slope of the green.

The calm, observant manner in which he made sure of his two putts on the 72nd was a succinct sample of the intelligence that had steered Willie Macfarlane through many rough passages from the first hole on. On the last green Willie paid close attention as his partner, Francis Gallett, with practically the same ticklish 40-footer as Willie, sent his approach putt slowly down the dip and saw it keep on sliding until it was well past the cup. Willie would have played his putt just that way, had he not been able to profit from Gallett's example, but now he hardly stroked his downhiller, barely nudged it on its way and let it crawl down the slope and peter out a foot from the cup. Willie still had a golf shot left, for in marking his ball before Gallett putted again, he noticed that his ball had ended up in a pitch-mark left by some player's approach. Willie thought it wisest not to use a putter from that indentation, for the ball might hop off-line as it came out. He took his midiron and hit it into the cup.

Without his glasses, tall, gaunt, aquiline Willie Macfarlane looked like a country schoolmaster, and when he wore his rimless glasses, he looked like a professor of poetry at Princeton. Willie had no love for tournament golf, preferring to play the game for the fun of it. But when he did enter the New York area tourneys at the coaxing of his pupils at Tuckahoe, he always gave a fine account of himself and occasionally went off on mad streaks that brought to mind the purple patches of Old Jock Hutchison. Willie didn't mind if it got around that he could play in the 90s lefthanded and in the 80s with one hand, but this was the extent of his vanity. He had entered the Open because it was one of the few tournaments he liked to play. He had no dreams of winning it. When the opportunity for winning did present itself, however, Willie made the most of it.

The playoff at Worcester was as exciting as the championship proper. Macfarlane appeared to be on his way to victory over the regulation eighteen-hole route. As the players came to the fourteenth green, Willie had a stroke lead and was in a position to pick up another stroke, or maybe two. After his second shot, Willie's ball lay eight feet from the cup, and Bobby was playing his third out of the rough fifty or sixty feet away. Bobby struck his chip smack into the cup. Willie missed his 8-footer and had lost his lead instead of going two or three strokes up. But Macfarlane was a placid operator and kept right on stroking the ball. He quickly took the play away from Bobby and made the young man can a 5-foot sidehiller on the eighteenth green to come out of the morning round all-square and force the match into a second eighteen holes. In the afternoon Jones slowly drew away from the Scot. At the halfway mark, when Bobby had built up a four-stroke advantage, the gallery concluded that it was all over except the handshake, since no one could ever hope to make up four strokes against Jones in nine holes. Willie picked up five. The break came on the long fifteenth, where Jones, forgetting his friend Old Man Par, attempted to shut off Willie's rally by pressing his second shot to the green and setting himself up for a birdie. Instead, he wound up with a 6. Willie went evenly on his way. His 33 home included two 2s. Scores: Macfarlane 75-72, Jones 75-73.

The 1925 Amateur, on the other hand, was one of the dullest tournaments in the history of that championship. Some parties had objected to the old tournament form as taking too long, so something new was tried in 1925 at Oakmont, north of Pittsburgh: only sixteen players would qualify for the match play, and the matches would all be over the 36-hole distance. On paper, the innovation did not look too bad. If a good percentage of the leading amateurs succeeded in qualifying, there would be no scary 18-hole matches in which they could get knocked out before they were warm by some reputationless upstart playing way over his head; ultimately, the two best golfers in the field would meet in the final. Well, it didn't pan out that way. Jess Sweetser, Jesse Guilford, George Von Elm, and Jones were the only name players to sneak under the qualifying wire, and Guilford and Sweetser were eliminated in their second-round matches. Perhaps if the new system had been tried out on some course other than Oakmont, it would have stood up better. On that penal institution, with its abundant hazards, one or two bad shots could always ruin an otherwise adequate round, and the Fowneses never seemed to think that Oakmont was sufficiently maddening. When word was received that Oakmont had been awarded the championship, they had toughened the course up once again. Several new traps were added, which was like carrying coals to Newcastle. Nine heaping railway carloads of sand from the Allegheny River were spilled into one excavation on the eighth that was thought to be the largest trap in the world.

The unyielding sternness of the new-and-improved Oakmont not only kept many of the best amateurs out but conspired against the chances of those who were in for giving Jones any competition. In winning his matches by scores of 11 and 10, 6 and 5, 7 and 6, and 8 and 7, Bobby finished 32 up on his opponents and had an even easier time of it than at Merion, where he had been 36 up over his span of five matches. The championship would have been little more than a string of sad statistics had Watts Gunn not introduced a chunk of human interest. Watts was Bobby's protégé, a small but well-knit twenty-year-older who had attracted Jones' attention by shooting a 69 at East Lake and a 67 at Druid Hills. Jones had persuaded Watts' parents that some seasoning in the Amateur would do the boy a world of good. At Oakmont, Watts vindicated Jones' faith in him by qualifying in fifth spot, and got hotter and hotter. He slaughtered his first opponent 12 and 10, winning *fifteen holes in a row* after he had stood 3 down at the eleventh. He went out in the wind and the rain against Sweetser and shot himself a 71, which on Oakmont is the equivalent of a 65 on the average non-championship course. Watts accounted for Jess, 11 and 10. He cooled down a little in his semi-final match with young Dick Jones but took it 5 and 3 to enter the final with R. T. Jones Jr., his friend and idol.

For a while in the final Watts Gunn acted as if he had forgotten that Jones used to give him three or four strokes during their informal matches in Atlanta and all week long at Oakmont had watched over him like a father. Watts went out in 35, and it was all Jones could do to keep up with that terrific pace. Watts took the tenth, and Jones had to fight and fight hard to save the eleventh and the twelfth. Then the senior Atlantan called on his great reserves. On the last six holes of the morning round and the first two in the afternoon, Jones had a relatively short putt for his birdie on each green, helped himself to five 3s, and won seven of these eight holes to go 6 up. This majestic burst of power settled the contest. On the 29th green Watts broke out into a big smile and walked across the green to congratulate the winner.

The year 1926 turned out to be Bobby's biggest to date, but it began quite inauspiciously. Tuning up in Florida in the winter, Bobby was scoring as well as usual and hitting the ball crisply when he and Walter Hagen were matched in a 72-hole exhibition between "the amateur and professional champions," the first thirty-six to be played over the Whitfield Estates Country Club at Sarasota, where Jones had been stopping, and the second thirty-six at Hagen's course in Pasadena, Florida. Walter put it all over Bobby. The final score was 12 and 11 as Walter moved out in front early and continued to add to his lead by his own ingenuity on some holes and Jones' errors on others. One of Hagen's more productive rounds prompted the crack that Walter had gone around in 69 strokes and Bobby in 69 cigarettes.

As this was the year that Walker Cup matches were set for St. Andrews, Jones had to do something about the weaknesses in his game that the overwhelming defeat by Hagen had uncovered, and he had to do it fast. Bob had first realized at Skokie in '22 that his iron play was liable to periodic depressions, and against The Haig his irons had been more off-color than the rest of his game. He put himself in the hands of Tommy Armour and Jimmy Donaldson, Tommy's assistant at Sarasota, and they quickly diagnosed the illness. Bobby had been playing his irons with too much right hand in the shot. Jimmy, in particular, worked with Jones on left-hand control, bringing the club down and through the ball with the left hand in charge and the right hand simply supplying momentum. Bobby began banging his irons on line again.

The British Amateur that year preceded the Walker Cup congregation, and with the other members of the American squad, Bobby Jones went up to Muirfield to see what he could do about winning for America the old mug that had never left the island since Travis' day. Bobby moved along, taking good care of himself in the treacherous 18-hole matches that constituted the British Amateur all the way to the final, where thirty-six holes were decreed. On the morning of his fifth-round match with Andrew Jamieson, a steady golfer from Scotland's West Coast, Bobby woke up with a stiff neck. As the day grew warmer, the knots loosened up—Bobby's stiff neck was not an alibi; it was a stiff neck—and Jones shot about the same brand of golf he had been playing in his previous victories, only this time Jamieson played even better. Over fifteen holes the young Scot, a very tidy pitch-and-run artist, posted thirteen pars and two birdies and was never behind and never flustered. So Jones went out, 4 and 3, and Jess Sweetser of the Walker Cup team went on to win the final from the chap who had taken care of Jamieson in the semis.

In the 1926 Walker Cup Match Bobby won his singles from Tolley 12 and 11 (a score that must have brought back memories of Florida) and teamed with Watts Gunn to defeat Tolley and Jamieson in the foursomes in which partners play alternate strokes and drive from alternate tees. He had his passage back to the States, and the U.S. Open, booked on the *Aquitania,* but at the last moment Jones canceled his passage and stayed on for the British Open. His decision was compounded from the still-rankling memory of quitting in the Open at St. Andrews in 1921 and from the desire to show the British golfing public that he could "sometimes play good stuff." Jones had never quite got going in Britain. His subsequent performance in the Open was all that he wanted it to be.

In the qualifying round of thirty-six holes in which Bobby was one of the entries assigned to the Sunningdale course, the Georgian smashed all records for that test with a 66 and a 68 for 134. The 68 was all right. The 66, in the opinion of the British critics, was definitely the finest round of golf ever played in their country. It deserves close inspection. First of all, Sunningdale is a testing course. While no figures from the back tees are available, it must have stretched to somewhere in the neighborhood of 6,500 yards. Whatever its exact measurement, it was long enough to compel Jones, who was a fairly long hitter, to play all but three approaches over his thirty-six holes with a 4-iron or more; twice he hit his second shot with a mashie (a 5-iron) and once he was able to get home with a mashie-niblick (a 7-iron). A 66 over such a layout is great going, no matter how you get it, but it was the way in which Bobby manufactured his 66 that set it apart from middle- and low-60 scores of earlier and later years. On every hole except the short thirteenth, Jones was *on the green* with the shot that should have been on—that is, on every par 3 (except one) he was on in one, on every par 4 he was on in two, and on the four par 5s, where on-in-three would have been regulation, he was also on in two. His one slip from perfection on the thirteenth, a 175-yarder, was a 4-iron he pushed into a bunker off the edge of the green. By chipping six feet from the cup and holing his putt, Bobby kept his card free from bogeys. Here is his card for that round.

	OUT				IN			
Par	554	344	434—36		544	353	444—36—72
Jones	444	334	434—33		434	343	444—33—66

Had "Calamity Jane," Bobby's putter, been functioning that round, Jones' 66 would have been at least several strokes lower. Bobby missed several banal 5-footers, and a 25-footer on the fifth was the only putt of any length that went down for him. On seventeen of the eighteen holes he was putting for birdies, or, more accurately, for eagles on four and birdies on thirteen. He used 33 shots going out and 33 back; he hit 33 putts and 33 tee-to-green shots. There was not a 5 or a 2 on the card, just 3s and 4s.

Bobby was not able to carry this streak with him when the qualifiers assembled at the Royal Lytham and St. Annes course for the tournament that marked the lowest ebb in Britain's golfing fortunes. At no point in the tournament was a Briton in the picture, and seven of the first nine finishers were Americans. Bill Mehlhorn, the venerable Freddy McLeod, and George Von Elm were contenders until the last nine holes, and Walter Hagen refused to be counted out until he had missed holing his approach to the 72nd green, yet the 1926 Open, in effect, narrowed down to a fight between Jones and Al Watrous, the young professional from Grand Rapids who had gone over with the Ryder Cup team. Jones, with two 72s, held a two-stroke lead on Watrous when they were paired to play the last thirty-six holes together. Watrous put together a grand third round, 33 out and 36 back for a 69 that took him from two strokes behind Bobby to two in front. Bobby was lucky not to have yielded more ground, for he was scrambling all morning long. During the noon intermission, Bobby and Al went back to the room Jones and Keeler shared in the Majestic Hotel to grab some rest. Bobby stretched out on his bed and Al on Keeler's. They removed their shoes and gabbed away until the tea, toast, and cold ham that O. B. had ordered were sent up. Keyed up as he was, Al managed to get down a slice of the ham. Then it was time to return to work, and the two friendly rivals put their shoes back on and tried to shake off their nervous tiredness.

Bobby hit his shots with more authority in the afternoon, but, as often happens, when the zip returned to his tee shots and his irons, his putting began to slip. On three greens on the first ten holes Bobby required three putts, and yet he chopped a stroke off Watrous' two-stroke lead. Realizing only too vividly how much a victory in the Open would mean to his career, the husky blond pro was beginning to tighten up. He made one last offensive thrust by tying together three neat shots and a nice putt for a 4 on the thirteenth (or 67th) to go two ahead on Jones again, but he three-putted away one of these strokes on the next hole and the other on the fifteenth. All even now. Watrous looked rickety in halving the sixteenth, but it was Jones who broke on the seventeenth tee, hooking his drive into the stretch of loose sand at the angle where the fairway breaks to the left on that 411-yard dogleg. Watrous hit an easy, safe, straight tee shot and played his approach onto the front edge of the green. Considering that it could have been partially buried in the sand, Jones' ball was lying well. Jones could still keep up with Watrous if he played a strong, perfect shot off the sand, although, on second thought, by picking the ball up cleanly and hitting it hard enough to carry the 175 yards over the dunes to the green, the only way the shot could be played, there was bound to be a lot of run on the ball and it would probably bounce on over the hard green into trouble—a minor type of trouble, to be sure, but sticky enough in a situation like this when anything higher than a 4 would lose the championship. He would have to play it blind, too, but . . . there was no other shot to play. He selected his mashie-iron—sort of a strong 4-iron—and the old frown of concentration came over his face. Then, into that deceptively lazy pivot, and into the ball. He got the ball, all of the ball, on the face of the club, and it came whistling out in an arching arc and sailed over the duney rough toward the green. The shot was high enough so that the wind held it up a helpful fraction, and when it came down on the green it had far less legs on it than Jones had anticipated. It curled up inside of Watrous' ball. Once again, Watrous took three putts after misreading the speed of the green. Jones got down in two for his par. He was in front again. Watrous dropped another stroke on the last hole but that was inconsequential.

Jones' winning total at Lytham was 291—72, 72, 73, 74—a more than creditable job despite the fact that only on the final eighteen had he hit the ball with approximately the same precision he had at Sunningdale, and then he had messed up his tee-to-green play by taking thirty-nine putts.

Bobby sailed for home, the British Open Champion, fairly well pleased with himself and unable to find anything much wrong with the world. His family and closest friends met him at Quarantine, and with Jimmy Walker as chaperone, Bobby rode in triumph down the canyons of New York to City Hall, and the band played "Valencia."

Two weeks later Bobby was back at work. Stale as he was after two full months of tournament golf, he announced his presence at the Open at Scioto, in Columbus, Ohio, by firing an opening 70, two strokes under par. He was a machine, an errorless machine, the reporters exclaimed, so Bobby went out and shot himself a very wild and very human 79. His 7 on the last hole was superhuman. Fighting to rescue a 76 with a birdie 4, Bobby pressed his drive into the rough on the right, slashed the ball twenty yards down the rough foolishly trying to get home with his 2-iron, hooked the ball clear across the fairway without changing clubs, fell short of the green with his pitch, rolled a chip five feet from the cup, and missed the putt. On that round, however, Jones did one of those little things that endeared him to the public and which explained, in part, the adulation that was showered on him wherever he went. On the tenth hole he had incurred a penalty stroke when his drive ended up against a stone wall that was ruled part of a water hazard. He had rallied after this bad break and was rolling to a probable 74 when he reached the fifteenth green. He placed his putter in front of the ball, as he always did to square the blade, but in doing this he cut off the breeze that had been holding the ball on the grade, and the ball moved a scant, unnoticeable fraction of an inch. Jones promptly called a penalty stroke on himself.

A third round of 71 put Jones back in the running, three strokes behind the pacemaker, Joe Turnesa, a very pretty swinger and the most accomplished member of that family of fine golfers growing up in Westchester. Joe was a good front-runner, and with only eighteen holes to go, he would take some catching.

Turnesa started out two pairs ahead of Jones and, playing steadily, increased his lead to four shots when Jones, for the fourth time in four rounds, failed to par the short ninth. Turnesa got his 4 on the tenth . . . and his 4 on the eleventh as well, Jones gathered from the applause that came from the eleventh green as he walked down the tenth. Jones matched those pars, and came to the twelfth with his first big chance to whittle away some of Turnesa's lead. Joe had taken a 6 on that 545-yard par 5 when his brassie second had lacked the distance to carry a bulge of the rough he tried to bite off. Joe hadn't wilted, not by any means. Maybe he was wrong to have gambled when he was ahead, but the alternative to gambling was playing conservatively, and Joe was wise enough to know that aggressive golf is usually winning golf. Jones slammed a long drive into the wind on the twelfth and followed it with a low, long brassie that rolled to the apron of the green. A chip and an 8-footer, and he had his birdie. Now with six holes to go, Jones was only two strokes down.

Turnesa meanwhile had played the 445-yard thirteenth. He drove nicely into the cross-wind, keeping his ball on the fairway. He played his spoon second for the right-hand corner of the green, trusting that the strong wind, blowing from right to left, would coddle it into the pin. It didn't take. The ball bounded into a green-high trap, and Joe took a 5. Jones' second on this hole finished up in a shallow trap at the left of the green. Using his bean, Bobby elected to roll the ball out, brushed it up and over the flattish face of the trap to within four feet of the cup. He sank the putt, and now he was within one stroke of Turnesa. A hole-and-a-half ahead, Turnesa knew exactly how he stood.

No blood on the fourteenth. Or the fifteenth. But Jones caught his man on the sixteenth, where Turnesa had missed a 9-footer for his 4 after a delicate downhill chip. Jones was on with his second and down in 2, for his seventh 4 in a row. And then Jones went out in front with a 3 on the seventeenth. Here Turnesa had made his only real mistake; he had been short with his iron, and his chip had not been close enough. But Turnesa had showed his mettle by playing a birdie 4 on the 480-yard eighteenth, making up for a pushed second by pitching out of the rough eight feet from the pin and holing his putt. To win, Jones would have to duplicate that birdie.

Jones hit a beauty off the tee, almost 300 yards down the fairway. (Under tension Bobby made it a practice to lengthen his backswing a notch to counteract the tendency of the under-pressure golfer to hurry his timing.) There was no mistake about Bobby's iron either. It came up to the green as big as a grapefruit, on the pin all the way, and finished about sixteen feet past. Bobby stuck his first putt up close and tapped in the winning shot.

In the privacy of his hotel room, the strain finally got to Bobby. He sat down and cried—he was that exhausted from the demands that the week of high pressure and the final chase had made on his nervous system. The spectators at Scioto would never have guessed that the man who had played sub-par golf down the stretch with such consummate grace was, inside, as keyed up as a playwright on opening night. Jones was high-strung by nature and during some tournaments became so nervous that he couldn't get his fingers to unknot his tie. But before a shot, he somehow drew himself together, and the average spectator received the impression that Bobby was all placidity. Jones was one of those great athletes who could never exterminate his basic nervousness but who controlled it and made it work for him and extracted from it an extra-something his more phlegmatic rivals were denied. But controlling one's nerves taxed an athlete severely, and sometimes he ended up, when the battle was over, crying in a hotel room in Columbus.

After Scioto, the Amateur Championship should have been a breeze for Bobby. He made his way to the final, where he met George Von Elm, the slick, blond challenger from California. In two prior bouts with Bobby, George had been made to look like just another amateur, and he wasn't just another amateur. Along with Jones, Von Elm was the only non-professional whom Hagen and Company had to watch out for, a player with all the shots. At Baltusrol, George came onto his game gradually, and in the final was under par for the thirty-five holes he needed to defeat Jones. With Von Elm's victory, for the first time a national championship trophy was taken west of the Rockies.

Bobby's 1927 campaign got off to a slow start when he finished eleventh in the Open at Oakmont, lengthened to 6,915 yards and so extravagantly trapped by the Fowneses that you couldn't see the greens for the bunkers. Jones may have treated his preparation for this tournament a trifle too cavalierly, may have been guilty of regarding his competition too lightly because of the success he had been enjoying against the pros in "their tournament." After the amateur had again led the field at Scioto the year before, Hagen, the natural leader of the pros, had told off his colleagues in no uncertain terms. They were losing face by letting Jones romp home in front so regularly, he lectured them. Once he (Hagen) had played himself out of the running, the other pros seemed to lose their fight. It was about time they stood their ground. It may have been Hagen's appeal to their sense of pride—it certainly wasn't his last two rounds at Oakmont—that spurred the pros on to leaving Jones far in in their wake for once. Or it may simply have been Jones' mediocre play. He turned the 3-pars into *faux pas*. Not once did he hit the short sixth, and when he took a 6 on the short thirteenth on his third round, he was done for. Bobby's aggregate of 309, and a tie for eleventh, contained no round under 76.

Jones' loose golf at Oakmont deeply disconcerted his best friend, O. B. Keeler, and his severest critic, Bobby Jones. In the two championships that remained on his itinerary for 1927, Jones drove himself relentlessly in his determination to make up for Oakmont. He was rewarded with one of the finest scoring sprees of his career. In the British Open and the United States Amateur, Jones played 224 holes, the equivalent of more than twelve rounds, in seventeen strokes under par, and, in the process, carried off both championships.

In successfully defending his British Open title, Bobby fulfilled one of his strongest desires: "to win a championship at St. Andrews." Along with most foreigners, Bobby's first estimate of the hallowed Old Course was that it was grossly overrated. Walker Cup warfare revised his opinion, and by 1927 he had learned to love St. Andrews like a native and to play it like one. Bobby began his defense with a 68, which equaled the competitive record for St. Andrews, and turned the tournament into a one-man show by adding a 72, a 73, and a 72 for 285, six strokes ahead of the second man and a new record

The eighteenth green at St. Andrews, close by the majestic clubhouse. Jones is about to sink the final putt on his opening 68 that gave him a lead he never surrendered in the 1927 British Open. By winning a championship played over the ancient course, Jones fulfilled one of his dearest ambitions.

for the championship. After holing his putt on the 72nd green, Jones received a terrific ovation from the Scottish spectators, the most astute golf galleries in the world, since golf to them is an extension of their lives as natural and as implicit as jazz is for Americans. They cared little that Bobby had taken St. Andrews apart on a week in which the Old Course wasn't really itself, the fairways baked hard by the sun and with hardly so much as a breeze stirring the whins. They were delighted that Bobby was the one who had done it, for in the judgment of the Scots he was the perfect player. In their minds they had conjured up the faultless golfer, in about the same way a man has his ideal woman, and when Jones came along they knew right off the reel that here was their dream-golfer. With a modicum of oral interchange, the Scottish galleries and their idol shared the bliss of complete communion. On the course the Scots knew instinctively when to let him alone, but once the tournament was over, they mobbed him and hoisted him high on their shoulders and carried him tenderly but triumphantly to the R. & A. clubhouse. Jones made a charming speech of acceptance when the cup was presented and then insured an everlasting place for himself in the hearts of the nation by signifying that he wished the trophy to be left in the keeping of the R. & A. If the Scots recognized their perfect golfer when they saw him, Jones was no less adept in sensing that they were his most intelligently enthusiastic admirers.

Splendid playing conditions also collaborated in the dazzling rounds Bobby turned in en route to his third victory in the U.S. Amateur Championship. After studying the weather conditions that prevailed during the fifteen previous summers and discovering that the third week in August invariably offered the coolest weather, the committee at Minneapolis' Minikahda Club, which had been awarded the tournament, settled on the week of August 22nd. Sure enough, the weather was delightful all week, almost sweater weather. Minikahda's famed "Sea Serpent" sprinkler took care of the patches that had been burned brown by the summer sun.

After qualifying easily, Jones got a bad round out of his system, a 78 that was no more than sufficient for an eighteenth-green victory over Maurice McCarthy, Jr. He was even par in taking Gene Homans, and then he really turned it on. In his morning rounds against Harrison "Jimmy" Johnston, Ouimet, and Evans, he shot a 68, a 69, and a 67, and coasted in to lopsided victories—10 and 9, 11 and 10, 8 and 7. Chick Evans, returning to the scene of his first national triumph eleven years earlier, was playing his irons with a much shorter backswing but getting the same beautiful results. He went all the way to the final, and, against Bobby, Chick gave a demonstration of mashie-play that might have got him home against any other amateur but Jones.

There weren't as many tournaments in the Twenties as there are today, when the various circuits are in action almost the year round except for a short layoff between Thanksgiving and New Year's. Nevertheless, the big guns had a fairly full calendar to shoot at—the California and Florida tournaments in the winter, the mid-continent affairs in the summer. Jones, however, rarely entered the lists. While his legal work did demand an increasingly large slice of his time, he could have probably sneaked off from the office had he not been convinced that there was such a thing as too much tournament golf. Some observers felt that Bobby might have been able to sharpen his game even finer if he played in more tournaments, but he remained steadfast in his view that continual competition would take too much out of him and leave him dried up and dull-edged when the major events came along. In 1928 he passed up defending his British Open Championship and confined himself to the two big domestic affairs.

Olympia Fields, that colossal installation below Chicago called a country club, was host to the Open. A glance at Jones' four rounds—73, 71, 73, 77—would forward the inference that Bobby, who tied for first, had tossed it away on the last eighteen. There was a bit more to it than that. During the championship proper and the first half of the playoff with Johnny Farrell, he was decidedly off his game. His driving, ordinarily one of his strongest points, was erratic, and Jones was perpetually struggling for his pars. By the fourth round he was so tired that the pupils in his eyes were drawn to pinpoints, and he felt more like flipping a coin with Farrell than going out the next morning to settle the tie via a 36-hole playoff. Farrell won. He threw a 70 at Jones over the first eighteen and held on bravely in the afternoon when Bobby, for the first time in the week at Olympia Fields, started to hit the ball and forced the slim Irishman to finish in birdies to win by one stroke.

The pros had managed to stop Jones two years in a row but among the amateurs he was still the boss. The field through which he made his way at Brae Burn, west of Boston, was a rather strong one, too. In addition to the players of the Ouimet–Evans generation and George Von Elm, it included new stars like Don Moe from Oregon, George Voigt (who had taken the Long Island Open from the pros), Phillips Finlay, Ducky Yates, and other young men with ambitions of their own. The British Walker Cup team was also entered, and Phil Perkins, the number-one man, was itching for a chance to square accounts with Jones for that 13 and 12 shellacking he had received in the Cup Match. At Brae Burn, Bobby had his customary close calls in his eighteen-hole matches, but once he was safely into the double-eighteens, he was as good as home. John Beck of Britain was a beaten man on the 23rd green; Phil Finlay was able to carry Bobby only one hole farther; and in the final Phil Perkins, who had earned his chance for another shot at Bobby, was stampeded almost as badly. Up to 1924, Jones' opponents in the Amateur had, more often than not, played over their heads. Now, with rare exceptions, they played "under their heads," if there is such a phrase, and, in any event, never seemed to be able to do themselves justice when they faced the great Atlantan. Perkins, for example, had used only 52 strokes over the fourteen holes of his afternoon round against Voigt. Against Jones, over the same distance, Perkins needed 66 on the morning round, and went down 10 and 9.

Had all matches been over the 36-hole route, the mature Bobby Jones might never have known what it was to *watch* a United States Amateur. However, in the very first round of the 1929 Amateur at Pebble Beach—the first national championship, incidentally, to be staged west of Minneapolis—Jones came up against a dogged youngster from Omaha named Johnny Goodman who jumped off to a lead over the first nine, hung on grimly as Jones came back, staved off Jones' last assault with a magnificent spoon shot to the green on the dangerous seventeenth, and succeeded in halving the eighteenth and winning the match 1 up. For years Jones had been frightened of being eliminated in the early 18-hole matches, and now that it had happened, he felt relieved, though at the same time it took him a while to get used to the idea of being a spectator in what had become his personal championship. He saw himself an interesting tournament in which

Jones' appearance in a national championship was the signal for thousands of his idolators to inundate the course and "play" each shot along with the incomparable Atlantan. Here the gallery at the 1929 Open swarms around the eighteenth at the Winged Foot Golf Club as Bobby plays his third shot from off the edge. Jones blew a four-stroke lead on the last four holes, but won in a playoff.

the oldtimers more than held their own against the youngsters. The average age of the semi-finalists—Jimmy Johnston, Doc Willing, Francis Ouimet, and Chandler Egan—was thirty-nine. Johnston from Minnesota and Willing from Oregon won through to the final where the thirty-four-year-old Johnston, the baby of the quartet, outsteadied the steady dentist.

The Amateur, as usual, had been held later in the year than the Open, and Jones' upset at the hands of the unknown Goodman was all the more shocking since Bobby had again captured the Open. For the fourth time he finished in a tie for first, this time with Al Espinosa. On the thirteenth tee of the last round, no one would have given an enchilada for the chances of the slow-moving Spaniard from Monterey, California. Starting out before Jones, Espinosa had to make up four strokes on the Georgian but fell further off the pace with a 38 on the first nine. After taking an 8 on the 66th, Espinosa, believing that he had kicked away his opportunity neatly and completely, played out the rest of the holes simply as a matter of routine. With no pressure to distract him, he covered the last six in 22 strokes and was startled to discover that, for all his blunders, he had the best four-round total among the early finishers. Jones meanwhile was marching along with par until he was trapped on his approach to the eighth green. He exploded clean across the green into another trap, then exploded out of that trap across the green and back into the first trap. He ended up with a 7 and was understandably trap-shy after this experience. Over the rest of the route, Bobby managed to stay out of the traps that guard the typically Tillinghast narrow-opening greens at Winged Foot, though this protective type of golf was not getting him any birdies. However, with four holes to go, he had pars in for a 75, a three-stroke lead over Espinosa's comparative figures. Then, on the 69th, a not particularly rough par 4, the Georgian completely lost his concentration. He punched his third shot much too forcefully into the wind, and the ball bounded well over the green. He chose to loft it back, over a little knoll, and flubbed his pitch smack into the knoll. The galleries that had come out to watch the flawless Jones play a 69 as he had on the first round watched an embarrassed man take his second three-over-par 7 of the day. They saw him throw away what looked like a sure birdie by three-putting the 70th from twenty feet. They shuddered for him when he left himself a touchy 12-footer on the 72nd to tie with Espinosa.

If Bobby Jones had failed to sink that putt on the 72nd green at Winged Foot, he would have blown a three-stroke lead on the last four holes, and there is no knowing how such a collapse might have affected a golfer as hypercritical of himself as Jones. There are many who think that the career of Bobby Jones would have tapered off then and there, that there certainly would have been no Grand Slam had he missed that curving 12-footer. He sank it, of course, borrowing perfectly off the slope and sending one of his "dying ball" putts into the exact center of the cup. Bobby Jones had won a reprieve. He went out the next day and shot two great playoff rounds of 72 and 69 and overwhelmed Espinosa by twenty-three strokes. Bobby Jones remained the champion of champions.

In chart form Bobby's major tournament record from 1923 through 1929 would look like this:

THE AGE OF BOBBY JONES 1923–1930

	BRITISH AMATEUR	BRITISH OPEN	U.S. AMATEUR	U.S. OPEN
1923			eliminated 2nd round	1 (playoff)
1924			1	2
1925			1	2 (playoff)
1926	eliminated 5th round	1	2	1
1927		1	1	tied for 11th
1928			1	2 (playoff)
1929			eliminated 1st round	1 (playoff)

Emperor Jones' appearance in a national tourney was the signal for five to eight thousand golfing fanatics to inundate the course and form a tense, idolatrous, noisy, frenetic, marshal-mangling gallery. Each person in the thousands wanted to touch his hero. Fans who couldn't get to the tournaments and who followed Jones' triumph by newspaper or radio felt an almost equal closeness to their hero. During the week of a national championship, the residents of every golfing community in the United States acted as if it were Atlanta. Bobby's victories were their victories, and his defeats were their defeats.

For a man who exerted so compelling a magnetism over American sports fans, Jones was an exceptionally restrained performer. He did not dramatize himself like Tilden or Hagen. He made no appeal to primitive human emotions, like Dempsey. He was no happy extrovert like Ruth. Jones' stupendous popularity—unprecedented in what had been a minor sport until he emerged—rested partially on a skill so apparent that it needed no showboating, and partially on the type of man he was.

There was a clear, cold aesthetic thrill in watching Jones hit a golf ball. The other leading players had excellent form that a duffer could appreciate, and they got results that spoke for themselves. Compared to Jones, though, they didn't look so finished. You noticed a little bumpiness in their backswing, a vague departure from the blueprint at impact, the expenditure of brute force in the followthrough. You looked at Jones and you saw the copybook form that you and two million other American golfers were striving for. You saw a one-piece swing in which the man had somehow incorporated every "must" your pro had enumerated—the left arm straight but not rigid on the backswing; the weight shifted from left to right going back and then gradually returned to the left side again as the club started down and the hands moved into position to unleash their power; the hit *through* the ball; the finish with the weight entirely transferred to the left side and the hands high—the million other integrated contributions of the chin, the hips, the balls of the feet, the knees, the grip, the left shoulder, the right ankle, the wrists, the eyes. If you could buckle down and remember to do all those things, then you, too, would play like Jones. No, you couldn't at that. You would always lack that something which lifted Jones above mechanical perfection. It was hard to put your finger on it. It had to do with a certain *je ne sais quoi* quality that made Bobby's swing so rhythmically singular, made it appear so effortless though you knew it was built on effort. Bernard Darwin came as close as anyone to tagging the genius of Jones when he said, without any gingerbread, that there was a strain of poetry in Bobby.

Dissected position by position, Jones' swing was, of course, not markedly different from those employed by the other stars. He did stand with his feet closer together than most of the other champions in order to facilitate the freest, fullest body turn the game has ever known. The shifting of weight is a very unglamorous facet of correct form to the average golfer. He would much rather hear that the key to playing par golf is the sturdy left elbow at contact or the machinations of the big toes. But Jones intimated that if there was any one most-important "secret to his success," it was that mundane, colorless chore, the free body turn, on which the correct execution of his shots depended.

A picture-postcard golfer like Jones had few idiosyncrasies. He teed the ball on his drive opposite his left arch, a bit farther forward than most players, since he preferred to hit his wood shots at the beginning of the upswing. He teed the ball high since he inclined toward woods with deep faces about four degrees straighter than the average clubs. He was of the opinion that his pitches from 60 to 125 yards were the weakest department of his game, but none of his rivals noticed this foible. If he had a weakness, it was his periodic unsureness at fading an approach. The shots he thought he hit best were the 3- and 4-irons.

Around the golf course, Jones, who could have gotten away with vanities and eccentricities, behaved as if he were just another golfer. A few soured also-rans griped that Bobby was always given the preferred starting times at the big tournaments. This was true, but it was the doing of the U.S.G.A. officials, who naturally were aware that Jones was an unrivaled drawing card. Jones' galleries were a trying lot, but no matter how deeply or how often he was disconcerted by individual gestures of love and devotion tendered at the wrong times, he never addressed a rebuking word to the offenders. His rivals were confounded by his regard for their feelings. The first word that came to Tommy Armour's mind in describing Jones was *considerate*.

Jones had rather simple tastes. There were stretches when he liked to be alone, such as tournament weeks. His evening ritual at these times consisted of two drinks (the first swallowed as he luxuriated in a hot tub), a relaxing dinner with Keeler and one or two other close friends, some conversation or a few chapters in a book like Papini's *Life of Christ* before retiring. But there was nothing prissy about Bobby—or Bob, as he preferred to be called. He loved the atmosphere of the locker room. He enjoyed a good story and told a good story. He used a man's language in expressing his emotions and had a nice gift for inventing phrases to describe his golf. (A hard, dangerous shot, for example, was one which demanded "sheer delicatessen.") Bobby was an intelligent person—he had studied at Harvard for two years, after getting his B.S. degree in mechanical engineering at Georgia Tech, and he later prepared for his legal career at Emory Law School. He was a man of many interests, to say the least. He was a good husband, a good father, and a good son. He and his father, "The Colonel," got a real kick out of each other. Paul Gallico, one sportswriter who never called a spade a sable instrument for delving, wrapped up Robert Tyre Jones, Jr., as well as anyone when he said of him: "I have found only one [sports figure] who could stand up in every way as a gentleman as well as a celebrity, a fine, decent human being as well as a newsprint personage, and one who never once since I have known him has let me down in my estimate of him."

The American sports public didn't know the intimate personal habits of Jones, but what they saw of him was an accurate index of the man. They liked the way he acted in competition. They liked the way he looked—clean-cut, boyish and grown-up at the same time. A decade or so before they had flocked to Ouimet because he was a young American they understood and admired, and it may not be at all excessive to say that they worshipped Jones, and formed an enduring enthusiasm for the game he played, because, of all the heroes in the Golden Age of Sport, he stood forth as the model American athlete.

THE
MASTER
BUILDERS

On the fairway Americans tried to keep up with Jones, and off the fairway they were busy keeping up with the Joneses. The Joneses were going in for golf in a great big way, more avidly, even, than they pursued the latest bridge systems, the inside story on murder trials, the new subterranean address the indispensable Tony had moved to, Clara Bow's formula, and a college education for their fair-haired progeny. The Joneses liked golf and would have stuck with the game once they took it up for the right good reason that it fascinated them. But there were other reasons for playing golf, more right and better. The fact that the Joneses were able to spend so much time at the course marked them as a family that was doing all right financially. Then, too, if they "made" an exclusive country club, a snazzier bazaar than the Smiths belonged to, they need not bow their heads to anyone socially. Membership in an *exclusive country club*—on rare occasions the three words were not yoked together—was the salient badge of distinction in the Twenties. Mrs. Jones was happy about it, for her kiddies' sake, she said. Mr. Jones was more honest. He got as much business done in the locker room and on the course as he did at the office. It was the environment that he favored as well for those hours when his second business, that wonderful invention called the stock market, made money for him even as he carded his 46 on the back nine with his new MacGregor Chieftains.

As the country club came of age in America, the Joneses and Americans of greater and less equilibrium puffed the ranks of the nation's golfers. Now there were over two million of them. Each year they spent $10,000,000 for caddies, bought about 24,000,000

balls and about $20,000,000 worth of implements, and contributed toward the $120,-
000,000 that went into new mowers, seeds, watering systems, and other equipment
requested by the green committees. Some of them furnished their golf bag with all the
items Hagen carried in the British Open: in addition to clubs and balls, they were
fortified with an umbrella, ball-cleaner and brushes, thermometer, clock, a case for tees,
wind gauge, rule book, a second pair of shoes, an extra sweater, and a caddie whistle.
Also a second pair of argyles, one of the 6,876,192 pairs of golf hose Americans
purchased in a single year. There was hardly enough room to carry around that Pivot-
Sleeve jacket—the one Ph. Weinberg and Sons had shown for years in the *American
Golfer*—but jackets were going out anyway. The old golfers had been blinded by
tradition when they had persevered with the jacket; obviously, the smart thing to wear
with knickers and cap was matching sweater and socks, like that sharp checkered
combination George Von Elm had on at the Amateur.

Room had to be found for the new thousands who wanted to play golf, and from
seacoast to seacoast kidney-shaped traps were scooped out and oaks were felled and split
for tee benches as the country went back-to-the-soil. By the middle Twenties, the
300,000 Oregonians living in Portland had twenty courses to choose from. Seattle had
only seventeen, but they were all within thirty minutes drive of the totem pole in the
center of town. Miami and Miami Beach were building new courses at the rate of over
one a year. The size of the community, though, was of small importance. The folks in
York, Nebraska, had twice attempted to finance a golf course and twice the project had
died on them, but they wanted a golf course and on the third try they made it. Enough
$100 bonds were sold in three drives to purchase forty-three acres of blue grass and
clover turf cut by a snaky little brook, and to add a modern frame clubhouse for $15,000.
George Ade, the humorist and a golf pioneer, had his own course in Hazelden, Indiana,
with a rustic clubhouse fashioned from three hundred burr oaks. Almost a hundred
towns in Kansas had their golf courses. Cloudcroft in New Mexico built one nine
thousand feet above sea level. By the late Twenties there were more greens in the
United States than savings banks and libraries.

The clubs with a problem were the pioneer layouts near the larger cities. At the turn of
the century the land purchased by the syndicates had been truly rural, fifteen or twenty
minutes from the heart of the city. Now, as the cities spread out, many of these old
clubs found themselves hemmed in by houses, stores, and factories, their land no longer
ample enough to take care of the holes they wished to build or remodel to keep up with
the livelier golf ball, their locations uncongenial to the commodious clubhouse their
members were discussing. Most of the time these clubs solved their problem by buying
new land farther out in the country and selling their old plot to the city. Municipal golf
courses were a paying investment. Norfolk, Virginia, for illustration, constructed nine
holes at the cost of $1,500. The green fee for a day's play was only fifteen cents, but six
months after the course had been opened, it had paid for itself and returned the city a
clear $2,000 profit. Norfolk then decided to extend the course to eighteen holes, and

soon after this, started work on the first of three public courses on a 575-acre farm owned by the city. San Antonio could boast of the $45,000 clubhouse, modeled after a farmhouse of the Marie Antoinette period, which it had ordained for the Brackenridge Park municipal course over which the Texas Open was played. Port Townsend, Washington (population 3,300), had a private club but the town officials at length gave in to the demands of that golf-happy community for a public course, and never regretted it. Everyone wanted to be a golfer, and if the man in the low-income bracket was stymied in joining an exclusive country club, thanks to the public course he could still play the same game that hypnotized his boss and after a good round he could experience that "g-r-r-rand and gl-l-l-lorious feeling" Clare Briggs had delineated in his matchless cartoons. Over five hundred non-private courses mushroomed across the country, some just unkempt acres with flags on the flattest spots, others too short for a long-hitter and overcrowded on weekends, but a fair percentage of them excellent tests of golf.

Looking for *lebensraum*, the wealthy clubs pushed deeper into the sticks. The little towns of America, Ade commented dryly, had succeeded in foisting Prohibition on the large cities but now they were being shackled with golf in retaliation. No land within thirty-five miles of a large city was safe, and if it had a winding stream and a hill suitable for a spreading clubhouse, it was as good as under construction. The golf architects went to the country and went to town. A. W. Tillinghast built his imaginative and pleasant-to-play courses in all parts of the country. Donald Ross had gotten away from his penchant for placing his greens on the crowns of graded hills and for sticking his traps so close to the greens that very often the average golfer was better off if he made a sizable error and not a wee one. Of the later courses Ross designed—and he was undoubtedly the busiest architect in the country—one of the most interesting was Oyster Harbors, reclaimed from a Cape Cod swamp at considerable expense, one hole running to $26,000. Devereux Emmett, another oldtimer, worked with W. H. Follett on the Women's National, the fine course in Glen Head, Long Island, financed by and operated for women exclusively. Marion Hollins, the former women's champion who had spearheaded the promotion of the Women's National, called on Dr. Alister MacKenzie when she fell in love with California, and MacKenzie did two first-class jobs for Miss Hollins—Pasatiempo at Santa Cruz and Cypress Point on the Monterey Peninsula. In the astonishing range of its beauty, Cypress Point stands almost alone among golf courses—green forests edging down to the blinding whiteness of the sand dunes, cypresses fringing the craggy headlands that drop with an awful suddenness into the blue Pacific. MacKenzie wisely winked at the principles of golf architecture when the rugged terrain suggested untraditional measures, such as two par 3s in a row. The fifteenth is a pitch over an inlet that is Stevenson's pirate cove come to life. The sixteenth is a carry (which must be all of 210 yards) across a deep elbow of the Pacific to a green that is a miniature Heligoland. MacKenzie and Robert Trent Jones, the young man who with Stanley Thompson did the thrilling courses at Banff and Jasper Park, were not showboat architects—indeed, quite the reverse of it. They share the credit for bringing back into American golf-course architecture the natural dune bunker and for replacing the multitude of penal headaches with a few strategically positioned hazards that punished a poor shot in direct proportion to its inaccuracy. They were also the first to realize the role that sharply contoured greens with several pin positions could play in making courses stiffer for par golfers while rendering them no more difficult for the average player.

One of the great courses of the world, Pine Valley, was the work of a non-professional architect, George Crump. One day when Crump was out hunting in the harsh stretches of sand and pine in western New Jersey, the idea came to him that this was the perfect land for building a golf course that would be fundamentally fair and yet be a course that would stand up to the wizards who were making scores in the 60s seem as prosaic as brushing your teeth. A few years later, Crump, a successful Philadelphia hotel man, turned all of his exceptional energy into making his dream come true. He engaged H. S. Colt, the highly respected English architect, to help him with the plans for his undertaking, and moved into a bungalow he built on the property. For eight years he lived practically the life of a hermit, hunting in the odd moments he wasn't occupied with turning his primeval domain into the most carefully planned golf course in the history of the game. George Crump died before he had completed his project, but he had finished fourteen of the holes, and his estate and a generous friend from Morristown furnished the necessary funds for carrying out Crump's plans for the last four holes. (These holes were executed by Hugh Wilson, another remarkable amateur architect from Philadelphia and the creator of Merion.) Pine Valley emerged the course George Crump had visualized—just about the toughest layout in the world, "an examination in golf," as Bernard Darwin phrased it. In 1922 George V. Rotan succeeded in getting around in 70, and down through the years, in the face of innumerable assaults by the best golfers, that 70 remained the lowest score made in competition at Pine Valley until 1939, when Ed Dudley played an astonishing 68.

The courses designed in the comparative country were handsome and ingenious, and yet at many of the country clubs the course was somewhat in the same position as the juggler who made the mistake of hiring a female assistant of such incandescent beauty that no one had the vaguest idea if he were twirling Indian pins or dishes. The clubhouse, of course, was the assistant that became the star of the show. Starting as Stanford White's modest lounge and locker room at Shinnecock Hills, the clubhouse had now become the center of the social life of America's middle-middle, upper-middle, and upper classes. At the clubhouse you lived with the people you wanted to associate with, played your bridge, drank your gin rickey, ate your guinea hen, danced your foxtrot, traded your tips on stocks, and gave your daughter away in marriage. Home was where you brought your dirty laundry—although the country club, in time, came to offer laundry service, valet service, a complete barber shop, a masseur, a dancing instructor. . . . Just name what you wanted and your country club had it. It was like some magnificent luxury liner that someone had forgotten to launch.

The fabulous sixteenth at Cypress Point. The green on this par 3 lies across 210 yards of the Pacific. Women, children, and timorous males can play safe to the left and then pitch to the green on their second. Cypress Point is one of the several spectacular courses on California's Monterey Peninsula. The oldest is Del Monte, which dates from the late 1890s. The toughest is Pebble Beach.

Bigger and better installations went up all over the country. The members of the Birmingham Country Club in Alabama spent over $300,000 on their new place in Shades Valley but they believed it gave them the most spacious clubhouse in the South. $250,000 was about par for a new clubhouse, and then there were the fixings—tennis courts, bridle paths, dancing pavilion, swimming pool, perhaps a polo field, and yes, a golf course or two. In Chicago, a thousand Shriners, building the Medinah Country Club at a cost of $1,500,000, planned to have the whole works, plus toboggan slides and ski runs. The Los Angeles Country Club had one of the largest memberships—three thousand. The Glen Oaks Country Club, occupying the former mansion of William K. Vanderbilt, had one of the nicest nooks, a sunken Italian garden. The richest was the Detroit Golf Club, founded in 1906 and still sticking with its original course, since its 212 acres now formed the heart of the city's residential district; the land was now valued at $100,000 an acre, and a Class A membership (entitling the holder to stock and voting power) went for $7,500. The most snobbish was Chevy Chase, outside of Washington, which barred local businessmen on the grounds that they were "persons engaged in trade."

Olympia Fields was the daddy of them all. Conceived in 1914, this gargantuan retreat in the woods below Chicago was at length completed in 1925. "The world's largest private golf club" was the first to offer its members seventy-two holes of golf. (Over two thousand caddies were enrolled.) The clubhouse was a liberal translation of English Tudor with a dining room seating eight hundred, a café seating six hundred, only one outdoor dancing pavilion but five hundred feet of veranda. The club operated its own ice-making plant and its own hospital. One hundred families owned cottages in the dells of the club's 692 acres. Through some oversight Olympia Fields never made provision for its own college and a major league baseball team, but it was possible to live out your life there if your wants were not exotic.

More and more celebrities played golf—Charlie Chaplin, Pola Negri, Uncle Joe Cannon, Harold Lloyd, Vilma Banky, President Harding, Douglas Fairbanks, to name just a few of the stars of stage, screen, and government. Magazines and newspaper editors never tired of photos showing Babe Ruth twisted like a corkscrew after smashing a drive, or Aileen Riggin, the reigning pin-up girl, bestowing her come-hither on a mashie, or cartoonist Rube Goldberg inventing some zany stroke at the Artists and Writers annual tournament. Earl Sande, the hero of the race tracks, became a convert. So did Ty Cobb, except during the baseball season. Frank Craven was impatient for the Broadway run of *The First Year* to end, for he had been neglecting his game. Rex Beach, a fairly good player, made a hole-in-one and won a free case of Canada Dry, among other things. John D. Rockefeller's spontaneous statements to the effect that golf was the best insurance of longevity sold more people on the tycoon's humanity than the artful campaigns of his publicity man, Ivy Lee.

The *American Golfer*, now a glossy job thick with advertising, tastefully edited by Grantland Rice and Innis Brown, conducted a "contest" in which various celebrities were asked to respond humorously to the question: What do you find the hardest shot in golf? Many of the boys came through nicely:

GROUCHO MARX: I find the hardest shot in golf is a hole-in-one.

RING LARDNER: I am undecided as to which of these two is the hardest shot in golf for me—any unconceded putt or the explosion shot off the first tee. Both have caused me more strokes than I care to write about.

W. C. FIELDS: I am stumped when it comes to saying which is the hardest shot in golf for me, but I know the easiest one—the first shot at the Nineteenth Hole.

Hot Springs, Virginia. This fashionable resort helped to fulfill Americans' desire for both golf and scenery in the grand style. In the Twenties, Americans carried their clubs with them wherever they went; it was debatable whether the toothbrush rated a higher priority as a travel companion than the putter.

Golf humor was no longer "society stuff." The office boy knew the game:

BUSINESS MAN TO OFFICE BOY: When people want to see me, do you know what to tell them?

OFFICE BOY: Sure. I've worked for business men before. When you're playing 9 holes, you're out-to-lunch—18 holes is in conference—27 holes, sick—and 36 holes is out-of-town.

As always, some of the best humor was unintentional. When Los Angeles was host to the P.G.A. Championship, the movie luminaries decided to give the tournament that extra Hollywood touch; before each twosome went out, a Hollywood star introduced the players to the gallery. Fay Wray, whose job it was to introduce Hagen and his partner, was doing fine in her breathless way until she referred to Walter as "the Opium Champion of Great Britain."

To play good golf was a gilt-edged social and commercial asset, so Americans beat a path to the door of the local pro, the doctor who could trim three strokes off anyone's game, maybe more if the instruction could be hammered home over a long series of lessons. In the Twenties the career of the average golf pro was no longer a precarious one, and the boys who had made a name for themselves in tournament golf had drawing rooms on the gravy train. The Open title was now worth about $25,000 to the winning pro, and after his victories in the Open and the P.G.A. in 1922, Gene Sarazen parlayed them into many more thousands by an astute understanding of the public's appetite. In addition to playing the numerous exhibition and special matches that every champion comes into, young Sarazen cashed in on his big year by opening a golf correspondence school in New York, signing with the Wilson Company to promote and design clubs, endorsing his favorite golf ball (and the cartridge the Open Champion liked to lock in his barrel when he went trap-shooting), making movie shorts, putting out an instruction book, and accepting the highest salary ever offered a professional to go with Briarcliff Lodge, Chauncey Depew Steele's combination country club and resort in Westchester.

As the money became easier, some of the top golfers chose to spend the winter as resident pros at select spas in Florida rather than follow the tournament caravan winding from California across the Southern states and up to the Carolinas with halts for $1,500 and $2,000 tournaments. To lure the likes of Sarazen and Hagen to their tournaments, the sponsors had to increase the prize money. The $6,000 San Antonio Open, once the richest pot on the winter march, began to look rather emaciated as the Los Angeles Open upped its prize money to $10,000, Miami countered with $15,000, and Agua Caliente placed the maraschino on the sundae with a $25,000 affair. (It was rather characteristic of Sarazen to come onto his game just in time to carry off the first-place check in the first Agua Caliente Open.) One reason why Bobby Jones faced so little competition in the amateur field was that nearly every young golfer of promise without a private income no longer hesitated to turn professional. Hagen had led the way in wiping out the old social stigma of being a professional, for one thing, and a tidy living awaited the young man who could shoot his way to a place among the nation's top twenty. Whole families of golfers became pros, the two outstanding examples being the Turnesas and the Espinosas. Six of the Turnesa boys were pros—in order of seniority, Phil, Frank, Joe, Mike, Doug, and Jim. Abe and Al were the only two Espinosas who earned national reputations, but Romie, Henry, Raymond, and *Annette* all made golf their career.

By 1929, the Joneses of America were playing golf on over 4,500 courses and were members of clubs whose collective real estate was valued at over a billion and a half dollars. The Joneses who lived in some small towns, in the Middle West in particular, belonged to clubs that remained free from arbitrary social distinctions, such as the one in Sheffield, Illinois, where the holes had been laid out by John Stapleton, the chauffeur for the town's leading banker and his boss' equal in the shower room and the sand trap. But by and large the class-conscious country club was the thing, and the Joneses were

The Westchester-Biltmore Country Club, one of the sprawling country palaces that answered the golfer's cry for bigger and better retreats. John McEntee Bowman, who built the Westchester-Biltmore, was reported to have invested almost five millions in its 400-room hotel, its 36 holes, its 540 acres, and its beach club.

seldom resentful, and then only if they were left out, as the spirit of the country club cut deeper and deeper into the mores of the country, obliterating, for everyone except Rodgers and Hammerstein, some of the healthier attitudes of non-metropolitan America. The Joneses liked to hear that private companies, like the Cudahy branch in Kansas City, had opened golf courses for their employees. This was Progress, and, besides, the Joneses were all set to spend the summer occupying two of the four hundred rooms at the Westchester-Biltmore's hideaway in Rye. They saluted golf as the great common denominator when the final match of the Cleveland District Amateur Championship

Rex Beach, Grantland Rice, Rube Goldberg, and Frank Craven—Knickers 3, Trousers 1.

brought together Ellsworth Augustus, the scion of a very affluent family, and Eli Ross, his gardener—and didn't think the perfect story had been sabotaged when Augustus trounced his gardener 10 and 8.

The Joneses read everything that was written about the game they doted on. They got a big bang out of the cranky scorn of a Mr. Quale, the Federal Director of Prohibition Enforcement in Minnesota, who declared that golf "encourages idleness, shiftlessness, and neglect of business as well as family responsibilities; that it deprives many wives of their husbands, and children of their fathers, and that it tempts hundreds of young men into extravagance that sometimes leads to crime." They knew why they played golf: it was a good game, a damn good game that took you outdoors—a damn fashionable game, too, and you didn't have to be a three-letter athlete to play it. Nevertheless, they ate up any and all dissertations by the posse of scholars who were hunting basic sociological explanations for the craze. The Joneses were delighted when Charles Merz in "The Great American Bandwagon" released his theory that golf had created a new frontier for the bored, frontierless modern world, that plus-fours were a substitute for leather chaps, and loud argyles were "the war paint of a nation." In their rude fortresses the Joneses and other frontiersmen ordered soda water at a dollar a bottle and talked about the lighter arts. Broadway was readying a show with a golf background, *Follow Through*. Indefatigable William Haines had included golf among the many sports he played so well on the screen. In *Spring Fever* he had won the girl by holing a full brassie shot on the last hole, just when things looked blackest. (When it was remade into a talkie with Robert Montgomery and called *Love in the Rough*, Montgomery's heroics were sublimated to making an impossible recovery shot and negotiating a stymie.) The Joneses planned their trips abroad to include golf in romantic locales and made gay references to Cheops' Pyramid as the oldest tee in the world. They attended indoor golf schools, if they stayed north for the winter, and turned up at the National Golf Show to study the exhibits on country club layout, caddie welfare, clubhouse structure, green committee work, etc. The country club had come to stay, and rain or shine the Joneses could always be found at Bubbling Bay. At seven-thirty sharp, Mrs. Jones was at her regular table in the café—not the dining room or the informal grill, but the café—reading a few of the two million words sent out over the wires to describe the Open at Olympia Fields. Mr. Jones was detained a moment. He was down at the putting green watching his star salesman practice missing the short ones.

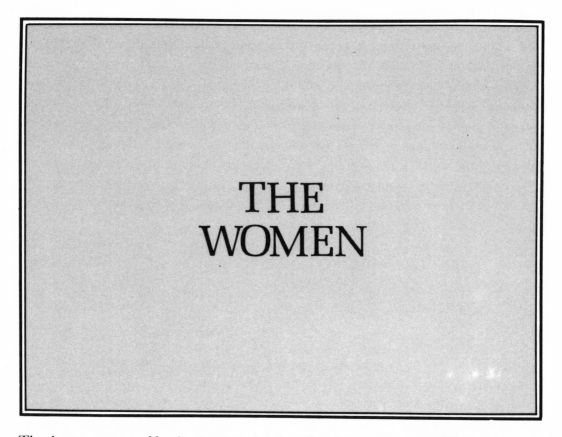

THE WOMEN

The best woman golfer in America in the Twenties was a graceful, strong, and appealing girl from Rhode Island with the euphonious name of Glenna Collett. In christening Glenna "the female Bobby Jones," the apostles of apposition were paying the logical tribute to Glenna's comparable dominance over the field of women golfers. Yet, if you pushed the analogy further, it stood up surprisingly well. Glenna was like Bobby in many ways. She came from the same stratum of society, took advantage of her assets with the same sensible determination to succeed, and reached her goal after the same painful but invaluable passage through the shoals of despondency. As a champion, like Jones she was more than the best in her business. She exuded quality. Young men wrote poems about her infinite charms as she stood silhouetted against the horizon at Pebble Beach; older men claimed that she was the exact type William Dean Howells had in mind when he had stated that the crowning product of America was the American girl; and women had a good word for Glenna.

Like Bobby, Glenna liked all sports. Blessed with a fluid coordination that set her apart from the other girls in her neighborhood in Providence, she was an accomplished swimmer and diver at nine. At ten, she drove her first auto. Mrs. Collett, with a mother's natural concern for her daughter's tomboy predilections, tried to steer her into tennis when Glenna began to blossom as a star on her brother Ned's baseball team. Glenna did develop a promising tennis game to please her mother but continued to play on Ned's club. The girl could throw a ball farther than most of the boys. One afternoon in 1917, when Glenna was fourteen, her father took her along when he went to the

Metacomet Golf Club for a round with his cronies. This was Glenna's first meeting with golf. She watched the men for a few holes, and then asked if she could hit one. Not knowing how ornery a game she was trifling with, Glenna banged a beauty straight down the fairway. The men smiled uncomfortably at each other and asked her to play along. Her score was nothing to post in the ladies' locker room, but Glenna came off the course both excited and sobered by the strange feeling that she was meant to be a golfer. Mr. Collett, a famous bowler and a former national cycling champion, went out of his way to see that Glenna had every assistance possible in improving her game, and there were times when he might have overdriven the girl in his desire to have another champion in the family. Mrs. Collett was relieved. She didn't care if her daughter went in for golf rather than tennis as long as it kept her off third base.

Glenna discovered that it took more than good coordination to play good golf. She chopped her score down from 150 to 130 but that was as low as she could get that first summer. It was all rather discouraging; the harder she concentrated on doing everything the pro told her, the worse she hit her shots. She was beginning to yearn to take-two-and-hit-to-right with Ned's gang when she went over to the Wannamoisett Club one afternoon to watch Alexa Stirling and Elaine Rosenthal team up with Jones and Adair in a Red Cross exhibition match. Elaine was in fine form that day, and Glenna stood silent and admiring as she shattered the woman's course record with an 80. Alexa impressed her even more strongly. Glenna had never seen anyone who hit an iron as crisply as the little Atlantan, and when it came to holing the crucial putts, Alexa stepped up to the ball as cool as a cantaloupe and plunked it in. The afternoon at Wannamoisett was just what the doctor ordered. The next day Glenna went out, and throwing off the encumbrance of a thousand *don'ts*, shot a 49 for nine holes.

The following summers Glenna worked diligently on the practice fairways, looked becoming in the red picture-hat she wore in tournament play, fell apart in competition, and retreated to the practice fairways. Her father had arranged for her to take two lessons a week from Alex Smith, then the pro at Shennecossett, and in the winters the Colletts followed Alex south to Belleair. Old Alex, the man who had made Jerry Travers, taught Glenna how to "miss 'em quick" on the greens with a compact putting stroke, cut down the backswing on her irons, squinted at her in mock anger until she learned to control her clubhead in her brassie and spoon play, and polished up her driving although Glenna had always looked like a 75-player off the tee.

At least once each season Alex's pupil would get going in a tournament, but, invariably, the day after she had looked like the most promising girl who had struck American golf in a decade, her game would fold like an Arab's tent and Glenna would silently steal away to brood over her chronic disappointments. There was the year—1919—when Glenna was the only member of the Boston Griscom Cup team to win her match against the Philadelphia powerhouse, and then, in her next important test, she had been humiliated 9 and 8 in an eighteen-hole match by Mrs. Barlow, and had barely been able to fight off her tears until she reached the clubhouse. And there was 1920,

Mrs. Dorothy Campbell Hurd and Miss Alexa Stirling, the two finalists in the Women's Championship in 1920. Mrs. Hurd, greatest of the early women golfers, played her first round in 1888 at North Berwick in Scotland at the age of five. Alexa, a childhood friend of Bobby Jones', won three national championships.

when she had astounded experts by defeating Elaine Rosenthal in the final of the Shennecossett tournament only to lose to Elaine when they met again in the second round of the U.S. Women's Championship. The same story in 1921—an 85 at Deal in the qualifying round of the national championship that was fast enough to tie for the medal and built her up to a painful letdown, a sound defeat in the first round by Edith Leitch, a sister of the English champion, Cecil.

Some of life's darkest moments come just before the floor-show goes on. Glenna followed the women's circuit from Deal to the Huntingdon Valley Country Club outside of Philadelphia to play in the Berthellyn Cup competition. When she found that she had drawn Cecil Leitch in the first round, Glenna prepared herself to accept another defeat. The safest means of carrying Cecil a respectable distance, Glenna decided, was to forget about winning holes with impossible shots and just go out and fight for a half on each hole. Cecil was a little off her game, and Glenna, sticking to her plan, halved one hole after another and was completely astonished when she found herself not only still in the match as they came to the eighteenth but actually protecting a 1-up lead. On the home green she had a 10-footer for a half, and the match.

The importance of this victory over Cecil Leitch cannot be overemphasized. Almost overnight Glenna became a different golfer, a confident golfer. She started to hit out, to strike her shots as forcefully as she did on the practice fairway. She carried off the Berthellyn Cup. And from that time on, Glenna was the woman to beat.

In 1922 the seasoned nineteen-year-old star captured the North and South, and then the Eastern, averaging 82 for her three rounds in the latter championship. She looked like the class of the field by several strokes. Golf writers composed psalms about her swing and told their readers that they could see no one else but Glenna winning the U.S. Women's Championship. It was all happening a little too rapidly for Glenna to be tranquil about her new eminence. Glenna was not dangerously close to that line where an athlete is too sensitive and too intelligent for his or her own good, but the superlatives frightened her. She was happy that at last she was playing winning golf, but she wasn't as good as all that. She realized how cardinally important it was to be confident about whatever she undertook, but super-confident people had never appealed to her, regardless of whether or not they were successful, and she found it vexing to adjust herself to the frame of mind she desired: to be able to think reasonably well of herself and yet to stop many stations south of conceit. Fortunately, her sensibilities were somewhat dulled once she was on the course. Glenna wasn't an icebox like Helen Wills, but she cultivated a restraint that led many of her friends to accuse her of being a "cold woman" and in turn brought passionate protests from Glenna to the effect that it was just a pose designed to help her control the tautness and tension she always felt in competition.

In a warm-up round at the Greenbrier Club in White Sulphur Springs, West Virginia, two days before the 1922 Women's Championship, Glenna scored a 75. The evening previous to this round, she had eaten lamb chops, string beans, and creamed potatoes for dinner, and she continued with this menu while the tournament lasted, half laughing at herself for being so superstitious but hoping that somehow it would preserve her 75 form. For the same reason she stuck with the hat, sweater, and skirt she had worn on the hot round. It was silly, but it seemed to work. Glenna won the medal with an 81. She won her first three matches without extending herself. In the semi-final she met one of the most stunning girls who has ever graced American sports, cool, blonde Edith Cummings. "She has Marilyn Miller and Julia Sanderson beaten a mile for sheer beauty," raved one smitten writer. Edith could also play golf. In match play she was cocky and aggressive, and played hard to win. In her match with Glenna, Edith picked up three holes on the out-nine but had to give them back one by one as Glenna fought back. The two were all even coming to the seventeenth. Edith found the rough with her drive on that hole, and Glenna went 1 up. Glenna also won the short eighteenth when Edith was stymied, and was safely into the final.

The final against Mrs. W. A. Gavin was something of an anticlimax. Mrs. Gavin was an old-school woman golfer, a short-hitting control-player. Against Glenna, Mrs. Gavin couldn't find her groove, and Glenna, powdering her drives twenty-five to fifty yards farther than her opponent, built up a 6-hole lead at lunch. Mrs. Gavin played considerably better in the afternoon, but one hole was as much as she could win back, and the match was over on the fourteenth green. Glenna Collett, 5 and 4.

The new champion was undeniably attractive—a nice-looking brunette with an easy outdoor manner. Many of the women sports champions who had preceded Glenna had been fairly slim and feminine, but their charms had been successfully camouflaged by the apparel with which they were afflicted, and sports fans had chosen to remember the bulkier champions and to generalize that every woman athlete looked like Stanislaus Zbyszko. Glenna came along when a more liberal post-war attitude and the new emphasis on the country club had altered men's ideas about the place of women and women who played sports. If their wives and daughters turned out no worse than Glenna or the California tennis players—let them play. They would anyway.

The sports fans of the country began to follow Glenna. They liked a consistent winner, and Glenna was that. In 1923 she won the North and South and the Eastern again, and defeated her girlhood idol, Alexa Stirling, in adding the Canadian Championship. In 1924 she won fifty-nine out of sixty matches! She was a thrillingly long hitter for a woman; she once belted a tee shot 307 yards. And that manner! In a match she was businesslike and capable. She threw no tantrums and had no affectations. In addition, she possessed a good sense of humor and a superb social instinct. Mention Glenna Collett to any reporter who covered her matches and he smiles as he sighs, "Glenna . . . Now there was a real girl."

Through their interest in Glenna, Americans became acquainted with the other women who were playing tournament golf, and a very good group they were: Edith Cummings, from Lake Forest, Illinois, who provided the photographers with a field day when she won the national title in '23; Marion Hollins, champion in 1921, a course promoter, and a talented all-round sportswoman; Alexa Stirling, of course; Ada Mackenzie, a gritty competitor from Toronto; Bernice Wall, a pretty girl from Oshkosh who

The Bobby Jones of women's golf, Glenna Collett. Glenna won the U.S. championship six times between 1922 and 1935. One of those girls who take to athletics the way most girls take to athletes, Glenna was an accomplished diver, rider, and tennis player, and, until her worried mother intervened, a budding baseball star.

Edith Cummings, the victor in the 27th
renewal of the Women's Amateur in 1923.

Virginia Van Wie, the winner of three
consecutive Women's titles, 1932–1934.

could putt; Edith Quier, the nicest sort of an aristocrat, from Philadelphia, like so many
other top-ranking women golfers; Miriam Burns, who as Mrs. Horn became the first
divorcée to win the title and was, by any name, the woman with the most sex appeal in
the judgment of the galleries. In the later years of Glenna's rule, the ranks were
augmented by many other good golfers—Helen Payson, Glenna's sidekick, a tall blonde
from Maine; golf's hard-luck girl, Maureen Orcutt, who could win everything but the
national championship; Mrs. Leona Pressler (later Cheney), from the West Coast, and
Mrs. Opal Hill of Kansas City, who took up the game at thirty on the advice of her
physician; Peggy Wattles, a child star from Buffalo, and petite Virginia Wilson, from
Onwentsia, who was an expert horsewoman; long-hitting Helen Hicks, the first champion to turn pro; Glenna's successor as our top woman player, Virginia Van Wie, a fine-
looking swinger who had been too sickly to attend school and was a walking advertisement for the wonders worked by the outdoor life.

The public came to know the old champions who were still active, like Mrs.
Clarence Vanderbeck, Mrs. Caleb Fox, over sixty and the grandmother of ten, and the
great Dorothy Campbell Hurd, who had earlier dominated international golf as authoritatively as Glenna did American golf in the Twenties. A native of North Berwick,
Scotland, Mrs. Hurd, as Dorothy Campbell, had extended her rule from Scottish golf to
British golf and then to American golf as well. She had won the national championship
for the first time in 1909 and repeated the following year when she also took the first of
her several Canadian titles. After her marriage in 1913 to J. B. Hurd of Pittsburgh (and

Oakmont), Mrs. Hurd went into semi-retirement. When she returned to the tournament whirl in the Twenties, she recognized that her old sweeping style, with the club held in the palms and the wrists stiff, was obsolete. She went to George Sayers, an old townie of hers from North Berwick, then a Philadelphia pro, and changed over to the Vardon grip and a semi-modern swing. In a very short time Mrs. Hurd was right up with the pacemakers again, mainly because she retained all the magic of her short game. She chipped with "Thomas," a goose-neck mashie with a small face, and putted with "Stella" who had been with her since 1909. At the Augusta Country Club, in Georgia, thanks to Thomas (who chipped in twice) and Stella (who couldn't miss anything), Mrs. Hurd used only 19 putts on eighteen holes, lowering by two strokes Walter Travis' record for putts-in-one-round.

Glenna was the outstanding woman golfer during 1923 and 1924, but in neither year did she win the U.S. Women's Championship. In '23 Mrs. Vanderbeck eliminated her in the third round; Glenna played erratically over the first eleven holes, went 4 down, and the run of pars she finally unleashed did not worry an experienced campaigner like Mrs. Vanderbeck. (Edith Cummings beat Mrs. Vanderbeck in the semis and Alexa Stirling in the final.) In '24 Glenna was apparently on her way to the championship—she hadn't lost a match all year—when Mary K. Browne upset her in the semis. Mary was better known as a tennis player. She had won the United States Women's Singles Championship three times, and only two weeks before the 1924 national golf championship, Mary had made her way to the semi-finals at Forest Hills and given Helen Wills a real battle before going down 6–4, 4–6, 6–3. Mary had been one of Glenna's childhood idols, and it was a big moment in that hero-worshipper's life when some friends had introduced her to Mary at Forest Hills after the Wills–Browne match. The knowledge that it was Mary K. Browne whom she had to beat bothered Glenna throughout their match. Glenna started slowly and found herself thinking more about Mary's game than her own. Down the stretch, though, Glenna did gain a one-hole lead, and that looked to be a safe margin when Mary's drive on the eighteenth rolled into a thick tangle of rough. Mary, however, was not conceding defeat. She went after the ball with her brassie and succeeded in slashing it to the vicinity of the green, where it caromed off the bough of an apple tree and bounced to within fifteen feet of the cup. Mary squared the match and forced it into extra holes. On the 19th, both women lay three on the edge of the green, Mary on the front, Glenna on the back, a few feet farther away. Glenna almost holed her fourth but it died on the edge of the cup. Mary stroked her fourth carefully. For a moment it seemed as though the putt had the perfect line but then it began to veer off the slightest bit, toward Glenna's ball. *Click!* It kissed off Glenna's ball and ricocheted into the cup.

Mary Kimball Browne lost to Mrs. Hurd the next day, but in reaching the semi-final round of the national tennis championship and the final round of the national golf championship *in the same year* she had displayed an athletic virtuosity that has never been equaled. Many other tennis stars—René Lacoste, Vincent Richards, Ellsworth Vines,

Althea Gibson, to name just a few—have turned to golf and attempted to duplicate their success on the courts. Their splendid coordination and battle-born competitive temperaments helped them to become skillful golfers in one-fifth the time it took the average novice to become mediocre, and yet they never developed into champion golfers. Striking a stationary ball with a club from a stationary stance calls for a different genius for timing than stroking a moving ball with a racket. Ellsworth Vines manufactured himself into one of the nation's top fifteen pros and was capable of winning a major championship, but Vines' shots on the golf course somehow seemed to lack the authenticity with which he struck a tennis ball.

In 1925 Glenna fulfilled Walter Hagen's definition of a true champion: a person who is able to win a national championship more than once. Previous to reclaiming the U.S. Women's title at the St. Louis Country Club in early October, Glenna campaigned in Europe, and rather successfully for the most part, since she won the French Championship at La Boulie and made Joyce Wethered play magnificent golf to oust her from the British Ladies' Championship. Glenna and Joyce met in the third round at Troon. For nine holes Glenna managed to stay on even terms with the great English stylist. As a matter of fact, Glenna was only one over par in the wind for the fifteen holes of the match, but what could you do when your opponent played four pars and six birdies over ten consecutive holes? You could congratulate yourself on having stood up as well as you did against the most correct and the loveliest swing golf had ever known, and thank your lucky stars that there was only one Joyce Wethered and that she lived in England.

Glenna had two close calls at St. Louis. After qualifying with a 78 (a stroke higher than Alexa Stirling Fraser) and having no trouble with Mrs. Caleb Fox in her first-round match, Glenna met the always-dangerous Canadian, Ada Mackenzie. A rainstorm saved Glenna. Ada had a two-hole lead on the fourteenth tee and was going well when the rain came. Glenna was wearing spikes, but Ada preferred rubber-soled shoes on a dry course and, not expecting a shower, had left her spikes in her locker. She sent someone to the clubhouse to fetch them but by the time he caught up with the players on the seventeenth, Ada, handicapped to some degree by the slippery footing, had lost three holes in a row and, as it turned out, the match. Glenna took Fritzi Stifel 3 and 2 in the third round, but in the semi-final against her favorite rival, Edith Cummings, Glenna had all she could do to pull out another 1-up victory. The final against Alexa Fraser saw Glenna in an invincible mood. She played a superb 77 in the morning and maintained that pace through the 28th green, when the holes ran out for Alexa—9 and 8. The girls decided to play out the bye holes, and Glenna finished the round in 75.

A review of the scoring at St. Louis helps to explain why women golfers were now viewed with respect, and occasionally with awe. The eighty-five entrants there played better golf than 99 percent of American male golfers. They had come a long way since Mrs. C. S. Brown had won the first championship meeting at Meadow Brook in 1895 with 132 for eighteen holes, only twenty strokes less than Glenna had compiled over thirty-six in the final against Mrs. Fraser. Limiting the comparative figures to the previous decade underlined the women's improvement almost as effectively. In the 1915 championship, more than half of the qualifiers had failed to break 100, and Mrs. Vanderbeck had won the medal with an 85. Ten years later, nine qualifiers carded 85 or lower, Mrs. Fraser cracked all records with a 77, and three women who played 93s failed to get into the match play. After the qualifying round at St. Louis, the quality of play grew even better. There is nothing degrading about an 85, but if that was the best a player could score at St. Louis, she lost her match. Glenna, for example, was carried to the home green in two matches, and yet her average score for her seven completed rounds was 78. Her performance at St. Louis was the finest golf that had ever been played by an American woman. (It would not be irrelevant to bring out that the women frequently played much tougher and longer courses at this period than in later years, when the women's professional golf circuit sought to encourage low scoring by holding its tournaments on short, hazardless layouts.)

Again there was a two-year hiatus for Glenna between titles. Little Virginia Wilson ousted her in the semis at Merion in '26, the year Mrs. G. Henry Stetson, nervously followed by two daughters who towered above her, defeated another matron, Mrs. Wright D. Goss, in the final. In '27, Miriam Burns Horn's year, Alexa Fraser defeated Glenna 2 and 1 when they met in the *second round*. (Perhaps the seeding was faulty, but by 1927, with so many playing so well, placing thirty-two stars with malice toward none had become a tough proposition.) Glenna won her third crown the next year on the Cascades course at Hot Springs, Virginia (13 and 12 over Gino Van Wie), repeated at Oakland Hills in '29 (4 and 3 over Leona Pressler), and in 1930 became the first modern golfer to win an American championship in three consecutive years when she beat Gino again, 6 and 5 this time, at the Los Angeles Country Club. Glenna took three more cracks at the British Ladies' crown. In 1927 Mabel Wragg defeated her in the fourth round. At St. Andrews in 1929 she bowed in the final to Joyce Wethered after a titanic seesaw struggle in which both champions shot sensational golf. Glenna played the first eleven holes in 41 strokes and at one time had a 5-up lead, but she could not hold it against Joyce's furious counter-charge. The following year, when Joyce did not defend, Glenna's chances appeared very favorable, and particularly so after she had edged by the formidable Enid Wilson in the semi-finals, but in the final she was upset by young Diana Fishwick. It remained for the phenomenal Babe Didrikson Zaharias to wrest this last championship away from the British some seventeen years later.

In 1931 Glenna married Edwin H. Vare, Jr., of Philadelphia. With her new responsibilities demanding more of her attention, Glenna played less competitive golf than before, but she did make her way to the semi-finals one year and twice to the finals the three times she entered the championship. And then in 1935 at Interlachen, Glenna, now the mother of two children, came back to defeat the newest meteor, Patty Berg, and to win her sixth and last national title.

Glenna's popularity with her friends, her colleagues, and the public was achieved in an era when the art of public relations was in its comparative gutta-percha period. The reasons why she cut ice with everyone, not just with one class or group or set or sex, were extremely simple ones: first, she was a beautifully consistent performer, a repeating champion; secondly, her attitude toward sport tallied exactly with the general conception of how an American girl should go about a career in sport. Glenna was popular with men, naturally. Any girl would have been, if she were good-looking and intelligent, able to smash a wood to the green like no other woman, and gifted with a conquering graciousness. She had a fine sense of humor at her own expense, she added verve to a party with her high spirits, and she was that very rare thing, a good winner.

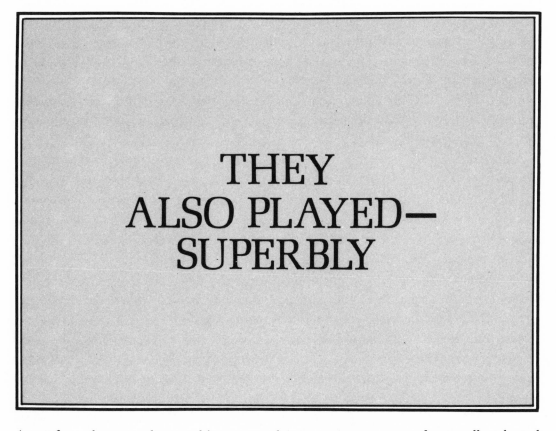

THEY ALSO PLAYED— SUPERBLY

Apart from the man who gave his name to the era, a score or more of unusually talented golfers flourished in the Age of Bobby Jones. Some, like Jock Hutchison and Jim Barnes, had seen their best days. Others, like Denny Shute and Johnny Goodman, were only starting out and would come into their own after Jones' retirement. Hagen and Sarazen and Ouimet, who had won championships before Bobby arrived, would win championships after Bobby had gone. There was also a considerable group of players whose peak years coincided too perfectly with Jones' to allow them to grab much more than the crumbs he left on the table, although they possessed the equipment to have become champions, and sometimes multiple champions, had there been no Jones in the Age of Bobby Jones.

Jones and the indomitable Walter Hagen did such a thorough job of dovetailing in the British Open that in only one year between 1924 and 1930 was another golfer able to break through their joint monopoly. That was Jim Barnes, the Cornishman who had moved to America years before; he won at Prestwick in '25, a year neither Hagen nor Jones was entered. It was a curious victory all around. Jim was well past his prime when he won. His scoring was very high, even for a British Open; after an opening 70, he fell off to 77, 79, 74. What Jim actually did was slip in through the back door in a tournament that seemed like Macdonald Smith's from the second round on.

Old Mac had started off with a 76, but had vaulted into the van at the halfway mark with a beautifully played 69. It looked as if Mac's years of coming close were at long last to be terminated, and on the last day every Scot who could get there poured onto the course at Prestwick to watch the Old Carnoustie lad in his hour of triumph. Mac's 76 in the third round could have been several strokes lower with any luck on the greens, but it did give him a five-stroke lead on Barnes, the closest man, and that was, after all, what counted. Barnes had brought in a final 74 just as Smith was starting out on his last eighteen, and so Mac knew exactly what he needed: a 79 would tie, a 78 would win— and a 78 for a golfer like Mac Smith was as simple as stirring sugar.

That afternoon one of the most tragic chapters in the history of championship golf was written. Too intent on not being careless, Smith began to overstudy his shots and fussed away one stroke after another until he had used up 42 of them on the first nine. His enormous, all-too-devoted gallery, swarming over a course that was not made for galleries, pressed in closer on their hero, reassuring him that they knew he could play back in even 4s, completely forgetting their usually instinctive regard for a player's feeling because they wanted so much for Mac to win. They killed old Mac with their ardor. Whatever chance he might have had for coming home in 36 was smashed in the unruly rush of the unmanageable thousands, strangling the pace he wanted to play at, forcing him to wait ten minutes and more before playing a shot until they had filed across the narrow foot bridges and pounded through the bunkers ahead and grudgingly opened an avenue to the greens. Despairing but impotent, Macdonald Smith played out his nightmare of a round, posted his 82, and then, all too late, was finally left alone.

The one other American victory in a British championship was Jess Sweetser's in the 1926 Amateur, a triumph that was notable not only in that Sweetser was the first American-born golfer to capture that reluctant title but also in the intense personal drama that accompanied the breakthrough.

Jess Sweetser may have been the best American amateur, Jones always excepted, in the early and middle Twenties. While an undergraduate at Yale—where he had run the quarter mile in a shade over fifty seconds—this broad-shouldered, powerful, frigidly aggressive young man from Siwanoy had taken the U.S. Amateur in 1922 at Brookline, defeating Jones and three ex-champions with the most dynamic golf ever exploded in the tournament. He was on the threshold of repeating his victory the next year when Max Marston, benefitting from the second of two stymies, ended a nerve-racking final on the 38th green. Jess was justly celebrated for his match-play temperament. When he opened up a lead on an opponent, he played with the unsocial determination that most players can capture only when they are behind. Splitting the fairways with his three-quarter-swing drives, punching his spade-mashie and his versatile 4-iron close to the pins, he never gave his opponents a chance to recover their balance. Even when he had a match all wrapped up, Jess would stride pugnaciously to his next shot tossing his jaw from one side to the other in an audible fight talk. In between fight talks he hummed popular songs to himself when he discovered by experimentation that this exercise took up his mind and relaxed him and that he played well. Galleries admired rather than liked Sweetser. They attributed his great match-play record to his killer instinct, but

Jess Sweetser plays an approach with his favorite club, his 4-iron, during a four-ball match at Asheville. Jess spent a full year recuperating at that Carolina health resort following his complete physical breakdown in Great Britain in the spring of 1926. That year, Sweetser had become the British Amateur Champion.

Jess always believed that a considerable share of the credit for his temerity and his success rested on the warmup regimen arranged for him ten days or so before the big championships by Tommy Kerrigan, the pro at Siwanoy. Kerrigan would get two other New York area pros, say Sarazen and Farrell, to fill out the group, and Jess would play several matches against them at Quaker Ridge, Wykagyl, and other nearby courses. When he found that he could hold his own with these stars, a tremendous confidence would come over Jess as he headed for the amateur tourneys. He knew that no one played better than these pros, and since he could stick with them, he could stick with any amateur. He was like the fighter who trains with extra-heavy gloves and weighted shoes before a bout and then goes into the fray feeling that his arms are as light as feathers in the regulation gloves, his legs full of drive in the lighter shoes.

The odd thing was that Jess, the strong boy, won his British Amateur crown when his body was wracked with flu, and incipient tuberculosis. No man has ever won a major athletic contest in poorer health. It was quite a saga of courage.

Jess had married in February of '26. Happiness and regular meals at home plus a modicum of golf had put some extra pounds on him. He planned to work them off by exercising in the gym aboard the ship that was carrying the Walker Cup team to Britain. Sweating pleasantly after one workout, Jess decided to take a dip in the pool . . . and his miseries began. His sinuses began to kick up, and he spent the rest of the passage stretched out on a deck chair, hoping that he would snap back once he was on land again. He didn't. In the raw air of early spring in England and Scotland, his cold was aggravated into an enervating flu. At Muirfield, where the American team was entered in the British Amateur previous to the Cup Match at St. Andrews, Jess got in only two practice rounds and stayed in his room the remainder of the time trying to nurse himself back into shape. He felt so rotten on the morning he was scheduled for his first-round match that, much as he wanted to play in the championship, he felt that there was no other course than to default. He stayed in the tournament only because his opponent chose to default before Jess did. After lunch—there were times during the tournament when Jess could hold hardly more than orange juice—he forced himself to go out and play his second-round match. He managed to win and staggered wearily into the clubhouse.

Day after day it was the same story. A masseur from Edinburgh, contacted by Henry Lapham of the American party, would work up Jess' circulation before he went out against his morning opponent. At lunch Jess would drink fruit juices and try a slice or two of beef, and push himself out to the tee for his afternoon match. He did no partying in the evening—took a hot bath and went straight to bed. His attitude was good. He wasn't expecting to win and he didn't worry when it took him six or seven holes to warm up. He kept hitting his shots, and eventually he caught and passed his opponents, although quite a few of Jess' matches went to the eighteenth hole. He defeated Ouimet on the eighteenth by pumping a beautiful second shot through the mist to the green. Against Robert Scott, he played another clinching approach on the home hole, toeing in his favorite 4-iron and punching it low and hard. Jess didn't have the energy at Muirfield to goad himself on with fight talks, but he hummed to himself as he went along, usually "Somebody Loves Me." He kept on winning.

In the semi-final round Jess came up against the Honorable W. G. Brownlow (later Lord Lurgan), a good golfer albeit a chap of weird sartorial tastes. Brownlow played in a small peaked cap, a long clerk's coat, and black silk gloves. Jess, for once, started fast and picked up two holes on Brownlow early in the match, but he could make no further headway against his opponent's neat if not spectacular golf. On the seventeenth, however, this two-hole margin became dormie for Jess, and the match looked as good as over when he laid his third twelve feet from the pin with Brownlow forty-five rolling feet away in the same number of strokes. The game young Irish dandy had been putting, and putting well, with an orthodox blade putter. Now, as he eyed his long route to the cup, he switched to a wide-soled, wooden-headed Gassiat model and proceeded to hole his cross-country putt. Jess then missed his, but was still dormie one with the home hole coming up. Once again Jess played the eighteenth perfectly. He was nicely inside Brownlow on the green, eighteen feet away to his opponent's thirty-five. His half seemed certain. And then the incredible Brownlow took his Gassiat in his black silk gloves and sent his ball trickling over the subtle rolls of the home green and into the very center of the cup. Jess made a courageous try for his putt but it slid by the rim of the cup.

The American team that defeated the British at Worcester in 1927 in the inaugural Ryder Cup Match. In the usual order: Al Watrous, Wild Bill Mehlhorn, Leo Diegel, Johnny Golden, Captain Walter Hagen, Al Espinosa, Gene Sarazen, Johnny Farrell, and Joe Turnesa. One of the more curious aspects of the international matches is the success the Americans have continually enjoyed in the foursomes, a type of match in which partners play alternate strokes and drive from alternate tees.

By this time the match had taken on an unreal atmosphere, Jess exhausted by the sudden turn of events, Brownlow unnaturally serene, both of them performing as if they were caught in the webbing of a dream. On the first extra hole, Brownlow had a big opening when Jess found a trap on his second, but Brownlow misfired with his Gassiat, taking three from twenty-five feet after slipping fifteen feet by on his first. On the 20th Jess went ten feet past the cup on his approach putt but Brownlow, timorous after his error on the 19th, fell nine feet short on his. Jess knocked in his 10-footer, and Brownlow stepped up and coolly holed his 9-footer. On the 21st tee the young Irishman finally cracked. He looked up badly on his drive. Jess smashed his two hundred and sixty yards down the fairway, and his faultless approach closed out the dramatic duel between two dead-game golfers.

The final between Jess and Archie Simpson, an East Coast Scotsman, was bound to be a letdown after the Sweetser–Brownlow match. Simpson didn't play nearly as well as he had against Andrew Jamieson in the semi-finals, and Jess won 7 and 6 after a dull match in which the outcome was never in doubt.

Jess' condition became worse after he was driven to St. Andrews on a very cold day. He asked to play and managed to win both his singles and foursome in the Walker Cup Match with a continuation of his impeccable golf, and then suffered a severe chest hemorrhage. Jess pleaded with the doctors to let him sail—he was frightened that he might not get home alive—and the doctors at length gave in. They shot him full of heroin and gave O. B. Keeler instructions on how to inject the drug if Jess suffered a relapse on board ship. Jess did have one more hemorrhage, but the heroin kept him going. . . . He reached home so utterly shattered that only after a full year of convalescence at Asheville did he begin to look and feel like the Jess Sweetser of old.

The one U.S. Open that Jones had nothing to say about was the 1927 event. Five good golfers came down the final nine at Oakmont with an equal opportunity to lead the field—Emmett French, Gene Sarazen, Bill Mehlhorn, Harry Cooper, and Tommy Armour. Oakmont licked three of them—French, Sarazen, and Mehlhorn. Harry Cooper licked one of them, Harry Cooper, when he three-putted the 71st from eight feet. One man licked Oakmont—Tommy Armour. After taking a 7 on the famous twelfth, the 66th hole of the tournament, Armour had to play the last six holes in 2 under par to tie with Cooper, and did this by cracking a 3-iron ten feet from the pin on the 72nd and holing his putt. In 1927 neither Harry nor Tommy Armour had earned the reputations by which we think of them today. It was the first time in the spotlight for both of them—Cooper, the brilliant consistent golfer who could never win a major crown: Armour, the brilliant inconsistent golfer who at one time or another won the U.S. and British Opens and the P.G.A., the three big professional championships, as well as the Western, three Canadians, and his share of the non-prestige tourneys. Cooper was just a kid then, a twenty-three-year-old naturalized Texan of English descent who played his shots without a moment's hesitation and walked so rapidly between shots that he came into the sobriquet of "Light Horse Harry." As for Armour, he had turned professional after coming to the States in the early 1920s as an unheralded amateur. Tommy had lost the sight of one eye during World War I, and in his left shoulder he carried several mementos of his front-line service—eight pieces of shrapnel. Armour was reputed to have been the fastest man with a machine gun in the entire Tank Corps, and his fine, strong fingers and his superlative coordination of hand and eye were helping him to come to the forefront in his peacetime profession. The long irons he drilled to the pins at Oakmont nailed down once and for all the reputation Tommy had gradually been acquiring as one of the very best iron players in the business.

In the playoff Armour came from behind to win. He caught the Light Horse with a

Tommy Armour, the iron master. The slim Scot came to the States after World War I as an aspiring young amateur. He made golf his profession, improved enormously, and before finishing his active career won all of the big professional titles—the United States Open in 1927, the P.G.A. in 1930, and the British Open in 1931.

50-foot putt for a 4 on the fifteenth and went in front by two strokes on the 226-yard sixteenth when Cooper shot boldly for the pin and caught a guarding bunker. Cooper stuck his approach to the seventeenth a foot and a half from the cup, and then the nerveless Armour showed his mettle by dropping his approach eight inches inside of Cooper's. That was the championship.

The 1927 U.S. Open probably decided more championships than just the 1927 U.S. Open. Had Harry Cooper not three-putted the 71st green, he would have galloped through to victory in his first real chance in a major championship and that might have been all that magnificent shot-maker needed to have become several-times-a-champion in name as well as in ability. Tommy Armour, on the other hand, would have probably broken through in some other year had he been repulsed at Oakmont. Whenever the Silver Scot played himself into a contending position, he always seemed to have that extra something that was the difference between barely losing and barely winning. He was singularly unaffected by the pressure of the last stretch. His hands were hot but his head was cool—one of the accidental rewards that only too rarely catch up with a war hero.

The one championship in which Jones could not play, the P.G.A., became Walter Hagen's personal tournament, the way the Amateur was Bobby's. Walter took the P.G.A. in 1921 and then in '24, '25, '26, and '27, winning twenty consecutive matches from the most talented players in the country. Some of Walter's victories were normally wrought: he outthought and outplayed his man. But an alarming number of Hagen's victories came in matches he should have lost and would have lost if that certain something in Walter's personality had not defeated his opponent for Walter. A few centuries before and he would have been burned as a disciple of the devil.

The manner in which Hagen won the 1927 P.G.A. was in character. He was 4 down to Johnny Farrell at lunch—Farrell could eat none—but won five of the first nine holes in the afternoon. Hagen, 3 and 2. Against Tony Manero, who had putted Bobby Cruickshank out of the tournament, Walter put on an exhibition of green play that stampeded the young man. Hagen, 11 and 10. Armour was a different proposition. Walter played under wraps, just well enough to keep close to Tommy but giving the impression that he was far off-form that day and that no one would have to hurry to beat him. Then The Haig stuck his nose out in front and strategically poured on the pressure now that he had Armour down. Hagen, 4 and 3. Next it was Al Espinosa. Hagen played poorly and he wasn't fooling. He was 1 down with one to play, and all Espinosa had to do to win was sink a yard putt on the 36th green. Hagen, 1 up in extra holes. The opposing finalist was Joe Turnesa. Joe was 2 up at lunch, 3 up after the first hole in the afternoon, playing with confidence and smoothness. Hagen, 1 up.

The Twenties produced some remarkable bursts of scoring, though, like today, most of the sacrilegious sixties were fashioned in tournaments other than the major championships.

Johnny Farrell, the handsome Irishman from Westchester, renowned for his graceful swing and his haberdashery. Johnny looked so impressive in winning the 1928 Open that many critics predicted that he would become a second Bobby Jones. Farrell, however, never quite recaptured the brilliance he displayed at Olympia Fields.

There were the brilliant rounds: Hagen's 62 at Belleair in the West Florida Championship . . . Virginia Van Wie's 74 at Ormond Beach . . . Leo Diegel's 65 on a bitter cold day at Moortown in 1929 in the second Ryder Cup Match . . . The two 66s young Horton Smith, the Joplin Ghost, put together in winning the French Open that year . . . The 66 Mac Smith played in the *third* playoff for the Metropolitan in 1926 after he and Sarazen had matched 70s and 72s in the first overtime stretches . . . Watts Gunn's 71 at Oakmont, and that 69 by Watrous at Lytham . . . A 67 and a 68 by George Voigt in consecutive rounds on long, tree-lined Pinehurst #2 . . . Miriam Burns Horn's 74 at Pebble Beach . . . That final round of 63 which won the $15,000 LaGorce Open for Johnny Farrell . . . Hagen's 59 on a short resort course in Switzerland . . . Harry Cooper's 60 on a course measuring 6,100 yards.

There were the torrid patches: Francis Ouimet's gallant finish at St. Andrews in his Walker Cup match in '23 with Roger Wethered, a 3-4-3 against a par of 4-5-4, which enabled Francis to halve with Roger after he had seemed hopelessly beaten standing on the 34th tee, 2 down and three to play . . . Watts Gunn at Oakmont in his first Amateur, taking one hole after another in his first-round match until he had made it fifteen holes in a row and could go on no farther since the match was over . . . The comeback by Roland MacKenzie, the teenage protégé of Freddy McLeod's, against George Von Elm in the Amateur of '24. Roland refused to quit when he was 8 down at the 23rd, kept plugging until he had cut away the last hole of Von Elm's lead on the 35th, and then had to go and lose the 37th . . . Al Espinosa's 22 for the last six in the 1929 Open when he had resigned himself to losing . . . Glenna against Mrs. Harley Higbie in the '29 Women's. Four down with four to go, Glenna swept the last four and then won on the 19th . . . Willie Macfarlane's 33 against Bobby on the last nine at Worcester, featuring two beautiful deuces . . . Diegel's informal 29 at Columbia when he was betting that he could break 30 . . . Willie Klein's out-of-this-world finish in the Shawnee Open of '25. The young assistant pro from Garden City needed a 29 on the last nine to tie for first place, and played in 3-4-2 4-4-3 3-4-2—29.

There were the bright flashes of form for the duration of a tournament: Armour's 273 at Ozaukee in the Western, and Diegel's 274 at Shreveport . . . Mac Smith's duplicate rounds of 35-35—70 over Charlie Macdonald's hazardous Lido course in a sectional qualifying round for the Open . . . Seventy-two easy, even holes by Billy Burke at Clearwater in '27, the first indication that the ex-iron molder from Naugatuck might have a champion's game . . . Old Abe Mitchell's victory in the Seminole Open (and the Englishman's relish for the sound of his new title) . . . Gene's 277 at Miami Beach and Walter's 275 at Wolf Hollow . . . Cooper's last-round 67 for a 279 in the Los Angeles Open . . . Leo's 65 for 274 in the Canadian, which he felt should have been lower.

And the streaks that carried through several tournaments: Walter's average of 70.5 for twenty-four rounds in the grapefruit belt in 1923 . . . The winter rush the next year by Joe Kirkwood when the Australian couldn't hit a crooked shot and carried off the Opens at San Antonio, Houston, Corpus Christi, and New Orleans . . . Mac Smith, elegant Mac Smith, playing consecutive tournament rounds of 68, 70, 70, 73, 70, 70, 70, 70, 71, 69, 71, 70, 70, 68, 73 . . . Johnny Farrell's spring harvest in '27—the Met, the Shawnee, the Eastern, the Massachusetts, the Pennsylvania, the Philadelphia . . . Mehlhorn, not listed as potential Ryder Cup material for 1929, confounding the selectors by adding a 277 in the Texas Open to his 271 in the El Paso Open, piling up two 66s, two 67s, a 68, and a 69 in the course of eight rounds . . . Horton Smith's sensational debut in the bigtime on the winter circuit of '29. In winning seven tourneys and running-up in four, the handsome twenty-year-older cleaned up a record $14,000-plus.

And there were the great moments, the unforgettable pictures: Jimmy Johnston on the white sand at Pebble Beach, waiting for the waves to ebb so that he could play his recovery to the green . . . Chandler Egan at the same tournament, hitting the ball sharper than a quarter of a century before when he had twice won the Amateur . . . The heartbreaking collapse by Roland Hancock on the last two holes of the Open at Olympia. Young Hancock needed only to play a par and one-over-par, two 5s or a 4 and a 6, to edge out Jones and Farrell. He took two 6s, and never again came close . . . The passing of Walter J. Travis. In his last years the Old Man, the first great American champion, allowed his beard to grow again; no longer was it the black frame that went so well in 1900 with the Old Man's menacing eye; it was white—as white as the dunes at Sandwich . . . That lesser oldtimer, Sandy Herd, was still going strong. At fifty-eight he captured the British equivalent of the P.G.A. . . . There was frail Cyril Walker playing the 72nd at Oakland Hills in a safe, smart 5 as Tet nodded her head . . . And Wiffy Cox, Brooklyn's leading pro, erupting on the greens with the choice epithets he had assimilated when he served as a fireman on the U.S.S. *Nevada* . . . Glenna buttonholing the experts and seriously asking them how she could get over being "social rather than savage" in her matches . . . Stewart Maiden rushing from Atlanta to Worcester in '25 on the eve of the Open, answering an urgent call for help from an out-of-the-groove Jones. Stewart watched Bobby hit out two batches of practice balls without saying a word, dourly sniffed, "Why don't you try hitting the ball with your backswing?," and walked away . . . Carl F. Kauffmann, "The Poor Man's Jones," who won three consecutive U.S.G.A.-sponsored Public Links Championships from '27 through '29 . . . The to-do in Texas when the unpredictable Mehlhorn, perched high in a tree by the eighteenth green, needled Bobby Cruickshank as the little Scot was about to stroke a thousand-dollar putt . . . Johnny Goodman, a stout-hearted kid from Omaha, traveling by cattle car to New York on a drover's pass to play in the Open at Winged Foot . . . The ridiculous hue and cry after the 1923 Amateur that Max Marston stymied his opponents on purpose. The alacrity of the newspapermen, many of whom Marston had antagonized by his lofty manner, in pointing out to the public that any golfer with skill enough to stymie an opponent could hole out with far less trouble . . . Oscar Baun Keeler shepherding Jones at every tournament, recording the feats of his hero in such faithful detail that the golfing literati began to refer to Boswell as Sam Johnson's Keeler . . . Mrs. Hagen pouncing on Walter after his roaring finish in the 1924 British Open, and their big open-air kiss. The mellow scene when Walter filled the old cup and Vardon, Braid, Taylor, and the other old giants all came up and lifted it to their lips . . .

And there was always Jones.

THE GRAND SLAM

In 1930 Bobby Jones won the British Amateur, the British Open, the United States Open, and the United States Amateur Championships. Jones' clean sweep of the four major titles—what George Trevor neatly termed "the impregnable quadrilateral"—was, of course, the crowning achievement of his career, and, very probably, the greatest exhibition of skill and character by any individual athlete, bar none, since the beginning of recorded sports history.

In the winter of 1930 as he conditioned himself for his annual campaign, Bobby Jones had no presentiment that he was embarking on a historic year. His feelings about his potential in any one tournament season were about the same as they had been in 1927 when, in collaboration with O. B. Keeler, he had published his autobiography, *Down the Fairway*. The chapter on 1926, when Bobby had won two major crowns for the first time, was entitled "The Biggest Year." He was overjoyed with having trounced the percentages in 1926 "because I'll never have another chance to win both the British and American Open Championships in the same year."

Bobby, however, was looking forward to 1930 with more than his usual enthusiasm. It was a year when the Walker Cup Match was scheduled to be played in Great Britain, and this meant that after two years of strictly domestic activity, Bob would have another shot at the British events, and particularly the British Amateur, the one major championship that had eluded him. During the winter Bobby, who put weight on rather quickly, kept in trim by playing "Doug," a combination of tennis and badminton evolved by Douglas Fairbanks, who had sent his friend the paraphernalia. From the first day that he began his light workouts on the golf course, it was evident to everyone who watched him that, for one reason or another, Bobby had something that he had never had before. Noteworthy, too, was the fact that, departing from his habit of tuning up informally, he entered two minor tournaments, the Savannah Open and the Southeastern Open, held at Augusta. At Savannah Jones finished second with 279, a stroke behind Horton Smith, the winter wonder. But at Augusta, Jones' 72, 72, 69, 71 for 284 was not only tops but thirteen full strokes ahead of Horton, the runner-up. After taking in Bobby's display at Augusta, Grantland Rice, who had studied the Georgian closely over a long period of years, expressed the opinion that Jones was playing discernibly better golf than ever before, and Bobby Cruickshank exploded with an indecently accurate prediction: "He's simply too good. He'll go to Britain and win the Amateur and the Open, and then he'll come back over here and win the Open and the Amateur. He is playing too well to be stopped this year."

Never one to enthuse about his own game, Jones confided to his intimate friends that he felt much more confident than in any previous year, that he was hitting every shot in the bag. Even those little pitches between 50 and 125 yards that had frequently displeased him were behaving properly. Psychologically, as well, Bobby was fit. His strong showing against Espinosa in the playoff for the Open the year before had not by any means erased from his mind the near-disgrace of kicking away a six-stroke lead on the last six holes and leaving himself a 12-footer to tie. The memory of Winged Foot would be a salutary spur. He was also rid of that mental block about eighteen-hole matches. At Pebble Beach he had lost the one he had been frightened of losing for years, and now he could go into the British Amateur free from any defensive phobia.

In Britain, before the stars of two continents convened at St. Andrews for the Amateur, Jones shot some of his best stuff in the Walker Cup Match at Sandwich. Partnered with Doc Willing, he won his foursome 8 and 7 and took his singles from Roger Wethered 9 and 8. As the captain of the American team, Jones could have placed himself in the number-one singles spot, for which his record logically qualified him. It was typical of Jones that he awarded the honor of playing number one to Jimmy Johnston, the Amateur Champion, and dropped himself to the second slot . . . And then on to St. Andrews and the one championship he had never been able to win—the British Amateur.

Right off the reel Bobby walked into a match he could have easily lost. Syd Roper, an ex-coal miner from Nottinghamshire without a clipping to his name, played one 5 and fifteen 4s over the sixteen holes of his match with Jones. On the very first tee Bobby seemed to divine what was coming on, for he got right down to business and knocked in a 20-footer for a birdie 3. He added a 4 and a 3, and on the fourth he holed out a 150-yard spade-mashie from Cottage Bunker for an eagle 2. Bobby's 5-under-par burst for the first five holes gave him only a three-hole lead, and this was the extent of the impression he was able to make against the amazing Mr. Roper.

In the fourth round Jones came up against Cyril Tolley, the defending champion, and a bitter battle ensued. Tolley's topped drive off the first tee was about the one mistake the long-hitting Englishman made for eighteen holes. At no time was either player able to edge ahead by more than one hole. They were all even as they came to the seventeenth, the famous Road Hole, a dogleg to the right that ordinarily required two good woods to reach unless the player elected to risk cutting the corner over Auchter-lonie's drying sheds and carrying the deep out-of-bounds elbow. Neither Tolley nor Jones thought this was the day for flirting with the straight-line route. Both drove out safely to the left, Jones far to the left. The shot Bobby elected to play for his second was a high spoon, cut just a fraction so that it would hold after landing on the back edge of the green. It didn't quite come off. The ball carried the vicious Road Bunker that guards the entrance to the middle of the green from the left, but instead of plopping itself down obediently, it kicked up like a colt and might have run on into trouble had it not struck a spectator standing on the back fringe. With this timely assist from Fortune, Jones was able to get his 4, and he needed it, for Tolley pitched two feet from the cup after playing short of the green with an iron on his second. They halved the eighteenth in 4. The match moved into extra holes. Both got off the 19th tee well but Tolley clubbed his approach off-line and it cost him the match. His chip was not stone-dead and Bobby, putting up on his third, laid Tolley a stymie he was unable to negotiate. (The entire population of St. Andrews seemed to stream from the town onto the links whenever Jones was playing, and on the day of the Jones–Tolley match the town was so deserted the novelist Gerald Fairlie selected that afternoon as the time when the villain in one of his mysteries committed murder in downtown St. Andrews and, though marked with the stains of his crime, was able to make his way unnoticed down the empty streets.)

Had it been Jones who had been confronted with jumping a stymie on the 19th to keep the match alive, there is every reason to believe that he would have done it successfully. A confirmed fatalist in his attitude toward golf tournaments, at St. Andrews Bobby was visited by the strange and wonderful feeling that he simply could not lose, whatever he did. After the Tolley match, in which Jones had been outplayed but had gotten the breaks, O. B. Keeler was beginning to share this queer sense of fatality, and as the tournament moved on and Bobby escaped from two more ferocious matches that could have gone either way, Keeler was convinced that some large and intangible Providence simply would countenance no other person's winning the 1930 British Amateur. It was an odd way, a very odd way, to feel about a golf tournament, but for Keeler there was no other explanation for the things that were taking place at St. Andrews. In several of Jones' matches a single bad shot at numerous junctures could have changed the entire picture, but as O. B. remarked, Bobby stood up to the shot and performed what was needed with all the certainty of a natural phenomenon. By the semi-final round, the feeling that Jones' triumph was mystically inevitable had communicated itself to many of the spectators. When Jones was 1 down to George Voigt with only three holes to play, Sir James Lieshman, a Scottish fan, declared, "His [Jones'] luck is as fixed as the orbit of a planet. He cannot be beaten here." On the very next tee Voigt drove into a bunker and lost the hole.

The struggle with Voigt followed a distressingly close scrape in the sixth round with Jimmy Johnston. Jones was 4 up on Jimmy with five to play, but Johnston won two of the next three holes and took the Road as well. A win for him on the eighteenth would have forced the match into extra holes, and Jimmy came within a hair of doing it. Both players took precautions to hit their approaches firmly enough to carry the Valley of Sin, and both ended up on the very back edge of that huge green, Johnston about ninety feet away from the pin, Jones not much closer. Playing the odd, Johnston putted up beautifully, inches from the cup, for a sure 4. It was up to Bobby to get down in 2 to save the match. His first putt began to slow down as it took the final dip toward the hole and died eight feet short, leaving Jones with a nasty sidehiller. He holed it precisely, just as Von Elm and Ouimet, watching from the balcony of the Grand Hotel, knew he would.

In the semi-final, Voigt, playing the finest golf of his life, sticking his irons inside of Jones' and putting very well indeed, had accumulated a two-hole advantage as he and Bobby prepared to play the fourteenth. There is an old golf fable that the man who is 2 up with five holes to play will lose the match. More often than not, the fable folds, but it holds up just often enough to perpetuate itself. Voigt, 2 up with five to play, cut across his tee shot, and the strong wind blowing from left to right tossed it out-of-bounds. Jones played safely down the left and won the hole. The fifteenth was halved. Up first on the next tee, Jones, who knew St. Andrews as well as he knew East Lake, played his drive fifty yards to the left of the center of the fairway to make certain he avoided the bunkers. Voigt, aiming for that patch of fairway to the left of the Principal's Nose, once again underestimated the force of the cross-wind and was blown into the bunker. Jones' hole. Hauled back to even now, Voigt made a brave counter-charge on the seventeenth. After two splendid shots had carried him to the front edge of the green, George all but holed his approach putt. To halve Voigt's 4, Jones had to hole an 18-footer. The weird sensation that someone was taking care of him was never stronger than when Bobby bent over his ball. He felt that no matter how he hit it, the putt would go in. It did. On the home green Voigt failed to get down his 6-footer for a par and Bobby had won the match from an opponent who had been 2 up with five to play.

Roger Wethered was Jones' opponent in the final and faced the hopeless task of staying with Jones when Bobby was in one of his most determined moods. There was only one moment during the match when Jones was not patently in command. On the very first hole, after his drive had set him up with the easiest of pitches, Bobby looked up on his shot and missed it so badly that it didn't even make the burn cutting across the fairway twenty yards ahead. He chipped up close with his third, went down in one putt for his 4, and took nothing over a 4 until he squandered a miraculous recovery from the Road Bunker on the seventeenth by muffing a 2-footer. He finished the morning round 4 up.

Francis Ouimet, who walked back to the Grand Hotel with Bobby at lunchtime, could not figure it out when Jones began pacing his room, obviously burned up about something.

"What in the world has got into you, Bobby?" Ouimet finally asked. "You're four up."

"Did you hear what that official said on the first tee?" Jones asked.

Francis thought a moment and then remembered that before Jones had teed off, an official had remarked that in all the years that the greatest golfers in the world had been playing the Old Course, no one had ever succeeded in going around with nothing higher than a 4 on his card.

". . . And I," Bobby said in disgust, "I had to go and miss a two-foot putt to be the first man ever to play St. Andrews without taking a five."

Bobby had turned an innocent conversational sally into a personal challenge. He had been playing St. Andrews rather than Wethered.

In the afternoon, the scent of victory, that long-awaited victory, was sufficient to insure a continuation of Bobby's aggressive play. The strain began to tell on Roger and he began missing the 4-footers. Jones added one hole and then another to his lead, and the match ran itself out on the 30th green. Then, fifteen thousand mad Scots, who had been waiting all week for this moment no less anxiously than Jones, converged on their idol. In the wild stampede Henry Lapham was knocked into a bunker and converted into a trestle; the crowd attacked the policemen guarding Jones with the fury of bobby-soxers; and the band that was to play the victor in was scattered in the mêlée and played not a note. Keeler finally made his way to the side of the young man whom he had followed for fourteen years through twenty-four championships. "Honestly, I don't care what happens now," Bobby smiled at O. B. "I'd rather have won this tournament than anything else in golf. I'm satisfied."

There was no mysterious presence walking hand in hand with Bobby Jones at Hoylake. Jones won the British Open by the normal expedient of bringing in the lowest four-round total in the field. He did it the hard way, as he had at Lytham in '26, outscoring through sheer stick-to-itiveness a handful of fine golfers who were on their game when Bobby was not. He was neat around the greens. He was lucky in playing his bad shots when they hurt him least, and he managed to pull off the best shots in his repertoire at the critical moments. St. Andrews had been touched with destiny. Hoylake was manual labor.

The understandable contentment he derived from his victory in the British Amateur made it hard for Jones to buckle down to belligerency as the date of the British Open approached. He had twice before won the British Open. Furthermore, he had no Grand Slam on his mind. Bobby was taking things easy, and his indifference brought back to Keeler the similarly flat frame of mind Bobby had acquiesced to when he was preparing for the United States Open at Oakmont in '27. Then, he had never been able to rouse himself and had floundered into his worst showing in a major tournament since he had first become a champion. The English critics had no Oakmont as a touchstone, but they noticed the letdown in Jones' attitude and in his game. He looked stale.

Once the practice and qualifying rounds were over and the championship proper was underway, a change came over Jones. His desire to win reasserted itself. It drove him to an opening round of 70 and a second round of 72, although his game remained as imprecise as it had been when Bobby hadn't cared. "I simply don't know where the darn ball is going when I hit it," he said impatiently to O. B. "I guess I'm trying to steer it, and of course that's the worst thing in the world to do. But what can I do? This is a tight course. You can't get up there and slam away and trust to freedom of action to take care of the shot. You simply have got to exercise some control of the ball. And it's the most hopeless job I've ever tackled. I've never worked so hard before." Jones' 74 in the third round began with a par on the first when he escaped a bunker by inches. He went 1 over on the second, and instead of getting that stroke back on the 480-yard third, an easy birdie hole, Bobby took a 6 and lost another stroke. Then he settled down and fought. 3-4-4-3-4-4 gave him a 37 for the out-nine, and 3-3-4-3 braced him for the killing finish at Hoylake, five holes averaging 457 yards. 5-5-5-5-4 was not too sharp—another 37 for a 74, which dropped him from first to a stroke behind the pacemaker, Archie Compston. Compston had led off with a devastating rush of 4-3-4-2 and completed as fine a round as has ever been shot at Hoylake in 68.

Jones set out on his last round fifty minutes before Compston was called to the tee. Bobby began with a par 4, and then on the 369-yard second sliced his drive hectically to the right. The swerving ball bounced wildly off the head of a steward and careened a full forty yards forward into a bunker off the fourteenth fairway. Considering where the drive would have ended up without the intervention of the petrified steward, it was an incalculably lucky break; Bobby was fifty yards off-line but only 140 yards from the green and lying well in the bunker. He stroked a pitch onto the center of the green, holed his 20-footer, and had come out of the hole with a birdie 3 when he would have settled for a 5. A short while after this had happened, Compston was striding across the first green full of confidence. A putt of eighteen inches would give Archie his regulation 4, an adequate opening for the bright round the rawboned giant felt was coming on. Compston tapped his wee putt, and, in almost the same motion, bent over to pick the ball out of the cup. It wasn't in the cup. It was still on the lip. Compston straightened himself up and stood staring at the ball, bewildered and unbelieving. He was never the same afterwards. His confidence had been cut away before he reached the second tee, and lurching like an injured vessel, he needed fourteen strokes more than he had taken in the morning to get around the same course. Nothing could snap Archie out of it, not even the early report that on the eighth, a 482-yard 5 that Jones was expected to birdie, Bobby had blown himself to a big 7. Just off the green in 2 with a prosaic chip up a bank to the green, Jones stubbed his chip short, was ten feet away on his fourth, slid a foot by on his fifth, and missed that 12-inch kick-in. Bobby's 38 meant nothing to the broken Compston, but the reports of this wobbly first nine filtered back to Diegel and Mac Smith and pricked up the ears of those two great hard-luck golfers.

Bobby battled his way home. Two 4s on the short holes didn't help. Then into that backbreaking final five. A 4 and a 5. So far, so good. A 4 on the 532-yard 70th, thanks to a great out from a trap by the green with the 25-ounce niblick Horton Smith had got for him. Another 4 and a final 4. A 37. A 75. It could have been worse, a great deal worse, but would it be good enough to win? Bobby relieved his exhaustion with a good stiff drink. He sat nervously in the clubhouse, using two hands to steady his glass, as he sweated out the news on Leo and Mac.

Diegel, two strokes off Bobby's pace at the 63rd, turned it on. He picked up a stroke on Bobby on the first short hole coming in, picked up another on the second short hole. He came to the 70th, tied with Jones. Throwing every ounce of his power into his shot off that tee, Leo smashed out a long, hard drive. The direction might have been better. The kick might have been, too. The ball caught the corner of a trap. Leo did not give up, even after he had missed a short putt for his 4 on that hole, but it was no use. The Dieg couldn't do it.

Nor could Mac Smith. Starting six strokes behind Jones, the grim old bloodhound had made up four of those strokes but, to tie with Bobby, Mac had to play those last five holes in one-under-4s. It was an impossible task. Mac's chances for a tie at length simmered down to holing a pitch for an eagle 2 on the eighteenth. As that pitch danced past the pin, Bobby took one hand off the glass he was holding.

At Hoylake Bobby had won through patience and guts and philosophy and instinct.

The United States Open was played in early June at Interlachen in Minneapolis. A hot sun beat down on the parched fairways where $40,000 worth of perspiring fans—it wasn't so much the heat as the humanity—walked restively after Bobby Jones. There was no question about Bobby's goal, now that he had won the two British championships. He had his sights set on a Grand Slam now. This would be the tournament. If Bobby could get by the pros at Interlachen, only the Amateur, the comparatively placid Amateur, would remain.

In many an Open Bobby had led off with fast rounds and had shaken off all but one or two of the pros before they could get going. At Interlachen Bobby started well with 71-73 for 144, but the big names were right along with him at the halfway mark— Horton Smith in front with 142, Cooper at 144, Mac Smith at 145, Armour at 146, and Hagen, Farrell, Golden, and others still close enough to pull out in front if they could get in a blazing third round.

It was Bobby who played the great third round. One of the earliest starters, he went out hard and handsomely, making no errors of commission or omission until he slipped one over par on the ninth. Even with that bogey, he had shot the first nine in 33 and was well on his way toward achieving the objective he had set for himself: to play so hot a round that he would demoralize the opposition and take a comfortable margin with

New York greets a returning hero. Showered by streamers and the cheers of his admiring countrymen, Bobby Jones rides in triumph down the canyons of Manhattan following his double victory in the 1930 British Amateur and Open. Bobby had a week or so to rest between docking at New York and the U.S. Open at Interlachen.

him into the final eighteen. At Interlachen there are seven holes of the drive-and-pitch variety, and Jones was flicking his mashie-niblicks right at the pin. Three times he came within inches of holing 100-yard pitches, the ball, directly on line, pulling up less than a foot from the hole. Six strokes under par for sixteen holes, Jones could not maintain that pace over the last two, the 262-yard seventeenth and the 402-yard eighteenth. He went a stroke over par on each of these holes, but his 68 was sufficiently low to have the desired harassing effect on his rivals.

The news of Jones' 68 quickly reached Horton Smith, Tommy Armour, Mac Smith, and the other contenders. It sent them off on the hunt for birdies, forced them to go for everything . These tactics cost them more strokes than they saved. Mac Smith's 74 put him seven strokes behind Bobby; Horton's 76 put him six strokes behind. Jones started on his final eighteen with a five-stroke lead over his nearest rival, Harry Cooper, who had added a relatively low 73.

Nine to ten thousand well-meaning, annoying fans, the largest gallery that had ever hounded a golfer in an American championship, shrieked and groaned and sometimes applauded as Bobby went to the turn in 38, added three orthodox pars, and then played the last six holes in a bizarre blend of beautiful and bad golf. He went two over par on the 194-yard 67th, his second double-bogey of the round on a short hole. He rallied with a birdie 3 on the tough 444-yard 68th, parred the 69th, and got himself another birdie 3 on the 70th after a pin-splitting approach. Then, almost home, almost completely safe from the gallant last-round challenge of Mac Smith, who had picked up four strokes and was still coming, Bobby again messed up a short hole, the 262-yard 71st. He hit his tee shot on the heel of his club and the ball sliced off in a dipping parabola and skidded into the water hazard past the rough. A penalty stroke, a chip, two putts—his third 5 of the round on a par-3 hole. Now it was imperative that he play the last hole right.

Bobby pulled himself together. He took a nice full cut at his drive and sent it down the fairway toward the large home green 402 yards away. His iron was on nicely. He holed a 40-footer. 75.

That final birdie clinched it. Mac Smith, the only challenger who did not wilt, finished with a 70, one of those supremely elegant rounds Old Mac could always play when it was too late, but it still left him two strokes off Jones' mark of 287.

By nightfall the radio and newspapers had carried the good news to the fans in the countless Atlantas from Portland to Portland who had been fidgeting like first-time fathers. The wait was harder on the Jonesmen living in foreign countries who had to go until the next morning before learning of the outcome. Bernard Darwin's ordeal was characteristic of the plight of thousands. Bernard came down to breakfast, and his heart stopped beating when he caught sight of the morning newspaper lying on the table. He ripped it open as fast as he could to the sports section—for good or for bad, he would know soon. This would be the page . . . Phew! The old boy had done it . . . Bernard settled down to a slow, wonderful breakfast.

Two months after his burst in the third round had won the Open for him, Bobby Jones headed for the Merion Cricket Club and the Amateur. Merion—it looked like a good augury. Fourteen years before, when Bobby had been a pudgy, club-heaving fourteen-year-older, he had played in his first national tournament at Merion and given the golfing world a startling preview of the shape of things to come. Six years before at Merion—Bobby had won so many titles between 1924 and 1930 that the Amateur of '24

September 22, 1930. The Merion Cricket Club near Philadelphia. The qualifying round of the National Amateur, the one championship standing between Bobby Jones and the Grand Slam. Jones cracked a drive down the middle and never looked back all week. He won the medal with rounds of 69 and 73; then, in six matches, his slimmest margin was 5 and 4. And that was it.

seemed like paleolithic times—the Georgian had marched to his first Amateur Championship. It was historically right that Merion, which had twice served as a milestone in Jones' career, should be the battlefield for Bobby's climactic performance.

Three down and the Amateur to go! What had appeared impossible five months before was now palpably achievable. Bobby could do it, the golfing world was sure . . . if he survived the qualifying round . . . and didn't run up against some unconscious stripling in the two rounds of eighteen-hole matches. . . and had the stamina to play

Jonesworthy golf in his big matches. He was so close now on the eve of the tourney that these and other trepidations annexed themselves to the fervent hopefulness of golf fans, the way the lurking danger of a lucky hit tightens up a baseball crowd that has been in on a no-hitter for eight innings. Multiply the tension of the no-hitter by fifty. There have been many no-hitters. There had never been even the prospect of a Grand Slam before. No-hitters are spun in less than three hours. Jones had been working for four months on his Grand Slam, on two continents, in all sorts of weather, in all sorts of form.

Each evening Americans squirmed in their chairs by the radio waiting for the word from Merion.

Tuesday evening: Jones had qualified. More than that, he had won the medal with a record-equaling 69-73—142 and would have broken the record had he not overpitched the last green with his spade-mashie. Bobby was evidently in good form. Five former champions—Johnston, Guilford, Marston, Egan, and Herron—had failed to qualify, and this was strangely comforting news. One of them might have given Jones trouble.

Wednesday evening: Bobby had got by his eighteen-hole matches safely. In the morning against the sound Canadian stylist, Ross Somerville, he had turned in 33 and had run out the match 5 and 4. That was the same count by which he had eliminated another Canadian, Fred Hoblitzel, in the afternoon. Bobby had played a wavering first nine of 41, but had started in 4-3-4-3-4. He seemed to be pacing himself intelligently, playing mediocre but winning golf when his opponent was playing downright poor stuff, stepping up his game when his opponent began to find himself. A bit of a relief, too, that some of the men who had the best chance of beating Bobby had run into some hot golf. Doc Willing, Phil Perkins, Francis Ouimet, and young Goodman had fallen in the first round. Voigt had been stopped in the second, and so had George Von Elm, a real threat, after he and Maurice McCarthy Jr. had battled stubbornly and brilliantly for *ten extra holes.*

Thursday evening: Yes, Bobby had won his first 36-hole match, defeating Fay Coleman of California 6 and 5. He had the match securely under control all the way.

Friday evening: And he had got by the semi-final round. Jess Sweetser had been far off form, and Jones had coasted to a 9 and 8 victory without having to shoot his best golf. But he might have to in the final, for Gene Homans, the lean, ministerial-looking chap who would be opposing him, had played very well in defeating Lawson Little and Charley Seaver (Tom Seaver's father).

It was much cooler on Saturday morning than it had been all week, and a gusty wind blew over Merion. It was apparent from the outset that Gene Homans was nervous, decidedly uncomfortable that he now represented the one obstacle between Jones and the Grand Slam. Gene went six holes before he played his first par, and it was surprising that Jones, wind or no wind, had picked up only three holes. When Homans settled down, Jones, as he had in his previous matches, accelerated his own game. Bobby played the second nine in 33 and boosted his lead to seven holes. It was no longer a question of whether or not Bobby would win but how soon he would win. In the

Bobby and his Boswell, O. B. Keeler, after the Grand Slam, when all was over.

afternoon he climbed to 8 up, to 9 up, and then, believing that he had built up a formidable reservoir of holes, permitted the deep tiredness he felt to show through in his play. He three-putted the 25th and took two shots to get out of a trap on the 28th, but Homans could win back only one hole and Jones was dormie 8 as they came to the 29th tee. The thousands of spectators, sensing that the great moment could be postponed no longer, fought for positions of vantage around the 29th green. Both Bobby and Gene were on in two. Bobby laid his approach putt up close to the cup. To keep the match alive, Homans would have to hole his long one. He stroked it carefully but as soon as he saw it swerve off-line, Gene started over to be the first to congratulate Jones.

Before Homans reached Jones, the first standard shrieks and howls had crescendoed into a mighty, heartfelt roar. The cheers of the thousands were not for the Homans match. It had been a dull contest, an irritating, drawn-out anticlimax. And the cheers were for the Amateur Champion only inasmuch as the Amateur was the last quarter of the stupendous whole—the Grand Slam. The cheers were for May, June, July, and September, for St. Andrews, where the Grand Slam had several times hung by a thread, for Hoylake, where courage and perseverance had nurtured a faint possibility into a fair probability, for Interlachen, where Jones had risen to his full powers on his third round and scattered the field with his 68. And yes, dull match or no dull match, tame tournament or no tame tournament, the cheers were also for Merion, where Jones had not only completed the last leg of the impregnable quadrilateral but had done it with such concomitant authority that never once did he allow an opponent or a break or the strain of four months the smallest opening to destroy the chance of a lifetime.

Protected by a Marine bodyguard, which had dashed onto the green the second the match was over, the authentic hero walked thoughtfully to the clubhouse, acknowledging as best he could the respects his thousands of rejoicing subjects were paying him, unable to digest the fact that the Herculean task he had set himself was actually accomplished, tired, very tired after pushing himself all week, and happy, so very happy, that at last it was all behind him. The walk to the clubhouse seemed to take days, and it seemed weeks before the hordes of friends and admirers were finished shaking his hand and telling him how overjoyed they were, but at length, everyone had the good sense to clear out of the locker room and give Bob a few minutes alone with his dad, the old Colonel. The great friends let themselves go completely, and in the furious outpouring of heart and head, Bobby finally washed himself clean of the strain he had been carrying around for months.

There were no worlds left to conquer for Bobby Jones.

PART FOUR

THE CHANGING OF THE GUARD

1930–1941

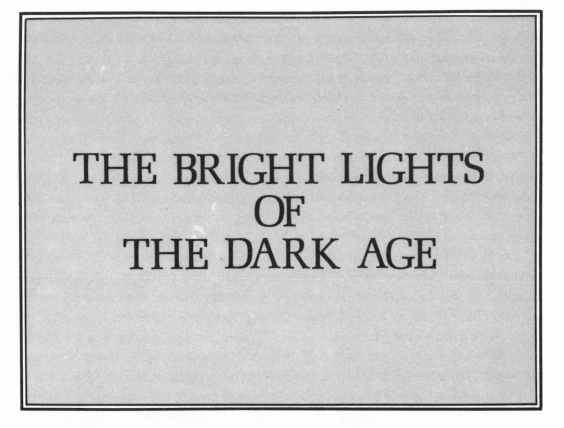

THE BRIGHT LIGHTS
OF
THE DARK AGE

Shortly after he had achieved his Grand Slam, Bobby Jones announced his retirement from tournament golf. The Emperor's abdication came as a colossal shock to the sports fans of the nation. Golf without Jones would be like France without Paris—leaderless, lightless, and lonely. But as they acclimated themselves to a Jonesless season, the fans could appreciate why Bobby had chosen to retire. He was still a very young man, twenty-eight years of age, but for fourteen full years, exactly one half of his life, he had been engaged in competitive golf; unreasonable as it may seem at first, there are few occupations that try a man's physical and mental stamina as harshly as year-in, year-out competitive golf. For years Bobby had felt his love of golf slowly eroding as the game came to mean to him the hyperadulation of his exuberant fans, the bitter strain of tournaments, the violation of his private life. It was a vicious circle: the more often he won, the more often he was expected to win, and the more he had to give of himself to win. Now that he had scaled the pinnacle that had loomed inaccessible, now while he was the quadruple champion and had more than satisfied his ambitions in golf, Jones decided to get away from the pressure and the publicity and rediscover the joys of a game that had become joyless for him. It was an altogether sagacious decision. Few champions have the foresight to retire when they are at the top of the heap, but those who do live on as champions in the hearts of sports fans and not as ex-champions pitifully struggling against the laws of nature.

By retiring when he did, Jones was able to cash in with unprecedented success in the various entertainment media. For years the entrepreneurs of entertainment had been conscious of Jones' powerful hold on the American public, the non-golfing as well as the golfing public. Their offers had been fancy, but Bobby had not been interested; while he remained a competitive golfer, he chose to remain an amateur golfer. However, when he had made up his mind to retire, Jones did accept several handsome offers. He agreed to design Jones-model clubs for Spalding. Along with his alter ego, O. B., he went on the air with a weekly half-hour radio series, a flavorsome chat-and-dramat re-creation of the highlights of his career. He signed a contract with Warner Brothers and made two series of "shorts," among the very finest of the species ever produced. For the first series of twelve, Bobby received $120,000 with a share of the profits if the series grossed above $360,000, which it did. For the second series of six, Bobby received $60,000. Jones' haul was pretty hard on the pros whom he had beaten as an amateur and now again as a professional.

As Bobby rearranged his life, he was able to give his legal and business interests in Atlanta the time they demanded, but he never got very far away from golf. On Sunday mornings he was out with his old cronies at East Lake. He usually turned up for the national championships, walking unobtrusively among the galleries. At Augusta he began work with Alister MacKenzie on the Augusta National course, where in future years he would make his one annual appearance in tournament play. Jones never won the Masters or threatened to. Once he dropped out of regular competition, he discovered that he could not regain the super-concentration required of the tournament golfer.

Jones' departure hurt championship golf. There were other interesting personalities still operating, but without Jones the Open seemed colorless and the Amateur lost its stature. No longer did the country lean forward anxiously during the weeks of the championships to see if Bobby could do it again, and the galleries that turned out were comparatively sparse and almost entirely local. When Bobby was doing his stuff, both the Open and the Amateur regularly returned big profits; without its ace drawing card, the U.S.G.A. was now lucky if the take equaled the expense of staging the tournaments.

The sharp slump in gate receipts at the championships the next few years reflected not only the Joneslessness of the tournaments but also the depression that had rocked the country. By 1931 the full impact of non-prosperity had struck home. Golf, like all the appendages of basic living, was hit and hit hard. A number of the mammoth country clubs gave up after only a brief struggle. Expenses were as high as they had ever been, but club incomes had dropped as much as 65 percent. Men who had formerly belonged to two or three clubs now had to save up before blowing themselves to a round of miniature golf. Only a few Bubbling Bays had built up a healthy reserve through astute optioning and selling of new and old property, and a great many clubs, intent on maintaining the integrity of their holdings, found themselves saddled with a steadily rising tax base and heavy fixed maintenance charges. The banks came in and became the residuary legatees of a good percentage of the crippled clubs, and in some cases, although public golf had also declined, the salvation was to sell out to the city or the state. The better-managed, more resourceful private clubs succeeded in riding out the storm although the solutions varied with the individual problem and inclination of the club. One method was to take in more members, if you could find them, and if the board of governors did not mind fraternizing with the men they had blackballed in the good old days. Another method, if an increase in members seemed the way out, was to offer several types of less expensive memberships to the prospective joiners, golf memberships for those who were solely interested in golf, social memberships for those who had no intention of playing golf but liked the environment. Some clubs discovered that they could keep going if they cut away the tennis courts, the polo field, the swimming pool—everything but the golf course; other clubs got back in the black by opening other sports facilities—bowling, squash, badminton, table tennis. Generally, however, retrenchment was the route. The valet and the masseur and the other janissaries of metropolitan-style service had to go. So did the money-losing dining room, or dining rooms, which a few years earlier had been cavalierly regarded as a necessary loss. Country clubs became golf clubs, and golf saw them through. When the gradual recovery, and Repeal, gave them the strength to restore some of the non-golfing attractions, the clubs wisely remembered to spend something more than thirty cents on the dollar, the old Bubbling Bay ratio, on the upkeep of the golf course.

With Jones no longer around to dominate and demoralize, the big tournaments regained their old unpredictable character. One year, for example, there were twelve co-favorites for the Amateur, and the Open was really open. The man who eventually won out was the man who had been solidly on his game during the vital week and additionally blessed with a hot putter and the breaks that decide championships when there are a number of equally equipped contenders. In the next few years the honors were divided among an amazing motley—veterans from the pre-Jones era striking again in stirring comebacks, moderately young men who had developed their games in the Twenties but whose light had been hidden beneath Jones' bushel, very young men, a horde of them, whose ambitions had been sparked by the deeds of the Georgian. In the spring of 1930, five Atlanta friends of Jones' had placed a wager with Lloyds of London that Bobby would carry off all four major crowns, a long-shot chance if there ever was one, but in the early Thirties a bet on the Grand Slam began to look as though it had been a sure thing, so bewilderingly formless was the form. Anyone could win—the gray or the crewcut, the tortoise or the hare, even the favorite, just often enough to be disconcerting—everyone, that is, except Macdonald Smith and Leo Diegel, who had to do it then or never.

It is not easy to fix an arbitrary date as to when the patternless period of transition was terminated by the arrival of a new crop of consistent winners and form-abiding champions. Perhaps the closest one can come is the spring of 1934, when Lawson Little emerged as a great, not just a good, amateur, and when the monopoly of our pros in the British Open was broken after ten straight years by that excellent messiah, Henry Cotton. At home, after Cotton's triumph, our veteran pros continued to be influential on the circuit and in the Opens, but the newcomers, the Picards, the Runyans, the Revoltas, were striding briskly into the limelight and laying the groundwork for the coming of Guldahl and Snead and a new age of professional golf.

Because of this very absence of predetermined winners, the tournaments of the early Thirties possessed an abundance of excitement, their own especial spontaneity, and the charm, however accidental, of intimacy. They also produced some of the warmest human-interest stories in the entire chronicle of American golf.

The youngsters did fairly well in 1931. Twenty-year-old Helen Hicks took the U.S. Women's, Tom Creavy the P.G.A. But the veterans did better. Tommy Armour won the British Open, Billy Burke the U.S. Open, and a chap called Ouimet—the name brought back the rumble of the horse and buggy—captured his second Amateur after a brief hiatus of seventeen years.

Armour's victory was gained at Carnoustie, not far from the Braid Hills of Edinburgh where Tommy had grown up. There was only one other golfer whom the Carnoustie gallery would have preferred to have won the championship, old Macdonald Smith, a native son returning to the course whose fame his and his brothers' exploits had helped spread throughout the New World. As the field entered the final eighteen holes at Carnoustie, Old Mac appeared to have the better chance of the two homegrown favorites; he was only two strokes off the pace set by the dapper little Argentinian, Jose Jurado, and Tommy was a full five strokes away. Tommy had the advantage of getting out early, and the 71 he carved with his great powerful hands gave the later starters a tough mark to shoot at in the high wind blustering over the long layout. Jurado came to Carnoustie's renowned finish, the last three holes, needing three pars, 3-4-5, to edge out Armour by a stroke. On the 71st—although it was learned afterwards that Jurado (who spoke only Spanish) did not know of Armour's score—the pressure caught up with the Argentinian and he plopped his tee shot into the Barry Burn, which coils like a serpent across the last two holes. He could still tie by birdieing the 72nd, but Jurado's unfortunate ignorance of what he had to shoot misled him into playing his second purposely short of the burn before the green, and his final 5 left him a stroke behind Armour. As if Jurado's finish were not heart-rending enough, along came Mac Smith, needing 3-4-5 to tie with Armour, and failing once again, only failing a shade more pathetically this time, with a 6 and two 5s. It was a cruel and piteous spectacle, Old Mac's seemingly inevitable collapse in front of his hometown admirers.

Billy Burke, the 1931 Open winner, was actually a youngish man, in only his fifth season as a professional with a reputation; but there was a rather old look in Billy's kind, calm eyes, his movements were deliberate and plodding, and he gave the impression that he had been around for years. Born Burkauskus, of Lithuanian extraction, Billy had worked as a puddler in the iron mills of Naugatuck, Connecticut, before turning to golf. In a mill accident the fourth finger of his left hand had been clipped off at the second joint and the little finger damaged, and Billy took to inserting a sponge inside his glove in order to increase the pressure of the grip with his injured hand and so counteract the tendency of his right hand to overpower the left. After gaining minor prominence through his steady play in the South in 1927, Billy had settled into his pro job at Round

Hill, Connecticut, and 1931 marked the first year he had done any campaigning to speak of. His consistent scoring in the Ryder Cup qualifications tests earned him a place on the American team, and he had borne out Hagen's confidence in him by winning both his foursome and singles matches. At Inverness in the Open, Burke played his four rounds in an average of 73, and unexciting as those figures were, only one other entry was able to match them.

George Von Elm, the man who had tied with Burke via a 10-footer on the last green, was also an easy person to root for. On the eve of the 1930 Amateur, the sleek Californian had announced that this would be his farewell appearance as an amateur. Amateur golf, he elaborated in a formal announcement at the close of the tournament, was too expensive a pursuit for him, and in the future he would play as a "businessman golfer," depending on golf for his living and not for his hardware. He had exceeded his rosiest expectations in his first season as a professional, earning just short of $8,000 in January and February alone. Like Burke, George had won a sentimental hold on the public. It was difficult for most fans to align themselves against either Billy or George. They would have liked to have seen both of them win.

Von Elm had a proclivity for getting himself involved in marathon matches, with his match at Merion against Maurice McCarthy that went to the 28th green—ten extra holes—being the example that comes most readily to mind. The Von Elm–Burke playoff was set for thirty-six holes, but when both men totaled 149 over this distance, another thirty-six was decreed. Over the seventy-two holes of the playoff, Burke and Von Elm engaged in a terrific give-and-take. At one point, Von Elm, four strokes back, played four birdies in a row and turned his deficit into a two-stroke lead. Then Burke came churning back. That is how it went as the two battled on, Von Elm, the dashing swatter, outdriving his opponent by twenty to thirty yards but losing his advantage around the greens, Burke, the cigar-chewing plodder, sinking his head at the start of his swing, then bobbing it up as he seemed to lift the clubhead back with both hands, but, for all his transgressions of the copy book, keeping the ball very straight.

As they entered the fourth and final eighteen, Von Elm, who had added a 76 to his 75 and 74, led the tortoise by a stroke and tried to pull away. Burke, and Von Elm's own putting, wouldn't let him. On that last tour George required thirty-five putts. (In Bobby Jones' opinion, thirty-one putts approximate "par putting" for a tournament golfer.) Into the breach stepped Burke, with one superb iron after another. Billy came to the 72nd green with two putts for his par and a 70. With a two-stroke lead over George, however, Billy sensibly closed in on the cup with two approach putts and left himself an unmissable tap of one or two inches for the decisive stroke.

After playing 144 holes at Inverness, Burke and Von Elm had ended up only one stroke apart. During the five grueling days, Von Elm had lost nine pounds, and Burke, amazingly enough, had picked up two.

In 1931 the U.S.G.A. introduced the sectional-qualifying system, which had worked out well in the Open, into the operation of the national Amateur. In previous years a golfer with the requisite handicap status mailed in his entry blank and résumé to the U.S.G.A. and entered his first qualifying test at the scene of the tournament. Each year the same old faces, who could arrange to get away from business or local golf for the week, were on deck for the Amateur, and while there was nothing wrong with this annual convocation of the older hands, the system discouraged many promising young golfers from trekking to the championship when it was held in parts of the country remote from their homes. The new system didn't cut down travel expenses nor did it excuse the sectional qualifiers from the national qualifying rounds, but the young man who had succeeded in gaining a place in one of the twenty regional sections designated by the U.S.G.A. was able, more likely than not, to gain the active sympathy of his boss and/or the interest of his club members, now that he had given the definitive local proof of his ability.

In 1931 a stream of beardless youths, sectional qualifiers, converged on the Beverly Country Club in Chicago for the Amateur. Not only Jones and Von Elm were absent, but many others who always "made" the Amateur as regularly as their class reunions had been unable to hurdle the sectional tests. Of the thirty-two players who qualified at Beverly, seventeen were entering the match-play brackets for the first time. Chandler Harper from Virginia Beach and Billy Howell from Richmond, two who got in, were the first Virginians ever to qualify. It was a great thing for American golf, this fusion of the youngsters into the big leagues, although it was rather mystifying at first for the oldtimers like Ouimet to walk through the locker room and find so few of the old faces around.

Francis always came to the Amateur meaning business. Five times from 1921 through 1929 he had made his way into the semi-final round, but each year he had been ousted, and ousted usually by stern margins. Francis' friends used to kid him about being "just a semi-finalist," which he could appreciate, but he did not agree with their judgment that at his age he just didn't have the stamina to stand up to a full week of championship golf. Francis' own opinion was that he had simply been outplayed by his semi-final opponents and that whatever weariness he had shown was the weariness that always afflicts the golfer who is not doing well, whether he be seventeen or thirty-seven. It was a little hard to believe that Ouimet was only thirty-eight in 1931, since Taft had been in the White House when Francis had first tried to qualify in the Amateur. He had married the game when he was very young, but, still, thirty-eight years were in those days a heavy load for an athlete to cart around.

After qualifying adequately, the old campaigner came up against John K. Shields, a twenty-two-year-older from Seattle. Francis outsteadied the young man 4 and 3, and moved on to Frank Connolly, a twenty-year-older from Mt. Clemens. Connolly had none of the fire he had shown in the morning when he had played a 71 against Gus Moreland, and Ouimet won 5 and 4. An older man, Paul Jackson, who had just turned twenty-one, was Ouimet's opponent in his first 36-hole match. Jackson was a pink-cheeked boy, no more than five-feet-five in height, and as he walked down the fairway with Ouimet, who was graying at the temples, the curious picture they made prompted one spectator to remark, "This looks like a father-and-son tournament." The father beat the son with plenty to spare, and once again Ouimet had reached the semi-finals.

His opponent was Billy Howell, a nineteen-year-old Virginian, a blue-eyed, sandy-haired boy, slim almost to the point of fragility, with a luxurious way of drawling "Yas, sah" that led the reporters to ask him more questions than they had really intended in order to get him to talk some more. The Howell–Ouimet match was the match of the tournament. There was nothing fragile about the golf that Billy shot that day. He was 1 up at lunch, and after he had given ground in the early part of the afternoon's play, he pulled off some courageous recoveries and evened the match on the 28th hole. On the 30th, Billy rolled in a putt for a birdie 2 and went one hole up. Francis got it back on the 31st. It is difficult to think of a better clutch-putter than Ouimet; the one he dropped on the 31st was a good twenty feet. They halved the 32nd; still all even. On the 33rd Francis holed a 15-footer for a win. The next hole was halved, and Francis teed up on the 200-yard 35th 1 up and two to play. He hit the green with his midiron shot, the ball finishing twenty feet from the cup. Billy sliced his iron into a trap beside the green, but the Virginian was not conceding defeat. He took his time studying his lie in the trap and came up with a gorgeous explosion inches from the cup. The gallery began to hurry for places along the last hole, but it was unnecessary exertion. Francis gauged the skiddy surface perfectly and holed his 20-footer for the match. The old guy who just didn't have the stamina had played the last ten holes in three under 4s.

Ouimet's opponent in the final was Jack Westland, who had accounted for Sam Parks, George Dunlap (the Intercollegiate champ), Ducky Yates (who had slimmed down to 270 pounds), and Junior McCarthy. Compared to the boys whom Ouimet had met in the earlier rounds, Westland was an out-and-out Methuselah, a doddering twenty-seven. Ouimet rushed off with a brace of birdies and stayed in front all the way. He was 4 up after nine, 5 up at lunch, dormie 6 after the 30th, and victorious on the 31st, 6 and 5. It was the identical margin by which Francis had beaten Jerry Travers in the final at Ekwanok seventeen years before to the day, almost to the minute.

1932 was Gene Sarazen's big year. Gene took the British Open and the United States Open to become, along with Jones, the only golfer to annex both titles in the same year. Bobby Cruickshank, who finished second to Gene at Fresh Meadow, had been hit much more directly by the Depression than any of the other name-golfers. The club at which Bobby had been the professional had gone under, and the courageous Scot *had* to win prize money in the Open. To a far lesser extent, Mac Smith, who finished second to Gene in Britain, also felt the pinch of the times. In winning his third Los Angeles Open, Mac's slice came from a pot that had been reduced from $10,000 to $7,500. Nearly all of the tournaments were cutting down, and a few of them had been suspended indefinitely.

Once again the Amateur, at Five Farms outside Baltimore, exceeded all expectations, except at the box office. The old tourney record of 31 for nine holes, created by Jerry Travers and equaled by Jones at Minikahda, was shattered by none other than Francis Ouimet. Francis went out in 30 in his match against George Voigt, and had par in, for a 64 when he closed out George on the fourteenth green. But Ouimet's friends were right this year; their man was just a semi-finalist. Johnny Goodman, Ouimet's conqueror, was apparently on his way to the crown in the final against Sandy Somerville, but, standing 2 up on the 27th, Goodman missed four vital second shots and they cost him the championship, 2 and 1. For the first time since Harold Hilton had outlucked Freddy Herreshoff at Apawamis away back in 1911, the Amateur had been carried off by a foreign threat. Somerville, who was twenty-nine and trying the Amateur for the fifth time, was a versatile games-player, not far behind Lionel Conacher as the finest all-round Canadian athlete. Sandy had been a regular on the Toronto rugby team, bowled for the all-star Canadian cricket team that toured Britain, and played center-ice for London in the Senior Ontario Hockey League. He was a very pretty golfer with a fine free swing off the tees and a dash of Armour in his irons. At Five Farms, Somerville hit the greens more often than anyone else, which is just another way of saying that the man who won the tournament deserved to win it.

Though Johnny Goodman had not won the Amateur, he had reached the final and on his way he had the warm satisfaction of beating Seaver, McCarthy, and Ouimet. This trio had been on the 1932 Walker Cup team, and for some reason, known only to the selectors, Goodman had not been included. The spokesman for the selectors answered the storm of protests that followed the slighting of Goodman with references to his defeats in early rounds in the Amateur, but it wasn't good enough. It was a matter of record that Johnny had twice been a first-round casualty in the Amateur, but the books also showed that in the 1930 Open Jones had been the only amateur who had outscored Goodman, and in the 1932 Open Goodman had been the top amateur. The oversight by the Walker Cup selectors made Goodman's supporters wonder if it wasn't Johnny's lack of social qualifications that had kept him off the team.

Johnny was the fifth of ten children of a poor Polish-American family who lived in the packing-house district of Omaha. He had bumped into golf at the age of twelve. One morning he and his gang had walked down the railroad tracks farther than they had ever gone before. Their hike took them by the Omaha Field Club. They stopped and watched the members playing by, and got a tremendous kick out of it. None of the kids had ever seen a golfer before. At home they dug up some poles and some balls, and simulated the motions of the men they had watched. Then they got the bright idea to walk down the tracks again to the Omaha Field Club and see if they could get jobs carrying those bags for the men.

Johnny caddied for four years. And then life, which had never been kind to the Goodmans, became very rough. Johnny's mother died, and with her death the children were virtually orphaned. Their father had deserted the family and his whereabouts were unknown. Johnny's older brothers had troubles of their own, and the burden of supporting the five youngest children fell on Johnny. He quit school and went to work, but the seventeen-year-older couldn't swing it. The family was broken up. Three of the youngest children were placed in an orphanage, and homes with families were found for

Closing in on one of the most stunning upsets in the history of the Open. Johnny Goodman, the upstart amateur from Omaha, fighting grimly to hold his lead, plays a perfect recovery from the short rough during the final round of the 1933 championship at North Shore. Goodman won by a single stroke over Ralph Guldahl.

the others. Johnny went to night school for one summer and was able to rejoin his class and achieve his ambition of graduating from high school.

The night of graduation, the minute after the ceremonies were concluded, Johnny and a couple of his friends jumped in a jalopy and headed for the Broadmoor course in Colorado Springs, where the twenty-seventh annual Trans-Mississippi Championship was being staged. Following the death of his mother, Johnny had been able to play golf only on odd weekends, but as a caddie he had developed a short, compact swing, the antithesis of the rhythmic but loose style most caddies come into, and it took him only two or three rounds to find his groove. Despite the infrequency of his play, the stocky boy had established himself as the best golfer in Omaha in the city tournaments. In 1927, when he had returned to high school, Johnny had the opportunity for the first time to devote his afternoons and evenings to working on his shots. He had come along rapidly. At Broadmoor he played with increasing finesse as the tournament progressed, and astonished the mid-Western golfing world by taking the Trans-Mississippi. Omahans were delighted. They were well acquainted with the story of Johnny Goodman. On the day the spunky eighteen-year-older returned from Colorado, the market center in South Omaha declared a half-holiday and greeted Johnny with a parade and a banquet. The next year a friend who worked for one of the packing houses arranged for Johnny to travel technically as a drover on a cattlecar when the young man signified his intention to go to the West Coast and try the Amateur at Pebble Beach. He catapulted himself to national fame in that tournament by outplaying and defeating the great Bobby Jones in the first round, and started on four years of campaigning, sectional and national, that convinced just about everyone but the Walker Cup selectors that he stood among the nation's top half-dozen amateurs.

Scarcely nine months after Somerville's rally on the last nine holes had denied him the 1932 Amateur, Johnny Goodman won an even more important championship, the Open. At North Shore, on the rim of Chicago, Johnny led off with a 75 and then left the pros far behind with a blistering 66 on which he used only twenty-five putts. He bolstered his position with a 70 and carried so sturdy a lead into the final round that his 76 was not calamitous. Hagen, in one of his oldtime finishes, tore the course apart with a 66 (which included an out-of-bounds penalty) but Walter had started too far back. The one man who might have caught Goodman was a large, slope-shouldered, unexciting and unexcitable twenty-one-year-old graduate of a Texas public course, Ralph Guldahl. Six strokes behind Goodman when he began his last round, nine strokes behind after fifty-seven holes, the big Texan, playing pars and birdies where the tiring Goodman had played bogeys and pars, made up one stroke after another until he had wiped out eight of them, and loped onto the 72nd green needing to hole only a straight 4-footer to tie with Johnny. It slid by on the left.

Goodman's victory was the biggest upset in the Open since little Cyril Walker had won at Oakland Hills. The pros were furious with themselves for letting an amateur show them up once again, but when the first sense of outrage had worn off, they joined with the rest of America in taking their hats off to a boy who had stood up to the hard blows of life like a man and had fought his way past one barrier after another to the top.

The Open champ was eliminated in the first round of the 1933 Amateur when he bumped into a 70 by Chandler Egan. George Dunlap—who had to play off for his place at Kenwood, in Cincinnati—went on to defeat the rejuvenated Max Marston in the final. Virginia Van Wie, swinging more impressively every year, won her third consecutive Women's Championship and then decided that she had had enough of the strain. In the spring Denny Shute had won the British Open to become, as it turned out, the last invader who would twist the lion's tail for thirteen full years.

Denny was a well-schooled golfer but a hard person to warm up to off the links as well as on. He was about as loquacious as Calvin Coolidge, and there was also a similarity in their attitudes toward matters financial. A West Virginian of Scottish

Walter Hagen takes his boys across for the 1933 Ryder Cup contest: Hagen (at extreme left), Craig Wood, Denny Shute, Ed Dudley, Paul Runyan, Horton Smith, Gene Sarazen, Olin Dutra, Leo Diegel, Billy Burke. The large carnival crowds at Southport seemed to upset the younger players, and the oldtimers shot the best golf.

lineage, Denny could never forget that the people back in Scotland could join the local golf club for a full year by smacking five shillings on the counter. Had Denny not married a vivacious girl with a flair for conversation, the most that anyone might have learned about his views on life was his considered opinion that the soft turf of American courses made it more difficult for U.S. players to hold the shots they hit off the hard British fairways.

The most important shot in Denny's early career, unfortunately, was the 3-foot putt he missed that would have knotted the 1933 Ryder Cup Match. A week or so after the Ryder, the British Open got underway at St. Andrews. Nobody paid Shute much attention as he played his staid succession of 73s, but the men who seemed to be winning the championship—Sarazen, Cotton, Kirkwood, Easterbrook, and, to be sure, Diegel— all ran into one form or another of disaster, with Diegel's, of course, the cruelest, and Craig Wood was the only one of the mid-tournament gallopers whose total matched

Shute's 292. On the first hole of the playoff, Wood put his second into the Swilcan Burn and chose to remove his shoes and socks and play the ball from the water. The wisdom of resorting to such desperate measures with thirty-five holes to go was open to question, and particularly when Wood, for all his pains, was not able to do better than a 6. He dropped two strokes on that hole, two more on the second, and after that there was not much to choose between Wood and Shute. Denny did pick up one more stroke and won the playoff by five.

Shute's victory at St. Andrews made it a full decade since the British Open had been won by a resident Britisher. Following Havers' victory in 1923, Hagen had taken the old mug three times, Jones three times, Barnes, Sarazen, and Armour once apiece. Just when it looked to the despondent British fans as if a messiah would never come, Henry Cotton appeared on the scene. In 1934 at Sandwich, Cotton, who had taken a post-graduate course in the States on the inside-out swing, led off with a 67, added a great 65, and ultimately won by five strokes. The big parade was over.

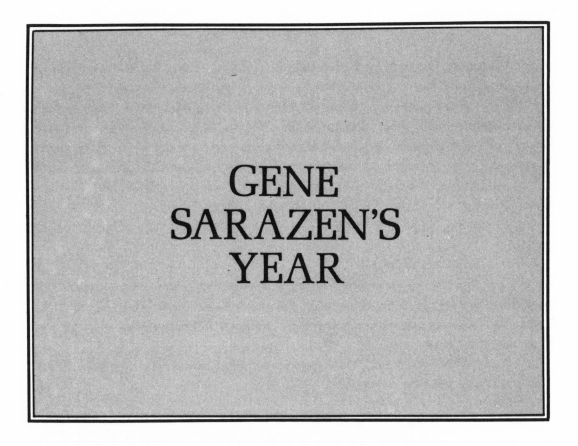

GENE SARAZEN'S YEAR

In the spring of 1928 Walter Hagen and Gene Sarazen were stretched out sleepily on adjoining deck chairs watching the blue-gray Atlantic heave and duck, talking leisurely and frankly of their friends, their families, and their golf. The two friendly rivals were on their way to England to play in the British Open at Sandwich, and as the conversation turned to that tournament, Gene angled his head a bit more directly toward Walter and, in a tone appreciably more ardent than he had been using, confided that his ambition in golf was to win a British Open Championship.

There was nothing startling about this confession. Walter, and many other persons not as close to Gene, had known for five years that he would never be wholly happy until he had triumphed in a British Open. In 1923, on his first visit to Britain, Gene had received a colossal jolt to his self-esteem at Troon. Hailed by the British press as the brightest star in a decade to flash on the American horizon, lauded as the reigning United States Open and P.G.A. Champion and the victor over Hagen in a 72-hole duel, young Sarazen did not succeed in even qualifying for the British Open. He felt disgraced. He vowed he would be back again, even if he had to swim across, but he had never done anything to atone for his failure, and it weighed heavily on the mind of this young man who was not accustomed to being unsuccessful. Better than any other golfer, Hagen could understand Sarazen's humiliation at Troon. The same thing had happened to Walter in 1920 when he had arrived at Deal for *his* first British Open, press-agented as the golfer who would show the British a thing or two. Walter had showed them four rounds in the eighties and had finished a lurid fifty-fifth.

"All you need is one thing to win the British Open, Gene," said the man who had rebounded from his degradation at Deal to carry off the British Open in '22 and '24.

"What's that?" Gene was hoping Walter wouldn't come up with some bromide about patience or the breaks, not that Walter dealt in clichés, but from 1923 on, when Gene's golf had begun to go sour and he became understandably fretful about his continuing slump, hundreds of well-intentioned folks had chirped up with their free advice, and it always boiled down to something beautifully unhelpful, like "Slow down your hip action, Gene" or "You've just got to be patient."

"All you need to win the British Open," Walter continued, "is to have the right caddie."

"And who's that, Walter?"

"The old fellow I'm going to have caddie for me at Sandwich—that is, if you don't want him. Daniels's his name. He's an old fellow but he knows Royal St. George's like a book. I'd like to see you win one, Gene. It'll cost you two hundred bucks, but if you want him, you can have him."

"Okay, Walter, you're on," said Gene pressing his lips into that tight grin. "What did you say my man's name was?"

"Daniels."

Daniels turned out to be the article described by Hagen. He was well along in his sixties, old even for a British caddie, and British caddies are regarded as immature apprentices until they have passed forty. When Gene first saw his weather-beaten prize, he wondered if Old Dan would have the strength to carry his big bag. Dan could not only do that, which is the least important contribution a good caddie makes, but he got onto Gene's game quickly and could call the correct club without a moment's hesitation. He knew when to sympathize without uttering a word and when a compliment would perk up his man, and he buoyed Gene's confidence with his own honest confidence that "we" could win. It is always *we* for the professional British caddie.

Sarazen and Daniels played three good rounds in the Open but they played one relatively poor one, the second. They were purring along nicely on that round until they came to the fourteenth, the redoubtable Suez, a par 5, 520 yards long, where a fence along the right separates the hole (and the course) from the adjoining course, Prince's. On the fourteenth, playing away from the fence and out-of-bounds, Sarazen hooked his drive into the high rough. Dan counseled an iron—the important thing was to get out. Gene shook him off. Tough rough or not, he wanted to go for distance with a wood and be in a position to play his third from up close to the green. Daniels looked again at Gene standing in the alien corn and tapped the head of an iron. Gene thought for a moment, of Daniels' knowledge of the course, and then of Hagen striding down the fairways ahead of him, and took his spoon. The high grass snuffed out the shot before it got up, and the ball expired a short way ahead, still in the rough. Sarazen impetuously lashed at the ball again without changing clubs, and hit a second bad shot. He ended up with a 7. By not heeding Daniels' advice, Sarazen had thrown away the championship. He finished two strokes behind the winner, Hagen.

The galling disappointment of coming so close and then tossing it away on a bonehead play only redoubled Sarazen's determination to win the British Open. He tried it again at Muirfield in 1929, but the best he could do was a tie for eighth, eleven strokes behind the man who knew how to win that championship, Hagen. He tried it once more in 1931 at Carnoustie, finished third, two strokes behind Armour, might have won if the wind had not changed between the morning and afternoon rounds twice in three days, handicapping him and benefitting Armour on both occasions. Gene was not planning to go to Britain for the 1932 Open. Things were rough then, what with the Depression, and much as he wanted that title, the two thousand dollars which his expedition would cost him seemed too high a sum to risk on three days' play. His wife Mary persuaded him to give it another try.

The 1932 British Open was scheduled for Prince's, a flat, wind-swept course measuring almost 7,000 yards, adjacent to Royal St. George's in Sandwich. Gene arrived at Prince's early. Daniels was waiting for him. Four years before, after they had failed so brilliantly at St. George's, Daniels had told the crestfallen runner-up, "I'm going to win this championship for you if it's the last thing I do before I die." He reminded Gene of that promise as they renewed their acquaintance, and it made what Gene had to tell Dan that much harder to say. Daniels was approaching seventy now and the past four years had exacted a heavy toll. His eyesight was almost completely gone. Friends of Sarazen's advised him against taking the old man. It would be folly, they had argued, to allow sentiment to interfere with his excellent chances of winning. Gene had decided they were right, but breaking the news to Dan was one of the hardest things he had ever had to do. He finally got it out, as delicately as he could, and walked away from the old caddie feeling like a heel.

Gene engaged a young caddie he had met at Stoke Poges. They did not get along at Prince's. Gene was in a frame of mind in which he could easily be irritated. He was training like a boxer for the Open, exercising to get rid of ten pounds he didn't want, practicing daily in weather that drove the less industrious challengers to the fireplace, swinging a 36-ounce driver an hour each day to strengthen his wrists. But this intensive preparation was doing Gene no good. He wasn't hitting the ball, he wasn't scoring. The young caddie was getting on his nerves, calling the wrong club, Gene thought, and then arguing that it wasn't his fault, that Sarazen had not hit the shot right. Old Dan had come around to the club nearly every day, shaking his head rather dolefully when he heard about Sarazen's poor form. Gene, of course, was expecting to snap out of the doldrums, but as the opening day of the championship grew closer and his game showed no signs of improving, he decided that something drastic had to be done. He fired the young caddie and told Daniels to grab his bag.

The old man straightened his celluloid collar and pulled his cap down lower over his old eyes, and Sarazen and Daniels went out to see what they could do about things.

It was almost magical the way Gene reacted to his old partner's presence. He stopped fighting his caddie and himself, and before he knew it, he was on top of his game. Dan couldn't see very far, but when he called a club, much as Gene wondered how he could do it, it was always the right club. Daniels knew golf, he knew Sarazen's game, and he knew Prince's like Sinclair Lewis knew Sauk Center. After his practice rounds with Daniels, the odds on Sarazen went from 25–1 to 6–1 on the eve of the tournament.

It was a runaway for Sarazen and Daniels. They opened with a 70 on the par-74 course. They added a 69. On that crucial third round they didn't slip—they got another 70. They had a 35 out on the last round, faltered for a few holes in their tiredness, but roused themselves with two fine shots to the home green that gave them a par 74. They were five shots ahead of the second man, 13 under par for the seventy-two holes. Their record total of 283 was twice tied later but remained unbroken until Locke compiled his 279 at Troon in 1950.

Old Dan had given Gene everything he had. Early in the morning on the last day, long before the players went out, he had walked through a fifty-mile gale over Prince's noting the new positions of the flags, pacing out their distances from the edges of the greens so that his man would know just what alterations to make on his approaches. His stride had never flagged once in the entire tournament. He kept his promise. He won the championship for Gene. It was the last thing he did. For a few months he walked around happily in the polo coat Sarazen had given him, talking about how they had done it, and then Old Daniels died.

There are many other chapters in the career of Gene Sarazen that read like fiction— his first win in the United States Open, his repeat performance ten years later, his triumph in the Masters, to name just a few. This patina of fiction was merely the residue of sweat. Few athletes have worked as strenuously as Gene Sarazen did to become a leader and to stay a leader in his chosen profession. Forthright, realistic, and as shrewd as David Harum, Sarazen enjoyed his success but did not let it rub out the hard facts he had learned when a boy and a hick pro. As he acquired money and polish and the opportunity to express his considerable charm, Sarazen did not change fundamentally. The hero of the Sarazen stories is a man who knows the way of the world.

The boy was born in Harrison, New York, in 1902, the son of Saraceni, an Italian carpenter-contractor. The Apawamis Golf Club was practically next door, and young Sarazen gravitated to the caddie ranks at an early age. He was caddie #99, a pleasant, knowledgeable kid, the personal caddie for Frank Presbrey, one of the founders of the U.S. Seniors Championship. Gene was adept at all sports and outstanding as a basket-ball forward. He was a squat youngster but in those days a basketball player didn't have to be seven feet tall.

Gene became a professional golfer quite by accident. He had come down with pleurisy shortly after going to work in a factory in Bridgeport. His vitality was so low after the illness that he figured that the wisest move would be to find some outdoor work. His friend, Al Cuici, who had caddied with him at Apawamis, sent him over to see George Sparling, the pro at Brooklawn, a club on the edge of Bridgeport. Sparling took Sarazen on as an assistant clubmaker. The new assistant clubmaker had the privilege of playing once a week. In a short time he could outdrive, if not outscore, the pro, and Sparling helped him to improve his game. Gene was ambitious to get ahead, however, and he felt that as long as he remained close to home he would always be regarded as an ex-caddie and not as a golf professional. When he was offered the position of assistant professional at a club in Fort Wayne, Indiana, he lost no time in accepting it. One of the advantages of his new post was that he could get away periodically and test himself in competition against the ranking pros. He qualified for the Open in 1920, when he was eighteen, and again the following year when he had switched from Fort Wayne to a club in Titusville, Pennsylvania. His showings in the Open were creditable. He attracted some passing attention by defeating Jock Hutchison in an early round of the 1921 P.G.A. and by winning the New Orleans Open the following winter. That spring he took over as the pro at the Highland Country Club in Pittsburgh. Sarazen, nevertheless, was almost a complete unknown when he arrived at Skokie, near Chicago, for the 1922 Open. One of the big-name stars declined to practice with the young pro from Highland.

Gene had a premonition he might surprise the Open field and he practiced hour upon hour at Skokie during the week preceding the tournament. His first two rounds, a 72 and 73, put him up with the leaders, but a spotty 75, which included eight 5s, dropped him four strokes behind Jones and Mehlhorn with eighteen holes remaining to be played. No one was looking for any fireworks when Sarazen, paired with another unknown youngster, Johnny Farrell, started off on his last leg. Gene was shaky on the first hole and he choked badly on the second; he had no chance for a par 3 and was lucky to salvage a 4. He wasn't going to overhaul Jones and Mehlhorn by being timid—that was obvious. On the third green, after reaching that 450-yarder in two, he turned to Farrell and said, "I might as well go for everything now." He made sure he got his 40-footer up to the cup, and it went in. On the next hole, twenty-five feet from the pin after his drive and pitch, Gene looked the line over carefully. "I'll give this one a chance, too, Johnny," he said hopefully as he returned to his ball. He got that one, too. These two long putts restored Sarazen's confidence. He kept on hitting out, blocking his ears to the sirens' song of safety and going for everything. On the 72nd he smacked his second with a driver onto the green and earned a final birdie, which gave him a 68 for the round. He was rather pleased with himself, as he had a right to be. People would now know that Gene Sarazen was a damn good golfer, even if one of the players out on the course beat his 288. He felt fairly confident that his mark would stand up. When one of the clubhouse jockeys suffixed his congratulations with the reminder that Jones or Mehlhorn or Black or Hagen might come in with a 288, Gene took his big black cigar out of his mouth. "That's possible," the youngster nodded, "but I've already got mine."

Hagen took 291, Mehlhorn 290, Jones and Black 289. The fresh kid had been right. He had his 288 and it was the winning total. His 68 had stolen the championship right from under the noses of the big guns. The story was a natural—*Unknown Pro Wins Open*—and the press played it to the hilt.

The Open champ did not remain at Highland long. Everyone wanted to see this new fellow, this Sarazen, and he was deluged with invitations to play exhibition matches. When he was accorded the privilege of selecting his opponent from a list of several name-pros offered by the sponsoring club, he made it a point to select the golfer with the biggest reputation. He was out to show that he was no flash in the pan. He bolstered his standing by winning the P.G.A. and challenged Hagen to a special 72-hole match for the unofficial world championship. Not the least bit cowed by Walter's reputation as a killer in match play, the cocky kid trimmed The Haig 3 and 2. In the space of a few months Gene Sarazen had shot from obscurity to nationwide fame.

The stringent circumstances of Sarazen's boyhood had taught him that money did not grow on trees. He had a chance to make money now and he intended to leave no angle uncalibrated. He endorsed clubs, balls, and cartridges. He established a golf correspondence school and made movie shorts. He played countless exhibitions. He turned down lucrative contracts from seven clubs in the metropolitan area of New York and waited until Briarcliff Lodge offered him a record sum to become its professional. Gene was making hay while his star shone, but within a year his star was definitely on the wane. He perceived it himself early in 1923, when he had attempted to add the British Open to his list of conquests. At Troon he had followed a 75 with an 85 played in a fierce gale, and had failed to qualify. He did succeed in holding his P.G.A. crown at Pelham, but that was the one tournament in which he hit the ball with the flaming confidence he had exhibited the year before.

After his second P.G.A. victory, Sarazen did not go into total eclipse. He won respectable chunks of the purse money on the tournament circuit, bobbing up occasionally in first place. But his golf, which had been so consistently topnotch in 1922, was now hot, cold, and in-between. There were mornings when the tidy, olive-skinned campaigner was putting for birdies on fifteen or more of the eighteen greens, but it was not unlike him to follow such a round with a highly exasperating struggle to keep his drives straight and his approaches out of the hazards. Gene had lost his groove. When he had won his first important tournaments, he hadn't been bothered by how he got his pars as long as he got them. He was a natural swinger. When he was hitting the ball, he was hitting the ball, and that was that. When he was off, well, he kept practicing until the feel and the timing came back. But after his banner season in '22, Gene had been visited by the idea that he could improve his game if he took the time to study it. He had run into the usual troubles that beset a person who tears down something he has been doing naturally, almost instinctively. Horton Smith, for another, was not content to leave well enough alone after his record-breaking campaign in 1929. Bill Mehlhorn had a few shots he didn't have, Horton thought. In trying to acquire these strokes, Horton had lost that first flawless groove and never entirely recaptured it. Dissection can be a very dangerous process. Sometimes the dissector comes out of it more skilled than before. Sometimes he doesn't.

Gene Sarazen was in midstream and changing horses every week. He couldn't put his old swing back together again and he couldn't manufacture a swing that would give

Gene Sarazen's admirers hoist the new champion to their shoulders. The unknown young professional captured the 1922 Open by playing a sturdy 68 on the nerve-wracking final round. Gene finished early, and his 288 withstood all challenges.

him equally sound results. One week he would think he had himself all straightened out—why hadn't he thought of taking the club back with the *right* hand before?—and then, wham! he would run into a 78 on which it seemed a physical impossibility to put the ball within forty feet of his target. The next week it was the grip—the change from the interlocking to the Vardon—but that wasn't it either. He became involved in other men's theories. Jock Hutchison had played many exhibitions with Gene, and Jock, who prided himself on his exhaustive knowledge of theory, enthusiastically mixed Gene up a little more. Other fine shot-makers, long-armed and almost a foot taller than Gene, made sincere efforts to help the appealing, impatient young man, but in their zeal to be the doctor, they overlooked the fact that the patient was of a quite dissimilar physique and that the cure did not necessarily lie in imitating their style of play. It was a slow, tedious crawl, and it led down many blind alleys on the way, but Sarazen, after four years of worry, at length made his way out of his slump. There was a conscious casualness to the swing he settled for. Gene held his hands in close to his body, brought the club back a little flatter than taller men with a longer hitting arc, threw his right side furiously into the shot, and let himself take a step forward or a step to the side if he felt like it at the finish. The informality of this finish, plus the calculated abandon with which Gene stepped up to his shot once he had made up his mind how he was going to play it, was a striking contrast to the super-deliberate, super-refined methods most of the pros were striving to master. Gene's wasn't the better style. But it was better for him. Then he began to work on his grip—making sure that it did not slip or become unglued at the top of the backswing—and that really helped.

By the late Twenties, Sarazen was again a factor in the major tournaments as well as in the subsidiary outings. In the 1930 U.S. Open, he was back in the ruck, tied for 28th, but with that single exception, he was a steady contender in both the U.S. and British Opens. He hadn't won, though, and now that he was striking the ball with conviction again, Gene began to speculate on the idea that there might be some other ingredient in that curious amalgam, the winning golfer, he might have overlooked. Sarazen had always felt that his size had militated against him, and this led him to investigate the possibilities of counteracting his physical limitations by experimenting with the *equipment* a golfer used. In 1931 he discovered the reminder-grip on some clubs he saw lying around a Wilson storehouse. Wilson had never used the grip. Gene tried it, liked it, and adopted it for his own sticks. The next year he struck on a far more valuable idea. Gene had never thoroughly conquered his fear of traps, and trap shots in many tournaments are the difference between first and second place. No niblick would ever be disaster-proof, but wasn't it feasible to evolve some variation on the conventional niblick that would cut down the percentage of error? During the winter of 1932, he worked out his idea in a machine-shop in Florida and fashioned the club that later became known as the sand-iron or the dynamiter or blaster or sand-wedge. Using this new heavy-soled, flanged sand-iron, Gene became the most proficient trap-player in the game almost overnight. To demonstrate to his fellow pros the wizardry he could wield with his new club, he used to invite them to place a batch of balls anywhere in a trap and bet that he could blast them all within ten feet of the pin—including the balls the pros always buried in the sloping back edge of the trap. The faithful Daniels, of course, made the chief contribution to Gene's victory in the British Open a few months later, but it should be noted that when Gene's years of drought were at last ended, he was carrying a sand-iron in his bag.

In the last week of June, a short time after he had returned to the States after his glorious gallop at Prince's, Gene took himself to Long Island to tune up on the Fresh Meadow course, the site of the Open. Fresh Meadow was a "second-shot course"—plenty of room to clout a drive but plenty of trouble around the greens. Gene had at one time been the pro at Fresh Meadow, and in the hundreds of informal rounds he had played over it, he had never been able to break 67. He had a wholesome respect for its pits and pitfalls; it was his contention that a topflight golfer could, with no trouble at all, drop five strokes to par over the course of nine holes. Perhaps Gene had too much respect for Fresh Meadow. Warming up in practice rounds with Bobby Jones on the Monday and Wednesday before the Open, he revealed to Bobby that he planned to play cautiously to the greens, to shoot for the openings rather than for the pins, to be a little short, if anything. Gene's set strategy surprised Bobby. Gene was best when he banged, Bobby felt, but if Gene wanted to play this one close to his vest, it was his business. Had the information been generally circulated that Gene was going to forsake his old give-it-everything tactics, a great many other golf enthusiasts would have shared Jones' surprise. Gene had admitted several times that he was temperamentally unsuited to playing cute golf, and on top of this he had intimated that now that he had built up a new confidence in his bunker play, there was one less reason for him to play conservatively. Why be frightened about getting into traps when you knew you could get out of them? Three years later in the Open at Oakmont, Sam Parks, Jr., using the same tactics that Sarazen had adumbrated to Jones, walked off with the championship, but Oakmont was a much different physical problem than Fresh Meadow, to begin with, and Parks was no Sarazen.

Gene's first cautious round gave him a 74, his second, a 76. Tidiness around the greens was the only thing that saved him from soaring higher. Nevertheless, he persisted with his plan on the third round until he found he had a 3 on the ninth for a 38 out. That was enough of that. He played his 7-iron boldly for the pin, rolled in his 12-foot putt for a 2, and threw caution to the winds. He began to lash his woods with his normal fury. He hit his irons extra hard, punching a 6-iron, for example, where a 5-iron looked like the shot, or even a 4. On the greens he maintained that nice easy stroke that had kept him alive during his first two rounds. The result was a 32 on the second nine, which gave Gene a 70 for the round and put him back in the running. The leaders had been finding Fresh Meadow obstinate. Bobby Cruickshank was the only contender who beat 70 on the third round, and most of the scores were high. Philip Perkins, the former

Sarazen drives off the first tee at Fresh Meadow. Ten years after his victory at Skokie, Gene came back to win his second United States Open. Again success rested on a par-shattering finish, a 66 that obliterated all records for a final round of the Open. Gene won by playing the last 28 holes in 100 strokes.

English amateur who had become an American pro, had used up 74 strokes on his third round, and his 219, the low total at the three-quarter mark, was only one better than Sarazen's. Cruickshank was another stroke behind.

Perkins played a 70 on his last round—289. Cruickshank added a 68 to his morning 69—289. Many holes before he knew the exact score he needed to win—a 68—Sarazen realized that he would have to clip several strokes off par. Attacking on every shot, he went out in 32—4-5-3 2-5-3 4-4-2. He kept pushing himself—4-4-3 4-3-3. Going to the 70th he was 7 under even 4s. Three stiff holes lay ahead—a 5 that was not a birdie hole, a tricky 4, and a long 4. One error he was determined he would avoid: he wasn't going to try to outsmart the topography. He kept hitting the ball hard and was rewarded with three firm pars and a wonderful 66.

Ten years after he had first astonished the golfing world at Skokie, Gene Sarazen had come back to win his second U.S. Open with the most inspired charge ever unleashed in the championship: He had played the last twenty-eight holes in an even 100 strokes.

Gene Sarazen had won two national championships in 1932. He was not destined to win another. Three times he came painfully close, once in Britain, twice at home.

The year that Shute and Wood tied at St. Andrews—1933—Sarazen was only a stroke behind. He played far and away the best golf in the field. Ironically, the great bunker-player kicked it away in the bunkers—in two, to be specific, Hill and Hell. Gene had made no mistakes of consequence on his second round until he buried his tee shot on the short eleventh in the sidewall of Hill, a deep pit to the left of the green. He clambered into Hill and braced himself for an explosion shot. He took a terrific cut at the sand behind the ball and succeeded only in dislodging it. He shoveled his feet into a firm stance, snapped his clubhead into the sand again, and semi-topped the ball; it rolled up the face of the bunker and then back to its original position. Looking up at the lip of the bunker, he shook his club belligerently at it. Gene hadn't bargained for this trouble. His fourth shot was on, sixty feet from the cup. Two putts and a 6. As if it wasn't upsetting enough to report a 6 on a par 3, Gene's count was challenged by the official in charge of marshaling the gallery. The marshal, who had been standing near the green in such a position that he could not see Sarazen in Hill Bunker but only the flailing motion of Gene's club, said that he had seen Sarazen take seven shots on the hole. Gene counted them again. He was certain it was 6 and he turned for corroboration to the person whose job it was to know, the official scorer. She happened to be a former Scottish Ladies Champion. She had counted 6. The marshal, who was technically outside his province now, insisted it was 7. He had seen Sarazen take four to get out of the bunker: the first shot from the buried lie, the second shot up the face and down again, that wild swing with his club, and . . . That was no wild swing, Sarazen interrupted. He had simply shaken his club at the lip in that conventional threatening gesture, the way a woman shakes a rolling pin at her husband. The marshal was sorry, but he had counted 7, and advised Sarazen that he would so report to the Championship Committee. Even with this black cloud weighing on his spirits, and a 6 (but not a 7) on his card, Sarazen kept control of his concentration and finished the round in a par 73. He would be in the thick of the battle on the last day if he was not disqualified. He was instructed that a decision would be made that night.

That evening Sarazen was summoned to the clubhouse of the Royal and Ancient

Golf Club of St. Andrews, the *sanctum sanctorum* of golf. He was shown into a small room where twelve men sat expressionless around a table. Gene was nervous and depressed. The tournament was not what he was worried about. He had won enough of them. But should these men—the Championship Committee—see fit to accept the report of the marshal who had questioned Sarazen's word and disqualify him from the tournament, they would be placing a black mark beside the name of Sarazen, and Gene valued his good name above everything. He was asked to give his side of the story. He was brief. He had taken six shots. The official scorer had counted six shots. That was the story. He asked to be excused, if that was all they wanted of him.

The marshal's protest was thrown out by the committee, but after his ordeal that night, it was an unstrung golfer who started out on the final thirty-six of the Open. Once on the course, warming to the task at hand, Sarazen was able to keep the unpleasant incident far enough at the back of his mind so that it did not interfere with his playing. He had a 73 on his morning round and was percolating along in fine fashion in the afternoon until he came to the 68th hole, the Long Hole. His drive was out there nicely. He decided to go for his birdie, to take the direct line toward the green over Hell Bunker and put himself in position for a little pitch and a putt for his birdie. Considering the closeness of the championship and the penalty if the gamble did not come off, it was perhaps an error in judgment. It did seem so, of course, when Sarazen's brassie failed to carry Hell Bunker and the ball thudded into the hazard. It took him two to get out, and when he reached the green, he three-putted. It was an 8. He pulled himself together once again and dashed down the last four holes, but the damage had been done.

It was a tough championship to lose by one stroke.

Gene lost by one stroke to Olin Dutra in the 1934 Open at Merion. One bad hole cost him the title, the 65th. On this hole, the eleventh, the Baffling Brook cuts across the fairway from right to left and then twists sharply back to the right and almost encircles the green. Both the drive and the approach take some figuring out. On the third round Sarazen had played an iron off the tee safely down the fast fairway and punched his approach safely onto the promontory green. He decided to play the hole the same way on his final round. Something went drastically wrong with his tee shot. The ball curved far to the left in a roundhouse hook and bounded into the Baffling Brook. He lifted and then played his third into a bunker to the left of the green. His fourth skidded over the green, and it took him another three to get down. Sarazen's 7 on that short par 4 simply left him too much to do.

Sarazen provided a great thrill on the last round of the Open six years later when he roared down the last nine at Canterbury in 34 to tie with Lawson Little. But in the playoff the young man shot a 70, and this was too good for Gene, three strokes too good.

The veteran's greatest victory in his later years came in the second Masters tournament at the Augusta National in 1935. That week Gene played some of the best golf of his career. Over the testing layout designed by Jones and MacKenzie, Gene totaled 271 for his four warmup rounds. He had not taken a 6 during this streak, and he didn't take a 6 for the four rounds of the tournament, yet, with four holes to go, despite a 68, a 71, a 73, and fourteen adequate holes on his last round, Gene seemed fated to be second. Craig Wood had also been on his game, very much on his game, and his final round of 73, after 69-72-68, had given him a total of 282. Wood's score was relayed to Sarazen as Gene stood on the fifteenth tee. He figured it out. To tie, he would have to play birdies on three of the last four holes.

The fifteenth at Augusta—then 485 yards long, now 525—is not a hard hole to birdie, and it is also pretty easy to wind up with a 6 on it. It all depends on the second shot. Unless the wind is unfavorable, the golfer who belts a long drive can reach the green with his second, and the green will hold a wood. But the golfer who is going for his birdie must make sure to be up or else he is in the soup—the pond Jones and MacKenzie created by widening the brook before the green. Gene was out 250 yards on his drive, on the right-hand side of the fairway. He inspected his close lie and selected a 4-wood. He took a quick look over the hill to the distant green, and then rode into the ball. It shot up like a streak and fled for the green. The spectators, grouped in a crescent around the back edge of the green, saw the ball coming. It was a good-looking shot. It would carry the water hazard with yards to spare and give Gene a very useful birdie. They saw the ball alight on the front section of the green and pop off the turf on a line for the pin. Say, Gene would have a crack for an eagle! And then they watched the ball slow down to a walk and roll dead for the hole, as if the cup were a magnet. The ball rolled straight into the cup. Gene had holed that 235-yard spoon shot for a deuce, a double-eagle! With a single shot—one of the most sensational ever played in tournament golf, if not *the* most sensational—Gene had, in effect, made the three birdies he needed on one hole. He still had to play the last three holes in par to tie with Wood, but after the double-eagle, he felt he was in. It had been a well-played shot, but well-played shots don't drop in the cup unless a golfer is playing in luck, and Gene interpreted this as a sign that he was meant to win. Whenever Sarazen got the idea in his head that he was the chosen man, he could usually do what had to be done. He played three sound pars for his 282. The next day he went out and put together a 71 and a 73 to win the playoff from Wood by five strokes.

Whether he was winning or losing, coming close or straggling back in the pack, Gene Sarazen has always been an enchanting player to watch and one of sport's most attractive personalities. After his victory at Fresh Meadow, although he was only thirty at the time, in the mind of the golfing public Sarazen was an oldtimer, along with Hagen a glorious survival of the Happy Twenties. Until Walter began to slip badly after the '36 Open and his tournament appearances became increasingly rare and decreasingly serious, Gene and Walter, with the occasional addition of cryptic Tommy Armour, formed the romantic old guard. The men who had watched them scale the heights in the Twenties found that they could not get as excited about the newer stars. They pointed out their heroes to their sons, told them to watch how Walter cut that one out of the rough and how Tommy played that spoon from the trap. They took an intense pride in Gene's scoring—"See, Gene's still right up there with the boys." The sons, while not as blind to the merits of the new champions, discovered that the old men knew what they were talking about for once. There was no getting away from it—the old boys executed their shots with an *éclat* few of the new scoring machines could approach; the old boys had golf in them right down to their fingertips.

For their part, the veterans relished the roles in which they were cast. When they were on their game, and putting, they could still give the young pups a lesson or two. When they were out of the running, there was nothing to fret about and a lot of fun to be had. Gene, who was about ten years younger than Walter, used to give him the grand-old-man treatment, and Walter retaliated with some amusing gags, like sending a rocking chair out to Sarazen as he staggered down the final nine holes of the 1933 Open. In many ways the two great professionals were as unlike as Asia and Europe, but they shared an equally realistic philosophy about the twentieth century, and they had a genuine affection and respect for each other.

And then it was only Gene. Until the advent of Bobby Locke, he was the only one of the crowd who regularly wore knickers. You could spot him two fairways away—the slicked dark-brown hair, the olive complexion so deeply tanned that there seemed to be some purple in it, the knickers, usually some off-shade of brown, the complementary sweater and socks, the quick step away from his ball almost before he had slapped himself into his followthrough. And he could still play golf. The new champions were longer off the tees and could out-putt him, but when it came to hitting one shot and then another shot and another shot, there was not much to choose between Sarazen and the Sneads and the Nelsons and the Hogans.

Sarazen had ordered his life wisely. When he had set out to be a golfer, the boy from Harrison, New York, was thinking in terms of a lifetime career. Golf was a game, but it was always for Gene a full profession and a continuous business. Success, he appreciated, depended on being a winner, and from the beginning he believed implicitly in his ability to win. After Skokie one person summed up Sarazen's credo like this: "All men are created free and equal, and I am one shot better than the rest." He made winning golf do for him what a smash hit does for an actor or a specialized process does for a shoe manufacturer. He cashed in when his irons were hot, and adroitly kept himself a leader in the eyes of the public even in the periods when he was not winning. Gene had an understanding of publicity superior to that of any of his colleagues. There was always some innovation in the Sarazen-model clubs—the reminder-grip, the sand-iron, the 4-wood that he popularized with his double-eagle. He knew the value of dissenting. He once plumped for an 8-inch cup; he criticized the selection of the Ridgewood course for the 1935 Ryder Cup Match; he had qualifying clauses whenever he discussed the heroes of the day. His tours were theatrically sound. His partners were always drawing cards in their own right—Kirkwood, the trick-shot artist; Babe Didrikson, when that colorful all-round phenomenon first turned to golf in 1935; Ed Oliver, immediately after Oliver had been disqualified from tying with Little and Gene in the 1940 Open because he had started out on his last round before it was officially his starting time.

From the people he met through his golf, Sarazen, who absorbs like a Cronkite, picked up a solid education that he has supplemented by extensive travel. He is still going strong today. During the winter he is the golf director at Marco Island, in Florida. The rest of the year he lives with his wife at a farm in New London, New Hampshire, near their married daughter and her family. He likes the life of the country squire. It is what he has always worked for: the strong sense of security, the privilege of picking his friends and associates. He is a remarkably honest person. His manner is as direct as a left jab. In conversation he is lively and very entertaining. He is a voracious acquirer. If he hears a phrase or an idea he likes, he adopts it instantly. His natural intelligence makes him at home in all strata of society.

Gene Sarazen has come a long, long way. Golf has given him a very great deal, but it works both ways. Gene has also given golf a very great deal.

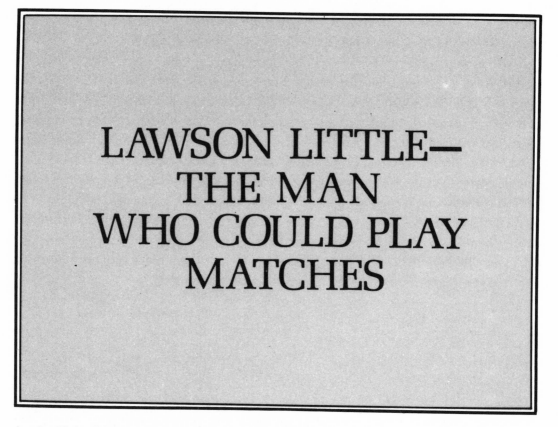

LAWSON LITTLE—
THE MAN
WHO COULD PLAY
MATCHES

As the United States Open Champion, Johnny Goodman could not very well have been left off the Walker Cup team that was selected to oppose the British at St. Andrews in May 1934. Goodman was not only on the team, but it was almost a foregone conclusion that, barring a complete reversal of form, he would be accorded the number-one post. Johnny was playing gleaming good golf, and compared to some earlier Walker Cup personnel, his team mates were not a distinguished group. They were competent amateurs, each of whom had done one or two things in the previous eighteen months, or earlier, which had lifted him a rank higher perhaps than the host of other competent amateurs. Max Marston's place on the 1934 team depended almost solely on his play at Kenwood in the 1933 Amateur, when Max briefly flashed his old form and reached the final. George Dunlap, the perennial Pinehurst paragon who had won at Kenwood, was, of course, on the club. In addition to Dunlap, there were three other holdovers from 1932: Francis Ouimet, returning as captain; Jack Westland; and Gus Moreland, the lean, graceful Texan who continued to play amazing golf in the sectional tournaments and to flop annually in the Amateur. The side was rounded out by one oldtimer, Chandler Egan, and two youngsters, Johnny Fischer and Lawson Little. The choice of Egan, then a full fifty years old, was largely sentimental and conditioned by the fact that a comparable graybeard, the Honorable Michael Scott, had automatically earned himself a place on the British side by his extraordinary triumph in the British Amateur at the age of fifty-five. Fischer, a Michigan law student, had lasted only one round at Kenwood, but his qualifying mark of 141 had broken the old record of 142, which he had equaled the year before at Five Farms. Little was a bull-necked slugger from Stanford University who had looked like a golfer of promise when he was eighteen and, in the minds of not a few authorities, would probably continue to look like a golfer of promise until he was eighty.

Of all the Walker Cuppers, Little unquestionably had the least impressive over-all record. He had appeared in the Amateur on five occasions. At Pebble Beach in '29, he had beaten Goodman in the second round, 2 and 1, in the afternoon following Johnny's stunning upset victory over the great Bobby. He had played a lot of golf in his third-round match against Ouimet, and while he eventually lost on the 36th green, he had made old Francis drop a 35-footer for a birdie to keep out of extra holes. At Merion in '30, Little had given a further demonstration of his staying powers by beating Doc Willing in twenty holes, but Gene Homans took him into camp in the second round, 4 and 2. The next year at Beverly, he failed to qualify. In '32 at Five Farms, he was defeated quite roundly by Fischer in his very first match. Just when most golf critics were ready to give up on him, Lawson finally came to life at Kenwood and showed that he could do something more than hit a golf ball a country mile. He made his way into the third round for the first time in four years and there outgeneraled Sandy Somerville in a thriller that went to the 35th green. Dunlap ended his march in the semis, 4 and 3. It was the resourcefulness of his play against Somerville that had won Lawson his place on the Walker Cup squad, plus the dearth of outstanding amateurs in a decade when most of the talented young men were turning professional for the right good reason that they could not afford to play non-profit-making golf. Lawson was not a bad golfer, mind you, but he certainly had given no forenotice of the wonders he would perform once he reached Scotland in the spring of '34.

In the practice rounds at St. Andrews before the international match, Lawson turned in one good score after another, and what was more important, he was not slugging and scrambling but playing a succession of fine golf shots. At Kenwood his iron-play, though effective from the standpoint of results, had been anything but a delight to watch. When he had a 5-iron to play, for example, he habitually took one or two clubs less and pressed his shot with the exaggerated inside-outside swing young golfers were in the habit of adopting to gain that vain distinction, extra distance. He played his irons off his right foot, a style that can produce shots of beeline accuracy and also some frightening errors when a player's timing slips the merest fraction. After Kenwood, Little had taken a series of lessons in iron-play from Tommy Armour, and for the first time began to look like a first-class golfer once he had an iron in his hands. Lawson's woods had always been tremendous, but at St. Andrews he appeared to have absolute control over where they were going. He was not only hitting them long and straight but he was dropping them on the particular patch of the fairway he had selected as the best spot from which to play his second. Ouimet was properly delighted with the young man's form. He placed him with Goodman in the leadoff foursome and in second position, the notch below Goodman, for the singles. Goodman and Little won their foursome from Wethered and Tolley 8 and 6, and Little crushed Tolley 6 and 5 in their singles match. Lawson was immense against Tolley, outdriving the famous long-hitter by ten to twenty yards and outplaying him in every department. As they shook hands after the match, one Scottish admirer of Little's turned to a friend and winked, "Tolley's thanking the lad for the lesson."

Lawson's golf had such a convincing air about it that when the bookmakers offered him at 14 to 1 in the Amateur at Prestwick, many Scots and Englishmen who had watched the Walker Match could not resist buying a little of Lawson. It proved to be just about the best investment many of them would ever make in their lives. In his seven 18-hole matches on his way to the final, Lawson was in danger only once. In the semi-finals, Leslie Garnett stood firm all the way, and 1 down to the pulverizer on the 18th proceeded to hole a lengthy putt for a win. Lawson, showing no signs of discomfiture, finished Garnett on the 19th. Meanwhile, as Lawson was winning his one scrap with Garnett and coasting in his other matches, in the other half of the draw great fratricide was going on, Americans against Americans, Scots against Scots. Moreland, for illustration, put out Ouimet. Then Fischer put out Moreland. Jock McLean, a Scottish star who would later meet Fischer in the final of the 1936 U.S. Amateur, then stopped Johnny's bid by playing seventeen holes in 2 under 4s. In the sixth round McLean met his countryman, thirty-year-old James Wallace, and became the fourth Walker Cupper—Egan, Tolley, and Eric Fiddian had preceded him—to fall before the straight shooting of the unimposing and unheralded carpenter from Troon. In the semis, Wallace accounted for his fifth Walker Cupper, George Dunlap, 3 and 1. Little was favored over Wallace in the final but he was expected to have no walkover. Wallace had been steady as sin in going through by far the sterner half of the draw, and in his match with Dunlap he had been 3 under 4s for the seventeen holes of the match.

A half hour before he and Wallace were scheduled to begin the 36-hole final, Lawson spread out his equipment on the practice area. The shafts of his clubs felt light in his hands and the clubheads seemed to be loaded with power. He was hitting his shots exactly the way he wanted to, and began to watch anxiously for the signal to proceed to the first tee so that he could get to work on Wallace while he was in that mood where hitting a golf ball seems the simplest thing in the world. He chafed at the momentary delay on the first tee as the formalities were taken care of. He walloped his opening drive far down the fairway and walked after it with, for Lawson, unusual speed.

Lawson's par was good for a win on the first hole when Wallace nervously three-putted. After they had halved the second in 3's, Lawson tied together two terrific woods on the long Cardinal and dropped a 34-foot putt for an eagle. The unlucky Wallace had played a birdie. Now 2 up, the burly Californian moved quickly to the fourth tee. He was in a hurry. There was no knowing how long this hot streak would last, and he wanted to play each shot as fast as he could and win as many holes as possible before he cooled off. He won the fourth, the fifth, and the sixth, this last with another breathtaking putt. He walked a little slower after this but he didn't cool off. He followed his 33 out with a 33 in for a 66. (Since Little's 66 was made in match and not in stroke play, Mac Smith's 71 still stood as the official record for Prestwick.) In the face of this ruthless golf—Little had plucked one eagle, four birdies, and had barely missed a half-dozen other birdies—poor Wallace never had a chance to get back into the match. The wrinkled Scot walked in to lunch bewildered and *12 down*.

When play was resumed, Little continued his brutal attack. On the first hole he dropped a 36-foot putt for a 3, added still another hole with still another birdie on the fourth, and wound up the slaughter on the fifth—*14 and 13*.

Hundreds of Scottish fans arriving at Prestwick to take in the afternoon portion of the final were astonished to find that all the golf that was going to be played that day had already been played. Their astonishment mounted when they were informed of what Little had done—played the 23 holes in *ten under 4s* with *twelve 3s* on a card that read like this:

		OUT				IN		
(Approximated)	Par	435	434	445—36	535	544	444—38—74
	Little	433	433	544—33	435	434	343—33—66
(Approximated)	Par	435	43				
	Little	334	33				

If Little had given Wallace half a stroke a hole, he would still have been 3 up!

In recent American history there have been frequent examples of young men and women of talent, theatrical or athletic for the most part, who first became known to their countrymen by their successes in Europe—on Wimbledon's center court, in Olympic competition, in the tiny night clubs of Paris, in the opera houses of Germany and Italy, and on the waters of the Thames at Henley. American authorities who scarcely knew-them-when cannot wait to pass judgment on the young men and women returning home with European reputations. In 1934 American golf critics wanted to see this Lawson Little and find out for themselves if he had played way over his head in Scotland or if he was really the amateur of the decade who had suddenly discovered the full range of his powers. In the 1934 Amateur, at The Country Club in Brookline, Little provided the skeptics with a very definite answer.

The face of the Amateur was lifted once again in 1934. The sectional qualifying tests had made the Amateur seem thoroughly *national*, and in 1934 the U.S.G.A. decided to grant even more importance to these sectional preliminaries. The 188 golfers who succeeded in gaining one of the varying number of positions allotted to the twenty-four districts from New England to Hawaii would *not* have to qualify for the match-play rounds once they unpacked at the championship proper. All 188 of these sectional qualifiers would enter directly into the match play. Six rounds of eighteen-hole matches plus two rounds of thirty-six—it was bound to be a battle-royal and it would not be in the least surprising if by the time the quarter-finals were reached, the survivors would be golfers whose names would ring no bells even for the enthusiasts who could reel off the middle initial of every golfer who had ever succeeded in winning a first-round match in the Amateur.

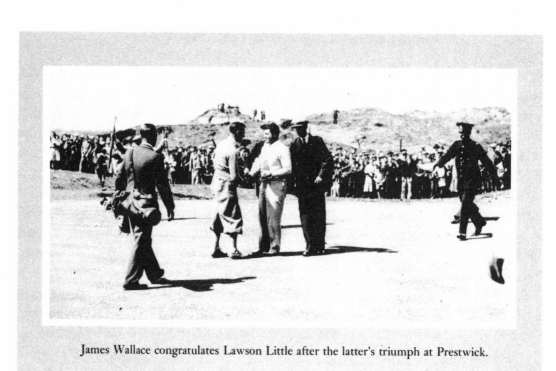

James Wallace congratulates Lawson Little after the latter's triumph at Prestwick.

The new Amateur was not the kind of a tournament that favors the favorites. The big names were ousted early. In the first round Ouimet fell before an eighteen-year-old boy from Detroit with the vaguely familiar name of Bobby Jones. Goodman drew a bye in the first round, but in his first match he was eliminated on the 19th by Bobby Jacobson, a sixteen-year-older. The defending champion, George Dunlap, met his downfall in the third round at the hands of Willie Turnesa, the youngest member of that prolific golfing tribe. In the quarter-finals the last of the ex-champions, Chick Evans, who had started his Amateur campaigning a full quarter of a century before, was put out by Don Armstrong of Illinois.

All of the favorites had found the going too hard—all of the favorites but Lawson Little. Round by round the burly one advanced. His scores were not spectacular but there was a rock-bound quality to his golf. His opponents could find no crevices, and Little wore them down, one by one, by the fifteenth or sixteenth green. In the quarter-finals against Willie Turnesa, Lawson was called on to play sub-par golf to wrest the advantage away from a young man who had been striking the ball as well as anyone at Brookline. Lawson was equal to it. A 34 out gave him a three-hole lead, and he protected it by sticking even with par on the in-nine until the holes ran out for Willie on the sixteenth. He had a 73 in the morning against his semi-final opponent, Don Armstrong, and staved off Armstrong's rush in the afternoon by staying one shot under par until he had the match won 4 and 3. Lawson's physique was proving itself to be an invaluable asset. He was scoring better and better as the killing tournament progressed, and would probably carry a good reserve with him into the final.

While Lawson was taking care of Armstrong, two young friends from Texas, Dave "Spec" Goldman and Reynolds Smith, were battling it out in the other semi to

244

determine which of them would have the honor of facing the British Amateur Champion in the final. Goldman, a metal-lathe worker, and Smith, a clerk for an oil company, had qualified together at Dallas. They had traveled to the Amateur together, hooking a free plane ride as far as Cleveland and then hitchhiking the rest of the way. In Boston they had found quarters in a rooming house on Beacon Street and had spent their evenings wondering if their joint fund, forty dollars, would take care of their expenses if they kept winning their matches. Of the two, Smith looked to be the crisper golfer. A pleasant fellow with a face like Mickey Cochrane's, Smith had established a record for winning extra-hole matches on his pull toward the semi-final. In the second round he beat Billy Howell on the 19th with a birdie. He won his next match from Ernest Caldwell on the 20th, also with a birdie. In the fourth round against Somerville, Reynolds drilled a 3-iron three feet from the pin on the 19th to win that one. Winfield Day then took him to the 20th before Smith came up with yet another bird. Right after this he went into overtime against Ernest Pieper, and on the twenty-third hole the bantam-sized Texan won his *fifth consecutive extra-hole match*. When the two roommates, Smith and Goldman, met in the semis, Smith's energy was about spent. Neither of them played particularly bright golf, and Goldman, the steadier golfer that day, accounted for his more colorful sidekick, 4 and 2.

Spec Goldman played better in the final but it made little difference. Lawson was in one of those not-to-be-trifled-with moods of his, as he had been against Wallace at Prestwick. Goldman was 5 down at noon to Little's 69, and did very well to carry the match to the 29th green. Over that distance Lawson was 3 below par, bagged six birdies, was in only one bunker, and did not three-putt a green.

The double Amateur Champion had shown himself to be a golfer with great confidence in his ability to perform and with great ability to perform. Off the tees he was overpoweringly long, this barrel-chested, broad-shouldered young man, this "Andalusian yearling bull," as Bob Davis described him. Little's was a deceptive build. Until you actually stood beside him and discovered that Lawson was only of average height, you would have wagered that he stood at least two inches over six feet. He was a shut-faced hitter, but his control of his length was something that Craig Wood or Jimmy Thomson and the other bombers of the professional brigade had reason to envy. His iron-play was strong and steady now, and he had developed, for a man who had once built his game on distance, a wonderful touch around and on the greens. Jones, who had looked Lawson over at Brookline, thought that he was the equal of Hagen when it came to canning the 12-footers for birdies.

Beyond this, Lawson Little was blessed with a majestic competitive temperament, a fine fusion of phlegm and fire. The fire burned at all times and his opponents felt the heat, but at no time in a match did Lawson allow the fire to show through. He took an inordinate amount of time over his shots, and acted as if there were no one on the course but Lawson Little. If you were a fan of Lawson's, you called him a painstaking craftsman who wanted to leave nothing to chance; if his personality nettled you, you called him a maddeningly slow player. He walked down the fairways swinging his arms emphatically, with his large head thrust forward, concentrating fiercely, his forehead serrated in a scowl, a brooding dullness in his eyes, no expression whatsoever around his tight mouth. A gallery to Lawson was an enemy, not a friend—a collection of people who might get in his way and mar his concentration and, if he wasn't careful, influence the progress of the match. Lawson wasn't trying to make friends, he was trying to win, and when a spectator or group of spectators bothered him, he could be as surly as a New York waiter. Much as they respected the new champion's ability, most golf fans found it impossible to take him into their hearts.

Lawson's background went a long way in explaining his attitude and his manner. The son of a colonel in the Medical Corps of the Army, he had grown up in a military environment at bases in the States and in China and had acquired some of the less attractive characteristics of that way of life: a humorless seriousness about himself, an inability to relax with "outsiders," a bearing that was at all times rigid and could be quite condescending on occasion. (Later, when Lawson turned professional, he became a much more regular fellow, though he never could be accused of geniality. The verdict of his colleagues was that he was a nice enough guy, and after his fourth martini a very nice guy.) His boyhood environment undoubtedly assisted Little in developing many of his praiseworthy traits: an unshakable self-reliance, a furious will to combat, physical and mental endurance. Lawson thought of a golf course as a battlefield, or, rather, as eighteen battlefields. Before opening fire, he surveyed each of these battlefields with infinite attention to detail. In his mind he marked the position on each hole where each shot should be played. He recorded the facts about each green, with special emphasis on the greens of the one-shotters. He reviewed his eighteen battlefields, and selecting five or six holes where the risk was at a minimum and the possibility at the maximum, charted these holes for birdies. The secret of good golf, he believed, was good brains. "It's all mental," he once remarked. "The man who doesn't plan out every shot to the very top of his capacity for thought can't attain championship form. I say this without any reservations whatsoever. It is impossible to outplay an opponent you can't outthink."

In the spring of 1935 Little went to Britain to defend his title at Lytham St. Annes. A course that rewards long drives and forcing iron-play, Lytham should have been ideal for Little, but the fact of the matter is that Lawson never quite got going in the steamroller style he had evinced at Prestwick the year before. He was lucky not to get beaten in his first-round match. Lawson played a ragged 80, but his opponent, T. H. Parker, conveniently played a slightly worse round, and Lawson won out on the eighteenth green. After that scare, Little began to control his matches with more of the authority one had come to expect of him. While he played some very beatable golf en route to the final, none of his opponents was able to take full advantage of his lapses, and Little could always summon a timely shot to break the back of their belated rallies. Despite the lackluster quality of his play, he was an odds-on favorite to take the final from Dr. William Tweddell and to take it by 7 and 6, 8 and 7, or some similarly secure margin.

Dr. Tweddell had won the British Amateur in 1927. He was a consistent low-70s

Lawson Little in 1935, when that bull-like young man from California completely dominated the amateur field. That season Little took both the British and the United States Amateur Championships for the second consecutive year. In 1936, the year he turned pro, Lawson failed to qualify for the Open.

shooter although, at first glance, he looked like a golfer who would have his work cut out to break 85. His arm action was stiff, and on his irons especially he aimed far to the right of his target and allowed for lots of draw. In 1935 he was playing hardly any tournament golf and might not have entered the Amateur had the week of the championship not coincided with the vacation the doctor's doctor had ordered him to take. Tweddell lost to Little, but it is difficult not to think of him as the hero of their exciting match.

Little started off as if he were going to make even shorter work of the doctor than he had of Wallace. He carried off three of the first four holes by dint of some remarkable iron shots into the wind, and would have taken the fifth hole had he gotten the breaks on a short putt. And then Tweddell turned around and made it a match. He refused to let the Californian go more than 4 up on him and started hacking away at Little's lead with his old wooden putter. At lunch, though he had scored an excellent 73 in the gusty morning, Little had only his original margin of three holes. In the afternoon Tweddell won the first two holes on Little's errors and was on the verge of making it three in a row when he failed for the first time to sink a holeable putt. With his margin reduced to one hole, Little's expression changed not the slightest whit, but he dug in with increased determination and by the 26th hole (the eighth of the afternoon) he had regained his three-hole margin. Tweddell then launched a brilliant counter-attack. He carried off the 27th with a birdie 2, and after halving the 28th, took the 29th with another birdie and squared the match on the 30th, a difficult short hole, with a fighting 3. On the 31st, Tweddell had a 12-footer for a win and 1 up, but his putt died on the edge of the cup. Still outwardly unconcerned by the surprising fight Tweddell was putting up, Little called on himself for everything he had. He won the 32nd and the 33rd to go 2 up with three holes to play, and once again set himself up in what seemed an invulnerable position. However, he had to hole from eighteen feet to get a half on the 34th, and he lost the 35th when Tweddell exploded from a bunker and sank a long one for a 4. Tweddell could square the match if he took the 36th.

The doctor made a brave attempt. He had his par 4 all the way, but when Lawson played a courageous recovery onto the green after pushing his drive into the high rough, Tweddell's chances narrowed down to holing an 18-footer for a 3, and this was something that valor could not do all by itself. Tweddell made a game try, but the putt was wide, and Lawson Little had successfully defended his British crown.

Little arrived at the Cleveland Country Club in early September in fighting trim for the United States Amateur. Behind him was a string of twenty-one consecutive victories in championship matches, and in front, another battle-royal. Two years later the U.S.G.A. reverted to a national qualifying test with the 64 lowest scorers entering the match play, but in 1935 the tournament was patterned after 1934, and the 201 sectional qualifiers constituted the largest field ever to start out in match play in the Amateur. The odds were against Little's going all the way again.

Nineteen-year-old Rufus King, Little's first-round opponent, had won the Grand American Handicap at trap-shooting as a boy of fourteen, but he had attained comparatively little distinction in the few years he had been concentrating on golf. Against the defending champion, young Rufus started off sedately with a par for a half. His birdie halved the second. He won the third with a birdie, the fourth with a birdie, and the fifth with a birdie. A golfer of less mental stamina than Little might have thrown up his hands then and there and comforted himself with the rationalization that no one could blame him for losing an 18-hole match to a kid who was 4 under for the first five. Little placidly went about his business, and at the tenth tee he had drawn level with King. Little went ahead for the first time and, in retrospect, won the match with his birdie on the 580-yard twelfth. The twelfth was as birdie-proof as a par 5 can be. It is a dogleg, but the break to the right occurs about 500 yards down the fairway, and the longest hitters are forced to use three shots to reach the green—two woods down the fairway to the opening and then the tight approach almost at a right angle. Lawson had not charted the twelfth as a birdie hole, but the closeness of the match called for extreme measures and the 330-yard drive he crashed out was all the immediate encouragement he needed to go for his 4. He squared away on the pin with his 4-wood, and imparting a slight cut to the ball, banged it high and hard over the tops of the elms in the angle of the dogleg. The ball came down on the bank a few yards short of the green and kicked back into a trap. Unfazed by this harsh punishment, Little recovered neatly from the trap and holed a fair-sized putt for the birdie he wanted. King continued to play impressively, but Lawson, 2 up on the sixteenth tee, produced another spectacular birdie to win that hole and the match.

After getting by King, Little's pilgrimage to the final was without serious incident until he met up in the semis with his old Walker Cup partner, Johnny Goodman. The Goodman–Little duel was a humdinger. Both men were distinctly on their games. After the morning eighteen, Little held a slight lead, but Goodman cut loose with a dazzling 32, 4 under, over the first nine holes in the afternoon, and the two stalwarts were all square as they walked to the 28th tee. Johnny had made a bold bid for the lead on the 27th, a 148-yarder. He had planted his tee shot close to the cup, but Little had followed with a three-quarter 5-iron to the green and holed for his birdie, and for the second time the rivals had halved the ninth in 2. It was Lawson, however, who came up with the irresistible rush down the stretch. He threw four birdies at Johnny in winning four of the next six holes, and the match, 4 and 3.

Another tough competitor lay ahead of Lawson in the person of Walter Emery, a law student from Oklahoma. Emery won the first three holes of the final and made Lawson fight a hard rear-guard action to gain them back by lunchtime. Taking his time, mapping his shots with massive deliberation, Lawson struck back in the afternoon. By the 28th he had built up a three-hole lead, and only eight remained to be played. Emery wasn't through, though. He took the 29th, the 30th. Only 1 down now, his confidence repaired, Emery meant to keep going. Little would not allow it. He played a 4, a 3, and another 3 to win back the two holes he had lost. On the 520-yard 34th, he smashed a long drive into the teeth of the wind, smashed a spoon all the way to the green, and holed an 11-foot putt for an eagle 3 . . . 4 and 2. He was still the champion.

No other golfer has ever done what Lawson Little did in 1934 and 1935: sweep both the British and United States Amateur Championships in two consecutive years. No one else, as a matter of fact, has even come close to this historic double double. From Prestwich to Cleveland, William Lawson Little won *31 consecutive matches* under the rigors of championship play, 25 of them over the eighteen-hole route in which upsets are not uncommon. Thirty-one consecutive match-play victories, and 32 if you count his triumph at St. Andrews against Tolley when the rugged Californian first came into his own. It is one of the few golf records that approaches the Grand Slam in its invulnerability.

Lawson Little had everything a great match-player needed: golf, guts, stamina, a contempt for the breaks, an unquestioning belief in his ability to beat any other amateur golfer. There was something of the strong adaptability of Joe Louis in Lawson Little. He could cope with all types of challengers, all turns of events. He could come from behind and wear down an opponent who had rushed off to an almost forbidding lead. He could be merciless when in front, as poor Jimmy Wallace knew. He could win when he was off-form through fortitude of spirit and a champion's extra-something, that unique capacity for hitting and not missing the blow on which the outcome of a match depended. There was no one like him for counter-punching, taking three birdies on the jaw and losing a lead, shaking it off and sailing right back with three birdies of his own and an eagle for good measure. He had, as he demonstrated most forcibly against Goodman and Emery, a last-ditch reserve that few golfers could begin to match. He was always the aggressor, tirelessly stalking his opponent, measuring him, hitting him where it hurt the most, and finally putting him away.

In 1936 it was time to select another Walker Cup team. Johnny Goodman was on it, and Johnny again played number one, for Lawson Little, the man who could play matches, had turned professional.

THE
TRAGEDY OF
HARRY COOPER

Whenever there are winners, there must be losers. In golf the winner is the man who brings in the lowest score, in stroke play, or who scores lower on more holes than his opponent, in match play. Nine times out of ten, scores are very just bases on which to judge the respective merits of golfers. The sharpshooter who lips five cups one day often finds all the side doors open the next day or the day afterwards. The stroke that is lost when a perfectly played approach kicks into a bunker invariably comes back through the hooked drive that ricochets back onto the fairway, the bellied iron that rolls through a trap, or some other undeserved chunk of luck. The unpredictability of the game is one of its bittersweet charms, and in the end the breaks even up fairly well.

Three of the greatest scorers in the full course of American golf were Macdonald Smith, Leo Diegel, and Harry Cooper. Their scores won them tournaments galore and huge percentages of the prize money. But above and beyond their aptitude for sub-par scoring was the method by which they got their pars and birdies. They were superb shot-makers. Smith and Cooper, according to many critics, deserve to be ranked among the top dozen tee-to-green golfers of all times. Diegel could put his second shots closer to the pins than any other golfer in his day, and he played in an age of giants. They were golfers' golfers, Smith, Diegel, and Cooper, and among them they probably hit as many exquisite shots as any other trio that might be named.

For all his skill, Macdonald Smith never won a national Open championship. Neither did Diegel, nor Cooper. Season after season one of the three was on the brink of victory in a national championship, but they always found a way to lose. In the long run their victorious deeds in the other tournaments have been forgotten and they are remembered by their failures in the Opens. When their names are mentioned, which is all too infrequently, there is almost invariably a shade of sadness in the speaker's voice, the sadness that accompanies names of men who are remembered not as winners but as losers.

There is no knowing the heights Mac Smith might have scaled in major championship play if he had seized his first golden opportunity in 1910. A par on either the 71st or the 72nd would have won the Open for the gauche twenty-year-old boy, but he went one over on each hole and landed in a tie with his big brother Alex and Johnny McDermott. In the playoff young Mac finished six strokes behind Alex, who had a 71, and two behind Johnny. No one went in for elaborate condolences. Macdonald was just a kid. He had plenty of time. Before he was through he would probably win more national titles than the rest of the Smiths rolled together. Harry Vardon thought so too. Harry had a look at the young man in 1913—another year when Macdonald came close—and pronounced him the best golfer he had seen in America.

Macdonald continued to win his share of the prizes until he went to work in a shipbuilding plant in 1918. After the war was over, he stayed away from golf for a few seasons, but in 1922 or so he drifted back to the game and in no time at all was right back where he had left off—winning the small ones but letting the big ones get away. *Nine times* in all Mac finished within three strokes of the man who won the United States or British Open, yet there was always something that prevented him from winning, a ghastly round early in the tournament that he couldn't make up, an inspired finish by an opponent, or—this is where the heartbreak enters—a tendency to fall utterly to pieces when he was within sight of the promised land.

Why was it that a golfer of Mac Smith's caliber cracked wide open with an 82 on his last round at Prestwick in 1925 when even a 79 would have seen him through? What lay behind that other stupendous collapse, his 6-5-5 finish at Carnoustie in '31, when he was going after pars of 3-4-5? Why was it an impossibility for him to play his best golf in an Open Championship? Was it his nerves? No, not exactly. Mac was less prey to pressure than many players who won major championships with heroic finishes. Was it temperament? No, not that either. Tommy Armour spoke for many when he declared that Mac had "the most ideal golfing temperament Providence ever put in a man's bosom." Could it have been lack of guts in the clinches? The records say otherwise. Mac was a very strong finisher who time after time in the lesser championships uncorked his sub-par streaks precisely when he had to. When he won the Los Angeles Open in '34, to give but one example, he started with a 73 and a 70 and then raced hard with a 69 and a final 68. Was it his personal habits? Mac was a pretty heavy drinker, but it would be as false to construe his fondness for whisky as the reason for his downfalls in the Opens as it would be to claim that his drinking explained why he was off the fairway or green only twice over the seventy-two holes of the 1933 Western. Was he a bad putter? No, he was a good putter and at times a beautiful putter. Then, why did he fail in the Opens year after

Macdonald Smith, perhaps the greatest golfer who never won a major championship. Mac tied for first in the U.S. Open in 1910, losing to his brother Alex in the playoff. Eight times after this initial disappointment, Mac came within three strokes of the winning figure in the British or U.S. Open.

year? Perhaps the best explanation is that Mac was harried in these events by some psychic injury sustained in his first mishaps that, fed by his subsequent failures to produce in the Opens, grew into a complex of such obstinate proportions that the harder he fought to defeat it, the more viciously it defeated him. John Kieran summed it up lucidly with his comment that achieving and not achieving certain things, for Mac Smith and for others, resolves itself into a basic personal equation.

Whereas Mac Smith was the nearest thing to a male counterpart of Joyce Wethered when it came to style, Leo Diegel was not a particularly graceful golfer. Leo hit from a rather flat-footed stance, and there was a sudden lurch to his backswing. But his arms, wrists, and fingers were powerful and sensitive, so beautifully attuned to the close timing of striking a golf ball that Leo could stand on one leg and regularly break 75 for eighteen holes. His contemporaries were sold on The Dieg. When he was on his game, they felt, no one, not Jones or Hagen or Sarazen or anyone else, could hit shots that could compare with Leo's. Willie Macfarlane believed that Leo, if given a week's time, could break the record on any course in the country. Leo struck Bernard Darwin, a sterling judge of golfers, as being "in a way the greatest golfing genius I have ever seen."

Like Mac Smith, Leo labored under a defeatist complex in national championships that prevented him from playing the golf he demonstrated he could play in all other tournaments. He never got over his experience at Inverness in 1920 in the first Open in which he played. With a victory in the Michigan State Open as his top reference, the keen-eyed, nervous, affable young man played three lovely rounds and lay only a stroke behind Vardon, the leader. When Vardon faltered in the gale and the other front-runners also ran into varying degrees of trouble, the gates were open wide for Leo. He had a 37 for his first nine. If he could have played a 39 back, he would have tied with Ray, and a 38, of course, would have won. And then on the fourteenth, with only five more holes to go, the keyed-up youngster succumbed to two upsetting incidents. He missed his drive, though not harmfully, when a spectator coughed as he was starting down from the top of his backswing. Right on top of this, when he was lining up his second and concentrating on hitting a brassie that would make up for what he had lost on his drive, a well-meaning brother professional fought his way through the gallery to tell Leo of some minor misfortune that had befallen Ted Ray. Under the circumstances, Leo could be excused for dashing his brassie to the ground and pleading to be left alone to play his own game, but after that untimely interruption, the young man was done for. He blew to 40 for his last nine, and this was a stroke too many.

With several hardening campaigns behind him in 1925, Diegel was not expected to collapse the way he did as he neared the tape in the Open at Worcester. Leo was 3 under 4s for the first twelve holes of his final round. Even par on the last six holes would have given him a 69 and a total of 287, which would have beaten the field by four full strokes. Ordinarily, Leo could have played six pars standing on one leg, literally. But over those last six holes, and they are not terrors, Leo lost no less than nine strokes to par. He lost four of them on the last hole through an awful 8. (This 8 on the 72nd hole of an Open naturally brings to mind Sam Snead's similar calamity in the 1939 event. The wonder is not so much that Sam took an 8 but that, after this disaster, he was able to come back and win a national championship, the 1946 British Open. Sam deserves a great deal of credit for doing what the other great hard-luck golfers could not do.)

All in all, Diegel came close eight times in the Open in the United States and in Britain. His last, and without a doubt his most pathetic, failure came at St. Andrews in 1933. He had only to play 1-over-par golf on the last five holes and the crown was his for the taking. Leo looked as though he was going to do it this time, for on the 68th he successfully atoned for an error that might have got him down; after leaving himself five feet short with a timid approach putt, he holed that worrisome 5-footer. He should have been all set after that, but on the 69th Leo needed three shots to get down from the edge of the large green. He got by the 70th all right, but on the 71st he three-putted from forty feet. On the last hole he had two putts for a tie with Shute and Wood. He rolled his tricky approach putt nicely up to the hole . . . and missed the short one.

Leo's weakness was his temperament. He was the high-strung, worrying type of player. On a golf course he could never stand still. He wanted to race, race, race. He couldn't wait to hit his next shot, and there are stories about his climbing tee boxes so that he could see the lie from which he would be playing his second. Usually, though, he limited himself to jumping in the air to get his preview. There were days, too, when Leo could talk himself out of winning by persuading himself that he was not in the proper frame of mind. On the other hand, he could talk himself into unbeatable moods. He felt that he was invincible in any tournament staged in Maryland, and since he was, it was entirely inconsiderate of the U.S.G.A. not to have selected some Maryland course as the Open battleground during Leo's heyday.

No one was more aware of Diegel's too-mercurial disposition than Leo himself. After he had lost two Opens he should have won, he set about eradicating the physical and psychic jitters that had brought on his fiasco. He made himself walk slower, and won a number of tournaments . . . but not the Open. He had himself psychoanalyzed and played like a new and freer man for a spell, trouncing his old nemesis, Hagen, in a series of matches . . . but he tied up in the Open. Another and undoubtedly the best known of his experiments was the contorted putting style he adopted. Under pressure Leo had been stabbing the 4-footers from the normal putting stance and, theorizing that the elbow nerves should be steadier than the wrist nerves, he switched to that singularly uncomfortable-looking style in which his chin rested almost on top of the shaft of his putter and his elbows were extended straight out like the wings of a plane. For a while he got improved results with this out-elbows push, but it wasn't too long before he began missing those all-important 4-footers with his old consistency . . . especially in the Opens. He was sold on his theory, however, and could never be persuaded to change back to the orthodox method. Like Mac Smith, Diegel regularly confounded the critics who accused him of lack of guts with his Hagenesque sprints down the stretch in the lesser tournaments in which he overtook and passed the same golfers whom he let beat him in the Opens. He could be immense in match play. It was Diegel who finally stopped Hagen in the P.G.A. after Walter had run off twenty-two consecutive victories. He did it by rifling a mashie to the 34th green and holing a 42-foot putt for a birdie 2. Yet in 1928 and '29, the years in which he ousted Hagen and carried off the P.G.A., only one of the eight rounds Diegel played in the U.S. Open was under 74.

In the end Leo Diegel had to settle for two P.G.A. titles and a slew of Canadians, much more meager honors than his exceptional talents warranted.

Harry Cooper didn't come close and then lose as often as Smith and Diegel, but, in a way, his experiences in the U.S. Open—Cooper never played in the British—were of an even more tragic character. Smith and Diegel were at least spared the anguish of believing that they had won. Harry Cooper twice thought that he had become the Open Champion.

Harry was a curious cross, an Englishman who grew up in Texas. His father, Sid, was a golf professional who, at the time young Harry started to win, was affiliated with Tenison Park, a municipal course in Dallas. In 1926 Harry culminated a year of coming up by leading the field in the rich Los Angeles Open. His total was an eye-catching 279, and best of all he had finished with a 67. He looked like a fine under-pressure golfer. On the greens he reminded one California sportswriter of a perky robin. Light Horse Harry, as they called the twenty-two-year-old pro because of the speed with which he played his shots and chased after them, was a happy extrovert. He bubbled with confident conversation. He loved galleries.

Twelve feet of turf at Oakmont changed Harry into a much more sober young man. He had the Open of 1927 as good as won when he placed his approach eight feet from the cup on the 71st green. He had been putting well up to then, and it was a better than even bet that Cooper would drop that downhiller for his bird. He went for it aggressively, missed the corner of the cup, and ran four feet by. An expression of worry and regret invaded Cooper's face. It was stupid to have been that bold, he was musing. He should have been up, of course, but he should have left himself no more than a tap of a foot coming back if he missed. There was nothing of the perky robin about Harry as he sighted the line on his 4-footer and checked it from all angles. Satisfied with his survey, Harry crouched over the ball and tapped it. The line was fine, but in his preoccupation with direction, Harry had babied his putt. The ball stopped an inch or two short of the hole. Harry had taken a 5 when he had had a grand chance for a 3 and a simple, sure 4.

This misadventure on the 71st eventually meant the championship. For a while, though, Harry's 301 seemed safe, and with only Armour to come in, Harry was instructed to change into his best clothes and be ready for the cup presentation. The new champion went about dressing gaily, and finished just in time to watch Armour sink a 10-footer on the home green for the birdie that earned him a tie with Cooper. In the playoff, Tommy defeated Harry decisively.

It was a stinging disappointment, reminiscent of Smith's and Diegel's in their first Opens, but Harry got over it. He worked hard on his game, practicing on the average of two or three hours a day. He cut down the length of his swing, and was the steadier for

Leo Diegel's unorthodox putting form. This contorted, elbows-out method, would, Leo believed, cure him of his fatal fault of stabbing the short ones under fire. The fact that Leo continued to miss many simple putts probably accounted for his style's remaining exclusively his own. Three-putting cost him several titles.

it. He kept himself in the best physical shape. Although he was never as carefree after Oakmont, the confident dash slowly came back to his game, and in the Thirties he was year in and year out among the top professionals in stroke-average and purse totals. His record in the Open was irregular, but he was fourth in 1930, tied for seventh in '32, and tied for third in '34. For no good reason, Cooper seemed to do better in the even years, but numerology had little or no connection with Cooper's being made the outstanding favorite for the 1936 Open. Harry Cooper was simply the best golfer in America, and he was overdue.

The 1936 Open was held on the Upper Course of the Baltusrol Golf Club, in Springfield, New Jersey. The course was playing very fast during the three days of the tournament, and the long-hitting stars made it seem decidedly shorter than its measurement of 6,866 yards. Taking advantage of the added distance they were gaining off the tees and the trueness of the greens, the pack opened up with the hottest pace in the history of the tournament.

Three men broke 70 on the first day, and Cooper could easily have been a fourth had he not been unlucky on the thirteenth. A spectator darted out of the crowd just as Harry was swinging into his drive. Harry flinched slightly and hooked his shot into the side of a ditch. He elected to play it rather than lift and incur a penalty stroke. His recovery was a good one, long and not too much off-line, but the ball ended up snuggled against the trunk of a low fir tree whose function was intended to be purely ornamental. Harry again elected to play the ball where it lay in preference to lifting for a two-stroke penalty. Twisting himself under the low branches, he flailed at the ball with the back of his club, and missed it clean. He tried it again, and this time he banged it clear. In an admirable display of self-control, he lofted a 7-iron two yards from the cup, sank his putt, and had escaped with only a 6. He finished with a 71.

At the halfway mark, Ray Mangrum and big Vic Ghezzi were out in front with 140. Cooper was a stroke behind. His 70 was Harry at his best. He was splitting the fairways with his drives, and his straight, arching approaches were leaving him little to worry about on the greens. He went over par on only one hole, the 213-yard seventh, and filled out his round with three birdies and fourteen pars.

The Light Horse stuck his nose out in front on the third round when he added another beautifully played 70 for 211, a new record for the 54-hole mark. He threw a scare into his supporters on the sixteenth hole of this round, however. Lying two in the clumpy grass in the fringe of a bunker by the green, he had to chop at his ball and succeeded only in knocking it into the bunker. But he played his fourth with great poise, and holed it. The ball was rolling for Harry. When he followed with a 45-footer for his bird on the seventeenth, there was a quiet understanding among the spectators at Baltusrol that this was Harry Cooper's tournament. The uncrowned champion was going to win himself a crown, and it was pleasant to be in on it.

Harry's 211 gave him a lead of two strokes on Ghezzi, three on Denny Shute, and four on Clarence Clark, Tony Manero, Henry Picard, and Ky Laffoon. Between rounds

"Light Horse Harry" Cooper in 1936, adding them up after a round in the rain. That was the year the Light Horse set a new record for the Open with 284 at Baltusrol. The record lasted for about an hour—until Tony Manero galloped down the stretch with a 67 for a total of 282. Once again, Cooper had failed.

Harry ate only a sandwich. He stretched himself out on a bench in the locker room and tried to relax, but he felt fidgety. He was anxious to get going again.

At thirty-two Harry Cooper looked years older than his age. His light-brown hair had thinned, he had taken to wearing glasses, and there was a drawn, pinched look to his face. During a tournament his pulse leaped twenty beats above its normal rhythm, and as he started on his final round, the fans who followed him could almost feel the terrific nervous strain under which Cooper was playing. On the first nine of his last round, he made nearly as many errors as he had on the three rounds previous when he had hit 49 of the 54 greens, but he managed to produce enough of those lovely shots of his to turn the nine in 35. His eagle on the first cushioned the three putts he required on the second. He missed the green on three par 4s in a row with his second shots, but each time he got down in two, playing a particularly brilliant cut-shot from a trap on the sixth. He went one over on the tough seventh but got it back by birdieing the eighth. He was holding up gallantly. Apart from a few conversations with his trainer, Harry was keeping pretty much to himself and his task.

On the 340-yard twelfth, Harry hit another one of his fine drives and dumped his short iron about four feet from the hole. There was a feeling among the gallery that if Harry seized this opportunity, the title would be his. Bobby Jones, leaning on a spectator-sports-stick behind the green, studied the Light Horse closely, as if he, too, thought that the 4-footer was Cooper's test. Harry seemed almost too painstaking about his putt, but he stroked the ball firmly into the cup, and that appeared to be it. Practically all the other contenders had faltered on their last round—Ghezzi had an 81—and Cooper now had a safe margin for error. He did peter out discernibly after that birdie, going one over on the fourteenth and fifteenth, and he went over once more on the eighteenth when he took three to get down from the apron. But it was a 73 and Harry was to be congratulated for bearing up so nobly to the strain. This 73 gave him a total of 284, two strokes lower than the previous Open record of 286, held jointly by Evans and Sarazen. As Harry headed off the last green, the gallery around the clubhouse, as jubilant over Cooper's apparent victory as he was, broke out in the resounding volley of applause that greets the champion.

As Harry made his way to the locker room, well-wishers slapped him on the back and yelled that wonderful phrase, "Hi ya, champ." The reporters and photographers and radio men were waiting for him. The reporters asked a few questions, and then began pounding out their stories about Cooper's victory. The photographers scurried around looking for the cup so that they could photograph the new champion smiling at his trophy. The radio men led him to the microphone and asked him to tell the world how it felt to be the champion. "I haven't won this thing yet," Cooper said cautiously. "There are several men out there on the course who may catch me. Better wait a while." Cooper was fairly certain that his 284 could not be beat, but he hadn't forgotten Oakmont.

Harry Cooper had not been in very long when the word came over the grapevine that Tony Manero was 4 under par at the twelfth. There was some confusion as to who was 4 under. What was that name? Manero? Well, if this Manero had a chance, the only thing to do was to go out and watch him come in. The spectators plodded back onto the course, forcing themselves to dogtrot, asking each other questions about Manero as they headed for the fourteenth fairway. Someone knew that Manero had started only four strokes behind Cooper. Somebody else wasn't sure but thought Manero came from the same neighborhood in Westchester that had produced Sarazen, Joe Turnesa, and the other fine golfers of Italian lineage. No one could recall any important tournament this Manero had ever won. Panting heavily as they converged on the fourteenth fairway, they saw a small, slight, dark man with a neat little mustache walking briskly down the fairway with Sarazen, his playing partner. Charter members of the gallery brought the newcomers up to date. Sarazen had gone out in 33, and this had given Tony something tangible to beat. He had shot a 33 himself. Gene had started back poorly, but he was out of it anyway. Tony had kept right on going with two pars and a birdie on the twelfth. He had knocked in another birdie on the thirteenth to put himself 5 under par. On the fourteenth the swelling gallery watched the diminutive pro play a safe iron to the green and hole out in two safe putts that gave him a 4 and the exact figure Cooper had totaled for 68 holes. One over par for the last four—Cooper had missed his pars on the 69th and 72nd—would win the Open for Tony Manero.

On the deceptive, downhill 140-yard fifteenth, Tony failed to gauge the distance correctly and his tee shot voomed into a trap before the green. He blasted out and two-putted for a 4, which wasn't costly since Cooper had also missed his 3 on that hole. Sarazen three-putted after being on with his tee shot, and the gallery began to wonder if he had purposely passed up his 3 so that Tony, a short driver, would retain the honor and not be tempted to press. (Sarazen has often received credit for "bringing Tony in," but Gene disclaims any credit for doing more than setting a hot pace going out and being as helpful as he could to a fellow he liked who had a chance to win. He did not purposely three-putt.) Tony teed up nervously on the sixteenth (70th) hole, a straightaway 439-yard par 4. Addressing the ball off the heel of his club, as was his odd and unattractive method with his woods, he hit a drive that was not long but useful. An iron twelve feet from the hole gave him a crack for his birdie. He sank it. Now he was one stroke ahead of Cooper.

On the 563-yard 71st Tony played three careful strokes to the green and would have had another birdie if he had holed a 7-footer. It was just about the only putt he missed all afternoon. Cooper had taken a 5 on the 71st, so Manero was still one stroke to the good with the home hole to be played. On the last tee Tony had a trying ten-minute wait. Sarazen filled in with conversation until the twosome ahead was out of the way and the officials had finally cleared the excited spectators from the route to the green on this long two-shotter. Tony kept his drive straight, which was the important thing, and played a cautious iron to the front edge of the green. (The spectators immediately encircled the green and Sarazen was forced to play his second over their heads.) As Tony came walking with quick steps down the fairway, the largest gallery since the days of Jones saluted him with a long round of applause. Tony had the presence of mind to acknowledge the ovation by tipping his flat white cap toward the spectators sandwiched on the steps and verandas of the clubhouse. It was a very winning gesture. A way was made for him to the green, and he saw for the first time exactly where his approach had ended up. He was about forty feet short.

Tony's up-putt could have been stronger. It finished about five feet below the hole. Cooper had taken a 5 on the 72nd, so Tony could take two from five feet and still win. He could have been excused if he had elected to take two cautious putts, but Manero finished like a champion by dropping his 5-footer. His 67 gave him a total of 282, two shots better than Cooper's and four under the old tournament record.

And what about Cooper? A few weeks later Harry competed in the St. Paul Open, which he had previously won three times. A 63 on his third round helped him to tie with Dick Metz, and a 66 and a 69 won the playoff handily for Harry. He finished the year among the top money-winners, as usual, and compiled the second lowest strokes-per-round average. The next season, 1937, was Cooper's best. He had the lowest strokes-per-round average, and his earnings, $13,573.69, were almost $4,000 more than his closest rival's. His 1937 campaign featured his second triumph in the Canadian and a 274 in the Los Angeles Open, in which the Light Horse cantered home in 66. There was no question about it: he was a superb golfer with all the requisites for winning the Open. But like Mac Smith and Diegel, of whom he was a compound, Harry Cooper was a champion whose name is not inscribed among America's national champions.

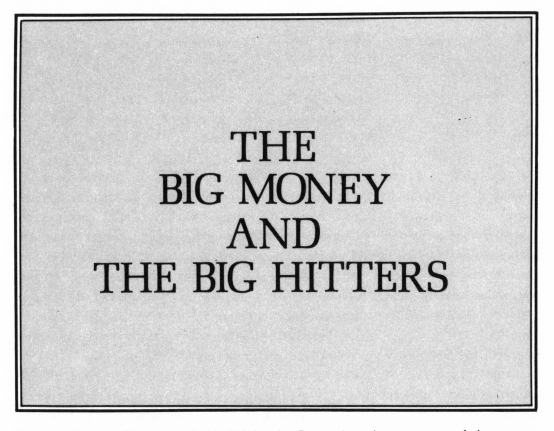

THE
BIG MONEY
AND
THE BIG HITTERS

In 1936, the year Cooper made his bid for the Open, Americans were on their way out of the Depression and looking for sports heroes with whom they could fall head over heels in love. Baseball would soon offer them a suitable idol in Joe DiMaggio, and football with a number of qualified candidates, Larry Kelley and Whizzer White, to name two. In boxing there was Joe Louis, in tennis Don Budge, in track Jesse Owens, in basketball Hank Luisetti. While most of the new heroes could compare favorably in ability and spectator appeal with their precursors in the Golden Age of Sport, golf was not quite so fortunate in the personalities who had taken the places of Jones, Hagen, Farrell, Diegel, Armour, and the other attractive figures who had made golf a major sport. There was no denying the skill of the young men who had become the leaders in professional golf, but when it came to color and the ignition of personal ardor, the new stars couldn't hold a mashie to the old boys.

Early in 1937, the P.G.A. released the figures on the division of spoils among the professional pack during the year extending from January 1, 1936, through December 31, 1936. The top twelve money-winners were the following:

Horton Smith	$7,884.75
Ralph Guldahl	7,682.41
Henry Picard	7,681.00
Harry Cooper	7,443.00
Ray Mangrum	5,995.00

Jimmy Thomson	5,927.00
Jimmy Hines	5,599.00
Gene Sarazen	5,480.00
Byron Nelson	5,429.00
Johnny Revolta	4,317.00
Tony Manero	3,929.00
Ky Laffoon	3,592.00

This is not, to be sure, a ranking of the professionals. If it were, several changes in the lineup would have to be made. Room near the top would have to be found for Denny Shute, for example, the winner of the P.G.A., whose name does not appear since he participated in few winter and regional tournaments. Moreover, many golf fans and authorities would have argued for the inclusion in the top twelve of Craig Wood and Paul Runyan, maybe Ed Dudley or Jug McSpaden or Dick Metz, all of whom had experienced lean seasons in 1936 but who ordinarily were in the thick of the competition. The list merely tabulates the leading money-winners of 1936 and how much they won. Beyond this, it serves as a fair introduction to the post-Depression pro pack with its four new faces for every one old face surviving from the Age of Jones.

Apart from Sarazen and Cooper, the one veteran professional with a place among the top dozen money-winners of '36 was Horton Smith. At twenty-seven Horton was the same wholesome, overlogical, studious, finicky, and handsome young man who seven years earlier had come out of Missouri to dominate the winter season as no debutant had ever done before him. In that first fine careless rapture, the Joplin Ghost had won seven tournaments and finished second in four others. With the coming of summer his game had slumped, not disturbingly but appreciably nonetheless, and he had not been the factor in the big tournaments that his winter record had implied he would be. In the years that followed, Horton continued to capture a heavy share of the winter loot and to lose his scoring touch when the prestige tournaments came along in June and July. As assiduously as he worked on it, his swing was not the simplified and correct thing it had been in 1929. In attempting to add several new shots to his repertoire, Horton had lost that first compact groove. He had to battle a tall man's tendency to overswing, and even when he periodically cut down the length of his arc, it did not always follow that he corrected a certain looseness in his swing. He compensated for his increased number of tee and fairway errors by improving a short game that had always been remarkable. In the long gamut from Travis to Trevino, there have been few golfers in the same class with Horton as a consistently great putter. On the practice green he did not try to see how many putts he could hole. He would select a stretch of cupless grass and concentrate on stroking the ball correctly, checking his grip, his backswing, the position of the blade, the followthrough, the way the ball rolled. Horton was a brilliant exponent of the theory that the man who strokes the ball correctly is bound to hole more than his share of putts. In 1936, when he won his second Masters—he had taken the maiden Masters in 1934—he holed a 43-footer on the 68th, an 8-footer

Horton Smith. Year after year Horton collected heavily on the winter circuit, but never quite fulfilled the promise he had shown on first joining the pack in 1929. In 19 tournaments that year, the twenty-year-old·sensation won seven, finished second four times, and came out worse than fourth only four times.

on the 69th, and a 16-footer on the 71st on greens drenched by a torrential rain. Horton Smith continued to campaign for many more years, but his two victories in the Masters remained the zenith for this "unseasonal" golfer whose birdies flew away when the warm weather came.

Horton Smith, the precocious veteran, was extremely popular with the galleries because of his splendid appearance and polished golf and, additionally, because he was a reminder of the glamorous giants of the Twenties. The Great American Golf Fan found that as much as he wanted to identify himself heart and soul with the more recently arrived stars, he couldn't. They were lacking in those qualities of charm and magnetism that transform a golfer into a personality with easy access to an enthusiast's emotions. The Great American Golf Fan who had died a thousand deaths with Hagen and shared in Jones' moments of exaltation and dejection could not immerse himself in the tides of fortune that washed for and against the new stars. From a technical point of view, of course, the newcomers were magnificent. As scorers, they were incredible. They lowered one record after another until a score in the 70s seemed like a nightmare. Into golf reporting came those distracting phrases: "He blew to a 71" and "He soared to a disastrous 73." But for all their sabotage, the new stars failed to make contact with the sympathies of the sideliners, and golf began to take on a flat, mathematical flavor.

The Great American Golf Fan knew a few facts about each of the newcomers to the pro pack. These were the set squibs, repeated with little variation in all the reports of the tournaments, adhering to the individual whether he lost, won, scrambled, rebounded, or floundered to a dismal 72: Ray Mangrum was The Human One-Iron. He lacked stamina. . . . Ky Laffoon liked to wear bright yellow socks and canary-colored sweaters with his knickers. He was of Irish-French-Cherokee ancestry, and had traveled from Kansas to Oklahoma in a covered wagon at the age of six. . . . Ed Dudley was a slow Southerner with a languid swing. . . . Johnny Revolta was a gnarled-faced young man with an obdurate marcel who had been encouraged to take his fling at the circuit when he had beaten the best-ball of Sarazen and Armour during their tour of the North Woods country. He and Picard made a redoubtable combination and seemed to win the Miami Four-ball every year. . . . Henry Picard was a tall, clean-cut Yankee from Plymouth, about as gregarious as Greta Garbo. He took fewer chances than any of his brethren when it came to shooting the works for birdies. His first important victories were scored when he was playing out of Hershey, and he was called The Chocolate Soldier. . . . Ralph Guldahl was sensationally dull to watch, but steady as a rock. He had been an automobile salesman. . . . Paul Runyan was the shortest hitter of the pack, but what he lacked in distance off the tees, he made up in the accuracy of his long approaches. He could sweep a spoon shot closer to the pin than his opponent's 5-iron, and on the greens he could be murderous. He was a dapper dresser, and it took some believing when you heard he was only a few years away from milking cows on his father's farm in Arkansas. . . . Dick Metz came from Arkansas too. He was always "handsome Dick Metz." Wavy black hair and a cowboy's complexion. Liked deep-sea fishing. . . . Byron Nelson, one of the newest faces, was a Texan whom George Jacobus

Henry Picard, nearing the top of his backswing on a 2-iron shot. Three weeks before the 1938 Masters, which he won, Picard changed his grip. Having injured his left thumb, he adopted an interlocking grip that got the thumb off the shaft and out of the way. Picard was a pupil of Alex Morrison's.

had taken on as assistant pro at Ridgewood in New Jersey. Nelson was winning more tournaments and more money each year. . . . Harold "Jug" McSpaden, from Kansas City, was "brilliant but erratic." Dangerous in match play. . . . Jimmy Hines was also brilliant but erratic. Probably the best of the pros situated on Long Island. A long hitter. . . . Craig Wood's golf was like the little girl who had a little curl right in the middle of her forehead. He was very handsome. Called The Blond Bomber. . . . Jimmy Thomson was the longest hitter in the pack, longer than Wood, Hines, Little. (With the exception of winning the Canadian Open with four rounds in the 60s, Lawson was finding the going rough among the pros.) Thomson, golf's Babe Ruth, averaged about 275 yards from the tees, and had thrilled the galleries at Oakmont by reaching the green in two on the 621-yard twelfth. That was in the 1935 Open, when he had finished second. Jimmy was married to Viola Dana, the actress. . . .

Every man in the pack was an accomplished shot-maker. Over the long run, three of them emerged as distinguished golfers—Byron Nelson and Ralph Guldahl, of course, and Henry Picard, whom many of the best golfing minds esteem one of the really fine swingers of all time. As 1937 got underway, though, only one of the newcomers had attained a hold on the public's fancy of sufficient strength to have made him a successful attraction had he chosen to set out on an exhibition tour. This was Jimmy Thomson. The Great American Golf Fan would have traveled a good many miles to see whether Jimmy hit them as long as they said he did.

The members of the pro pack had their individual fortes and weaknesses, but they shared a large number of things in common. With the exception of Runyan, they were wickedly long off the tees. Hypodermic injections, stepping up the internal pressure of the golf ball to the neighborhood of 800 pounds per square inch, gave the ball lots of carry when it was properly struck. The steel shaft—steel had been approved in 1924 by the U.S.G.A., but the Royal and Ancient withheld its sanction until 1930—had been perfected, and was also a major factor in the added yardage the golfers were getting. With steel-shafted clubs eliminating the torque and torsion of the hickory, a strong-wristed golfer could put everything he had into a shot, for a slight departure from the perfect coordination of hands and clubhead resulted in errors far less acute than with the wooden shafts. With this wider zone for an error in timing, the advantages of the swinger over the hitter were considerably reduced. Walter Hagen, who was regarded by his contemporaries as a hitter, was a rippling swinger compared with the stars of the new generation. Some of the newer crop were out-and-out sluggers; they tore into the ball almost exclusively with their hands. Few of them were caressers of the Mac Smith school. The best golfers lay halfway between the two poles. They had grooved swings that made provision for an accentuated hitting action.

Once they were off the tee and down the fairway, the golfers of the Thirties had a generous range of perfectly matched clubs from which to choose. In the earlier periods golfers built up their sets by discarding clubs whose weight or balance was not precisely to their feel, and gradually assembled sets that were interbalanced from the driving-iron to the niblick. This experimentation was now passé with the coming of age of the scientifically wrought and pretested steel shaft. (To their matched sets the pros added a liberal number of pet clubs, in-between clubs, trouble clubs, and clubs that were useful for only one extreme and exotic type of shot, until some of them were carrying around close to thirty weapons. From this vast armory, the pro, and the professional amateur, could select the club that would give him just the distance he needed if he hit a full shot.

Those delightful half-shots and three-quarter shots, by which you could distinguish a true golfer from the men who played golf, were fast disappearing and might have vanished entirely had the U.S.G.A. not invoked in the winter of 1937 a regulation limiting to fourteen the number of clubs a golfer could carry in his bag. Some of the real oldtimers, remembering that Vardon had six times broken 70 playing with only six clubs, lobbied for a further reduction of armaments, but the adoption of fourteen as the maximum was generally hailed as a sage and sound compromise.)

Around the greens the new pro pack displayed astonishing skill. In the eyes of the reactionaries—who were reluctant to admit that the newcomers could do anything better than Jones or Hagen—the improved quality of the professionals' bunker play could be explained by the new agents of excavation, the sand-iron or the blaster or the dynamiter, depending on the trade name stamped on the super-niblick by the various sporting-goods manufacturers. In the previous decade the golfer who got down in 2 from a trap by the green believed that he had saved himself a stroke. By the middle Thirties, the pro who failed to put his recovery from a trap ten feet or less from the cup felt that he had tossed away a stroke. The new clubs greatly simplified the problem of getting out and getting up close, but it still took nerve and decision to execute the shot correctly under pressure.

On the greens the pros, as a group, were definitely ahead of the earlier performers. The equipment for putting hadn't changed. Indirectly, though, the improved irons and wooden clubs were more germane to the superior standards of putting. With the greater length they had gained, the pack turned all but the longest layouts into drive-and-pitch courses. A hole measuring 410 yards, for instance, which formerly demanded a drive and a 4-iron or so, could now be reached with a drive and a 6-iron or even a 7. Everyone was getting on in 2, and the premium on tee-to-green play, consequently, was not as high as it once had been. More than ever before, putting was the department of the game that separated the winners from the losers. The pro who finished tenth or fifteenth in a tournament might have used no more shots to reach the seventy-two greens than the pro who finished first. The knowledge that the gulf between $1,000 and $50 could be bridged only by putting better than the other fellow drove the professionals on to acquiring their phenomenal skill on the greens. In time, after the players had created for themselves higher and higher criteria, a putt of five feet came to be regarded as a short putt that a golfer had to hole if he had financial aspirations. Because the pros were so uncanny on the greens, particularly on the flat tables of the courses over which many of the winter tournaments were played, any fan who had watched their performances could almost sympathize with the lobby who wanted putts to be counted half a stroke and thus re-establish the value of the other shots in golf.

Intrinsic as were the peppier ball, the steel shaft, and the sand-wedge to the new assaults on the old marks, in the opinion of many students of the game the rash of record-breaking performances resulted not so much from the refined equipment as from the changes that came over the golf courses themselves. Golfers may say that they don't care how well they score as long as they hit the ball well, but the fact of the matter is that every golfer is concerned with his score. At almost every club in the Thirties, as now, pressure was brought to bear on the green committee to fill in traps, thin the rough, and, all in all, muzzle the terrors that transformed possible 89s into actual 97s. The cry was answered. Architects were called in to remodel the sterner holes and the greenkeepers were informed of the new standard of maintenance required. In the Thirties for the first time the greenkeepers at the wealthy clubs had at their disposal machines like the seven-gang mower which could domesticate a course and keep it scoreable. The clubs that could not afford the new machinery manicured their courses as best they could. American golfers got what they asked for: easier courses and lower scores. The average golfer cut four to seven strokes off his score now that bunkers were scaled down and their lips removed, fairways groomed to resemble a hairbrush, and roughs reduced to such a state of obedience that women could play a brassie from them.

The professional golfer as well as the average golfer benefitted from the New Look of the nation's golf courses. He, too, received better lies in the fairway. More important, he did not have to sacrifice a shot when he found the rough. In fact, he could play almost the same shot from the rough as he did from the fairway; a soft green might still hold a shot even if it carried no backspin. In time, as the soft, watered green became the rule and not the exception, the pitch-and-run approach practically vanished from professional golf in America. Just as instrumental as the new construction of greens in the lower scoring, if not more instrumental, were the new grass strains introduced for the putting surfaces. Quite a number of golf authorities, architects predominantly, give the improved texture and uniformity of the greens 100 per cent of the credit for the advanced standards of putting and 65 per cent of the credit for the reduction in scores.

One reason why it is important to talk about the changes that made lower scoring possible for the professionals of the Thirties and afterwards is that too many fans today dismiss the champions of the first three decades of the century with a flip comparison of scores. Jones and Hagen, they state categorically, couldn't have been particularly good golfers. They were rarely in the 60s and often in the middle and high 70s. They won with totals that would not even place them in the money today. They just happened to be around when the competition was seedy. That isn't quite right. Golf was a different game in the Twenties than it is today, a much harder game, just how much harder it is impossible to gauge.

On the other hand, by explaining the less arduous conditions under which the new stars performed, one runs the danger of detracting, inadvertently, from the abilities of these later champions. To begin with, the record-breakers of the Thirties and Forties were golfers of very high talent. On top of this, the ever-surging competition forced them to discover new peaks of efficiency and new styles of play. In the Twenties, for example, a tournament golfer was content to get his drive out by the 225-yard marker except on the extremely long holes. Since the rough was rougher and the penalty for an off-line drive much stiffer, the earlier golfers placed high value on straightness. The idea was to keep the ball in play off the tee and to postpone any thoughts about a birdie until the birdie shot presented itself. These tactics rapidly became obsolete in the Thirties.

Sam Parks, one of the darkest of all the dark horses who have figured in United States Open history, crouches over his winning 2-footer on the home green at Oakmont in 1935. Parks won by two strokes from the powerful Jimmy Thomson.

The hunt for the birdie began with the drive—the longer the drive, the shorter the approach; the shorter the approach, the easier the putt. A golfer attacked with every shot.

If some of the old masters appeared to have "more golf in them" than their heirs, it can be argued that it only seemed that way since the new stars made the game look like a science rather than an art.

During the Depression and the years of slow recovery, some of the winter tournaments had been forced to give up, and there was, naturally, a halt in the race between tournament sponsors to see who could offer the highest prize money. But, all things taken into account, the winning pros were still well paid for their efforts. For example, statisticians computed that Paul Runyan received $1.61 per stroke played during his sixty-one tournament rounds in the winter season of 1934 when Paul picked up checks totaling $7,026. The leaders usually made between $5,000 and $7,000 with the rest of the tour checking in between $2,500 and $5,000. When a top pro's salary at his home club was added to this figure, plus his gleanings from instruction, endorsements, and his fee from the manufacturer whom he "advised," his yearly take was quite respectable. Fighters, of course, outearned him, as did a few of the outstanding baseball players and newly turned-professional tennis stars, but compared with most professional athletes who flourished in the bad times, the winning golfer received a generous compensation for his skill.

With things brightening up somewhat by the end of 1936, both the well-heeled stars and the penniless "dew sweepers" who slept in autos were hoping that some of the new money would blow their way. As things turned out, due to a number of circumstances more or less beyond their control, the pros were entering upon a period far more lucrative than they had dreamed it could be. For, beginning in 1937, professional golf graduated into Big Business.

An energetic, imaginative Irishman from Boston, Fred Corcoran, was one of the "circumstances" behind golf's big boom. Corcoran had been around golf all his life. He began as a caddie at the Belmont Country Club. In 1918, when he was thirteen, he became the caddie-master. He moved on to the position of handicapper with the Massachusetts Golf Association, where his amiability and his progressive ideas about such items as scoreboards and publicity brought him to the attention of the U.S.G.A. and other organizations that ran golf tournaments. Richard Tufts, the head of Pinehurst, asked Fred to take charge of press relations when that North Carolina resort was host to the P.G.A. Championship in the late fall of 1936. Fred's systematic methods at Pinehurst sold George Jacobus, the P.G.A. president, on the advantages of having in his organization a young man who could transform "dirty work" into bright columns on the sporting pages of the country. After a three-month tryout, Corcoran became what amounted to tournament director of the P.G.A., succeeding Bob Harlow, who had been shepherding the pros wisely and well for almost a score of years.

Well stocked with sincerity and figures, thoroughly sold on his product, Corcoran invaded the offices of organizations he thought he could interest in sponsoring tournaments, concentrating on the Chambers of Commerce of ambitious cities and the publicity bureaus of resorts. How well Corcoran succeeded in imposing his factual enthusiasm on his customers is best illustrated by figures: In 1936, the year before Corcoran took over, the touring professionals played about twenty-two tournaments a year; ten years later they were lined up for tournaments during *forty-five* weeks of the year. Where tournament purses had totaled $100,000 in 1936, the pros in 1947 were shooting at prize money exceeding $600,000. During the ten years that Corcoran had been promoting the pros, the size of the galleries had increased 300 per cent.

Corcoran is the first to admit that it was the times and not the tournament director that was responsible for the boom. However, Fred is deserving of copious praise for the shrewdness with which he diagnosed his problem and the drive with which he followed it through. Fred's work did not end with selling prospective sponsors the idea that a golf tournament would not lose money and would insure them more publicity per dollar invested than any other means of attracting attention to their fair city or spa. He won the cooperation, and space, of the newspapermen covering golf by obligingly reeling off the statistics, color, and anecdotes that columns are made of, rescuing the boys from blank sheets of paper on many rainy days. Realizing that it was not so much the competitive angle of a tournament as the in-person stars that brought in the customers, Corcoran

The Los Angeles Open, a regular feature on the winter circuit. West Coast fans cluster around the tenth tee at the Riviera Country Club for a close-up inspection of Sam Snead, the spectacular shot-maker from the Virginia hills.

watched carefully over his troupe of golfers, a restless combination of Barnum, Mrs. Wiggs, and Pygmalion. There were times when he oversucceeded and experienced the qualms of a Frankenstein, for every so often one or two of the professional stars, taking their write-ups too seriously, would demand special courtesies that Louis B. Mayer would have been reluctant to grant Lana Turner. By the time Fred left his P.G.A. post in 1948 to turn to newer promotions in golf and other sports, he had made the American public extremely circuit-conscious.

A great many of the golfers Corcoran trumpeted into pseudo-personalities were as drab as a comedian in his own home. But hardly had Corcoran stepped into his job when there arrived on the scene, with no advance notice, a golfer who exuded color from every pore and who, far more than any other professional, was responsible for the tremendous resurgence of interest in tournament golf. This newcomer was a lean, supple, fluidly coordinated twenty-four-year-old pro from the mountain resort town of Hot Springs, Virginia, making his first tour on the winter circuit. His golfing background was not exceptional. During his school vacations he had caddied to get away from plowing and milking on his father's farm. He was no great shakes as a golfer when he was in high school. He won a driving contest held in conjunction with a high school golf tournament but finished no better than eighth in the tournament. His sports were baseball, football, and basketball, and he played them well enough to receive scholarship bids from two West Virginia colleges. What turned out to be his big break was the broken left hand he suffered in a football game during his senior year in high school. Golf, it seemed to him, helped him in recovering the use of the hand, and for the first time he devoted the bulk of his free time to the game. After graduation in 1933, he landed himself a job in the pro shop at the Homestead course as assistant caddie-master and handyman. He found himself a better job shortly afterwards at the Cascades course down the road. Three weeks after his switch, he played a record-breaking 68 over that hilly 6,800-yard layout. He returned to the Homestead course a year later as assistant to Freddie Gleim, but stayed only one season. His play in a local tourney had caught the eye of Fred Martin, the manager of the Greenbrier Golf Club in White Sulphur Springs, and the young man, now twenty-two, spent the next two years attached to that rival spa in West Virginia. In 1936 he won the West Virginia Open and P.G.A., scoring a 61 in the latter tourney, and gained further confidence by outplaying Lawson Little, Billy Burke, and Johnny Goodman in an exhibition four-ball match at White Sulphur Springs. (He had filled in at the last minute when Jack Davison could not make it.) He tried the Hershey Open, and when he succeeded in finishing a good sixth, thought himself ready to battle for the big money. His club felt that he deserved the chance and backed him for a swing around the circuit in the winter of 1937.

The smooth-swinging mountaineer's first start was the $10,000 Miami-Biltmore tournament. He finished in tenth place, which was not as noteworthy as it might appear at first glance, since most of the name-players had been lured away from Florida to compete in the California tournaments. He joined the pack on the West Coast in January, still such a total unknown that when he finished sixth in the Los Angeles Open the newspapers misspelled the name "Sneed." They learned to spell the name right when Samuel Jackson Snead caught fire during the Oakland Open, shooting 69-65-67-69 for a winning total of 270.

Many of the golf writers knew more about James K. Polk than they did about Samuel J. Snead. Fred Corcoran filled them in on Snead's background as best he could, and the writers who had been energetic enough to leave the press tent and follow the young man for a few holes could supplement the hillbilly angle with enthusiastic reports on this fellow Snead's fine swing and his extraordinary length. Sam was bewildered by his overnight fame. When Corcoran showed him the photo *The New York Times* had run along with its account of the Oakland Open, Sam cocked his head to one side and said in his worried Appalachian drawl, "How'd they ever get my picture? I ain't never been to New York."

Following his breakthrough at Oakland, Sam Snead built up his bio by winning the Rancho Santa Fe Open (sponsored by Bing Crosby) and carrying off his share of the spoils as the caravan swung cross-country to Florida and up the Atlantic coast. A suitable name was coined for him—"Slamming Sammy." All the world loves a long-hitter, and Snead could really powder that apple. In the driving contest held at the P.G.A. Championship, Sam averaged 307 yards on his three tries and won in a walk. Perhaps Jimmy Thomson hit them a bit farther when he really caught hold of the ball, but Jimmy could not compare with Sam in consistency. Or method. The marvelous thing about Snead was that he hit his tee shots with one of the sweetest, soundest swings golf has ever known. For many discerning students of the game, Sam Snead was simply in a class by himself when it came to the mechanics of hitting a golf shot. In the excitement over Snead's proficiency with his woods, his iron-play received less attention than it merited. Like most golfers who strike the ball decisively on the downswing, Sam could run into error on his irons when his timing was off, but he played them with the same smooth compactness that characterized his woods. Without pressing, relying on the perfect coordination of his pivot and his hitting action, Snead could drill a 4-iron to tight greens over two hundred yards away. (On par 5s he had room to use a 4-iron.) If there was a weakness in Snead's game—although it was not so apparent at the time—it was his putting. He was a fair birdie-holer, but by professional standards he was erratic on his short putts. The 2-footers bothered him even when he made them.

Wherever Sam Snead played, he made a fan of every person in the gallery who subconsciously was waiting for another Jones. In personality and manner, Sam and Bobby were miles apart, but when it came to that indefinable quality called magnetism, the shambling mountaineer had it. Spectators ignored the proven stars to give the newcomer the once-over, and after they had seen him hit one or two shots, they found it was impossible to leave. Snead's shots were far more beautiful than the raving sports-writers had claimed they were. Watching him, like watching Jones, provided an aesthetic delight. Here was that rarity, the long-hitter who combined power with the delicate nuances of shot-making, this slow-speaking, somewhat timid, somewhat cocky young man from the mountains.

Sam Snead did not cool off. In the 1937 Open, his first big test, he finished second. A strong finish by Ralph Guldahl was all that kept Snead from winning the crown in his first crack. The sensational freshman made the Ryder Cup team, and won his match from Dick Burton 5 and 4. He finished the year in fourth place among the money-winners with a take of $8,801. His sophomore season was even more successful. Included in his list of victories were the Nassau Open, the Miami Open (via a spectacular 30 on the last nine), Bing Crosby's 36-hole tourney at Del Mar (72-67—139),

Sam Snead, always in perfect balance, puts the sweet swing to a mashie-niblick.

Ralph Guldahl, winner of consecutive Open Championships, leans into a tee shot.

the Canadian, the first Goodall, and the Westchester 108-hole tourney. His total winnings between the first of January and the fifteenth of October climbed to $17,572.83.

Two or three bad tournament days did disclose, much to the chagrin of Snead and his most ardent supporters, certain chinks in Slamming Sammy's armor. In the Pasadena Open, after a first-round 76 had made him cantankerous, Sam threw down his clubs after batting one out-of-bounds on the twelfth hole of his second round, and walked into the clubhouse. His subsequent apology for this childish petulance helped a bit. In the 1938 Open at Cherry Hills, he finished far back; after a ragged start, he had no comeback. In the final of the 1938 P.G.A. he was routed 8 and 7 by Paul Runyan, whom he was outdriving by fifty yards, and outputting by several yards as well. It was the widest margin ever run up in a P.G.A. final. When he was off his game, Sam was prone to sulk rather than hang in there like a Travers or a Hagen and think his way out of the wilderness. But Snead was mostly on and was regarded as the coming golfer, the next great champion. 1939 would undoubtedly be his year. Ralph Guldahl could not go on winning the Open indefinitely.

While Slamming Sammy Snead was setting the golfing world agog in 1937 and 1938, an immeasurably less attractive golfer, Ralph Guldahl, was colorlessly going about the job of doing something that only three men before him had been able to do—win two consecutive United States Open Championships.

Guldahl had reentered the professional picture in 1936, two and a half years after he had blown a chance for quick fame by missing the 4-footer that would have tied Johnny Goodman in the 1933 Open. The big, tousled Texan was a much improved golfer. Olin Dutra had helped him to change from a palm grip to finger control in 1935. Through long hours of practice he had corrected his principal bad habits, picking the clubhead up too early and cutting across the ball from the outside in. On his last two rounds of the 1933 Open, Ralph had taken 35 and 36 putts, but he had remedied this defect of his game as well. In that unexciting but important department of putting, rolling the long ones close to the hole, Ralph was now unsurpassed. The new Guldahl, however, was no more electric in action than the old Guldahl. In 1936, the year in which he won the first of three consecutive Westerns, the Radix trophy for low average, and $7,682.41, he was paired on the final day of the Open with Paul Runyan. For the gallery, Runyan was the attraction. The heavy slouching fellow in the sloppy white cap and rumpled trousers was merely the golfer who was playing along with Paul. When the spectators studied the final standings on the board, they discovered that Guldahl had compiled the same total score as Runyan, 290, and a tie for eighth. This puzzled them elaborately. The big fellow seemed to have been playing about 77 golf. They could think of ten or twenty stylish shots that Runyan had played, but try as they would, they could not remember one brilliant shot by Guldahl.

A year later, 1937, Guldahl won his first Open, at Oakland Hills. Even in winning, Guldahl was partially overshadowed by the runner-up, Snead. Ralph was regarded more or less as "the other man," the fellow who beat Snead. It was grossly unfair to Ralph, since he won at Oakland Hills by playing a 69 on his final round, holding up sturdily under the pressure of knowing that he would lose unless he could match the 71 Snead had brought in on his last round. For seven holes Ralph was even 4s. On the eighth he chipped in from sixty-five yards for an eagle 3. On the ninth, a rugged par 3, he was on with a 2-iron and holed from twenty-five feet for his 2. These two sharp thrusts carried Ralph to the turn in 33. With nine holes to go, he was two or three strokes lower than he had figured he would be. He could drop one stroke to par on the last nine, a par 36, and still nose out Snead. This was not asking too much of a man who would be champion, and Ralph felt exactly that way about it. "If I can't play this last nine in thirty-seven strokes," he said on the tenth tee, "I'm just a bum and don't deserve to win the Open."

He dropped a stroke to par on the tenth. He dropped another on the eleventh. The spectators began to speak in whispers, the way they always do when a crack-up seems imminent. Ralph brought them to life again with a birdie on the twelfth. On the thirteenth he all but holed his tee shot for an ace, and his easy birdie brought him back to even par on the back-nine. The fourteenth was routine, but on the next hole the pressure of the Open began to tell on Ralph. He hit his second shot very poorly, but was lucky. As it was about to bounce into the heavy rough, the ball struck the foot of a spectator and was diverted into a smooth trap by the green. Ralph played his wedge just right, and dropped his short putt. Harry Cooper, Guldahl's playing partner, nursed him along with skillful conversation as the bulky Texan managed his par on the sixteenth. Still even with par coming in. A stroke to spare on the last two holes. On the short seventeenth Ralph belted a low iron ten feet from the cup but nervously jabbed his putt. He holed his second putt for his 3 and was all for racing to the eighteenth tee when Cooper slowed him down by making him take his 10-footer over three times. It helped to relieve the tension. Going to the last hole, a par 5, Guldahl still carried his safety stroke, but he was comfortably on with his third shot, fifteen feet from the cup, safely home. He got down in 2 for his par. He had played the last nine in 36. He was not a bum and deserved to win the Open.

At Oakland Hills, Ralph Guldahl had put together rounds of 71-69-72-69 for a record-breaking 281. Thereafter he was profoundly respected as the magnificent stroke-play virtuoso he was, but he did not catch hold of the affections of the public. He went about his golf most of the time in a solemn, sluggish way that was utterly lacking in showmanship. When he felt sullen, he made no effort to conceal it, and even his grouchiness lacked the theatricality that would have turned him into a character whom Fred Corcoran could have billed as "The Scrooge of the Fairways." He had no idea what the galleries wanted in a champion. Where Tony Manero had won hearts by doffing his cap as he walked to the 72nd green, Ralph had paused a moment before his final 15-footer at Oakland Hills and combed his hair.

In 1938 Snead, Picard, and the other boys gobbled up the lesser tourneys, and the publicity, but when it came to the Open, the unglamorous champion again ran away from them. At Cherry Hills, in Denver, Guldahl won as he had at Oakland Hills, by playing a 69 on his last round to overtake the leader. Apart from Guldahl, only Dick Metz had completed his first three rounds without one score in the high 70s. Metz's 73-68-70 put him four strokes ahead of the defending champion, and only a fifty-foot chip by Guldahl smack into the cup on the 54th had prevented Metz from assuming a more commanding lead. Playing just in front of Guldahl, Metz ran headlong into a series of mistakes on his last round. Guldahl stalked his man with four deliberate 4s, all pars. On the fifth Ralph ran down another 4 for a birdie. At this point he caught Metz. On the sixth he went out in front by two strokes, picking up a birdie 2 where Metz had taken a 4. Metz was unable to get going, and the big unemotional man behind him pulled farther and farther away to win by six strokes, the widest margin that had separated an Open winner from the runner-up since Barnes had spread-eagled the field at Columbia in 1921. Ralph made only two errors on his machinelike 69, one on the eighth and the other on the eighteenth, where his spoon-shot ran over the green.

In joining Jones, McDermott, and Willie Anderson in that exclusive fraternity, winners of two consecutive Opens, Ralph had played his eight rounds in eleven under 4s—281 at Oakland Hills, 284 at Cherry Hills.

LOST:
A WALKER
CUP

The primary purpose of the Olympic Games is, of course, to promote international understanding. Whether or not the past Olympics have created more friction than friendship is a highly debatable topic. But sidestepping the moral issues involved, or not involved, and focusing on the contests themselves, the Olympic Games and other international rivalries have provided many of the most dramatic moments in sports, for the very good and obvious reason that whenever the representatives of different nations meet in competition, the air is supercharged with a tingle and electricity that strictly domestic rivalries cannot engender. Players and fans alike who pride themselves on being blasé about such things find a sense of patriotism—or simply a sense of involvement—tightening the throat and heightening the pulse beat. Track and field sports would be immeasurably poorer were there no Olympic Games, as tennis would be without the Davis Cup matches, soccer without the World Cup, and so on. Where international sports are concerned, there are few isolationists.

In golf through the years a keen though friendly rivalry has flourished between the Americans and the British. They have invaded and carried off our championships. We have retaliated. The international aspect, as goes without the saying, was what made the feats of Travis, Ouimet, Hagen, and Jones seem so momentous to us, and made the British, for their part, so unanimously relieved when Henry Cotton (and, later, Tony Jacklin) revived the oriflamme of Vardon and Ray.

In addition to the personal sorties of Americans and Britishers, the players of the two countries have contended against one another in three sets of team matches, the amateurs battling for the Walker Cup, the pros for the Ryder Cup, the women for the Curtis Cup. The first of these competitions to get underway was the Walker. Shortly after World War I, America developed able golfers in numbers for the first time, and a victory by a side of American amateurs over a British side in an informal match in 1921 dispelled any doubts among the Britishers that they still held a superiority that would make an international team match uninteresting and one-sided. In 1922 the top British and American amateurs met in the first official competition for the cup donated by George H. Walker, a past president of the U.S.G.A. Four years after the Walker Cup Matches were inaugurated, the groundwork for a similar transatlantic rivalry between American and British professionals was laid during an informal match at Wentworth in England in which, incidentally, the Americans took a terrific lacing. Samuel Ryder of St. Albans, a wealthy English seed merchant, provided a trophy, and in 1927 a British squad journeyed to America for the first official Ryder Cup Match. In 1932, five years after the Ryder had gotten started at the Worcester Country Club, the top women golfers of the two countries met at Wentworth, outside London, in the maiden match for the cup donated by the Curtis sisters, Margaret and Harriot, two early champions. All three competitions were held biennially, in alternate countries, the Curtis and Walker in the even years, the Ryder in the odd. Taking their cue from the Walker Cup pattern, the Ryder Cup Matches consisted of four foursomes followed by eight singles; the Curtis modified it to three foursomes and six singles.

Before World War II canceled their outings, the women had met in four Curtis Cup competitions. Three times the Americans were victorious after hard-fought battles, and once, in 1936, at Gleneagles, they were held to a $4\frac{1}{2}$–$4\frac{1}{2}$ tie when Wee Jessie Anderson won the vital singles by holing a 60-footer all the way across the home green. The standard of play in the Curtis Cup has been exceedingly high, and the atmosphere surrounding the matches has been ideal—serious, but not overserious, pleasantly warm but not gushy.

The Ryder Cup competitions, considering the wealth of colorful golfers who have been participants, have never been the events they should have been. The P.G.A. has shown less savvy than the U.S.G.A. (which supervises the Curtis and the Walker) in mounting the matches held in America; and in handling their end of the deal, the British professionals' organization has not upheld the reputed British genius for administration. To insure large galleries and healthy gate receipts, the British P.G.A., after selecting Moortown for the first match played in Britain, fastened on the mediocre course at Southport as the Ryder Cup stamping grounds. Southport became a stamping grounds in a most literal sense, for the seaside vacationers who formed the huge galleries carried their Coney Island *joie de vivre* with them onto the links. The marshals and the bamboo bearers were swept helplessly aside, concessionaires blatantly hawked their wares, while, amidst this confusion, the golfers did their best to bear up under the distracting carnival. Until 1937, when the Americans triumphed 8 points to 4 at Southport, neither side had been able to win a match on a foreign course. An odd sidelight was that a

British victory in the Ryder Cup Match was invariably followed by an American victory in the British Open.

American teams, through 1974, won twenty-one of the twenty-four Walker Cup Matches, tying in 1965 and bowing only in 1938 and 1971. Though a bit more one-sided than the Ryder feud, the Walker, paradoxically enough, has been the more successful series—more tastefully presented, played on better courses, altogether higher-pitched. An amateur is less apt to "lose" his nationality than a professional, and even when the Matches were farcical from the standpoint of team totals, the Walker retained its aura of a serious but civilized international rivalry. The series has abounded in colorful incident. The "hero" of the first Match was none other than Bernard Darwin. Bernard, the great and the lovable, accompanied the British team to Charlie Macdonald's National in 1922 in the capacity of a reporter for the *Times* of London. When Robert Harris, the British captain, fell ill on the eve of the Match, Bernard stepped coolly into the breach, played creditably in his foursome, and won his singles from Bill Fownes 3 and 1. Jones was unfailingly superb in Walker Cup play. Bobby won all five of his singles by wide margins and four of his five foursomes, his one defeat coming in 1924, when he and Fownes were beaten on the last hole. Foursomes being a peculiarly British addiction, the Americans' aptitude in winning a type of match they play only during the Cup series came as a distinct surprise. Except for the 1923 and 1938 Matches, up to the outbreak of World War II the Americans were never outscored in the foursomes.

That meeting in 1923 at St. Andrews—until 1925 the Match was held annually—was won by the American team 6 points to 5 (with one singles halved) after one of the most thrilling team finishes on record. Trailing by two points after the foursomes, with two singles irretrievably lost and only one singles definitely going their way, the Americans seemed hopelessly beaten, and then, at the last moment, one courageous rally after another snatched the victory away from the British. George Rotan swept eleven out of twelve holes and won easily. The other matches were closer. Standing 2 down with three to go against Wethered, Ouimet played birdies on the 34th and 35th, and earned a split in his match by holing from eighteen feet for a third birdie when he was partially stymied on the 36th green. Bob Gardner capped his comeback by sinking a 5-footer on the 36th for the hole and the match. Fred Wright, 2 down with three to go, evened his match by carrying the 34th and 35th, and won it with a birdie on the 36th. The winning or the losing of the cup eventually hung on the match between Willie Murray and Doc Willing, and Willing struck the decisive blow on the 35th by holing a 10-footer for a birdie.

The American team won the 1926 Match at St. Andrews by that identical score, 6–5, but thereafter the Matches were runaways for the Americans. The new and unseasoned players who replaced Jones and his crowd were as dependable as the veterans when it came to rising to the occasion. Don Moe, for example, shot the finest golf of his career in his first international competition, the 1930 Match. Out in 32 at Sandwich, the young Oregonian found himself 1 down to James Stout, who had collected six 3s. At lunch Moe was 4 down, and after the first three holes of the afternoon, 7 down. Stout continued to play well and his card for the afternoon round was 72, but Moe beat him. All square coming to the 441-yard 36th, Moe played his second shot from a tough sidehill stance to within a yard of the cup and took the crucial hole. His 3 gave him a 67, a magnificent performance.

But while the American newcomers were turning the Walker Cup Matches into a springboard to fame, the Britishers who took over for the aging were far weaker competitors than the Tolley–Wethered generation. Only Tony Torrance had the stuff that wins singles matches. Torrance's 1-up victory over Chick Evans saved his side from the ignominy of a shutout in the '28 Match at the Chicago Golf Club. In 1930 he accounted for half of the British points by submerging Ouimet 7 and 6 at Sandwich. Tony received the symptoms of support in 1932, when he halved with Ouimet, for Stout and John Burke also halved their matches and Leonard Crawley actually won his. But in 1934 it was the same sad story, Torrance alone rising above the inferiority complex that now gripped the British side and winning his singles once again in his last appearance as a Walker Cupper.

In their efforts to assemble a team that would at least lose by a respectable score, the British selectors resurrected veterans, dug up more Scots, gave youth a chance, and became a little less blinded by the social stripes of the Old School Tie. When their teams continued to lose by vast margins, the selectors resorted to even more desperate measures and included in their 1936 squad a teenage schoolboy champion (John Langley), a left-hander (Laddie Lucas), and an Irishman (Cecil Ewing). The 1936 British team at length succeeded in gaining the distinction the four previous teams had been flirting with, a coat of whitewash.

The 9–0 humiliation at Pine Valley in the 1936 Match shocked the British into cleaning house from the cellar up. The old selectors were excused, and a new board installed. In studying the form of the players who looked to be Cup timber for the 1938 Match, the new selectors covered the geographical areas in more detail than their predecessors. They gave proof that they meant business when they invited a large number of candidates to come to St. Andrews in late May and play in tryout tests on which the final selection of the team would be based. Jettisoning all social distinctions, they named to their squad Charley Stowe, a hulking ex-coal miner, one of the unprettiest technicians on the island but a golfer who got results. A major problem the selectors and the team captain, John Beck, knew they faced was ridding their players' minds of the myth that the Americans were supermen. At the tryouts at St. Andrews, Jimmy Bruen, an eighteen-year-old boy from Ireland, accomplished this invaluable service for the selectors and Beck. Aggressive, strong, and with a brilliant flair for the game, young Bruen reeled off a succession of sub-par rounds. Bruen's scoring bred a feeling among the British players that for once their side had a leader who could match any American star, and this confidence in Bruen kept on enlarging until the British players came to believe that as a side they were just as good as the Americans. In addition to Bruen and

Stowe, the British team was made up of Hector Thomson, the 1936 British Amateur Champion, an amateur with a professional's poise; Gordon Peters and Alex Kyle, like Thomson, from Scotland; Cecil Ewing from Ireland, the runner-up to Charley Yates in the 1938 British Amateur; Frank Pennink, a steady Oxfordian; Leonard Crawley, a pupil of Cotton's, ex-schoolmaster and cricketer, a natural competitor, and the proud possessor of a ginger mustache and an antique mustard-colored sweater; and Harry Bentley, a merry Lancashireman, the comedian of the team. Bentley, who had won the French Amateur and always played well in France, got a great boot out of referring to France as "my country" and in muttering phrases like *"C'est difficile"* to relieve the seriousness of a match.

The American team that Francis Ouimet shepherded to Britain was a fairly well-balanced young team composed of four Walker Cup veterans and four novitiates. The man expected to play number one was Johnny Goodman, now an insurance salesman and at twenty-eight the oldest man on the squad. Goodman had finally won the Amateur at Alderwood in Portland, Oregon, in 1937. The one other veteran of two Walker Cup Matches was Johnny Fischer. After helping to apply the whitewash at Pine Valley in 1936, Fischer had taken the Amateur, at Garden City Golf Club, by coming from behind in the final to overhaul Jock McLean with a birdie on the 36th green and to win out with a birdie on the first extra hole. Reynolds Smith and Charley Yates, who had won their matches handily in 1936, were back again. The four freshmen had the following credentials: Freddy Haas, from New Orleans, had captured the Intercollegiate and the Southern; Charley Kocsis, from Detroit, had a sound all-round record in sectional, collegiate, and national tournaments; Ray Billows, the kingpin in the New York area, had reached the final of the 1937 Amateur; Marvin "Bud" Ward, from Tacoma, had an adequate sectional record and in the 1936 Amateur had fought a fine semi-final with Goodman before losing. (Ward's credentials were not too formidable, and the followers of Frank Strafaci, Harry Givan, and Wilfred Wehrle let it be known that they thought their men had been done dirt.) The 1938 team was certainly not up to the standards of the 1922 team, for instance—every member of the '22 team won at least one national championship—but the American golfing public had become so accustomed to lopsided victories over the British that the possibility of losing the tenth Walker Cup Match scarcely entered their minds.

Ouimet was able to get a line on his boys during the British Amateur, which was held at Troon just before the Cup Matches. On the strength of what they showed at Troon, Ouimet was led to make several changes in his batting order. Goodman, far off his best form (and displeased with himself for losing to Kocsis in an early round), was dropped to the second spot, and Charley Yates was promoted to number one. Yates had hit the ball wonderfully well in winning the British Amateur. Everything was coming into his strenuous swing at the right time, and several Scots who had witnessed Charley's impressive march were almost convinced that what was holding back British golfers was that they didn't dip their knees as Yates did when he hurled his right side viciously into his shots. The Scots cottoned on to Yates as soon as they heard he was a fellow-townsman of Bobby Jones', and Charley's forcing golf and rich sense of humor made him the most popular man in Scotland.

The third of June, the first day of the two-day meeting at St. Andrews, brought good weather for golf. A light breeze off the bay was stirring the whins and the air was agreeably cool as the rival captains, Ouimet and Beck, watched their charges tee off in the four 36-hole foursome matches. Seven hours later, for the first time in fifteen years, a British team was out in front after the first day's play—2 points to 1. Pennink and Crawley, in the fourth foursome, defeated Smith and Haas 3 and 1 in a match that was not as close as the score implies. The British team was always in command, and Crawley's irons and Pennink's putting abruptly halted the periodic attempts of the Americans to get back into the match. Peters and Thomson, the Scottish combo, raced off to a lead against Goodman and Ward in the second foursome and were never seriously threatened as they went on to a 4 and 2 victory. Goodman, still off his game, was conspicuously irritated by his own errors and Ward's, and his attitude did not make it any easier for his less experienced partner to settle down. Because of the many criticisms of his selection for the team, Ward had felt that he was on the spot before he sailed for Scotland, and his poor play at Troon, where he was fighting a quick hook, gave the anti-Ward society further fuel for its second-guessing. Ward was handicapped by being overdetermined to "show them," it seemed, and Goodman was certainly not the steadying influence he might have been. The American victory was racked up by the team of Yates and Billows, who had their match against the third British pair, Kyle and Stowe, under control at all times. The feature foursome, which pitted Fischer and Kocsis against Bruen and Bentley, was definitely the hardest-fought and best-played match. At the close of the morning round, in which they had dovetailed for a 72, 1 under St. Andrews' par, Fischer and Kocsis were 3 up on the British pair. Though not playing badly, Bruen was not up to the brilliance of his practice rounds, and it had been Bentley who had prevented the Americans from gaining a larger lead. The British did not win a hole all morning, and while they were the aggressors in the afternoon, not until the 27th did they break through with a win. Had the British wanted to be technical, however, they could have claimed the 21st. On this hole, after Bentley and Bruen had made their 4, Fischer lined up the 10-footer for a birdie 3 that Kocsis' approach had set up. Johnny babied the putt. It stopped a foot or so short of the cup. It would have been a routine half in 4s if Johnny, momentarily upset by being unforgivably short on the birdie putt, had not walked up to the ball and tapped it into the hole. By tapping the ball, Fischer had played out of turn. It had been Kocsis' shot. Bruen, impatient to get going, was all for demanding the hole on Fischer's infraction of foursome rules. Bentley was just as eager as his young partner to win a hole, but the cool Lancashireman did not choose to win one this way. He finally calmed young Bruen with his explanation that he had conceded the Americans their foot putt before Fischer had tapped it, and waiving any claim to the hole, assured his partner that he thought they were playing good enough golf to win the match if they stuck to their knitting. On the

The team that lost the Walker Cup: Johnny Fischer, Charley Kocsis, Captain Francis Ouimet, Charley Yates, Bud Ward, Reynolds Smith, Johnny Goodman, Ray Billows, and Fred Haas. The British won by 7 to 4 on their home court, St. Andrews.

27th, still 3 down, Bruen and Bentley won their first hole of the day when the Irish boy holed for a birdie from eighteen feet. On the 29th they won another with a birdie 2, Bruen once more dropping a sizable putt. Fischer and Kocsis stopped this rally when they took the 30th, and the Americans' lead of two holes loomed larger and larger as the 31st, 32nd, and 33rd were halved. Then the British pair struck back with a gallant last-ditch drive. On the 34th Bentley put his chip inside of Kocsis', and Bruen holed for a win that cut the Americans' margin to one hole. On the 35th, Bentley squared the match by knocking a 45-footer into the can for an eagle 3. Bentley's sharp approach to the 36th gave Bruen a crack for a birdie that would have beaten the Americans, but the young man's putt was wide of the mark, and the hole and the match were halved. It was probably a fortunate thing for the Americans that Walker Cup Matches do not go into extra holes, for Bentley and Bruen, who had used only 68 strokes on their afternoon comeback, were getting hotter and hotter whereas Fischer and Kocsis were fading fast.

In Walker Cup Matches at this time, no points or fractions thereof were given for a halved match, hence the 2–1 lead the British carried into the second day of play. Insignificant as the British margin seems on paper, that one-point difference backed the Americans against the wall. A split in the eight singles matches would result in a British victory. To hold the Cup, Ouimet's boys could afford to lose no more than three of the eight singles.

At noon things didn't look too rosy for the Americans. Johnny Goodman had been thoroughly outclassed by Hector Thomson's 69, and stood 6 down. Fischer was 4 down to Crawley's 71. These two matches seemed as good as lost, and that wasn't all. The outcome of four matches—Smith versus Peters, Haas versus Kyle, Billows versus Ewing, Kocsis versus Stowe—was still undetermined after the first eighteen, but any of them could go to the Britisher as easily as to the American, and the loss of just one would be disastrous. Only two matches were going the way of the Americans. Charley Yates had a slight lead in his scrap with Bruen, and there was a feeling that he would be able to match anything the Irish whiz threw at him; Charley was playing confidently. Ironically, the much-maligned Ward was the one American who had his match virtually won after the morning round. In an exhibition of very great shot-making, the grim tax accountant from Tacoma had whirled around St. Andrews in 67 strokes and was 9 *up* on the hapless Pennink.

In the afternoon the tide of battle seemed to be turning. Once more the Americans appeared to be off on one of those team rallies that had so often overcome the British challenges in the past. Charley Yates successfully protected his thin lead over Bruen and registered his victory on the 35th. Bud Ward, piling it on, took three of the first seven holes from Pennink to win 12 and 11, and here was another point for the Americans. Kocsis, the report came in, was getting the upper hand over Stowe, and, most heartening of all, a match that had been chalked off as lost was won. Standing 4 down to the man with the ginger mustache, Johnny Fischer had turned his battle with Crawley inside out by shooting six consecutive 3s from the 25th through the 30th, and closed Leonard out on the 34th green.

Most of the spectators had been following the exciting Fischer–Crawley match. When it was over, they lingered around the sixteenth green exchanging information on the matches that were "in" and rumors on the matches that were still in progress. Thomson had finished Goodman, Peters had trounced Smith, and some hasty addition disclosed that each side had now garnered four points (including the foursomes) with three matches yet to be decided. Fischer's remarkable recovery had raised the hopes of the handful of American spectators and sobered the spirits of the British. By taking two of the three matches still out, the Americans could win.

And then the tide of battle swung back to the British, suddenly and dramatically. Kocsis and Stowe were coming into sight on the sixteenth tee, the 34th hole of their match. The last definite word on this pair was that Kocsis was 1 up on the ex-coal miner as they left the 29th green. But Kocsis carried no lead as he and Stowe walked set-faced down the 34th. Kocsis was 2 down. Stowe had taken the 30th, the 31st, and the 32nd. The spectators picked up this match and followed it to the 35th green, where Stowe tucked it away 2 and 1. His victory put the British team in front by a point. Haas would have to beat Kyle, Billows would have to beat Ewing, or else the British were in.

Nobody seemed to know how Haas and Kyle, the last starters, were coming along. They would be somewhere around the thirteenth, and rather than chase after them, the majority of the spectators backtracked a hole to pick up Ewing and Billows on the sixteenth. Beyond the fact that these two fighters were locked in an extremely tight give-

and-take, nothing more was known for certain. Billows was seen to be driving first off the 34th, and it was soon discovered that he had won the honor by birdieing the 33rd. But it was also discovered that he was 1 down to Ewing. Ewing batted one out-of-bounds on the 34th, and Billows squared the match. They moved on to the Road Hole, both men patently worn from their furious duel. Billows put his second into the deep bunker by the green and would have to fight hard for his half . . . and then, as the thousands tensely watched Billows enter the bunker, over the hill came Kyle and Haas preceded by the small gallery who had watched their match. It was good news for the British and it spread across the fairway like wildfire. Kyle had defeated Haas on the 32nd.

That was it. Great Britain had won the Walker Cup. For the first time!

The Billows–Ewing match didn't matter now. Ewing did win the 35th, guarded his one-hole advantage on the 36th, and this made the final count Great Britain 7, United States 4.

The British had been the better team at St. Andrews. When the better team wins, it is not so hard to lose. The Americans quickly got over the sting of losing a cup they had held without interruption since 1922, and joined with the overjoyed Britons in celebrating the successful conclusion of their sixteen-year vigil. On the steps of the Royal and Ancient, the cup changed hands as thousands smiled. The Scottish majority in the crowd began calling for Yates, their favorite, who had gone undefeated in eleven matches in Scotland, and with very little coaxing the uninhibited Georgian sauntered onto the "stage" wearing that cockeyed grin of his. Completely at home with his friends, Yates passed up speechmaking in favor of leading the crowd in an old Scottish song: With Gordon Peters helping him out, Charley bellowed his way through "A Wee Deoch and Doris." The high-spirited community-sung chorus ended on a happy note, and so did The Walker Cup Matches of 1938. It would have been grand to have won, but if you had to lose, where else would circumstances have made defeat so sweet?

ALL
GOOD
THINGS

After he had won his Walker Cup match 12 and 11, Bud Ward stayed out on the course to see how his team mates were faring. An American fan, spotting Ward on the fringe of the gallery following the Fischer–Crawley match, walked over to Bud and congratulated him on his splendid victory. How much had he won by, the fan asked. "Twelve and eleven," was the stern-voiced answer. The American went on to say that he had watched Ward on his morning round and knew about the marvelous 67, but how well had he scored in the afternoon? "I had four-four-three-three-six-four-four," Ward answered. When Ward had come to the 6, the American had smiled one of those smiles meant to imply that he understood—sooner or later a bad hole must creep onto the card of every golfer, even if he be the man who has just taken St. Andrews apart like no amateur before him. The smile offended Ward. "I would have had my par on the fifth if I hadn't three-putted," he said testily. "I hit three good shots. I three-putted, that's all."

In his attitude toward the game's camp followers, Bud Ward bore the marks of the severe beating he had taken before his crashing victory over Pennink had silenced his detractors. He brushed off compliments and declined to cultivate the little courtesies that would have made him popular with the galleries, for he had learned the painful way of the fickleness of sports fans. Win and you're a great guy, lose and you're a monkey. On the golf course Ward tended strictly to winning. The social amenities could wait until later when he was among his friends.

But if Ward's experiences in the spring of 1938 had put acid in his attitude, they had also put iron in his self-confidence. In vindicating himself so gloriously against

Bud Ward lofts a short approach from the rough. This stern, unsmiling competitor from Spokane scored notable victories in the 1938 and 1947 Walker Cup Matches, won the U.S. Amateur in 1939 and 1941, and, all in all, proved himself the top amateur of his day.

Pennink, Ward had acquired an unshakable belief in himself that changed him from a fair golfer into the outstanding amateur in the four-season stretch between the last pre-war Walker Cup Match and Pearl Harbor.

In the qualifying round for the 1938 Amateur, at Oakmont, Ward tied for second place with Willie Turnesa and Dick Chapman, two strokes behind the medalist, Gus Moreland. Some very hot golf by Art Doering, however, was too much for Bud and he went out in the first round, 3 and 1. (Turnesa, the quiet, smooth swinger, took the title by defeating Pat Abbott 8 and 7. In the final Willie gave an amazing demonstration of blaster-play from Oakmont's furrowed bunkers and one-putted no less than fourteen of the twenty-nine greens.) The next year, 1939, Ward crashed through. In the Open he matched the best professionals stroke for stroke. *Ifs* do not count, of course, but if Ward had not hooked a tee shot on a short hole on the last nine and ended up with a 5, he might have won the Open. As it was, his 285 (69-73-71-72) was one stroke above the winning mark shared by Nelson, Wood, and Shute. Ward's showing in the Open made

An aerial view of the Oakmont Country Club, outside of Pittsburgh, as that bunker-scarred battleground awaited the invasion of the nation's best amateurs in 1938. Founded in 1903 and continually revised by the Fownes family, Oakmont is without a doubt one of the most rigorous tests of scoring in the world.

him a heavy favorite to take the Amateur at the North Shore Country Club, near Chicago, some three months later. In the semi-finals he got his revenge on Doering, 2 and 1. Against Ray Billows in the final, played in a twisting, gusty wind, Ward was 1 under par for the thirty-one holes he required to win the match.

The hard-boiled champion took it on the chin when he attempted to defend his title at Winged Foot a year later. Bud appeared to be on his game as he took care of Ellis Knowles, Freddy Haas, and Pat Abbott on his way to the quarter-finals, but there he ran into a wild streak, and Ray Billows defeated him with no more trouble than the 4 and 3 count suggests. (Ward's successor was Dick Chapman, the son of a wealthy man who had raised his boy to be a golf champion. It was curious that Chapman, who had sat before the most celebrated instructors in golf, and Joe Ezar as well, won the Amateur when he was employing a swing so awkward and unrhythmic that it looked as if he had never taken a lesson in his life. But at Winged Foot—which, incidentally, was one of

Dick's home courses—he was getting results, and was an unpressed and deserving winner.)

Ward regained his crown in 1941, and in doing so defeated not only some capable opponents but also some of the most hostile galleries a golfer had faced since Travis at Sandwich. The Omaha Field Club, where the Amateur was held, was not in the best of shape—the fairways scorched by the summer heat, several of the greens mottled with bare spots. Many of the competitors were unhappy about the conditions, and Ward, according to the hometown newspapers, had called the Omaha Field Club "a cow pasture." Ward denied having made this statement, but some of the proud people of Omaha, affronted by the general slurs against their leading golf course (and additionally upset by the elimination in the first round of their favorite son, Johnny Goodman), decided, under the influence of the dogstar, to square accounts with Ward. If he had lost, all would have been forgiven, most likely, but the man they wanted to see lose, this sour, unrepentant, businesslike competitor from Spokane, was too good for his opponents. He reached the final, where he was opposed by Pat Abbott, who had been a finalist against Turnesa three years before.

In the morning round the gallery of three thousand Omahans looked on with displeasure as the genial Abbott, an actor by profession, fell farther and farther behind the man they wanted him to beat. In the afternoon Abbott revived their hopes when he struck a streak of chipping and putting that reduced Ward's lead from five holes to two. Ward was on his way to winning or halving the 24th hole, or rather, Abbott had apparently halted his own surge when his iron approach, played from a downhill lie in the coarse rough, hit the green with no stop on it and was heading for the steep bank behind the green. It was at this moment that some members of the raucous anti-Ward gallery, as Bill Richardson of *The New York Times* reported it, decided that the time had come for more demonstrative participation. As Abbott's ball was running fast over the green, six spectators on the far apron moved in front of the ball and stopped it short. It may have been an accident. Then, as the partisan gallery unwound itself from Abbott's ball, a marshal kicked the ball nearer the pin as accidentally as the six spectators had stopped it. At this juncture, Harold Pierce, the president of the U.S.G.A., walked to the center of the green and addressed the gallery. "We all know what is happening here today," Mr. Pierce began slowly, and he went on to request an immediate cessation of the conduct that was making a travesty of a national championship. After this censure, the spectators did not touch Abbott's ball again, but in spirit they remained unchastised. On the 31st hole, for instance, Ward hit an approach that was much too strong. "Let her through. Let her through," yelled some members of the gallery who were fearful lest their colleagues clustered behind the green inadvertently prevent Ward's shot from carrying over the green into trouble. Despite the gallery and competent golf by Abbott, Ward built up his lead again and ended the match on the 33rd green. The gallery then swooped in on the loser and hoisted him triumphantly to their shoulders.

It was not one of the shining chapters in American sportsmanship.

As close as Bud Ward came to winning the 1939 Open, Sam Snead came closer, much closer. With only two more of the seventy-two hells of the grind to endure, the popular man from the mountains had the title in the bag. Pars on the 71st and 72nd would give Sam 282, two strokes better than the total at which Nelson, Wood, and Shute had tied. Sam looked shaky, very shaky, in dropping a stroke to par on the 71st, when he fell a full foot shy on his putt from six feet, yet there was no cause for alarm. Hitting a golf ball under pressure, the spectators knew from their own experience, takes it out on a man's nerves more vehemently than any other effort in sports. Nearly every member of the gallery at one time or another in his life had stood on the eighteenth tee with a chance to win the Saturday tournament and had found that his vertebrae shivered like a marimba and kept on shivering when he tried to relax and laugh at himself for becoming so keyed up at the prospect of getting his name in the paper and winning an electric clock. The 90s-golfers and the 107-golfers watching Snead knew that nearly every other athlete has an incalculable advantage over the golfer under tournament pressure. The football or the hockey player can get rid of his nervousness by bodily contact, the old releaser, and even the ping-pong player can *move*, and the act of moving does wonders for the athlete under tension. But the golfer, stationary before a stationary ball, is helpless. No one jars him out of his introspection with a left to the jaw. He cannot run three steps to the left and by that physical motion assuage the rat-tat-tat of his nerves and banish that indigo foreboding that he will be fifty yards off-line if his hands fail by a fraction of a second to do the right thing at the right time. What other sport punishes a minuscule error by the *fingers* so savagely? What other sport gives a player less chance to wipe out an error? Double-fault in tennis; you have lost only a point in a game of a set of a match; win a point and you're often as well off as you were before your error. Miss a lay-up in basketball; you have a dozen other opportunities to atone, and scoring is merely part of a player's efficiency anyhow. Throw wild to first base, and it may not hurt at all, but if it does, you can play the next ball hit to you as if nothing had happened. Compared to golf, other sports are lenient with the transgressor. But golf—roll your wrist before your swing is ready for it and the ball flies madly into the rough . . . and you don't tee up again and say to yourself that that was a bad one and you'll make up for it by hitting a good one now. Golf does not revert to a set situation. There is no fresh restart. Each thing you do you are stuck with. When the ball flies wildly into the rough, on your next shot you pay the immediate penalty for your error, and error breeds error. More than the terror of knowing you must beat forty players and not a single player, more than the always-varying, ever-unpredictable character of the terrain on which the game is played, more than the unreasonable proportion with which a small error in muscular control is often punished, it is the knowledge that there is no recourse from a bad shot plus the unrelenting accumulativeness of shot on shot that makes tournament golfers old before their time and that made a seasoned golfer like Sam Snead shiver like a marimba as he teed up his ball on the 72nd hole of the Spring Mill course of the Philadelphia Country Club in the United States Open Championship of 1939.

There was no cause for alarm, however. All Sam Snead had to do to win was to

Snead in trouble. At the top, Sam explodes expertly from a trap on the 7th hole at the Spring Mill course, the 61st hole of the 1939 U.S. Open. However, below, bunkered on the 72nd, praying for another such recovery, Snead faltered pathetically. He needed two strokes to extricate himself from the sand and staggered to an 8 that cost him the championship. A par 5 would have won for Sam.

play the 558-yard eighteenth in five strokes, par. An expert like Sam would not take a 6 on a fairly easy par 5, but in the event that he did, he would still tie for first.

Snead hit his drive squarely, but his right hand apparently turned over too quickly, for the ball hooked into the trampled rough. Snead elected to play a wood from the rough. Maybe it would have been smarter to have taken an iron. Anyhow, Sam played a brassie in an effort to eat up as much distance as possible, and he pushed it off into a bunker about a hundred yards before the green. He was worried now, and his face and his walk showed it. He failed to get the ball out of the bunker on his third shot, and now he was lost. He played his fourth before he had thought the shot out, and barely extricated the ball from the bunker. He made the green with his fifth. He putted once, to three feet. He putted again. He putted once more.

Sam Snead walked like a man hypnotized through the stunned, muttering crowd. He sat silently in the clubhouse trying to adjust himself to the unreal fact that he had taken an 8 and blown the championship. He didn't want to speak to anyone, least of all to the reporters.

Outside the crowd was still muttering. Few of them had seen Diegel take his 8 at Worcester or Hancock his two 6s at Olympia Fields. Most of the spectators had never before witnessed a crackup of this dimension. They talked it over and tried to puzzle it out, as if it had been caused by something occult and mysterious. And one well-known professional, recalling the transfixed look in Sam Snead's eyes as he had walked away from his nightmare, shook his head and said, neither cruelly nor sentimentally, simply said, "Snead will never be able to get over this. He will never be able to win an important championship after this. He'll never be the same."

Had the sympathies of the sports fans of America not been drained dry by Sam Snead's tragic collapse, they might have been more affected than they were when Craig Wood, after tieing for first place with Byron Nelson and Denny Shute, lost still another championship playoff in the 1939 Open.

Wood had made the playoff through a courageous finish. On the last hole he had busted his second shot all the way to the green and got the birdie he realized he had to get. In the extra round to decide the first triple tie in the Open since the historic Ouimet–Ray–Vardon playoff in 1913, Shute fell by the wayside early. Nelson and Wood fought it out tooth and nail to the eighteenth green, and there Wood could have ended it had he holed an 8-footer. He missed, so Craig and Byron went into a second playoff, and this time Byron had it and Craig didn't—70 strokes for Byron, 73 for Craig.

By losing the Open playoff Craig Wood ran to three the championships he had lost after tieing for the top. In 1933 Shute had beaten him in the playoff for the British Open. In 1935 Sarazen had snatched the Masters away from him by holing that double-eagle and then outplaying him over the extra thirty-six. The only one of the four big professional championships that Wood had not lost in a playoff was the P.G.A., and in 1934 Wood had been defeated by Runyan in the final of that tourney. Considering the gall and wormwood he had swallowed, the manner in which Wood took his latest and

Craig Wood. Craig started his professional career with a curious combination job: during the summer months he served as the pro at a nine-hole course in Manchester, Kentucky; in the winter he was assistant bookkeeper in a tobacco warehouse.

most bitter disappointment was thoroughly to be admired. He was not downcast. He would have liked to have won, but he salvaged some satisfaction in knowing that at Spring Mill he had played the finest golf of his life.

Craig wasn't getting any younger. He was thirty-seven when he lost to Nelson, and after they have reached thirty-five, most golfers have passed their peak and are on the way down. In the 1940 Open, however, Wood came through with another excellent performance. He totaled 289 for his four rounds over the stiff Canterbury course and finished fourth, two strokes behind Little and Sarazen, a stroke behind Horton Smith (making his last strong bid for a national championship), a stroke ahead of Nelson, Guldahl, Ray Mangrum's brother Lloyd, and the sensational Ben Hogan, who had cleaned up on the circuit and was starting out on a prolonged streak of superlative golf that would carry him into the money in fifty-six consecutive tournaments. (Snead, by the way, the-man-who-had-taken-an-8-on-the-72nd-hole-of-the-Open, had an 81 on his fourth round when a 72 would have won for him. It was rather pitiable.)

Craig Wood philosophically readied himself for another campaign in 1941. It proved to be the year that amply rewarded his gameness and his patience.

In the spring Wood won the Masters. The situation at Augusta was tense from the moment Wood posted his first-round score, a 66. Here was the best chance he had ever had. No gallery ever pulled harder than the gallery at Augusta was pulling for Craig. A brace of 71s gave him a three-stroke edge on the field with a round to go. So far in the tournament, Craig had not suffered any of his usual bad breaks, and when his caddie caught a rabbit that had been scooting across the fairway, Craig instructed the young man to carry the good-luck omen the rest of that final round. Despite the four rabbit's feet, Craig lost his lead by the 63rd. He had needed 38 strokes going out, and Byron Nelson had burned up the nine in 33. With nine holes to go, Nelson and Wood were exactly even. But Wood did not buckle. He came home in 34, and when Nelson slipped to a 37, Wood had scored the most notable triumph in a career that went back to the Kentucky Open of 1925.

Wood's dreams of going on to take the U.S. Open received a rude jolt two weeks before the big event. On the morning of May 22, Craig was preparing to shave. As he was reaching in the cabinet for his razor, he suffered an excruciating muscle spasm in his back, in the lumbo-sacral region near the fifth vertebra, as a specialist later informed the worried veteran. To enable Wood to walk and hit his shots without pain—Craig had his heart set on playing the Open—the specialist prescribed a heavy and involved corset belt. Working out in his harness on the course of the Colonial Golf Club in Fort Worth, the Open site, Wood felt uncomfortably restricted, but when he removed the belt, the pain was intense and he could not concentrate on his shots. He put the belt on again.

Colonial was not then a course worthy of the Open. It was too young a course, barely six years old. Two holes were being played for the first time. Under perfect conditions, Colonial would have been somewhat of a trial; in the weather that prevailed during the Open, Colonial was a quagmire. The ground was not porous enough to drain the many inches of rain that electric storms and a steady downpour cast on the course. Fairways and greens were puddled with water. Traps were almost unplayable. The most impervious stretches of Colonial were turned into muck and mud as the golfers sloshed toward the greens. Wood, oddly enough, profited from the inundation. His strong legs and Mehlhornesque shoulders made him a consistently good mudder, and even with a corset restricting his swing, he met the conditions at Colonial more successfully than the younger, haler pros. A 73 and a 71 placed Craig in a tie for the lead at the halfway mark. His woods were straight, as they had to be in the narrow fairways, and he was fading his irons elegantly into the pin. A 70 put him in the van by two strokes after fifty-four holes. Another 70 made it conclusive. There was no challenge. Wood's was a striking, clear-cut, three-stroke triumph.

Thirty-nine when he won in the marshes of Fort Worth, Craig Wood was the oldest American to win our most important championship. (In later years Ben Hogan took the 1953 Open at forty and Julius Boros the 1963 Open at forty-three.) The gamester in the corset had finished like a colt. On the 72nd he had slammed out his best drive of the tournament. He had faded a 7-iron eighteen feet from the cup. Then he had rammed in his putt for a birdie.

What had happened to Guldahl? This was the question that golf fans were asking more and more insistently. When Wood won at Colonial, Guldahl was not even among the first twenty. It was not a momentary slump, not one of those bad weeks that punctuate the good ones. In 1941 Ralph Guldahl, the masterful medalist, did not have one week in which he performed like the golfer who had swept three successive Westerns, two successive Opens, and the 1939 Masters. What had happened to Guldahl?

Ralph Guldahl didn't know. He was still trying to hit the ball the same way he had in '37, '38, '39. He hadn't monkeyed around with his swing. It wasn't his personal habits, for Ralph was a clean liver, didn't drink or smoke. He was baffled when he found that he could not shake off his slump. He asked his friends among the pros for their suggestions. None of them knew for sure what had happened to Guldahl. They stood by as Ralph hit hundreds of balls off the practice tees, checking each position of his hands, his clubhead, and his body, but they could not spot what he was doing wrong. Ralph had slow-motion pictures taken of his "slump swing" and studied them along with the pictures shot at Augusta when he had triumphed in 1939. As far as he or any of his friends could make out, the two swings were identical, fundamental for fundamental, detail for detail. But, obviously, they weren't. If they were, Ralph still would have been playing winning golf and not struggling to break 76. His shots would have had that sharp click and not sounded as though Ralph were hitting a soggy pudding-bag.

Although no one could point out what had happened to Ralph Guldahl, there was no dearth of theories. A popular one was that the invisible, infinitesimal error in Ralph's timing was caused by his breathing. Another well-supported theory blamed it on the hands; an upright swinger, Ralph, who used the merest suspicion of a pivot, might have thrown too heavy a burden on his arms and hands; his was, therefore, the easiest kind of a groove to lose and the hardest to rediscover. Sam Snead, as close to Guldahl as anyone, didn't claim to know what Ralph's trouble was but Sam thought he knew when it had begun—in the tail end of the winter of 1940. Partnered with Snead in the annual Miami Four-ball, in one match Ralph had hit only three greens in eighteen holes. Sam's views on the Guldahl mystery synthesized the opinions of most of Ralph's colleagues. "When Ralph was winning," Sam once commented, "he had some peculiar habits, like all of us.

His left elbow used to be stuck out a bit. He used to toe in his irons. He drew the ball a little. But those small things didn't amount to anything. When Ralph was at his peak, his clubhead came back on the line and went through on the line as near perfect as anyone I've seen. I don't know what happened to Ralph."

Nor does anyone, even now.

The outbreak of World War II in September 1939, as this survey of the highlights of the 1938–41 stretch may imply, did not put a damper on sports schedules and sports enthusiasm in the United States. However, the Ryder Cup Match, planned for Ponte Vedra, Florida, in November 1939, had to be called off, as did the other Anglo-American competitions. Johnny Bulla, the clouter who played the drugstore ball, could not try to better the runner-up position he had gained in the 1939 British Open. There was no French Championship for Dick Chapman to recapture. International golf, what there was of it, was inter-American. (The winner of the Argentine Open of 1941 was Jimmy Demaret, a Texan who had jumped to the forefront by taking the 1940 Masters.) But in the United States, since it was life-as-usual, it was golf-as-usual, making minor allowances for the increase in griping among the Scotch-drinking clique in the locker room, the threadbare look coming over the tweeds of the tweedy, and the unflinching despotism of club pros as they doled out their shrinking supply of good balls. But after December 7, 1941, the United States was in it, and there were some changes made.

PART FIVE

THE ADVENT OF THE MODERN ERA

1941–1948

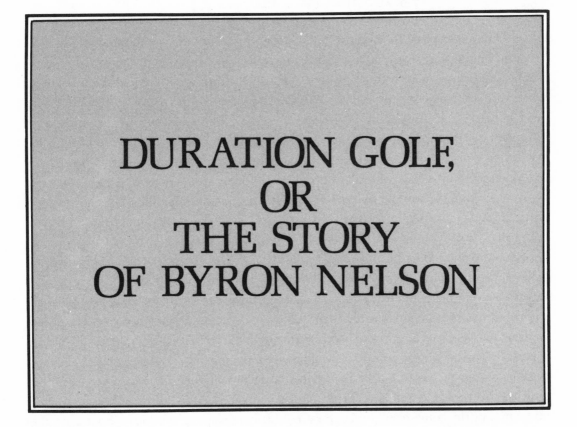

DURATION GOLF,
OR
THE STORY
OF BYRON NELSON

When war came for the British in 1939, sports were immediately and completely abandoned. In total war, or the approximation of total war which lasted from September 1939 to September 1945, the pursuit of sports was ranked at first with sumptuous unrationed parties, long-distance trips on bootlegged gas, and soft-berth manipulation as a harmful, unpatriotic anachronism that would hinder the war effort. The British dug deep pits the breadth of their fairways to destroy their value as possible landing strips for German gliders, and unless they were in uniform, few Britishers of sound body and military age ventured on the links. After the Battle of Britain, however, and the removal of the immediate threat of invasion, the British perspective on total war altered and it began to be realized that proper relaxation, far from prolonging the war, was the best insurance that men and women, working harder than ever before in their lives, could continue to back the men behind the guns. The English, the Scots, and the Welsh returned to their golf courses and, absolved from the fear of condemnation, benefitted from their golf and almost as much from the anticipation of a pleasant round on their next day off from the factory.

In the United States people went through a somewhat similar cycle. The threat of an enemy landing being much smaller, the first expulsion of sports and our subsequent easing back into them were not as extreme as they were in Britain. But during the dark days when the Japanese were marching unhalted throughout the South Pacific and the Germans were rolling toward Stalingrad and the Suez, Americans who played golf made certain that in their community their part in the home-front effort was well enough known to place them above apologizing for taking their recreation so publicly. With the landings in North Africa and Sicily and the stabilization of the situation in the Pacific, Americans who wanted to play golf usually did. Most consciences were clear when War Manpower Commissioner McNutt told the nation's golfers, officially, to get out and play—golf was not an unpatriotic diversion. Three-quarters of the clubs in the United States remained open throughout the war. Few of them took up the U.S.G.A.'s suggestion that part of their roughs be turned into victory gardens, and the members of the Wykagyl Golf Club were almost alone in ploughing up their first two holes and allotting a plot to be worked by each of the fifty-five member families. The ingenuity of most clubs was directed instead toward ways and means of overcoming the shortage of golf balls. The Westchester Country Club engaged professional divers to scour the bottom of its pond. The Black Rock Club in Atlanta drained its lake and rescued 16,000 balls for reprocessing. Reprocessed balls went ten or fifteen yards shorter than the pre-war jewels, but the home-front golfer realized that he was fortunate to be playing at all, and could not manage much more than a *sotto voce* grumble when his car pool kept him waiting, his caddie (if he got one) barely came up to the top of his bag, and his pro smiled superiorly and added the gesture of Kismet when the inevitable subject of golf balls was broached. Courses could not be maintained as they had been in peacetime, for power mowers had broken down and the strong-bodied minions of the greenkeeper were in uniform, but the home-front golfer, for all of his handicaps, played just about as well as he had in 1941 except when members of his draft board were in the foursome immediately in front or behind him.

Shortly after the declaration of war, Ed Dudley, the president of the P.G.A., called a special meeting of his executive committee. The P.G.A. heads decided to send a wire to Washington and ascertain the government's point of view on the position of golf tournaments in wartime. Professional golf was never given the green light like baseball, but the P.G.A. was instructed by officials in Washington to encourage its stars to give exhibitions at service hospitals and to play in as many tournaments as possible for the War Bond drives. A fair percentage of the tournaments scheduled for 1942 were put on—Snead at last won a big one, the P.G.A. Championship, before going into the Navy—but after that the circuit folded, since most of the stars had entered the service and those who remained could not get the gas to go from tournament to tournament. At one Knoxville Open only eighteen players turned up to compete for the twenty prizes.

After Pearl Harbor, Porky Oliver, who had been drafted early in 1941, soon lost his distinction of being the one name-pro in uniform. Jimmy Thomson went into the Coast Guard, Henry Ransom into the Merchant Marine. Little, the son of an Army colonel, became an officer in the Navy. Other Navy men included Snead, Jimmy Demaret, and young Lew Worsham (stationed together at Bainbridge), and Herman Keiser, who put in a good thirty months at sea. Craig Wood, set to become a captain in the Marines, was rejected because of his back. Lloyd Mangrum, Jim Turnesa, Vic Ghezzi, Dutch Harrison, Horton Smith, Clayton Heafner, Jim Ferrier, and Ben Hogan were in the

Army. Smith, Heafner, Ghezzi, and Mangrum got overseas. Mangrum's contact with war was by far the most direct. In the Battle of the Bulge, Lloyd was wounded twice.

Horton Smith and Ben Hogan had perhaps the most ironic encounter with the environment of their peacetime profession. During their periods at the Army Air Forces Officer Candidates School at Miami Beach, Smith and Hogan spent many hours on the old Bayshore golf course, which had been converted into a drill field and obstacle course. It was not so pleasant shooting for their bars instead of their pars, and Horton and Ben could put plenty of feeling into their voices as they marched to the Bayshore day after day with the other beleaguered officer-candidates, singing an appropriate set of lyrics to the tune of "Take Me Out to the Ball Game":

> Off we go to the golf course.
> We ain't gonna play golf.
> Gone are the caddies around the place,
> Gone are the balls that we once used to chase.
> For they've leveled off all the sand traps,
> Closed up the bar and the grille.
> No, it's not for golf that we're out,
> It's a goddam drill.

In 1944, with the initiative secured in both the European and South Pacific theaters, the home-fronters were in a mood to enjoy their hours away from work, and turned out in droves for every sporting event in sight. The quality of the sports they watched was necessarily low. The best athletes were in the service. The big league baseball teams were manned by 4Fs, youngsters awaiting the call from their draft boards, and graying veterans recalled from their gas stations and bowling alleys. The most powerful football teams in the country were Army and Navy outfits, and the few college teams playing better than high school ball were the ones who had received a quota of the experienced stars now involved in the Navy's training programs. In the lesser sports, the one athlete measuring up to pre-war standards was Gundar Haegg, the touring Swedish miler.

It was during this period, when the nation was hungering for first-class athletic performances but expecting none, that Byron Nelson and Jug McSpaden came to the fore. To win the tournaments slowly being revived, Nelson and McSpaden (rejected by the services for hemophilia and sinusitis respectively) did not have to outshoot much of a field. But in golf there is always Old Man Par to test the caliber of the players, and in 1944 Nelson and McSpaden did things to par no golfers had ever done in the Age of Jones or when the post-Depression pack roared fifty-strong around the circuit. The sports-starved fans became extremely excited about the scores turned in by the Gold Dust Twins, as Nelson and McSpaden came to be called, as they triumphed in tournament after tournament.

Nelson, the calm, mechanical Texan, played his seventy-two holes of the Los Angeles Open in 5 under par. In winning the San Francisco Open, Nelson was 13 under, and he maintained this pace as the duration circuit-chasers swung through the South. At the end of ten tournaments, Nelson was 60 under par. His old friend McSpaden—Byron was the godfather of Jug's son—had been even hotter. The big crasher with the dark glasses had beaten par by 69 strokes. Jug's putting began to slip after this, and a decline in his scoring followed, but Nelson continued to travel at a better-than-par clip. When the P.G.A. Championship was renewed at Spokane, ten thousand fans, the largest attendance in the history of the tournament, turned out to watch Nelson in action. On his march to the final, Byron showed them impeccable golf, but in the final his putting touch deserted him. Byron missed three 2-foot putts and bowed to Bob Hamilton, an unknown pro from Evansville playing his first big tournament. Byron's performance at Spokane displeased him mightily, and he declared that he would take the next three tournaments to make up for it. He was as good as his word, winning George S. May's Tam O'Shanter carnival and the Nashville and Dallas Opens. Before he was finished for the year, Nelson had won War Bond prizes amounting in cash value to $35,005, almost doubling the previous record high for total winnings in one year set by Sam Snead in 1938. He did this by averaging 69.67 for his eighty-five competitive rounds. In the Associated Press' nationwide poll, Nelson was chosen Athlete of the Year.

But 1944 was not Nelson's peak. In 1945 he was to go on a tournament rampage the likes of which may never be equaled.

John Byron Nelson, Jr., was the son of a Texas grain and feed merchant. The Nelsons lived in a house adjoining the Glen Garden Country Club in Fort Worth. Byron began caddying at the age of ten. His first golfing hero was Walter Hagen. He followed Hagen around during a P.G.A. Championship in Texas, and when the steaming sun forced the great man to borrow a hat from a person in the gallery, it was young Nelson who stretched his cap out first. Nelson scored 117 the first time he played eighteen holes, and he developed into one of the two best caddie-golfers at the club. The other was Ben Hogan. Theirs was a friendly rivalry, and the two youngsters were not displeased when they tied in the final of the caddie championship and were each awarded a golf club. In 1930 Byron won his first important tournament, the Southwest Amateur. He qualified in his section for a place in the U.S. Amateur the next year, but failed in the national qualification test at Beverly. He turned professional in 1932 and earned $12.50 for his labors on the circuit. Discouraged about his chances of making a living through golf, Byron gave up the game and went to work in Texarkana for J. K. Wadley, an oil man. Wadley was very fond of the quiet six-footer and could sense that his heart still lay in golf. He wangled Nelson the job as pro at the Texarkana Country Club. Nelson's run of good luck continued. He married a fine girl named Louise, whom he met in Sunday school.

Byron Nelson's first promising showing in a big-league tournament came in the 1934 San Antonio Open. His 136 (66–70) put him in front of the visiting name-stars at the halfway mark. Then the young pro succumbed to tournament jitters, and dropped to second place with two 74s. In the Galveston Open, he finished second to Craig Wood.

These two red ribbons were all the encouragement he needed to prepare for another shot at the circuit the next winter. This time he made it. (Nelson and McSpaden, two young aspirants with no sponsors to stake them to coffee money, formed their firm friendship at this time.) Nelson won no tournaments on the circuit but he was regularly in the money, winning over $2,000 in all. More important for the struggling young pro, George Jacobus, then president of the P.G.A., took him on as his assistant at the Ridgewood Country Club in New Jersey. At Ridgewood, Byron had an opportunity to improve his golf and learn to curb his skittish disposition in competition far more strenuous than Texarkana could have afforded. He came along rapidly. By 1936 he was good enough and mature enough to capture his first sectional tournament, the Metropolitan Open. In 1937 he arrived. He won the Masters. With seven to play, Byron was four strokes behind the pace-setter, Ralph Guldahl. Guldahl caught Rae's Creek on the twelfth and an arm of the creek on the thirteenth, went 3 over par with a 5 and a 6. Byron birdied the twelfth in 2, rolled in an eagle 3 on the thirteenth, and picked up six strokes on Guldahl on these two holes. He clinched his victory by playing par golf the rest of the way in.

Byron was now one of the big boys. He was a member of the Ryder Cup team that for the first time defeated the British on British soil. In the foursomes, he and Ed Dudley won the key match from Great Britain's leading tandem, Cotton and Padgham. In the singles, however, Dai Rees, the little Welshman, turned him back on the 35th hole. (Nelson's direct, uncomplicated style received a good press from the British writers, who were favorably disposed, to begin with, toward any man bearing two such glorious English names as Byron and Nelson.) At Carnoustie in the British Open, Byron led all of his Ryder teammates, although he finished no better than fifth. Back home he boosted his earnings for the January–November push over the $6,000 mark by taking the high-pursed Belmont Match Play Open tournament. He was all but ousted in the first round by an amateur, Johnny Levinson, but then he played the best man-to-man golf of his career. In the final he defeated Picard, thanks to his putter. On fifteen of the thirty-two greens, Byron found the cup with his first putt.

The next year, 1938, was not an especially lucrative one for the ambitious Texan, then proing at the Reading Country Club in Pennsylvania. He won the tourneys at Hollywood, Florida, and Thomasville, Georgia, but apart from this, his play was a disappointment to him. He spent many hours working on his swing, trying to break his habit of cocking the left wrist at the top of his backswing; this "deliberate" cocking, he believed, was mainly responsible for inconsistency. He practiced a fuller body turn. All in all it was an effortful, lean season for Nelson, with but one happy note. In his earlier shots at the Open, his best mark had been a tie for twentieth. At Cherry Hills he moved up to a tie for fifth.

Byron Nelson climaxed his long pull to the top in 1939, when he won the North and South, the Western, and the tournament that really makes the difference, the U.S. Open. Byron did not hit the ball at all well the first two days at Spring Mill. His 72 and 73 were manufactured by stubbornly sticking to his guns, like Hagen at Muirfield and

Jones at Hoylake, redeeming mistake upon mistake through courageous recoveries and putts. He came back on his game on the Saturday. Where he had been struggling, he was now playing easily and well, and his 71 in the morning left him fresh for the payoff round. Out early, unharried by knowing more than was good for him, Byron went around in 68 blows and gave the rest of the field a mark of 284 to shoot at. Snead, with the best chance to beat 284, crumbled like a sand castle, but Craig Wood and Denny Shute matched Nelson's total by bringing in 72s. Shute went out on the first 18-hole playoff when Craig and Byron tied with 68s. On the third and fourth holes of the second playoff, Nelson won the Open. On the 384-yard third, he lofted a lovely pitch next to the pin for his birdie. He hit a smooth, straight tee shot 240 yards down the fourth, a 453-yard par 4, and followed it with an absolutely perfect shot with the hardest club in the bag, the 1-iron. Playing it with a slight intentional draw, Byron hammered a low, buzzing approach that climbed onto the green, hopped dead for the hole, and wedged itself between the edge of the cup and the pin. When he reached the green, he tenderly removed the pin and the ball eased itself into the cup for an eagle 2. Byron had a lead he never surrendered.

With his shrewd head for business, Byron quickly caught on to making the adjustments, pronunciamentos, and dollars customary for top-drawer champions. From the clubs bidding for his services, he selected Inverness in Toledo. He arranged for the usual endorsements and "advisory" functions. Thinking about a series of exhibitions, Byron was hopeful that his old crony, McSpaden, would take the P.G.A. so that they might tour the country together. Jug wasn't equal to it. As it turned out, Byron all but won the P.G.A. himself; he stood dormie 1 on Henry Picard in the final, and then fell before two pressure birdies. Following the practice of earlier Open winners, Byron picked an all-star team in which he showed an almost unnatural respect for his elders: driver—Thomson; brassie—Little; #1—Shute; #2—Picard; #3—Picard; #4—Shute; #5—Cooper; #6—Macfarlane; #7—Runyan; chipper—Horton Smith; sand-trap shots—Revolta; putter—Horton Smith.

It was interesting, in the light of this listing, that the only two men who out-averaged Byron the following year were Ben Hogan and Sam Snead. After his ordeal at Spring Mill, Sam was very wobbly for a time, and then he came back, after a rest and a lengthy visit with his dentist, a far more relaxed and congenial competitor. As for Hogan, after several successful but not spectacular whirls around the circuit, Ben started to blaze in 1940. He finally snapped out of his runner-up role, and thrived on winning. Ben, in fact, definitely took the spotlight away from Byron in 1940 and did not relinquish it until he was called into the service after his 1942 campaign. Nelson annexed the 1940 P.G.A. and the 1942 Masters (beating Hogan in the playoff), and while Ben had no major victories to show for his 1940–1942 stretch, the 135-pound gamecock led the pros in total prize money and strokes-per-round average in 1940 and '41, and he was showing the way again in these departments in 1942 when he went into the service. Ben also carried off the Hale America tournament, the ersatz U.S. Open of 1942, with rounds of 72-62-69-68, which put him seven strokes ahead of Nelson. Both Byron and

Nelson strokes the winning putt in the 1937 Masters tournament, his first victory in an important event. In the space of two holes on the final nine, Nelson made up six strokes on Guldahl, playing birdie-eagle while Ralph went three over par.

Ben had their legions of faithful frenetics who were ready at any hour of the day to unload their carloads of facts, figures, and syllogisms to prove that their man was the best golfer in the world. As excellent as Nelson's play had been, the records would have given the nod to Hogan's corner.

1943 was a quiet year, and then in 1944 Byron Nelson, a tired thirty-two with a nervous stomach, began his premeditated assault on par in particular and golf records in general. He had no Hogan to contend with, no Snead. His challenges came from an emaciated pack led by McSpaden, Wood, Sam Byrd, the old Yankee outfielder,

Ellsworth Vines, and Toney Penna, with occasional appearances by Dutch Harrison and Jim Ferrier. The competition was not what it might have been but there was no contesting Nelson's record-breaking average of 69.67 strokes per tournament round. It is impossible to assay how Hogan would have stood up against Nelson's rush in 1944 . . . or in 1945, when, with Snead to push him, Byron Nelson went on his historic rampage.

The record-shattering performances of Lord Byron were compiled over a backbreaking number of tournaments, hunched one upon the other, week after week. The surest method for appreciating Nelson's wondrous consistency is to travel the same tormenting grind that he did, tournament for tournament, trial for trial, total for total.

The first tournament of 1945 was the Los Angeles Open, a four-day event, like most of the tourneys, beginning on the fifth of January and ending on the eighth. Los Angeles, however, was not the first stop on the winter circuit. The caravan always began to move about Thanksgiving time, and in late 1944 the nomads had pitched their tents at Portland (Ore.), San Francisco, Oakland, and Richmond (Calif.) before moving on to Los Angeles' Riviera Country Club. In those four meetings in November and December, Sam Snead, discharged after twenty-six months in the Navy because of a slipped vertebra, gave notice that he was going to make things a shade more interesting for Nelson, his injury and his prolonged absence from competition notwithstanding. The Slammer showed the way at Portland with 289 in his first start, and after Nelson had won at San Francisco and Ferrier at Oakland, Sam led the field home at Richmond. At Los Angeles, Sam began the New Year right. His 283 nipped Byron by a stroke.

On to the Arizona and Texas stands. At Phoenix, Nelson won his first tournament of 1945—the first of the nineteen he would win—by steaming home in 32 for 274, 10 under par. In both the Tucson Open and the Texas Open in San Antonio, Byron brought in totals of 269, a figure that would have commanded the front page a few years earlier but then was not even good enough to win. Ray Mangrum edged him out at Tucson with a 268, and Sam Byrd had the same mark in winning at San Antonio. Short courses with fast fairways and demure roughs made these figures possible, but the boys were also hitting a few golf shots. In the Corpus Christi Open, Byron got back in the win column by shooting a 16-under-par 264. In compiling this total, Byron had the advantage of preferring his lies on the stubbled fairways; consequently, Nelson's score did not enter the record books as equaling the record low total for a 72-hole tournament, Craig Wood's 264 in the Metropolitan Open, earned without benefit of winter rules and over a much tougher course.

Next stop, New Orleans. Byron made it two in a row by outshooting Jug McSpaden in the playoff, 65 to 70, after they had tied at 284. On his 65 round, 7 under par, Byron went out in 32 but had to take a mediocre 33 back when he three-putted the fifteenth. In the Gulfport Open, Byron's bid for his third straight was stopped by Snead. Locked at 275, Sam and Byron had 71s on the first eighteen holes of the playoff, and the match moved into sudden death. On the 19th Byron caught a ditch with his drive, and Sam picked up all the marbles with a simple par. Sam then went off on a little

Byron Nelson, whose golf in 1944 persuaded thousands that he was at least the peer of the immortal Bobby. In 1945 Lord Byron averaged an incredible 68.33 for 120 rounds of P.G.A. tournament play, winning 11 straight events in one stretch. The breaks, good or bad, never influenced this disciplined competitor.

streak of his own. He was 21 under regulation figures in winning the Pensacola Open with 267, seven strokes ahead of Nelson, the runner-up. At Jacksonville, Sam was 22 under. Nelson was far in the ruck, for him, his 275 being nine more than Sam took and good only for sixth.

At this point, as the boys headed for the Miami Four-ball, Snead held a 6–4 lead over Nelson on the winter circuit, a 4–3 lead in the tournaments staged in 1945. Nelson closed the gap by teaming with McSpaden to take the four-ball final 8 and 6 from Byrd and Shute, and then he really began to sizzle. . . . March 16–21. The Charlotte Open at Myers Park. With 70-66-68-68—272, 16 under, Nelson was tied with Snead after seventy-two holes, still tied with him after ninety, when they both took 69s on the playoff round. In the second playoff Sam needed 73 blows, and Byron coasted in with a 69. He was off on his legendary streak. . . . March 23–25. The Greensboro Open at the Starmount Country Club. Nelson defeated his nearest rival, Sammy Byrd, by eight strokes. His 271 was 13 under par. . . . March 30–April 1. The Durham Open. At the Hope Valley course. Most of the boys complained that the hard, unwatered greens made it impossible to hold an approach, hence their disgustingly high totals in the 280s. Nelson was a stroke over par himself for his first three rounds but avoided disgrace by playing his last round in 65, 5 under. . . . Then the Atlanta Open, last stop on the winter circuit. On the Capital City course, par 69. Nelson was 13 under for a record-breaking 263. In view of the shortness of the layout, it was wisely decided to enter Nelson's 263 in the books with the asterisked notation that, as far as championship-length courses went, Craig Wood's 264 was still tops.

A brief rest and the boys went back to the grind in June, Nelson and Snead a week earlier than the rest so that they could decide in man-to-man match and medal play who was the "world's best golfer." On May 26 they met at Fresh Meadow for thirty-six holes of medal play, and Snead's 143 (70–73) was one stroke better than Nelson. Byron was off on the greens. The next day, in thirty-six holes of match play, Nelson reversed matters by running up a six-hole lead over the first thirteen holes and ultimately winning 4 and 3. The split in the weekend matches didn't help to clarify the situation, but Nelson did when he rejoined the pack. . . . June 7–10. The Montreal Open. At the Islemere Country Club. Nelson won his sixth consecutive tournament, his 268 placing him ten strokes ahead of his closest challenger, McSpaden. . . . June 14–17. The Philadelphia *Inquirer*'s Invitation tournament. Played at the Llanerch club. McSpaden finished with three 66s, and all it got Jug was a commendable second. Nelson nosed him out by burning up the course with a last round of 63 (seven birdies, eleven pars) for a total of 269. . . . And then the Chicago Victory Open, at the Calumet Country Club, June 27–July 1. A 69, two 68s, and a 70 added up to 275, 13 under par, seven better than the runners-up, McSpaden and Laffoon. Snead was no longer around to push Nelson. Sam had broken his right wrist playing softball at Hot Springs and was sitting the summer out on an enforced vacation.

July 9–15. The P.G.A. Championship. Match play for a change. At the Moraine

Country Club in Dayton, Ohio, against the largest field ever to contend in the championship. Nelson felt terribly overgolfed after his succession of tournaments. His back was lame and bothered him considerably. "I feel like I'm a hundred years old," he sighed heavily as he prepared for the qualifying round, and then went out and played his thirty-six in 6 under par to tie with Revolta for the medal. He won his first match, 4 and 3, over Sarazen. Then he ran into a tartar, Mike Turnesa. Mike threw a 68 and then a 67 at Byron. With four holes to go, he had a seemingly safe lead of two holes. Nelson won the 33rd with a birdie, the 34th with a birdie. On the 475-yard 35th, Turnesa battled back with a bird, but Nelson beat it with an eagle 3. A quaint par on the last hole protected Byron's 1-up lead. Byron had no comment to make, other than that his back was still hurting a bit. Turnesa had words for the press. "I was seven under par," he groaned. "I don't see how *anyone* can beat him." The rest was easy: 3 and 2 over Shute, 5 and 4 over Claude Harmon, 4 and 3 over Byrd in the final. Byron was 37 under par for the 204 holes he played.

Nelson passed up the St. Paul Open in favor of resting, but was on deck for the richest tournament in golf, George S. May's All-American Open, in which each player—including a man in kilts and a masked marvel—was asked to wear a number on his back, the better to be recognized by the thousands of fans attracted to May's conception of a super golf tournament. Nelson won it, for the fourth time in five years. He totaled 269, 19 under par, eleven better than the two men tied for second spot, the venerable Sarazen and Lieutenant Ben Hogan. In racking up his tenth tournament win in a row, Byron produced a best-ball of 55 from his four rounds. . . . Over the border again to Toronto's Thornhill Golf Club for the Canadian Open, August 2–5. On this tricky course, with distances extended and par cut to 70, the best Nelson could do was equal par with a symmetrical 280—68-72-72-68. This, however, was four strokes better than anybody else did, and Byron had won his eleventh straight.

Then Nelson was stopped. In the Memphis Open, Freddy Haas, then an amateur, posted an 18-under-par 270 to become the first amateur to capture an important circuit tournament since 1936. Nelson's 276 was good for no better than a tie for fourth, and the longest consecutive tournament winning streak in golf history was over. Nelson had beaten the old mark, three consecutive wins, by eight.

Byron Nelson then resumed his old habits, winning the meeting at Knoxville labeled the Supreme Open with 276, ten strokes ahead of Byrd and eleven ahead of Ben Hogan, out of the Army and burning to make up for the time lost away from work. In the Nashville Open, Ben blazed around the Richland course with all of his old authority. Leading off with a 64, he was 19 under for 265, four strokes better than Nelson and Bulla, who split the second- and third-place money. It was quite evident from Ben's attitude, as well as his golf, that he did not countenance with pleasure the preeminence Nelson had gained in his absence. Hogan played the Dallas Open, the next stop, although he was weak with flu. Ben's 285 put him in fourth spot, behind Snead, McSpaden, and Nelson, in that order. Sam's victory was his first since rejoining the caravan after his wrist had mended. Snead, with a 277, again took the play away from Hogan (286) and Nelson (288) in the Tulsa Invitational, and then the players headed for autumn in the Northwest.

Nelson won at Spokane with 266 (66-70-66-64). Hogan and Snead tied for third. . . . Hogan then cut loose with four tremendous rounds at Portland. Refusing to be disheartened by a second round of 69 after an opening 65, Ben added a 63 and a 64 for a total of 261, smashing all records for seventy-two holes. Nelson, only 13 below par figures, was a poor second, fourteen strokes behind The Blazer. . . . In the Tacoma Open, Nelson looked tired. He slid to a tie for ninth with his 283. Ben was off, too. His 281 placed him in a tie for fifth. The winner, with 275, was Jimmy Hines. . . . Then, scarcely two weeks after Hogan's 261 had erased Nelson's mark of 263, Byron retaliated in kind. At Seattle, over the Broadmoor course, Nelson busted Ben's mark off the books with rounds of 62-68-63-66 for a total of 259! The nearest man was thirteen strokes away, Ben a full twenty. In fairness to Hogan it should be mentioned that Nelson's 259 was made over a par-70 layout, Ben's 261 over a par-72.

Satisfied with his performance at Seattle, Byron decided to rest his weary bones for a spell. The Nelsonless field re-formed in early November in Virginia for the tournament in Richmond. Hogan took it with 289. In the North and South Open at Pinehurst, a twenty-three-year-old Army dentist, Lt. Cary Middlecoff, carded 280 and became the first amateur to win that tourney in its forty-four-year history. At Durham another meteoric newcomer, and another amateur to boot, Frank Stranahan, sank a 12-foot putt on the last green to edge out Porky Oliver by one stroke and Hogan by two. (A thousand miles away, Nelson was grinning. Twenty-three-year-old Frank Stranahan had been one of the boys he had taught at Inverness.) Into the deeper South, with Dutch Harrison winning at Mobile, Hogan at Montgomery after a playoff with the Jug, Hogan at Orlando with 270, and the veteran Picard, returning to the golf wars, showing the youngsters a fine 267 in taking the Miami Open.

Byron, looking less peaked after his rest at home but no less gray around the temples, joined the tour in mid-December for the Fort Worth Open played over Glen Garden, the course where he and Hogan had caddied as boys. On the way to the tournament, Byron was shaken up in an automobile accident, but apparently it had no effect on his rested nerves. Finishing with a 66 and a 70 for 273, Byron, 11 under, was seven strokes in front of Jimmy Demaret.

The victory in the Fort Worth Open brought to nineteen Byron Nelson's wins in 1945 in P.G.A.-sponsored tournaments. During the year he had collected $66,000 in War Bond prizes, the largest chunk being the $13,600 for winning at Tam O'Shanter. The cash value of his take, $52,511.32, replaced his 1944 total of $35,005 as the all-time high. The man with the aching back had been in the money in every tournament he had entered and was on his way to doubling the previous record set by Hogan of finishing in the money in fifty-six successive tournaments. Assuming that par on the courses he played averaged 71, Byron was about 320 under par for his year's work. (Charlie Macdonald probably rolled over in his grave at this irreverence, and must have winced at

Bing Crosby and Byron Nelson, two men who could afford to rest on their laurels.

that tennis eyeshade Byron had taken to wearing.) Many of Nelson's rounds were fashioned on short courses with easy roughs, lightning-fast fairways, uncontoured greens, and occasionally with some help from winter rules, but, even allowing for the favorable conditions for par-pummeling under which he played, Byron's average score for eighteen holes over his 120 tournament rounds, 68.33, was unquestionably the most amazing feat by any golfer since the Grand Slam. It was small wonder that Byron Nelson had thousands of admirers who believed that he was the greatest golfer the game had ever known, greater than Jones, greater than Vardon.

Though competing with Hal Newhouser and Doc Blanchard, two great athletes starring in sports with a hold on the public surpassing golf's, Byron Nelson was voted Athlete of the Year by the writers of the Associated Press for the second year in a row.

Nelson was a miracle of consistency. At his peak Byron erred so infrequently that it could be boring to watch him. He made good golf look as easy as Vardon did, although he lacked the grace of Harry, and of Jones as well. Byron was a proficient rather than a pretty golfer. Lack of error was what he aimed for and achieved by reducing shot-making to a minimum of fundamentals. He did not believe in endangering a proved

The Gold Dust Twins, Nelson and McSpaden. Byron won a record $52,511.32 in 1945.

groove by playing different shots different ways. Having arrived at the swing that fitted him, he merely modified its length to suit the club he was playing and the distance he desired. He did vary his stances for the various shots, playing his woods from a slightly closed stance, his long irons from a square stance, his medium irons from a slightly open stance, and his short irons from an open stance. His style offered few idiosyncrasies: he believed in waggling the club once or twice to relieve the tightness in the fingers before starting the backswing; his hands were unusually high at the top of his backswing and gave it the illusion of shortness; he used a variation of the standard grip on the greens, the reverse-overlapping grip. He was a competent putter. As regards Nelson's temperament, it suffices to say that one opponent declared that a person receiving a transfusion from Byron would come down with pneumonia.

Off the links Byron was friendlier and more animated than when at work, but generally speaking, Nelson the person was very much like Nelson the golfer, calm and efficient rather than colorful. He thought his moves out well in advance, and let no impulses throw him off his line. Byron Nelson, deliberate, pleasant, gentlemanly, and definite, a specialist in an age of specialists, always knew where he was going.

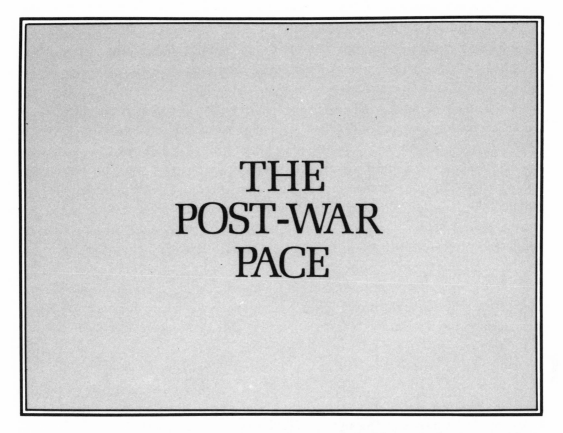

THE
POST-WAR
PACE

Golf had turned in a first-rate job during the war. It had been the one sport able to supply the short-rationed sports fans the quality performance of peacetime, thanks to the adventures of Lord Byron Nelson, Childe Harold McSpaden, and company. Through golf tournaments and exhibitions, over $600,000,000 worth of War Bonds were sold—a figure that speaks for itself. In the realm of exhibitions, there was no one quite like the Messrs. Crosby and Hope. They were herculean. Besides easing the strain on the hard-working home-fronter, golf, in its own small way, was a good friend of the men in the service. Rather early in the war, the game's restorative powers came to be appreciated by the air commands in Britain; fliers returning from missions were encouraged to get out on the course immediately. American soldiers and sailors found the game almost everywhere they traveled, and when there was no course available, they improvised one. In the hurry-up-and-wait intervals between action, Army and Navy men played golf around the globe, from the desert courses of North Africa to the rice paddies of China. Golf continued to do a splendid job for the servicemen during the period of rehabilitation.

After its wartime successes, golf's prospects in peacetime were enormous. Hundreds of thousands of new enthusiasts wanted to play the game, and fans in every section of the country wanted to see the low-scoring pros in action. Fred Corcoran, the manager of the P.G.A.'s Tournament Bureau, had a product that needed no salesmen. Corcoran's office was besieged with offers from individuals, committees, and companies desirous of sponsoring tournaments. The companies generally lost interest when they were informed that the wire services would not cover a tournament bearing the name of the auto or the beer the sponsors were marketing, but the other potential customers—publicity bureaus for individuals, hotels, and resorts, Chambers of Commerce and Junior Chambers of Commerce—were sold on the promotional value of a golf tournament and their ardor was not at all dampened when Corcoran explained that the minimum prize money offered by a sponsor now had to be $10,000. Well before the 1946 season got underway, the touring professionals were booked solid forty-five weeks out of the fifty-two, the extra seven held open, at their request, so that the travelers could go home and pick up their mail and be reintroduced to their children. In order to fulfill all the demands for tournaments, Corcoran toyed with the idea of setting up two distinct tourney schedules, one set of sponsors to get the dates during the even-numbered years, the other set in the alternate years.

The three golfers Americans wanted to see, of course, were Nelson, Hogan, and Snead, and particularly the arch-rivals, Byron Nelson and Ben Hogan. Without corning up their relationship, Hogan and Nelson, it must be said, did not feel the same affection for each other they had in 1937, for example, when Byron had two 14-ounce drivers made up and had given one to Ben. The new club helped Ben subdue the hook that had been holding him back. A good drive is the foundation of good scoring, and Ben for the first time had become a splendid driver and a splendid scorer. In 1945 it was different. The post-war rivalry between Hogan and Nelson never burst into declared warfare, but there was no love lost between the two Texans. The Nelsonites said that Ben's actions and insinuations had made it very clear on a number of occasions that he resented the esteem and fortune that Byron had earned during the war years; under the circumstances, there was no other course open to Byron than to show Ben that he was still the boss. The Hoganites had another interpretation. Ben, they believed, was naturally ambitious to regain the number-one position he had held in 1942, and being the combative type, he could not behave like a buddy toward the man who stood between him and his goal. Some personal animosity might have crept in, the Hoganites explained, but Ben just happened to be built in such a way that he hated to lose to anyone.

Byron and Ben had about a year in which to prove who was the better golfer—from August 1945, when Ben was discharged from the Army, until August 1946, when Byron went into semi-retirement on the ranch he had bought in Roanoke, Texas. Their year of grim-faced competition proved that a steady diet of tournament golf does a terrific job on the nerves of men who act nerveless, that 275 and not 288 approximated par for four rounds on a circuit course, and quite a few other things about modern professional golf, but it did not prove who was the better golfer, Hogan or Nelson. It would be unfair to either golfer to say that the other had demonstrated even a slight superiority. When Hogan did something remarkable, Nelson invariably came up with a matching performance, and vice versa.

Hogan, for instance, shot that record 261, and two weeks later Nelson broke it with that 259. Considering the length and difficulty of both courses, the two totals were equally fantastic. There were periods in the year when each man seemed to be leaving the other in his dust. Nelson, for example, started 1946 by sweeping the Los Angeles and San Francisco Opens, with Ben five strokes behind him in the first, ten in the second; in mid-summer, riding another streak, Byron corraled the Columbus Invitational and the Chicago Victory Open. But, on the other hand, it was Ben who flourished in Florida, winning the St. Pete Open and the Miami Four-ball, assisted in the latter tourney by The Wardrobe, Jimmy Demaret; and just before the Open, Ben outdistanced Byron en route to successive victories in the Colonial Invitational, the Western Open, and the Goodall Round-Robin. Over the course of their year of feuding, Hogan won more purse money than Byron, but then Byron, his nerves frayed and his back aching and his mind on his ranch in Texas, took three- to five-week rests from the grind and did not enter as many tournaments as Ben. Byron, however, had the lower strokes-per-round average. Because of Byron's periodic absences from the field, the chances of their locking horns in an epochal struggle were arithmetically reduced, and they were further reduced when the cumulative pressure told on Hogan as well and he began to absent himself from tournaments in favor of fishing and resting. As circumstances ordained it, in no tournament were Hogan and Nelson joined in a match that brought out all the inherent drama and fire of their smoldering rivalry. They met only twice in match play. Hogan scored a 1-up victory in their 18-hole match in the Goodall; partnered by Demaret in the Inverness Four-ball, Ben shared the satisfaction of trimming Nelson and McSpaden by one hole. In the rare medal tourneys that turned into two-man fights, it was Nelson who enjoyed the edge. At New Orleans he started his final eighteen two strokes off the pace Ben was setting; Byron not only overtook his man with a 66 but won going away, by five strokes. At Houston the situation was reversed and it was Byron who took the two-stroke lead into the last round; he met Ben's challenge by firing a 68, the same score Ben did. Neither of the strong, silent Texans won a big championship over the first eleven months of their duel. Hogan, burning to win the Masters and his first prestige tournament, had only to two-putt the 72nd green to tie with Keiser. He three-putted. Ben had a second agonizing experience on the last green at Canterbury in the first post-war Open. He blew the 5-footer he needed to get into the playoff with Ghezzi, Lloyd Mangrum, and an old friend of his, Byron Nelson. Byron lost out in the second playoff to Mangrum, 73 to 72, and so, like Hogan, he had missed a big boat by a single stroke.

A few weeks before the 1946 P.G.A. Championship at the Portland (Ore.) Country Club, Byron Nelson made up his mind that he had definitely had his fill of the grind that had made him a bone-tired man at thirty-four. He announced that this championship would mark his farewell appearance as a regular member of the tour and that only on special occasions, like the Masters, would he leave his ranch in Texas. Nothing would have pleased Nelson more than to quit the arena in a blaze of glory by carrying off the P.G.A. Hogan, too, had special reasons for wanting this tournament. For all his steady brilliance, Ben had never been able to win one of the three leading American tournaments, and Nelson, as Ben knew only too well, had one Open, two Masters, and two P.G.A.s to his credit. Ben was impatient to break through, and in the weeks before the championship was due to get underway, he practiced every shot in the bag hour after hour. Nelson and Hogan were placed in different sections of the draw, and had they made their ways to the final, the nation might have seen the fierce hand-to-hand struggle it had been waiting for. But a showdown, once again, was not in the cards. In the quarter-finals Nelson was beaten 1 up by Porky Oliver, and it was Oliver and not Nelson who traveled through the upper bracket and met Hogan in the final. For a while it seemed as if Ben was going to have to wait until next year. Oliver was 3 up after the morning round. Then Ben regained his putting touch. He holed one from seventeen feet and two from twelve feet to wipe out Oliver's lead. He staggered Oliver by rushing to the turn in 30, and by the 31st had played himself into a five-hole lead. The two drives down the 31st were so evenly matched that Ed Dudley, the referee, tossed a coin to determine which man would play first. Hogan won the toss. He then ended the match by fading an iron three feet from the pin.

A year after his return to the gold fold, Ben Hogan was the undisputed king of the pros. He had won the prize he had been shooting for, his first important crown. The one man skilled enough to dispute his dominance was farming fifteen hundred acres in Texas. With Nelson's departure, of course, the Hogan–Nelson rivalry died out . . . but not entirely. When Byron came out of retirement to play in the 1947 Masters, his purpose was primarily social. He wanted to see the old crowd again. However, in his first start in six months, Nelson was only two shots behind the winner, Jimmy Demaret.

The new king, Ben Hogan, was a hard man—a hard man to know, a hard man to beat. He hated to lose and drove himself harder than any of the pros to develop a game that would win for him. In his warmup sessions before a tournament round, Hogan was not content to get the feel of his clubs in a leisurely twenty minutes of practice. He put more concentration into his warmup than many pros put into their rounds on the course, cracking each shot down the practice field as if the outcome of the tournament rode with the flight of that ball. When a tournament round was over, were it a 66 or a 72, Ben was out on the practice field again, pumping each shot for all he was worth. On the golf course, permitting himself not so much as a flicker of relaxation, Ben Hogan pursued his purpose, beating the other fellows, with the burning frigidity of dry ice. He never smiled. He rarely talked, and then only to address his caddie or opponent. He lit one cigarette after another. Masked by the set scowl of the card player, Ben Hogan was concentrating every second he was at work, concentrating on lashing his 135 pounds into his drive so that it would be out by the 265-yard mark and give him the shot he wanted to the green, concentrating on playing his approach so perfectly that it would leave him a tap and not a putt, concentrating on holing out every chip, every putt he played. His unsparing demands on his mental, physical, and nervous energy seemed to leave Ben untouched. His expression never changed. His walk never changed. His silence never changed. But it did have an effect on Ben. There were times when the dry-

Ben Hogan blasts out of a trap. Dour, detached, and determined, Hogan never relaxed for an instant when on the course. In 1948 Ben won his second P.G.A. and his first Open Championship, with a record-breaking total of 276. A magnificent shot-maker for over two decades, Ben must be considered one of the very greatest ever.

iceman had to release all the terrible tension that he, no different from any other golfer, could not escape. In these sessions, following a disappointing round or a defeat, Ben took it out on himself in the privacy of his room. Then Ben was ready to enjoy a brief burst of indolence and was cordial and pleasant. But Ben allowed himself these periods of relaxation all too rarely. Some observers predicted that Ben would burn himself out long before his time if he did not slow down his pace and temper his attitude. In 1947 he began to increase the number of the rest periods he took between tournaments, but once at work there was no sign of letup in his white-hot concentration. It was the only way Ben could play winning golf, as natural for him as it was for Demaret to confide in his gallery.

Ben Hogan was perhaps the best golfer pound-per-pound who ever lived. He was a thrilling golfer. He expected perfection from himself and was always thinking in terms of the flawless shot, not the good shot. The green was not his target on his approaches nor the quarter of the green around the pin. The flag was his target, and he drilled for it. He fully intended to be inside of the other man on every shot. The astonishing distance he gained was the result of perfect timing, exchange of weight, and the almost incredible speed at which Ben accelerated his clubhead as it entered the hitting area. Hogan's all-out shots with a wood or a long iron were the ultimate development of the steel-shaft swing that had grown up in America.

Ben Hogan and Byron Nelson were too wrapped up in American tournaments in 1946 to take time out for the first British Open since 1939. Samuel Jackson Snead, however, decided at the last minute to take a fling at the old mug. Walter Hagen gave him a quick lesson in putting, Fred Corcoran hustled him a passport and a place on a transatlantic plane, and Sam was off to try his luck at St. Andrews. This was Sam's first look at the cradle of golf and, like most visitors, his first reaction was astonishment that eighteen such ordinary-looking holes could have gained the reputation they held throughout the golf world. He learned to like the course as he caught onto its subtleties on his practice rounds, and one thing in particular about St. Andrews appealed to him as worthy of duplication on more American courses—the huge greens. Putting had always been the weakest part of Sam's game. In the opinion of a number of critics, he might have been the greatest of modern golfers if he could have putted as well as most of the other top pros. There were countless occasions on which Sam had been beaten because he could not hole his 3- and 4-footers as consistently as his rivals were holing putts twice that length. (The same malady, a generation before, had afflicted another superb shot-maker, Chick Evans.) But on the huge greens at St. Andrews no golfer was going to putt himself into the title. Sam believed that he could win the Open if he shot good stuff from tee to green.

Playing the most intelligent golf of his career—and, for once, playing his own game—Snead started with two 71s. This left him in a favorable position, two shots behind the leader, Henry Cotton. (Cotton, a paragon of the Hagen school, was driven to the club in a Rolls-Royce and regularly massaged after his rounds in his suite in Rusack's

Hotel.) On the last day the course was swept by a wind so fierce that it blew downhill putts clean off some greens. Cotton played himself out of the lead on his third round. Under the conditions Snead's 74, 1 over par, was commendable golf. It placed him in a tie for the lead after fifty-four holes with Johnny Bulla, Dai Rees from Wales, and Bobby Locke, the South African champion. Snead had the golf in him to win, and the only question was how Sam, who had never won a big championship at medal play after his ordeal at Spring Mill, would bear up to the crucial last eighteen holes.

Sam was the last of the contenders to go out. This meant that he would be playing under the added strain of knowing the figures he would have to get in order to win. He was wise enough to play "the next shot" and not the scorecard, even when he ran into all sorts of trouble going out—two three-putt greens, a harsh 6, and a miss from two feet on the ninth when he needed that birdie sorely. It added up to a big 40. After the ninth, Sam began to hear reports on Locke, Bulla, and Rees. They were all having a time of it in the wind, running into higher figures than Sam was. He continued to play his own game and had reached the sixteenth green before he knew the exact scores he had to get to win. Richards Vidmer, the former sports columnist then covering a European beat for the New York *Herald Tribune*, gave Sam the dope: 6-6 on the last two holes would tie for him, 6-5 would win.

On the Road Hole, the 466-yard seventeenth, which breaks to the right, Sam did not change to conservative tactics. He cut the corner with a daring drive, and played a fine, full 4-iron onto the green. He got his 4. Feeling much more sure of himself than he had ever imagined he would on the 72nd tee of a major championship, Sam enjoyed the cheering comments of the gallery and grinned back at one old codger who had called out that Sam could use a putter and still win. Sam's tee shot sailed far up the eighteenth fairway. His pitch onto the carpet was a firm one. He went down in two putts for his par and a 75 and 290, a good four strokes ahead of Locke and Bulla.

Sam Snead had done what they said he would never be able to do: he had won an Open championship. Furthermore, he hadn't done it the easy way—scampered home early in the afternoon before he knew what he was up to. *He* had been the late starter, the strain had fallen on *his* shoulders. Nobody had *lost* the championship. He had *won* it.

The news of Snead's victory caused great rejoicing in America. It would have been tragic if a golfer of Sam's talents were to have passed from the game without his name emblazoned on at least one of the two great cups in golf. That unpleasant and ever-increasing posssibility had been scourged. A champion had finally won a championship he was worthy of.

For the amateurs the big week began on the ninth of September. Bud Ward, winner of the last Amateur held before the war, had not been playing a great deal of serious golf following his return from a long siege in the South Pacific, and his chances of retaining his title at Baltusrol were held to be moderate at best. The field that Bud would have to wade through contained, in addition to such established stars as Chapman and Turnesa, some unusually talented and colorful newcomers headed by Smiley Quick, Cary Middlecoff, and Frank Stranahan. Quick, who had captured the Public Links title in July, had been everything from a circus performer to a high-tension linesman in his earlier youth, and infused his golf with a raw, unrestrained vigor. Stumpy and heavy-muscled, Quick looked and acted more like a marathon runner than a golfer. He had a lurching style and all but swept himself off his feet on his more powerful swipes. Appearances can be deceiving, and in Smiley's case they certainly were, for he had long proved himself a talented golfer. He did not suffer from an inferiority complex. Cary Middlecoff, a Memphis native, had first attracted attention by outplaying the professionals in the North and South Open while on leave from the Army, in which he had served as a dentist. Cary was a tall, clean-featured young man, and on the links he comported himself in a very appealing fashion, businesslike and well-mannered. Walter Hagen was of the opinion that Cary was potentially one of the finest strikers of a golf ball the country had produced.

Frank Stranahan, like Middlecoff, made his mark by beating the pros at their own game, first at Durham and later in the Glen Garden and Kansas City tourneys, shooting spectacular golf on each occasion. Frank, the son of a millionaire spark-plug manufacturer from Toledo, had been in and out of as many colleges as a wartime halfback. He settled down considerably when he hitched his wagon to the golf-star. He was the Ben Hogan of the amateurs in his devotion to the principle that practice makes perfect. To build up his physique, which was good to begin with, Frank went in for weight-lifting exercises. (An old Stranahan gag was to carry his heavy dumbbells in a flimsy-looking suitcase and stand by in feigned amazement as unwary porters struggled to lift the bag off the floor.) Besides developing strong shoulders and a huge pair of arms, young Stranahan, under the coaching of Byron Nelson, developed a sound, methodical golf game. The stabilizing effect that golf had on Frank's life made his father only too happy to advance his son's career in that sport. In time Mr. Stranahan's aspirations for his son to become a champion outstripped Frank's own ardor, and perhaps that was not such a good thing for the young man. He was apt to try too hard to fulfill his father's ambitions. Frank flew off the handle on several occasions of stress. One year, for example, when he went over for the British Amateur, he accused his caddie of purposely giving him the wrong line to the hole early in the match he lost to the veteran Gerald Micklem. Frank was essentially a likable man, warm in his affection for his friends, if a little too inexperienced in handling unusual situations properly.

With three such personalities as Stranahan, Middlecoff, and Quick augmenting the veteran contenders, the forty-sixth Amateur promised to be one of the most exciting if the favorites succeeded in surviving their early tests and clashed in the last three rounds. The luck of the unseeded draw squelched this possibility. Chapman, Stranahan, and Bud Ward, for illustration, were bunched in the third quarter of the draw. Ward met Stranahan in the second round, and Frank went out 2 and 1. Skee Riegel, the medalist, was also eliminated that early, 1 down to Quick. In the third round, two more favorites fell, Ward to Charley Lind, Chapman to Ted Bishop, the New England star who had

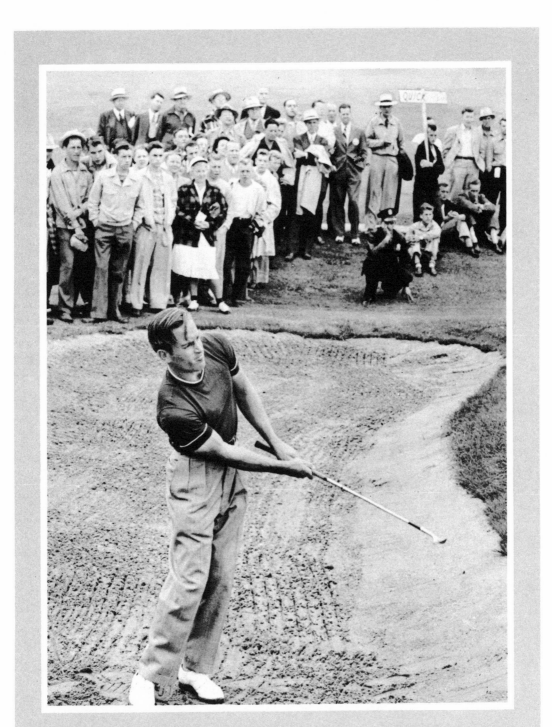

The most colorful of the post-war amateur stars, Frank Stranahan, whose perseverance at length paid off in the 1948 British Amateur. Frank erred in his public relations, but there was no arguing his courage and his ability.

once been a pro for a short spell. Middlecoff went out in the fourth, 5 and 4 to Freddy Kammer. So, before the 36-hole matches had been reached, all the stars who had been expected to add punch to the climax of the championship were on the sidelines, with the exception of Quick. That barrel-chested antic-man took care of Kammer in his semi-

Ben Hogan, Playing Captain
of the American side,
warms up for the Ryder Matches.

final test and was a strong betting favorite to triumph over Ted Bishop in the final. At one point in their match, Smiley owned a 3-hole lead on Ted. He lost it all in the afternoon before Bishop's precise, dogged play. All square after thirty-six, Bishop and Quick were launched into sudden death. The end came quickly. On the 37th, Smiley Quick, who had been remarkable on the greens throughout the championship, flubbed the 2-footer he had to get to keep the match alive.

As for the women, their first post-war champion proved to be a new face in the realm of amateur golf, but it was a face that required no caption. Even before Franklin D. Roosevelt had begun his first term, the country had been well acquainted with the athletic genius of Mrs. Mildred "Babe" Didrikson Zaharias.

THE
BABE

The outstanding performer in the 1932 Olympics was a nineteen-year-old girl, a lithe, smooth-muscled, deep-jawed Texan named Didrikson, Mildred "Babe" Didrikson. On the opening day of the games, Babe created a new women's record in the javelin when she tossed the spear 143 feet, 4 inches. She followed this by breaking the record in the high hurdles in winning her heat, and in the finals she lowered the mark again. In the high jump, after she and Jean Shiley had cleared 5 feet, 5¼ inches but could go no higher, the judges halted the jumpoff for first place by disqualifying Babe for "diving"—leaping over the bar head first. This surprising decision, so dismally typical of the aberrations of the big moguls of sport, forced the Babe to content herself with two firsts and a second.

Mildred Didrikson was a bronzed, sharp-featured girl who wore her hair like a boy and whose coordination had in it none of the jerks, the halts, the feminine wrinkles that often creep into the form of even the finest female athletes. She was the sixth of seven children born to Mr. and Mrs. Ole Didrikson, natives of Oslo who had migrated to Port Arthur, Texas. Encouraged, or rather left alone, by her sports-loving parents, Mildred—or Babe—played all the seasonal games with her three brothers and the kids in the neighborhood. She was more than a tomboy; she was a splendid athlete, judged by the strictest criteria. When the Didriksons moved to Beaumont, she won herself a spot on the Beaumont High School basketball team, and it was here that the saga of Babe Didrikson began to acquire momentum. Her shooting and floor work caught the eye of an official of a Dallas insurance company that kept its name in front of the public by sponsoring athletic teams. He told the Babe to be sure and look him up after graduation. She did. In her first year as a typist and a forward on the company's girl quintet, Babe was merely unbelievable. She polished off a few of her rough points in her second year and was selected as a forward on the All-America team. She began to test her skill in other sports, and became an accomplished swimmer and diver, a softball pitcher with a man's fluid delivery, a good bowler and tennis player. Her virtuosity in track and field sports was perhaps more arresting. Two weeks before the Olympic Games in '32, Babe entered seven events in the National A.A.U. Track and Field Championships held at Dyche Stadium in Evanston, Illinois. She won the javelin throw, the baseball throw, shot put, broad jump, and eighty-meter hurdles, tied for first in the high jump, and picked up a fourth in the discus. This satisfactory afternoon's work made it hard for the Babe not to be disgruntled when the Olympic ruling, limiting a competitor to three events, allowed her no opportunity to show the folks what she could do when she was really warmed up.

On the final day of the Olympics, everyone in Los Angeles was still talking about Babe Didrikson. In the press box, Grantland Rice was telling a group that included Damon Runyon, Westbrook Pegler, Paul Gallico, Braven Dyer, and Will Rogers that the Babe could hit a golf ball like no woman they had ever seen, that she had the makings of becoming a wonder in that sport too. There was some dissension; Granny was letting his enthusiasm run away with him. To put the skeptics in their place, Rice called the Babe up to the press box and asked her how she would like to play some golf the next day. The Babe said she'd love to. She hadn't played for over a year, but if someone could dig up some shoes and clubs for her, she'd love to play.

At the Brentwood Country Club in Santa Monica the next day, with the nation's toughest sports critics watching her every move, Babe took nine holes to get the feel of the clubs borrowed from Olin Dutra and then showed the gentlemen a nice 43 on the back-nine. On the seventeenth, 523 yards into the wind, she banged two woods to the apron and barely missed her birdie. Rice was delighted. "Babe, how do you do it?" Granny beamed at her after she had whaled her tee shot 250 yards down the eighteenth. "Man," the Babe smiled back, "I just can't help it."

The wonder girl turned professional shortly after the Olympics. For $3,500 a week, she started on a tour of the vaudeville palaces of the country, dancing and playing the harmonica and letting her curious countrymen take a good look at her. (Beginning at the age of seven, Babe was for three years a featured harmonica soloist over a Texas radio station. She was a first-class tap dancer.) After a few weeks, Babe walked out on her tour. She was an outdoor girl. The four-a-day was not for her. She cashed in on her publicity instead through exhibitions of her versatile athletic prowess, including a tour as a pitcher with the House of David baseball team. She pitched an inning for the Brooklyn Dodgers in an exhibition game against the Phillies, and if Larry MacPhail had been in the saddle in Brooklyn at this time, there is no knowing what shape Babe's future athletic career might have taken. As it was, she exhausted her potential as a baseball attraction, and in 1934 turned her talents to golf, the game Rice believed she could play better than any other member of her sex if she gave it the time and concentration. In the summer of 1935, partnered with Gene Sarazen, she went on an extensive tour of the country. Her golf was not altogether impressive. The public wanted to see how far this super-woman could smash a golf ball; they weren't interested in how well she played the game. A good showman, Babe gave the patrons what they wanted. She cracked her tee shots past the 250-yard marker, and farther when she pressed, as she did too often. On a few tees, as a fillip to her driving exhibition, she would tee up, walk a few yards behind the ball, take her sight on the line, and sauntering casually into the ball, whale it as she kept on walking. It was a stunning demonstration of advanced coordinative powers, but it wasn't golf. She was overly concerned with distance in her iron play, too, and slapped her shots so far that the rumor (unfounded) went around that Babe's 4-iron was stamped a 5, her 5-iron a 6, and so on. She hit those irons erratically on her best days. Her chipping was juvenile and her putting could be peevish. If she harbored the ambition to become a champion golfer, and she frequently stated she did, the Babe had a long way to go.

Settling down in southern California and adjusting herself to what was, for her, the sedentary life, Babe Didrikson gladly gave golf the time and tears it exacts from the man or woman who would excel. Two years later she had improved her game sufficiently to be a threat in the tournaments, but the proven stars were equal to her challenge. Babe hit many breathtaking golf shots but she still mis-hit too many simple shots to have the consistency demanded of a champion. She was not discouraged, this girl who continually had refuted the interviewers who wanted her to say that she was just a natural athlete who never had to practice. She prevailed on Tommy Armour to give her a series of lessons, and practiced every morning and every afternoon to make certain that she absorbed Tommy's theories so thoroughly that she did the right thing instinctively. She practiced so strenuously that her hands became raw. She soaked them in brine, bandaged them, and kept on practicing. She began to look like a golfer.

In 1938 the Babe, always a sure-fire attraction, was asked to appear in a golf benefit in Los Angeles. The promoter, thinking of Babe as a muscle moll, as most Americans did, thought it would be a bright idea to team her in a threesome in which the other players would be a mountainous wrestler and, for contrast, a minister who was a professor of religion at Occidental College. The wrestler, George Zaharias, better known to the scholars of his art as "The Crying Greek from Cripple Creek," enjoyed his frantic afternoon on the course very much. His sense of humor appealed to the Babe and she accepted his invitation to talk over their round during an evening date. A short while later they were thinking of getting married, and hearing this, the third member of their old threesome, the professor from Occidental, offered to officiate at the ceremony. Babe backed out of the idea at the last moment, but after Zaharias had chased her around the country, she finally succumbed to his persistence in St. Louis.

Her marriage was the important event in Babe's life. It gave her confidence in herself as a woman, a normal woman. As an unpretty girl watching her more lissom colleagues walk off with the males' attention and the males, the Babe had compensated for this blow to her vanity by stressing to herself, and her sistren, her athletic superiority. After her marriage, there was no need for forcing an equalizer, and the Babe was also free at last from the insinuations of quack anthropologists. She relished the opportunity to live like a human being and not a legend. She made a fine home for George, showing a delicate hand in decoration and a powerful hand in the kitchen. She let the womanliness she had always felt assert itself in her appearance and her manners. One day a sportswriter whom she had known in her rougher era began kidding her about the smart new dress she was wearing. "I made this dress myself and I've got silk underneath," Mrs. Zaharias retorted, "and what's more, I like it."

The Babe had simply expanded; she hadn't changed. Sports—winning at sports—meant as much to her as they had before her marriage. At one time she contracted the tennis bug, and in her eagerness to master that game began to neglect her domestic duties. George put his foot down firmly. However, where golf was concerned, as long as Babe didn't overdo it and turn him into a grass widower, George was all for his wife's realizing her ardent ambition to become the best woman golfer in the world. He was her number-one booster as she sedulously developed a short game and an iron game that matched her mighty woods. (One day, helped by a strong following wind, the Babe hit a drive 408 yards.) During the war years the Babe began to play *golf*. In War Bond exhibitions on the Coast, partnered or solo, she regularly defeated the combined efforts of the former champion of the Lakeside Golf Club, erstwhile pigeon of the mysterious John Montague, and sectional qualifier for the 1940 U.S. Amateur, Mr. Harry Lillis Crosby, and Mr. Crosby's friend, Mr. Leslie Towne Hope. Returning to the Brentwood course nine years after she had flabbergasted Rice's colleagues, she tore it apart with a 65. Over the testing, treacherous layout at Cypress Point (men's par 72) she shot successive rounds of 77-77-76-76. A double-eagle on a par 5 hole enabled her to catch Clara Callender in Los Angeles' Mid-Winter tournament in 1943 and to go on to win. The sole female starter, she played in the 1944 Southern California Open, and very creditably: 74-74-74-70—292. In 1945 she won the Western Women's Open for the third straight year.

As a professional, Mrs. Zaharias was not eligible to compete in the United States Women's Amateur and the British Ladies', the two championships that in those days, before women's professional golf took hold, officially determined the best women golfers in the world. The Babe applied to the U.S.G.A. for reinstatement as an amateur. Her request was approved in 1944, and two years later when the U.S. Women's Amateur was revived after its wartime suspension, Babe Didrikson Zaharias was on the firing line.

In 1946 many of the excellent women golfers who had graced the game during and after the reign of Glenna Collett had retired from active competition. The Babe would not have to worry about Jean Cothran, Kathryn Hemphill, Virginia Guilfoil, Mrs. Leona Pressler Cheney, and that consistent Curtis Cup heroine, Charlotte Glutting, to name a

Patty Berg,
1938 U.S. Women's
Champion and one
of the many stars
who turned pro.

handful of the stars of the interim who had gone into retirement. The 1938 champion, Patty Berg, the red-haired tomboy from Minneapolis, had turned professional. So had Betty Jameson from San Antonio, who had won the U.S. Women's title in 1939 and '40, and the last pre-war champion, tiny Betty Hicks Newell, one of the many topflight women golfers who swung the clubhead in the manner prescribed by Ernest Jones, the renowned theorist and instructor. Babe could expect most of her competition to come from six experienced campaigners: Estelle Lawson Page, the 1937 champion; the veteran Maureen Orcutt; Helen Sigel, a slip of a girl from Philadelphia who had made the final in '41; Clara Callender, now Mrs. Sherman, a socker; Dorothy Kirby, from Atlanta, runner-up to Betty Jameson in 1939; and Louise Suggs, also from that golfing province, Georgia, a supple youngster who could develop such clubhead velocity that she was rightfully termed the Ben Hogan of women's golf.

The women convened on September 23 at the Southern Hills Country Club in Tulsa, a pretty, undulating course, 6,232 yards long, with a ladies' par of 75. For the first time, the qualifying round of the tournament was extended from eighteen to thirty-six holes. The Babe's 156 put her in with shots to spare. The medal went to Dorothy Kirby's 77-75—152, and her townswoman, Louise Suggs, with two easy 77s, confirmed the pre-tournament consensus that she stood perhaps the best chance of stopping Mrs. Zaharias. But in the first round Louise was eliminated; Mrs. Dan Chandler caught her on the sixteenth and defeated her by jumping a stymie on the 19th. Dorothy Kirby was a first-round victim as well, falling before Grace Lenczyk 4 and 3. In the second round there was another upset, though not as startling as the defeats of the two Atlanta favorites. Clara Callender Sherman, the six-foot Californian, rallied after being 2 down to Mrs. Page at the turn and pulled out the match on the home hole.

Meanwhile the Babe was winning her first two matches by piling it on during the first nine holes. Against Peggy Kirk, she was out in 35 and coasted to a 4 and 3 victory. She was 5 up at the turn on Betty Jean Rucker, and again ended it 4 and 3. The Babe was at a disadvantage at Southern Hills. A high percentage of the holes were doglegs, and if she used her driver off the tees, she was past the corner and in the rough. On many of these holes she switched to driving with an iron. Babe expected to be pressed much more closely by her third-round opponent, Maureen Orcutt, and made up her mind to give that formidable competitor no chance to turn the match into a stretch duel. Babe took the first hole with a birdie, and went 2 up when Maureen missed a shortish putt for a half on the third. A birdie on the fourth, a par on the fifth, and a par on the eighth boosted the Babe to 5 up before Maureen won her first hole, the ninth. The two halved the next four holes, and on the fourteenth the Babe applied the crusher by dropping a long one for a birdie 2.

In her semi-final-round match, Babe met Helen Sigel, the conqueror of Grace Lenczyk. The Babe was very nervous. She had her heart set on winning this championship, and now the nearness of realizing her ambition was beginning to frighten her. She hooked her drive off the first tee, pushed her iron across the fairway into a trap but scrambled out for a half in 5s. On the second the Babe belted one into the brook, but again she salvaged a half by holing a 10-footer. Helen had wasted her opening by underclubbing herself on her approach, an error she was to repeat on several holes when the Babe's fidgety wildness gave the little Phiadelphian good opportunities. On the third the Babe moved out in front with a par. She added the fourth by recovering adroitly after another hooked drive, and went 3 up at the fifth when Helen, with a big chance, underclubbed into trouble. There was no more action until the ninth, when Helen canned a 20-footer for the hole. The next three were halved, and then Helen cut the Babe's lead to one by holing from ten feet for a birdie on the thirteenth. The Babe fought back to take the fourteenth. She nearly lost the fifteenth when she shanked her second into the roadway, but recovered to the apron of the green and popped her chip into the cup for a half. Standing 2 up with three to play, the Babe closed out the match by getting down in 2 from a trap off the sixteenth green for a winning 4.

Clara Sherman was no match for Mrs. Zaharias in the final. The Babe had got all of her nervousness out of her system in the Sigel match. Mrs. Sherman did succeed in squaring the match at the sixth in the morning—the Babe was never down to an opponent during the entire tournament—but after the tenth it was a runaway. Babe was five holes up at noon by virtue of a round of 76. She made it 6 up by birdieing the 19th and kept percolating. On the 25th she holed out a 9-iron from 120 yards for an eagle 2. Anxious to finish the match as soon as possible, she did it on the 27th by planting an iron eight feet from the cup. The score, 11 and 9, was the largest margin that had ever been registered in the final of the championship.

Clara Sherman, standing at the edge of the green, watches Babe Didrikson Zaharias drop a 9-footer on the ninth hole in the final match of the 1946 Women's Amateur Championship, at the Southern Hills Country Club in Tulsa. The Babe drew away after six holes and won the match on the 27th green, 11 and 9.

Mrs. Zaharias' triumph in the Women's Championship was one of the fifteen straight tournament victories she peeled off in 1946–1947. In many of the tourneys Louise Suggs made the Babe step on it, but the Babe, relaxed and confident after her victory in the big one, could always lift her game the necessary notch. Her husband, whom the Babe had persuaded to give up wrestling, followed her around the tournaments and became a circuit character in his own right. The big, garrulous, open-hearted fellow, whose thighs were broader than most men's shoulders, also attended many tournaments on the men's P.G.A. tour and became more or less the father-confessor to the host of young men taking the bumps as they tried for fame and fortune. At the end of each tournament day, big George would wander into the bar, and one after another the youngsters would seek him out and pour their troubles into George's cauliflowered ear and be the better for their session with that pleasant and helpful man. He and the Babe were never embarrassingly demonstrative, but their pride in each other and sincere mutual affection were unusual for a couple married nine years. It was hard on them both when the Babe sailed for England in May 1947 to see whether she could do what no American woman had been able to do before—win the British Ladies Golf Championship.

The Babe made an instantaneous hit with the Scottish crowds who went down to Gullane to watch the highly touted American work out on the links on which the championship would be decided the second week in June. Babe had been in front of crowds nearly all of her thirty-four years, and when she liked them, as she did the Scots, she enjoyed speaking her thoughts aloud and keeping up a running conversation with the gallery. The remark of hers that received the widest circulation came in response to the question, "What do you do on your drives to gain that tremendous distance?" "I just loosen my girdle," the Babe replied, "and let the ball have it." Her quality wisecracks and her "big game" destroyed any animosity the Scots might have felt toward the person who was visiting them for the express purpose of taking home the one British trophy that had never made the trip across the Atlantic. When it became known that Babe's wardrobe contained no clothes heavy enough for the severe Scottish spring, well-wishers in every corner of the island asked for the Babe's measurements (five-foot-six, 140 pounds), and the warm garments they sent the popular challenger filled the lobby of the clubhouse at Gullane.

Throughout the championship Babe played beautiful golf, probably the finest golf of her career. She sailed through her first four matches 6 and 5, 4 and 2, 6 and 4, 6 and 5, outclassing her opponents so markedly that a British observer complained in high admiration, "It seems cruel to send our girls out against a game like that." In the fifth round Babe outdrove Frances Stephens by as much as a hundred yards, but the young English player chipped and putted defiantly and prolonged the match to the sixteenth. This victory brought Babe to the semis and to Jean Donald, the Scottish Champion, a long-hitter compared to anybody else but the invader. Fond as they were of the friendly American, the Scottish gallery found that it could not root against its own champion. The Babe forced the Scots to cheer for her by the very brilliance of her play. Out in 34 for a 4-up lead, back in even 4s through the thirteenth, she defeated Miss Donald 7 and 5. Over the thirteen holes of the match, Babe had used only twenty-one putts.

In the final, deferring to the occasion and the first sunny day of the tournament week, the Babe dispensed with the blue corduroy slacks she had been wearing in favor of "some refined clothes," white blouse, yellow brushed-wool sweater, gray flannel divided skirt. It may have been that this outfit hindered the Babe from playing her regular game or it may have simply been that her opponent, Cotton-taught Jacqueline Gordon, pounced on the Babe's errors like a kitten on a ball of yarn. Whatever the reason, the Babe was 2 down after the thirteenth and had to execute several risky shots to win back these two holes by the halfway mark. Both women had 75s.

During the intermission the Babe changed into her faded blue slacks. She did not regard these slacks as her "lucky clothes," as was generally reported. Her reason for changing was far more mundane. Sun or no sun, it had been bitter cold on the links and her ankles had been almost numbed. She tied her slacks close around her ankles with string, and was ready for work. She took the 19th, the 20th (with an eagle), the 21st, the 23rd, the 24th, smashing the ball with renewed confidence. Miss Gordon was able to

Mildred "Babe" Didrikson Zaharias. The Didrikson legend made her out to be a female Paul Bunyan. Actually, the wonders Babe performed were based on study, tedious practice, and self-discipline. Once, when Babe was a member of a championship basketball team, she missed a key foul shot, and her team lost. For the next five weeks, Babe forced herself to practice shooting fouls, 300 a day.

win back only one hole, the 28th, and then lost the 29th to go 5 down again. Three halves, and the match was over, and Mildred "Babe" Didrikson Zaharias had become the first American to win the British Ladies Golf Championship. The Scots cheered the happy champion all the way to the clubhouse, a tribute to her personal charm and her skill. Babe had been off the fairway with only three drives on her eight rounds at Gullane and had visited only three bunkers. She had holed out one of those bunker shots, and on the other two was left with "gimme" putts.

Louise Suggs, another of the great golfers from Georgia. Louise succeeded Babe Zaharias as our national champion in 1947, and as the British champion in 1948. Rather small as golf stars go, Louise was Hoganesque in style and temperament.

The Babe had promised her British admirers that she would be back to defend her crown in 1948, but two months after her return to the States and her beaming husband, she turned professional again by accepting an offer of $300,000 to make a series of movie shorts. She had achieved the ambition she had nurtured over thirteen years: she had become the best woman golfer in the world. The one topic left unsettled was the comparative greatness of the Babe, the virulent, explosive par-shatterer, and Joyce Wethered, that dream of grace who could also score. It is one of those controversies that can never be settled, like who was the better man, Tilden or Budge, Jones or Hogan, Dempsey or Louis.

When the rough, rugged girl from Texas had first skyrocketed to prominence in the 1932 Olympics, erudite critics were of the opinion that she was probably the finest woman athlete who ever lived. If there were any dissenters then, the Babe's subsequent performances in golf cured them of their heresy. In fact, remembering her unapproached ability for becoming a champion in every sport she tried, an ever-increasing number of fans and writers believe that the finest athlete of the twentieth century was The Babe.

THE
REVIVAL OF
INTERNATIONAL
GOLF

In 1947 international sports got back to "normal," anticipating several slightly more important facets of civilization in this respect. In golf, the traditional team rivalries between the United States and Great Britain were renewed in Walker and Ryder Cup play, and plans were formulated for resuming Curtis Cup competition in 1948. American golfers invaded the austere island, Britons repaid their visits, and everyone was glad to be going overseas again with a city and not an A.P.O. as his address.

The first-time-ever character of Babe Zaharias' conquest of the British Ladies Championship elevated it above the successes scored by American amateurs in Britain in the spring, but the youthful invaders gave an excellent account of themselves. At St. Andrews, Francis Ouimet's well-balanced Walker Cup team recaptured, 8–4, the cup that had been lost in 1938, winning six of the eight singles after splitting the four foursomes. Each member of the team contributed to the eight points, Bud Ward, Smiley Quick, Dick Chapman, and Frank Stranahan taking their singles, Freddy Kammer and Ted Bishop playing on winning foursome teams, and the stars of the meeting, Willie Turnesa and Skee Riegel, emerging victorious in both their singles and foursome. (Middlecoff, named to the team, had turned pro.) As it so happened, the two two-point men in the Walker Cup triumph, Turnesa and Riegel, went on to carry off the two important amateur championships, Skee winning the United States Amateur at Pebble Beach in September, Willie the British Amateur at Carnoustie a week or so after the Walker Cup.

On his route to the final, Turnesa was pushed to the seventeenth green on five of his seven eighteen-hole matches. Two of his closest ones were with Stranahan and Ward, but the unruffled, contained amateur from the family of pros consistently played the crucial holes better than his opponent. He was as deadly with his blaster in the wet bunkers of Carnoustie as he had been at Oakmont nine years before. His putting was lethal, and this was somewhat surprising, since the British ruling against center-shafted implements had forced Willie to leave his favorite putter at home and do-or-die with the blade model he had borrowed from, of all people, his mother-in-law. Dick Chapman made his way through seven matches in his half of the draw, and for the first time in the sixty-two years of the British Amateur, two foreigners had the final all to themselves. Turnesa's temperament and his putter proved to be the deciding factors in a well-played, stirring match. Five holes down to Dick's 34 after the first nine holes, Willie drew back to even by lunch on the strength of an errorless 35 and Chapman's careless-ness. They halved the first eight in the afternoon in par. Willie played another par on the 27th, and it was good for the hole when Chapman drove into the heavy rough and couldn't make up the stroke. With only nine to go, Chapman poured everything at his command into his shots. He played four stalwart pars in succession and then a birdie, and was still 1 down. At length the strain of chasing an opponent who wouldn't crack told on Chapman, and he missed a 6-footer on the 33rd to go 2 down. Turnesa terminated the match and his unmerciful exhibition of putting when he holed for his par from ten feet on the 34th, the eighteenth time Willie had gone down in one putt.

For the British, still struggling with food, clothing, coal, and other shortages, the lack of native athletic heroes was hard to take. They saw their trophies carried off one by one by the invading Americans, and an American victory in the British Open would have left the cupboard bare. The cash of the domestic tournaments, however, out-weighed the glory of winning the British Open in the minds of the leading professionals, and Vic Ghezzi and Johnny Bulla were the only two pros who turned up at Hoylake in 1947. The third American contender was Frank Stranahan, who made a second trip to England after returning to the States following the British Amateur. In command of his emotions at all times and courteous to the galleries and his playing partners, his pugnacity directed solely toward overcoming a disheartening series of bad breaks, Frank stuck by his guns and came within one shot of catching the winner, Fred Daly of Northern Ireland. Daly had posted a total of 293. After playing his 292nd stroke, Frank was still a good 165 yards from the 72nd green, but he was conceding nothing. He took his 5-iron and hit a great golf shot that almost did achieve the miracle he was fighting for. The ball finished seven inches from the cup.

The following year Stranahan captured a major title, the British Amateur. Over the old Royal St. George's course in Sandwich, little changed since the days of Travis' historic victory, Frank played sound, deliberate golf in every match and always had the reserve he needed to shake off a troublesome opponent. In the final, he went to lunch all even with Charley Stowe but ripped the match apart by taking five of the first six holes in the afternoon. In 1950 he repeated at St. Andrews, defeating a field of 324 entrants that included H. L. Crosby of the Bel-Air C.C. Frank was never as successful in the U.S.

Amateur, his one strong bid coming in 1950, when he made his way to the final and lost on the 39th green after a terrific match with Sam Urzetta, a fine young player from Rochester. Late in the summer of 1954, Stranahan turned professional. He enjoyed moderate success on the professional tournament trail.

The transatlantic traffic was not all one way in 1947. Dai Rees and Charley Ward, two top British professionals, followed our P.G.A. circuit for a few months, finishing in the money in several tournaments but concentrating on observing the American stars in action and trying to learn wherein their superiority lay. Ward and Rees came over a second time as members of the British team that renewed the Ryder Cup competition in early November after an interval of ten years. The American team was expected to win without too much exertion, but few people looked for as devastating a rout as took place on the muddy fairways of the Portland (Oregon) Country Club. The American pros virtually won the cup on the first day of play, when they swept all four of the foursomes. They completed the humiliation by taking seven of the eight singles, to make the final count 11–1, the most one-sided victory in Ryder Cup history.

Though Fred Daly's victory in the British Open constituted the sum and total of their triumphs in international golf events, the British could draw solace from the performances of two Commonwealth golfers on American soil. Jim Ferrier was a naturalized American citizen when he took the 1947 P.G.A. Championship, but by birth, and by swing, he was an Australian. The other was, of course, that singularly successful visitor from South Africa, Arthur D'Arcy "Bobby" Locke.

Locke came to the States in early April, known to the American golf fans merely as that South African fellow who had beaten Sam Snead that winter in twelve of the sixteen matches they had played in Bobby's homeland. (Snead had been invited by Locke to visit South Africa when they met at St. Andrews in the 1946 British Open.) Bobby, however, had been a luminary for a decade in British golfing circles. The son of a successful sports-outfitter in the town of Vereeniging, forty miles from Johannesburg, young Bobby had won everything there was to be won in South Africa by the age of seventeen. The next year he had made his first attack on the tournaments played in Great Britain, and while he had never managed to bring off a victory in the big affairs, the young man made it very warm for Cotton and his crowd. He turned professional at an early age, and, backed by wealthy and chauvinistic South Africans, Bobby increased his reputation as a steady, nerveless competitor by his play in several big-money matches, particularly in the scraps he and his countryman Sid Brews had with Cotton and Reg Whitcombe. Sam Snead persuaded Locke to fly to America with him upon the conclusion of their series of exhibitions in South Africa, and considering the job Bobby did on the circuit in the States, it is a wonder that Snead's colleagues didn't stop talking to him.

Americans got their first look at Bobby Locke at the Masters. They saw no slim boy wonder but a large, big-boned man who looked at least ten years older than his age, twenty-nine. Bobby's physique and face had altered markedly during his wartime service in the South African Air Force; he had flown over a hundred Liberator missions out of Foggia. This oldish-looking fellow with the weather-beaten complexion of a sailor was not an overwhelmingly impressive swinger at first inspection. By current pro standards, he was as old-fashioned as the knickers he wore. His swing exaggerated the inside-out arc. There was nothing crackling about his hooky woods, but they went a long way and they ended up on the fairway. There was nothing crisp about his irons, but they were accurate. At Augusta, on a new type of grass for him, he did not do the outstanding things with his wooden-shafted, rusty-headed putter that Snead promised he would, but then he was just off the plane. As far as tactics went, Locke reminded one a bit of Horton Smith, declining to gamble when a slightly imperfect shot would mean a peck of trouble, relying on his putting to make up the difference. Locke's total for his four rounds in the Masters was 289, 1 over par. Everything taken into account, it was an admirable debut. But no one looked for Locke to drive Hogan and Demaret, the two leading money-winners, onto the practice fairway.

Locke did some quiet tuning-up in North Carolina after the Masters, and then stepped out without any advance fanfare and captured four out of five tournaments from our supposedly peerless touring pros. He won the Carolinas Open. He won at Houston with 277. His putting touch—the American pros were now studying Bobby's technique—deserted him temporarily at Fort Worth, where he tied for third, but he won the Philadelphia *Inquirer*'s tournament and then the Goodall. At Philadelphia, Ben Hogan had been as hot on his first two rounds as only Ben can get. Hogan's 132 placed him five strokes ahead of Locke as they started out together on the last thirty-six in the unseasonal cold rain and fog. On the morning round, with a methodical 70, Locke made up seven strokes on Hogan, whose erratic play seemed to bear out the contention of some observers that the dry-iceman was bound to crack unless he tempered the intensity of his tournament golf. Hogan played better in the afternoon, if not up to the form one had come to expect of him, but his 73 was three more than the South African required for his round. At Charles River, outside Boston, in the Goodall, Locke, putting magnificently, set the home brigade back on its heels again. On the last four holes the red-hot visitor snagged the three birdies he needed for a winning total of plus-37.

For the first time since the final tour of Vardon and Ray, a foreigner had busted wide the monopoly American pros had taken for granted to be theirs in their home-soil tournaments. And for the first time in a score and more of years, American golfers were beginning to wonder if the profuse refinements our pros had made in technique were in reality the improvements they had accepted them as being. Locke, for all the deceptive antiquity of his methods, hit the ball as far as the average long-hitting pro and he hit it down the fairway. His other shots had the same chronic excellence. He wasn't winning those tournaments solely on the greens, though he was also outputting our best putters too.

Locke, who at this point felt that he had accomplished enough to permit himself the privilege of comment, made the usual complimentary statements about the standard of golf played by American pros, but added a rather provocative thought: His type of swing, he believed, was the *natural* golf swing; the swing developed in the States had certain artificial elements in it. There was no getting away from the wonderful shot-making this American type of swing produced, Locke went on, but to hold that unnatural groove demanded continual practice and the strictest kind of concentration, and even then, our pros were subject to lapses. His type of swing, Locke believed—and he was talking with a modest objectivity—didn't have to be oiled daily. He needed only to knock a batch of balls down the practice fairway to be as tuned up as he wanted to be. He felt American pros overpracticed, and, speaking for himself, he always had a fear that if he practiced too much, he would leave too many of his best shots behind him on the practice fairway. (Ouimet, incidentally, had felt the same way about practice, but Francis was of a different generation from the men against whom Locke was competing.)

As far as putting went, Locke blasted another illusion we had held about our golfers. The British press had abetted the American press in emphasizing that the superiority of Americans on the greens went a long way toward explaining our golfers' over-all superiority: There was nothing wrong with that observation in itself, but many fans had added, quite unconsciously, another Gimbel-like step: nobody but nobody could putt like an American pro. Well, Locke could. And furthermore, he expected to. At Charles River he was short of the cup on one approach putt, and though he had only shaken his head on the green, in the locker room he was quite cut up with himself when the subject of his minor slip was introduced. "It was an unforgivable blunder," he said emphatically. "I am never short on a putt, *never.*" This was not conceit; it was a confession of the standard of putting Locke expected to produce and which he did produce. It was this confidence in his putting that shaped the conservative strategy Locke employed. To illustrate this point, on one par-3 hole, a long one requiring a 3-iron and sometimes more, most of the players had banged for the pin positioned behind the trap guarding the right-hand corner of the green. Some of the pros had faded expert shots around the trap, setting themselves up with short putts for their birdies; as many others had found the trap. Locke, almost alone, had gone for the center of the green. Didn't he go for birdies? he was asked. Of course he went for birdies, Bobby replied, but no foolhardily from the tee when there was a sizable chance that he would lose his par as well as his birdie if the difficult shot failed to come off. "And suppose I had cleared the trap and my ball had ended up seven or ten feet from the pin, what advantage, really, would I have gained? My shot, my safe shot as you call it, left me no more than twenty or twenty-five feet from the hole. If I am putting, I figure to make the twenty-five-foot putts as regularly as I would make the eight-foot putts. One putt is not more difficult than the other. The only difference, old boy, is that one putt is longer than the other."

Not only did the string of victories the South African scored rock the American golfing public, but his manner on the golf course was equally provocative. Most of our leading pros, chill and unbreathing as mannequins when they were playing well, frowning and fretful when off their game and easily upset by the chirping of some ignorant sparrow, had made tournament golf seem the most serious occupation in the

Arthur D'Arcy "Bobby" Locke, the most successful invader since Harry Vardon. In 1947 this poised and precise South African earned over $20,000 in prize money, even with missing the first three months of the U.S. professional circuit.

world. (Demaret was the shining exception.) As golf became Big Business and first place came to mean thousands and not hundreds of dollars, the element of the *game* had vanished from tournament golf. Golf stars were much more temperamental than opera singers, racehorses, and even tennis players. And then along came Locke, recalling not only in his knickers and his swing but in his deportment that earlier era when golf was a friendly game and not a dry run for Purgatory. When galleries applauded after a well-hit shot, this strange man smiled and tipped his cap. When he missed a holeable putt, he did not act as if only the sternest self-discipline had prevented him from breaking the club in two over his caddie's knee right there and then. "Shaky, very shaky indeed," was his comment after blowing a short one at a critical juncture at Fort Worth. He was relaxed at all times, and appeared to be having a genuinely good time playing golf.

As can be easily understood, the commotion that Bobby Locke created among American golf fans did not sit too well with the men whose livelihood he was diminishing. One American professional was openly rude to Locke. He advised Bobby not to get the idea in his head that he was better than our best professionals just because he had won a few tournaments; it just so happened, he explained, that Locke had come to the States at a time when all of our best golfers were in a slump. Locke refused to take offense. "Well, if that is the case," he answered, "I'd better make it while the making's good, eh?" That professional's attitude, happily, was not typical of all American pros' conduct toward the South African whiz, though, as is understandable, they were a trifle resentful of this newcomer who was poaching on their special preserve.

The American pros of that era were as fine a group of golfers as the world had ever known, and quite a number of them were excellent fellows personally, but few of them had escaped contracting an occupational disease—venality. One recently arrived celebrity always answered telegrams collect. Another leader, who was employed at a fashionable golf club, was in the habit of ending his working day by playing Nassau matches for reasonably high stakes with the young members of the club, apportioning them a number of strokes to make up the gap between his skill and theirs; however, he made it a rather debatable practice to charge his opponents, under the entry of *Lesson*, for the time he devoted to taking their money in their Nassau matches. Another first-rank pro had the gold bug so bad that he had to play for something, be it a dime a hole, or else golf seemed a waste of time to him. These were disturbing traits that made the oldtimers, after they had asked a social question and received an economic answer, fume that some of the contemporary pros were just "overdressed caddies."

There is a difference, and a decided difference, between a man's earning all he can possibly earn and being money-mad. No one blames a top golfer for parlaying his talent as far as it will go—endorsing, teaching, advising, playing tournaments, playing exhibitions, and picking up a few thousand acting as a "contact man" for businessmen who have found that bringing a name pro with them to New York or Washington or Chicago makes it that much easier for them to gain a few hours with a client who happens to be golf-minded. The top pros have it coming to them. They are the leaders in their profession, and it isn't a secure profession, especially when the number of very good players is continually mounting. A pro must get it while the getting is good. It is the exceptional pro, the highly exceptional pro, whose career as a winner lasts longer than ten years. As far as the big side-dough is concerned, it is usually out of reach once a pro stops winning regularly. The anxiety complex that torments professional golfers under the circumstances does help to explain their susceptibility to the gold bug, though it does not excuse the venality that ensues upon its bite.

Bobby Locke, the man who provoked such trains of thought in the minds of the American sports public, was in time bitten by the bug himself, and some phases of his case were among the most acute of their kind ever observed. At first, Bobby's

Jimmy Demaret. Golf will always need personalities like this jovial, uninhibited Texan who enjoys having people around him and was always a prodigious favorite with the galleries. Jimmy was a clotheshorse of the first order.

conversion to American folkways took the form of removing his tie while on the golf course, calling the other pros "old buddy," and purchasing white-walled tires for the automobile in which he drove around with his business adviser, Neil Scott. But by mid-June the young man from Vereeniging thoroughly appreciated the fact that he was the man that American fans wanted to see and that his presence alone would insure the financial success of a tournament, as it did at George May's All-American, in which Hogan, Snead, and Demaret, the active big-draws, did not choose to participate. In order to play in May's tournament, Bobby canceled his original plans to go to Britain for the Open and had his American visa extended from ninety days to a full year. Money like the check for $7,500 May guaranteed him didn't grow on the veldt. Bobby, with his natural swing in the groove day after day, cleaned up in a succession of tournaments and by midsummer he had pocketed about $20,000 in prize money alone, right up along with Hogan and Demaret, the leaders, who had had the advantage of stocking up in the January, February, and March tourneys. What soured the American public on a golfer they had welcomed as a benign influence were the reports that Bobby was not willing to make his thousands and let it go at that. When reporters approached him with their questions, he stopped them short by saying that if the material they wanted was of an instructional nature, he was afraid he would have to charge them a fee of $100, old boy. Sympathies are easily turned, and when the converted Locke doffed his cap after an applauded shot, the action may have been as spontaneous in August as it had been in May but now it seemed as blandly commercial as the increase in Maurice Chevalier's accent the longer he remained in America. It was a shame that Bobby had changed, or had been ill advised, for he had the opportunity of becoming a triple threat—a salutary influence on our tournament manners and a highly popular sports figure as well as a prosperous golfer.

Locke won a host of tournaments during his profitable first visit to America but not the P.G.A. or the Open. In the P.G.A. he was toppled in the first round by Henry Ransom's birdie on the eighteenth before he had a chance to get rolling. Bobby played his usual neat, brainy brand of golf at the St. Louis Country Club in the Open. With nine holes to go he still had a fair chance of catching the leaders, but he missed his pars on the tenth, thirteenth, and fourteenth, and though he birdied the fifteenth, it was too late by then. Apart from Locke's challenge, the Open, an exciting Open, was a two-man affair. Sam Snead, needing a birdie on the final hole to tie with Lew Worsham, got it by holing a tough 15-footer. On the same green the next day he lost the playoff by failing to get down a putt that measured 2 feet, 6½ inches.

As was only logical after his sterling golf and dollar reward, Locke returned to the States for a goodish stay the following year, 1948, but after that his visits became briefer and less frequent. The reason for this was the marvelous success he enjoyed from 1949 on in the British Open, which for a South African like Bobby ranked as the premier championship. Locke came into his own at Royal St. George's in Sandwich in '49, defeating Harry Bradshaw, the portly Irish wizard, in a playoff. In his sixteen rounds in the next four British Opens, Locke was never over 74. He added two more champion-ships, in '50 and '52. By that time old Bobby's exchequer was in such a healthy state that American golf had understandably lost some of its fascination for him.

Among the features of the international picture in 1948 were young Peter Thomson's adumbrative feat of finishing top amateur in the Australian Open and the resumption of Curtis Cup competition at Birkdale. The favored American team won that match by a score of 6½ to 2½. Louise Suggs, who had dropped her foursome and barely halved her singles match, gradually came onto her game in the British Ladies Championship played the following week at Lytham. In the final she met Jean Donald of Scotland, and the two women waged a tremendous battle in the storm that blew off the Irish Sea. Trailing by a hole after the 33rd, Louise won the 34th, halved the 35th, and then carried the crucial home hole.

Once again, in 1948, the British Open was the one championship the British were able to retain. Henry Cotton won the old mug for the third time, at Muirfield. None of the American entries was near the English stylist, who hit the ball as sharply and as shrewdly as he had at Sandwich in 1934, when he snapped the skein of American victories in the British Open and became a national hero.

In the tournaments at home, it was Hogan, Hogan, Hogan. Ben won the exhaust-ing P.G.A. for the second time in three years. Then he rushed home to Texas to recuperate from the strain, vowing that he was worn to a frazzle and was thinking of giving up the whole nerve-wracking business. A few weeks later he won the U.S. Open, wiped his forehead, and sighed that he was all in. Then he teamed with Demaret to take the Inverness Four-Ball and won the Motor City Open, a very strong tired man.

Ben's victory in the national Open was long overdue, but it was worth waiting for. He was never more brilliant than in that Open, played at the Riviera Country Club, a 7,020-yard course made to order for Hogan's length and accuracy. (After Ben's victories in the 1947 and 1948 Los Angeles Opens at Riviera, the pros dubbed the course "Hogan's Alley.") Ben opened up with a 67, 4 under par. A 72 dropped him three strokes behind Snead, whose 138 set a new record for the halfway mark of the tournament. Snead's old bugaboo, his putting, began to take its toll and Hogan fought his way back into the lead after fifty-four holes with a 68. He started his last round with a birdie and ended it with a birdie and bore down on every shot in between for a 69.

Ben's total of 276 (67-72-68-69) clipped five full strokes off the old Open record established by Ralph Guldahl in 1937. In every respect his four rounds at Riviera were as impeccable a performance as an American national championship had ever produced.

MID-CENTURY
ARCHITECTURE

It is always difficult to know when an idea, a person, or an institution has reached maturity, and games are not one whit easier to evaluate. Baseball, the most complicated of all team sports, is just about the same beautifully balanced contest it was a hundred years ago. The game was born adult. Experimentation has only proved its original soundness. Lawn tennis tactics have widened, the equipment has been somewhat refined, but the basic rules and the playing area have remained fixed, and wisely, it would seem. But then, on the other hand, there are games like football and basketball, games not as old as tennis and baseball but with many years of development behind them, which are still in the throes of revision. All a fan can deduce is that the final form of these games has yet to be forged. As many of the alterations dismay him as please him. Naturally prejudiced toward leaving things alone, he has no way of knowing for certain if he is irked by a change that for the next generation will be the magic lantern, the motion picture, or the talking picture.

Of all sports, the most enigmatic to appraise is golf. It is the most "imperfect" of games, which is its strength. The change from day to day may be minute, but every golf course is a chameleon. No golf hole ever plays exactly the same way twice. No golfer has ever lined up two absolutely identical shots. Apart from the variations that Nature brings into play, golf courses have been constantly remodeled by golfers for numerous reasons: to eradicate ugly-duckling holes that improved standards of architecture have shown to offer no honest golf shots; to balance the improved techniques that have made some holes too easy; to keep pace with the improved equipment that has made some holes too short. When Bobby Jones and Alister MacKenzie built the lovely Augusta National in 1931–1932, for example, they made a really remarkable effort to construct a course without a single weak shot or weak hole, a course that would be as modern in the Seventies as it was in the Thirties. To illustrate—Jones had a violent distaste for drive-and-pitch par 4s, gift birdie holes. He believed that a two-shotter should demand two good shots, and accordingly eight of the par 4s at Augusta measured between 400 and 440 yards. As far as the par 5s were concerned, Jones, a strategic school man, held that a golfer should be physically able to get on or close in two but should be penalized severely if his second shot, the gamble shot, failed to measure up, even slightly, to the clearly stated challenge. To put as much value as possible on tee-to-green play, Jones and MacKenzie sharply contoured the greens at Augusta, especially on those holes where the "birdie shot" was a moderately short iron. These contours had the effect of reducing the holing distance to that area within twenty feet or so of the pin; or to say it the other way, the professional who failed to stick his approach within twenty feet of the pin, the pros' target area, had to abandon his thoughts of one-putting that green. Jones personally banged hundreds of shots down each fairway and onto each green to test the integrity of each yard at Augusta. The result was a stiff course but a thoroughly fair one. If a player hit the ball correctly on the Augusta National, the course was ready to reward him. Jones himself shot a 63 in one of his warmups before the first Masters.

The Augusta National has stood up fairly well. The 279 made by Ralph Guldahl in 1939 and equaled a decade later by Claude Harmon remained the record low total for four rounds until 1953, when Ben Hogan took astute advantage of perfect playing conditions and compiled a fantastic 274. Hogan's mark stood up until 1965, when Jack Nicklaus brought in a four-round total of 271. However, in most years four rounds in par, 288, will usually place a player in the money; in 1954 and 1956, no player in the entire field matched 288. At the same time the course has already shown signs of obsolescence. Although Jones and his aides continually revamped tee positions and hazards and green decks—and the course in the process has been lengthened until it now extends to about 7,020 yards from the back tees—a number of the holes are now not as testing for the pros as they were intended to be. Under ideal conditions, at least five of the two-shotters now play as drive-and-pitch holes. Two of the par 5s can be birdied by the pros a shade too regularly, without requiring brilliant shots. The added length the present-day tournament golfers have cultivated has made the difference.

Along with Robert Trent Jones, that able architect, Robert Tyre Jones, Jr., prepared late in the 1940s a new and much lengthier course on the outskirts of Atlanta, the Peachtree Golf Club. From the front tees, which the average golfer plays, Peachtree measures 6,300 yards. From the backs, in order to make each par for the pros the examination that par is supposed to be, Peachtree plays about 7,000 yards long, and if the extreme back tee on each hole is used, 7,400 yards.

Seventy-four hundred yards is a lot of golf course. The average length for each hole, counting the par 3s, would be over 410 yards. And the question is simply this: Is this the end or will Peachtree be merely a continuation of the race in which the golf course tries to keep up with advances, technical and otherwise? In other words, will Peachtree become outmoded in the years ahead and a 7,600-yard course be necessary to test the ability of a topnotch golfer?

The consensus of the experts is that 7,400 yards should hold firm and can hold firm if the game's American watchdog, the U.S.G.A., guards against further "rabbiting" of the ball and is properly wary about accepting new "inventions," such as shafts made of new materials, which also promise greater yardage. Improved techniques—and golf techniques will continue to improve—will not by themselves make 7,400 yards an obsolete workout. . . . Mind you, this is 7,400 *strategic* yards. A far shorter course of penal design can defeat low scoring but it also defeats good golf.

If 7,400 yards proves enduring and golf for its finest exponents becomes a somewhat fixed game, the experts believe this will be all for the best. They assert that they are not non-progressive. They are anxious only to prevent some unnatural elongation of the game, not to stunt it. Golf, in their opinion, has attained approximate maturity. Allowing scientific developments to alter the game further would be as unwise as if baseballs were permitted to be hypoed and bats chemicalized and then, to counteract the new overpowering distances, bleachers built 600 or 700 feet from home plate. The vigilance of baseball's leaders has kept the game fundamentally the same for over a century. The enviable result is that baseball is the possessor of a majestic tradition. What happened in 1900 still means something by today's standards. One cannot emphasize too strongly that golf will benefit immeasurably if, proceeding naturally but with judgment, it remains essentially the same game that was played by Charlie Macdonald, Jerry Travers, the young Ouimet, and their followers, so that the wonders they wrought will always have a contemporary application, a continuing pertinence and vitality. The golfer in 2030 should be able to recognize instinctively the genius that fashioned the Grand Slam.

One is compelled to think of a sport's tradition in terms of the men who break the records, but there is also the average golfer to be considered. What about the fellow who plays 98? How does he fit into the "big picture"? Rather easily. Golf for the average player is already a mature game. The fact that some fourteen million Americans want to play golf is the briefest and the best argument that the game provides a fascination, a test, and an over-all enjoyment superior to any other all-ages game. It didn't with the feathery, nor with the guttie. It was too difficult. But the rubber-cored ball was the last revolutionary step needed to make golf a game that had basically found its true expression. The average golfer will always hit a few shots each round that will compensate for his inability to play each stroke like a Nicklaus or a Hogan. One or two of his drives will zoom 225 yards down the fairway, and his pleasure in "the long drive" will give him that gr-r-rand and gl-l-lorious feeling. A 225-yard drive is long enough. The thrill is there.

One very big step forward was taken in 1954 when the fairways for the Open Championship at Baltusrol were entirely roped off, a practice the R. & A. had earlier found to be the best of all solutions. The roped-off course proved to be so popular with

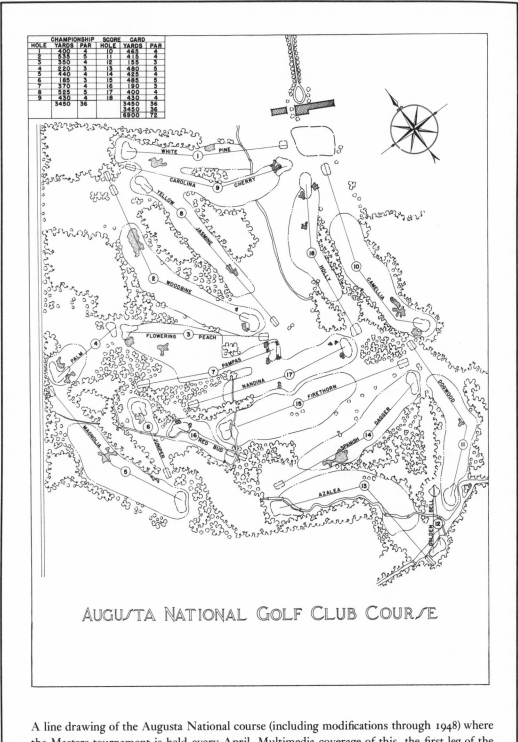

AUGUSTA NATIONAL GOLF CLUB COURSE

A line drawing of the Augusta National course (including modifications through 1948) where the Masters tournament is held every April. Multimedia coverage of this, the first leg of the modern Grand Slam, has acquainted a majority of American golfers with the finest elements of strategic design, as reflected by Augusta.

both spectators and players that it has since been regularly employed by the U.S.G.A. for the championships it conducts and has also been taken up by the Masters, the P.G.A., and an ever-increasing number of other tournaments. Another solution advocated by Robert Trent Jones and other progressive thinkers—it is admittedly a visionary idea but one well worth attention and thought—resides, to begin with, in building for some established tournament (like the P.G.A.) a course over which that tournament would be played year after year. Then the money required for the extra spectator-aids becomes a natural extension of the project. The primary design of the course would have to be of the "loop" type—nine holes marching out in a relatively straight direction from the clubhouse, nine holes marching back. A high road would be built entirely around the perimeter of the course, bordering the rough. This elevated roadway might be built with three levels, for example. The lowest level would be for spectators who choose to walk. Provision would be made for vantage points, both fixed and variable, near tees and greens and along fairways so that the spectators could "move in" on the players at these junctions and get the feel of nearness without blocking the views of the fans on the two upper levels. The middle level would be for vehicles—open trucks fitted out with tiers of seats. In a match-play tourney, these trucks would be assigned to follow particular matches, say Miller versus Player or Jacklin versus Trevino. At the first tee the spectator would buy a ticket for the match he wanted to take in, and clamber aboard the mobile bleacher. And on the topmost level, according to the rough blueprint, a track would be laid for an observation train similar to the type that follows a crew race. This observation train would be for the spectator who prefers, at the moment, to take in the play of the entire field. He would sit with his friends, relaxed and omniscient, as the train slowly crawled around the perimeter during a sixty-minute run. Under such a plan, with the players, caddies, and referees the only persons on the course, every spectator would have a perfect position for watching the action.

Golf is no different from any other sport in the added color and tingle it takes on when international stars compete. Throughout the world there are a surprising number of Gary Players and Peter Thomsons and Takaaki Konos and Sukree Onshams and Roberto DeVicenzos, and it is always very good to see them. In little more than a century the old Scottish game has found its way to every corner of the world. Wherever it has been introduced it has flourished—not that this has been too surprising. After all, as every golfer in every land will attest after a good round, it may well be the best game ever invented.

PART SIX

THE AGE
OF
HOGAN

1948–1955

THE CHAMPION WHO CAME BACK—A GREATER CHAMPION

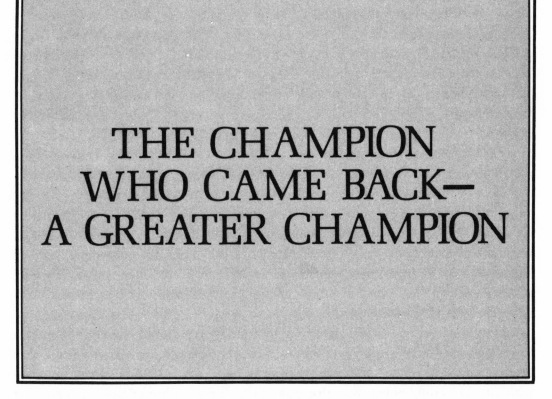

THE CHAMPION
WHO CAME BACK—
A GREATER CHAMPION

As January gave way to February in 1949, Ben Hogan and his wife Valerie were driving back to their home in Fort Worth from Phoenix for a few weeks' respite from the attritive tournament-a-week winter circuit. At thirty-six, finally the reigning United States Open Champion a hard twelve years after he had first qualified for that event, Ben had started his winter no differently than usual by entering four consecutive tournaments. In the Los Angeles Open (which Lloyd Mangrum won), he had played loose and disappointing golf. He had come back with all of his undetourable determination to win The Crosby and the Long Beach Open, and then, after tying for the top, had been defeated by Jimmy Demaret in their playoff for first place in the Phoenix Open. The edge was beginning to come off Ben's game, and a vacation was in order before catching up with the caravan again, perhaps when the pros hit Houston, perhaps later when they rolled into Florida, depending on how hungry for action he felt.

On the morning of February 2nd, as the Hogans were pushing eastward on the highway beyond the town of Van Horn in western Texas, a Greyhound bus traveling in the opposite direction swooped out of the ground haze and smashed head on into the Hogans' automobile. A second before the collision, in an effort to protect his wife, Ben had flung himself across the seat in front of her. It was a fortunate thing he did, for the awful impact of the crash jammed the steering wheel through the driver's seat. As it was, Ben suffered a double fracture of the pelvis, a fractured collarbone, a broken inner bone in his left ankle, and a broken right rib. It was questionable if he would ever recover sufficiently from these injuries to be able to play competitive golf again.

About a month later, in the Hotel Dieu Hospital in El Paso, to which he had been moved, Ben's condition took a sudden turn for the worse. Blood clots had formed. On March 3, in order to halt the phlebitis causing these clots, the doctors attending Hogan performed a two-hour abdominal operation and tied off the principal veins in his legs. The operation saved Hogan's life, but there was a stern possibility that he would be a lucky man indeed to be able to walk normally again, let alone resume the toil of tournament golf, where the invariable strain on a man's physique, his legs in particular, can be a terrible thing even for the hardiest of young men. After lying flat on his back for fifty-eight days, Ben was strong enough to go home to Fort Worth. Knowing the man, golf devotees around the world—and millions of people who ordinarily did not concern themselves with golf—could appreciate that the game was almost the whole of Ben's life and that he would expend every ounce of his being in order to return to it, but they also appreciated that it was extremely doubtful if even as doughty a character as Hogan would be able to make it. There are some circumstances that just don't yield to anybody's will. If there was a vague silver lining to the cloud, it was that Ben, long entitled to the formal distinction of being the national champion, had at least, and at last, won the Open the previous spring.

Hogan not only came back, which in itself was something of a miracle, but once he had his legs under him again, he demonstrated that he was a discernibly better golfer than he had ever been. Shortly after his return, he set off, at first tentatively and then with an accelerating momentum that came to have the quality of irresistibility, on a succession of triumphs in the major tournaments that recalled the dominance of Bob Jones in the Twenties and of Harry Vardon around the turn of the century. Some seventeen months after the accident that had almost crushed the life out of him, Ben won his second U.S. Open, at Merion. The following year, in 1951, he carried off his first Masters and, a few months later at Oakland Hills, his third U.S. Open. His performances in 1952, when he lacked the final push to pull through in both the Masters and the Open after he had played himself into "the perfect position for Hogan," seemed to indicate that at thirty-nine he was slowing down. So, as confounding as ever, the man who was over the hill came back in 1953 to enjoy the greatest of all his campaigns: he took the Masters, the U.S. Open, and then the British Open, in that order, a prodigious feat that had never before been accomplished. Ben was on the verge of winning yet another Masters in 1954—he ultimately lost by a stroke to Snead in the playoff—and a year later barely failed in his ambitious bid to become the first golfer ever to win the U.S. Open five times when he was defeated in another playoff, this time by that most unknown of unknowns, Jack Fleck. Following that 1955 championship, Ben announced that he was entering semi-retirement. He emerged from it the following spring to play in the Masters and to try once again for his fifth Open title at Oak Hill in Rochester. He all but made it, finishing just one stroke behind the winner, Cary Middlecoff. It was clear that for many more years, if he started a tournament with two sharp rounds that put him into the thick of the battle, Ben Hogan would remain one of the most vigorous, combative, unretired competitors who ever stalked a figure he had to get.

The Champion Who Came Back—a Greater Champion

At the same time, something did change after the 1955 Open. A period had come to an end. For the first time since 1948, when the Age of Hogan had begun, Ben had gone two years in a row without winning at least one of the major championships—either the U.S. Open or the British, the P.G.A., or the Masters. Over that span, Ben had perennially been the first factor to be reckoned with in every championship, the man who had to be beaten. Just as it had been the field versus Jones in the Twenties, it had been the field versus Hogan. Time after time he had outgolfed and outthought and outfought and outlasted the stiffest competition, and had established himself in the process as not only the outstanding golfer but the outstanding athlete of the postwar decade, the acknowledged peer of the genuinely superlative athletes of all times, immortals of the stature of Ruth, Thorpe, Jones, Tilden, Nurmi, Cobb, Morenz, Johnson, John L. Sullivan. In his chosen sport, he had gained the ultimate honors: an equal eminence with Harry Vardon and Bob Jones as the greatest players in the history of the game, a man who dominated his age as completely as was humanly possible and whose record would arouse a sense of awe and disbelief among future generations, who would wonder how any one man could have played so well so consistently and won so many important championships so often.

HOGAN'S RECORD 1948–1956

	U.S. OPEN	MASTERS	P.G.A.	BRITISH OPEN
1948	1	tied 6	1	
1949				
1950	1 (playoff)	tied 4		
1951	1	1		
1952	3	tied 7		
1953	1	1		1
1954	tied 6	2 (playoff)		
1955	2 (playoff)	2		
1956	tied 2	tied 8		

The road back to golf and these wondrous achievements was a fretfully slow one at first. Back home in Fort Worth after his release from the hospital in El Paso, Ben carefully mapped out a program of convalescence. In order to build up the strength in his legs, in which the smaller veins were forced to carry more blood than they normally would now that the larger veins had been tied off, he began by doing some walking every day, at first fifty-five "laps"—a lap consisted of once around his living room—and then an additional five laps each ensuing day. The weather on the sixth of April was balmy and bright, and, clad in his pajamas, a topcoat, and a cap, Ben tried his legs out of doors for the first time. Not until late August, however, did he pick up a golf club, and it was December before he essayed his first faltering round, walking some of the holes but riding most of the way in an electric golf cart. A week or so after this, his legs encased from the ankles to the thighs in elastic bandages to facilitate circulation, he trudged his first eighteen holes. It took so much out of him that he immediately went home and to bed, further depressed by the thought that he might never be able to recondition himself for tournament golf. He decided, though, to file his entry for the Los Angeles Open scheduled for mid-January at the Riviera course, the old alley where Hogan had always scored well and where he had won the 1948 Open. "It's a possibility I'll play," he remarked as he boarded the train to the Coast, "but right now I can't say. I honestly don't know myself. I'll just have to wait and see how I'm feeling and how my game is working. One thing I can tell you for sure: I'm not going out there and shoot in the eighties."

Hogan's first round in the Los Angeles Open was a 73, 2 over par. This was a much lower score than was expected of the warrior so newly returned to the wars, and golfers everywhere were exceedingly happy over this more than respectable showing. Give Ben a few months more, so went the consensus, and who could tell—he might be fighting it out with the boys again. When he followed his 73 with a pair of 69s, the golf world was ecstatically stunned. There he was, as if he had never been away, in a position actually to *win* the tournament if he could fashion one more good round. And he did, yet another 69. When Ben's total of 280 was posted, there was only one man still out who had a reasonable chance of matching that mark—melodramatically enough, Sam Snead, Hogan's ancient rival. To do this, Sam would have to play the last four holes two strokes under par. He parred the fifteenth. He parred the sixteenth. On the seventeenth, Snead, the celebrated poor putter, dropped a 10-footer for his birdie. On the home hole, a long par 4, he fired his approach eighteen feet from the pin and stroked his putt into the cup—280. Only this superb finish by Sam prevented Ben from walking clean off with the tournament that was supposed to have served merely as a mild warm-up to ascertain whether or not he could stand up to eighteen holes on four consecutive days.

Hogan's amazing and heart-warming comeback was front-page news. There were few Americans who had not followed his progress in the tourney and who were not now anxiously interested in whether or not he could cap the whole incredible sequence by defeating Sam in their playoff. As it turned out, the dramatic crest had already been reached. First of all, a torrent of fine California weather forced the playoff to be postponed a week. Then, before Snead and Hogan did get together, Hogan's mediocre, terribly tired play during the intervening week in the Crosby had made it clear that he was still not altogether his old self again. Snead, never behind at any stage, captured the delayed playoff by a comfortable four strokes.

Hogan's next start of any consequence was in the Masters early in April. He got off well with a 73 and a 68, he followed this with a 71, but on the final day he answered the question on everybody's mind—Did he have the old stamina and the old shots?—by taking a shaky 76. (Demaret, with a closing 69, became the first three-time winner of the Masters.) Some two months later the Open rolled around. Despite the fact that Ben had in the meantime won the four-day tourney at White Sulphur Springs (and won it with a total of 259, equaling the record score for seventy-two holes on a par-70 course), and despite the magic that the name of Hogan had begun to connote, the game's unsentimental observers did not rate his chances of taking the Open too highly. On the final day of the Open, the field played those taxing thirty-six holes, and this grind, they believed, would probably be just too much for Ben. There was no way of knowing, of course, since he had not attempted two rounds in one day since his accident.

On the eve of the final thirty-six, Ben was in the position that golfing tradition has long decreed the ideal spot: two strokes behind the leader—in this case, E. J. "Dutch" Harrison, the Arkansas Traveler, whose 139 had been compounded of a 72 and a 67. (The 67 would have seemed much lower than it did, particularly since it had been made on the time-resisting East Course at Merion, had not a jobless young pro from Alabama, one Lee Mackey, Jr., shattered all records for a single round in the championship with an opening 64, 6 under par. Mackey, unfortunately, needed seventeen shots more than that to get around Merion the next day, and his brief moment of glory was over.) As for Hogan, his first two rounds, a 72 and a 69, had revealed that his game was perhaps a shade sounder in all departments than it had been at Augusta. Though he walked at a very slow pace and limped quite badly on his left leg, this aftereffect of his accident appeared to be no impediment to his concentration or to his execution of his shots once he was over the ball. He was playing careful, painstaking golf, and on Merion that always looks good. A stroke behind Ben lay the veteran Lloyd Mangrum and Cary Middlecoff—Cary defending his title won at Medinah the June before. A stroke in front of Ben were Jim Ferrier, the transplanted Australian who had taken the P.G.A. Championship in 1947, Johnny Bulla, and Julius Boros, a new convert to the professional ranks whose manner was so untheatrical that he gave the impression that he was simply serving as the playing companion for whomever he was paired with and, usually, unobtrusively outscoring.

Until mid-afternoon on Saturday, the day of the third and fourth rounds, there was no knowing for certain what was taking shape as the endless merry-go-round of golfers made its solemn double circuit of the subtly exacting course. At the three-quarters mark, Mangrum had taken over the leadership with a 69 for 211, a stroke ahead of Harrison (73), two strokes ahead of Hogan (71), Middlecoff (71), and Johnny Palmer (70), three strokes ahead of Ferrier (74). A fine last round would have won for any of these contenders, but one by one they began losing strokes to par and found it next to impossible to pick up the birdies that would have given them a new lease on a confident mood. Mangrum could do no better than a 76, nor could Harrison. Palmer and Middlecoff, both off balance from the start of their final rounds, eventually wound up with 79s. When it began to become apparent as the afternoon wore on that inflation was the order of the day, two developments assumed increasing importance. First, the total of 287 turned in by George Fazio—the former Canadian Open Champion, practically unobserved, had added a 70 in the afternoon to his 72 in the morning—slowly but surely changed from a commendable effort into a hard figure, the more so when Mangrum succeeded only in tying it. And second, as Hogan was making his way up the twelfth, or 66th, fairway, only 1 over par for the round, it was suddenly realized that his own steady if unspectacular progress and the comparatively high scores of the other leaders had quietly combined to place the tournament right in the palm of his hands. If Ben could fend off his weariness long enough to play the last seven holes in 2 over par, he would be in.

On the twelfth, Ben dropped a shot to par when his approach bounded over the green and he missed a 5-footer after chipping back. He made his pars in regulation fashion on the thirteenth and fourteenth, and needed only to sink a 30-inch putt for his par on the fifteenth. He missed it. On the sixteenth, the famous Quarry Hole, a 445-yard par 4 where the sway-backed fairway is separated from the elevated green by a broad, deep, bush-and-sand-filled quarry pit that somehow escaped from Pine Valley, Ben had his 4 all the way. Then, almost home, he failed to get his 3 on the seventeenth. Here, after his tee shot had finished in a trap off to the left of the upper deck of this terraced green, some 230 yards from the tee, he had put his sand shot within five feet of the cup only to miss the putt. It was his third bogey in six holes. Now it was a different story altogether. Winning was out of the question. To tie Fazio and Mangrum, Ben would have to get his par 4 on the eighteenth.

A 4 on Merion's eighteenth is never an easy matter. Two first-class shots are required to get home on that 458-yarder, a big drive and then either a fairway wood or a long iron that must hold the line unwaveringly to end on the mildly plateaued green. Hogan belted just the drive that was asked for, long and straight. He elected to play his second with a 2-iron. It seemed to the thousands of spectators lining the length of the fairway and stacked behind the green that Ben took a bit more time than usual to think the shot out, but it may have been only the suspenseful atmosphere that stretched the seconds out. There was a lot of gauze in the air in Merion at that moment, the soft mood of twilight in so tranquil a setting accounting for some of the unreality and, in another and entirely different way, the inward recognition by each spectator that he was witnessing a truly dramatic moment without knowing quite what to make of it. Hogan shuffled his heels a little, reset his palms, and moved into the shot. He hit it with admirable decisiveness. The ball took off in a low trajectory toward the left side of the green, but for some time it was hard to tell where it had finished, for hardly had the shot become airborne when the huge gallery broke from the edges of the fairway and blocked out all view of the ball as they raced for positions around the green. Cheers had started up from the spectators behind the green, many of the shouts unleashed almost as soon as the shot was struck, so there was really no telling from that evidence whether the fans were roaring their delight at the excellent results of the long iron or were just roaring as galleries will because they had come to roar. Actually, the ball ended up just where it had looked it might—on the left side of the green some forty flat feet away from the cup

Hogan at Merion. To tie for the top in the 1950 Open—his first start in major championship play following his accident—Ben had to get his par 4 on the hole that was probably the most difficult on the course, the 458-yard 18th. After a long tee shot, he burned a superb 2-iron to the green and calmly made his 4.

set to the back and right. Ben rolled his approach putt about a yard past the hole. He tapped the short putt in, firmly. He had tied for first.

In the playoff, displaying no signs of enervation, Hogan made his comeback complete when he outplayed both Mangrum and Fazio, his 69 being four shots better than Mangrum and six better than Fazio. The outcome was determined on the Quarry Hole, the sixteenth. At this point Hogan was leading Fazio by three strokes but stood only a shot in front of Mangrum. On the sixteenth green, Hogan lay about eight feet from the cup after two beautiful shots. Mangrum, who had missed his drive, was twelve feet away in three, thanks to a lovely pitch. He holed his 12-footer and Hogan missed his 8-footer, but the scores on that hole were a 4 for Hogan and a 6 for Mangrum. When Fazio had been lining his putt up, Mangrum had marked his ball at Fazio's request since it was in his line. He had then replaced the ball. This procedure, of course, was legal and customary. But then, when Mangrum stepped up to play his putt, he noticed a bug on his ball, whereupon he picked the ball up and blew the bug off. In those days the rules called for a penalty of two strokes if a player lifted and cleaned his ball when it had not been stipulated before the round that balls could be cleaned on the green. Under the circumstances, since cleaning the ball was not permitted on this playoff round, there was nothing for the U.S.G.A. officials to do but to impose a two-stroke penalty on Mangrum. On the short seventeenth, Mangrum made his par and Hogan rapped a 50-footer up and over the steep dip and into the cup for a birdie 2. This made everyone feel a great deal better, for it counteracted the bad taste that the inflicting of a technical penalty at a crucial juncture inevitably must bring with it, and it reinforced the clean-cut character of Hogan's triumph. Ben parred the eighteenth. He was not only back, he was back on top.

There was an entirely different emotional content in the air the following year, when Hogan rang up two more major victories, in the Masters and in the Open at Oakland Hills. Whereas in 1950 there had been widespread doubt whether Ben would ever regain his full powers, in 1951 no one, certainly not his competition, had any lingering qualms about that. If anything, it was becoming more and more obvious that Ben was a surer shot-maker and a more obdurate tournament player than he had been before his enforced absence from the lists. His appetite for victory had abated not one swallow, and he had picked up something he hadn't had before: a marvelous ability to gauge and pace his golf to fit (1) the requirements of the course at hand, (2) the probable efforts of his rivals, and (3) the 72-hole total he deduced he would need to outscore them. Hogan came to refer to this ability as "management" and to claim that it accounted for 80 percent of his success, his technical talent for a mere 20 percent. Be that as it may, in the 1951 Masters he provided one of his most memorable demonstrations of how to win a golf tournament by using your head as well as your hands.

On the final day of that Masters, Ben was the last of the leaders to go out. When he made the turn on that final round, everyone else in the running had finished, and he knew for a fact that all he had to do to beat the lowest total, Skee Riegel's 282, was to play the last nine holes in even par. There is water in front of or flanking five of the

Lloyd Mangrum stares down a long one on his way to wrapping up another L.A. Open.

greens on that perilous last nine at Augusta, plus a number of other physical and psychological obstacles that have contributed over the years to the collapse of many experienced golfers down the stretch. Hogan, however, nursed the ball so artfully over the terrain that you wondered why that back nine had ever given anyone the least bit of trouble. On the tenth, twelfth, fourteenth, sixteenth, and seventeenth he was the epitome of orthodoxy: on in the regulation number of strokes, down in 2. On the eleventh and eighteenth holes, his tactics were ultra-conservative. On the eleventh, an extremely dangerous par 4 on which all the trouble lies to the left—a bulge of Rae's Creek curves around that side of the green—he played his second wide to the right, then chipped up and holed his putt for his par. On the eighteenth, which he had learned from galling experience was terribly easy to three-putt if you planted your approach above the pin on the upsloping green, he purposely lobbed his approach short of the green, then got down in a chip and a putt for his par. By the time he had made this decision on the home hole, Ben was already the assured victor. He had needed no birdies on the last nine, save for their insurance value, but he had come up with two of them anyway on the long holes, the thirteenth and fifteenth. On each of these par 5s, a water hazard (an arm of Rae's Creek on the thirteenth and a pond on the fifteenth) guards the approach to the green, but a player can carry the hazard on his second shot, reach the green, and set himself up for a probable birdie if he follows a long, controlled drive with a well-played fairway wood or long iron. Although Hogan poked out sufficiently long drives on each of these holes to have warranted his gambling on going for the green on his second, he chose in both instances to play safely short of the hazard before the green with a medium iron. On the thirteenth he flicked his third, a little pitch, stiff to the pin with his wedge and holed for his birdie; he repeated this procedure on the fifteenth. Most members of the gallery who followed Ben on his watertight march were disappointed by his eschewing the spectacular shots they had come to watch, but they will probably never see a finer exhibition of how to play solid, heady, sticking-with-par golf.

The 1951 Open called for bolder measures. Like every golfer in the field, with the one possible exception of Paul Runyan, the short-hitting star of the Thirties, Hogan was bothered and confused by the revised Oakland Hills layout. Recognizing that the course had grown obsolete as a championship test, the tournament committee at Oakland Hills had called in Robert Trent Jones to revitalize the holes and generally restore some of the meaning that par had held back in the old days. (In 1924, for example, Cyril Walker had been the lone player among the eighty-five starters who had broken 300 in the Open at Oakland Hills.) Trent Jones' major move was to fill in the defunct old traps flanking the fairways 200 to 220 yards out from the tees, which the modern pros with their advanced equipment could carry with ease, and to carve new flanking traps some 220 to 250 yards out. To increase the premium on accurate tee-shot play, the fairways were narrowed, particularly in the "landing area," that section of the fairway in which the pros' average tee shot landed. Admittedly, these wasp-waisted, trap-flanked fairways constituted a rigorous examination of a pro's ability to control the ball, but then perhaps this is what should always obtain in a national championship, where the point is not to see how many men can take a course apart but to test their mastery of all the shots. One or two of the fairways might have played a little too tight and there were a couple of new greenside traps whose virtue was debatable, but as the course proved during the tournament, it would respond to the golfer who played it with courage and skill. Oakland Hills in 1951 very possibly was the most difficult assignment the country's top golfers had ever encountered in the Open and very possibly it was also the best over-all test of championship golf we had had in this country in a long, long time.

To have voiced a complimentary opinion of the course to any contestant during that tournament, however, would have meant sure death to the ambitions of anyone who aspired to become the Dale Carnegie Man-of-the-Year. The pros, unable to smash out their drives with the immunity offered by the circuit courses to which most of them had become habituated, fearful of finding either a trap or the heavy rough if they strayed off-line, rode off in all directions at once. Some of them began steering the ball, though, to be sure, this was not their intention. Others thought they would outfox the course by using brassies and spoons and even irons off the tees and thereby keep short of the trouble. When they did this—Oakland Hills measured 6,927 yards—they found that they left themselves such long and wicked approaches that they couldn't hit the greens. One way or another, as Walter Hagen remarked regally from his dais in the clubhouse, the boys were not playing the course, they were letting the course play them.

Hogan started with a 76, 6 over par. He was grim about it. He had overclubbed himself on a couple of approaches, played to the wrong sides of several fairways and greens, and committed one or two other mistakes of management that incensed his driving, perfectionist nature—all the more so because he was really on his game, feeling every inch of his swing. Before the start of the tournament, he had been in a saturnine mood—he had protested that the rough was too high—and standing tied for forty-first place after his opening round did not have the effect of filtering any sunbeams into his disposition. He managed, however, to do some correct thinking, which was like him, and, what was at least as characteristic, he managed to utilize his irritation constructively, almost welcoming its entrance into the chemistry of his attitude (the way old Walter Travis had welcomed the affronts of the British at Sandwich in 1904), since it could serve him as a goad to his goal.

On the second day, Ben started to make his way out of the pack—not that he was pleased with his 73, but 149 kept him within five shots of the leader, Bobby Locke, who was over once again to share a few golden moments with his friends in the land of opportunity. Dave Douglas, a slim circuiteer, was a shot behind Locke; Lew Worsham, the ageless Runyan, and Clayton Heafner were three shots back; Boros and Demaret were four back along with young Fred Hawkins. Then came Hogan and Mangrum along with Snead, who had led after the first day with a 71 and then for the nth time had foozled away a splendid chance in the Open with a second round of 78. No one had broken par, 70, on either of the first two rounds, and, in fact, only two players had equaled it.

Saturday was a lovely June day. The growing national popularity of golf and Hogan's immense personal popularity attracted over twelve thousand spectators, a new record attendance for one day of the Open. Locke, as the leader, carried a sizable gallery with him. Dressed in white shoes, white socks, white knickers, white shirt, and white cap, the large South African called to mind the White Rabbit in *Alice in Wonderland* as he came pattering down the fairways, all neatness and dispatch. He was having trouble staying out of the bunkers, but he was recovering with remarkable finesse and getting his figures, and he gave the impression that he would probably go on doing so. For any of the other leaders to catch him at the 54-hole mark was obviously going to require a round of the first order. On the fourteenth tee, Hogan seemed on his way to just such a round: he was 3 under. He had to give one of these strokes back on the fourteenth when he took three to get down from off the edge. On the comparatively easy fifteenth, a dogleg to the left 392 yards long, he tossed away those other two strokes when he pushed his drive into the rough, hooked his approach clear across the fairway in a dinky little parabola, then came out of that rough with another feeble shot that plopped into the bunker before the green. Standing motionless on the green with his hands on his hips after holing out for his 6, Hogan scowled into the distance for a moment, then ducked his neck and walked moodily to the next tee.

On the last three holes, Ben went 1 over par to finish with a 71, an excellent score but a most disappointing one all the same, since he had been on the verge of coming up with a round so dazzling that it would have had the effect of taking the heart out of his opposition and leaving them muttering to themselves the old threnody that Hogan just wasn't human. His 71, nevertheless, had moved him to within two strokes of Locke, who had taken a 74, and Demaret, who had come up with a 70 to share the lead at the three-quarters mark with 218. Boros and Runyan stood at 219, Heafner along with Ben at 220. A quick lunch, then back to work again.

In the afternoon, sullen with determination, Hogan made the turn in even par, 35. He went 1 under on the tenth, 448 yards, perhaps the ruggedest par on the course, when he drilled a 3-iron four feet from the pin on the slope-top green. He got his par on the eleventh. His par on the twelfth. He went 2 under after the short thirteenth, where he knocked in a 15-footer. Back to 1 under after a 5 on the fourteenth. On the fifteenth, which had been his undoing in the morning, he carried the bunker in the middle of the fairway with his drive, lofted a 6-iron four feet from the hole, and dropped the putt. Again 2 under. A wedge over the water to within six feet of the pin after a whale of a drive on the sixteenth gave him a crack at still another birdie. No dice. A blueprint par on the 194-yard seventeenth. Still 2 under. Though nothing is ever certain in golf, Ben knew as he prepared to play the eighteenth, a heavily bunkered dogleg to the right that measured 459 yards and had been assessed a 4 for the Open, that a par there would probably see him in with a stroke or maybe two to spare. Of the early-starting challengers he had to watch, Demaret had faded quickly on the last round, Boros had not gotten going, and only Heafner had been traveling at a pace at all comparable to Ben's. As for Locke, the South African was playing about nine holes behind Ben and finding the going rough.

On the eighteenth, or 72nd, with a following wind making the risk worth the taking, Ben attempted to carry the bunkered ridge in the angle of the dogleg, and did so. He had only a 6-iron left, and threw up a towering shot that landed in the middle of the green and ended some sixteen feet from the stick. He rolled the putt gently up to the cup, giving it a chance to catch the high corner, which it did: 35-32—67, 3 under par.

At this precise moment, Locke, the one man who still could overhaul Hogan, was standing composedly by on the tenth tee waiting for the cheers from the gallery around the eighteenth to subside. Out in 37, Bobby now needed three birdies to tie Hogan's total of 287. He got one at the tenth. He barely missed another on the twelfth. Trying to nip the ball close to the pin on the short thirteenth, he failed to give the shot quite enough to carry the front bunker, and the White Rabbit's chase was over.

Ben derived colossal satisfaction from his victory. He had improved his score round by round: 76-73-71-67. He had not only conquered the field but, to his way of thinking, a hostile course as well. In later years he came to refer to his final 67 as the greatest round of his career, and perhaps it was, since Heafner's finishing 69 was the only other sub-par round of the tournament. But the figures by themselves do not give a true indication of the brilliance and belligerence of Hogan's shot-making throughout the final day. For illustration, after he had taken that double-bogey 6 on the fifteenth hole in the morning, tournament-tough as Hogan was, there was naturally some speculation as to the effect this would have on him. His answer, if such it was, was a crackling drive to the edge of the lake on the sixteenth. It could not have been hit more fully and it could not have been placed more perfectly if it had been dropped by hand. A good iron-shot away

Julius Boros, the least theatrical
and one of the soundest
of the post-war paragons.

across the small lake, the green noses well out into the water. The pin was set that day over to the right of the green, the most dangerous position. A quick squint at its location had persuaded most of the golfers that discretion was the better part of valor, and player after player was happy to settle for a cautious approach to the left or safe side of the green and a prudent par. Not Hogan. He smacked his iron approach right at the stick, stopping the ball only five feet away. He played that shot as if he had every confidence that his swing was so dynamically sound that it would produce the result he desired ten times out of ten, like a piece of tested machinery. Furthermore, he played that shot as if he had every confidence that he could execute his swing correctly ten times out of ten. He was as formidable as that.

From time to time after Ben's recuperation from his accident there had been indications of a "new Ben," a "mellower Hogan." Up to a point this was true. When there was no golf to be transacted, his manner was more outgoing than it had been formerly and his conversation revealed a warmth and depth that, if they had been there before, he had kept well concealed. At the same time, whenever the starch of competition was in the air, Ben was much the same as he had always been, all intensity, all detachment, all business. In the autumn of 1949, when he had gone to Britain as the non-playing captain of the American Ryder Cup team, for example, in his vigilance to perform the job right up to the hilt he may have made too much of an issue over the question of whether or not the grooves in the faces of one of the British player's irons were scored so deep as to be illegal. At the presentation ceremonies following his triumph in the Open at Oakland Hills, he might well have been expected to glow with the euphoria that follows a hard job well done. Not Hogan. "I'm glad," he stated sternly and with more than a pinch of vindictiveness, "that I brought this course, this monster, to its knees." These incidents and others served as eloquent reminders that as long as he remained a competitive golfer Ben would probably never be so "new" or so "mellow" that the chip on his shoulder would entirely disappear. He seemed to like it that way, or maybe it would be more correct to say that he continually translated any opposition, mineral or vegetable or animal, into a personal challenge and gained an abiding gratification from responding to that challenge with all the sense and sinew at his command.

When Bob Jones retired in 1930 after his Grand Slam, he was twenty-eight. At that same age, Ben had only been beginning to make his presence felt in the world of golf. Born in 1912 in the town of Dublin, Texas, the son of the local blacksmith, his first contact with the game came when he was twelve, shortly after his mother had moved the family to Fort Worth following her husband's death. Ben became a caddie at the Glen Garden Country Club when he learned that the boys received sixty-five cents for a round, more money than he could make selling newspapers at the Union Station. Like nearly all caddies, he fooled around with golf clubs and began to play, but no one thought the undersized, terribly taciturn boy possessed any special aptitude for golf. It came as a considerable surprise to everyone at Glen Garden, when, at fifteen, Ben somehow managed to tie for first in the annual Christmas Day caddie tournament with Byron Nelson, a boy who had shown himself to be a natural golfer and who regularly went around the course close to par and sometimes below it. Not long after this, Ben started to enter amateur tournaments in all sectors of the state, trying to keep up with Nelson, Guldahl, and the numerous other young players who were growing up in Texas, that rough and ready incubator of so many of our foremost players. He wasn't bad, but a chronic tendency to hook cut into his consistency. At nineteen he turned professional and the next winter audaciously set out for Los Angeles and the tour with less than a hundred dollars in his pocket, counting on winning enough prize money to keep afloat. He lasted a month. The following winter, 1933, he took another shot at the circuit, lasted a little longer, and then had to come home again. The next four years he stayed around Fort Worth, supporting himself with odd jobs here and there, working day in and day out on his game, refusing to alter his intention to make golf his career. In 1936 he qualified for the Open at Baltusrol but failed to "make the cut"—that is, he did not finish among the low 76 scorers after the first two rounds and so was not eligible to play the last thirty-six holes. In 1937—by this time he was married to Valerie Fox, a wonderful woman, and particularly for Ben—he set out on the circuit once more and demonstrated himself to be an improved but still far from a winning golfer. In 1939 he qualified for the Open again, succeeded in making the cut this time, but finished in a tie for sixty-second place. He was almost twenty-seven at this time, an age when a golfer must expect some measure of success or else get out of the profession. In a way, it would not have been too illogical if the name Ben Hogan had never become better known to the sports public than the names George Slingerland and Frank Gelhot, the only two men who played the final thirty-six holes at the 1939 Open who did not bring in lower totals than Hogan's. In short, Ben was anything but a born wonder. No athlete ever worked harder or waited longer to become a champion. It explains an awful lot about the man.

In the circuit tournaments in 1939 and 1940 Hogan's tenacity showed definite signs of paying off. He began to win money regularly and then to finish closer to the top regularly. Everyone was wondering when he would finally break through and win a tournament—it would have to come sooner or later; he couldn't end up second or third forever. It came at length in the North and South Open at Pinehurst in April 1940. Then, as he graduated into the most consistent low scorer and leading money-winner on the circuit, golf fans began to wonder when he would make the next step upward and capture one of the major championships. In the 1940 Open, he finished only three shots behind Little and Sarazen. In the '41 Open—despite a 77 in the second round, typical of this one-bad-round period—he tied for third, five shots behind Craig Wood. In the 1941 Masters he tied for the top with Nelson, but Byron came up with some of the best golf of his life in the playoff and defeated him by a stroke. Midway in 1942, Ben entered the Army Air Corps, in which he served for three years. When he returned to civilian life and combat golf late in 1945, he quickly reaffirmed his position of standing with Snead and Nelson as the country's best. In 1946, he succeeded in winning his first prestige tournament, the P.G.A. He played like a killer in the afternoon of the final in defeating Porky Oliver, and he played that way many afternoons afterward, for earlier in 1946—and one can imagine the depths of anguish and self-recrimination a person like Hogan underwent—he had taken three putts on the 72nd green in both the Masters and the Open when two putts would have enabled him to tie for first. After these crucial disappointments, Ben seemed always to be reminding himself not to relax for an instant, to make every shot and every thought count, to show the other fellow (and himself) no mercy.

The Hogan of this period, just prior to his initial victory in the U.S. Open in 1948 at Riviera, was a better golfer than the pre-war Hogan, as his success in itself made clear. Technically, he was well on his way to mastering a slight but critical alteration in his method of striking the golf ball. He referred to this alteration as his "secret" and for several seasons before he finally revealed what it was, trying to guess it became a sort of junior national pastime. If one meant the exact movement or movements Ben introduced into his swing in order to impart a controlled fade to his shots, then no one knew his secret. If one meant more generally doing everything to retain his power and yet everything to guard against a hook, then everyone knew what Hogan was up to. The swing he arrived at and learned so well that he could execute it flawlessly under fire varied somewhat in its details from season to season but it had as its features, bypassing Hogan's true fundamentals of perfect balance and his wide "forward" arc, such anti-hook staples as the right hand riding high on the shaft, the slightly open stance, the thrust of the right forearm at the beginning of the downswing, and the maintenance of an anything-but-shut clubface as he biffed through the ball. Hogan lost some roll as a result of his slight fade, but what he gained was ten times as valuable. When he failed to meet his drives and his other full shots just right, the ball did not hook into trouble but merely veered a few yards to the right in a far safer and "slower" arc than a hook describes. Before effecting this change, when Ben had played an unbroken competitive stretch he had been prone to tire near the end of a tournament. When he was tired, he hooked. When he hooked, he incurred punishing lies in the rough and, sometimes, penalty strokes. When he incurred these extra strokes, it defeated him. His revamped swing gave him margin for unpenalized error and proved to be the difference between his becoming a great champion and remaining simply a great golfer. (When Hogan announced his semi-retirement from competition in the summer of 1955, he confided in a magazine article what his "secret" was. It boiled down to pronation plus two accompanying adjustments, placing the left thumb down the center of the shaft and—and this was the heart of the matter— locking his left wrist so that it could not roll over as he came into and through the ball, locking it by cocking the wrist backward at about a ten-degree angle at the top of his backswing.)

Contrasted with a swing like Snead's, the swing Hogan built through years of practice, trial and error, and practice was not a picture-postcard lyric. But Hogan's swing, when he had the time to tune it up properly and the physical reserve to maintain it as he wanted it, was so functional and assertive that it had a smooth, efficient, kinetic beauty of its own. Behind it, to be very sure, lay Hogan's exceptional will to accomplish. On the course, totally absorbed with producing his best game and a game calculated to win, Ben necessarily had precious little to say. His trenchant silence was only one of the elements that made up the memorable picture of a "man at work" that no one who watched Hogan was ever likely to forget.

There he is, moving up to his approach shot, walking with that little waggle, his eyes fixed straight ahead down the fairway like a man heading for a spot in the woods where he has marked an errant shot. He wears the straight-visored white cap over his tanned countenance. It is a countenance—the mouth set as ever in that locked grin which should never be mistaken for a sign of Ben's enjoyment of the morning air, the devotion of his gallery, or the shot just played, however "right" it may have been. The mind is moving ahead, thinking out the next step in the big picture, filing through this checkpoint and that checkpoint to make certain the next step is the wise step. He stands beside the ball, hands on hips. He examines the lie, studies the type of grass, looks up and sizes up the wind. He discusses inwardly the best position on the green to place that approach in order to set up the most holeable putt, thinks out the type of shot he will play, the club he will play it with. He takes his time, walking ahead sometimes as much as thirty yards as he ponders his decision. (Other players went through somewhat the same motions, but they seldom gave the impression Hogan did that he was genuinely thinking about what he was doing.) Then, the mind made up, there is that light practice swing, the meticulous settling into his stance, the always-decisive stroke. If it is a good shot, there is no expression on Hogan's part to show he acknowledges it as such. However, after he plays a poor shot at a stage of a tournament when it might be costly, there is a change of expression. The grin becomes ironical and his cold, gray-blue eyes widen until they seem to be a full inch in height, and when you look at this man, so furious with himself, he is, as his colleagues refer to him, "The Hawk."

No athlete, perhaps, ever set himself a higher standard of performance than Hogan did. What trying to achieve this standard would have taken out of the average tournament golfer no one knows, but it is probable that few others would have had the stamina to find it tolerable for long. A total giving of one's self was required. What Hogan didn't give to his golf, he didn't have to give. Without any question, no other golfer ever dedicated himself so totally to the game.

The exploits of Ben Hogan were viewed bifocally by the American public, some of whom saw him primarily as a scientist-golfer working miracles of precision, others of whom saw him primarily as the man-who-came-back hero of a heart-warming human-interest story, and all of whom saw him in their different proportions as both golfer and man. The interest Hogan aroused had a great deal to do with the gigantic new boom golf was enjoying in America in mid-century. There were other notable factors. For instance, whatever remained to be done to remove the last traces of the average man's carefully nurtured prejudice against a game originally linked with the wealthy and the aloof was done by President Eisenhower. Probably few men in the long history of the game have ever been bitten by the golf bug quite as badly as the President. As the public came to associate this most regular of fellows with the practice swing on the White House lawn, the quick dash out to Burning Tree for that late afternoon round, vacations in the Little White House right off the practice green at the Augusta National course, and summertime rests in Denver, where golf was given the priority over the time-honored Presidential predilection for fishing, Ike's undisguisable relish for golf made the 3-wood seem as traditionally American as the old fishing pole. As a matter of fact, there was more than a little consternation on the part of baseball's drum-beaters that the President was undermining their game's historic status as the national pastime.

In a way, the trepidations of the baseball men were justified: golf was coming to be more and more an intrinsic part of the lives of millions of Americans. Golf's special appeal is that it is fundamentally a participant sport and the participant can be male or female, eleven or sixty-five, athletic or of only fair coordination, gregarious or dour, and still find the game inexplicably playable and fascinating. A much broader cross-section of the public than ever before turned to the golf course for its recreation, a migration facilitated by the shorter working hours and the additional time for leisure which most Americans enjoyed. Reading the handwriting on the scorecard, an increasing number of the large industrial firms built golf courses for their employees, and, in this general connection, numerous small towns, hopeful of landing a large firm that was looking around for a rural site for a new branch plant, took the counsel of the National Golf Foundation and constructed a course in order to enhance the attractiveness of what they

Down the first fairway of the Augusta National, two days after the conclusion of the 1955 Masters tourney, walk a somewhat more than typical foursome. Left to right, President Dwight Eisenhower, Clifford Roberts, chairman of the Masters since its inception, Billy Joe Patton, and the 1955 Masters champion, Cary Middlecoff.

had to offer. Golf, in fact, became such a common denominator that on occasions, when an aged-in-the-wooden-shaft golfer went to a driving range to patch up the old slice, he came home grousing that at the driving range the old poolroom crowd had found a new hangout. Well, it was an altogether baffling age and perhaps the driving range was a good thing. Maybe slapping out a bucket of balls built character as the old bromide said golf did, and, anyway, it kept the kids momentarily away from the rock-and-roll records in the jukebox.

In an effort to provide facilities for the burgeoning army who wanted to play golf, cities and states constructed more and more public courses, but the supply was destined to fall far short of the demand. A man who did not belong to a private club had, as always, to rise practically in the middle of the night on the weekend in order to snag a favorable starting time. For all the new construction of both public and private courses, their total number increased only slightly until the 1960s, for as suburbia continued its inexorable spread, real-estate developments devoured tens of courses that had been "deep in the country" when they were originally plotted. Of the new courses that sprang up, some of the most imaginatively designed were located in Florida, the Caribbean area, and other sectors of the winter-vacation territory, poised for the jet age, when golfers living a thousand and more miles away would be able to hum south for a "long weekend" of sun and supination. The development of improved grass strains capable of withstanding the burning heat of the south and, just as important, the experienced eye of professional golf architects made many of these new Southern courses a far cry from the short, scraggly, nine-hole nothings that had long made the term *resort course* synonymous with better-bring-your-tennis-racquet-and-a-good-book.

The face of American golf was changing in mid-century in countless other ways. Shorts, which the U.S.G.A. had banned from its female competitions in one of its periodic retreats to the propriety of the Jane Austen era, were the natural warm-weather garb for women with trim figures (like Barbara Romack, the 1954 champion), and they came to be officially recognized as such. The electric and gas-operated golf cart came in, an undeniable boon for the aging who still wanted to get in their round of golf but in other respects a problem, since in some locales it became almost as accepted a badge of "arrival" for a man to own a two-toned golfmobile as a cream-colored Rolls. In the opinion of many golfers, playing the game via this shot-to-shot transport ruined the lovely natural tempo of golf: it didn't give you enough time to figure out your next shot or, for that matter, enough time to brood about your last one. Senior golf tournaments and senior regional organizations—a golfer usually became eligible for senior golf and a new crack at the crockery when he was either fifty or fifty-five—shot up all over with the indiscriminate speed of pizza palaces. The boys seemed to be playing for a new title each week, and the high caliber of their golf and close-to-par scoring was downright unnerving. In this boom period, organizations desirous of promoting golf for young players (or simply desirous of promoting themselves through golf) conducted such a slew of tournaments for boys and girls in every age bracket that a stranger visiting an unfamiliar course had to dig down as low as the eight-year-olds before he could be reasonably certain that that youngster on the practice tee had not recently returned from a trip to the Continent, where he had sturdily beaten off the best that the junior champions of Britain, France, and Andorra had been able to throw at him. Whereas in the Twenties the ability to shoot an excellent game of golf had presaged for a young man a promising career as a salesman, by the Fifties it presented young men with the opportunity to go to college on a scholarship, for many seats of learning were not stubbornly averse to the publicity that accrued to them via the feats of their golf stars as well as their football heroes. In this age of excesses, one of the most lamentable trends was the coast-to-coast infatuation with wagering (both in "friendly" games and on official tournaments) that was all out of proportion. Calcutta pools that surpassed $75,000 became hardly uncommon. Hustlers sprang up like weeds. In the summer of 1955, as was inevitable sooner or later, it was discovered that the winners of an invitational four-ball event at a prominent Long Island club were playing with grossly false handicaps and, moreover, that one of the two players was masquerading as an entirely different person. Golfers were appalled by this scandal and felt that it gave their game a black eye. In truth, however, breaking when it did and exposing the evils before they became widespread, it turned out to be one of the best things that ever happened to American golf.

If a spiraling number of young Americans hoped to stake out a career for themselves in professional golf, and many did, it was indeed understandable. The successful pro, a Hogan or a Snead or a Middlecoff or a Demaret, had become a tremendously enviable figure. There he was—if you shut some of the hard qualifying facts from your mind's eye—following the sun, ladling in oodles of dough as the prize money mounted higher and higher, and enjoying the status of a celebrity, part athlete and part entertainer. The hard fact of the matter was that less than two dozen of the pros on the circuit could make money or break even as they followed the dust and the pressure as well as the sun. Nevertheless, just as few hopeful young actors can stay away from Hollywood and New York and a shot at fame and fortune, so too did hundreds of young men aspiring to a career in golf hie themselves to the circuit each winter. Each winter one or two of them, a Gene Littler, a Mike Souchak, or a Dow Finsterwald, did succeed in breaking into the select company of the substantial money-winners—Middlecoff, Mangrum, Demaret, Ted Kroll, Doug Ford, Jack Burke, Jr., short-hitting Jerry Barber, long-throwing Tommy Bolt, Julius Boros, Bob Toski, and the other well-established circuit riders like Ed Furgol, Shelley Mayfield, Ed Oliver, Jim Turnesa, Chandler Harper, Dick Mayer, Johnny Palmer, Bo Wininger, Freddy Haas, Art Wall, Bud Holscher, Fred Hawkins, and Marty Furgol. While its inducements were not so golden, and certainly more complex, the relatively new Ladies Professional Golf Association's circuit held a similar lure for young women who preferred to earn their livelihoods in golf. Pioneered by Babe Didrikson Zaharias and the other members of "The Big Four"—Patty Berg, Louise Suggs, and Betty Jameson—the big attraction for the public was, naturally, the Babe. In 1954, this altogether gallant woman won her third U.S. Women's Open at Salem, a long, stiff course, with rounds of 72-71-73,75, an achievement all the more re-

Dr. Cary Middlecoff, that happy refugee from subgingival curettage, had hardly turned professional when he carried off the 1949 Open at Oak Hill. An intense, terribly talented player capable of blistering hot streaks, Middlecoff employed a unique swing rhythm, pausing markedly at the top before swinging down.

markable since she had made her way back to the fairways after recovering from a cancer operation. There has never been anyone quite like her.

In a period when professional golf could be so lucrative, amateur golf had its troubles keeping its champions for long. Sam Urzetta and Billy Maxwell, who won the Amateur in 1950 and '51 respectively, turned professional not long afterward. Gene Littler and Arnold Palmer, the victors in 1953 and '54, left the fold within a few months of their coronation. Despite these defections and the loss of several other ranking players, the American Walker Cup teams continued to have it much their own way in international competition with Britain's best amateurs. In 1949 at Winged Foot, when Francis Ouimet served as captain for the sixth and last time, the Americans dropped only two of the twelve points. (The star of the British side was Ronnie White, a solicitor from Liverpool, who, as he had done previously in the 1947 meeting, took both his singles and his foursome. White remained undefeated in the singles until 1955.) In 1951, when Willie Turnesa took the American team over to Birkdale, the British provided much stronger opposition, losing only 6-3 (with three matches halved) after a protracted duel that could have gone either way. In the next two meetings, however, the American team, led by Charlie Yates at Kittansett, Massachusetts, in 1953 and by Bill Campbell at St. Andrews in 1955, won by very decisive margins, 9-3 and 10-2. The one-sidedness of these frays prompted fans on both sides of the Atlantic to suggest that the Cup had lost its meaning and that the competition should be terminated. While this is not likely to happen, the sharply different socio-economic conditions in Britain and America seemed to argue that the disparity in the quality of the amateur golf played in the world's two great golf communities would continue, if anything, to widen and that it would take forty-eight hours of inspiration for the British side to win a Walker Cup Match on its home soil and a blooming miracle for the British ever to win in the States. This same general conclusion seemed to hold true for that other ivied British-American team match, the Ryder Cup. While the outcome of none of the first three post-war Ryder Cup Matches held in America was seriously in doubt at any time, the British pros were a tough bunch to beat in their own backyard and, with a little twist of fortune, might well have carried the day both at Ganton in 1949 and at Wentworth in 1953. In 1957, however, the British brought off a tremendous upset in the Ryder Cup Match at Lindrick, in Yorkshire. After trailing 1-3 in the foursomes, they sent their unbelieving supporters into raptures by climbing all over the Americans in the singles, winning six of the eight and halving another, to capture the match 7½-4½. Then, the following year, 1958, the British, who held the Curtis Cup by dint of a 5-4 victory at Prince's in 1956, kept possession of the trophy by gaining a 4½-4½ tie at Brae Burn, in Newton, Massachusetts—the strongest performance a British Curtis Cup team had ever given in the United States. Mrs. Frances Smith, it should be added, won the critical singles for the British both at Prince's and at Brae Burn.

With golf on the sports calendar nearly fifty weeks of the year, it became well nigh impossible to keep up with all the events, all the winners, all the noteworthy achievements. Sam Snead still could not win the Open but he did win two more P.G.A. crowns

Above, on the home green of the Oklahoma City Country Club in the final round of the 1953 Amateur, Gene Littler watches his 18-foot birdie putt fall in the cup to give him a 1-up victory over Dale Morey. Five months later, Littler turned pro, becoming one of the first to follow the circuit in a house trailer.

The transatlantic scene in 1955. Above, the American Walker Cup team that triumphed at St. Andrews: Patton, Cherry, Conrad, Yost, Jackson, Cudd, Morey, Ward, and Captain Campbell. Below, the British Ryder Cuppers warm up in the unfamiliar heat of Palm Springs before falling to the American side, 8 to 4.

and three Masters. Two men who obviously thrived on match play were Chick Harbert and Walter Burkemo. Each reached the final of the P.G.A. Championship three times and won it once. The 1949 Open Champion, Cary Middlecoff, always a formidable competitor, came back after a six-year absence from the winner's circle in a major tournament to take the 1955 Masters and the 1956 Open with the most impressive golf of his career. The son of the Texas professional who had tied for second in the 1920 Open, Jack Burke, Jr., an engaging player who seemed doomed to be remembered as the perennial rookie-of-the-year, at length broke through in a big one, the 1956 Masters, when Ken Venturi, a twenty-four-year-old amateur from San Francisco, yielded to the strain on the final round and tossed away a seven-shot lead. Venturi's inability to hold on marked the second time in three years that an amateur had led the Masters during the last round but had failed to seize the opportunity of a lifetime. In 1954, in what may have been the most spectacular edition since 1935 of that inveterately exciting event, an unheralded amateur from Morganton, N.C., Billy Joe Patton, chatting amiably with his gallery and charging the pins with his approaches, stayed with Snead and Hogan for three rounds, caught them during the final round with the help of a hole-in-one on the sixth, and finished only a stroke behind them even after his all-out tactics had cost him penalty strokes in two different water hazards on his hectic last nine. The most heart-warming victory scored by an amateur was Dick Chapman's ultimate triumph in the British Amateur in 1951; the veteran from Pinehurst had twice earlier reached the final and gone down to defeat. The most talented amateur of the decade, no question about it, was Harvie Ward, a consummate stylist from North Carolina. Archaically relaxed on the golf course, Harvie won the British Amateur in his first try in 1952, was runner-up when he went back to defend, won the Canadian Amateur, spearheaded two successful Walker Cup teams, and after eight vain attempts in our Amateur at length attained the championship in 1955 at the Country Club of Virginia with a week-long exhibition of how to hit the fairway, the green, the hole. In the final, which he won 9 and 8, Harvie was off the fairway only twice and 7 under even 4s. He successfully defended his title at Knollwood outside Chicago in 1956.

If so few of the country's gifted professionals won major championships in the late 1940s and the early '50s, it was because Ben Hogan won so many of them. However, 1952 was a year he won none. In the thick of the contention in the last round of the Masters, he soared to a 79, his poorest performance on a critical round since he had launched his comeback. He seemed to be on his game again some two months later, when he led off in the Open, held at the Northwood course in Dallas, with a pair of 69s that gave him a two-stroke lead, but he wilted in the 96-degree heat on the last day. A pair of 74s dropped him to third place, five shots behind the winner, Julius Boros. Customarily a solid tee-to-green player but not a particularly good putter, Julius—or Jay, as the new champion was called by his friends—fashioned his winning rounds of 68 and 71 most atypically. Frequently in trouble, he used only eleven shots on the hard-baked greens over the last nine holes of his morning round. On his final eighteen, he

Harvie Ward. The graceful Carolinian was America's ranking amateur star of the '50s.

Augusta National, 1954. Patton eyes the situation at his Waterloo, the par-5 13th.

used only twenty-nine. Hogan gracefully accepted the disappointment of not winning his fourth Open in four starts, but the old perfectionist was quite unhappy about his lackluster play on the final day. There was a wonderful little exchange between Ben and a member of his gallery as Ben made his way to the clubhouse when the grind was over. "I sure enjoyed it," the fan told him. "Thank you," Ben replied agreeably. "You're easily pleased."

During the ten months between the 1952 Open and the 1953 Masters, Hogan stayed away from competitive golf. This was not unusual, since it was his practice to husband his energy and concentration for the major events. When he showed up at Augusta, as always the first member of the field to begin his preparation, a few of the game's experienced observers predicted that he would undoubtedly regain his top form and win many more championships, but the majority opinion was that Ben had lost something in 1952 and at forty years of age was not likely to regain it. A threat, yes, but a beatable threat. The field would quail no longer at his mere presence.

Hogan, to be brief about it, won that 1953 Masters with rounds of 70, 69, 66, and 69. His 274, five strokes in front of the runner-up, Ed Oliver, was also a full five strokes below the previous record total for the Masters, which had been set by Ralph Guldahl in 1939 and equaled nine years later by Claude Harmon. Ben made one or two minuscule errors over his four rounds but, really, his golf was about as forceful and as flawless as golf can be—his tee shots long and straight, his approaches so sure and accurate that there was almost a monotony about his play. Eternally his own harshest critic, even Hogan himself was exhilarated by his performance and, releasing a rare smile of contentment, acknowledged that it was "the best I've ever played for seventy-two holes." Continuing in this fine fettle, he proceeded to win the Pan-American Open in Mexico City and the Colonial Open in his home town, Fort Worth . . . and then he was ready for the main event, the U.S. Open.

The 1953 Open was staged at Oakmont. That old graveyard for low scoring—Sam Parks had been the one contestant who broke 300 when the championship had last been held there in 1935—had been humanized to a noticeable degree. Sixty of the traps had been covered over and some of the fairways had been widened. In addition, the increased length modern golfers had acquired drastically reduced the truculence of several holes on which a par had formerly been a mighty tough prize. For all of this, Oakmont remained quite a test, and its celebrated lightning-fast greens had lost little of their old menace: tap a 5-footer just a fraction too hard and you had a 6-footer coming back. After his first two rounds, a par 72 and a 69, Sam Snead, turning on all of his mountaineer manner, allowed as how he reckoned he'd figured out how to play the critter. "You gotta sneak up on these holes," Sam volunteered. "Iffen you clamber and clank up on 'em, they're liable to turn around and bite you."

Sam's 141 for the first two rounds placed him two shots behind the leader—who else but Hogan! The two decisive rounds on a mild Saturday were, in effect, a duel between the old familiar adversaries. Playing some five holes behind Hogan, hitting the ball as handsomely as he ever hit it but frustrating his own momentum by missing his invariable quota of short putts, Snead closed the gap between them to one shot with a 72 to Hogan's 73 in the morning. Sam had lost a golden opportunity to make up that one outstanding shot when he had three-putted the seventeenth from thirty feet after smacking his drive all the way to the green on that odd-size (292 yards) uphill par 4. In the afternoon, both made the turn in 38. Half of the spectators went with Snead to see if the greatest golfer who never won the Open could pick up that one stroke, maybe more. Half went with Hogan to see if the man who knew how to win would once again respond to the occasion as he strode down the stretch. On the 598-yard twelfth, a hole that offered him one of his best chances for a birdie—Hogan had earlier parred it—Sam mis-hit his fairway wood, and when he reached the green, three-putted for a bad 6. Hogan, meanwhile, after going one over on the fifteenth, where he overclubbed himself on his long approach, took off on one of his most irresistible finishes. A superb wood found the center of the green on the sixteenth, 234 yards to a relatively small target. Two putts and a par. Ben added another 3 with a birdie on the seventeenth, flying his drive into the opening between the traps and onto the green, then getting down in two putts from about the same spot Snead had taken three in the morning. On to the eighteenth, a stout par 4 some 462 yards long. A colossal tee shot—it kept rising higher and higher and took ages to come down—left Ben only a medium 5-iron. A crisply struck approach sat down nine feet past the cup. The putt found the cup—another 3. 38-33—71. After this burst, it mattered not at all that Sam was unable to get rolling after muffing his chance on the twelfth. He ended up with a 76 for 289, six shots off Ben's pace. With this victory, Hogan joined Willie Anderson and Bob Jones as the only four-time winners of the Open.

Weeks before Hogan's triumph at Oakmont—in fact, right on the heels of the Masters, when it had become evident that the true-tempered Texan was playing the finest golf of his life—a clamor arose that Ben should go to Great Britain for the British Open scheduled for Carnoustie in early July. Ben had already earned his place as one of golf's authentic immortals, but, as the game's internationalists pointed out, what a shame it would be if a player of his genius did not, while at the peak of his powers, take a crack at the old and honored championship that for so many decades had served as a measure of the greatness of the great golfers before him. It would be a marvelous thing, of course, if Ben happened to make a first-class showing and so prove that he could adapt himself to the completely different British conditions, that "other kind of golf." But win or lose, finish close to the top or down the list, he owed it to himself and to golf to go—so went the argument. Shortly before our Open, Ben sent in his entry for the British Open. When he was assured of accommodations within comfortable range of the Carnoustie course, he made definite plans to go across.

Some ten days before the morning of the first qualifying round, the most dedicated invader since old Walter J. arrived at Carnoustie. He started his preparations instantly. On his first familiarization round he found that there was a lot he would need to learn about the 7,200 yards of the heavy-turfed duneland course close to the gray water where the Firth of Tay and the North Sea become indistinguishable. As had become his custom, on most of his practice rounds Ben hit three balls off each tee, one down the center of the fairway, one down the right, one down the left—a neat trick in itself—in order to find out which side of the fairway opened up the most favorable shot to the green. Early in these practice sessions, he discovered that the ground, so ungiving compared to the lush, soft American fairways, jarred his wrists painfully when he sped the clubhead into the turf on his irons. He decided that the best solution, the only solution, would be to take the ball a bit more cleanly than he normally did. ("He ended," Sir Guy Campbell remarked, "taking the ball exactly like the great Scottish golfers had done years and years before.") Ben had no trouble adapting himself to the smaller British ball—the same weight as the American ball (1.62 ounces) but .06 of an inch smaller in diameter (1.62 inches). Nevertheless, that seemingly unimportant difference could make all the difference in the world, especially in a heavy wind. However, there were a number of things that did bother him. The weather, for instance, was penetratingly cold, and to keep warm Ben had to wear more, and more constricting, clothes than he liked. There was also the condition of the fairways. A public course accustomed to heavy traffic, Carnoustie's fairways were pock-marked with divot holes; there had been a long spell of dry weather, and no new grass had grown in. This gave Ben some concern, for he was afraid that some of his drives might end up in these divot holes and present him with recovery shots instead of ordinary approaches. And then there were the greens, much heavier and slower than ours. Ben was apprised that they would be fast enough when they were cut just before the tournament, but he was not sure that they would suit him even then. In his determination to make a good showing—in Hogan's dictionary a good showing means to finish higher than second—Ben was disturbed by all these insolubles. He let it be known. For example, anent the greens he had this to say: "You can't putt on putty," and, at another time, "I've got a lawn mower back in Texas. I'll send it over." The Scots were affronted by Hogan's brusque criticism of a course they were deeply proud of, and, brusque folk themselves, they let it be known that golfers had always been able to adjust to Carnoustie—champions, that is. Hogan, characteristically, went right on with his practice and his evening seminars in "learning the course." After dinner each night he walked the links in the long Scottish gloaming. The better to memorize the subtle conformations of the terrain and the distances to the greens from key points on the fairways—the absence of trees on most of the holes made it harder to arrive at a handy set of distance markers—he walked the course "backwards," from the greens to the tees, charting the undulations and the hazards. He had the eighteen holes pretty well under his belt by the time the qualifying round was at hand. He knew, for example, that there were six holes on which there were fairway traps that had to be carried off the tee in order to get home on his second shot, and that a large number of the greens did not incline toward the golfer but fell away and so could not be attacked in the American style but had to be approached more measuredly, with the type of shot where the bounce and run of the ball had to be taken into account. And somewhere along the line, as the austere American went about his appointed rounds of preparation, the Scots, perceiving him as the direct, absorbed perfectionist he was, forgot about his initial rudeness and began to admire the challenger and to refer to him as "The Wee Ice Mon."

Hogan qualified with plenty to spare, not exerting himself unduly. On Wednesday, the eighth of July, the tournament proper got underway with a colorful and truly international field on the firing line: Bobby Locke of South Africa, who was not only the defending champion, but also had exceeded his ambitions by winning the British Open in 1949, '50, and '52, and would win again later in '57; Peter Thomson, the personable young Australian who was to win the British Open in '54, '55, '56, '58, and '65; Roberto DeVicenzo, a powerhouse, and Antonio Cerda, a small, compact stylist, both from the Argentine; along with Hogan, Lloyd Mangrum and Frank Stranahan from the United States; Van Donck from Belgium; Hassenein from Egypt; Grappasoni from Italy; Dai Rees from Wales; Henry Bradshaw and Fred Daly from Ireland; a large Scottish band, including Eric Brown, Hector Thomson, John Panton; a sizable English delegation headed by Max Faulkner, Arthur Lees, Harry Weetman, John Jacobs, young Peter Alliss, and old Sam King. It had rained the night before the tournament, and the fairways were fine. The greens had been cut, and while they remained a touch on the slow side, they were in excellent shape.

Considering the wind and the cold and some occasional hail, the scores on the opening day were quite low. Stranahan led the field with a 70. Playing very well as usual in Britain, Frank was out in 37 against the par of 36, back in 33 against the par of 36. A stroke behind him with a 71 was Eric Brown. Locke, Rees, Thomson, and DeVicenzo had 72s, Hogan a 73. Ben appeared to have a much better round than that going for him but had wavered on Carnoustie's renowned finish: the 250-yard sixteenth; the 454-yard seventeenth, where the drive must be placed within a "cape" of land formed by the Barry Burn as it winds across the fairway and coils back; and the burn-cut eighteenth, a short par 5, a potential birdie hole and yet a troublous passage under pressure. One shot under par after fifteen holes, Ben went 4-5-5, not 3-4-4. He failed to get down a 9-footer on the sixteenth after finding a bunker on his tee shot. He was wide with a 3-footer on the seventeenth. He was bunkered on his drive on the home hole and finally missed an 8-footer there for his birdie.

On the second day, almost no wind was abroad and there were only patches of rain. Continuing to hit the ball effectively from tee to green but constantly short on his putts, Hogan was around in 71. His 144 put him two strokes behind the leaders, Brown (71-71) and Rees (72-70). DeVicenzo was 143, Stranahan and Peter Thomson 144 (along with Hogan), Locke and Faulkner 145. With so many able and tournament-tested players bunched so closely, and many others capable of winning still within striking distance, on the eve of the last thirty-six the 1953 British Open was, as the old saying goes, "anybody's tournament." The weather for the final day was a typical Angus mixture of cold winds, gray skies, some rain, some sunshine. Trained down to 149 pounds, some twenty pounds below his winter weight, Hogan had picked up a touch of flu in the Scottish "summer." He took a protective shot of penicillin before setting out for the course. It was thronged with people who had traveled from all corners of the island to watch the legendary American make his bid. By midday over 20,000 keyed-up spectators were traipsing excitedly over the rolling course.

On his morning round, Hogan was 70. It was a round somewhat similar to his opening 73 in that it had the aspect of being a much lower one until the finishing holes. Four strokes under even 4s with the seventeenth and eighteenth coming up, Hogan needed a par 4 and a birdie 4 for a 68 and the undisputed lead. On the seventeenth, however, he shoved his second shot into a greenside trap and took three putts after a mediocre out for a 6. He got his 4 handily on the eighteenth. His putting, as on his earlier rounds, was a disappointment to him—he was not getting up to the cup—but his wooden-club play, which had been potent from the very beginning, had come on some. He was swatting the small British ball close to 300 yards off some tees. In his pre-tournament practice, having deduced that on long Carnoustie length off the tee was one of the prime requisites, Ben had devoted the bulk of his time to his woods, and it was certainly paying off.

With his 70, Hogan was tied for the lead after fifty-four holes with Roberto DeVicenzo at 224. Like the American's, the Argentine strong man's round, a 71, had been marred by one bad hole, the ninth, where he had hit one out-of-bounds. Locke, at 229 after a 74, and Faulkner at 228 after a 73, were four and five shots behind now; all things being equal, they would not have to be watched too closely. Neither, in a way, would Stranahan and Brown, both at 227, three strokes back, Frank after a 73, Eric after

Peter Thomson holds his daughter Deirdre. At noon on the final day of the 1954 British Open, the young Australian, sensing he might win, had his wife leave to fetch "Dee," then only nine months old, so that she could be on hand for the big moment, should it arrive. It did. Thomson repeated four more times.

a 75. But as the Wee Ice Mon returned to work in the afternoon after munching his box lunch, he knew that, in addition to DeVicenzo, he would have to keep well posted on the progress of three other contenders: Rees, Thomson, and Cerda. They stood only one stroke behind him, and each had the stuff in him to stick with the pressure.

Ben got off on his final round with four orthodox pars, 4-4-4-4. After he had putted out on the fourth, one of his friends who kept him informed on the scores of the other top contenders reported that Cerda had just birdied the third. Calculating their respective scores against par, that made Cerda and Hogan all even. The fifth at Carnoustie, 388 yards, bends mildly to the right. Hogan's approach here landed on the edge of the green but kicked off a slope toward the bunker at the left. It stopped rolling at the very edge of the sand, "held by two blades of grass," as Ben later described it. It left him with an extremely delicate shot. He would have to stand with one foot in the bunker and one on the bank. He would have to hit the ball decisively to get it up the slope of the green to the pin some thirty-five feet away but still not so boldly that it would run yards past the stick and leave him with a skiddy downhiller coming back. He chose to chip the ball. He contacted it cleanly with his 9-iron, it landed nicely up the slope, started to run fast for the hole, kept running, hit the back of the cup, jumped three inches in the air, and came down in the hole. This well-played and fortunate stroke gave Ben a birdie 3 and set up his winning mood there and then. It put him a stroke ahead of Cerda again and three in front of DeVicenzo who, Ben learned at this juncture, had gone out in 38, two over. For the first time in the tournament, Hogan was in the lead.

Holding not an ounce in reserve now, he birdied the long, long sixth after smashing two terrific woods to the edge of the green. He parred the seventh, eighth, and ninth to turn in 34, 2 under. By this time he knew that Stranahan had finished with a 69 for 286, that Rees was in with the same total after a 71, that Thomson was headed for about the same total. Par in would give Ben 284. "The only thing I had to worry about," he later said, "was holding what I had and keeping track of Cerda right behind me."

Four holes later he was in an even better position. He had matched par on the tenth, eleventh, and twelfth and had dropped a 14-footer for a birdie 2 on the short thirteenth to go 3 under par when he received word that DeVicenzo had posted 287 and, more important, that Tony Cerda had fallen back to even par on his final round following a bogey 5 on the twelfth. That put Cerda three strokes behind Ben for the round and four strokes behind in all. Ben made his pars on the fourteenth and the fifteenth, and marched home in absolute control with a very good par on the sixteenth, another on the troublesome seventeenth, and a concluding birdie on the eighteenth as the huge gallery crowded along the home fairway and cheered the Wee Ice Mon, expressionless as ever, on to his epochal triumph. Hogan's finishing birdie gave him a 34 in, a 68 for the round (a new competitive record for Carnoustie), and a total of 282, four strokes lower than the quartet who tied for second, Cerda, Thomson, Stranahan, and Rees.

In Britain Hogan's immensely popular victory inspired a spate of accolades, written and verbal, saluting his capability, temperament, and courage, and pronouncing him the peer of any golfer who ever lived. Bernard Darwin, as ever, put his finger on the man's particular genius more surely than anyone else. "If he had needed a 64 on his last round," Bernard commented, "you were quite certain he could have played a 64. Hogan gave you the distinct impression he was capable of getting whatever score was needed to win." In America, Hogan's victory was viewed as nothing less than a national triumph. His progress had been followed round by round by millions of non-golfers as enthusias-

The morning of the final momentous day of the 1953 British Open. His caddie behind him and a Scottish policeman close by, Ben Hogan makes his way through the cold drizzle at Carnoustie. Two wonderful closing rounds, a 70 in the morning and a 68 in the afternoon, brought Hogan home, the victor by four shots—the greatest golf victory and the most exciting sports story of that period.

tically as it was by veteran addicts, and there were arguments on countless main streets between green-to-golf citizens, each man claiming that he had been the first to spot Hogan's gift for the game or had first announced his conviction that Ben would win in Britain. All in all, it was hard to imagine a victory that could have been more completely victorious. Perhaps that is why it had scarcely been achieved when it began to have the ring of a legend to it. The day after it was all over, Hogan had quietly left the scene of

The exploits of Hogan and Snead gave
distinction to the Masters.
Snead (above) won the tournament
in 1949, 1952, and 1954.

his conquest. Since he had never entered a British Open before and since it was probable
that he would never do so again, what had happened—his arrival in a strange land, the
perfect completion of the task he had set himself, his succinct departure—seemed to be
sealed off from all other events, suspended as it were, in a separate and somehow unreal
land of its own, so that if it were not known for a fact that there had been a 1953 British
Open on that remote stretch of duneland in Angus, you might have thought that the
whole story was the concoction of a garret-bound author of inspiration books for
children who had dreamed up a golfing hero and a golfing tale that he hoped might catch
on as had the exploits of Frank Merriwell in the days before golf was considered the
proper vehicle for the dreams of glory of the red-blooded American boy.

Since Ben Hogan could never hope to improve on 1953, *his* 1930, there was widespread conjecture as to whether or not he would retire from competition, either completely or partially, and devote his extraordinary energy and drive to some of his newer projects, his golf club-manufacturing plant, for instance. He found that he could not stay away from the big ones, the Masters and the Open. The story of his next three years is the story of his fortunes in six tournaments, three Masters and three Opens.

A poor second round put Hogan out of the running in the 1956 Masters and he eventually tied for eighth, but the two previous Aprils he had finished second and had come very close to hanging up his third victory in that event—in 1954 especially. That was the year that the upstart amateur, Billy Joe Patton, crashed what had all the earmarks of another exclusive Snead–Hogan party. Patton's slashing last-round rally forced Hogan to do something no professional had ever pushed him into doing: to make a costly tactical mistake. It came on the eleventh hole, that 445-yarder where the left half of the sunken green is girded by the waters of Rae's Creek. Hogan customarily played his approach to this green off the carpet to the right, satisfied to settle for a chip-and-putt par. In fact, he once confided to a fellow professional, "If you ever see me on this green in two, you'll know I've missed my second." On that final round in '54, unaccountably uninformed that Patton (playing three holes in front of him) had taken a 2-over-par 7 on the thirteenth, thinking that he had to begin banging for his birdies immediately to overhaul the all-or-nothing amateur, Hogan gambled on drawing his iron into the flag on the eleventh. He hooked it into the water hazard instead and took a 6. Patton's 6 on the fifteenth and Ben's subsequent birdie 4 on that hole put Ben a shot ahead of Patton, which is how they finished. Had Ben managed to get down a 5-footer he had for his birdie 3 on the seventeenth, he would have, despite his double-bogey on the eleventh, also moved a stroke ahead of Snead, who had come in early and unattended after a dismal start had apparently destroyed his chances. Tied at 289, Ben and Sam played off the next day. Sam came up with the better golf—Ben's cultivated fade was breaking anything but slightly and killed his distance off the tees—and Sam, with a 70 to Ben's 71, deserved his victory.

At Baltusrol in '54—Ed Furgol was the winner—Ben made a rather disappointing defense of his Open title. On the greens he putted with much less confidence than the year before. His irons had a tentative air about them. His wooden-club play carried none of the pow it had at Oakmont and Carnoustie. He ended up in a tie for sixth, and this he accomplished mainly through the skillfulness of his management. A year later, when the Open field convened at the Olympic Club overlooking the white city of San Francisco, Ben was hitting his shots more positively, but he was not in the form he had reached in 1953. Going with a short, tight swing, he was controlling the ball deftly nevertheless, keeping it down the middle and avoiding the matted, punishing rough that hemmed in the fairways and ringed the small greens. Steady, straight play produced rounds of 72, 73, 72, to which he added a rousing 70 that was much better than the final-round efforts of the handful of challengers who had not earlier succumbed to the rigors of the rough. He was in with 287, with shots to spare, it seemed. As Ben sat resting before his locker, his spirits buoyed up by the knowledge that his fifth victory in the Open was all but officially wrapped up, word filtered in that a golfer named Jack Fleck was halfway through the last nine and had not yet shot himself arithmetically out of contention. Up to that moment, practically no one had taken Fleck into account, for the thirty-two-year-old professional from Iowa had never given any indication on the circuit that he possessed a champion's game or the nerves to hold up under the pressure of an Open. After fourteen holes on his final round, Fleck still had to bag two birdies and two pars in order to tie Hogan. This was a stupendous order, and so it was no disparagement of the lean, Lincolnesque Iowan that the people gathered around Hogan in the locker room awaited with only a modicum of anxiety the seemingly inevitable report from the field that Fleck had run into a bogey or into one par too many and that his chances had run themselves out. That report never came. Playing like a man "touched" by fate, Jack Fleck holed a good-sized putt on the 69th for a birdie 2. He barely missed holing a chip on the 70th and then a long putt on the 71st, either of which would have given him that second and all-important birdie. But he got it on the 72nd. On this straightaway 337-yarder to an elevated, heavily trapped green that tips severely from back to front, he laid his 7-iron second hole-high, eleven feet to the right of the cup. Neither rushing the putt nor bestowing on it the extra-thorough research usual in such momentous situations, Fleck tapped the ball off the sidehill break and into the center of the cup.

After this glorious finish, Fleck went out the next day and, the picture of calmness, defeated Ben by three shots in their playoff. A stroke in front after eight holes, Jack birdied the ninth with a 25-footer, birdied the tenth with a 17-footer, and increased his lead to three strokes. Ben fought back, cut away one stroke of Fleck's margin on the fourteenth, another on the seventeenth. On the eighteenth tee, just as Fleck had been faced with birdieing that hole the day before to tie Hogan, so now was Hogan faced with birdieing it to tie Fleck. Up first on the tee, Ben's foot slipped on his drive and he hooked it off the fairway into a growth of Italian rye about two feet high. That settled it, for Fleck had his 4 all the way and Ben required three shots merely to get out of the rough: one to uncover the ball, a second to cut a path for it, and the third to wedge it laterally back to the fairway. On his approach, he did the only thing he could do: he hit it well up to the pin, since—you never could tell—the ball might go in. It sailed past the pin and finished some thirty-five feet beyond, near the top of the sloping green, a position from which everyone had been taking three putts to get down throughout the tournament. His dreams of winning his fifth championship conclusively dashed and the probable humiliation of three putts and an 8 staring him in the face, Ben limped onto the green. His face was ashen. When you looked at the old warhorse, his energy and his hopes exhausted, he appeared to be much smaller and infinitely thinner than he ever had been before. Then he did something that had the hallmark of a champion. He collected himself before his putt as if everything depended on it. He barely touched the ball, and it slipped down and down the slope and tumbled into the cup. A 6. That wasn't so bad. A 72. Creditable. After Fleck had putted out for his 69, Hogan made a tremendous effort to get a smile onto his face as he walked over to congratulate the new champion. He managed to get that smile out and once he did . . . why, it was easier than he thought it would be. A moment later, looking much more like himself, he was grinning easily and, so unlike the gray-grim Hogan, fanning Fleck's hot putter with his cap as the photographers closed in on them. In victory he had never been more magnificent than he was that afternoon in defeat.

When Middlecoff won the 1956 Open at Oak Hill in Rochester, Hogan was second again, a stroke behind, the stroke he dropped when he failed to sink a $2\frac{1}{2}$-footer on the 71st green. (After 1953, Ben lost a good deal of his former certainty on the greens that had made him probably the finest holer of all the great tee-to-green golfers in the game's history. Indeed, lamenting his lapses one afternoon, he announced ruefully that he would not be at all averse if instead of having to putt out, golfers simply fired their approaches or their chips into enormous funnels positioned over the target: "You'd just sock the ball into the funnel on, say, the seventh, and it would roll out of a pipe at the other end onto the eighth tee.") At Oak Hill, trying a new blade putter—Ben had dismissed his old brass-headed model after the 1956 Colonial Open—he missed a number of short ones he would have gobbled up during his peak years, but he did get down a number of fairly long ones, including a 14-footer on the fifth green on the last round that saved him his par and that, had he missed it, would have placed him 3 over par and four shots behind the front-running Middlecoff. That putt gave Ben just the inspiriting juice he needed. Two hours later a scene that had taken place many times before and that looms as one of the most distinctive signatures of postwar American golf was repeated again.

Down the sixteenth fairway marched the familiar figure in the white cap, walking intently after his ball, still in the hunt long after most of the favored contenders and current hotshots had gradually frittered away their opportunities or collapsed all at once. Year after year, at Olympic, Baltusrol, Carnoustie, Oakmont, at the Augusta National, Northwood, Oakland Hills, at Merion, Riviera, and so on and on, he had always been there, in the thick of the battle when it raged the hottest. Many times he had pulled it out, and sometimes he hadn't, but he was always there, bobbing after the ball, playing with great heart and great skill, year after year, as if time had stood still. That is how we will remember this transcendent champion.

PART SEVEN

PALMER, NICKLAUS, PLAYER, AND A NEW ERA

1955–1975

ARNOLD PALMER, THE MAN WHO MADE CHARISMA A HOUSEHOLD WORD

THE GOLDEN HOURS OF THE GOLDEN BEAR

GARY PLAYER AND THE OTHER NEW CHAMPIONS

THE SCENE CHANGES

HIGH DRAMA IN THE SEVENTIES, AT HOME AND ABROAD

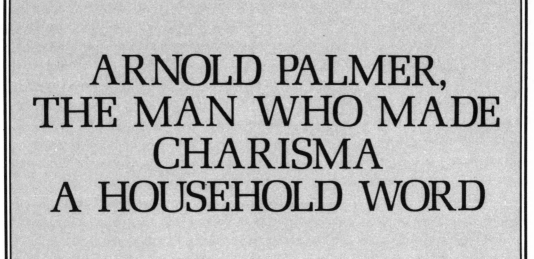

ARNOLD PALMER, THE MAN WHO MADE CHARISMA A HOUSEHOLD WORD

It was Ben Hogan's ambition to become the first man ever to win the United States Open five times. Accordingly, the year following his near miss at Oak Hill in 1956, he prepared with his characteristic thoroughness for the championship, which was scheduled for Inverness for the first time since 1931 and the memorable marathon playoff between Von Elm and Burke. On the eve of the opening round, Hogan had the misfortune to come down with neuralgia of the chest wall. Reflecting on his ailment, he concluded that he had probably gotten this "cold in the back"—that is how he thought of it—when he had practiced for two hours that afternoon in a puffy wind and, after working up a sweat, had neglected to put on sufficient protective clothing. That night, to relieve the painful binding in his chest, he doctored himself with ointment and heating pads, but it did little good. When he tried to warm up on the practice tee the next morning, he could not raise his arms above his chest without wincing with pain. When he hit a 3-iron, it would only go a hundred and forty yards. The U.S.G.A., in an unprecedented move, pushed back Hogan's starting time from 9:36 to 10:32 to afford him an opportunity to see a physician, which he did, but no miracle therapy was forthcoming, and when Hogan returned to the first tee shortly before 10:32, it was to inform Dick Tufts, the U.S.G.A. president, that, most reluctantly, he would have to withdraw. "I'm sorry," he said to Tufts. "I just can't make it."

Ben was back on the firing line the next year when Southern Hills Country Club, in Tulsa, was host to the Open, but after an opening 75, he was never in contention and ended up in a tie for tenth, eleven strokes behind the winner, Tommy Bolt. In 1959 at

Winged Foot, in Westchester, it was different: he was very much in the fight. With a round to go after three crisply played eighteens of 69, 71, and 71, he stood only three strokes behind the pacemaker, Billy Casper, a rotund, quietly self-assured young man from the San Diego area who had enjoyed five very productive years on the tour but had never before made a serious thrust in a major championship. Interestingly, the fourth round that year was not played as part of the usual double-round on "Open Saturday." Early that Saturday morning, Winged Foot was hit by punishing rainstorms that forced play to be suspended for two hours; eventually, since the entire field would not have been able to complete two rounds before darkness set in, the fourth round—for the first time in history—was moved forward to the next day. Sunday turned out to be wild and windy. The sky was oyster gray, the air had a Novemberish chill, and in early afternoon some of the swirling gusts of wind approached gale velocity. Hogan was the first of the contenders to go out, teeing off just after two o'clock when conditions were at their worst, the wind blowing dead against the players on the first four holes. Thereupon on the first three holes he played five classic golf shots in a row, and those who saw this exhibition of shot-making are not likely ever to forget it. On the 442-yard first hole, he sent two woods boring through the wind: a drive down the center of the fairway, followed by a 4-wood twenty feet to the left of the flag. Two putts for his par. The second is a par 4 of 415 yards, which swings to the right. Hogan ripped two more low, knifing woods into the wind, again finding the middle of the fairway with his drive, then hitting the green with a 4-wood, twenty feet past the pin. Down in 2 for his par. The third at Winged Foot is a par 3, 217 yards long, to a difficult green bunkered tightly on both sides. Here Hogan whipped a 4-wood through the narrow opening and onto the green, only to take three putts from thirty-five feet. Though the wind was now beginning to die down, on the 435-yard fourth he still required two woods. Hogan's second shot was pulled slightly to the left of the green, and it brought to an end his skein of impeccable shots. It also brought him a second straight bogey. After that, Ben never got moving in high again, and, before long, he began to let strokes slip away from him on and around the greens. He wound up with a very disappointing 76 to finish in a tie for eighth with Snead, four strokes behind Casper, the winner.

Although Hogan was now approaching fifty—he turned forty-seven in August 1959—his hopes of winning that fifth Open remained very much alive. In 1960 at Cherry Hills, in Denver, he made a tremendous bid for it. On the final day he was paired with the reigning Amateur champion, Jack Nicklaus, an up-and-coming player twenty-seven years his junior. With eighteen holes to go in what was perhaps the most rambunctious Open since Worcester in 1925, no fewer than ten men still had a good shot at winning: Mike Souchak, Arnold Palmer, Julius Boros, Jack Fleck, Dow Finsterwald, Don Cherry, Dutch Harrison, and Ted Kroll along with both Hogan and Nicklaus. A birdie on the short twelfth, the 66th hole of the tournament, put Nicklaus out in front, a stroke ahead of Boros, Palmer, and Fleck, but the youngster quickly fell back by three-putting the next two greens. On the fifteenth, a par 3, 196 yards long, Hogan, after a fine iron twenty feet from the pin, holed for his birdie. Suddenly he was very much in the picture—in a triple tie for the lead with Palmer and Fleck, both of whom, incidentally, were playing behind him. Throughout the arduous double-round, Ben's golf had been magnificent. In fact, up to this point he had hit every green—all thirty-three of them—in the regulation stroke. However, apart from one 10-footer, the 20-footer on the fifteenth was the only putt of any length he had made all day.

On the sixteenth Hogan missed another makeable birdie putt, this one from twelve feet. On to the seventeenth, a par 5, 548 yards long, on which a stretch of water about twenty feet wide separates the fairway from the green, part of a small island in a lake. Since reaching the green in two was out of the question, Hogan laid up with his second some twenty-five yards short of the water. The pin was positioned close to the front on this very fast green, and the only way to get near enough to it to have a relatively short birdie putt left was to drop a soft pitch only a yard or two beyond the far bank of the hazard. Throughout his career Hogan had made it a rule never to gamble in a make-or-break situation and to take his chances that his opponents would run into a crucial error. This time, possibly because he felt that Palmer or one of the other challengers behind him would almost surely birdie the seventeenth, he went boldly for his 4. He cut up a little wedge pitch that looked as though it would be perfect, would just carry the water. No! It caught the far bank inches from the top and trickled down into the water. Hogan played the ball out of the hazard and onto the green, then took two putts. A 6 and not a 4. The gamble had failed. As it transpired, it did cost him the championship or, at least, a tie for first—for Palmer, who, after outlasting the other challengers, was informed, of course, of what had happened to Hogan on the seventeenth, forthwith played the hole for a sure, safe 5 that sealed his victory. It was irrelevant that Hogan took a triple-bogey 7 on the home hole, hooking his drive into the lake and finally taking three putts. As Nicklaus later expressed it, after Ben's gamble on the seventeenth had failed, "He just went flat. He was completely drained—of drive, energy, concentration. It was all he could do to finish the round."

As it turned out, this was Hogan's last serious bid for the Open. At Oakland Hills in 1961, he tied for fourteenth. In those days only the top ten finishers, and ties, automatically qualified for a place in the starting field in the next year's Open. To be sure, a man who had won the Open was exempt from qualifying for the next five years, but this no longer applied to Hogan, whose last victory had come in 1953. In the spring of 1962, faced with qualifying for the championship for the first time since 1941, he was readying himself for the sectional qualifying test when bursitis of the shoulder forced him to pass it up. When he made no move the next few years to enter the sectional qualifying round, the rumor circulated that he felt someone who had won the event four times should not have to qualify. Whether or not this represented Ben's feelings, in 1966, when the Open returned to Olympic for the first time since 1955 and his dramatic playoff with Jack Fleck, he was quick to accept the special invitation tendered by the U.S.G.A. to play in the championship. He turned in a highly commendable performance, ending up twelfth after a strong closing round of 70. This gained him a place in the starting field at Baltusrol the next June, for the rule had been modified and now the top fifteen finishers, and ties, earned automatic qualification. At Baltusrol, playing appreciably better than suggested by his scores, 72-72-76-72—292, Ben tied for thirty-fourth, seventeen strokes behind the winning total. This marked his last appearance in the Open.

Hogan did not retire from competition until 1970, although he made relatively few appearances during the 1960s. He played in the Masters whenever fit, in the P.G.A. Championship in 1960, 1961, and 1965, and in occasional tour tournaments, such as the Colonial in Fort Worth, and the Houston International, held at the Champions Club, founded and operated by his two closest friends in golf, Jimmy Demaret and Jack Burke, Jr. From tee to green he was still the old nonpareil, but on the greens it was now a different story, and a somewhat pathetic one. In the late 1950s, Hogan, who had always been a good, reliable putter if not an outstanding one, started to experience difficulty in drawing his putter back from the ball. Sometimes he would remain frozen over a putt for twelve or fourteen seconds, and sometimes longer, before he was able to begin his stroke, and, understandably, the stroke he then made was more of a tentative push than a rhythmic, confident rap. Had his putting not disintegrated, Ben might have kept on winning long after his banner season of 1953, but the fact of the matter is that after that year he won only two more tournaments: the individual competition in the World Cup (then the Canada Cup) at Wentworth, in England, in 1956—he and Snead also captured the team competition—and the Colonial Open in 1959, in which he defeated Fred Hawkins in a playoff with a superb 69.

In the middle Fifties, when it was becoming apparent that Hogan was probably past the peak of his powers, the golf world was filled with endless speculation as to who would emerge as his successor. Some students of the game wondered if it might not take a decade or two, or even longer, before a player would come along who would bestride the tournament scene with comparable authority, but other golf fans had an idea that one of the young men traveling the tournament circuit might well turn out to be the new Hogan. Early in 1955, the most likely candidate seemed to be Gene Littler, the quiet, polite, clean-cut young man from San Diego, and San Diego State College, who had won the U.S. Amateur in 1953, and the following January, just before becoming a professional, had outdistanced all of the touring pros in the San Diego Open. Later in 1954, Littler had made a very impressive showing in the Open, at Baltusrol, barely missing the 7-foot sidehill putt he had on the 72nd green to tie Ed Furgol for first. The next year, 1955, he had started like a house afire, winning the tour tournaments at both Los Angeles and Phoenix, and had ended the campaign as the fifth leading money-winner. Littler had his critics, who felt that he did not hit the ball long enough and that he also lacked the inner fire to become an outstanding champion, but his supporters believed that his pacific temperament was actually one of his most reliable assets, as intrinsic to his success as the beautifully slow tempo of his simplified, grooved swing and his sound, unhurried putting stroke. The professional insiders, who didn't want you to forget for a moment how close they were to the name-players, liked to point out another plus of Littler's that the average enthusiast might have missed: for a man of only average size, he had an enormous pair of hands—when you shook hands with him, your wrists disappeared from sight. In any event, Gene was definitely worth watching. He might well prove to be the next great player.

During that same season—1955—another neophyte on the tour began to be boosted as a possible heir to Hogan. This was Mike Souchak, a burly young athlete who had played end for Duke University. He came from a golf family; his older brother Frank had finished ninth, and low amateur, in the 1953 Open at Oakmont, his home club. Mike could hit the ball a ton—George Bayer, six-foot-five, 240 pounds, and very well coordinated, was the only touring pro who could hit it farther—but, more importantly, he could play all the shots up to and including the little touch stuff around the greens. Souchak's first tour victory came in the 1955 Texas Open at Brackenridge Park, that scarred and almost grassless battleground in San Antonio. He opened with a 60, which tied the record low score for a single round in an official P.G.A. tournament. His 27 on the second nine that day set a new P.G.A. record for nine holes. He followed with rounds of 68, 64, and 65, which gave him a 72-hole total of 257 and another new P.G.A. record. The next week Souchak won the Houston Open by bringing in a final round of 65. Later, when the tour was moving through Florida, he led the individual scoring in the 36-hole Seminole Pro-Am, a regular stop on the winter trek in those days. He went on to do well in the big ones that year, too, tying for fourth in the Masters and for tenth in the Open. In 1956, enjoying another fine season, Souchak won four tour events. He obviously had a very big future—just how big, one would have to wait and see. As it turned out, Mike played a lot of good golf over the next ten years, but he never fulfilled the immense promise he had shown in those first two seasons. Under pressure in the big championships he was never at his best. For example, three years in a row— 1959, 1960, and 1961—he played himself into an excellent position to win the Open, and each time he failed to seize his chance. His policy in those situations, it appeared, was to concentrate on not tightening up, and he didn't, but in his preoccupation with hitting through—"releasing"—the ball, he often played critical irons too hard, over the back of the greens, and this was just as damaging in the end as less assertive and less "admirable" forms of error. For some curious reason, the one competition in which Mike always rose to the occasion was the Ryder Cup series.

The next golfer to be heralded as the heir-presumptive to Hogan was Ken Venturi. The son of the manager of the pro shop at the Harding Park municipal course in San Francisco, Venturi, slim, handsome, emotional, and imaginative, first came to national attention in 1956 when, as an amateur, he just failed to win the Masters. Out in front by four strokes with a round to go, he finished with a jittery 80 (which could easily have been a 76 or 77 if a few 5- and 6-footers had dropped), and this allowed Jack Burke, Jr., who closed with a 71, to beat him by a shot. Later that year Venturi turned pro. He not only fared well financially but soon came to be regarded by many of his colleagues as the most talented golfer on the circuit. He had a highly personal style. He set up at address with his hands fairly low and took the club back in an upright arc made up of three rather distinct segments, but when he arrived at the top of the backswing his hands and his body were in such a perfect position that a little forward flick of the hips was all that was needed to initiate a wonderfully integrated and precise movement down into and through the ball. Most of the golfers on the tour at that time hit every shot the same way and hit every shot full, but Venturi tailored his irons to fit the flow of the terrain, the wind and the weather, and the position of the pin that particular day, riding a low 3-iron with a little fade into this green, tossing a climbing three-quarter 7-iron with a little draw on it into that one, and so on and on—the instinctive artist. Some knowledgeable golf critics hold that Venturi at his best was the most accomplished iron-player they have ever seen, better even than his teacher, Byron Nelson.

Because of his painful failure at Augusta in 1956, the tournament that Venturi wanted to win above all others was the Masters. In 1958 he came terribly close again. In the last round he and Arnold Palmer, the two front-runners, were paired together, and they waged a rousing duel until, with six holes to go, Palmer slowly drew away. Two years later, in the 1960 Masters, it looked as if Venturi had at last achieved his goal. After fighting a tense head-to-head battle with Dow Finsterwald down the last nine holes, he edged into first place by a stroke on the 72nd when Finsterwald took a bogey 5. In the clubhouse he took off the flat white cap he always wore on the course—Dick Mayer and Gardner Dickinson, Jr., also followed the example that Hogan had set in headgear—and sweated out the one man on the course who could still catch him, Palmer. Palmer not only caught him with a birdie on the 71st but swept by him with another birdie on the 72nd. After this heartbreaking loss, Venturi played quite well the rest of the season, although the Milwaukee Open was the only event he actually won. The next three years, however, he won no tournaments at all. Very much like a baseball pitcher who has lost the hop on his fast ball, his game grew progressively ineffective, due in part to a succession of physical setbacks. By 1963, frazzled and unconfident, he was scarcely recognizable as the dazzling technician who had thrilled the galleries only three short years before. Where his earnings in prize money in 1960 had topped $40,000, in 1963 they fell to less than a tenth of that amount. Ken was still a relatively young man—thirty-two—but, to be realistic, it was questionable if he would ever again be able, in the argot of the tour, to put it all together.

To round out the picture, two other young golfers were occasionally mentioned, though with less exuberance, when the subject of Hogan's successor came up—Dow Finsterwald and Billy Casper. For five straight years, from 1956 through 1960, Finsterwald, a methodical Ohioan, finished fourth or better on the list of money-winners; he took the P.G.A. Championship in 1958 when that event was held at stroke play for the first time; he had a nicely tuned golf swing, and on the greens he could rap in those 5-foot "character builders" with unblinking regularity; and yet, for most people, he was not an exciting golfer to watch, mainly because he always played the percentage shot. Casper, like Finsterwald, annually was one of the top money-winners. Early in his career he was not the superior driver he was to become, and on some courses his penchant for playing his irons on a low trajectory with a touch of draw caused him trouble, but from the start he was a rather sturdy tee-to-green golfer. This was frequently lost sight of because he could do magical things with his putter, and, as so often happens in these cases, he became celebrated almost exclusively for his mastery of that one club. In winning the 1959 Open, Billy gave one of the most sensational exhibitions of putting in the history of the championship on Winged Foot's hard-to-read greens, taking a total of only 114 putts over the four rounds. (Bothered by the high winds at the start of the last round, he held on by one-putting the first, second, third, fourth, fifth, seventh, and ninth greens.) A fast, disciplined player, Billy did not exactly throb with color, but he could certainly compete, and if he kept on improving, there was no telling how far he might go.

In 1960, almost before anyone had quite realized it, Hogan's successor had arrived on the scene. He was Arnold Palmer. His name had, of course, been mentioned in some quarters when the talk had turned to the possible heirs to the throne, but he had not been rated among the leading candidates. In 1960, however, Palmer, a handsome, clear-eyed, thirty-year-old Pennsylvanian, gentle in manner, rugged in build (five-foot-ten, 170 pounds), established himself practically overnight as an exceptional player by winning the Masters and the Open and then failing by the narrowest of margins in his first crack at the British Open. In addition, he also won five tour events (the Palm Springs Classic, the Texas Open, the Baton Rouge Open, the Pensacola Open, and the Mobile Sertoma Open), and his official tournament winnings—we can't forget those, can we?—came to a record $75,262, almost thirty-five thousand more than the second man's haul. After 1954, the year he captured the Amateur and then had turned professional, it was generally appreciated that Arnold Palmer was a good, strong golfer, but, for some reason or other, his play during his first five seasons as a pro did not evoke the feeling that he was destined to become one of the game's historic figures. Consequently, his multiple triumphs in 1960 and the dashing, histrionic manner in which he carried them off came as something of a surprise.

Two years before, when he had won his first big championship, the 1958 Masters, Palmer had demonstrated a remarkable self-control under tournament stress, but at the same time, hard as it is to believe in the light of the prodigious popularity he was to achieve subsequently, his course personality was regarded as rather bland and undistinctive. His naturalness and the boy-next-door friendliness that were to make him everybody's hero simply did not project themselves then the way they did two years later. For another thing, he was not yet the golfer he would be in 1960. His driving, conspicuously dependent on arm and shoulder force, was not the prettiest thing to behold; his long irons were erratic; his chipping and putting, while improving, still needed plenty of work, and more than once his putting let him down in the clutch. For example, when most golfers discuss how Palmer lost the 1959 Masters, when he seemed to be on his way to a second straight victory in that event, the one shot they invariably recall is his 6-iron to the short twelfth, or 66th, hole, which kicked down the bank before the green into Rae's Creek and cost him a triple-bogey 6, his lead, and, ultimately, the tournament. They do not remember the two 4-foot putts he missed on the 71st and 72nd greens, which, had he holed them, might well have changed the outcome of that Masters. (Art Wall won it by birdieing five of the last six holes.) Later that season Palmer muffed a chance to tie for first in the Houston Open when it took him 3 to get down from just off the edge of the 72nd green. Then, in the Western Open that summer, he missed the 2-footer he had on the 72nd for a tie for first with Souchak. These things would never have happened to the Palmer of 1960. Apart from having become a much abler golfer, he had also become destiny's favorite. His trademark was pulling off the incredible, preferably at the eleventh hour. His ability to accomplish these wonders was based on the firm conviction that they were not wonders at all. He simply felt that, if it was necessary for victory, he could birdie any hole—the heavier the pressure, the better. If his confidence was unbounded, to the young man's credit there was not a drop of arrogance in it. In the best sense of the word, he was a plain man essentially, an extraordinarily sound and uncomplicated person. He had been preparing all his life to be an outstanding golf champion, and now that he was, he handled his position, with all its demands and obligations, as if it were nothing at all.

Arnold Palmer was born on September 10, 1929, in Latrobe, Pennsylvania, a steel-mill town about thirty miles east of Pittsburgh. Arnold was the oldest of the four children of Doris (Morrison) and Wilfred Palmer; his mother was of English descent, his father of Scotch-Irish. Mr. Palmer, a solidly built, down-to-earth man known to his friends as "Deacon" or "Deke," had spent some time working in the local steel mills before taking over as the greenkeeper of the nine-hole course of the Latrobe Country Club in 1926. During the Depression he was also named the professional, a temporary appointment that turned out to be rather permanent: the Deacon is still the pro. In 1964, the course was expanded to eighteen holes, and since 1971 the club has been owned and operated by Arnold Palmer Enterprises. The purchase price was reported to have been in the neighborhood of a million dollars.

Arnold began swinging a golf club at the age of three, using a set of sawed-off clubs that his father had made for him. The Palmers lived in a white frame house alongside the third fairway, and when Arnold had outgrown the yard as a practice ground, he began exploring the third hole, then the fourth, and so on. When he was seven, he played the nine holes in one continuous circuit for the first time. (By that age, seated in his father's lap, he could also "drive" the club tractor.) He had a natural aptitude for golf. At twelve he broke 40 for the first time, and at fourteen he shot a 71 in his first high school match. His approach to the game reflected to a good degree his father's approach, which was somewhat less intellectualized than Alex Morrison's or Percy Boomer's. The Deacon stressed the fundamentals. "Start deliberate and bring the club back slow," he would tell his pupils, "and then give it everything you have." However, the Deacon departed from the traditional touchstones of instruction in a few interesting ways. For instance, he encouraged Arnold, who loved to hit his shots just as far as he could, to keep swinging hard at the ball. After all, distance was an important asset for a golfer. In his pursuit of yardage, Arnold developed a swing that featured a very wide stance and a hook grip (the right hand tipped under the shaft), both of which habits he later had to break in order to develop a sounder swing and more control. As a boy, though, with the wonderful timing of youth, these faulty exaggerations caused him little or no trouble, and he won the Western Pennsylvania Junior Championship three times. From the start he was a splendid putter. During his days as a junior golfer, he used the simple, comfortable putting method he had picked up from watching his father, who happened to be a very good putter. Years later, when Arnold had evolved his highly individual knock-kneed, locked-in putting style, the Deacon could never understand it. "Sure he gets results," he once said in his best no-nonsense manner to Pat Ward-Thomas, the noted English writer, "but why he thinks he must get himself all twisted up like a pretzel, well, that's beyond me."

When he was growing up, Arnold gave little thought to going to college. He would fulfill his military service requirements and then become a professional golfer—that is how he saw his life in outline. What changed the picture was that his best friend, Bud Worsham—he was the younger brother of Lew, then as now the pro at Oakmont—received a golf scholarship to Wake Forest, in North Carolina, and then proceeded to sell the golf coach on arranging a scholarship for Arnold. (They had met playing in Hearst junior tournaments.) At Wake Forest, Arnold more than lived up to Worsham's glowing advance notices. Few college golfers—and by this time nearly every shining young prospect ended up on some campus or other under the elms or the sycamores or the cacti—could match Palmer's slashing power with both the irons and woods, not to mention his overall promise. Then, in 1950, Bud Worsham was killed in an auto accident. Palmer was deeply affected by his friend's death, and it took him a long while to absorb the shock of it. He dropped out of Wake Forest during that time and enlisted as a yeoman in the Coast Guard. Early in 1954, when his three-year hitch was up, he returned to Wake Forest for a short period, but finding himself totally disconnected from college life, he went to work as a salesman for a paint supplies company in Cleveland, where he had been stationed during most of his tour of duty. (In 1961, Palmer established a golf scholarship at Wake Forest in Bud Worsham's memory. The general provisions of the scholarship are to make financial aid available to the student golfer who possesses the qualities to represent the school and the program in a spirit that reflects Buddy Worsham's approach to life. The money in the scholarship has been principally donated by Palmer, who plays exhibitions specifically for that purpose, but donations have also been made by Arnie's and Buddy's friends. Candidates are recommended to the scholarship committee, and the selection of the recipient is made by Palmer and Jesse Haddock, the Wake Forest golf coach. Until recently the scholarship supported only one person at a time—first Jay Sigel, then Jack Lewis, Lanny Wadkins, and Eddie Pierce. Now it has reached that degree of health where it can help two student golfers each year for four years.)

Arnold's plans for 1954 also called for lots of serious golf. He felt he was now a mature enough player to hold his own in the top amateur tournaments. His first taste of that kind of competition had come in 1948, when he had entered the North and South

Amateur, at Pinehurst. He had done very well, reaching the semi-final round before losing to Harvie Ward 5 and 4. The next year he again got to the semis in the North and South, only to be overwhelmed by Frank Stranahan, 11 and 10. In 1950 he had won the Southern Intercollegiate. Aside from his excellent record in collegiate competition, his top achievement, as he moved hopefully into the 1954 season, were the five victories he had piled up in the Western Pennsylvania Amateur between 1948 and 1952. He soon eclipsed this. In early August 1954 he led all the amateur entrants in George S. May's All-American Tournament at Tam O'Shanter, near Chicago, finishing nine shots ahead of Stranahan. The following week, in May's World Championship of Golf, he was the second low amateur, a shot behind Stranahan. In that brief fortnight, Palmer had jumped from relative obscurity into a "name golfer" known to most of the country's committed golf fans. When the United States Amateur got underway the last week in August at the Country Club of Detroit, Arnold D. Palmer (D. for Daniel) was looked upon as a dark horse who would bear plenty of watching in the championship.

The two hundred qualifiers who gathered at the Country Club of Detroit comprised one of the strongest fields in the history of the Amateur. One indication of this was the dispatch with which players of reputation were ousted, frequently by unknowns. In the first round, for example, three former Amateur Champions were eliminated—Ted Bishop, Charlie Coe, and Sam Urzetta. Another ex-champion, Willie Turnesa, went in the second. Billy Joe Patton went in the third. In that third round the unpredictability of the draw brought Frank Stranahan, who had made eight unsuccessful attempts in the Amateur, up against Harvie Ward, who had just captured the Canadian Amateur. After Ward had squared the match by taking the sixteenth and seventeenth, Stranahan's par on the eighteenth was good enough to win it. In the fifth round, one of the sentimental favorites, Bill Campbell, who earlier in the year had lost the final in both the British and Canadian Amateurs, was stopped. In that round Palmer met Stranahan. Arnold had just scraped by, 1 up, in his first two matches, but by the time he met Stranahan he was playing much better golf on the long, flat, heavily trapped course originally designed by Harry Colt, the able English architect, and recently remodeled by Robert Trent Jones. Palmer won their grim battle 3 and 1. That afternoon he defeated Don Cherry 1 up after standing 2 down with seven to play. He was now in the semi-finals. On his route there he had smother-hooked a few drives and messed up several bunker shots, but on the whole he had acquitted himself well.

When the news reached Latrobe that evening that his son had made the semis, Deacon Palmer rounded up his wife and they drove through the night to Detroit, pausing for only one pit-stop—three hours of sleep—in Lodi, Ohio. They arrived at the Country Club of Detroit just as Arnold was teeing off in his 36-hole match with Ed Meister, a thirty-eight-year-old publisher of trade papers for the fruit industry who had been the Yale golf captain in 1940 and had kept his aggressive game in very good shape. Throughout that long, hot August day, neither man could make much headway against the other, but down the stretch it was Meister who played the better golf. Four times— on the 35th, 36th, 37th, and 38th—he had victory at the tips of his fingers but failed to

While Ed Meister looks on stoically, Palmer holes for the winning birdie on the 39th green in their semi-final match—Palmer's closest call in the 1954 Amateur.

hole successive putts of ten, fourteen, five, and sixteen feet, which he had to make to win these holes. To gain his half on the 36th and send the match into extra holes, Palmer, after firing his approach over the fast, up-sloping green, had played a marvelous little wedge pitch seven feet from the cup and then holed the putt. After his series of fortuitous escapes, on the 39th, a 510-yard par 5, he finally took command, cannonading his drive so far down the fairway that he was able to reach the green with a 2-iron. He two-putted for a winning birdie, and the longest semi-final ever played in the Amateur was over.

In the final Palmer faced Bob Sweeny, a tall (six-foot-three), slim, graying, forty-three-year-old member of the international set, an American who spent half the year in London, the headquarters of his family's investment banking business, and the other half in New York and Palm Beach, where he worked hard on his game and opponents at Seminole, Deepdale, and Meadow Brook. An Oxford man who had organized the Eagle Squadron of the R.A.F. in World War II, Sweeny had won the British Amateur in 1937. He had never won anything of importance in the States, however, and now that he was on the verge of correcting that oversight, he meant to make the most of his opportunity. He rushed off to a three-hole lead in the final by sinking birdie putts of forty-five, fifteen, and twenty feet on the second, third, and fourth greens. Palmer, frequently outdriving Sweeny by as much as forty yards, got back to even by winning the eighth, ninth, and tenth. That is the way it went, a deliberate battle of attack and counter-attack, with Palmer never quite able to stick his nose in front. Sweeny, who had finished the morning round 2 up, still led by a hole after the 29th. Then Palmer came on again, and this time he made it, squaring the match on the 30th, going out in front for the first time on the 32nd, and then moving to 2 up with a birdie on the 33rd, where he put his approach with his pitching wedge seven feet from the flag. Sweeny fought back to win the 35th, but Palmer held him off with a perfect par 4 on the home hole. Arnold D. Palmer, 1 up. As composed as if he had finished just another Saturday afternoon round, he was piped to the clubhouse to the strains of "To the Victor" by Mr. Finzel's twelve-piece military band, an old Detroit institution.

Before the year was over, the new champion had not only turned pro but had made one of the most intelligent moves of his life by marrying Winifred Walzer, a pretty and gifted girl from Coopersburg, Pennsylvania, where her father headed a small canning company that produced the Pennsylvania Dutch brand. It is hard to know why so many golf champions, widely different in personality, have exhibited such a high talent in selecting their wives. The mention of Winnie Palmer brings to mind the many exceptional women who have been married to prominent golfers—Mary Jones, Mary Sarazen, Estelle Armour, Louise Nelson, Valerie Hogan, Edith Middlecoff, Vivienne Player, and Barbara Nicklaus, to name just a few.

It took Arnold until 1958 before he won his next important tournament, the Masters. In the intervening three years, he had done extremely well on the pro tour, and the only possible rap against him was that he had never been a true contender in the big prestige tournaments, the ones that, when all is said and done, determine a golfer's stature. In that 1958 Masters, a 68 in the third round placed him in a tie for the lead with Sam Snead at 211. On the final day, as alluded to earlier, he was paired with Ken Venturi, who stood at 214. As they came to the short twelfth, Palmer was the undisputed tournament leader, Snead having faded early, but Venturi had made up two strokes on him and now trailed by only one. The twelfth, 155 yards long, can be a delicate and dangerous affair when the pin is positioned at the far right-hand corner, which it was, and when there is a puffy wind to take into account, which there was. The golfer wants to be sure to take enough club to carry Rae's Creek, flowing at a traverse before the green, but not so much club that his ball carries the thin, diagonal green on the fly and lands in the steep bank of rough rising behind it. Venturi and Palmer both hit their tee shots over the green and into the bank. Venturi's ball kicked down onto the far side of the green, presenting him with a probable 3, which he went on to make. Palmer's ball struck low on the bank, about a foot or so below the bottom rim of a bankside trap, and embedded itself. It had rained heavily during the night and early morning, and parts of the course were very soggy. For this reason the tournament committee had invoked for the final round a local rule permitting the players to lift, clean, and drop without penalty any ball that became embedded in its own pitch-mark "through the green." Since that term takes in all parts of a course except the tees, greens, water hazards, and sand traps, it clearly applied to the rough in which Palmer's ball had hit and stuck. However, the official who was patrolling the area behind the twelfth either did not know this local rule was in force or was confused in his interpretation of it. After a long and unsatisfactory discussion with this official, Palmer played the half-buried ball as it lay, chopping it out two feet forward with his wedge. He chipped close to the pin but missed the putt. That was a 5. Then, in a puzzling move, he returned to the spot in the bank where his tee shot had been embedded, dropped an "alternate ball" over his shoulder, and played out the hole again. He put his chip stone-dead and sank the putt. That was a 3. Now the question was: What was his score on the hole, a 3 or a 5?

This dilemma was still hanging in the air heavy and unresolved when, after both players had driven on the thirteenth, the 475-yard par 4 that doglegs to the left, Palmer played the shot that, in retrospect, won him the tournament. Venturi, well behind Palmer off the tee, had chosen to lay up with his second short of the creek before the green and to take his chances on getting down in 2 for a birdie. (He did this.) Palmer, however, was out far enough on his drive to go for the green on his second. To make sure that he had enough stick to carry the creek, he took a 3-wood, going down the shaft a half-inch or so with his grip for better control. He settled into his sidehill stance, moved into his swing smoothly, and came through with a magnificent shot. It started out a little to the right of the pin, but as it rose in its fairly low trajectory, one could see that there was a helpful bit of draw on it that was carrying it away from the twist-back of the creek to the right of the green. The ball carried the hazard with yards to spare and finished hole-high, eighteen feet to the left of the cup and slightly above it. On his walk to the green, Palmer spent several more minutes discussing the twelfth with a member of the Augusta National who was an expert on rules, but he took his time on the green, and not until he had fully collected his concentration did he begin to work on his eagle putt. Then he stroked it into the center of the cup. A clamorous roar went up from the thousands of spectators massed along the right-hand side of the fairway. On the fourteenth, more discussion with officials, but on the fifteenth Palmer was officially notified that his score on the twelfth was a 3 and not a 5. Now he stood well out in front.

Anticlimactically, Palmer finished his round rather loosely, missing his pars on two of the last three holes and winding up with a 73. This opened the door for two of his pursuers, Doug Ford and Fred Hawkins. Each of them had a chance for a tie if he could birdie the par-4 eighteenth; neither did, although each had a birdie putt of about fourteen feet. But the crux of that Masters, no question about it, was the resolution Palmer had shown on the twelfth and thirteenth—two holes that have so often decided the winning and losing of that tournament—first in insisting on his right to play an alternate ball on the twelfth, then in not allowing the incident to unsettle him and going on to bag that decisive eagle on the thirteenth. This was not lost on the perceptive students of the game, and they began to regard Palmer in a new light.

Though Palmer won three tournaments (and seemed to be on his way to winning a second Masters until disaster struck on the watery 66th), the 1959 season was somewhat of a letdown for him. He more than made up for it in 1960, the first of three fantastically successful seasons, one after the other, in which Arnold came into full bloom as a golfer and simultaneously made such a deep impression both on the golf world and the spikeless, markerless, capless outside world that he became, in effect, an instant folk hero. He had, as everybody informed everybody else, charisma—a term that had previously seldom been heard in the land, and certainly not in sports circles, until it became the accepted word to describe Palmer's singular appeal. It soon became so overused that in certain groups any man uttering it *in re* Palmer was subject to a two-stroke penalty. The penalty for using "a legend in his own time" was stroke and distance.

One reason why the galleries swarmed to Palmer, as earlier galleries had to Jones, was that they liked the looks of this broad-shouldered, compact athlete who had the build of a halfback or middleweight boxer, this handsome man whose face was so mobile that his moods and feelings were clearly registered for everybody to see. They also liked his manner—calm, assured, masculine, and American—plus the vast underlying drive and energy that early in a tournament were visible only in his love of forceful hitting and his long, reaching strides down the fairway, but which manifested themselves unforgettably during the decisive hours when he was taking off after the leader and holes were running out fast. At these junctures, he was temperamentally incapable of going with the safe shot and was forever gambling on the birdie shot, the super shot. Many times when he failed to bring them off, he kept his chances alive, as Hagen had done, by improvising daring recoveries and by holing long, serpentine putts.

Palmer was like Hagen in another respect. He had to count on his natural athletic talent to carry him a long ways, for his technique lacked the refinement of a great champion's. For example, early in his career, the face of his clubhead was in an extremely closed position at the top of the backswing. He derived his considerable power—until the advent of Nicklaus, no topflight player was as long as he was—principally from his arms and shoulders, and as he came flashing into the ball, the spectator was usually aware how hard he worked with his left hand and arm to block out the right hand and prevent it from taking over control of the hitting action. Whereas Hogan's technique was so assured that, as you watched him come into the ball, you felt that there was no other course for his shot to take than to fly straight toward his target—everything was that correctly interaligned—in Palmer's swing the movement of the body and the movement of the arms and hands always seemed to be a little out of "synch," and when he made contact with the ball, you didn't know whether it would sail far right or far left or straight down the middle until you actually saw it airborne. But there is much more to golf than pure technique, and that was what Palmer had in abundance. When he came tearing down the final holes— "charging" became the word favored by his fans—he made golf seem as exciting as any contact sport, and many sports buffs who had hitherto scoffed at the game became ardent converts after watching Palmer in action on television. When his fans met their hero in the flesh they were seldom if ever disappointed. He had the innate politeness and patience to treat people as individuals in handling their endless requests for autographs and answering their repetitive questions. (In dealing with difficult commercial problems, when in doubt he was wise enough to say "Maybe.") Success did not change him, and by remaining entirely himself, he was equally at home with Presidents, ad men, caddies, students, tycoons, farmers, and small-town radio interviewers eager to tape a closeup with him. He had always been very well liked by his colleagues on the tour, and continued to be.

If there was any one set of spectators who "discovered" Palmer, it was the folks who gathered regularly at the Augusta National early each April for the Masters. It was there that "Arnie's Army," as his fervidly responsive and vocal supporters came to be called, was born. New detachments sprang up like dragon's teeth wherever Arnold played, but none of them matched the faithful Augusta troops in size, decibel power, or ingenuity. (Some years a small plane would drone around the perimeter of the course tugging a banner with the injunction, "Let's Go, Arnie." At several of the large leaderboards, members of the crew posting the hole-by-hole scores found the time to post a special message: "Go, Arnie, Go.") Whether or not Arnie's Army had anything to do with it, Arnie almost always played well in the Masters. It was there, after four wins on the winter tour in 1960, that he really set up his first big year with a smashing victory.

After starting that Masters with a 5-under-par 67, Palmer led it after every round and entered the last day with a one-stroke lead. He lost this early in the round, however, and came to the last six holes trailing Venturi and Finsterwald, up ahead, by a stroke. As every old Masters hand knows, the thirteenth and fifteenth are the most likely holes on the back-nine for picking up a birdie; 475 and 520 yards long respectively—par 4½s, as some people call them—they can usually be reached in two shots by a golfer who hits the ball as far as Palmer. In this taut situation, he failed to make his birdie on the thirteenth, where his 3-wood second bounded over the green into a bunker. He also failed to make his birdie on the fifteenth. Here, after a slightly pulled drive, he was stymied by one of the two pines on the left side of the fairway, and he was forced to play an intentional hook around it with a 1-iron, which didn't quite come off. With only two holes to go, he was still looking desperately for the birdie he needed to tie Venturi, now the sole leader. His chances of getting it on the seventeenth, a 400-yard par 4, didn't look too propitious when his 8-iron approach sat down much more quickly than he had bargained for and left him twenty-seven feet below the cup. Twice he walked away from the putt, distracted by the movement of spectators behind the green. Over the ball again, he rapped a firm putt that was right on line but which looked as though it might die at the lip of the cup. It did, and then toppled in. On the eighteenth, a par 4 of 420 yards, uphill all the way, the pin was set on the lower deck a bit to the right. With the wind in his face, Palmer, after a good drive, went with a 6-iron, punching it a shade to keep it low. The ball landed two feet to the right of the pin, almost hit the pin when the terrific spin on it sent it fizzing and fuming to the left, and subsided five feet from the hole and slightly below it. Palmer played the putt for the high left corner of the cup, and it dropped. It took him a moment to realize that by finishing birdie-birdie he had won the tournament. He retrieved the ball from the cup, walked a normal step, and suddenly began jumping all over the place.

Cherry Hills, in Denver, where the 1960 U.S. Open was held, is a majestically

Palmer's first big year came in 1960. Above, on the 72nd green of the Masters, the 5-foot birdie putt on which his victory rested is on its way to the cup. Below, on the 72nd green of the Cherry Hills Country Club, the scene of the U.S. Open that year, Palmer studies the putt for his par. He made it and won by two strokes.

sited course. In the distance rise the eastern slopes of the Rockies and, not far beyond, a higher snow-covered ridge looking for all the world like an old calendar or a new beer ad. From the outset, scores ran low for a national Open. In the thin air a mile above sea level, the ball could be hit a long way, and the course—the first nine in particular—played very short. During the first three rounds, Palmer's name was scarcely mentioned. He had not played badly. He had led off with a 72, 1 over par. He followed with a 71 and another 72. Nevertheless, with the field scoring very low, he had never been up among the leaders. When he began his final round on Saturday afternoon under a hot mountain sun, he trailed Souchak, the front-runner, by seven full strokes and seemed hopelessly out of the running. As he was heading out of the clubhouse for the first tee, Arnold turned to Bob Drum, a golf writer from Pittsburgh and an old friend, and said, with a smile, "I may shoot a sixty-five out there. What'll that do?" "That'll do nothing," Drum replied. "You're too many shots back."

Because of its historic dimensions, Palmer's start on the fourth round is worth describing hole by hole. He birdied the first, a par 4 only 346 yards long, driving the green and getting down in two putts from twenty feet. He birdied the second, a 410-yard par 4, holing a little run-up of thirty-five feet from off the edge. On the third, another abbreviated par 4, he picked up a third straight birdie when he put his second, a wedge chip, a foot from the flag. On the fourth, 426 yards, he stuck a full wedge approach about eighteen feet from the flag and made the putt for another birdie. He had to be satisfied with his par 5 on the long fifth after driving into the rough, but on the sixth, a par 3 of 174 yards to a banked green, he was off again. He hit the center of the green with a 7-iron and rolled in a curving 25-foot sidehiller. On the seventh, another short par 4, he played a pretty wedge approach to six feet, and when he ran that putt in he had made his sixth birdie in seven holes. His dash was halted on the eighth, a tough par 3, 233 yards long, although Palmer played two A+ shots on it: a low, hard 3-iron that was dead on line but caught the last foot of the front bunker, and a delicate sand-shot to within three feet of the cup. Then he went and missed the putt. A bogey 4. On the ninth he made his par 4, and this took him to the turn in 30. With this incredible burst he had practically turned the tournament inside out. He was now in a position to win it, and win it he did when he played the second nine in 35—only one birdie but all the rest solid pars—and outlasted Nicklaus, Boros, Fleck, and Hogan, his nearest competitors. His winning margin was two strokes, over Nicklaus. His 65 was the lowest final round ever shot by the winner of the Open, and his whole astonishing performance cemented the foundation of the Palmer legend once and for all.

When a man wins both the Masters and the Open the same year, he cannot pass up the British Open. He must see if he can sweep the Triple Crown, as Hogan did in 1953, and maybe even complete a Grand Slam of modern professional golf's four major championships by taking the P.G.A. Championship upon his return. Palmer probably would have played in the British Open anyway. First, it had already been arranged that he and Sam Snead would make up the American team in the Canada Cup Match scheduled for Portmarnock, near Dublin, two weeks before the British Open. (They won it.) Second, 1960 marked the centenary (pronounced cen-teen-ry) anniversary of the British Open, the first great championship, and the occasion had drawn a larger number than usual of foreign players. Naturally, the event was held at St. Andrews. During his practice rounds, Arnold worked hard to get to know the Old Course, poring over a map of it in the evenings. He played a very good tournament, especially when one remembers that this was his début in Britain and that he was facing for the first time such standard treats as heavy winds off the sea, cold rains, and hard-surfaced greens that made "target golf" out of the question. In addition, he had to cope with such specialties of the house as the Old Course's famous hidden fairway bunkers and colossal double greens. With a round to go, Palmer stood at 211 (70-71-70), three strokes under par but four behind Kel Nagle, the soft-spoken, manly Australian who up to this tournament had been best known as Peter Thomson's partner in the Canada Cup Matches. It had looked at one time as if Palmer would be much closer to the lead, but he had taken 3 to get down on the last two greens to finish the third round 5-5 against Nagle's 4-3.

Ordinarily the fourth round would have taken place in the afternoon after the completion of the third, but it had to be postponed until the next day when a wild storm broke early in the afternoon, depositing so much rain that two greens and several fairways were soon under water. When the final round finally began, Palmer rushed off as if he meant to repeat his exploit at Cherry Hills. He birdied the first two holes by putting wedge approaches less than two feet from the flag. He barely missed a 10-foot putt for another birdie on the third. Then the spark went out of his attack. He turned in 34, but so did Nagle, playing a hole or so behind him. Nagle had regained the two strokes he had lost to Palmer's early birdies by somehow contriving to birdie the seventh and eighth in the midst of a squall that brought down icy sheets of rain. Then things got closer. Palmer picked up a stroke with a birdie on the thirteenth, picked up another when Nagle three-putted the fifteenth. On the seventeenth, the renowned Road Hole, 453 yards long and bending sharply to the right after the drive, Palmer's approach trickled over the back of the green and down the bank of rough to the edge of the road. He had yet to make a par 4 on this hole, but he did this time after playing a skillful run-up with his putter close to the cup. This gave him a conspicuous lift, and he went on, as one sensed he might, to birdie the home hole, a short par 4 of only 383 yards. Now, in order to defeat Palmer, Nagle would have to finish with two 4s. The key stroke was the 6-footer he had for his 4 on the seventeenth; it had two little shimmer breaks in it. A wonderfully sound putter, Nagle read the line perfectly and tapped the ball into the center of the cup. It was all over when he put his pitch to the eighteenth a yard from the pin. Knowing he could afford to take two putts, he took them, for safety's sake. Palmer, despite a closing 68, had lost by a shot. He had enjoyed the championship, he had taken to the Scots (and they to him), and he had liked the whole British golf scene, but he found it hard to accept congratulations on his performance. "It wasn't good enough," he said time and again. "It just wasn't good enough."

The rest of the year was, in effect, a winding-down for Arnold, though he did win two more tournaments and was in contention in the P.G.A. Championship (which went to Jay Hebert) until he came up with a triple-bogey on the 52nd hole. It had been an immeasurably significant season for him. He had matured into a decisive, pure striker of the ball and into a worthy champion, not that this was what leaped into people's minds when they thought of Palmer. It was his heroics—that birdie-birdie finish at Augusta; that run of six birdies in seven holes at Cherry Hills; that birdie-birdie finish that almost saw him through at St. Andrews. Golfers in particular, since they knew from their own experience what a perverse, treacherous game golf can be, marveled at Palmer's capacity for playing his best when the pressure was most intense. At those rough moments, he seemed more relaxed than most men are lounging in their own den. In brief, a superlative athlete had arrived. Now when you said the name Arnold Palmer, it gave off a whole different ring than it had a few short months before.

The year that followed, the second of Palmer's three big years, was not as big as 1960 and a lot more uneven. Alongside 1961 in the record books a host of achievements are listed: victories in three of the first five P.G.A. tournaments he played that winter, and a season's total of five victories on the tour; prize-money earnings of over $60,000, placing him second to Gary Player in that category; in the major events, a win in the British Open, a tie for second in the Masters, a tie for fifth in the P.G.A., and a tie for fourteenth in the U.S. Open. It looks like one long sweep of topnotch golf, but there was much more complication to it than that. To begin with, in the Masters Arnold received the most stunning jolt of his career—one that would have scarred many players for life. It was not that he lost the Masters but how he lost it. Then, in neither the Open nor the P.G.A. was he truly in the fight, when one looked into it. In the Open, at Oakland Hills, he did not play good golf until it was much too late. Having barely made the 36-hole cut after a 74 and a 75, he was in the last group—a threesome—to go out on Open Saturday. It was testimony to his popularity that he still carried the day's largest gallery with him, and testimony to his mental stamina that he finished with a pair of 70s. Much the same pattern obtained in his jinx tournament, the P.G.A., back again at Olympia Fields after a hiatus of thirty-six years. Virtually out of the running after a 73 and a 72, he then came through with a 69 and a 68. It was a fortunate thing that Palmer won the British Open that July. It made up for everything else—particularly the Masters.

Throughout the winter of 1961, the one golfer contesting Palmer's preeminence had been Player, the little (five-seven-and-a-half), bright-eyed South African star—a zealot about physical conditioning, a born competitor, and now, at twenty-five, the possessor of an efficient American-style swing and the timing to make sharp, square contact with the ball. From start to finish, the Masters was a contest between Player and Palmer. The first day, under dull skies, Palmer had a 68 and Player a 69. The second day, in better weather, Player had a 68 and Palmer a 69, so they shared the lead. In the third round, Palmer, out first, carded a 73, Player a 69, thanks to a 32 on the front side. On Sunday the rains came. The tournament committee tried to get the fourth round in, but it had to be abandoned when the leaders were beginning the second nine. (The eleventh green and some others were pocked with deep puddles.) With the day's play washed out, Palmer and Player went at it again on Monday. Player at one stage widened his lead from four strokes to six, but then Arnold came on with some helpful birdies, and, simultaneously, Player, a couple of holes in front of him, began to encounter trouble. He bogeyed the tenth. He double-bogeyed the thirteenth. There, after driving through the fairway into the wooded rough on the right, he found his ball sitting on ground strewn with pine needles and also found that his straight-line route to the green was blocked by the branches of some pine trees. He chose for some hard-to-fathom reason to use a 2-iron on his recovery shot. It may have been his intention to manufacture a low, punched safety that would pull up short of the creek curling before the green. What he hit, in any event, was a ducking hook that broke across the fairway almost at a right angle and bounded into the creek, which runs parallel to the left side of the fairway at that stretch of the hole. A penalty stroke to lift out; a 3-iron to the back of the long green; three putts; a 7. Shaken, Gary also bogeyed the long fifteenth, where he failed to make a short putt. The situation by this time had changed so drastically that when Arnold came to the fourteenth, he had not only overhauled Gary but had moved in front by a stroke. Pars would see him through now, and it was clear from Palmer's play that his tactical plan was simply to try to match par hole by hole the rest of the way in. He made methodical pars on fourteen and fifteen. Another par on sixteen. Another on seventeen. On eighteen his drive was down the middle of the fairway. One more sound shot and he was in. He took a 7-iron. He meant to draw it a little, for the pin was positioned on the left side of the green, on the lower deck. The shot didn't have the right click at impact; it sounded thin and tinny. More to the point, the shot didn't come off as planned. The ball started out to the right, heading for the long sand trap on that side of the green; it stayed out on the right and came down in the trap, roughly pin-high. Arnold would have to work for that winning 4 now, but, at the same time, he would probably be able to get down in two from the trap. As a matter of fact, not so many minutes before, Player had.

Palmer got set quickly over the ball. The club met the sand, and out came the ball. Something had gone wrong. The ball was carrying too far, almost to the pin, and there was no spin on it. It took a couple of fast hops and rolled over the green and down the steep far bank—a good twenty-five feet over. The huge gallery that had gathered around the green to watch Palmer wrap up another Masters was shocked into a sepulchral silence. To *tie* Player, Palmer now had to get down in two from the foot of the incline. That wouldn't be easy. He took his putter, allowed for the upgrade and for a considerable left-to-right swing. The line was good, the distance wasn't—the ball slid fifteen feet past the cup. The putt for the 5 was never in.

If one shot had cost Palmer the Masters, one shot won him the British Open. The venue that year was Royal Birkdale, off the Irish Sea in Lancashire, not too far north of Liverpool. Accuracy pays off on this links, for many of the fairways are tucked between dunes covered with wiry rough and a bush called the willow scrub. Palmer, hitting everything hard nevertheless, was off with a 70. The next day, though he had to play a good part of his round when a fifty-mile gale was at its height, he had a marvelous 73,

Palmer at Birkdale in 1961. The previous summer he had made his debut in that event at St. Andrews and had lost by a shot. In 1961 he was not to be denied. From the start, Arnold's attacking golf made him a big favorite with the British galleries.

banging one low, screaming iron after another below the wind or through it. (This 73 included a most unlucky 7 on the sixteenth, where his ball moved just as he was in the act of trying to explode it from a bunker by the green. This not only cost him a penalty stroke but, since he had bellied the ball back over the green, three more strokes to get down.) Heavy rains on Friday made it necessary to postpone the third and fourth rounds. There were no bells on Saturday's weather either. It was wet and raw and windy. Palmer somehow managed to get around in 69 in the morning, thanks, among other things, to an audacious wedge shot whacked through a minuscule opening in a willow scrub close by the sixteenth green. Only one other player was close—the veteran Dai Rees. A master of the hard-hit, low-flighted shot, Rees, after a 71, was only a stroke behind. After the first nine in the afternoon, Palmer, playing in the pairing in front of Rees, led him by three, but Rees was still hitting the ball sharply, still coming on.

On the fifteenth, or 69th, Palmer's drive bobbled into the sandy rough off to the right of the fairway, the ball ending up deep in a growth of creeping blackberry bushes. It was questionable whether he would be able to do more than hack his way back to the fairway with a wedge, and even that would require a powerful blow. After a look at the situation, Palmer took a 6-iron and fidgeted himself into the best stance possible. He then whipped the club down and through the ball with such velocity that the shaft of the club was hardly visible. The ball shot out of the bushes and streaked for the flag 150 yards away. It found the narrow opening between the front bunkers and jumped onto the green. Palmer two-putted for his par. The importance of this miracle shot soon became clear. While Palmer was finishing with pars, Rees, needing four birdies to tie, birdied the fifteenth and sixteenth, barely missed his birdie on the seventeenth, and birdied the eighteenth. Talk about valor under pressure! This was, by the way, the third time that Rees, the best British golfer of this period, had been the runner-up in the Open. In that respect, and some others, he stands as the British counterpart of Snead.

The last of the three big years, 1962, started slowly. In the first four tournaments, as the tour wound through California, Arnold finished eighteenth, twenty-first, twenty-first again, and thirty-fourth. In order to succeed at tournament golf, as has long been appreciated, it helps a golfer to have little else on his mind except his golf. Palmer's concentration, however, was fragmented by a hundred different concerns. The combination of his championship golf game and his enormous personal appeal had made him one of the hottest commercial properties in the country—in the world—for companies searching for the right man with the right image to endorse their products. No one understood this more acutely than Palmer's manager, Mark McCormack, a bright, restless young lawyer who worked for an old and imposing Cleveland firm. A good enough golfer himself to have played on the William and Mary college team and to have qualified several times for the U.S. Amateur and once for the U.S. Open, McCormack had got into the business end of golf late in 1958 when he and a friend, Dick Taylor, who helped put on the annual Carling tour tournament, organized National Sports Management, an outfit that lined up exhibition matches for fifteen of the top professionals, Palmer among them. A year later, Palmer, harried by the ever-increasing amount of time he was having to give to business matters, asked McCormack to take over as his manager. McCormack really began to work with Palmer in 1960. From the outset he was prodigiously successful in persuading prestige companies that, to procure Palmer's services, they would have to pay much higher fees than had previously gone to any athlete. McCormack's pitch, in brief, was that Arnold Palmer symbolized dramatic vitality for millions of Americans, as he most certainly did. If anything, McCormack may have been too successful, for he soon had Arnold scheduled for so many exhibitions, luncheon talks, television appearances, sessions with clients, and so on and so forth that, even with his own plane and a personal pilot to split the flying with him as they zipped from one appointment to another, Arnold was forever pressed for time and had much too much on his mind. This was the basic reason why he had gotten off so poorly on the 1962 tour.

It took Palmer four weeks of diligent practice to get his swing and his concentration back in the groove. Then he was ready to move . . . January 31–February 4, the Palm Springs Golf Classic. Palmer, paired with Gene Littler, who started the fifth and final round three strokes ahead of him, took over the lead with a run of five consecutive birdies on the front nine, and went on to win by three strokes . . . February 8–11, the Phoenix Open. Palmer bolted out in front with a 64, added a 68, a 71, and a 66, and won by a full twelve strokes—the largest margin of victory in a P.G.A. tourney in many, many years. He eased up then until the Masters, April 5–8.

At Augusta, after going into the last round with a margin of two strokes over Gary Player and Dow Finsterwald—Finsterwald had won the P.G.A. in 1958 when that championship was changed from a match-play to a stroke-play event—Palmer contrived to throw away his lead with some wretched golf on the front nine. (Among his errors was a long iron to the short fourth that was mis-hit so badly that the ball plopped down like a dead duck after carrying scarcely halfway to the green.) After a double-bogey on the tenth, he trailed both Finsterwald and Player by two strokes. There was a fair possibility that he might be able to remedy this on the thirteenth and fifteenth, those two short par 5s that are eminently birdieable for Palmer. This time he birdied neither. His chances now looked grim, and all the more so when his 5-iron to the 190-yard sixteenth finished on the fringe at the back-right corner of the green. The pin was set on the tiny cape to the left, forty-five slippery feet away. Palmer chipped with his pitching wedge and, since the shot would be traveling slightly downhill, hit it very softly. Nicely on line, the ball kept rolling and rolling and did not stop until it had rolled into the cup and lodged itself between the flagstick and the rim. This sensational shot set off one of the loudest, maddest salvos of applause ever heard at the Masters. That birdie 2 changed things quite a bit. Palmer now needed only one more birdie to tie. All juiced up, he belted a big drive up the seventeenth and put an 8-iron pitch twelve feet from the cup. He sank the birdie putt. Another colossal salvo. A careful par on the eighteenth gave him a total of 280 and a triple tie with Player and Finsterwald.

In the playoff, Finsterwald got off badly and never was a factor. Player was in good form. As he began the second nine, he led Palmer by three strokes. Palmer then unleashed one of the most furious charges of his career. He had a birdie on the difficult tenth; another on the short, fearsome twelfth; another on the long thirteenth, after getting home in two; and still another on the fourteenth, this one via a fifteen-foot putt. In the course of five holes, this thrust had carried him from three strokes back of Player to four in front of him. In the end, he won by three, with a 68 to Player's 71. Perhaps it had been preordained, Palmer's third victory in the Masters. He had won the tournament in 1958, in 1960, and now again in 1962. Evidently he was unbeatable in the Masters in even-numbered years.

The week following the Masters, Palmer tied for fifth at Greensboro and then sat out the next event on the tour, the Houston Classic. His victory in the Masters was still the most popular topic of conversation across the land. People, young and old and in between, thought back to his feats at Cherry Hills and Birkdale as well as those at the Augusta National and wondered if in the long history of the game there had ever been a finisher in the same class as Palmer. Whereas most tournament golfers would have been content to have brought off just one heroic triumph in their lives, Palmer gave the distinct impression that he felt nothing was beyond his reach—and then proceeded to

Wherever Palmer played, "Arnie's Army" quickly mobilized itself. It was a force to be reckoned with, for its vociferous support unquestionably helped Palmer to work his miracles, and the sound of its salvos spelled discouragement for his opposition.

demonstrate what he meant. His self-possession in the clutch would have been outrageous had it not been suffused by his intrinsic modesty and the feeling he conveyed that he depended above all on being touched by the wand of inspiration.

When he returned to the tour, Palmer gave his idolatrous public further reasons to gasp . . . April 26–29, the Texas Open at Oak Hills Country Club in San Antonio. He won by a stroke after birdieing three of the last four holes . . . May 3–6, the Tournament of Champions at the Desert Inn Country Club in Las Vegas. Two shots behind Bill Casper, as tough a competitor as any on the tour, as they moved down the last nine holes together, Palmer birdied the 67th and 69th and came to the home hole, a hard par 4, tied with Casper. After Casper had chipped up close to the pin for his 4, Palmer, whose second shot had ended on the right-hand fringe of the green some twenty-five breaking feet away from the cup, stroked the winning putt into the middle of the hole. One had the eerie sensation that no other result was possible . . . May 10–13, the Colonial Open at the Colonial Country Club in Fort Worth. This is the sort of course, confining and penalizing, that Palmer was not supposed to be able to play. It requires pinpoint driving and very accurate iron-play, and the man who can move the ball both from left to right and from right to left has a definite advantage. For all of his skill, Palmer, lest we forget, still had to fight the tendency of all natural shut-face swingers to hook the ball, and no matter how industriously he worked to block out his right hand at impact, he remained susceptible to streaks of non-precision golf. Nevertheless, with a round to go at Colonial, Palmer held a three-shot edge over the nearest man. He got off to an indifferent start on the round, though, and this time there was no charge down the stretch. Even so, on the 72nd green the tournament was still Palmer's for the winning if he could hole a 12-footer for a birdie. Instead, he did something he almost never did: he left the putt short of the hole. This was interpreted by most spectators as a sign that Arnold had come to the end of his hot streak, whereupon the next day in the playoff against Johnny Pott he shot a fluorescent 32 on the in-nine to win by four strokes. He then decided to leave the tournament circuit and work off a little nervous energy by playing exhibition matches and practicing before rejoining the tour in early June, two weeks before the U.S. Open.

The 1962 Open was held at Oakmont. (Only one sizable alteration had been made in the old battlefield: the first hole had been changed from a short par 5 to a long par 4.) Oakmont lies in the heart of Palmer Country—less than an hour from Latrobe—and one was frequently reminded of this by the keyed-up galleries. As far as they were concerned, there was no other player on the course. On the first two days Palmer was paired with Jack Nicklaus, the Ohio strongboy, who had turned pro late in 1961. While Nicklaus had yet to win on the tour, at the same time he had been in the money in every tournament he'd played. Arnold began with a 71 and a 68, Jack with a 72 and a 70. This was a fair reflection of their golf: Arnold looked to be a bit the better, more polished player. His 139 gave him a share of the lead with Bob Rosburg at the halfway mark. On the morning of the third day—this was still the era of the double round on Saturday— the thousands traipsing after Palmer waited patiently for him to make his move. It came, at last, on the 53rd, or seventeenth, the mongrel par 4, 292 yards long, that ran up a humdrum hillside to a small green guarded by a ring of Oakmont's storied bunkers, not as deeply furrowed as for previous Opens but furrowed nevertheless. Palmer drove the green by bouncing a great tee shot through the tight entrance on the left, and then holed from twelve feet for an eagle, which put him out in front all by himself. Then, in an uncharacteristic lapse, he three-putted the last green when he muffed a 2-footer, and dropped back into a tie for the lead with Bobby Nichols.

Palmer's surprising botch-up of the 54th proved to be an augury of the unexpected turn his afternoon round took just when it seemed that he had the championship wrapped up. As he came to the ninth, he held a two-stroke lead on Nichols and Phil Rodgers, several holes ahead, and a three-stroke lead on Nicklaus, playing the eleventh. On the ninth, a 480-yard par 5, uphill all the way, Arnold had a chance to add to his lead with a possible birdie. His second had finished in malleable rough on the right, about fifty feet from the pin, which was situated on what Oakmont members call "the piano," a rise in the green roughly shaped like that instrument. Getting down in 2 would not be too hard. Well, it took Arnold 4 to get down. He fluffed his first chip only a few yards ahead, still in the rough. His second chip stopped seven feet short of the cup. He pushed the putt slightly. A 6 and not a 4. He had lost a stroke instead of gaining one. Now he led Nicklaus, the challenger who was to concern him, by only two shots. After Nicklaus birdied the eleventh, he led him by only one. On the par 3 thirteenth, Palmer was bunkered when his 5-iron hung out on the right, and there went the last stroke of his lead. Both men played an unbroken series of pars down the stretch, giving them totals of 283 for the four rounds. Over the final holes Palmer had had the best opportunity for victory—a 12-footer for a birdie on the seventeenth. He missed it by an eyelash.

Unlike most playoffs, this one was packed with interest. Nicklaus raced off to a four-stroke lead. Palmer then began one of his great rushes with birdies on the ninth and the eleventh, and added another when he got home with two Herculean woods on the 603-yard twelfth. The crucial hole was the short thirteenth. Once again Palmer bogeyed it, this time when he took three putts. That just about settled things. On the home hole Palmer missed an irrelevant tap-in, making the final scores 71 and 74. Putting had undoubtedly decided the championship. Palmer, the wizard of the greens, had three-putted the large, fast, undulating surfaces ten times in all. Nicklaus, rated a good but not exceptional putter, had three-putted only one green over the ninety holes—the first green on his fourth round. That kind of putting would have earned a mildly approving nod even from Walter Travis.

They say that you can tell a man's fiber by how speedily he recovers from a harsh setback. A month or so after Oakmont, in his next important start, Palmer won the British Open, successfully defending the title he had captured at Birkdale. In 1962 the venue was Troon, a rumpled old course along the Firth of Clyde that is replete with sandhills and brambles, hillocks and heather. As long as a golfer stays on the fairway, he hasn't too much to worry about. (Arthur Havers won at Troon in 1923 with 295, Bobby Locke in 1950 with 279.) Palmer, on the stick all week, not only dominated the '62 Open

Winnie Palmer, one of Arnold's
most valuable assets,
adds them up at Aronomink.

from beginning to end but wound up by breaking the old record low total for the British Open by two strokes.

That summer a month-long drought had burned Troon's fairways a tawny brown and made the ground so hard that the only way to stop an approach on a green was to land it a good distance short of the green and correctly gauge how many yards of bounce and roll it would get. Most of the players in a distinguished field couldn't cope with these chancy conditions. Palmer found them no bother at all. He also used the speed of the fairways, and his own extraordinary power, to reach in two shots par 5s that were out of range for practically everyone else. He won in a waltz. After the first two rounds he led the second man, Kel Nagle, by two shots. They were partnered on the final thirty-six. After a slow start on the third round, Palmer got it moving and really turned it on coming in with birdies on the thirteenth, fifteenth, sixteenth, and seventeenth. This gave him a 67, a new course record. At one point in the final round, before Nagle mounted a spurt of his own, Palmer's lead had grown to an unbelievable ten shots. Late in that final round there was an unanticipated complication. Hundreds and hundreds of Glaswegians on holiday, not deigning to buy tickets to watch the Open, clambered onto the course from the sandy beach along the Firth, entering through the "Aberdeen Gate," as it is called. These new spectators converged on Palmer and Nagle with moblike myopia as they played the last few holes, and it was a lucky thing, especially on the eighteenth, that neither of the players was injured in the violent crush that resulted. It was typical of Palmer that, after calming the crowd encircling the home green, he managed to drop a good birdie putt to finish the championship in style: 71-69-67-69—276. Nagle was six shots back, and the third man, Phil Rodgers, a full thirteen. It is easy to see why many golf cognoscenti consider this championship the acme of Palmer's career.

The following week, a little weary from it all, Palmer was on hand at Aronomink in suburban Philadelphia for the P.G.A. The splendor of his triumph at Troon had pushed the Palmer fever of the American golf fan up several degrees. The thousands who came out to Aronomink were not the least bit interested in the tournament. So Gary Player was out in front being chased by Bob Goalby. What else was new? They had come almost solely to see Palmer, to talk to him, listen to him, touch him, yell for him. Arnold coped with this whirligig of adoration as best he could, but with scarcely a moment to collect his thoughts and to think about his game, all he could do was go through the paces of playing golf. He was lucky to finish in a tie for seventeenth.

Later that summer, just to round things off, he won his last tournament of the year, the American Golf Classic, and won it by five shots.

About midway through the 1962 season, Americans everywhere began to speak of Palmer as "the most exciting athlete since Babe Ruth." The people who did this were sports fans, not golf fans pure and simple, and the fact that they felt this way seemed to demonstrate that golf was now accepted as a major sport. They had come to know Palmer because of the increased coverage television now accorded golf. These newcomers to golf were enchanted by Palmer—by the vigor he brought to a button-down game, this unaffected, friendly, smiling, decent, determined man. They even learned to enjoy his idiosyncrasies—the way he was forever hitching up his trousers, the way he was so contorted at the finish of a tee shot that he had to twist and bob his head to follow the ball, like a man craning his neck around the corner of a building. General Eisenhower and Ben Hogan had been responsible for enlarging the common-denominator quality of golf, and Palmer, whose personal popularity among its champions was unprecedented save only for Jones, widened this further. It is not excessive to say that everyone liked Palmer: children and grownups, the rich and the poor, men and women, country folks and city folks, doers and dreamers, Americans and foreigners, sports nuts and people who didn't give a damn about sports. Small wonder that political savants began to talk about Palmer's possibilities in that field when his golfing days were over.

In the two years that followed his three big ones, Palmer's standing among his admirers didn't slip one cog, although some of them may have noticed a slight falling off in the standard of his play—this despite the fact that in 1963 he led the money-winners for the fourth time in six years and that in 1964 he was nosed out in that race by Jack Nicklaus by a paltry $81. He won eight tour tournaments those two seasons. He was in the thick of several major championships. He barely missed winning another U.S. Open in 1963, losing a three-way playoff. He was unfortunate, too, in being edged out by Bobby Nichols in the 1964 P.G.A. after he had shot four straight rounds under 70 (68-68-69-69), but nobody could have beaten Nichols at Columbus that week—he improvised more unintentional trick shots those four days than Joe Kirkwood had come up with in a lifetime. On the other hand, Palmer kept his even-year record in the Masters going, winning again in 1964 with just about the most elegant and artistic exhibition of shot-making of his career.

Arnold Palmer, the Man Who Made Charisma a Household Word

Taking everything into consideration, his status and his glamour continued to take on new dimensions, if anything. One eloquent scene comes to mind. It took place in the press tent after Arnold had won the first Piccadilly World Match Play Championship in 1964 by defeating Neil Coles in the final at Wentworth, England. With his phenomenal memory for names, he was just as much at home there as he would have been at Augusta or Pebble Beach. "Arnie," a treble Midlands voice called out from the shadows of the tent, "were you bothered by the hardness of the greens?" "Well, Nigel," came the answer, "after the first day, no. Actually, I didn't think they were too difficult." An Oxford voice with another question was raised: "Arnie, can you tell us why you played the British ball here?" A brief pause and then the answer: "Well, Peter, I like the small ball, and since I do, I'd be silly not to play it, wouldn't I? I can always use those extra yards." And so, on and on. It was the same wherever he played. In short, Arnold Palmer had become a full-fledged international personality, like Ingmar Bergman, Willy Brandt, Joan Sutherland, Stavros Niarchos, Sophia Loren, and the Beatles.

But there *was* a change in Palmer's golf: he was no longer able to summon that sub-par burst or that unbelievable shot when he desperately needed them. For example, when he fell behind Julius Boros (the winner) and Jackie Cupit in their playoff for the 1963 Open at The Country Club in Brookline, the harder he tried the more poorly he played. When a badly hooked tee shot on the eleventh ended up in a tree stump deep in the woods, his chances were definitely over. (His score in the playoff was a 76.) In the Open the following year at Congressional, to cite another example, his old stamina was obviously lacking. After he had jumped into the lead with a 68 and a 69, he slipped way out of the running with a 75 and a 74—thirteen more strokes than the winner, Ken Venturi, required on that blazing Saturday.

Why this change? There were endless theories. One that made much more sense than most was propounded by a British doctor, a former Oxford golf captain, who regularly attended the British Open as a member of one of the R. & A. committees. After watching Palmer struggling with his game in the 1963 British Open at Lytham, this doctor said with a troubled shake of his head, "Unless I'm very wrong, Palmer's absolutely exhausted—that's why he isn't playing any better. As a matter of fact, it's a long time since I've seen a man as totally tired as Palmer. He needs a long rest—a minimum of three months." Yes, it was possible. After all, Palmer's many and varied enterprises made continual demands on his time and energy. The interstructure of these ventures under the Palmer umbrella was at least as intricate as the genealogical chart of an Ottoman dynasty. Since Mark McCormack's imagination and drive were almost boundless, included among Palmer's operations were organizations for the distribution of dry-cleaning franchises, a maid-service service, and over a hundred Arnold Palmer putting courses in the United States, Canada, Britain, South Africa, and Japan. There was also a short-lived chain of Arnold Palmer laundries, best remembered because of the wisecrack by Dave Marr they prompted: "The only golf pro I'd send my laundry to is Chen Ching-po." In addition to the usual annual expeditions to the British Open, there was an enervating number of other overseas trips to be made—to South Africa in 1962, to

Australia in 1963 and 1964, to Britain in 1964 (where he won the inaugural Piccadilly World Match Play Championship), to France in 1963 and to Hawaii in 1964 for the Canada Cup. Besides, he was now deeply involved in the production of filmed golf series for off-season showing on television, such as "Challenge Golf," in which he and Gary Player opposed other top-ranking pros in four-ball matches, and "The Big Three," co-starring Palmer, Player, and Nicklaus. Palmer loved being active, enjoyed engaging in certain aspects of business, and got a kick out of meeting new people and seeing new countries, but it took him a long while to realize that a man in his middle-thirties, however extraordinary his physical endowment, could not keep going from morning till night, day after day, without finally feeling its effects.

At the same time, Palmer's one major victory during the mild diminuendo of 1963–64 was almost a direct contradiction of this thesis. This was the 1964 Masters. The majority of the game's veteran observers had previously considered Palmer's four rounds at Troon as his finest tournament performance, but now this had to be revised; his golf en route to his fourth victory at Augusta had to be rated as equally impressive. At Troon the galleries had seen the dashing young champion at his gung-ho best. At Augusta they saw a much more mature Palmer. He played well within himself all the way, maintaining a proper balance between boldness and good sense in his tee-to-green play, thinking every step of the way about the tempo he wanted his swing to have, the kind of flight he wanted the ball to take. A typical Palmer shot, for example, was his 4-iron approach to the terraced green on the fifth, perhaps the hardest par 4 at Augusta, when he was on his way to a 69 and a share of the lead on the first round. It wasn't so much the result—he put the shot twelve feet from the hole—as the ease and restraint with which the shot was hit. Instead of trying to cream the ball just as hard as he could with those powerful hands, which was his usual style, Arnold played that approach with an unhurried, cohesive swing in which the movements of his legs, hips, shoulders, arms, and hands were fused so smoothly that the stroke really did seem almost effortless. The ball fluttered down on the green as softly as a snowflake—also something new for Palmer, since his medium and long irons came in smoking hot as a rule, and the heavy spin on the ball sent it hopping around like a jumping bean. It was clear on that first day at Augusta that he had been working hard to modify certain facets of his technique and that he had managed, after a disappointing winter, to bring his game to the perfect pitch at exactly the right time.

On the second day, Palmer, his swing still as rhythmic and integrated, birdied four of the last six holes for a 68 and a four-shot lead. A 69 on the third round pushed his lead to five shots, but there were two moments on the second nine that afternoon that sent cold shivers racing up the spines of his supporters; it was then that he hit his only two bad shots of the tournament, and they really were bad. The first was a 3-iron approach to the eleventh, which he snap-hooked into that arc of Rae's Creek that curves in front of the left side of the green. The second was his drive on the thirteenth, the dogleg par 5, where he hooked his tee shot deep into the pine woods. It was how he went about playing his recovery that filled his rooters with anxiety. It was evident that Palmer's only

One of the most popular features of the American landscape in the 1960s was Arnold Palmer in action, letting everything rip on one of his long, low-flighted drives.

opening back to the fairway from the thick woods lay behind him, in the direction of the tee, but even though he was in a position to sacrifice a shot in the interests of security, it was also evident that he was in no mood to accept a 6. After shuffling around and studying the branches at the top of the tall pines in front of him, Palmer switched from a 9-iron to a wedge, settled into his stance, and took a vicious cut at the ball. The members of his faithful Army saw it start up, then lost it in the pines, and didn't see it again until it dropped safely onto the fairway some seventy-five yards nearer the green. He got his 5 and was so exhilarated that he then rattled off three birdies in a row.

On the last day Palmer had a quiet 70 for a total of 276 (the same as at Troon) and a six-stroke margin over Marr and Nicklaus, who tied for second. In the hubbub after the tournament, an old friend of Arnold's cornered him for a moment and asked him about his recovery from the woods on the thirteenth on the third round. Had he really played a good shot there?

"It was the best shot I hit the entire round," Palmer answered emphatically. "I got that ball almost straight up in the air, which was what I was trying to do."

But why, his friend persisted, had he even thought of taking a gamble like that in the first place? It could have cost him four or five shots if it had failed to come off.

"I realized that," Palmer said. "I just felt sure I could make the shot."

THE
GOLDEN HOURS
OF THE
GOLDEN BEAR

In the winter of 1944, Charles Nicklaus, a Columbus, Ohio, pharmacist, injured his right ankle playing volleyball. The X rays disclosed no dislocation, but the foot did not heal well. Over the next five years it continued to give Mr. Nicklaus, a former Ohio State athlete who liked to be active, a good deal of pain and bother. In 1949 the ankle flared up badly, and this time the source of the trouble was finally discovered: a small bone, the calcaneus, had been chipped; a growth of bone had covered it, and arthritis had set in. A local orthopedic surgeon operated to fuse the ankle, then put the ankle in a cast for three months, and, upon removing it, counseled Mr. Nicklaus to give the foot regular exercise. Mr. Nicklaus, who had played some golf as a young man and had taken up the game again in 1948—two years before this operation—immediately thought of the game as the perfect answer. He quickly learned that it wasn't; he could play only a hole or two at a time before he would have to stop and rest the ankle. To his considerable disappointment, he was forced to tell his regular foursome at the Scioto Country Club that they would have to find a replacement. Since the idea of playing golf all by himself didn't appeal to him, he decided that perhaps the best solution would be to have his ten-year-old son Jack come out with him on his golfing expeditions. Since the boy was crazy about all sports, he would probably like golf too.

That summer of 1950, in addition to acting as his father's golfing companion, Jack Nicklaus joined the weekly Friday morning class for junior members that Jack Grout, the new pro at Scioto, had instituted. He also took a few private lessons from Grout. The first time he played nine holes he had a 51, the second time a 61, and then he got so

Jack Nicklaus at thirteen,
the year that the prodigy
from Columbus first broke 70.

bad he didn't even keep his score. Near the end of the summer, he began playing much better, and one day he had a 95 for eighteen holes.

The summer he was eleven, Jack got down to 81. His father had started him off with the interlocking grip, like Ouimet's and Sarazen's, and Grout experimented for a while with switching his promising pupil over to the more conventional overlapping, or Vardon, grip. After a couple of weeks he changed him back to the interlocking—he seemed more comfortable with it—and from then on Grout never again thought even for a moment of altering his grip. Jack attended Grout's weekly junior class that summer and the next one—1951 and 1952—and continued to take occasional private lessons with him. When he was twelve, he got down as low as 74, and a year later he actually broke 70: one evening when he was playing with his father, he rolled in a 35-foot putt for an eagle on the eighteenth for a 69!

Jack was a big fellow for his age—at thirteen he stood five-ten and weighed 165 pounds. He played center on the school basketball team (since he was the tallest kid in his class), he caught on the school baseball team, and, despite his bulk, he played quarterback on the football team. The Nicklauses had always been strong, brawny folks. The earliest Nicklaus to whom the family has traced its lineage was Peter Nicklaus, who lived in Alsace-Lorraine near the beginning of the nineteenth century. Old Peter's grandchildren were the first Nicklauses to come to America, dispersing and settling in Cincinnati, Columbus, and Wichita. (The Columbus branch, headed by Jack's great-grandfather, Charles Louis Nicklaus, has always pronounced the name

Nick-*lus;* the other two branches pronounce it Nick-*loss.*) Jack's great-grandfather founded the Nicklaus Boiler Works in Columbus, an important railroad junction. He had three daughters and seven sons, and all of the boys became boilermakers. This necessarily included Louis Nicklaus, Jack's grandfather, a tough-minded man who worked for the Pennsylvania Railroad, became secretary of the local railroad men's union, and in time felt so deeply aggrieved by the Pennsy management's handling of the long, bitter strike in the early 1920s that, rather than go back with that company after the strike was finally settled, he chose instead to work for the little Hocking Valley Railroad. He and his wife, Arkie Belle, had five children. Frank was the eldest, two years older than Louis Charles, Jr., Jack's father. The Nicklauses were hard workers. As boys in grammar school, Frank and Charlie—as everyone always called him—rose at four to load a vegetable wagon for a neighbor who was a house-to-house vendor. This still gave them time to whip through their morning paper route before school. In the evening they worked at Doc Mebs' pharmacy. Somehow or other, Charlie, a broad, big-boned friendly young man, still found the time to keep up with his studies and to play on the South High School football, baseball, basketball, golf, and tennis teams. (He played #1 on the high school golf team although he never had time to practice, and in his junior year at college he won the Columbus Public Courts Tennis Championship.)

Although he was offered several scholarship deals by Eastern colleges, Charlie Nicklaus decided to attend Ohio State University. O.S.U.'s College of Pharmacy was regarded as one of the best in the country, and he was quite sure that this was the field he wanted to enter. He played on the freshman football, baseball, and basketball teams, but the autumn of his sophomore year he had a tantalizing decision to make when he was hospitalized after his appendix had acted up midway during the football season: Should he have the operation the team physician suggested (and fall behind in his studies), or should he say to blazes with it? He climbed out of his hospital bed, never had the operation, and instead of playing football for Ohio State henceforth played pro football on Sundays under an assumed name for the Portsmouth Spartans, filling in for "Father" Lumpkin at linebacker whenever the famous Georgia Tech All-American needed a rest.

Seven years after Charlie Nicklaus received his degree in pharmacy in 1935 (and two years after his marriage to Helen Schoener), he purchased, with the help of his brother Frank, who was now a dentist, his first drugstore—an old Walgreen branch at the corner of High and Crittenden Streets, adjacent to the Ohio State campus. He prospered. By 1960 he owned three other pharmacies in the Columbus area. Later he sold two of them to employees of his. He wanted more time to enjoy life, and there is little doubt that nothing else filled him with more pride and happiness than watching his son play tournament golf. He was always in Jack's gallery at every major event. Until Jack went on his spectacularly successful diet in 1969, it was easy to spot Charlie Nicklaus. All you did was look for a middle-aged version of Jack, a husky, companionable, smiling man who always took the modest precaution of removing his name card from his tournament badge.

Interestingly, during Jack Nicklaus' high school days the sport closest to his heart was not golf but basketball, a peculiarity that has been known to occur among natives of the American Midwest. He was a starting forward for three years on the Upper Arlington High School team, a good all-round player—an effective outside shot, a fairly dangerous driver, and a dependable rebounder who in his junior and senior years was selected as an all-league forward in the Central Buckeye League. ("I was so deeply involved in basketball in high school," Nicklaus stated not long ago, "that even now I can tell you how many points per game I averaged my last two years—17.5 as a junior and 18 as a senior.") When the warm weather came, though, he turned to golf, as he had done from the start, with an almost matching exuberance. He began to compete in tournaments at thirteen, and the record he compiled would lead one to deduce that he was unquestionably the outstanding golf prodigy to appear in America since Bobby Jones. Here are some of the high spots of that record:

Age thirteen (1953). Won the Ohio State Juniors (for boys between thirteen and fifteen) . . . Won the Columbus Junior Match Play Championship . . . Entered his first national tournament, the U.S. Junior Championship (for boys seventeen and under). Won his first three matches and then lost to Bobby Ruffin.

Age fourteen (1954). Won the Columbus Junior Match Play Championship and the Columbus Junior Medal Play Championship . . . Was defeated in the second round of the U.S. Juniors by Hugh Royer . . . Was low scorer in the Tri-State (Ohio, Kentucky, and Indiana) High School Championship, carding a 64 in one round.

Age fifteen (1955). Again won both the Columbus Junior Match Play and Medal Play Championships. In the latter, held over the short (6,400-yard) Gray Course at Ohio State, shot two 63s . . . Won the Ohio Jaycees . . . Won the Columbus Amateur but was knocked out in the first round of the Ohio State Amateur . . . Lost in the quarter-finals of the U.S. Juniors to Billy Dunn . . . Qualified for the U.S. Amateur for the first time but lost, 1 down, in the first round to Bob Gardner.

Age sixteen (1956). Low scorer in Tri-State High School Championship . . . Lost in the playoff for National Jaycees Championship to Jack Rule . . . Lost to Rule, 1 down, in the semi-finals of U.S. Juniors . . . Lost in the quarter-finals of the Ohio State Amateur but won the Ohio State Open, defeating a very good field at the Marietta Country Club with rounds of 76, 70, 64, and 72. The structure of the tournament called for the last two rounds to be played on the same day, and Nicklaus has always believed that his third-round 64, which broke the tournament wide open, was due in good measure to the fact that the previous afternoon he had played an exhibition in Urbana, Ohio, with Sam Snead and had no doubt picked up a little of Sam's magnificent tempo. (Scores of the exhibition: Snead, 68; Nicklaus, 72.) . . . Eliminated in the third round of the U.S. Amateur by Ronnie Wenzler . . . Attempted to qualify for the U.S. Open for the first time, but failed to make it.

Age seventeen (1957). Won individual prize in Ohio State High School Championship . . . Won Ohio Jaycees . . . Won National Jaycees in his last crack at it, edging out John Konsek on the last hole . . . In his last crack at the U.S. Juniors was defeated in the third round by Larry Beck. (This was the one junior championship of any importance that Nicklaus did not win.) . . . Qualified for the U.S. Open but played two woolly 80s and came no place near making the cut . . . Was defeated in the fourth round of the U.S. Amateur by Dick Yost, at The Country Club in Brookline. Went out in 32 but still stood 1 down.

Since the America in which Jack Nicklaus was growing up was peopled with dozens of hotshot young golfers, anyone who did as well as he did had to be imbued with a formidable competitive spirit. He had one other tremendous asset. This was not his staggering power, though he was longer off the tee than anyone else in his age group, but the soundness of his swing. In Jack Grout he had one of the finest teachers in the country. Grout had been an assistant to Henry Picard, who in turn had studied with Alex Morrison, far and away the game's most *avant garde* scholar in the period between the two world wars. From his many hours of listening, reading, thought, and experiment, Grout had concluded that a correct golf swing rested mainly on the execution of three fundamentals. 1. The head had to be kept still throughout the swing, since it was the balance center of the swing. 2. In order for a golfer to move swiftly and correctly through the ball on the downswing, he had to have excellent balance. Balance depended on proper foot action, and proper foot action meant the correct rolling of the ankles—the left ankle rolled in on the backswing and the right ankle braced, with the reverse taking place on the downswing. (When Morrison first propounded this theory, he was ridiculed—he was that far ahead of his time.) 3. A golfer should try to develop the fullest possible arc by making the fullest possible shoulder turn. Like Deacon Palmer, Grout believed that golfers should be encouraged to hit the ball as hard as they could when they were young and their muscles were flexible and stretchable. They could work on control afterwards. This went headlong against the traditional advice given for eons to young players: Learn to control the ball first; distance will come later. How long, you ask, did Jack, when he had grown up, hit the ball? Try this one for size: In a warm-up round for the 1960 Open at Cherry Hills when he was twenty, on the 550-yard seventeenth, aided by a mild following wind, he was home in two on the island green with a drive and a 7-iron.

During Jack's years in high school, Grout was concerned with instilling in him certain approaches to technique in general that he felt would stand him in good stead as he encountered faster and faster competition on tougher and tougher courses. There were two chief points he emphasized to young Nicklaus. First, hit the ball high. Then when you have to play a long or medium iron to an exceedingly tight green, the ball will come floating down softly and will hold the green. (That came easy for Jack. He always held his head a little farther behind the ball than most golfers, and this promotes a high-trajectory shot.) Grout's second point was the value of hitting the ball from left to right as opposed to from right to left. Under pressure it could make all the difference in the world. At those times, if the right-to-left golfer—who normally hit a draw—lost his timing, the result would sometimes be a duck-hook; the ball would break so sharply

One of a series of superb stop-action photos of Nicklaus taken by Bill
Foley of Columbus when Jack, at nineteen, was a freshman at Ohio
State University.

because of its heavy side spin that it might finish yards off the fairway in the kind of
trouble that could cost the golfer two or three strokes. On the other hand, if a left-to-
right golfer—the educated fader—made the same degree of error, he would suffer a
much less damaging penalty, because the side spin on a slice is never as vicious as on a
hook and, as a result, the ball will not angle as radically and penetrate as deeply into
trouble. In other words, left-to-right was much the safer method, as Ben Hogan proved
so effectively after his changeover following his accident. One thing more: Grout
believed that a first-class golfer had to possess the skill to play the ball either from left to
right or from right to left, as the weather and the topography dictated.

Were it not for their desire to represent their country in the international Walker Cup
competition, nowadays the leading young American amateurs would turn professional
the day after graduating from college, having spent four years on a golf scholarship at
the old alma mater preparing for the P.G.A. tour. It was not quite so extreme in Jack
Nicklaus' day—amateur golf had much more vitality—but the goal of every young
amateur then, too, was to make the Walker Cup team.

The next meeting with the British was scheduled to take place at Muirfield, in

Scotland, in May 1959. As a freshman at Ohio State during the 1957–1958 season—he had never given a moment's thought to attending any other college—Jack was limited to playing on the freshman golf team. The better to call the attention of the Walker Cup selectors to his ability to play pretty fair golf, he undertook an ambitious summer schedule that stressed four big tournaments. He not only succeeded in qualifying for the U.S. Open, scheduled for Southern Hills, in Tulsa, but he also made the 36-hole cut. With rounds of 79-75-73-77 and a total of 304, he ended up tied for forty-first, but only three other amateurs—Charlie Coe, Jerry Pittman, and Harvie Ward—finished in front of him, so this had to be a plus. He then captured the Trans-Mississippi, one of the four top amateur tournaments in the country, winning the final at Prairie Dunes, in Kansas, from Richie Norville. Now if he could only make a creditable showing in the U.S. Amateur, set for the Olympic Club in San Francisco. That wasn't going to be easy: when the pairings arrived, he saw that he and Harvie Ward, the 1955 and 1956 Amateur Champion, would meet in the second round. The Ward–Nicklaus match was a humdinger. Outplayed by a wide margin from tee to green, Harvie held onto a small lead by dropping putts of six feet or longer on *twelve* greens and by chipping in from off the edge of another green. With Harvie standing dormie 2, Jack holed out a wedge chip on the seventeenth to get one hole back, but he still had to win the eighteenth, and he couldn't. The scores were 70 and 71. The selectors would keep that in mind. Jack also played in his first P.G.A. tournament, the Rubber City Open, on the old Firestone course in Akron. A 67 and a 66 put him right up with the leaders and rendered him so nervous that the best he could do on the third day was a 76. A final 68 enabled him to tie for fourteenth, not a bad showing at all for an eighteen-year-old kid. His summer campaign was not lost on the Walker Cup selectors. When the team was announced late in January 1959, at the annual meeting of the U.S.G.A., Nicklaus was named to it along with three other young players—Deane Beman, Ward Wettlaufer, and Tommy Aaron—and five veterans—Charlie Coe (the playing captain), Billy Joe Patton, Bill Hyndman, Bud Taylor, and Harvie Ward. (That spring, before the team flew over to Scotland in mid-May, Jack had added another prestige title, the North and South Amateur Championship, defeating Gene Andrews in the 36-hole final by one hole.)

The 1959 Walker Cup Match was expected to be a very close contest. The British had a seasoned, well-led team that, in the last previous Cup Match in 1957 at Minikahda, in Minneapolis, had actually held the lead at one time on the second day before going down to defeat 8–3. (In those days, four 36-hole foursomes were played on the first day of a Walker Cup Match, and eight 36-hole singles on the second. A victory was worth one point, but no half points were awarded for a tied match.) From the beginning, Bernard Darwin and the other British writers were thoroughly in agreement that the outcome of the 1959 Match would hinge on how well the four young members of the American team coped with Muirfield, a much franker test than St. Andrews and most linksland courses but, for all that, a very touchy piece of terrain that would be especially difficult to handle since it had gone ten days without a drop of rain and was as fast as a roadway.

Nicklaus and his one and only teacher, Jack Grout, work on the Scottish putter he brought home from the Walker Cup Match of 1959. He won his singles, his foursome.

Captain Coe paired Nicklaus and Wettlaufer, a beefy young man from Buffalo with a fine hitting action, as his fourth foursome team. (In foursomes the partners play alternate shots and drive from alternate tees.) The luck of the draw found them opposed by the youngest British pair, Michael Lunt and Alec Shepperson. The two Americans started off in jittery form—the occasion was more tensive than they had expected—but they rallied to win the sixteenth, seventeenth, and eighteenth and went to lunch only 1 down. In the afternoon they squared the match at the 20th, went ahead on the short 31st, where Wettlaufer cracked an iron four feet from the flag on the high plateau green, and closed things out 2 and 1 on the 35th. This victory just about decided the 1959 Match, for it gave the United States a 4–0 lead. Of the three other foursomes, the British had been overwhelmed in one but two had gone to the final green.

In the singles, Nicklaus, placed in the eighth spot, played W. Dickson "Dick" Smith, a congenial Scot in his early forties. A 70 in the morning put Jack 5 up, and in the afternoon he quickly won three more holes. Then Smith began to play, but his four birdies came much too late, and Nicklaus wrapped up the match 5 and 4. The score of the over-all Match was United States 9, Great Britain 3, and while the entire American side had played well, perhaps Harvie Ward and Ward Wettlaufer deserved to be singled out for special praise.

Two weeks later the British Amateur was held at Royal St. George's, in Kent. Driving erratically and finding the high rough much too often, Nicklaus was ousted in the quarter-finals by Hyndman, 4 and 3. In an all-American final, Beman outsteadied Hyndman 3 and 2.

As it turned out, that defeat at the hands of Hyndman was the only one Nicklaus suffered all season. There is no explaining it, really, but the experience of playing on a Walker Cup team—especially when the Match is held overseas—has been the making of many golfers. It was, to a large extent, the making of Nicklaus, though at the time no one sensed it, most people in golf being far more smitten then by the young man's disciplined violence off the tees than by the solidness of his game as a whole. But after the Walker Cup, Jack Nicklaus was a discernibly better, wiser, and more deeply confident golfer, as became clear that September in the U.S. Amateur Championship.

That 1959 Amateur was held on the East Course of the Broadmoor Golf Club in Colorado Springs, some seventy miles south of Denver. Situated 6,400 feet above sea level, the Broadmoor's two layouts are perhaps the highest championship-caliber courses in the world. In 1959, the East Course measured 7,010 yards, but because of the rarefied air it played more like 6,700 yards. It presented some problems. It took some acclimatization for a golfer to learn how to select the right iron for his approach—one or maybe two clubs less than he would have taken going by his perception of distance alone. Then he had to learn how to read the very tricky greens. At Broadmoor, knowing that the break is generally away from the mountains is somewhat analogous to knowing the first four letters of the alphabet. The real work, even on a relatively simple putt that at sea level would take only a glance to read, is to determine whether it is uphill or just appears to be, whether it will break two inches or two feet, and just how softly it needs to be tapped to cruise the sleek surface and die near the cup if it fails to fall in it. The design of most of the individual holes on the course has all the sparkle of a zircon, but with Broadmoor's built-in deceptiveness there is plenty to absorb the full attention of even the topflight golfer.

By the end of the week, the two hundred entrants had been whittled down to two—Jack Nicklaus and Charlie Coe, a thirty-five-year-old oil broker from Oklahoma who was the U.S. Amateur Champion in 1949 and 1958, a lean, laconic man with just about all the other attributes of the typical television sheriff. On their way to the final, Coe and Nicklaus each had one rough match. Up against Bill Hyndman in the quarter-final round, Coe stood 5 up after corraling five birdies on the first eleven holes. However, over the next five holes, Hyndman, playing one peerless shot after another, as he can when he is in one of his purple moods, cut away four of those holes. On the eighteenth, gambling for still another birdie, he caught the heavy rough with his tee shot, and that was that. Nicklaus, coming through the lower half of the draw, had his close call in the semis against Gene Andrews, whom he had barely edged by six months earlier in the final of the North and South. A heavy-set, painstaking, forty-six-year-old insurance man from California, Andrews, who had won the U.S. Public Links Championship in 1954, deserves the credit for being the first tournament golfer to make it a practice before each event to chart the distances to the pin from the drive zone on every hole and also to chart the rolls of each green. The Andrews–Nicklaus match swung on the 30th green, where Andrews, with a chance to go 2 up, three-putted and lost the hole. On the 35th green, Nicklaus, who was then 1 up, salvaged a crucial half by sinking an almost impossible putt. Between his ball and the cup twenty-five feet away was a small ridge, then a rather extended downgrade, and then, just above the cup, a right-to-left break. Nicklaus somehow got the speed perfect, and the ball came trickling down the slope just slowly enough to take the break and rattle into the cup.

The four thousand spectators who witnessed the final are not likely ever to see a better golf match. Coe, with that beautifully compact swing (and deceptive length) of his, led off with three straight birdies. This gained him only a one-hole lead, for Nicklaus also birdied the second and third. Right there and then, the imprint of the match was set. It maintained its quality and grew in tension and simmering drama all day long. Coe forged a 2-up lead on the morning eighteen with a two-under-par 69, was caught by Nicklaus at the 21st, moved out in front again with a birdie on the 24th, was overhauled once more on the short 30th, fell behind for the first time on the 32nd, and then came back to square the match on the long 35th, where Nicklaus hooked his tee shot into comparative Indian country, the one error the bull of a boy made throughout the afternoon.

All even, then, coming to the home hole. At that time the 18th on Broadmoor's East Course was a dogleg to the right about 430 yards long, with a small pond sitting in the middle of the fairway halfway between the long, upsloping green and the crown of the fairway where a well-placed tee shot would finish. Coe, with the honor, put his drive in position A. Nicklaus followed with an equally good drive perhaps two or three yards longer. With the pin set about twenty feet from the rear edge of the green, Coe elected to play an 8-iron. The ball was hit squarely and on line, but it was a shade too strong; it rolled over the green and into the clumpy rough at the base of a small bank. Here was a great chance for Nicklaus and he seized it with a brilliant shot, a 9-iron, not too high, dead on line, which sat down nine feet short of the pin. With his work really cut out for him, Coe took a few tugs at the bright red Oklahoma U. coach's cap (which his friend Bud Wilkinson had given him) and got the feel of his sand-iron in his fingers. He lobbed the ball softly onto the back edge of the green. It came rolling slowly, slowly toward the cup. It stopped on the very edge of it, literally one turn away. Coe and Nicklaus exchanged knowing smiles, and then Nicklaus began working on the 9-footer that would mean the match or extra holes. It was not an easy putt—slightly uphill with a faint left-to-right break near the cup. He rapped it into the middle of the cup and became, at nineteen years and eight months, the youngest Amateur champion in fifty years.

At nineteen Jack Nicklaus was a bulky, muscular athlete who stood five-feet-eleven and three-quarters inches tall and whose weight varied between 208 and 220 pounds. His shoulders were thick and his posterior was not negligible, but he carried a high proportion of his weight in his heavy legs and thighs. (His leg drive has always been the main source of his colossal power. Incidentally, he can punt a football fifty yards high and sixty yards long, in the air—a standard only the best pro punters attain.) At nineteen his face was full and round, which exaggerated the smallness of his features. His tow-colored hair was cut short, and what with his blue eyes and thickish neck, he was Central Casting's idea of the young Teutonic-American. At this time, and for quite a few seasons afterwards, Jack did not pay too much attention to his golf clothes. On the course a white or dark blue sports shirt and a pair of plain slacks sufficed, and he wore the golf version of a baseball cap, usually pushed well back off his forehead. During a tournament, he registered a minimum of emotion. He had been brought up by Jack Grout and his father to appreciate that golf was a game that required a player's undivided concentration, and he seldom let his mind wander even momentarily from the task at hand. Since he smiled so seldom and was businesslike to the point of grimness, he was not especially popular with galleries, except those which appreciated the quality of the clean, incisive, assertive golf shots he played. People who knew him well, however, liked him very much. His colleagues found him not only a friendly, pleasant opponent but also a marvelous sportsman. Jack didn't lose very often, but when he did, there was no one in the game who congratulated the man who beat him more quickly, more genuinely, and more graciously. (This admirable trait has never altered.) Off the course he liked a lighthearted atmosphere. He gravitated to people who had a good sense of humor and who knew their sports. He followed nearly all sports avidly himself. This was one of the reasons he was so close to his father, another insatiable sports fan. From the time Jack was six until he was twenty (and had to be in Philadelphia for the Eisenhower Trophy Match one September Saturday), he and Charlie never missed attending an Ohio State home football game.

Oddly, in 1959, when he won the Amateur, Jack had not played a stroke of golf for the Ohio State varsity team, for during his sophomore year his Walker Cup commitment had, of course, taken precedence. Then, having made his mark on the national and international scene, it was hard for him to get as steamed up about college golf as the average undergraduate. His golf during his junior year—1960—was inconsistent all the way. He played well in the Masters, tying for low amateur with Patton. In the Big Ten Championship he lost the individual title to John Konsek by two strokes. In the U.S. Open, at Cherry Hills, he had perfect control of his swing, and on the final day, paired with Hogan, he burst into the lead when he birdied the 66th, only to throw it away by taking three putts from twelve feet on the 67th and three putts again from forty feet on the 68th. (On the 67th he had been plain unlucky. He missed from eighteen inches when he had to putt across a badly repaired pitch-mark that twisted his ball off-line.) For all that, he finished second, and his total of 282 was the lowest ever posted in the Open by an amateur. The week after the Open, however, he was eliminated in the second round of the N.C.A.A. Championship. In the U.S. Amateur at the St. Louis Country Club, he lasted only until the fourth round, in which he was beaten 5 and 3 by Charley Lewis and six three-putt greens. (Deane Beman defeated Bob Gardner in the final.) What resurrected the year for Jack was his golf in the second World Amateur Team Championship for the Eisenhower Trophy, which was held at Merion the last week in September.

This competition, which takes place every two years, had been inaugurated at St. Andrews in 1958, where the Australian team had defeated the American team by two strokes in a playoff. The format is an interesting one: each nation's team is made up of four players, and its total for each day of the four-day tournament is the sum of the three lowest rounds of its four players; its grand total is the sum of its four daily totals. At Merion the United States fielded a very capable team: Nicklaus, Beman, Hyndman, and Gardner, with Tot Heffelfinger as the non-playing captain. Plenty of competition was expected from Great Britain and Ireland, Australia, South Africa, New Zealand, and Canada, but the American team ran clear away with the event. After the first round, the United States held a nine-stroke lead, which it increased to twenty strokes on the second day, to thirty-eight on the third, and finally to forty-two. There has never been so one-sided a victory in golfing history, and there may never be again—it was just one of those things.

The most likely explanation of the American rout is that Merion, with its high premium on correct placement of the tee shot and its subtly constructed, fast-breaking greens, was just too much for the visiting players to cope with. At the same time, in just about every respect, the Merion the world amateurs played was a much less demanding and harsh course than the one over which Ben Hogan had posted a four-round total of 287 on his way to winning the U.S. Open in 1950. The tee markers had been set forward so that the holes played shorter; the fairways were cut wider; the rough was shorter; the pins were placed in more accessible positions; the greens were considerably slower, and a run of moist weather made them very holding. These conditions should be mentioned, for otherwise there would be no comprehending how during the Eisenhower Trophy competition Jack Nicklaus returned a four-round total *eighteen* strokes below Hogan's mark by shooting four superlative rounds of 66, 67, 68, and 68— 269. For the first time the entire world of golf realized the full extent of young Nicklaus' endowments, particularly the players and administrators who were lucky enough to be at Merion that week. Every department of his game was under compelling control, but, as one would expect, it was his driving that made the deepest impression. There may have been a suspicion of lift to his backswing, but on the downswing and in the hitting zone there was such astounding coordinated timing between the movements of his body and his arms and hands that the ball fairly exploded off the clubface. Years afterwards, when people would enthuse to Charlie Nicklaus about how well Jack was hitting his tee shots, Charlie, while usually agreeing, would sometimes add if he knew the person well, "I could be wrong, but I don't think that Jack has ever been as good a driver as he was as an amateur—and particularly that week at Merion."

Nicklaus' senior year at college was different from the first three in one basic respect: he was no longer a bachelor, having been married in July to a classmate, Barbara Bash, the daughter of a mathematics teacher at South High School in Columbus. Jack had met Barbara, a tall, slim, blue-eyed blonde with brains and balance, their first week at college, and they had gone together since the February of their freshman year. Following their marriage they lived in a small house in Upper Arlington, and to pay the bills Jack devoted a fair share of his time to selling insurance. The previous spring, after he had completed the three-year pre-pharmacy course, he decided that he would prefer a career in business, and in his senior year he switched to the College of Commerce and a major in insurance.

What with so many changes, it was a sort of hectic year for Jack, and he did well to maintain a high standard of golf in his tournament appearances. He won the Western Amateur, which he used as a tune-up for the Masters. In *that* event, he tied for seventh, a somewhat misleading figure if it implies that he was even a peripheral contender at Augusta; he simply came on strong at the end. In the Big Ten Championship, realizing that his team's chances depended on his personal performance, he got down to business and won the individual championship by twenty-two strokes, and that extra effort did carry Ohio State to a five-stroke victory in the team championship. Later in the season, after the national Open, he won the N.C.A.A. Championship, defeating his O.S.U. teammate, Mike Podalski, in the final. A further word about the Open, held at Oakland Hills. For the second year in a row, Nicklaus was in a position to win this most important of all championships. A 69 and a 70 made up for an opening 75. Midway through the fourth round, as he stood on the twelfth tee, he was only one shot behind Gene Littler, the eventual winner, who was then playing the eighth and driving hard to overtake the leader, Doug Sanders, which he eventually did on the eleventh. However, as far as Nicklaus' chances were concerned, the twelfth, a 566-yard par 5, was the make-or-break hole. While he could not reach it in two—the raised green was trapped in front—it presented a reasonable birdie opportunity. Jack didn't even make his par, three-putting from thirty feet for a 6. In the end he finished in a tie for fourth, three strokes behind the winner.

The next big event on his schedule was the Walker Cup Match in late August at the Seattle Golf Club. He readied himself for this by playing, among other things, two P.G.A. tour tournaments, the Buick Open and the American Golf Classic. At Seattle he was in sharp form, winning his foursome in partnership with Beman and then trouncing Joe Carr in the singles as his contribution to an unhappily lopsided affair in which a weak British team was lucky to scrape up one point. Next, down the coast to Pebble Beach for the Amateur. Just as the Eisenhower Trophy Match had transformed 1960 from just a satisfactory season into a spectacular one, Nicklaus' play in the Amateur had the same effect on his 1961 campaign. From start to finish, his level of concentration and his technical execution at Pebble were every bit as extraordinary as at Merion. Over the 112 holes he played, he was 20 under par, which is something when you stop and reflect that Pebble (with its eight perilous, cliff-lined holes along Carmel Bay) may be nothing less than the greatest golf course in the world. In each of his matches, moreover, Jack was under par at the point where the match ended. After tight tussles against Dave Smith in the fourth round and Johnny Humm in the fifth, he was merciless in the 36-

hole semi-final and final, defeating Bud Methvin 9 and 8 and then Dudley Wysong 8 and 6. No one has ever played Pebble Beach better, not even Jack Nicklaus in winning the 1972 U.S. Open.

The week after the Amateur, the Nicklauses' first child, Jack William II, was born. Jack, who had returned to Ohio State to make up the three quarters of credits he lacked, began to think more seriously about the benefits of turning pro. After all, his income from his insurance work was only in the neighborhood of $6,000, and the pro circuit had become so rich that the winner's take alone in many tournaments was more than $6,000. In the summer he had set up a meeting with Mark McCormack, who managed Gary Player as well as Arnold Palmer, in order to explore what he might reasonably expect to earn as a professional. Now, in October, he arranged for a second meeting with McCormack, in Columbus, at which Mark estimated that Jack could undoubtedly make around a hundred thousand dollars in endorsements alone if he chose to turn pro. That was something to think about! He asked the opinion of a number of friends and, to be sure, his father. On November 7 he decided he would remain an amateur. On November 9 he decided he would become a pro—for one thing, it would be much fairer to his family, and, for another, only by making golf his profession did he feel that he might be able to realize his full potential as a golfer. Two days later he signed with McCormack and began the hundred and one preparations for joining the pro tour at the Los Angeles Open, the opening event of the new season. In the meantime he practiced daily at Scioto, but for the first time in a decade Jack Grout was not on hand. He had taken a new post at La Gorce, in Miami Beach, and had already gone South. Yes, everything was changing for Jack Nicklaus. No one needed to tell him that he would be starting out on an entirely different life.

In some quarters a curious misconception persists that, upon joining the tour, Nicklaus immediately dominated professional golf as authoritatively as he had the amateur scene. The fact of the matter is that, while Nicklaus did well from the very beginning, finishing in the money in every tournament he played his first year, in 1962 Palmer was the king of the professional world and would continue to be for quite a few more years. Palmer was warm and welcoming to the highly touted newcomer whom he had first met in tournaments in Ohio some seven or so years before. (Considering the keenness of the rivalry that grew up between them, their mutual regard and considerateness have been exemplary.) That first season, Nicklaus, like every newcomer to the caravan, had to get accustomed to a whole new set of situations and problems: traveling from week to week to a new tournament; going for weeks without seeing his wife or any other member of his family; living out of a suitcase in soul-sapping motel rooms; accepting the seemingly ceaseless routine of taking out and picking up his laundry and dry cleaning; adapting his game to mediocre courses that were in poor shape (in particular, the winter-tour courses with their wet, high fairway grass and their hard, unholding greens); learning to putt the slowish greens (and getting used to using a heavier putter); finding a dependable method for digging the ball out of terrible lies in the middle of fairways; learning how to get along with the press and the other media men; putting up with criticism (such as the allegation of certain savants that his "flying right elbow" would be his downfall); and, of course, continually pursuing the elusive goal of every hopeful young golfer on the tour: learning how to weed out the bad rounds. It all came in time. The week before the Open, he finished second to Littler in golf's first post-George S. May $100,000 tournament, the Thunderbird Open, winning $10,000 for his efforts. The next week he won his first tournament as a pro, the Open, when he defeated Palmer in a playoff at Oakmont. Before the year was over, he had won two tour events, the Seattle World's Fair Open and the Portland Open, and had run his official winnings to $61,869, which placed him third behind Palmer and Littler. Not too bad for a freshman.

As goes without saying, it was Nicklaus' victory in the Open that made his year. There are two or three comments about that championship that might well be made here. To begin with, the driving by both Nicklaus and Palmer over the full ninety holes was just about as good as one could ever hope to see on a long, rolling course like Oakmont, whose sweeping fairways were bordered by shaggy rough. No doubt, it was Nicklaus' superior putting that finally made the difference in the extended battle between the two men. In tying with Palmer in the championship proper, after Arnold had opened the door on the fourth round by taking his bogey 6 on the 63rd, Nicklaus, along with playing sound stuff from tee to green, made three key putts. None of them being very long, they are not the type that live on in the conversation or memories of most Open aficionados. The first was a straight 8-footer for a birdie on the eleventh, or 65th, that cut Palmer's lead to a single shot. The second was a 3-footer for a par on the par-3 70th; it was a putt that had him worried, since it was uphill on a slanting green. The third, and hardest, was the 4-footer he made to save his par 4 on the 71st. (By that time he and Palmer were tied for the lead.) On that mongrel hole, Jack had driven into the furrowed bunker before the green, exploded onto the front fringe, and then run his chip four feet past. The putt he faced had an insidious double-break: it tipped slightly to the left until a few inches from the hole, where there was a quick little reverse roll from left to right. Not daring to trust his touch on Oakmont's slick greens at this delicate moment, Nicklaus concluded that the safest tactic was to aim for the inside left corner of the cup and hit the ball firmly enough that it would get to the hole before either of the two breaks could influence it. He really hit that putt hard. The ball sped toward the left corner and dived in. If it hadn't, it might have rolled ten or twelve feet past.

In the playoff, after Jack had gotten off to a four-stroke lead, his equanimity saved him when, starting at the ninth, Arnold uncorked one of his celebrated charges that reduced Jack's margin to three, to two, and then to one. Under this barrage of birdies, Jack held on well and continued to play good golf shots. When Arnold three-putted the thirteenth, however, it turned the match around again. At that stage of a round, holding a two-stroke lead is entirely different from holding a one-stroke lead. Jack made no mistakes until he pulled his drive off the eighteenth, but by that time he was safely home.

The Golden Hours of the Golden Bear

After his breakthrough in the Open, Jack Nicklaus accomplished so much so quickly and so continuously that the only way one can hope to cover his multiple successes is simply to brush the high spots. This necessarily means concentrating to a large extent on the four major championships in modern professional golf: the Masters, the U.S. Open, the British Open, and the P.G.A., to list them in the order in which they are played. By emphasizing this quartet, some things are bound to be lost; they are not by a long shot the only competitions in which a top field gathers at an outstandingly good layout and produces, for any number of reasons, golf of the first order. At the same time, the ranking players tend to point for the four major championships, since a victory in any one of them is not only the most direct route to material prosperity but also satisfies the yearning of every serious, talented player to have his name go down in history alongside the names of the earlier champions. Out on the tour, with the exception of a few tournaments, the name of the game today is Money. In the major tournaments, there is much more on the line: money, prestige, and, as mentioned before, that certain, special, hard-to-define kind of homage that has always been paid to the men and women who have the head and the heart to be at their best on the significant occasions. That is why the feats of Young Tom Morris a century ago still mean something today to every informed golfer.

In Jack Nicklaus' case, it is oddly relevant if one concentrates on his golf in the major championships, for he has always believed that they are the ones that count. His goal since he was a very young man has been to try to win one major championship each year. His over-all goal was to see how close he could come to bettering Jones' record of thirteen victories in the major events. In any event, it was an unusual year when Nicklaus did not win at least one major championship. In 1963, he had an excellent chance to win three of the four. In the fourth he was so far out of the running that he didn't even make the 36-hole cut. This was the U.S. Open, in which, ironically, he was the defending champion. Some trouble with his neck the previous week had led him to experiment with his swing pattern, and the best he could do at The Country Club—a 76 and a 77—was a stroke too many. He made a great many friends, however, when, asked to come to the press tent after his expulsion, he walked in with a big smile on his face and said, "You guys have got to be crazy, talking to a 76 yesterday and a 77 today . . . What course do we play next year?"

Earlier in the year at the Masters, held during a stretch of very rough weather, Jack had been much more on his game. A 74 (in a high wind), a 66 (on the one nice day), and a 74 (in a punishing rainstorm) gave him the lead with a round to go—a shot in front of Ed Furgol, two in front of Julius Boros, three in front of Sam Snead and an up-and-coming star, Tony Lema. The story of the tournament is the story of the last seven holes. As Jack got ready to play the twelfth, he shared the lead with Snead, who, playing three holes ahead, had caught him with a birdie on the fourteenth. The next man, Boros, who was paired with Nicklaus, was two strokes behind them. With the honor on the capricious 155-yard twelfth, Boros hit a beauty twelve feet past the pin, set to the front of the green. Nicklaus' shot was not a good one. The ball just did get over Rae's Creek and thudded into the soggy front bunker. Permitted a lift and drop because of casual water, he hit what looked like a fine recovery from the sand, but the run on the ball carried it twenty-five feet beyond the pin into stubbly rough. Electing to go with his putter, Jack pushed the ball nine feet past. As he stood on the green trying to get a grip on himself and wondering if Snead would birdie the long fifteenth, Boros knocked in his birdie putt. Now, if Jack missed his putt, Boros would be a shot ahead of him. Jack played the putt to break a half-inch to the left just before the cup. It did. He had gotten out of it with a 4.

There are few cases in golf history when the man in the lead, overtaken and passed with victory in sight, has had the courage and the poise to fight back and recapture it. Certainly few young golfers have managed this. (Jack Nicklaus at this time had only just turned twenty-three.) Quickly assimilating the shaking experience of the twelfth, Nicklaus reached the long thirteenth with a driver and a 2-iron, and two-putted for a birdie. This put him in front of Boros again, but since Snead had meanwhile made his birdie 4 on the fifteenth, Nicklaus still trailed him by one. On the fourteenth, 420 yards, he made his par 4. On the fifteenth, the last par 5, a well-positioned drive and then a tremendous piece of good luck on his second. He made smashing contact with his 3-wood, but as the ball was carrying the pond before the green, its slight draw widened into a hook. It kicked off the left-hand bank of the green and scooted like a frightened hare toward the pond in front of the sixteenth tee. Ordinarily the ball would have bounded into that hazard, but on this day, because of all the rain on Saturday, the ball was stopped well short of trouble by the gumbo of mud churned up by the tramping feet of spectators along the narrow passageway between the two holes. Under a local rule, Nicklaus was permitted a free lift and drop, and made the most of it. His third shot was an exquisite chip-and-run with a 7-iron four feet from the flag. He missed the birdie putt but, everything considered, he could not feel too upset since he could have as easily taken a 6 or a 7 as a 5. More than that, he learned that Snead had failed to make his par 3 on the sixteenth—he had needed three from off the front edge—and this meant that Nicklaus was now tied for the lead. On the sixteenth he went out in front with a sterling 2. With the pin positioned on the dangerous upper terrace at the back right-hand corner, he hit a gorgeous, high, soft-falling 6-iron thirteen feet or so from the flag, and rolled in the putt. As he was walking to the seventeenth, he heard the news that Snead had finished with another bogey. A two-shot lead now—that would make things easier. On the seventeenth, after a drive down the fairway, a sudden shock—an enormous roar from the horseshoe gallery around the eighteenth green. In a moment, Nicklaus had been filled in: Lema, whom everyone had forgotten about, had topped off a strong finish by holing a rainbow putt for a birdie, a 70, and a total of 287. Quick arithmetic: to beat that figure, Nicklaus would have to make his pars on the last two holes. He made no mistakes and got them. He did not intend to throw this tournament away a second time.

Then came the fiasco at Brookline, and following that the British Open at Lytham and St. Annes. The previous summer, Nicklaus had made a somewhat less than sparkling début in that august championship at Troon, hitting the ball all over the place, never in the hunt. He did much better at Lytham, the most northerly of the run of Open courses along the Irish Sea. The site of the championship in 1926 (Jones), 1952 (Locke), and 1958 (Thomson), Lytham may be the least prepossessing of the links on the Open rota. Situated a good mile from the sea, which is never visible or even felt, the course, a rather flattish piece of terrain, is pretty much hemmed in today by rows of ugly, tomato-red brick houses. "Inevitably," as Sir Peter Allen has written, "the character of the course has changed in the process, as has that of so many of the great seaside links, and it has become much more 'inland,' softer, fatter, and lush." Were it not for its final five holes, which make for a fairly formidable finish, Lytham would have very little to recommend it.

As the 1963 Open took shape, a strange feeling enveloped the tournament. From the morning of the second round on—an opening par 71 had placed Nicklaus four shots behind the leaders, Peter Thomson and Phil Rodgers—everyone, almost without exception, had the feeling that the powerful young American was destined to be the winner. The story line, moreover, was as clear as the bright blue sky: he would gradually overhaul the leaders, assume the lead with a flourish on the last round, and finish in style. Well, a 67 on the second round moved Nicklaus three shots behind the leaders, still Thomson and Rodgers. In the third round, on the morning of the final thirty-six, he closed to within two shots of the new leader, Bob Charles. Early in the fourth round he gained another shot on Charles. Only one shot back now. It was uncanny how everything was following the scenario. On the seventh, a par 5 of 551 yards, Nicklaus vaulted into the lead with a thrilling eagle. The shot that set it up was the drive. The fairway of the seventh swings out to the left from the tee and then gradually veers back to the right and straightens as it runs toward the punchbowl green. It is one of those holes where each golfer must decide for himself how much of the abundant rough between the raised tee and the distant arcing fairway he should attempt to cut off. Nicklaus, a slight breeze behind him, took aim on a point where the fairway met the rough about 270 yards away. He wound up and slammed the ball high and hard right on the line that he had selected. He had gauged the distance perfectly. Carrying the rough only by a matter of yards, the ball came down on the right edge of the hard fairway, bounced fast, and ran a good distance. It had been a poke that left Nicklaus' playing partner, Tom Haliburton, over a hundred yards behind him. Jack hadn't actually hit that gigantic drive 350 yards—he had cut the corner—but it had left him within two hundred yards of the flag. He took a 5-iron for his approach and whipped the ball onto the green. It finished four feet from the cup. He holed the putt.

Entering the last five holes, Nicklaus held a one-stroke lead on Charles and Rodgers, and still did with three to go. A birdie 3 on the sixteenth (or 70th), a short par 4, gave him a valuable insurance stroke. On the seventeenth, the famous 472-yard dogleg to the left, something went wrong. After a 3-wood off the tee, Jack played a fine, straight 2-iron but the ball carried too far, landing in about the center of the hard-surfaced green and bounding over it into the high, gnarled rough beyond. He took 3 to get down from there. A bogey 5. Now, in terms of how they stood with par, if either Rodgers or Charles birdied the sixteenth—they were on that green now—he would then be tied with Nicklaus. Nicklaus took his time on the last tee, and hearing no shouts or applause from the sixteenth, assumed that neither Charles nor Rodgers had birdied the hole. Actually, both of them had.

On the eighteenth Nicklaus lost the championship when he hit a low hook off the tee into the last bunker on the left, the ball finishing close to the steep, lipped front face. He had no choice but to wedge out semi-laterally, ninety yards short of the green. It took him three to get down—a second straight bogey 5. Charles and Rodgers each made his par 4 on the seventeenth. Each then made his par 4 on the eighteenth. They had beaten Nicklaus by a stroke. The scenario had not held up after all.

The next day, in what may well be the last 36-hole playoff in golf history unless fools rush in, Charles, sinking one long twisting putt after another, defeated Rodgers handily and so became the first left-handed player ever to win a major championship.

The following Thursday, some five thousand miles away, the P.G.A. Championship got started in Texas on the course of the Dallas Athletic Club. A par 71 layout, 7,046 yards long, it had been carefully prepared for the event and stood up valiantly under the worst heat wave in which a consequential tournament has probably ever been played. In his three practice rounds, Nicklaus suffered through temperatures of over 100 degrees. Once the shooting began for keeps, conditions became even worse. For four consecutive days the thermometer climbed above 110 scorching degrees. When his daily round was over, Jack hurried to his air-conditioned car and drove to his air-conditioned hotel room, which he never left unless it was to go to dinner at some air-conditioned restaurant. Considering how woozy the players felt, the golf was more than creditable. After fifty-four holes, Bruce Crampton, at 208, was in first place, followed by Finsterwald at 210, Nicklaus at 211, and Dave Ragan at 212. The oppressive heat made the fourth round sort of a blur to Nicklaus. As he remembered it, Crampton, with whom he was paired in the last twosome, lost the lead on the twelfth when he got into trouble off the tee. Then, shortly after Nicklaus had birdied the fifteenth, word reached him that Ragan had hit a wild tee shot on the seventeenth and had subsequently bogeyed it. Anyhow, when Nicklaus teed up on the eighteenth, a 420-yard par 4 with a fairway-wide creek 290 yards out and the green perched on a high plateau, he held a two-stroke cushion. To make sure he was short of the creek, he played a 3-iron off the tee, but he let up on the swing and hooked the ball into the rough. He pitched safely short of the Styx, then lofted a 9-iron for the center of the green—all he wanted was a bogey 5. However, he made precise contact with the ball, and this, combined with the slope of the green from back to front, gave the ball a lot of backspin action, and where it had landed twenty feet past the pin, it spun back to four. Jack made the putt and so won by two shots. He had been around in 68. On the way to the clubhouse the security officer who had taken care of him all day collapsed from heat exhaustion.

The atmosphere at Dallas had been so uncomfortable, enervating, and unreal that during the tournament Nicklaus' thoughts never did get beyond immediate problems, like wiping his hands dry or finding a cold soda, and it wasn't until he was making his speech at the presentation ceremony that he fully comprehended that he had won a major championship. The 1963 British Open and the 1963 P.G.A. remain locked together in his mind. The championship he was sure he would win he threw away, and the championship he never gave any thought to winning he won.

For almost any other golfer but Nicklaus, 1964 would have been a year to savor. He won six tournaments in all, four at home and two abroad. He was a marvel of consistency: in six tournaments he was second or tied for second, and in another three he tied for third. It was not surprising that he gained that perhaps overfussed-about distinction of being the leading money-winner that year. Nicklaus, however, didn't consider it a good year because he had let the big ones get away—he did not win a major championship. To rub in the sting of this disappointment, he was second (by himself or in a tie) in three of the four. In the 1964 Masters, Palmer, in what was quite possibly the best tournament he has ever played in America, was never seriously threatened. Jack came as close as anyone. In the third round he was narrowing the gap a little when he shanked his iron on the short twelfth, which rather cooled him off. The next day he and Dave Marr finished six shots behind Arnold. In the P.G.A., Nicklaus came busting home on the fourth round at the Columbus Country Club with a 64, but all this did was gain him a tie for second with Palmer three shots behind Bobby Nichols. Nicklaus' other red ribbon came in the British Open. One scene, which those fortunate enough to have been on hand always refer to, cuts to the heart of the tournament. It took place on the third day, when Tony Lema, that lovely swinger, had played himself into the lead, although he had had the gall to fly into the face of tradition and to arrive in St. Andrews so late that he had time for less than two rounds of practice on the Old Course, which, as every golfer is aware, takes years to begin to know. On that third day of the Open, the day of the last thirty-six, Nicklaus, who trailed the leader by nine shots, was off on his morning round an hour and a quarter before the leader, Lema. Unlike the first two days, this one was dry and sunny, and Nicklaus, who had gotten the worst of the stormy weather on the first two days, was quick to take advantage of it. As he came down the thirteenth fairway—this is the scene—he stood 5 under even 4s for the round. Lema, going up the parallel sixth at the same time, took this in as he gazed across the fairway at Nicklaus' scoreboard. Simultaneously, as they passed each other, Nicklaus going south and Lema going north, Nicklaus squinted across at Lema's scoreboard and saw that he was 3 over even 4s for the first five holes. In other words, Nicklaus had made up eight strokes of his nine-stroke deficit. He finished with a birdie on the home hole for a 66. All of Nicklaus' heroics went practically for naught, though. The sight of Nicklaus' scoreboard was just the spur Lema needed to wake up and get going. From that juncture on, he made six birdies and never once went over par. A 68 for Tony, and instead of the slim one-stroke lead he had had when he and Nicklaus had passed each other, he was in front by seven full strokes. The afternoon was something of a repetition of the morning. Nicklaus was around in a flashing 68, but Lema calmly stuck to his knitting and brought in a well-played 70. It was a victory that deserved the champagne party that "Champagne Tony" threw.

This leaves Nicklaus' play in the U.S. Open to be accounted for. At Congressional, outside Washington, D.C., he was a good many rungs farther down the ladder than second—he tied for twenty-third. It was his putting that undid him. For example, he muffed three short putts, two of them under two feet, on the last three holes of the first round to tarnish a promising start. On the third round he failed to hole eight putts of four feet or less on the first seven holes. Finis.

By 1964 Nicklaus had his own plane, a twin-engine Aero Commander with a thousand-mile range. (Like Palmer, he took over the controls from time to time but had a regular pilot.) He was now an extremely busy young man, with a hundred and one subsidiary business interests at home and abroad. Incidentally, the two titles he won overseas that year were the Australian Open, at the Lakes Golf Club in Sydney, and the individual championship in the Canada Cup, at Royal Kaanapali in Hawaii.

At about this stage in his career, Nicklaus began to experience some trouble retaining the natural groove of his swing and he concurrently became more vulnerable to picking up small but injurious habits, such as exaggerating his open stance (to make sure he hit the ball from left to right), shutting his shoulders just before starting his backswing, not getting his hands back high enough, "crossing the line" with his club at the top of the backswing, and rushing into the downswing before he had quite completed the backswing. A couple of hours with Jack Grout usually straightened him out if he hadn't already corrected the error himself. His game was also going through a number of changes. For example, although he began to hole more long putts, he also began to miss more short ones. His pitching remained unreliable, and it was not a gag to say that he could put a 1-iron shot closer to the pin than a flip with his wedge. His most woeful new habit was the left-to-left drive, a long pull-hook that cropped up all too frequently when there were out-of-bounds markers along the left. While he mis-hit many more shots than he had before, Nicklaus by and large maintained his consistency as a scorer, because his middle and long irons remained dependable, because he learned to utilize his unmatched power to dig his way out of lies in the rough that would have been frankly unplayable for the average golfer, and because his fighting spirit would never allow him to quit no matter how hopeless the situation. In brief, there was less consistency to his golf. Some weeks it was just superlative, but there were others when he did not strike the ball with anything like the squareness and control one expected of him. By the way, no player in history probably has ever been subjected to as much criticism from his friends as Nicklaus, simply because they knew Jack's capabilities so well. They didn't march up to him and let him have it with an adjective to the jaw, but during his rounds as they followed him outside the ropes, they would shake their heads after an errant shot and expostulate, "What does that dummy think he's doing? Hey, wake up out there and start playing some golf!" That's the price that potential pays.

The Golden Hours of the Golden Bear

In 1965, for all his periodic lapses, Jack Nicklaus was not only the leading money-winner but also led the second man, Lema, by almost $40,000. He won four tournaments. In the major tournaments, his play showed wide fluctuation. In the U.S. Open, at Bellerive, he barely made the 36-hole cut and ended up in a tie for thirty-second. In the P.G.A., at Laurel Valley, he tied for second with Billy Casper, two shots behind Dave Marr. Jack had played some fantastic shots and a matching number of terrible ones. In the British Open, at Birkdale, where Peter Thomson won the crown for a fifth time, Jack finished eleven shots back in a tie for twelfth. He had not been impressive at all, but then British Open courses and British conditions, it could be pointed out, did not flatter Jack's strong points. He naturally flighted the ball high, and in those heavy, wet, swirling ocean winds, the lower you could keep it, the better off you were. He naturally hit the ball long, but as often as not in Britain his length got him in trouble in the thick, bush-laden rough fringing the bone-hard fairways. It seems pertinent to mention these points, because the one major title Nicklaus won in 1965 was the Masters, and after that victory whenever Nicklaus played well in the Masters, which was just about annually, the old refrain was heard that the course favored Nicklaus and the other long-ball specialists. This was true, with qualifications. As Bob Jones remarked, the long-hitter assuredly had an advantage provided he hit the ball in the right direction. For another thing, many golfers who were not powerhouses—Jimmy Demaret, Henry Picard, Claude Harmon, Jack Burke, Jr., and Art Wall, to name just a few—had won the Masters. That proved something. At the same time, it should be added that the man who can fly the ball 250 yards or more in the air gains immeasurable rewards at Augusta, for his drives will frequently carry beyond the crests of hills and will land on flat, hard upland stretches of fairway, adding yards to the run of the ball. After the way Nicklaus handled the Augusta National in the '65 Masters, one could see why the playing properties of the course were such a popular subject of conversation.

Nicklaus started off in that Masters with a 67. It had been perfect weather for scoring, and Player had begun with a 65. Friday brought wind and more difficult pin positions. Nicklaus had a 71, 1 under par, which placed him in a triple tie at the halfway point with the two other standout members of the McCormack A.C., Player and Palmer. A 64 on Saturday in ideal conditions gave Jack a five-stroke lead. He was worried that he might play too conservatively on the last round, but brought in a 69, the lowest score of the day. His total of 271, nine shots lower than Palmer's and Player's, was 17 under par and broke by three shots the previous record set by Hogan in 1953.

The pivotal round, of course, was the third. How can one best transmit the almost unbelievable standard of power golf that Nicklaus played that day? Probably by just setting the facts down plainly. Jack was out in 31 after going par, birdie, par, birdie, par, birdie, birdie, birdie, par. He came back in 33—par, par, par, birdie, par, birdie, birdie, par, par. In the light air he drove the ball improbable distances. He was home on the first, 420 yards, with a driver and a sand-wedge; on the second, 555 yards, with a driver (into the woods), a 3-iron, and a wedge; on the third, 355 yards, with a driver and

You can't stay down over the ball any better than the young Jack Nicklaus did. In 1962, his first year as a professional, he won the U.S. Open. The following year he took the Masters and the P.G.A. Then in 1965 he set a new Masters record of 271.

a pitching wedge; on the fourth, 220, with a 4-iron (from the front tee); on the fifth, 450, with a driver and a 6-iron; on the sixth, 190, with a 6-iron; on the seventh, 365, driver and pitching wedge; on the eighth, 530, driver and 3-iron; on the ninth, 420, driver and pitching wedge; on the tenth, 470 (downhill), driver and 8-iron; on the eleventh, 445, driver and 8-iron; on the twelfth, 155, 8-iron; on the thirteenth, 475, driver and 5-iron; on the fourteenth, 420, driver and 7-iron; on the fifteenth, 520, driver, 5-iron to the back fringe, and chip; on the sixteenth, 190, 6-iron; on the seventeenth, 400, driver and 8-iron; on the eighteenth, 420, driver and pitching wedge. Nicklaus hit every green in the regulation stroke except the seventeenth; there, his approach landed on the green, but the spin on the ball backed it off the green onto the front apron. He had thirty putts on the round, by the way. His 64 equaled Lloyd Mangrum's record low score that had been set a quarter of a century before. At the presentation ceremony, Bob Jones, in congratulating Nicklaus, was probably thinking primarily of the third round but no doubt had Nicklaus' incredible display of power golf on all four rounds in his mind when he said, "Jack is playing an entirely different game—a game I'm not even familiar with."

The following April, Nicklaus became the first Masters champion to successfully defend his title. He was lucky to win in 1966, for his golf at Augusta was as spotty as it had been solid the year before. It seemed that every time he fought his way into the lead, he would immediately fall back by unfurling an inglorious pull or push. Then he would rally again. With five holes to go, he looked to be out of it. He lay three shots behind Gay Brewer, who was playing two pairs ahead, and two shots behind Tommy Jacobs, just ahead. He closed the gap with birdies on the fourteenth and fifteenth, but this might have meant nothing if Brewer had parred the last hole. After going into the lead with a birdie on the 63rd, Gay, a very pleasant man whose swing is identifiable several fairways away because of its pronounced inside-outside loop, had rattled off eight straight pars. He was on the upper part of the home green in two but left himself a touchy 7-foot sidehiller for his par 4, which he proceeded to miss. This opened the door for Jacobs, who got his 4 on the eighteenth by firing a long 3-wood onto the green after his drive had hit a tree limb and had ricocheted back toward the tee. Brewer's bogey also opened the door for Nicklaus, who could have jumped clean into the lead if he had been able to hole a 3-foot birdie putt on the seventeenth. In the three-man playoff the next afternoon, the unfortunate Brewer soon fell far behind Jacobs and Nicklaus. Two putts decided their duel. On the eleventh Nicklaus ran in a 25-footer that put him in the lead by two strokes. On the long fifteenth he made a 15-footer that rubbed out the effect of a birdie there by Jacobs and kept him in front by two strokes, his eventual margin of victory.

Nicklaus won only one other tournament (the Sahara Open) at home that year, he was a distant twenty-second in the P.G.A., and he was never a factor in the Open—strictly a skirmish between Palmer and Casper—although he did wind up in third place, seven shots behind them. For all this, 1966 was a memorable year for him: he won the

The 1966 Masters brought a three-way playoff among Nicklaus (left), Gay Brewer (center), and Tommy Jacobs. They are shown driving off the first tee at Augusta.

elusive British Open and therewith joined Sarazen, Hogan, and Player as a member of that very exclusive club: golfers who have won all four of the modern major championships.

The 1966 British Open was played at Muirfield, and the importance this made to Nicklaus cannot be overstated. He knew the course well from having played the Walker Cup Match there seven years before; he had happy memories of that occasion; he liked the course, the most American and the least linksy of the top-class British seaside tests, and its well-knit turf was to his taste. It was a good thing that his affection for Muirfield went this deep, because the course he found on his arrival in 1966 was almost unrecognizable as the one he had remembered. Feeling that at 6,887 yards it would play too short for the top professionals, the Championship Committee of the R. & A. decided that the course would have to be made ultra-tight. Some 230 yards from the tee, the fairways were an ample thirty-five yards in width, but from that point forward they gradually narrowed, and some were no more than ten yards wide near the end of the driving zone. After his practice rounds, Nicklaus was persuaded that discretion was the better part of valor: he would use his driver as little as possible, for it was imperative to be on the fairway and not in the rough, an intimidating growth of stalky grass, going to seed, that was at least two feet high in spots and which, as it waved in the wind, called to mind, most disquietingly, not the hard-and-fast glories of Caledonian golf but Vincent Van Gogh's passionate landscapes of southern France.

The Golden Hours of the Golden Bear

At Muirfield, Nicklaus got off well with a par 71 and then added a 68 to lead by a stroke with thirty-six to go. (For the first time, the final thirty-six in the British Open was split into two days of play. The U.S.G.A., with possibly a little subconscious nudge from the wonderful world of television, had instituted this four-day format in our Open the previous year.) Nicklaus can be so awesome when he is playing well, which he continued to do in the third round, that when he reached the turn in even par, his gallery was sure that at any moment he would pop in a couple of birdies and begin to tear the tournament apart. Not at all. For no logical reason, Nicklaus fell into a succession of small but costly mistakes—a misjudged iron here, a wavering putt there. He bogeyed four of the last five holes for a 39 and a 75. Meanwhile, many of the golfers in contention had made hay on the second nine. Rodgers, for one, had come in in 30, Palmer in 32. Instead of a one-man show, it was now a tournament that any one of several players could win. Rodgers was out in front with 210, followed by Nicklaus at 212, Doug Sanders at 213, Palmer and Dave Thomas, of Wales, at 214.

It is a temptation to say that three holes decided the championship. The first was the first. Nicklaus was paired with Rodgers in the last pairing, and whereas Phil bogeyed the first, Jack birdied it by knocking in a 25-footer. Getting back into a tie for the lead this quickly revivified Nicklaus' confidence. He played errorless golf to reach the turn in 33, 3 under par. He started home with a par on the tenth, at which point he led Thomas by three strokes, Rodgers by four, and Sanders by four. (After hooking into the deep rough, Palmer had taken a 7 on the tenth, and now was out of the tournament.) For a moment it looked as though it would be a one-man show after all, but only for a moment. On the eleventh, Jack messed up a birdie putt of seven feet, then jabbed the 2-footer he had left himself wide of the cup. After that bogey, his play took on a discernible jitteriness just as it had on the second nine the day before. His par on the twelfth was a scramble all the way. He bogeyed the thirteenth and fourteenth, and then managed a shaky par on the fifteenth. By this stage, his entire lead had melted away. Thomas, with a brave effort, had finished with a 69 for 283. Sanders, on the eighteenth, needed a par for 283, and got it. It began to look like Lytham all over again. A good par on the short sixteenth helped to steady Nicklaus. Then, knowing that two pars would tie for him and that a birdie and par would win, he went and won the championship on the last two holes.

No other par 5 in the world resembles in basic pattern the seventeenth at Muirfield. Some 528 yards in length, it presents, in this order, a blind tee shot up a mildly rising greenish-brown fairway, a sudden turn of the fairway to the left, the reduction of the width of the fairway about a hundred yards from the green when a bulky, high ridge, cut with bunkers, plunges into it from the right, and, finally, a smallish green set in a hollow and hemmed in by heavy rough. The wind, out of the west, was almost directly behind Nicklaus on the seventeenth this day, and so he changed from the 1-iron he had been playing off the tee to a 3-iron. He hit it—remember, he was playing the small British ball—290 yards down the right-hand side of the fairway. Nicklaus, who measures off every course before the start of a tournament, knew that he was out 290, for his ball finished in line with the front edge of a bunker on the left that he had marked down as being 290 yards out. This meant that he was some 238 yards from the flag, which happened to be positioned close to the center of the green. He took a 5-iron, and aiming it a shade to the left of the flag, made a firm, smooth swing. The shot rose in a high trajectory—a wonderfully well-played shot that held its line as it flew over the bunkered ridge, landed in the narrow channel of fairway five yards before the green, and rolled up eighteen feet from the flag. He putted the ball cautiously to the edge of the cup to make sure of his 4. Now, after that birdie, all he needed to win was to par the last hole, a straightaway 429-yard 4 in which the driving zone is closed in by bunkers on both sides and where the long green is not only bunkered left and right but in front as well. It is a good, tough finishing hole. It runs perpendicular to the seventeenth, and so on this day the wind was coming from the right. That was perfect for Nicklaus, who loves to fade his long irons. Using the wind as a kind of bank to keep the ball on line, he hit two superlative irons, a 1-iron off the tee that split the fairway, then a 3-iron that dropped softly at the back of the green and stopped pin-high twenty-five feet to the right. His approach putt left him a tap-in of a foot. 70-67-75-70—282. In dealing with the 1966 British Open, future historians will no doubt stress the four great irons Nicklaus produced in the clutch on the 71st and 72nd, and they will be right. At the same time they would do well to emphasize Nicklaus' aplomb and wisdom in sticking with his "game plan" even when the situation had turned sour and unnerving. Over the four rounds, he used his driver only seventeen times, his 3-wood thirteen times, and drove with his 1-iron and 3-iron the rest of the way.

There were only a few weeks the following year—1967—when Nicklaus hit the ball as sweetly, as masterly, as he had at Muirfield. Twenty-seven years old that January, the Golden Bear now had five years as a professional behind him. During that period he had won six major championships and established himself, except with the diehard Palmer coteries, as the number-one golfer in the world. However, at exactly this stage in his career, when Nicklaus should have been bursting into full bloom, that tendency to let small faulty movements intrude into his naturally sound swing pattern began to reappear, and he started to play some of the most erratic and least effective golf of his career. There was a particularly bad patch in March that featured a tie for thirty-fourth at Jacksonville followed the next week by a tie for thirty-first at Pensacola. Nicklaus then skipped Greensboro to prepare for the Masters. There, after a 79 in the second round, he failed to make the cut.

What had happened to Jack? There were many different schools of thought. When he was home between tournaments in Lost Tree Village, north of Palm Beach, he seldom if ever practiced, and many people felt that the scrupulous attention he gave to his fishing was not the best way to cure what ailed his golf. Others were of the opinion that, as had happened to Palmer before, he was suffering from trying to do too many things—making television features, writing a daily column and a book, acting as a consultant to a golf architect, playing periodic exhibitions, and attending a slew of conferences with the reps from the several commercial outfits with which he was affiliated. Other people thought it wasn't all that serious: Jack was just going through a slump. What golfer hadn't!

In the spring, after adding a dashing tie for thirty-seventh in the Houston International and a tie for twentieth at the Memphis Open to his mystifying record, he started to hit the ball much better. Now his overriding problem was his putting. The week before the U.S. Open, when he was practicing at Baltusrol with his old friend Deane Beman, he picked up Deane's center-shafted Bull's Eye putter and began stroking the ball better than he had in months. Since Deane wanted to use the club himself, he arranged for a friend to lend Jack a putter that was identical except that the brass blade was painted white to prevent sun glare. The new putter helped, and so did a putting lesson from Gordon Jones, a pro Jack had known back in Ohio, who suggested that Jack use a shorter stroke and hit the ball harder. Baltusrol, by the way, is situated in Springfield, New Jersey, some twenty miles southwest of New York. An old club founded in 1895, it occupies a strip of gently rolling green land at the foot of Baltusrol Mountain. Today it looms as a veritable oasis to the traveler coming from Manhattan, since the drive out involves passing through the Jersey Meadows, the pungent seascape of Port Newark, on Route 22, and such shoulder-to-shoulder eminences of our advancing culture as the Rent-A-Tool Company, the Chez Pompeii Beauty Salon, and the Cheetah Flagship. The 1967 Open was the fifth hosted by Baltusrol but only the second played over the Lower Course designed in 1916 by the gifted Albert W. Tillinghast. (The first was the 1954 Open, won by Ed Furgol.) For this Open the course was in splendid condition, the fairways close cropped, the greens a bit more holding than usual. If there was a weakness, it was that an absence of sunshine had prevented the rough from attaining traditional Open height and thickness. Very low scoring was predicted, and resulted. Nine players broke par, 70, on the opening round. Marty Fleckman, a young amateur from Texas, was low with a 67. Nicklaus had a 71.

Holing a putt of some length not only saves a golfer a precious stroke but also does something else at least equally valuable for him: It gives him an immeasurable lift, and nine times out of ten he hits a fine shot on the next tee and is off and running. In the second round of the Open, Nicklaus, playing the fourth, a scenic 194-yard par 3 on which a pond extends to the edge of a slightly raised green, pulled a 3-iron (which he was trying to play left to right) over the back left corner of the green, and then slid his chip back eleven feet past the pin. Already a stroke over par for the round, he was now on the verge of dropping another, and the way the scores were running he might be out of the tournament before he knew it. He worked hard on that 11-footer and eased it into the middle of the cup. In retrospect, that may have been the critical stroke of the championship. From that point on, despite the ninety-six-degree heat, he played such an immaculate round that, although he wasted four opportunities for birdies from ten feet or less, he still birdied five holes. He was around in 67, and at the halfway mark found himself a single stroke behind the leader, Palmer. This was a championship Palmer wanted to win desperately to make up for his collapse in the Open the year before at Olympic, where he had blown a seven-stroke lead on Casper on the fourth round and a two-stroke lead on him in the playoff. Incidentally, after two rounds at Baltusrol, Casper was only two shots off the pace.

In line with the U.S.G.A.'s system of pairing the first-place and second-place men, Nicklaus and Palmer played together on the third round. They were followed by a large and over-exuberant detachment of Arnie's Army who urged their man on with raucous verbal support. In truth, they had few valid opportunities to cheer, for Arnold and Jack both misguidedly played each other rather than the course, and as a result they both produced such loose golf that neither made a birdie until the seventeenth. At the end of the day, Fleckman, after a second 67, was back in the lead at 209. Nicklaus after a 72, Palmer after a 73, and Casper after a 71 were all at 210. Since Casper had finished earlier in the afternoon than the other two, under the U.S.G.A.'s system of pairing he was placed in the last pairing with Fleckman on Sunday, and Palmer and Nicklaus were paired for the second straight day, just in front of them. On this fourth round Arnie's Army was not only in clamorous voice but came equipped with such psychological warfare equipment as cloth signs reading "Right Here, Jack" which were held up by cadres positioned behind a bunker or a water hazard. (The U.S.G.A. moved quickly to pass a regulation forbidding all such signs at future tournaments.) On that afternoon, there was little to choose between Palmer and Nicklaus from tee to green—they both played really fine golf. (After the first few holes, Casper and young Fleckman were no longer in it.) In his battle with Palmer—their first head-on collision in a major championship since Oakmont—it was Nicklaus' putting that made the difference, just as it had at Oakmont. On the third green he had a 12-foot sidehiller for a birdie that just caught the high corner of the cup on its last rotation. He holed from eighteen feet across the sloping fifth green for another birdie. On the seventh he got down a sliding putt of twenty-four feet, again for a birdie. In the lead by four strokes at the turn, on the in-nine he sank two short birdie putts set up by picture-postcard pitches, and climaxed this staggering display by holing a 22-footer for a concluding birdie on the 72nd. (How often the winner of a tournament, who has putted like an angel, has done it with a new putter he rescued on the eve of the tournament from his mother-in-law's ashcan or his psychiatrist's mobile!) Nicklaus' final putt gave him a 65 for the round—Palmer had a 69—and a four-round total of 275, a stroke lower than the old record low total that Hogan had set at Riviera in 1948.

Baltusrol seemed to clear up whatever had been plaguing Nicklaus. The remainder of the year he finished worse than third in only one tournament and carried off the Western, the Westchester, and the Sahara to again lead the money-winners. He finished second to Roberto De Vicenzo in the British Open and third behind Don January and Don Massengale in the P.G.A. For good measure he won the World Series of Golf and teamed with Palmer to take the Canada Cup in Mexico City.

It had been the Nicklauses' intention to make their permanent home in Columbus and merely to winter in Florida. Jack, however, loved everything about Florida, from the

On the thirteenth green at Baltusrol in the final round of the 1967 U.S. Open, Palmer has just missed his birdie putt, and Nicklaus steps up to try for his birdie, which he holed. Nicklaus' superior putting decided their confrontation.

climate to the incomparable fishing, and in the winter of 1965 he and Barbara rented a house in Lost Tree Village, a charming development that is built around a very good course and that places a decided accent on golf. Don Moe, the hero of the 1930 Walker Cup Match, and Betty Probasco, a first-class golfer from Tennessee, had homes there before the Nicklauses arrived, as did Cary and Edie Middlecoff, who lived in the house just to the right of the Nicklauses' on the shore of Little Lake Worth. Before they realized it, the Nicklauses were year-round Floridians. Jack's idea of bliss was to jump into one of his two boats and go fishing with his children, whom he introduced to the sport when they reached the age of three. In Lost Tree Village, though the first fairway was only a wedge shot from his house, he gave hardly more than a passing thought to golf, and while some people believed that sooner or later his game was bound to suffer unless he kept it tuned through regular practice on his vacations from the tour, in 1967, at any rate, he had turned the most worrisome slump of his life into a triumphant season on the strength of talent alone, and had reaffirmed his position as the finest golfer in the world.

GARY PLAYER
AND
THE OTHER
NEW CHAMPIONS

For quite a number of seasons after he won his last tournament, the 1961 Memphis Open, Cary Middlecoff made it a practice to return to the tour periodically. He did not do this simply for the pleasure of renewing old friendships. He seriously believed that, while winning a tour event was probably now beyond his powers, he could still play well enough to occasionally be a contending force, and, at least, finish in the money. One reason he felt this way was that he could still break par quite regularly on the course at Lost Tree Village, in Florida, where he made his winter home. That course was as long and as testing as many over which P.G.A.-circuit tournaments were held, and Cary felt that if he could shoot 67s and 68s at Lost Tree, there was no reason why he couldn't do the same on the tour. It didn't work out that way. On the tour it was a rare day when he scored as low as 70 or 71, and he had his share of much higher scores. "I don't know what it is," he said to a friend one day after a mediocre round in the Houston International. "Back at Lost Tree I've been playing very good golf. I just can't seem to get my game past the airport."

That statement applies to most golfers, whatever their age or handicap—they cannot get their game past the airport; they can play their best golf only at home. It also applies, in a slightly different way, to the world's best golfers: even in this age of constant international travel, comparatively few of them are able to play golf of the same high calibre in foreign lands as they do in their native country. Palmer, Nicklaus, De Vicenzo, Brewer, and Jacklin are five who have shown the ability to adapt their games to a wide variety of conditions and climes, but the golfer who has undoubtedly confected the most brilliant record for playing well away from home is Gary Player. The South African star won his first two British Opens in Scotland, at Muirfield in 1959 and at Carnoustie in 1968. He won the Piccadilly World Match Play Championship five times in ten years (1965, 1966, 1968, 1971, 1973) over the West Course at Wentworth in England, and, for that matter, he scored his first notable foreign victory in England when he won the 1956 Dunlop tournament at Sunningdale. He has won the three most important American tournaments: the Masters, at the Augusta National, in 1961 and 1974; the Open, at Bellerive, near St. Louis, in 1965; and the P.G.A. twice, at Aronomink, outside Philadelphia, in 1962, and at Oakland Hills in 1972. (As a result, he is one of the four golfers who have captured all of the world's four major championships.) He has won in Spain, taking the individual trophy and teaming with Harold Henning to take the team trophy in the Canada (World) Cup at the Club de Campo in Madrid in 1965. He has won in Egypt, where, on his first trip outside of South Africa, back in 1955, he paused en route to Britain to enter the Egyptian Match Play Championship and beat that old camel-driver, Harold Henning, in the final. Although he has made comparatively few appearances in Japan, he has won there too, leading the field in the tournament that opened the Yomiuri course and also winning the 1972 Japan Air Line Open at the Narashino Country Club, his total of 280 edging out Haruo Yasuda, Toru Nakamura, Lu Liang-huan ("Mr. Lu"), and Peter Thomson by a stroke. He has won in Brazil and he has won in the Philippines. He has flourished mightily in Australia, winning the Australian P.G.A. twice and the Australian Open no less than six times (in 1958, 1962, 1963, 1965, 1969, 1970, and 1974). He has won the Brazilian Open twice. As you might expect, Player has not done too badly at home, either. In fact, although South Africa has produced many capable golfers over the past fifteen years, there would be no South African circuit without Player's presence. In his country he has the status of Palmer and Nicklaus combined, and it is his box-office appeal that makes the tournaments go. He has won just about all the important African events at least once and the South African Open no less than nine times—in 1956, 1960, 1965, 1966, 1967, 1968, 1969, 1972, and 1975. All in all, he has won at least forty tournaments in South Africa. One can understand how the top practitioners of certain games have been able to adjust to the different conditions of different countries. For example, it is not surprising that a number of the very best tennis players have been able to complete the Grand Slam of the Australian, French, Wimbledon, and United States Championships, since the court dimensions are standard and the variations in surfaces and the other influences on play are not all that extreme. Golf, however, because it is the one game played over natural terrain in all kinds of conditions, is perhaps the most difficult of all sports for the traveling competitor to play well. Granting that a South African has to spend a greater portion of his time overseas than golfers who come from countries with a bigger and richer tournament schedule, and which offer lusher subsidiary benefits, the fact that Gary Player has been able to win (and win the significant tournaments) in Asia, Africa, Europe, North America, South America, and Australia stamps him as one of the genuinely great athletes of our age.

Player's accomplishments loom all the more impressive when one reflects that he is a relatively small man—he stands a little over five-seven and weighs about 160 pounds—competing against much bigger men in an era of out-and-out power golf. Nevertheless, it is only the super-long hitters like Nicklaus, Palmer, and Tom Weiskopf who crack the ball a good distance past Player. He is exceedingly strong, having realized many years ago that he would have to compensate for his size by building up his body. He has since devoted large periods of each day to lifting weights, or doing hundreds of pushups, or running in place for hundreds of strides, or executing whatever exercise he was dedicated to that particular season. Whether he is at his country farm outside Johannesburg or at his ranch at Magoembas Kloof in the beautiful rolling country 250 miles north of Johannesburg, he loves to take on hard physical chores, such as mending gates and fences, repairing roads, rebuilding barns and other shelters. His unrelenting search for sinew and stamina has also made him a health food devotee. His passions and discoveries run their courses. At one period he was sure that the master key to fitness was a regular intake of honey, but at other times he has been equally sold on the merits of wheat germ, fruits, raisins, nuts, black bread, and bananas. (Upon registering at their hotel in San Francisco for the 1966 Open, the members of the press received, along with their room keys, a bunch of bananas enclosed in a plastic practice bag, compliments of Gary Player and the Chiquita Banana people.)

While part of Player's strength results from his almost fanatical attention to the old *mens sana in corpore sano* approach, it is also due in equal measure to the fact that he has a fundamentally sound swing and is one of the game's most precise strikers of the ball. It wasn't always that way. Some people have helped Gary along the line, but he has had to do the bulk of the work himself. When he first appeared in international competition in the middle 1950s, the swing he had put together was extremely awkward-looking if not downright ugly. He had corrected his original four-knuckle hooker's grip but the linkage between his hands and his arms was stiff and strained. He used a wide stance—much wider than the width of his shoulders—for he had the mistaken idea that this would give him a firmer base to hit from. On his backswing he started the club back well but then rolled it onto a very flat plane. On the downswing he had a tendency to jump at the ball with a hooker's hand action because of his chronic concern for getting it out the maximum distance. As a result, he hit the ball left, right, and straight, impartially. In spite of all these transgressions, there was something strangely promising about Player. He had a supple body and his hand action was very "live," and if he was in a correct position when he arrived at the ball, he hit it far and well. For all of his errors, he could get the ball around the course. (He had two rounds of 64 in winning his first big event in England in 1956.) He was skilled at recovering from all kinds of trouble—practice never hurts—and he was excellent around the green. He had great touch on his chips and little pitches, and he stroked the ball so squarely on his putts that the rotation he got was almost as perfect as that of Bobby Locke, the hero of every South African golfer, who had started to pass his peak just as Player was coming up. Player has always been a formidable putter, but there are a number of golf scholars who think he has never since been quite as effective on the greens as he was as a very young man. At that time he putted almost all arms and shoulders, with hardly a suspicion of wrist action. This sounds like an ungainly method, but it wasn't, not the way Player managed it. Pleasantly relaxed as he addressed the ball, his alignment was so correct that it was no wonder that he struck the ball perfectly in the center of his blade on stroke after stroke and holed putt after putt. One more thing. In those days when he was somehow scoring in the low 70s with a low-80s swing, several astute judges of golf predicted a huge future for Player, because they sensed that he had the essence of golf in him and, furthermore, was the most determined young man to come along in years.

When Player made his first visits to the States in 1957 to play in the Masters and eight tournaments on the P.G.A. tour, he was twenty-one but hardly looked his age. He had a full, round face, dark brown hair neatly swept back, and large, luminous brown eyes. He brought to mind the boyish members of vocal trios featured by dance bands in the Twenties who stepped forward in brightly striped blazers and sang "Collegiate" or "Ten Little Miles from Town." As he grew older his features gained definition and character, but maturity did not dim the effect of those large brown eyes. They are inherited from Gary's great-grandmother, perhaps the most memorable of his ancestors. In the early eighteenth century, her family, French Huguenots, had settled in the Capetown area, and a century or so later, when friction with the British forced the Boers to find new lands to live in, she was in the Great Trek north from Capetown into the territory that is now Transvaal, Orange Free State, and Natal. She married an Englishman, James Power, and they had seven children. "In an era of great marksmen," Gary has remarked of James Power, "he was an outstanding rifle shot and was said to have a great knowledge of country, of the kind of country that it would be safe for wagons to go through . . . All South Africans have this powerful feeling for land, and this has come down through the generations, too. My father had a keen eye. He was very good with a rifle, very good with golf clubs, and had this feeling for the lie of the land . . . I do believe that I have some of it, in relation to golf . . . I certainly have a feeling for the drainage of a golf hole, the sheltering effect of trees, the feel of the surface soil under my spikes and so on."

Gary was born in Lyndhurst, a country town a dozen miles from Johannesburg, the third and youngest child of Muriel and Francis Harry Audley Player. When Gary was just a tot, the Players, who had earlier lived in Johannesburg, moved back to the city again. Mr. Player had been promoted to mine captain and assigned to the Robinson Deep Mine, a gold mine situated in a part of Johannesburg called Booysens, a working-men's district where the Players had lived before their shift to the country. The mining company provided the new mine captain with a house. After their taste of Lyndhurst, which in those days was an idyllic village, none of the Players liked Booysens, a clamorous, dusty suburb where the area around the mine was ringed with high mounds of light brown earth. The member of the family who minded Booysens the most was Mrs. Player. A small woman, a very active mother who found her chief diversion in reading, she had been ill for a long time. She became worse. In 1943, when she was forty-four, she died of cancer after undergoing several operations. Gary was then eight. Mrs. Player's death was a tremendous blow to her husband and three children, and they have ever since felt a deep responsibility to one another. At the time of her death, Ian, the oldest of her three children, was fighting in Italy with the South African Armoured Brigade. A serious, intelligent, tall young man—physically he and his sister Wilma take after their father—Ian had difficulty after the war finding a job he liked, until the opportunity to be a game warden came his way. He was for many years the Chief Game Conservator in Zululand of the Hluhluwe and Umfolozi game reserves, and earned an international reputation for his work in protecting the wildlife in his domain, the white rhino in particular. Now nearing fifty, Ian is still Chief Game Conservator, but presently works out of the main office in Pietermaritzburg, in Natal.

When he was growing up in Johannesburg, Gary attended the King Edward VII School, an outstanding public school. He was not an especially good student but, despite his size, excelled at sports. He was a standout in cricket, Rugby, swimming and diving, and track; he captained the soccer team; and he was awarded the trophy his last year as the school's best all-round athlete. He did not discover golf until he was fifteen, when his father asked him to play a round with him at the Virginia Park course. Mr. Player was a pretty good golfer—at his best about a 2-handicap. To his astonishment, Gary parred the first three holes, a par 3 and two shortish par 4s, and then fell apart. The game fascinated him and he set out to master it. At home he practiced his swing nearly every evening, swatting a rubber mat in the garden. Swinging without hitting a ball could be tedious, so some evenings he went to a nearby Rugby field and practiced hitting 8-iron shots through the goal posts. He played his rounds on the weekends. Then he made the step that was to change his whole life. He began to play steadily at Virginia Park. The professional there, Jock Verwey, had a son, Bob, and a pretty daughter, Vivienne, who were about Gary's age. The fact that Gary grew very fond of Vivienne may have had something to do with his zeal for golf, but, in any event, the three of them played regular matches. Each would put a shilling into the kitty at the start of the round, and the first one who broke 50 for nine holes—that day, the next day, or the next week—won it all. The kids improved rapidly, and breaking 50 soon was no challenge at all. As a matter of fact, after sixteen months at Virginia Park, Gary had made himself into a scratch player. When he finished his schooling, he went to work as an assistant to Jock Verwey and lived with the Verwey family. His salary was twenty-nine pounds (a little over eighty dollars) a month, which he supplemented by giving lessons at five shillings (about seventy cents). Verwey helped his young assistant with his game as much as he could. He changed his hook grip to a proper one, and he got him out of the habit of picking up his club at the start of the backswing. Once, after Gary had lost a match by his sloppy play around and on the greens, Verwey handed Gary his 8-iron and a shag bag of balls and told him to start practicing with that club and his putter until he could regularly get down in two from a hundred yards out. Only then would he give him back the rest of his clubs.

Gary stayed at Virginia Park until 1955, when he became the assistant pro at the

Killarney Golf Club, in Johannesburg. That year, although he had previously won only one tournament, the East Rand Open, and, furthermore, had failed that winter even to qualify for the South African Open, Player, at nineteen, made his first trip to Britain. His purpose was to learn by watching how the best players hit their shots and by studying the best courses to see the type of shots required. He learned enough to win the 1956 South African Open as well as the Dunlop tournament at Sunningdale on his second trip to Britain. At least as important was his fourth-place finish in the British Open. He was coming now. In 1957, on his first visit to the American tour, he picked up a nice third at Greensboro, and in a most commendable performance in the Canada (World) Cup at Kasumigaseki in Japan he tied for second with Sam Snead and Dave Thomas. He felt he was ready to take a crack at the U.S. Open, scheduled in 1958 for Southern Hills in Tulsa. By this time he was earning a respectable amount of prize money, but if he needed a helping hand financially—he had married Vivienne Verwey in 1957 and so his expenses had risen—he could always depend on his friend George Blumberg, a pacific, legato, well-to-do paper products manufacturer who played his golf at Killarney. A shrewd judge of golfers, Blumberg was convinced that Player had the ability and the temperament to become one of the top players in the world, and whenever it was possible, he and his wife Brenda were in Gary's gallery, at home and abroad, urging their young countryman on.

In 1958, when Player made his second visit to the States, he didn't get off to a very propitious start. In his first tournament, the Masters, he failed by a stroke to survive the 36-hole cut. Then he began to play golf. Two weeks after the Masters he won his first American tournament, the Kentucky Derby Open, in which rounds of 68, 68, 69, and 69 gave him a decisive three-stroke margin. A month or so later, in mid-May, he tied for first with Sam Snead in the Greenbrier Invitational, played at Sam's old stamping grounds in West Virginia. Snead won the playoff on the fifth extra hole. Three weeks after that, Player and Snead along with Julius Boros and Johnny McMullin tied for first in the Dallas Open. Snead again took the playoff, birdieing the first extra hole. All in all, in the nine tournaments Player entered between the Masters and the Open, he finished in the top ten in six. American golf fans naturally had come to have considerable respect for the young invader, but not to the degree where they regarded him as a serious threat in the Open. He gave it an awfully good shot, though.

Few Opens have been played under more exhausting conditions than the one in 1958 at Southern Hills. During the heat of the day, the temperature was rarely below eighty-seven and often a lot higher. The humidity was fierce. The gusty wind that blew in from the southwest, mainly on the day of the first round but on and off during the tournament, was a warm, smoky wind. For the first and only time in the history of the Open, the U.S.G.A. permitted certain greens to be syringed while play was in progress, for there was a real danger of losing several of them because of the terrific heat. In addition, the course, which was 6,907 yards long for the Open with par pegged at 70, played hard. It had been given the regular Open treatment. The fairways had been narrowed down a good bit, and the Bermuda grass rough, while not quite as high as an elephant's eye, had been permitted to grow tall and heavy. This created a problem, for when a ball is driven into tall Bermuda grass rough, it sinks to the bottom, and the only sensible course of action is to take a wedge and settle for just punching the ball laterally back onto the fairway. Under the prevalent conditions, it is questionable if any Open winner has ever played finer golf than Tommy Bolt did at Southern Hills. An opening 71 put him in a triple tie for the lead. Another 71 gave him a one-shot lead over the second man, Player. Refusing to be discouraged by a 75 on the first day, Player had rebounded with a marvelous 68, which he topped off by getting home in two on the eighteenth, a monstrous par 4, 468 yards long, where the first half of the tilted fairway runs downhill and the second half then climbs a gradual slope to a two-tiered green. Until Player brought in his 68 no one had broken 70, and the spectators were beginning to wonder if anyone would throughout the tournament. Accordingly, Player was cheered in the spirit of a St. George who had slain a dragon. However, the tournament belonged to Thomas Henry Bolt. There was little doubt of this after that very accomplished shot-maker—only Hogan and Snead among his contemporaries surpassed him for sheer technical artistry—brought in a 69 on Saturday morning to move four shots ahead of Player and three ahead of Littler, the closest man. Tommy held on strong in the afternoon with a 72. As he strutted home over the last four holes, an unprecedented scene took place: between shots Tommy kept up a running conversation with about fifty or sixty of his friendly enemies from the press corps, many of whom hadn't walked on grass in years but, regarding this as a special occasion, had come out to escort their ol' buddy home in his hour of triumph with a mixture of wisecracks, compliments, put-downs, and cheers. Player, after a 73 in the morning, added a 71 to finish second, his 287 placing him four shots behind the winner—a winner who for once was in perfect control of his geyser-like temperament every step of the way.

Among the things that Player showed the golf world at Southern Hills was an extremely good-looking, simplified swing. There is a temptation to make the categorical statement that no golfer has ever changed his swing so drastically for the better in six short months as Player did between December 1957 and June 1958. Now he was all orthodoxy and functional grace. The stance had been narrowed; the grip had been strengthened, the hands and arms firmly fused; he had more of a sitting-down position over the ball, like his hero, Hogan (with whom he had gotten to play a round in the Open); the tempo of his swing was much more uniform; the plane of his swing was not as flat as it had been; his hip action was smoother, and he now kept the upper part of his body over the ball longer during the hit; he followed through well and finished high. In a word, in a few short months he had somehow acquired a modern swing, a fundamentally sound swing that he could build on. How? Player has stated that the single most important factor in learning the correct movements was watching Hogan practice hour after hour. "I was able to make the necessary changes in my style," Player has said, "because I practiced very hard and was never complacent with just scoring well. When you practice hard, you can change things at a very rapid pace when you are young and dedicated."

Player deserved credit in another respect. Local conditions make a South African golfer value hitting the ball straight far more than flighting it enormous distances. He is used to playing on courses on which the ground is hard and the ball gets a good deal of run, and, besides, in the Johannesburg area, six thousand feet above sea level, the ball travels far in the light air anyway. What he wants to avoid is the rough, which is generally scrubby or tangled. He is used to playing to greens that have a base of clay and not of sand, and that, as a result, have little or no "give" when it comes to holding an approach shot. The grass on these greens invariably develops a nap that makes putting very difficult. Accordingly, when a South African golfer goes abroad, he must learn to make many adjustments. In America, where he must switch to the large ball, he must become a more assertive hitter off the tees and he must gain a feel for playing his approach shots right up to the pin on our soft, watered greens. Adjusting to the different demands of British seaside courses constitutes another problem, but Player had also handled this successfully. In the 1958 British Open at Lytham, he finished fourth, as he had at Hoylake two summers before.

In 1959 it was Muirfield's turn to host the British Open. Player, who had enjoyed a somewhat less gleaming spring campaign in America than he had the year before, arrived at Muirfield to begin practice ten days before the start of the Open, for he believed that he was now good enough to win the championship and that careful preparation might just possibly turn the trick. Contributing to his good frame of mind was the arrival of his wife and their first child, Jennifer, just two months old, at the charming Greywalls Hotel, situated just off the course near the tenth tee. The qualifying rounds went well for Player—in those days only the defending champion was exempt from qualifying—but his opening round in the championship was a 75. Finishing in the worst weather of the day, he had gone 4 over par on the last five holes. A par round of 71 on the second day placed him eight shots behind the leader, Fred Bullock, a pro from Prestwick who now operated a driving range there after his old course had been bulldozed away to make room for extending the runways at Prestwick Airport. Bullock, who made only rare appearances on the British tournament circuit, did not seem the sort of golfer who would be able to stand up to the strain of the double round on the final day, Friday. In what was an exceedingly weak field for the Open—this was the year before Palmer inaugurated the annual infusion of the best American players— Flory Van Donck, of Belgium, a seasoned internationalist who had finished second in the British Open in 1956 and had tied for third in 1958, appeared to be the best bet. At 140, he stood only two strokes behind Bullock. On the eve of the final thirty-six, although eight shots behind, Player, in a grimly earnest mood, said to Pat Matthews, an old friend, "Tomorrow you're going to see a small miracle. In fact, you're going to see a large miracle. I'm going to win the British Open." At dinner that night he told George Blumberg the same thing.

A 70 on the third round brought Player to within four strokes of Bullock and Sam King, an old-time Ryder Cupper who had bobbed up with a surprising 68. Van Donck was a stroke behind them. Six other players, including Reid Jack and Dai Rees, were also ahead of Player at the three-quarter mark, and this traffic jam, as much as anything else, convinced him that he would have to go for everything on the final round, that only something like a 66 would win for him. The break he needed came on the fifth (or 59th) hole, a par 5 of some 516 yards, which he eagled when he banged his second shot four feet from the flag. He had a chance now. He kept his momentum going by holing good putts for birdies on the tenth, the thirteenth, and the sixteenth. On the par-5 seventeenth, where he was over the green in two, a poor chip back left him twenty feet short, but he got the putt down. That was a very big stroke. Now if he could get his par on the eighteenth, the 427-yard par 4 long esteemed one of the best finishing holes in the game, he *would* have a 66. He elected to play a left-to-right tee shot, aiming it down the left side of the bunker-bordered fairway. The ball went dead straight and caught a corner of one of the three bunkers on the left. Player's second was a so-so recovery with a 6-iron. His third was another 6-iron that barely made the front part of the long, upsloping green. He took three inglorious putts. A 6. A 68 and not a 66. He had probably thrown the championship away. Player sat by himself for a long while in the locker room, hunched over, close to tears.

In those days, it was not the practice, as it is today, to group the leaders together at the end of the field, and Player, a relatively early starter, faced a two-hour wait before Bullock and Van Donck, the men he had to watch, would be in. Rather than brood to no purpose in the locker room, he went to the Marine Hotel in North Berwick with George Blumberg, and took a cold bath followed by a stiff drink. Blumberg at length persuaded him to return to the course. There they went up to the television room in the Muirfield clubhouse, which faces down the eighteenth, and from there watched Bullock and Van Donck play the last hole. Each needed a birdie 3 to tie Player's 284. Each made a bogey 5. His own 6 had not been fatal after all. Player had won the title that for a South African was the most prized in golf at that time, and perhaps is still regarded so today.

Two years later, in 1961, Player won his second major championship, the Masters. That year he had come to Augusta with the definite feeling that he had a chance to win there. For one thing, he had finished an encouraging eighth in the Masters the year before. He was learning how to handle the course. For another, he had departed from his usual schedule and had played the entire American winter tour, with marked success. He had won two tournaments, and the level of his play had been so high week after week that he was leading the whole parade—including Palmer, who had captured three tournaments—in the matter of prize money won. The 1961 Masters turned out to be a duel between Palmer and Player all the way. From another angle, up to a point, it recalled Muirfield and the '59 British Open: for a while Player thought that he had tossed away the championship by taking a double-bogey at a crucial moment on the last round.

To backtrack a little, Palmer (68-69) and Player (69-68) shared the lead going into the third day. A loose, untidy 73 by Palmer then gave Player, who was around in a well-played 69, a four-stroke bulge. The little South African was employing an exceedingly long swing, but with his gymnast's ability to coordinate intricate body movements, he had everything under control and was slamming his drives almost as far as Palmer or anybody else in the field. The fourth round on Sunday was washed out by driving rains after both men had turned in 35, incredible scoring under the conditions. When they went at it again on Monday, Player, out ahead of Palmer, went to the turn in 34, 2 under par, and still dropped a shot to Palmer. He lost another by bogeying the tenth and now led by only two shots. This is how things stood when he came to the thirteenth (or 67th), the 475-yard par 5, which doglegs sharply to the left about two hundred and fifty yards out from the tee. Here Player got himself in trouble by driving past the angle of the dogleg into the pines in the rough on the right. Prudent tactics were called for—under the circumstances a par 5 would be quite satisfactory—but Player, for some unfathomable reason, took a 2-iron, proceeded to duck-hook the ball across the fairway into the arm of Rae's Creek which parallels that side of the hole, and ended up with a 7 after three-putting the long green. That second, the hooked 2-iron, never got more than eight feet off the ground, and it was such an altogether weird shot that the spectators couldn't tell whether Player had intended to lay up short of the creek, which twists back before the green, or to try to carry the creek. Anyhow, that hole cost him the last two strokes of his lead. It also left him so flustered that he missed a short putt for his par on the fifteenth. That put Palmer in the lead. All that Palmer, that experienced stretch-runner, had to do now was to match par over the five closing holes. It seemed rather irrelevant that Gary, still wobbly but fighting hard, managed to save his par on the 71st by knocking in a 12-footer and then saved his par on the 72nd by getting down in 2 from the right-hand bunker with a splendid explosion shot to six feet and a firm putt.

This is the Masters where Palmer, after a long run of comfortable pars, came to the 72nd needing one more par to win, only to let the whole tournament twist in his hands. His approach to the last green hung out to the right and landed in the bunker, close to the spot where Gary's second had ended up. His bunker shot, hurried a fraction, carried too far, and the ball squirted over the green and down the steep left bank. He rolled his fourth with his putter fifteen feet past the pin. Now he needed to hole the putt for a tie. He missed it on the high side. With this shocking 6—Palmer was the last man one expected to see falter like this in the clutch—he had presented the tournament to Player. It was Palmer and not Player who had lost it with a double-bogey.

Before that Masters, when he was talking with some newspapermen, Gary had remarked that he was sure that God wanted him to win the tournament, and after his victory he declared that he had won only with God's help. Some Americans, who believe that a person's relationship with the Deity is essentially a private matter, were not too keen about Player's statement, but the majority of Americans undoubtedly approved of it. Generally, Player was very well received by American galleries. They appreciated his invariable politeness and liked the seriousness he poured into his golf. Indeed, he was far more popular in this country than in Britain, where many thought that his penchant for moralizing and his approach to the game were too intense. He was also disliked there, somewhat unfairly, for having become too American. They objected, for example, to his crewcut and to his adopting as his sartorial signature a playing outfit consisting of black shoes, black trousers, black sports shirt, and a white or black golf cap that was a variation on the baseball cap. They thought that Bobby Locke, with his knickers, his shirt and tie, and his old-fashioned cap, had the right idea about how a South African golfer should dress. (On the occasion of Locke's fourth victory in the British Open in 1957, Henry Longhurst opined that Locke, with his ornate aplomb, could easily have been taken for an archbishop's butler if not for the archbishop himself.) While the British coolness toward Player often seemed unreasonable, he was occasionally guilty of small breaches of taste that he should have known enough to avoid. At the centenary British Open, for instance, when he was the defending champion, Gary showed up one day at the Old Course wearing trousers that had one black leg and one white leg. Even Doug Sanders never went that far.

As golf fans around the globe gradually came to understand, Gary Player is an infinitely more complex person than he often appears to be. He has a definite bent for the mystical, as he first displayed in predicting that a miracle was in the offing in the 1959 British Open. There have been several subsequent occasions when he was visited by intimations of impending success, some of which came to pass. As Americans first learned in connection with the 1961 Masters, religion plays a large part in Gary's life. He reads the Bible daily and has a deep belief in the power of prayer. What throws one off is that this man of exceptional zeal and fervor is one of those rare people who can function on three different levels at the same time. If he has made appearances with Billy Graham's evangelical troupe, he has also stopped the Ed Sullivan television show with his rousing impression of Elvis Presley. An instinctive gentleman, he simultaneously possesses perhaps the most intrinsically theatrical temperament of any golfer since Walter Hagen and is "on" a good percentage of the time. Like Palmer, he has a sixth sense for knowing where every television or motion picture camera is hidden. His flair for dramatizing himself has led him to develop a set of physical exclamation points to punctuate his golf rounds. He is, for example, the inventor of the emphatically thrown punch aimed at the cup into which a long or important putt of his has just fallen—a gesture that has now become standard with most members of the tour. His explanation of why he dresses in black is pure Gary: "Black absorbs the sun's rays better than any other color and, consequently, transmits warmth and strength to the body." With his adeptness at public relations, he can be responsive to the point of corniness in handling certain situations, and this has led people who like him very much to observe wryly (taking their cue from Oscar Levant's famous crack about Hollywood), "With Gary, underneath the fake tinsel lies the real tinsel." These same people also are well aware that under the real tinsel lies a very warm heart. No one questioned Gary's sincerity when, after winning the 1965 U.S. Open, he donated his purse of $25,000 to the U.S.G.A.—$5,000 to be turned over to the cancer fund, his mother having died of that disease, and the rest to be used in assisting the development of junior golf in the United

Gary Player, the most successful golfer ever to invade our shores, togged out in his almost invariable outfit: black sports shirt and black trousers. The cap varied.

States. As he explained it, he wished to show his appreciation for all the wonderful things that his success in this country had brought him.

America has certainly been good to Gary, but it has also subjected him to some very rough moments: the South African government's apartheid policy has understandably displeased and angered many Americans, and a few individuals have taken it upon themselves to make life miserable for Player when he is competing in a tournament by yelling at him when he is in the act of playing a shot, by splashing soft drinks over him, and by other such disturbing actions. He has received letters and phone calls threatening his life, and has often had to be protected by a police guard during tournament rounds. He has kept on playing and sometimes, somehow, brilliantly. Great concentration, yes, but more than that—great courage. Player's civilized reaction to this hostility was to see to it that the South African government invited Lee Elder, the best black golfer in America, to be its guest during the 1972 tournament season. Elder played in one tournament, the South African P.G.A. "The thing that sticks in my mind," Player recalls, "is that when Lee walked onto that first tee—I was paired with him the first two rounds—everybody gave him a standing ovation. He played very well and proved, all in all, to be a great ambassador for America." Player and Elder also met in a special exhibition match in which Elder birdied the last two holes to halve an exciting duel.

Under the management of Mark McCormack, Player has made well over a million dollars. Unlike most persons in his bracket, he is capable of spontaneous favors, financial and otherwise, to his friends. He loves the limelight in small doses, he has become one of the most sophisticated travelers in the world, he still relishes the challenge of tournament golf, but he is never as fundamentally happy as he is when he is home with his wife and their children—there are six now: Jennifer, Mark, Wayne, Michelle, Theresa, and Amanda Lee—on his beautiful farm, raising thoroughbred race horses. The farm, on the outskirts of Johannesburg, covers a hundred acres, and the main house is called Zonnehoeve, which in Dutch means "Place in the Sun." Thirteen thousand feet square, the house has a grass roof, and each window and each fringed door faces a paddock, so that the family can look out and see the horses in that paddock—that was how the house was designed. At the Johannesburg farm, there are thirty-five stables for the race horses. They train them there, but the horses are bred at the Players' ranch, Magoembas Kloof, in the mountains north of Johannesburg. At Zonnehoeve, in addition to their horses, the Players have five dogs, a hundred pigeons, and a parrot.

Gary Player has done quite a job with his life.

In the summer of 1962, Player won his third major championship, our P.G.A., at the Aronomink Golf Club in the Philadelphia area. He had had a curiously uneven season. On our winter tour he had been no great shakes, but he had perked up at the Masters, where the tall upland pines and the ardent galleries seemed to have the same bracing effect on him they did on Palmer. A 67 followed by three 71s put him in a triple tie with Palmer and Finsterwald, but in the playoff Arnold was too much for him, leaving him well behind with one of his most Palmerian dashes—a 31 on the second nine. (Year in and year out, with few exceptions, Player was never far off the pace at Augusta. Beginning in 1963, over the next ten years he finished tied for fifth, tied for fifth, tied for second, tied for twenty-eighth, tied for sixth, tied for seventh, tied for thirty-second, third, tied for sixth, and tied for tenth—not bad on a course on which a very big hitter has a decided advantage.)

The British Open at Troon in July 1962 had seen Palmer at his best and Player at his worst. Arnold set a new record score for the championship, and Player failed to qualify for the last two rounds. He was playing so wretchedly that the whole idea of chasing back across the Atlantic to compete in the P.G.A. the next week seemed inane, but from the moment he arrived at Aronomink, not a noble test but just a nice old Donald Ross layout in a sylvan setting, his attitude changed completely and his golf game snapped back. This frequently happens when a man takes to a course. On his practice rounds Player noted that on a good many of the holes the fairway bunkering repeated the same pattern: there would be several large bunkers along the right, and then farther along in the driving zone there would be a large bunker on the left. Throughout the tournament he hit the fairways consistently by driving with his 4-wood and playing for a controlled hook. The draw on the ball swung his tee shots away from the bunkers on the right, and by using a 4-wood he didn't get the ball out far enough to reach the bunker on the left. After rounds of 72, 67, and 69, he was out in front, and on the last round he had just enough left to hold off a stirring rush by Bob Goalby. Muttering an incessant stream of encouragement to himself, Goalby birdied the 68th and 70th to draw within a stroke of the leader. On the last two holes Player held him off with hard-working pars, getting down in 2 from thirty-five feet on the subtly contoured home green. It had been neither a dramatic tournament nor a shining triumph, but a win is a win is a win, and it did a lot for Player. Mark McCormack, who managed the trio, began to publicize Palmer, Nicklaus, and Player as "The Big Three" and, among other things, to book them for exhibitions and television series around the world.

In golf, today's canny move can turn into tomorrow's costly weakness. Having succeeded so handsomely at Aronomink driving with his 4-wood and hooking it in, during several tournaments the next two seasons Player reverted to this tactic when he thought it suited certain courses. Before he realized it, by mid-1964 he had fallen into the habit of playing all of his full shots for a good bit of draw. (That is a very different thing from having your shots fall in slightly from the left or the right, an absolutely straight golf shot being almost as rare a phenomenon as Halley's comet.) As anyone knows who has been in the position of playing for some draw on every shot, it can be ruinous: you never know how far to the left the ball will move. Half the time when your plan is to aim for the trap to the right of the green and draw the ball into the flag, the draw doesn't take; and half the time when your plan is to aim right for the flag and block out your draw, something goes awry and you hook the ball wildly into the trap on the left. Forgetting about Bobby Locke, who was an exception to just about every rule, no golfer can expect to play championship golf if he is a chronic hooker.

What with his exceptional skill on and around the greens—just about everyone was now agreed that he was the best bunker player in the world—Player did not have a bad season at all in 1964, but after he had been beaten soundly (8 and 6) by Palmer in their semi-final match that autumn in the first Piccadilly World Match Play Championship, he knew that something had to be done. Driving with his 3-wood and playing for draw, he had sometimes found himself forty or fifty yards behind Palmer, who was using his driver, and he did not need to be told that no golfer could give an opponent of Palmer's caliber such an advantage and hope to stay with him. Player resolved there and then to junk his right-to-left hitting action. He spent the winter rebuilding his swing so that, except in special situations, he would be firing straight at the target on all his shots. It paid off for him. One big reason he won the United States Open the following June was that he did not hook one drive during the seventy-two holes of the championship proper; the only drives he hooked in the playoff were purposely played that way for strategic considerations.

The scene of that 1965 Open was the Bellerive Country Club, near St. Louis. A relatively new course designed by Robert Trent Jones and featuring the vast, weaving Cecil B. DeMille greens that are one of Jones' trademarks, Bellerive, with a par of 70, was stretched to 7,191 yards for the championship. This made it the longest course in the history of the U.S. Open and perhaps accounted for the fact that Nicklaus and Palmer, two of the biggest hitters, were heavy favorites to win. Palmer, with a pair of 76s, didn't even make the cut. Nicklaus, with a 78 and a 72, just sneaked in, but his presence was not felt. This was a case of Jack's simply playing rather mediocre golf, for he had prepared diligently for the event. He and Gary had arrived together at Bellerive the week before the Open and had played eight full rounds plus another nine holes for good measure. Gary, besides pacing off the distance to the greens from various points on the fairways where he would be likely to be playing his approaches, went to the trouble of sketching the undulations of every green on a pad, the better to study them in the evenings. Abrim with confidence and striking the ball meticulously, he was off with two 70s, which gave him a one-stroke lead over Kel Nagle and Mason Rudolph. A 71 widened his lead to two strokes over Nagle and Frank Beard. On the last day—this was the first time the Open was played as a four-day tournament with a single round on each day—Player, with nine holes to go, led Nagle by three strokes. He seemed to have the championship in his pocket.

However, no Player victory in a major event, it appears, is ever achieved easily. There is always some odd turn of events, some flurry, some crunch, that makes it a skittery thing. At Bellerive, Nagle, in the twosome just in front of Player's, lopped two strokes off his lead when he birdied the tenth, a long and difficult par 4, by sinking a ticklish downhill putt of fifteen feet just before Player bogeyed the hole by taking three to get down from the edge. Some fifteen minutes or so later, when Player was about to hit his drive on the twelfth—another long par 4, the action on the distant green is clearly visible from the high elevated tee—a disheartening sight greeted him: Nagle, putting for a birdie from forty feet, struck the ball, watched it roll for the cup, and then flung his arms toward the sky. He had holed it! Here Player showed his fiber. He split the fairway with a long, stinging drive, punched a 6-iron fifteen feet past the pin, and then holed the putt to recapture his lead. A half hour later, after Nagle had gotten into trouble on the fifteenth and taken a double-bogey, Player's lead was back to three strokes, and once again it looked as if the championship was surely his. Not at all. The sixteenth, a 218-yard par 3, was the critical hole. Player went with a 4-wood. It wasn't hit quite solidly enough, and the ball buried itself in the bunker cut into the front bank of the elevated green. He blasted out fourteen feet past the pin, but when he walked off the green only moments later, he had lost all three strokes of his lead: while he was taking three putts (and finally missing a 2-footer), Nagle was birdieing the par-5 seventeenth. Just like that—a new tournament. Nagle finished with a good par. Player, preserving his composure, just missed holing an 8-footer for a birdie on the seventeenth, and then parred the home hole after planting a handsome 5-iron approach twenty feet from the hole. He had not gone boldly for the birdie on his putt but had played for a tie, thinking that at twenty-nine he would carry into the playoff a greater physical reserve

Player at the Bellerive Country Club, outside St. Louis, where he won the U.S. Open in 1965 after a playoff with Kel Nagle of Australia. Throughout the tournament, held on the longest Open course in history, the little South African was as steady as a rock. He followed rounds of 70-70-71-71 with another 71 in the playoff.

than Nagle, who, although he didn't appear to be, was forty-four. (As Jim Murray of the Los Angeles *Times* expressed it, Nagle, bronzed and rugged, still looked like the classic Aussie from World War II, the man wearing a beret as he peered from the top of a tank.)

The playoff was all Player. After the ninth, he led by five strokes. Coming to the seventeenth, he still led by five. On the last two holes, he deliberately drove into the left rough, away from the out-of-bounds on the right. The final scores were Player, 71, Nagle, 74. With that victory, Player had completed his Grand Slam of the four major championships.

As the poet has written, always fear the Greeks when they come bearing gifts, or athletes who are gamely carrying on despite some physical disability. In the autumn of that year, 1965, Player, suffering constantly from pains in his left side that were thought to be brought on by pulled muscles but that finally proved to be caused by gout, went off on the greatest tear of his career. First, in Madrid, he and his old friend Harold Henning won the Canada (World) Cup for South Africa. Spain, the runner-up, trailed by eight strokes, the United States by eleven. Player also won the individual trophy, his 281 being three strokes lower than Nicklaus' total.

Moving on to England and Wentworth for the second Piccadilly World Match Play Championship—only eight players are invited—Gary defeated Neil Coles, the British Match Play champion, in his first match and went on to defeat Tony Lema in the semis and Peter Thomson in the final, 5 and 3. (All matches are over thirty-six holes.) His match with Lema was historic. In the morning, after turning in 34, 2 under, Player was 1 up. He lost the eleventh to a par. All square. He also lost the twelfth, thirteenth, fourteenth, fifteenth, sixteenth, and seventeenth, making it seven straight holes he had lost, five of them to birdies. He looked as though he would lose the eighteenth too, but he got down a 15-footer for a half in birdies. Around in 66, Lema was 6 up. After lunch Lema picked up where he had left off, birdieing the 19th to go 7 up. Then Player began to fight back. Birdies on the 20th, 21st (from eight feet), and 22nd (from nine feet) brought him back to 4 down, but he halted his own drive by blowing a 2-footer for a par and a half on the 24th. That would have settled it for most golfers. The next three holes were halved. Lema stood 5 up with nine to play.

Player then mounted another assault. He took the 28th with a par and the 29th with a birdie (from five feet). The 30th was halved. Holes running out now, though—only six left, Player still 3 down. On the 31st, after Lema had curled in a 40-footer to salvage a par 4, Player holed from ten feet for a 3. Halves on the next two holes—2 down and three to play. On the 34th, a narrow drive-and-pitch par 4 veering left through heavy woods, Player usually drove with a 3-wood, the placement of the tee shot being the paramount consideration; but that afternoon, thinking it might possibly put more pressure on Lema, he took his driver instead and really leaned on his tee shot. He hit a hard, low whistler far down the fairway. This bold move may have had some effect on Lema; in any event, he hooked his drive with his 3-wood into trouble, and lost the hole. Now his lead was down to 1 up, two holes to go. On the 35th, an odd, artificial par 5 which is 555 yards long, the fairway slurs to the left three hundred yards or so out and runs past a succession of country houses whose lawns or gardens edge down to the out-of-bounds stakes along the left side of the fairway. Lema, his timing on his fairway woods now conspicuously off, was well short of the green in 2, but he wedged to twelve feet and made the putt. To keep the match alive, Player had to hole from eight feet, and did. The home hole at Wentworth is a par 5, 495 yards long, on which a tournament golfer can get home in two. The second shot has to be accurately played. Tall trees overhang the fairway along the right, and a fairway bunker short of the green patrols the entrance on the left. After a good drive, Lema hooked a scuffy second short of the bunker. Now it was all up to Player. An acknowledged expert with the fairway woods, he settled on a 4-wood for his second. He caught it flush but it was pushed a fraction off the line he wanted. The ball got through the branches at the top of the trees, however, kicked left on landing, and rolled onto the green, ten feet from the pin. Lema's pitch left him with a longish putt which was never in. To win the hole, Player had only to get down in two putts for a 4, which he did. He had squared the match. He had come all the way back from 7 down by birdieing ten of those last seventeen holes.

The emotionally exhausted gallery moved on to the 37th, another shortish par 5 reachable in 2 for the professional golfer. The end came quickly. Lema once again hooked his fairway wood, this time into a bunker before the raised green. Player flew his second safely onto the front part of the green, and then got down in 2 for a winning 4.

On the wings of that definitive demonstration of guts and golf, Player flew to Australia for the Australian Open at Kooyonga in Adelaide, a course about 6,800 yards long. Worn out from his expenditure of nervous energy, and with his left side still bothering him, the last thing he felt like was seventy-two more holes of tournament golf. The best he could do on his opening round was a 62. It would have been lower if he hadn't bungled a couple of shortish putts near the end after turning in 28. He added a 71, another 62, and a final 69 to set a new record total of 264 for the championship.

After 1965—his "golden year," as Gary took to calling it—the edge seemed to come off his golf. Two humdrum seasons followed, during which his game, always subject to streaks, lost some of its old assurance, and the facets of his style that observant fans admired the most were not so steadily present. Instead of making his usual Cotton-sharp contact with the ball, there were weeks when he appeared to waft his irons on the upswing, and they were seldom on target. There were weeks, too, when he tried to hit the ball too hard and had trouble maintaining his balance at impact and at the finish of his swing. His putting declined a bit, though at times it seemed that he was more unlucky than anything else; no other golfer stroked as many firm, uncompromised putts that spun off the rim of the cup. When Player got off to another mediocre start in 1968, the general feeling was that he was probably over the hill. He was only thirty-three, but he had been pushing himself without letup for fifteen years.

Thereupon Player went out and won his second British Open, at Carnoustie. With eighteen to go, Billy Casper, making his strongest bid for a major foreign championship, was in front, a shot ahead of Bob Charles, two ahead of Player, four ahead of Nicklaus.

Holding on at Carnoustie.
On the 69th, Player reacts
as a 10-footer drops for a par.

On a gray day on which the wind off the North Sea became progressively stronger, Casper began with three bogeys on the first five holes and could never make up what he had lost. Player and Nicklaus, paired together just ahead of Casper, knew as they stood on the tee of the long sixth that once again it was anyone's tournament. Nicklaus, after hooking his tee shot out-of-bounds, had to settle for a 6 on the hole, but Player had a birdie 4. This propelled him into a lead that he managed to hold onto by dint of some fancy scrambling and a few superlative shots produced at timely moments. The most valuable of these was the wonderful 4-wood second on the fourteenth, a short par 5, which he flew over the twin bunkers called the Spectacles and onto the green four feet from the pin for an eagle that lengthened his lead over Nicklaus to three strokes. From there on in, with Jack cutting loose with everything he had and playing some colossal shots, it was a matter of holding on grimly for Gary. He matched Jack's par 4 on the fifteenth by getting down in two from a hundred yards out with a wedge pitch and a 10-footer. He dropped a stroke on the sixteenth, a 243-yard par 3 dead into the wind, which he couldn't reach with his driver. He got out of the seventeenth, a tough par 4, with a half in pars when he stroked a 70-foot approach putt over a series of slippery contours and up to the very lip of the cup. One more hole to go, the 525-yard eighteenth, smack into the wind again, coiling twice across the Barry Burn. A safe drive purposely out to the right onto the seventeenth fairway. A half-hit second that landed in the high rough 140 yards from the green. But then a superbly struck 8-iron that covered the flag all the way and finished twenty-five feet from it. That did the trick.

472

Gary Player and the Other New Champions

The power and the over-all fury of Nicklaus' attack down the closing holes is something that the Scots still talk about, but under the tremendous pressure at Carnoustie that afternoon, Player had brought off a few extraordinary shots himself. Yes, he would probably be around for a few more years.

During the dozen years between 1958 (when Palmer scored his first big victory) and 1970, many other championship-class golfers beside Palmer, Nicklaus, and Player performed some extraordinary exploits. They should be mentioned, however briefly.

In the 1959 Masters, after Palmer's triple-bogey on the 66th had turned the tournament into a free-for-all, one man finally took control. Art Wall, the quiet, introspective Pennsylvanian who had established himself as one of the best iron-players and putters on the tour, went birdie, birdie, birdie, par, birdie, birdie over the last six holes to edge out Cary Middlecoff by a shot. For all of the florid sub-par finishes we have been treated to in recent years, no winner has since equaled Wall's feat of birdieing five of the last six holes. He needed every one of those birdies, too, for Middlecoff, who was among the last players to finish, closed in quickly with an eagle on the fifteenth. As it turned out, this was to be Middlecoff's last real bid to add another major title to his two Opens (1949 and 1956) and his one Masters (1955). When he took control of the '55 Masters with a 65 on the second round, Cary, with at least ten thousand spectators ranged along the right-hand side of the thirteenth fairway, climaxed his rush by holing an eagle putt of eighty-six feet, practically the full length of the long green. For sheer volume, the shouts and cheers this putt engendered may never have been equaled at Augusta even by Arnie's leather-lunged Army.

Middlecoff was one of the few Americans in the field in 1957 when Arthur D'Arcy Locke, who had previously carried off the championship in 1949 at Royal St. George's, in 1950 at Troon, and in 1952 at Royal Lytham, won his fourth and final British Open at St. Andrews. Locke had not participated in much tournament golf over the previous few years, and he surprised everyone by leading by a stroke at the end of the first two rounds. Then he really bowled them over by playing a 68 and a 70 on the Friday to win by three shots over Peter Thomson. This is the Open where Locke, after stopping his pitch to the 72nd three feet from the pin, marked his ball either one or two clubheads from that spot so that his coin would not interfere with his fellow competitor's line to the cup. However, it was several minutes after Locke had putted out, holing for his 3, before it dawned on the officials that Locke had forgotten to return his ball to its original position when he replaced it. Whether or not the Championship Committee of the R. & A. technically could have penalized him, in any event it didn't.

Bobby Locke's career as a topflight golfer was ended after he was seriously injured in 1959 in South Africa when his auto collided with a train at a crossing. He still plays well but confines his conquests to minor affairs like the Vermont Open.

Considering the almost satanic personality it projected in 1951 when Hogan won there and "brought it to its knees," Oakland Hills, for some mysterious reason, never came to life when the Open returned there ten years later. On the afternoon of that Open Saturday, Central Casting rushed to the rescue of the moribund championship, and "The Nicest Guy in Golf," Gene Littler, outplayed the field with a 68 and won by a stroke. Littler took the lead when he holed a skiddy birdie putt on the 65th at almost the same moment that Doug Sanders, who had been leading, failed to hole a short putt for his par on the 64th. On that last round, Littler, the picture-swinger whom many had picked to be Hogan's successor but who had never quite lived up to the promise he had shown as an amateur and as a newcomer on the tour, set up his victory by playing one elegant iron after another to the difficult greens.

When pretty swingers of the golf club are mentioned—and, like the timber wolf and the whooping crane, they are an endangered species—Julius Boros, along with Littler, is always among the first players mentioned. As relaxed as a bowl of Jell-O, Julius long ago developed the helpful habit of staying constantly in motion from the moment he addresses the ball until he has hit through the ball. His style is deceptive. He seems to drag the club back almost unconcernedly along the ground, then he slides forward and sweeps the ball away with what appears to be an effortless stroke. Under tournament conditions, he maintains this unhurried, even tempo, and a sangfroid bordering on nonchalance.

While hitters frequently lose their timing after a few big years, swingers last. Boros certainly has. In 1963, eleven years after he had won the U.S. Open at Northwood in Texas—he had subsequently finished in the top five in five Opens—he appeared to be a little too far back to have a real say in the Open being held at The Country Club exactly fifty years after Francis Ouimet had made that corner of Greater Boston hallowed ground. However, Boros birdied the 70th and 71st and posted a 293, nine shots over par but the lowest total in. Arnold Palmer and Jackie Cupit later equaled this figure, but in the rough, windy weather no one beat it. (Cupit had looked like a certain winner when he came to the 71st needing two par 4s for 291, but after driving into a bank of clumpy rough just beyond the rebuilt Vardon Bunker in the angle of the dogleg, he took a 6. His play on the 72nd was just the reverse. Going with a 6-iron on his second after pushing his drive into the bristly rough, he tore the ball out and sent a super shot flying over the bunker before the plateaued green to within fifteen feet of the cup. He just missed the putt, grazing the edge of the cup. History was against him. No one has ever won the Open by sinking a sizable putt on the last green.)

In the three-man playoff, Boros, as tight-lipped and dour as he always is on the course, came up with his best round of the tournament, a 70. Cupit was 73, Palmer was 76. A control player of the Hogan school, Julius hit all but three fairways off the tee, and the ones he missed he didn't miss by much. Most of his irons were right on the flag, and whenever he missed a green, he came up with an expert wedge recovery from the rough hugging the greens. Ever since the 1955 Open, when the U.S.G.A. made a collar of

474

Gene Littler at Oakland Hills, where he won the 1961 Open by a stroke. Seven years earlier, in his first year as a pro, Gene had lost the Open by a stroke.

Behind Julius Boros' longevity lay his superb technique.

rough around the greens a standard part of its preparation of an Open course, it has been incumbent on the members of the field to be able to play a soft little chop shot with the sand-wedge from this greenside rough—a touch shot hit hard enough for the ball to land on the putting surface but gently enough for it to sit down before reaching the rough on the opposite side. Methods vary on just how this somewhat synthetic shot should be played, but, in essence, the technique resembles playing a bunker shot from a half-buried lie—you snap the club into the ground a good inch behind the ball and pop it out.

On the day he won the playoff, Boros, according to the game's leading actuaries, was forty-three years and a hundred and twelve days old. This made him the oldest American ever to win the Open but not the oldest of all Open winners. That distinction still belonged (and belongs) to Ted Ray, who was forty-three years and a hundred and thirty-eight days old when he showed the way at Inverness in 1920. However, when he carried off the 1968 P.G.A. Championship, Boros, then forty-eight, became that tournament's oldest winner, and there wasn't an asterisk in sight.

Of all the players of this period who had failed to win one of the big championships, the man whom golf fans felt most sympathetic toward was Ken Venturi. Where the even-numbered years had come to presage dramatic success for Palmer in the Masters, for Venturi they had brought heartbreaking defeats in that tournament. In 1956, when he was still an amateur recently returned from a tour of duty with the U.S. Army in Germany, the high-strung young Californian had decisively outplayed the field over the first three rounds at Augusta only to let his four-stroke lead slip away in the tricky winds on the last day and to lose eventually by one shot. In 1958, paired with Palmer, the pacemaker, on the last round, he had moved to within one stroke of the lead, but the delays and distraction occasioned by the embedded ball incident involving Palmer on the twelfth seemed to affect Ken's concentration far more than they did Arnold's. He took three putts on the fourteenth, fifteenth, and sixteenth, and, largely because of these lapses, finished two shots behind the winner. Then, in 1960, he suffered his cruelest blow at Augusta. On the opening round, after turning in 31, he suddenly got an attack of the shakes, and pulling irons, stubbing chips, and steering putts, staggered home in 42. The next day he silenced that group of critics who were declaiming once again that there was a weakness somewhere in Venturi's makeup and that he would always find a way to lose: he shot an errorless 69. He continued his determined play with a 72 and a 70 for 282, the lowest total in. It looked as if Ken had finally made it—until Palmer birdied the 71st and 72nd to nip him by a stroke. Bob Jones spoke for everyone when he said to Venturi at the presentation ceremony, "It is a very great pleasure to present to you the runner-up medal, and Lord knows it ought to be a lot more."

After that third disappointment in the Masters, something seemed to go out of Venturi. The quality of his golf steadily declined. In 1961, 1962, and 1963, he was, to be sure, hounded by a succession of physical ailments, ranging from a bad back to walking pneumonia, but even when he was feeling fit he bore little resemblance to the dazzling young shot-maker of the 1950s. His confidence was completely gone. In some way, this may have explained why Venturi appeared to have no idea that his old swing had disappeared almost totally and that his present swing was an anthology of bad faults: an exaggerated crouch at address; a hurried backswing; a loop at the top; a tendency to bring the club into the ball from the outside in and to cut across it. After 1960 he never came close to winning a tournament, and each year he collected less prize money, dropping to $3,848 in 1963. In the spring of 1964, however, he began to find his way back. In the Thunderbird Classic in early June, he tied for third, and the next week—the week before the U.S. Open—he tied for sixth in the Buick Open. The money helped, but the big thing was that he was setting up at the ball and smacking his shots like the old Venturi. He was not all the way back yet—he was still making some wild errors, and his putting stroke was flabby—but he was at least, and at last, on the right path.

Congressional, outside the nation's capitol, had gone through a couple of facelifts to ready itself for the 1964 Open. It measured over 7,000 yards for the championship and played harder than it was expected to. There was an awful lot of grain in the greens, a blend of Arlington and Congressional Bent, and the weather was blazing hot. Venturi got off with a 72, two strokes over par. He could have been a lot higher, for he played a number of holes loosely. He topped one bunker shot cold, fluffed another bunker shot completely, and on one hole where he heeled his drive into the rough, he didn't even get his wedge recovery back onto the fairway. On his second round he played much better golf en route to a 70. He sank some bothersome putts early in this round, which did his morale no end of good, and he was ripping into his irons with obvious authority. At 142, he was, technically, in contention—one shot behind Bill Collins, four behind Palmer, and five behind the leader, Tommy Jacobs, who had played a stunning 64 on the second day. Nevertheless, not even Venturi's most faithful supporters believed that, after all he had gone through, he would have the fire, the composure, and the shots to be a force in the winning and losing of the tournament.

The first surprise of the long, scorching double round on Saturday was Palmer's rocky start. Shooting overaggressively for the pins, he missed the first five greens. He hit the sixth, but then three-putted it to fall four shots behind Jacobs, his playing partner, who was moving along placidly and well. At this point, Venturi, playing with Raymond Floyd two pairs ahead, entered the picture by holing for a birdie on the eighth, his fourth birdie of the round. He had actually overtaken and passed Palmer. He kept on going. On the ninth, the Ravine Hole, a par-5 599 yards long, he laid up his second, a 1-iron, short of the ravine that begins its steep descent about 110 yards before the small green. He punched his third, a wedge, eight feet from the pin, and made the putt. Out in 30, 5 under par. On the twelfth, 188 yards, he hit his best iron of the morning—a full-blooded 4-iron that stopped hole-high sixteen feet to the left. He played the sidehill putt to break three inches, and it fell into the middle of the cup. That birdie put Venturi 6 under for the round, 4 under for the tournament. A nearby scoreboard carried the news that Jacobs had bogeyed both the eighth and the ninth; now he was only 3 under for the distance. It was hard to believe, but it was a fact: Venturi was leading the Open.

Venturi did not stay in front very long. Jacobs, mustering some fine attacking shots, played the second nine in 34, one stroke under par, to bring in a 70 for a fifty-four-hole total of 206. Venturi, after a 36 in for a 66, stood at 208. Near the end of his round he had wavered discernibly, missing a putt of eighteen inches on the seventeenth and one of thirty inches on the eighteenth, both for pars. During the luncheon interval, it was announced that Venturi had been near collapse from the heat on the last five holes. On the advice of a doctor, he spent the bulk of the fifty-minute interval resting. He drank some tea but ate no solid food. Then he took some salt tablets and headed for the first tee accompanied by the doctor, who walked the last round with him.

The final round had hardly started for Venturi when a double-bogey by Jacobs up ahead on the short second boosted Ken back into a tie for the lead. Drawn and pale, Venturi was walking slowly on stiff old man's legs, but he was hitting the ball with astonishing sharpness. After parring seven of the first eight holes, he came to the ninth, the 599-yard Ravine Hole, still tied for the lead with Jacobs. Here, after a satisfactory drive, he hit a perfect second, a buzzing 1-iron that hopped to within five yards of the edge of the ravine. He followed this with a wedge that spun itself dead nine feet past the pin. Faced with a delicate downhill putt, he played it just right: the ball caught the high corner of the cup and twisted in. With this beautifully engineered birdie, he had regained the undisputed lead, and, as it turned out, he not only held on to it the rest of the way but also widened it to four strokes.

The sun was beating down furiously all this while. On the fourteenth, where he had started to wobble in the morning, Venturi's slow walk decelerated into a painful trudge, and his head began to droop. He hung on tenaciously, though, and while he hit

His face lit with happiness and lined with fatigue, Ken Venturi has let his putter fall to the ground on the 72nd green after sinking his final putt in the 1964 Open. Once the most brilliant prospect in American golf, Venturi went into a terrifying three-year slump from which he extricated himself only weeks before the Open.

at least one very tired shot on each hole after that, some fortunate bounces and his own tidy work around the greens saw him safely through to the eighteenth, a long par 4 that slopes gradually downhill to a peninsula green projecting into a large pond. He needed only a 7 there to win. His tee shot was weak but straight. He blocked out his 5-iron approach to the right, away from the water, and the ball ended up in a bunker about forty yards from the pin. He played a much braver recovery than he had to—a daring floating wedge shot that sat down ten feet from the cup. He had been applauded all the way down the eighteenth hole, and now as he walked onto the green, his ashen face taut with fatigue and yet radiant with pride and happiness, the applause started again and slowly grew into a tumultuous ovation. It stopped when he reached his ball. He holed the putt. He had done it. He threw his hands in the air and exclaimed in ecstasy and disbelief, "I've won the Open." The most dramatic and moving championship since 1913, when Ouimet had beaten Vardon and Ray, was over.

In the 1950s life was made simpler for young men who aspired to become touring professionals. The time had arrived when more than a few American colleges had decided that having a winning golf team gave them desirable publicity and a cultivated image, and, as a consequence, promising golfers were recruited and given golf scholarships. At college these young men picked up a good deal of knowledge from daily practice sessions and from matches against students attending other "golf colleges." When they graduated, a fair percentage of them were able to make the jump directly from the campus to the tour and to enjoy considerable success without having to spend several years in the boondocks going through a gray, wearisome apprenticeship.

Others had to make it the hard way. One of these was Tony Lema. He was born and grew up in the workingmen's section of Oakland, California. His father had died when Tony was three, and so the four children had to pitch in and help their mother meet the family's bills. At twelve, Tony began to caddy at the Lake Chabot municipal course. He started to play the game and became crazy about it. In the summers, in order to play a round or two every day, he switched to working the night shift at the local food canneries.

After his graduation from high school, Lema, with no better options in view, joined the Marines. He spent the last eleven months of his two-year hitch in Korea—the war was over—as an observer in the artillery corps. Upon receiving his discharge at Camp Pendleton in 1955, he was driving home in his second-hand car, glumly accepting the prospect of returning to work in the canneries, when he learned from an old golfing friend, who was now a policeman in Heyward and had stopped Lema for speeding as he went through that town, that John Geersten, the pro at the San Francisco Golf Club, was looking for an assistant. Lema got the job. The San Francisco Golf Club has a very top-drawer membership, and it was there that Lema, a tall, slim, good-looking young man of sensibility and taste, acquired some of the polish that stood him to good advantage when he became "Champagne Tony," the bon vivant who sent a case of Moet & Chandon to the press tent whenever he won a tournament. Lema qualified for the U.S. Open in 1956, won the small Imperial Valley tournament (first prize: $1,000) in 1957, became the pro at a nine-hole municipal course in Elko, Nevada, where one of the rich, regular visitors agreed to bankroll him on the tour, did nothing much to speak of in the tournaments in 1958, 1959, or 1960, sparkled momentarily on the Caribbean Tour the next winter, broke through and won a couple of tournaments late in 1962, and at

Tony Lema—a lyrical swinger, an accomplished shot-maker, and a sturdy competitor.

length arrived in 1963, when he finished second in his first Masters and played a strong
Open at The Country Club in Brookline. In the opinion of many men who knew their
golf, Lema was the finest stylist of the Sixties, a solid technician with an inborn
gracefulness. Jack Nicklaus, one of his admirers, especially liked the way Lema never
just slammed the ball for yardage but, with his intuitive feel for the clubhead, brought it
into and through the ball with fluid precision. As Lema himself once explained it, he
worked on keeping his right shoulder moving under his head as he swung through the
ball, and he also emphasized extending his hands through the ball as far as possible.

In 1964 Lema won the British Open under the most unlikely circumstances. The
week before he had played in, and won, the Cleveland Open. The night the tournament
ended, he had flown to Scotland and then gone on to St. Andrews, arriving on Monday
evening. On Tuesday, he was able to get in only one round plus an extra ten holes of
practice on the Old Course before the Open began the next day. By all rights, since the
Old Course takes so long to get to know, he should have floundered around it misreading
the greens, visiting Hill and Hell and many of the other frightening bunkers, and
spending a little time in the gorse for good measure. On the first day, when it blew a
gale, Lema, with the assistance of his caddy, Tip Anderson, who is excellent with

Americans, got around in 73. On the second day, when conditions weren't much better, he had a 68, tacking his way around the Old Course as if he had grown up on it. The weather turned clement and bright for the last day. Nicklaus, the man Lema had to watch most closely, played a 66 in the morning and a 68 in the afternoon, taking the Old Course apart as no one had ever done before. This spectacular irreverence didn't quite accomplish all that Nicklaus had hoped it might, for Lema finished with two fastidious rounds, a 68 and a 70, to win by the comfortable margin of five strokes. The audacity of the man!

Two years after his storybook triumph at St. Andrews, Tony Lema died in the crash of a private plane the night of the conclusion of the 1966 P.G.A. It had taken him a long while to realize what a splendid golfer he was, and he was gone well before he had fulfilled his vast potential. It was a mild comfort to know that this attractive young man had won one of the imperishable championships and won it with great élan.

When he defended his British Open title at Royal Birkdale, Tony Lema, playing almost as well as he had at St. Andrews, was in the running until the last few holes when Peter Thomson, with whom he was paired, took command and carried off the championship. For Thomson, of Australia, this, his *fifth* victory in the Open within a span of twelve years, was the sweetest one of all. His four earlier successes—at Birkdale in 1954, at St. Andrews in 1955, at Hoylake in 1956, and at Lytham in 1958—had been registered before the best American players had begun to come over each summer for the British Open, and, as a result, there had been a tendency among many American fans to dismiss Thomson's triumphs as nothing special, having been scored over inferior fields. That could not be said about the 1965 Open. At Birkdale he had outplayed the full American brigade—Palmer, Nicklaus, Lema, *et al*.

Peter Thomson's story is, in a way, different from most golfers'. His first goal was to be a topnotch chemist. He won three scholarships to technical schools in his native city of Melbourne, studied applied chemistry, and worked as a rubber technologist for a major sporting goods company. Playing golf as an amateur during this period, Thomson, a sturdily built young man of medium height, found that he could keep pace with the pros in the big tournaments, and at twenty he turned professional. That was in 1949. The next season he was runner-up to Norman Von Nida, his friend and mentor, in the Australian Open. The season after that, he won it and was soon embarked on annual world tours that included visits to the United States and South Africa but which were centered on the British circuit and the British Open. After he had won that championship four times in five years. he was lionized in Britain as a player of the same rare quality as Locke, Cotton, Jones, Hagen, Braid, Vardon, and Taylor. (Queen Elizabeth conferred on him the honor of membership in the Order of the British Empire.) As the greatest golfer ever produced in Australia, he occupied a position of unusual importance in his own country. If you mentioned "Peter" in any conversation, there was no need to explain whom you were referring to; everyone knew, just as a few years later it was sufficient in this country to speak of "Arnie" and let it go at that.

Thomson didn't expect to be made a lot of in the States, but he was naturally hopeful of building a reputation and a following in this, the world's leading golf country. He didn't. For some reason or other, he never got going in America in a way that even began to suggest his exceptional skill. He won only one tournament, the Texas International Open at Brook Hollow, in Dallas, in 1956. He made only one forceful challenge in the U.S. Open, at Oak Hill in 1956, where he led after thirty-six, lost his lead on the 52nd (where a bad bunker shot cost him two strokes), and ultimately finished fourth. Similarly, he also made only one good showing in the Masters: in 1957 he was fifth. After a while he cut down on his visits to the American tour and spent more of his time on other projects, such as trying to get the Australian professional circuit on its feet and helping to develop the Far East or Asian tour from a competitive backwater into a collection of tournaments that now attract strong international fields and pack a surprising financial clout.

Why did Thomson play so disappointingly in the States? Was he, as some people said, an unmatched striker of the small British ball who never learned to play the large American ball? Possibly, but there are many people who play both balls effectively— Nicklaus, for one, De Vicenzo for another, Jacklin for a third. Others pointed out that American courses were not exactly designed for the strongest features of Thomson's game: exceedingly accurate driving and superb middle- and long-iron play on which the swing was smooth and compact and the ball was flighted low, helping it to hold its line in the wind. On the other hand, American golf places a high premium on three phases of golf that, ironically, were not strong parts of Thomson's repertoire: the ability to bash the ball a tremendous distance off the tee; the ability to improvise all kinds of shots with the wedge; and the ability to hole long putts. Thomson sometimes found himself in the position of hitting more fairways and greens in one round than people who outscored him hit in two rounds.

An intelligent, thoughtful, well-read man with a mind of his own and the stubbornness that usually accompanies this trait, Thomson is quite a different kind of person from the average American professional. This is one of the reasons why he has spent less time in the States in the last dozen years than many of us would have wished, but the truth of the matter is that this has been due to an unhappy combination of circumstances: his preference for the British approach to golf and sports in general, the rankling memory of his failure to do himself justice in our tournaments, and the wide variety of interests he pursues, to name just a few. He is still winning tournaments. For example, in 1967 he won both the Australian Open and the Australian P.G.A. In 1972 he won the Australian Open again, a mere twenty-one years after his first victory in that event. It takes a real player to do that.

The one statistic that lingered on after the 1959 U.S. Open at Winged Foot was that the winner, William Earl Casper, Jr., required only 114 putts. To break that down further, Billy took twenty-eight putts on his first round, a 71; thirty-one on his second, a 68, by far his best-played round; twenty-seven on his third, a 69; and twenty-eight on his fourth, a 72, on which he three-putted the 64th green, the first and only time he committed that delinquency during the championship. From the second round on, Casper, a friendly, heavy-set native of San Diego who in 1959 weighed about 215 pounds, was clearly the man to beat, and though his driving was inconsistent, he played some very useful irons when it counted, and his putting did the rest. (Golfers who have a gift for putting come to resent its being mentioned—the implication, at least in their eyes, being that it is the only thing they can do. They never quite understand the huge difference that being a good putter makes, and, like pretty girls, they tend to take their good fortune for granted.)

When he won the 1959 Open, Casper, at twenty-seven, was in his fifth season as a touring professional. He was well on his way to establishing himself as one of the best and steadiest players in the country. Beginning in 1956, he was among the ten top money-winners fourteen times over the next fifteen years, and there was a stretch in which he won the Vardon Trophy (for the lowest scoring average per round) five times in nine years. Casper kept working on his swing—from the outset he had fine natural hand action—and in time became an excellent driver with a very smooth execution. He could both fade and draw his irons, and the one trouble he ran into here was that his long irons were flighted so low that occasionally he had difficulty stopping them on small greens. A likable, family-oriented man, on the course he was a very stalwart competitor, hardly the man you wanted to have nipping at your heels. Many people in golf considered him to be in the same class with Palmer, Nicklaus, and Player, and they felt that it would have been much more to the point to speak of "The Big Four" than "The Big Three." On the other hand, the golf public found Casper somewhat on the dull side. On the course he played his shots swiftly and seldom emoted. The most colorful thing about him off the course was his love of fishing. In 1964 he finally became "copy": he went on an anti-allergy diet of exotic foods that dropped his weight from 220 pounds to 180, and whenever he burned up a course it was learned that he had breakfasted that morning on moose cutlet or filet of walrus or something of the kind. Life was moving along well, and Billy had no kicks to register, but in 1966, when he got off to a fast start in the Open at Olympic, in San Francisco, he needed no one to remind him that it was seven full years since he had won a big championship. He was not going to let this chance slip by if he could help it.

The other man involved in what was a two-man Open from the second day on was Arnold Palmer. He had come to Olympic in a most determined mood. It was six years since he had last won the Open. In the intervening years he had twice lost it in a playoff. The previous year he had suffered the indignity of failing to make the cut. He had had enough frustration. It was time to get back on the track and win the big one.

For the 1966 Open, Olympic measured 6,719 yards—nineteen yards longer than eleven years before, when Hogan had made his memorable attempt to win a fifth Open. Nothing much had changed. Par was still 70. There were still nine par 4s between 403 and 461 yards, and they played some twenty yards longer in the moist air off the ocean that filtered down fairways narrowed and elongated like El Greco faces and shut in by stands of eucalyptus, pine, cedar, and cypress. There *was* one difference: the rough was not as high or as thick as in 1955. A considerable test, nevertheless. On the first day, played in gray, damp weather, Palmer was around in 71, Casper in 69. On the second day the skies again were overcast but the air was drier. Palmer had a dazzling round—a 66 that could easily have been several shots lower. For example, he blew putts of under a yard on the last two greens. Casper brought in a scrambling 68, and so, at the halfway mark, they were tied for the lead at 137.

As the two players with the lowest scores, Palmer and Casper, in accordance with a new procedure introduced that year by the U.S.G.A., went out together on Saturday, the third day, in the last pairing. On the first nine, Casper quite uncharacteristically sprayed his drives all over the place. Palmer, on the other hand, was off with a controlled rush. As he viewed it, the secret to scoring well at Olympic was to get by the first five holes in good shape. On this round, he was 2 under par at the end of five, birdieing the long first and nailing another on the fifth, where he ran in a 25-foot putt. (Has there ever been another golfer who holed half as many 20- and 25-footers as Palmer?) On this warm, clear day, he looked to be at the very zenith of his powers on the first nine. As you watched the ball glinting white as snow as it caught the sun, it was hard to remember when Palmer had last hit his shots so squarely and with such verve. On the in-nine, he cut a number of his tee shots into trouble, which was both uncharacteristic and costly, but, collecting himself, he played the last five holes 2 under for a 70. Casper, with his flair for getting the ball "up and down," managed a 73. Mathematically, he was still very much in the game—only three strokes back—but there wasn't a soul in San Francisco who would have bet against Palmer.

On Sunday, Palmer and Casper, holding the two lowest totals, were paired again. Once more Palmer swept aggressively to the turn—out in 32, three strokes under par. As he walked off the ninth green, he had extended his lead over Casper to seven strokes. Many of the spectators, believing that the 1966 Open was as good as over, began to focus more of their attention on Palmer's chances of breaking Hogan's record Open total of 276 (Riviera, 1948) and Barnes' record nine-stroke margin of victory (Columbia, 1921). On the tenth, Palmer, somewhat carelessly, took three to get down from off the edge of the green and lost a shot to Casper's par. He lost another on the short thirteenth, where he pulled a 4-iron into a hollow of rough. The edge had obviously come off his game, but with only five holes to play, he still led by five. However, on the fifteenth, a fairly routine 150-yard par 3, he dropped two more strokes. With Casper well on with a 7-iron, Palmer, also going with a 7, just missed the right-hand edge of the green and caught the lateral trap. (This error evoked memories of the difficulty Palmer had experienced on the short thirteenth at Oakmont on the final round and in the playoff of the 1962 Open. There, as on the fifteenth at Olympic, it seemed as if he had meant to draw the ball into the flag only to have it fly relatively straight.)

In any event, Palmer bogeyed the fifteenth, and Casper, now putting with much more confidence than at the beginning of the round, birdied it by sinking a hard-to-read 20-footer that broke a good two feet to the right as it neared the cup. With his lead down

The incredible 1966 Open at Olympic. *Left:* After leading by seven shots with nine to play, Arnold Palmer, here on the 71st green, loses the last shot of that lead over Billy Casper by missing his short putt for a par. *Right:* On the 13th green in their playoff, Casper holes from thirty feet to move out in front for the first time.

to three strokes, Palmer, who had been playing his drives during the tournament to slide in from the left, decided on the sixteenth (or 70th), a par 5 of 604 yards that is shaped like a crescent and curves to the left, to go back to his old right-to-left method off the tee. His timing was way off, and he pull-hooked the ball sharply into the trees on the left; it dropped down into the rough about 150 yards from the tee. A 3-iron got snarled in the rough and went nowhere. Then he played a 9-iron back onto the fairway and followed it with a big 3-wood that rolled into the bunker before the green. A sand-shot to four feet, a good putt—he had escaped with a 6. And yet Palmer had dropped two more shots to Casper, who had birdied the hole; Billy's third, a 5-iron, had pulled up thirteen feet from the pin and he had coolly made the putt. On the seventeenth, a long 4 uphill, Palmer drove into the rough on the left again and lost the last of his seemingly impregnable seven-stroke lead when he didn't get his 5½-foot putt for his par up to the cup. He did well not to lose the championship on the eighteenth, a drive-and-pitch 4, for, with Casper down the fairway, Palmer, for the third time in a row, hooked his drive into the rough—into so dense and deep a growth that it didn't seem possible that he could slug the ball halfway to the green eighty yards away. With his colossal strength, he somehow got it onto the back of the green. He was down in two putts, the second a very tricky 4-footer. Casper, thirteen feet from the cup in 2, studied the slippery downhiller he had and decided he would rather take his chances on a playoff. He cozied a cautious third a foot from the hole and tapped in. Casper, a 68 for 278. Palmer, a 71 for 278. Hold onto your periscope.

The playoff had a curious *déja vu* quality, so closely did it repeat the pattern of the previous round. For nine holes Palmer played glorious golf. He turned in 33, and when Casper fluffed a short putt on the ninth—the result was his first three-putt green of the tournament—Palmer led by two strokes. The pivotal hole was the 430-yard eleventh. After Casper's long-iron approach had bounded through a sloping bank of medium-heavy rough along the left edge of the green and had ended up twenty-five feet from the hole, Palmer's almost duplicate approach got hung up in the rough. Palmer proceeded to take three to hole out, missing from six feet after Casper had curled in his long, twisting birdie putt. They stood all even after that, but not for long. On the thirteenth, another aggressive birdie putt by Casper, this one a 30-footer, put him out in front—incidentally, for the first time in the tournament. An hour or so later, when he finished his round with another birdie after sticking a gorgeous wedge a yard from the hole on the eighteenth, Casper had widened his margin to four shots. The scores were 33-40—73 for Palmer and 35-34—69 for the new champion.

The 1966 Open is generally remembered as "the Open Palmer lost," just as the 1961 Masters is remembered as "the Masters Palmer lost." But make no mistake about it—the 1966 Open took a lot of winning. For all of his faltering on the fourth round, Palmer might have avoided defeat had he been up against a less dauntless customer than Casper. How many other golfers in Casper's position on the fourth round would have had the stuff to birdie the fifteenth and the sixteenth? How many others, for that matter, could have hung on as tenaciously as Casper did all week and then have had the stamina to mount such an explosive rally in the playoff? From the seventh hole on that day, whenever Palmer peered ahead to the green, there was Casper's ball sitting on the carpet. Casper did not miss one approach shot over the last twelve holes. There is a lot of bulldog in him and a lot of golf.

The golf world had a great deal to think about after that championship, but the main area of speculation was this: What effect would this bitterly disappointing defeat have on Arnold Palmer?

In the Open the following June, which Nicklaus won at Baltusrol, a strange phenomenon took place: a player no one had ever heard of came in fifth. Moreover, he played four admirably solid rounds: 72, 70, 71, 70. His name was Lee Trevino, and he was a Texan of Mexican descent who was the assistant pro at the Horizon Hills Country Club in El Paso. Why hadn't anyone heard of him before? In interviews with Trevino some facts came out, but there were gaps, too. Evidently he had become a golf pro in 1960, when he was eighteen, but for some reason that was never made clear, he had never been accepted as a member of his local P.G.A., and without a P.G.A. card he couldn't get to play in any of that association's tournaments. He had tried the Mexican Open in 1965 and finished second. The next year he played in the U.S. Open at Olympic, all seventy-two holes, but he was so far back—he tied for fifty-fourth—that no one had been aware of him. At Baltusrol, after he had posted his third good round, many people made it a point to go out and watch this Trevino fellow play a few holes. They saw a chunky, light-brown-skinned young man with a black golf cap over his thick black hair. He was

A complete unknown twelve months before, Lee Trevino ignites his winning dash down the last nine by rolling in a 30-footer on the 65th green in the 1968 U.S. Open. In 1971 this gifted, garrulous Texan won his first British Open and his second U.S. Open. The following year he added his second British Open.

wearing scuba goggles over his eyes. In western Texas, he explained, a golfer had to contend with wind-blown dirt nearly all the time, and he had taken to wearing the goggles and had gotten used to them. Trevino was an amusing guy. He came down the fairway talking a mile a minute, patently relaxed and in high spirits. Periodically he would stop talking to his playing partner or his caddie and, stepping up to his shot with no ceremony, hit it. His swing was very flat but his shots were struck firmly and sharply. He proved to be no four-day wonder, this Trevino. After the Open, in which he won $6,000, he tried his hand on the P.G.A. tour and won over $20,000 during the next few months.

Snead had come up extremely fast, and so had Horton Smith, but no one ever rose to the top with the speed that Trevino did. The very next year, 1968, he won $132,127.32 in prize money and, more important, carried off the U.S. Open at Oak

Hill, in Rochester. From start to finish this Open revolved around three golfers—Trevino, Nicklaus, and Bert Yancey, a tall, blond, studious Floridian who probably knows more about the history of the golf swing than anyone else connected with the game. Yancey's own swing at that time was based on an ultra-smooth, rhythmic hip turn, and as he came flashing through the ball and finished on his left side with his hands high, the golfer he called most to mind was Jones. At Oak Hill he was in front after each of the first three rounds, following a 67 with a 68 and a 70. With the payoff round coming up, he led Trevino (69-68-69) by one stroke and Nicklaus (72-70-70) by seven. Why mention Nicklaus at all if he was so far back? Only because in winning the nine major titles he had collected at this date, Nicklaus had never played better golf from tee to green than he did at Oak Hill. His putting, though, was a disaster. On his opening nine we were given a preview of things to come: he missed five makeable birdie putts, three of them no longer than seven feet, and then three-putted the ninth.

On the fourth round, after an abbreviated rally by Nicklaus had petered out, Yancey, who had been having trouble off the tee on this round, lost the lead to Trevino when he failed to make his pars on the 62nd and 63rd. Some golfers panic at the realization that they are leading a championship. Trevino's reaction was to rap in a 30-foot putt across the 65th green for a birdie and then drop a 22-foot uphill putt for another birdie on the 66th. That just about did it.

When Trevino, clad in vermilion shirt, black trousers, and vermilion socks, came striding up the 67th fairway, the possessor of a four-stroke lead, he walked over to Joe Dey of the U.S.G.A., who was acting as rules observer, and slapping him heartily across the back of his navy-blue blazer, told him, "I'm just trying to build up as big a lead as I can so I won't choke." There is an ebullience to Trevino that even the strain of a very important occasion cannot stifle. Matching par over the last five holes, he brought in a 69, making him the first man ever to break 70 on all four rounds of the Open. His total of 275 also tied the new record low total that Nicklaus had set just the year before.

Prior to his victory in the 1968 Open, Trevino had already earned over $50,000 in prize money in the winter and spring tourneys. Piece by piece, the different segments of the amazing story behind his velocitous rise had become known and began to fit together like a mosaic. Born near Dallas, he had been raised by his grandfather; they had lived in a shack without electricity or running water. He had left school in the eighth grade and got a job helping out at a par-3 course. He then put in four years in the Marine Corps, mainly on Okinawa, and returned to his old job, where he stayed until he moved to El Paso in 1966. Few people can chip and putt like Trevino, and it is understandable when one recalls all the years he spent around that par-3 course taking on all comers for whatever they wanted to wager. To augment his income when his pigeons became wary, he would bet that he could beat them playing right-handed with left-handed clubs, which was a cinch for a fellow who could beat them using no other implement than a family-size Dr. Pepper bottle wrapped in adhesive tape. (He slapped the ball toward the green with the big end of the bottle and putted billiards-fashion with the neck end.) Now all those days of super-John Montague hustling were behind him, and ahead a great future. He would attract to golf a whole new section of the non-country-club public, widening the base of the pyramid much in the way that Gene Sarazen had when he broke through in the 1922 Open and moved to the front in a game that had been thought of as the almost exclusive domain of the moneyed Anglo-Saxon.

Looking back over the decade of the 1960s with its many engaging players and its spate of events with melodramatic climaxes, three tournaments not previously mentioned are deserving of comment. In the 1961 P.G.A., Jerry Barber tied Don January on the last green at Olympia Fields after what must be the most unbelievable series of pressure putts in golf history. On the 70th, Barber holed for his birdie from twenty feet. On the 71st, he holed for his par from forty feet. On the 72nd, he holed for a birdie from almost sixty feet. Barber then went out in the playoff and shot a 67 to defeat January by a stroke. (January had to wait six more years before he won the P.G.A.)

Second, there can be no disputing that one of the unhappiest moments in golf during that decade resulted when it was announced that Roberto De Vicenzo, instead of tying for first with Bob Goalby in the 1968 Masters, had lost by a shot on a technicality: he had signed a scorecard that incorrectly charged him with a par 4 on the 71st and not with the birdie 3 he had made. De Vicenzo's defeat would have been incalculably more tragic had the aging Argentinian not captured the British Open the previous year at Hoylake. At the time of that victory, De Vicenzo, forty-five years old, had won 140 tournaments all around the world but had never taken one of the four major championships. He certainly had come close enough in the British Open: third in '48, third in '49, second in '50, sixth in '53, third in '56, third in '60, third in '64, and fourth in '65. The big, handsome porteño had taken his defeats with a genuine sportsmanship matched by few men in the game, and the British galleries loved him for this. In 1967, when he had held off a fierce closing rush by Nicklaus by playing the last three holes flawlessly, De Vicenzo's victory was one of the most popular ever recorded in the old championship.

In his acceptance speech, De Vicenzo, as thoughtful as ever in his moment of triumph, told the mass of spectators gathered around him that he hoped that at the next championship the Open cup would be handed to a British player. That wasn't to be—it went to Player—but in 1969, for the first time in the eighteen long years since Max Faulkner had carried the day at Portrush, a British golfer won the Open. He was Tony Jacklin, a young man from Scunthorpe, in Lincolnshire. The son of a golf-playing truckdriver, Jacklin had turned pro at seventeen, won the British Assistants Championship at twenty-one, made his mark with little delay on the British tournament circuit, married a very pretty and very sensible girl from the Belfast area, gained his Approved Tournament Player card in the autumn of 1967 at the P.G.A. Qualifying School at Palm Beach Gardens, went on the American winter tour in 1968 and won the Jacksonville Open, and topped off the whole dizzying climb by winning the British Open at Lytham and St. Annes in July 1969. A self-confident, bouncy young man, more American in temperament than many Americans, at Lytham Jacklin moved into a two-stroke lead by posting a 70 on the third round, getting down in 2 from bunkers on both the seven-

Tony Jacklin was not able to carry the Thames with this drive, but that was about all he failed to do, this fine young English golfer who won the 1969 British Open.

teenth and eighteenth. On the day of the final round, he worked hard to wall himself off from the palpable excitement of the British galleries. He warmed up by hitting 7-iron shots exclusively to establish the tempo he wanted. On this last round, four veterans who were on the rim of contention—De Vicenzo, Nicklaus, Thomson, and Christy O'Connor of Ireland—fell further off the pace when Jacklin went to the turn in a relaxed 33. This left Bob Charles, the left-hander from New Zealand who had won the British Open in 1963, as the one remaining challenger. With four holes to go, Jacklin led Charles—with whom he was paired—by three strokes. He still led by two as they came to the eighteenth, a drive-and-pitch par 4, 389 yards long, on which the critical shot is the drive; it must be placed on a relatively small patch of fairway hemmed in on the right by shallow bunkers and on the left by deep ones. The moment Jacklin struck his tee shot on the eighteenth, the keyed-up thousands jammed round the tee and lining the perimeter of the hole erupted instantly, as one man, in a fierce shout of relief, admiration, and pride: Jacklin had belted a perfect drive straight down the middle. He was on with a soft 7-iron, twelve feet from the cup. When Charles, who was also on with his second, missed his try for a birdie from eighteen feet, Jacklin had won the British Open, and the nation's long wait was over. As it turned out, this would not be the last time Tony Jacklin would provide his countrymen with a good reason to shout for joy.

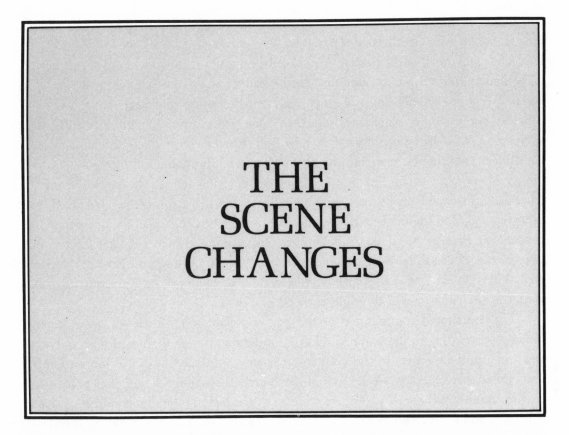

THE
SCENE
CHANGES

It was hard to imagine how America could become any more golf-conscious than it had been in the middle 1950s, when President Eisenhower chose the Augusta National Golf Club as the locus of his vacation White House, when Ben Hogan's appeal continued to burgeon until each tournament appearance he made evoked a reverence that recalled the response to Sarah Bernhardt on her farewell tours, and when a high percentage of members of the different strata of our prospering society found that golf was such a good game it was worth all the lessons, slow-poke foursomes, sports shirts, club dances, starting times, bar-room bores, club assessments, and other affiliated hazards. Nevertheless, in the 1960s and 1970s the popularity and gestalt of the game did continue to grow, remarkably so. The one-two punch behind this was television and Arnold Palmer. As far back as 1954, the United States Open had been televised nationally in a limited way, but it was not until the Sixties, when color television really arrived, that at least five million viewers—and in the Seventies an average of ten million—tuned in to the telecasts of the tournaments. With that sort of interest, one could understand why early in the 1960s the large companies made it a point to get into the golf picture. Beginning in 1961, the Shell Oil Company began to underwrite an annual series of television matches in which the outstanding American and foreign stars met on the great courses of the world, from Gleneagles to Gavea, from Banff to Royal Melbourne. This program was so well received that it lasted for nine years. (The largest audience ever to watch a golf telecast was the twenty-four million-plus who took in the 1971 Crosby tournament, but it should be noted that Bing & Co. came on the air directly after the conclusion of the Super Bowl telecast on the same network and may have picked up a viewer or two who already had the dial set.)

The second half of the parlay, Arnold Palmer, was a man with a kind of magnetism no computer could begin to calibrate. Arnold had a natural aptitude for "reaching" just about everyone—young and old, male and female, golfer and non-golfer, poet and peasant. For example, Americans who had been previously addicted only to contact sports and who had been introduced to golf by television liked this masculinely handsome, vital, honest man and the physical way he threw himself into golf, slashing his tee shots with every last ounce of power, devising incredible escapes from the Château-d'If's in which he was imprisoned after heroic gambles had failed. Palmer captured and held these bleacherites who had never worn an old school tie as they had cheered on Bronko Nagurski, Bill Dudley, and Jimmy Brown, Hank Luisetti, Bob Cousy, and Oscar Robertson, Joe Louis, Sugar Ray Robinson, and Rocky Marciano, Ted Williams, Stan Musial, and Henry Aaron. Like Henry V at Agincourt, it was a matter of the right man at the right time.

The accelerated continuation of the post-war golf boom made for some striking statistics, according to the National Golf Foundation. Where there had been only two and a half million golfers in this country in 1946 who played fifteen or more rounds a year, today there are close to eleven million. Nearly three million more play at least two or three rounds. Where in 1946 there were less than five thousand golf courses (private, daily fee, and municipal) in the United States, today there are over eleven thousand. (During this period, the number of golfers in the world has increased from eight million to over twenty million, the number of courses in the world from ten thousand to well over fifteen thousand.) Before the war the par-3 course was practically nonexistent; today there are over a thousand of them in the United States alone. All in all, the estimated capital invested in golf facilities in the United States as of 1973 was well over three billion dollars and the estimated annual cost of maintaining these facilities just about a half billion dollars. Two more items of interest: at last count there were 295,000 golf carts spread over the land, and 8,650 high schools (not counting church and private schools) had golf teams.

This enormous national involvement in golf was reflected in the growth of the professional tour. In 1947, when there was a total of thirty-one tournaments offering a total of $352,000 in prize money, Jimmy Demaret led the list of money-winners with earnings of $27,936.83. Contrast that with the 1973 tour: seventy-six events—forty-seven regular tour tournaments, twenty-six "satellite" or "second tour" tournaments, and three Caribbean tournaments—produced a total purse of $8,657,225. The man who took home the largest slice of this was Jack Nicklaus—$308,362. That season fourteen players in all made more than a hundred thousand dollars on the tour, and no fewer than ninety-three won more than the $27,936.83 that Demaret had hauled in back in 1947. For that matter, in 1973 fourteen women professionals on the Ladies' P.G.A. tour surpassed Demaret's mark, and Kathy Whitworth, who led the money-winners for the eighth time in nine years, surpassed it by something like $54,927.17.

One effective indication of the game's febrile rate of expansion over the past thirty-odd years is the fact that the U.S.G.A. has seen fit to establish four new national championships: in 1948, the Junior Amateur, for boys seventeen and under; in 1949, the Girls' Junior, for girls seventeen and under; in 1955, the Senior Amateur, for men fifty-five and over; and in 1962, the Senior Women's Amateur, for women fifty and over. In addition, in 1953, the U.S.G.A., at the request of the L.P.G.A., assumed the administration of the Women's Open Championship. These events have all flourished, and a few remarks about each of them seems appropriate.

The aspirants in the Junior Amateur must first qualify locally for one of the 150 places in the field. At the site of the championship, the field is winnowed down to sixty-four players after a qualifying round of thirty-six holes at stroke play. From there on in, match play takes over. Among the men who won the Juniors as boys are such well-known players as Gay Brewer (1949), Mason Rudolph (1950), Tommy Jacobs (1951), Rex Baxter (1953), and Johnny Miller (1964). Miller holds the record score for the qualifying round: 71-68—139. Jack Nicklaus, by the way, made five attempts in the championship but never got past the semi-finals. An idea of the tremendous lure this event holds for young players of ability can be gained from the high number of entrants. This reached its peak in 1963, when a total of 2,230 boys entered the sectional qualifying round.

The starting field in the Girls' Junior is limited to a hundred and twenty players. There is no sectional qualifying; the applicants with the lowest handicaps are selected for the field. At the scene of the championship, the structure of play is, essentially, the same as in the Junior Amateur. After a 36-hole qualifying round, the low thirty-two scorers then begin the process of match-play elimination. The roll of champions includes Marlene Bauer (1949), Mickey Wright (1952), and JoAnne Gunderson (1956). Judy Eller, of Old Hickory, Tennessee, pulled off the considerable feat of winning the championship two years in a row (1957 and 1958). This record was equaled by Hollis Stacy, of Savannah, in 1969 and 1970. Then in 1971 the remarkable Miss Stacy, a charming as well as gifted young golfer, won the title for a third straight time, defeating Amy Alcott in a smashing final with a birdie on the 37th hole. (From the third through the 30th, neither girl bogeyed a hole, and between them they had nine birdies.) Hollis was fifteen years and four months old when she won this title for the first time, but she is not the youngest champion ever. That distinction belongs to Nancy Lopez, from Roswell, New Mexico, who was fifteen years and one month when she won in 1972. (Miss Lopez was an old hand at precocious accomplishments. She had been her state's women's champion at twelve.) Two years later, she won the Girls' Junior again.

An estimated two million of the country's male golfers are fifty-five or over. A good many of the best and most serious players among them are members of the nation's oldest senior organization, the United States Seniors' Golf Association, which was founded way back in 1905, and meets each summer at Apawamis, in Rye, N.Y., and Round Hill, in Greenwich, Conn. The U.S. Seniors, however, limits its membership to a thousand, and this makes it much harder for a new senior to get into it than into, say, the Southern Seniors Golf Association, which has a membership of eighteen hundred. There are dozens and dozens of senior golf groups in this country today. Many seniors, being semi-retired or retired, have plenty of time for golf and never seem to get their competitive fill of it. People are simply younger for their age than they used to be. For all these reasons, in 1955 the time had come to hold an official national senior championship. Its format is like this: 132 players qualify sectionally; the championship starts with a 36-hole qualifying round; then the low thirty-two scorers continue on in match play. The first U.S. Senior Amateur was won by Woody Platt, a member of the American team in the unofficial Walker Cup match of 1921 but a man whose most lasting claim to fame was that he once played the first four holes at Pine Valley in 3, 2, 1, 3—birdie, eagle, eagle, birdie—after which he repaired to the clubhouse for a calming draft and never came out to finish the round. In recent years three well-known golfers have come to the fore in the Senior Amateur. The victor in 1970—the year of the record entry: 683—was Gene Andrews, a former Walker Cupper and the 1954 Amateur Public Links Champion. In 1973, after decades of frustration, Bill Hyndman, the amateurs' Sam Snead, won it—his first victory in a championship conducted by the U.S.G.A. Then in 1974 Dale Morey, a former Walker Cupper and the runner-up to Gene Littler in the 1953 Amateur, won it in his first year of eligibility.

The first winner of the Senior Women's Amateur was Maureen Orcutt, the Bill Hyndman of women's golf, since, in the 1920s and '30s, when her game was at its apex, she had won just about everything except the U.S. Women's, in which she was twice the runner-up. For good measure, Maureen won the new championship again four years later. The Senior Women's Amateur calls for fifty-four holes of stroke play. The field is limited to 120, the applicants with the lowest handicaps getting the berths in the starting field. The institution of the Women's Seniors was a marvelous thing for Carolyn Cudone, for many years an outstanding player in the New Jersey–New York area, where she had won twenty-two state and regional titles. (An accomplished shot-maker, in 1961, when she was in her forties, Mrs. Cudone finished in the first ten in the U.S. Women's Open, at Baltusrol.) When she became eligible in 1968 for the Senior Women's Amateur, she led the field by ten shots. She repeated her victory in 1969, 1970, 1971, and 1972—the first golfer ever to win a U.S.G.A.-superintended championship more than three straight times. In 1973 Mrs. Cudone's historic streak was brought to an end by Mrs. Gwen Hibbs, an English-born golfer who had won the Southern California Seniors six times.

After it took over the Women's Open in 1953, the U.S.G.A. made no major alterations in the old format, which called for seventy-two holes of stroke play. In 1965, when the men's Open was changed to a four-day affair with a single round on each day, so was the Women's Open, which had also previously concluded with thirty-six holes on the final day. Louise Suggs and Donna Caponi Young have won the Women's Open twice. Babe Zaharias won it three times, in 1948, 1950, and 1954, and Susie Maxwell Berning has also won it three times, in 1968, 1972, and 1973. Mickey Wright and Betsy Rawls have won it four times, Miss Rawls' victories coming in 1951, 1953, 1957, and

Among the great women golfers, Mickey Wright ranks at the very top level with Joyce Wethered and Babe Zaharias. Between 1958 and 1964 she won the U.S. Women's Open four times, but what set her apart was the sophistication of her technique.

1960, Miss Wright's in 1958, 1959, 1961, and 1964. In 1967 at the Cascades course at Virginia Hot Springs, Catherine Lacoste, of France, the daughter of the famous tennis champion, became the first and only amateur to capture the Women's Open. Two years later, Mlle. Lacoste, who had previously won the amateur championships of France and Great Britain, won our Women's Amateur at Las Colinas in Irving, Texas.

The most inspiring edition of the Women's Open was, without a doubt, the one held in 1954, at the Salem (Mass.) Country Club, in which Babe Didrikson Zaharias, back on the fairways after recovering from an operation for cancer, captured the event for the third and last time—by twelve strokes. (Over the four rounds, she didn't have a single 6.) The most tragic championship was the one held on the East Course at Winged Foot in 1957, in which Jackie Pung, after finishing with an almost flawless 72 to post a winning score of 298, was disqualified on the grounds that, while her total for her round was correct, she had signed a scorecard on which her fellow competitor and marker had improperly marked down a 5 for her on the fourth hole and not the 6 she had made. There are good reasons for the endless intricacies of the rules of golf, but there are times, such as the 1957 Women's Open, when legality and not justice is served by the questionable application of certain rules and a great day's golf is turned into a Lewis Carroll travesty. The best—and best-attended—Women's Open was the one played in 1961 over the Lower Course at Baltusrol and which was won by Mickey Wright with rounds of 72, 80, 69, and 72 on a difficult, heavily bunkered layout that measured 6,372 yards and played appreciably longer.

One could make out a good case for ranking Mickey Wright as the finest woman golfer of all time, but since there is no fair way to compare the stars of different eras, it is probably more judicious to say that she stands as one of the three greatest along with Babe Zaharias and Joyce Wethered, the tall, slim, English stylist of the 1920s who won nine of the twelve championships she entered in her abbreviated career. Mickey joined the women's tour in 1955, and from 1957, when she won three tournaments, until 1965, when she went into semi-retirement, there was no one who could touch her. She won something like sixty-five tournaments over that span. A tall, good-looking girl who struck the ball with the same decisive hand action that the best men players use, she fused her hitting action smoothly with the rest of her swing, which was like Hogan's in that all the unfunctional moves had been pared away, and like Jones' in that its cohesive timing disguised the effort that went into it. The daughter of a San Diego lawyer, Mickey used to drive with her mother up to the Los Angeles area when she was fourteen and fifteen to take lessons from Harry Pressler, the pro at the San Gabriel Country Club. Pressler emphasized three points for his young pupil to work on: at the start of the downswing, her weight should begin moving across from her right foot to her left; on the downswing, also, her right elbow should be tucked in close in front of the right hip; and, third, as her hands moved toward the ball, her wrists should remain cocked as long as possible. Mickey has adhered faithfully to these three principles throughout her career. An extremely self-critical person with impossibly high standards, she masks her feelings well on a golf course and presents a picture of unruffled calm. During the

A few well-chosen words
by Mickey Wright
after her playoff
with Ruth Jessen in '64.

decade when she dominated the L.P.G.A. tour, she had no interest in playing the role of royalty and went her way quietly both on the course and off. Her idea of a gala evening was to have dinner with a few friends, preferably of an intellectual bent, who were entertaining talkers. Between rounds and tournaments, she spent a good deal of her spare time listening to music—she carried a portable record player on the tour—and, in addition, she read exhaustively, studied French and the guitar, and occasionally went fishing. She was, like many of the women pros, fascinated by the theory of the golf swing, and loved to articulate her thoughts on it in long, rounded sentences.

To get back to her performance at Baltusrol in the 1961 Women's Open: At the halfway mark, because of her second-round 80, on which she had putted very poorly, Mickey was four strokes behind the leaders. On the third day, when the last thirty-six holes were played, she moved out in front with a coruscating 69 in the morning and then added a par 72 to finish six strokes in front. En route to her 69, she had no fewer than six birdies, but, in a way, her closing 72 was every bit as brilliant, for she was on all the greens except two in the regulation stroke. The difference was that she needed only twenty-eight putts in the morning but in the afternoon took two on every green. Eloquent as they are, these figures do not begin to suggest the near-perfection of Mickey Wright's play on that double round. Throughout the long day of pressure, she laced one long drive after another down the middle of the narrow fairways. For all of her length, she had to use a lot of club to get home on her approaches—3-irons, 4-irons, 5-irons, and 6-irons, for the most part—but on hole after hole, hitting very pure shots, she put the ball within twenty feet of the pin. Had she been sinking her putts in the afternoon, she could have been around in 66, easily. It is hard to think of a comparable exhibition of beautifully sustained golf over thirty-six holes in a national championship, unless it be Ben Hogan's last two rounds at Oakland Hills in the 1951 Open.

There were countless ways in which the expanding popularity of golf manifested itself, and one of them, certainly, was the steady increase in the number of entrants in the long-established national tournaments. In 1971 a record total of 10,780 players entered the U.S. Amateur, Open, and Public Links Championships. (Among the Public Links champions of this period who went on to gain considerable reputations and rupees on the pro tour were Dan Sikes, R. H. Sikes, and Bob Lunn.) In the glamour events the attendance figures kept on getting higher. For illustration, 88,414 spectators, a record for the U.S. Open, were on hand at Baltusrol during the four days of the championship in 1967. The Masters, overwhelmed in the early 1960s by daily crowds of around 30,000, inaugurated in 1967 a radical new policy whereby no tickets were put on sale at the gates during the tournament, the entire complement having been purchased that winter by men and women who had for years been regular patrons of the Masters. (A golf fan can, however, buy a ticket at the gate for one of the Masters practice days, if he is willing to spend five dollars. Actually, it is a good buy: he is apt to see a lot more of the play on a practice day.)

There can be no argument that television was a prodigious factor in this ever-increasing interest in golf. The number of nationally televised tournaments kept on mounting until by 1974 twenty-two were available on the tube, not counting a handful of women's tournaments or an occasional bonus like the delayed telecast of the British Open. Not that this is exactly in the nature of a scoop, but there have been quite a few things wrong with televised golf, ranging from wooden presentation by the networks to muddle-headed reaction by the viewing audience. For example, one of the most deplorable facets of American golf today is that it now takes close to five and a half hours to play a round, primarily because the average golfer, having watched on television the snail-like pace of the top pros, especially on the greens, has got it into his head that if he expends a similarly unrushed fastidiousness over his shots, he will suddenly emerge as the reincarnation of Horton Smith or Walter Hagen. Then there are viewers for whom the fascination of televised golf resides not in the golf itself but in the money at stake. "Hurry up, Monty," fan #1 yells to fan #2 who has gone to the kitchen to fetch two more cold bottles of Old Shimonoseki lager. "He's got this putt for fifteen thousand smackers." However, at least an equal number of faults are television's, such as the hoary pattern whereby one announcer, or pair of announcers, is assigned to cover a particular hole. When some fairly important players are about to putt on his green, this announcer comes on the air, describes the putts with suave banality, and then "throws it" to Lance or Alex, who is on another green where some putting is going on. (Sometimes three out of every four shots shown are putts.) Only infrequently does the combination of the cameramen, the announcers, the director, and the producer create the true atmosphere of a golf tournament.

The Scene Changes

As has been said innumerable times, television is so powerful a medium that it is almost impossible to overstate its influence. Some of the side-effects of golf telecasts are funny, such as the change that comes over a number of the veteran players, long-established as the game's ranking grouches, whose surliness is instantly replaced by sweetness and light the moment they come on camera on the fifteenth or whatever is the first televised hole. Then, too, some of television's side-effects are destructive. Because match play is such a precarious commodity to fit into a time slot, television has practically killed this form of golf, though it is the fault of the national organizations for not staging match-play tournaments anyhow and not worrying about how television might handle the problems they present. It has no doubt contributed to the U.S.G.A.'s decision to abandon the traditional double-round of thirty-six holes on the last day of the Open. Television will find a way if it wants to. On the plus side, it should be made clear that the payments by the networks for the right to carry the pro circuit events have given the game not only a much wider audience but almost a new financial dimension. Generally speaking, under the P.G.A.'s Tournament Players Division's contracts with the networks, each televised tournament receives a sum equal to a quarter of its prize money and each non-televised tournament a sum roughly equal to 16 percent of its prize money. Without television's contribution—to understate the matter considerably—we would not have seen the prize money on the pro circuit pass the eight-million-dollar mark.

When there is so much lucre and prestige to be garnered in pro golf, is it any wonder that a young man who is offered a golf scholarship by the old U. of Sunshine is delighted to accept the opportunity? What could be sweeter than four years of refining your game to the point where, after graduation, it is no real sweat to earn your Approved Tournament Player's card by finishing among the low scorers in the special tournament at the Qualifying School the T.P.D. runs annually to accredit new players for the tour. Bingo—you're in the big time, and if you have the stuff in you, all it takes is *five good years* and you're made financially for life. The only complicating circumstance that prevents the star college golfer from turning pro the moment he receives his diploma is the desire to represent his country in a Walker Cup Match, particularly if the upcoming Match is scheduled to be held in Britain. Every four years, as a result, a particularly imposing group of young amateurs leaves the amateur ranks after the Walker Cup meeting. For instance, four members of our 1967 team, which defeated the British at Royal St. George's—Bob Murphy, Ron Cerrudo, Marty Fleckman, and Jim Grant—then turned pro as fast as they could. Two other members of that team, Bob Dickson and Jack Lewis, followed them into the pro ranks not long afterward. As for the American Walker Cup team that bowed to the British at St. Andrews in 1971, three players—Lanny Wadkins, Steve Melnyk, and Allen Miller—turned pro without much delay, and Jim Simons and Tom Kite later joined them.

While the big payoff obviously comes after graduation, the world of collegiate golf, as it spins in the Seventies, is a very interesting milieu. For example, as of 1972, a number of colleges (including Nebraska, Arizona State, and Eastern Kentucky) were awarding as many as eight scholarships a year. Texas and Memphis State were doling out eight to ten, and Texas A. & M. twelve to fourteen. That borders on prodigality. At most "golf colleges," the average is two to three each year. A good percentage of the scholarships are for small or moderate amounts, hovering in the neighborhood of five hundred dollars. However, at some colleges, such as Wake Forest, Michigan, and Southern Illinois, the scholarships can be as hefty as three thousand dollars. At a few schools, such as Southern California, Florida, and Stanford, they can run even higher.

In the years following World War II, the first college to enjoy a dynasty of sorts was North Texas State, which won four N.C.A.A. Championships. The University of Houston, though, has been the Big Daddy of college golf, without a question. Since 1951, when David Glenwood "Dave" Williams, a professor of engineering, took over as the golf coach, Houston has taken twelve N.C.A.A. Championships. (Furthermore, six Houston golfers have captured the N.C.A.A. individual crown: Rex Baxter, in 1957; Phil Rodgers, in 1958; Richard Crawford, in 1959 and 1960; Kermit Zarley, in 1962; Marty Fleckman, in 1965; and John Mahaffey, in 1970.) One of the secrets of Williams' success is that he takes advantage of the depth of his squad. If one or two of Houston's starters have made a mediocre showing in their last match or tournament, during the following week they must compete against men on the second team; if they beat back their challengers, they retain their position as starters, but if they lose, they go to the bench. This policy is bound to keep a young man warm but motivated. It may also help to explain why, since the beginning of the Williams era, about sixty of his boys have gone on from the Houston campus to fruitful careers on the pro tour.

Speaking of the finer things of life, to assume that a golfer who earns, say, $87,500 in prize money on the tour picks up only a few bob and baubles on the side is a grievous mistake. A good rule of thumb for arriving at an accurate estimate of a touring pro's annual income is to double his prize money, or, if he is young, promising, and photogenic, to triple it. This additional income comes from the old, familiar subsidiary activities—exhibitions, product endorsements, royalties from the golf club manufacturing company with whom he is affiliated, his salary as the touring pro representing a club or resort, personal appearances, and so on—except that today the fees are much, much higher. The more the golfer achieves on the course, the more sought after he becomes for off-the-course activities and the more he can command for these services. To say it another way, a golfer knows when he's reached the top of his profession not when he wins the Vardon Trophy but when one of the big automobile manufacturers taps him to be its television spokesman. In time, what the successful golfer earns from his off-the-course ventures frequently far outstrips what he earns directly from his tournament play. That is merely the vestibule of the villa. After a while, a golfer who has been a consistent winner for a number of years plays only enough tournaments to meet the minimum-appearances requirements of the T.P.D. and to remind the public that he still has what it takes.

The man who has earned the most through golf is, to be sure, Arnold Palmer, whose net worth has been estimated to be in the neighborhood of twenty million—a very nice neighborhood, as the old saying goes. Palmer's annual net income is said to easily exceed a million, which is reasonable when it is also reported that the various world-wide companies developed around Palmer and his charismatic manner gross between fifty and sixty million dollars a year. The ubiquitous Mark McCormack, the perfect model of a modern mercantilist, has, through his parent company, International Management Inc. (offices in Cleveland, Johannesburg, London, Los Angeles, New York, Tokyo, Paris, Christchurch, Melbourne, and Barcelona), left few stones unturned in cashing in on Palmer's potential. In addition to Arnold Palmer Enterprises (which was sold in part to the National Broadcasting Company in 1966 for a reported figure in excess of fifteen million), McCormack has set up and brought along the Arnold Palmer Golf Company (recently merged with Professional Golf, Inc.), Palmer Golf Export, Palmer Apparel Export, the Arnold Palmer Golf Academy, the Arnold Palmer Putting Courses (which still number over a hundred and which operate not only in this country but also in Canada, Britain, and Japan), The Bay Hill Company (built around a splendid Dick Wilson course near Orlando), the Ironwood Country Club (another golf course development, in Palm Desert), and, lest we forget, Endel Visuals, a small photo-engraving plant located in the heart of the village of Youngstown, a few minutes from Palmer's home. Arnold performs promotional services for the companies with which he is associated, such as the Cadillac division of General Motors. He plays a fair number of exhibitions each year but nothing like as many as the twenty-two or twenty-three that he somehow worked in during the middle 1960s. He now gets $12,500 for an exhibition.

This quick description is a simplification of Palmer's commercial activities. (There are companies within companies within companies, and, of course, tax situations must always be kept in mind.) To facilitate his being in three places in one day if his schedule demands it, Palmer, since 1960, when he bought his first plane, a twin-engine Aero Commander, flies. He is a first-rate pilot—he soloed back in 1957—but he always splits the time in the left seat with a professional pilot. Since 1968, Palmer has flown a Lear jet, and unless a fuel crisis prevents it, his air mileage will probably continue to be well in excess of a hundred thousand miles a year. The Latrobe Airport, by the way, is less than a mile from Palmer's house.

We have lately been entering upon an era in America when the sports stars have supplanted the stars of the movies and other entertainment media as the most glamorous and admired public figures. The top men in every major sport are recompensed handsomely, and sometimes all out of proportion, it seems. Joe Frazier and Muhammad Ali, we are told, each banked over five million dollars for their two fights. Jerry West and Kareem Abdul Jabbar in basketball, Bobby Hull and Bobby Orr in ice hockey, Henry Aaron and Carl Yastrzemski in baseball, Rod Laver and John Newcombe in tennis, and Joe Namath and Fran Tarkenton in football are just a few of the superstars who have demanded and received stratospherically high emoluments for their services; they have also done all right when asked to say a good word about a brand of aspirin, applesauce, air-conditioner, or auto. Getting back to golf, according to Put Pierman, the head of Golden Bear, Inc., Jack Nicklaus' yearly gross income is around three and a half million dollars. The remarkable thing about Palmer, though, is that he still makes as much money as ever, although he has not won a major tournament since 1964. His continuing commercial success has refuted the old axiom that once a man stops winning, he is soon forgotten.

Over the years, Palmer's golf from tee to green has not changed very much. The main difference has been that this once great putter has become a very ordinary putter. At his peak he never hesitated to go for the cup no matter how long or dangerous the putt or how ticklish the situation. He felt he had a good chance of sinking any putt, and as a result he probably did sink more "impossible" putts than any golfer in history. Another thing: he was not afraid to go boldly for the cup, because he felt he could always make the 4-footer or 5-footer coming back—and almost always he did. When his putting began to slip in the middle-late Sixties, it wasn't the long putts he missed that hurt but those short ones, the ones he had always gobbled up. Putting is largely a psychological matter, and after Palmer lost his old confidence on the greens, he has never since been able to get it back, entirely. If he were still the master putter he was, he would still be winning tournaments. Off the course, Palmer's life has changed hardly at all. With his wife Winnie and their two daughters, Peggy and Amy, he lives in the same home in Latrobe he purchased in 1958. It was then a six-room ranch house, white with black shutters. Over the years the Palmers have put up a garage, converted the original carport into an office, twice expanded the cellar (into a large, comfortable game room), added a new dining room and kitchen, and extended the sleeping quarters. Now they live in an eleven-room, two-level house, white with black shutters. At regular intervals the Palmers debated the wisdom of building a new house on another site. Their decision to stay put was undoubtedly the correct one. Arnold Palmer lives precisely where Arnold Palmer should live. The view from his house takes in the first five holes of the Latrobe Country Club, where he learned the game, as well as the old clapboard house, alongside the third, in which he grew up. The biggest change, really, has been the erection of a good-sized office building up the slope behind the house on what was once the site of a stable in which the Palmer girls kept their horses when they were young. The building contains a large workshop in which Arnold can bang away working happily on his clubs, an office for the boss, and offices for his secretary and his ideal right-hand man, Donald Webster "Doc" Giffin, who was the Press Secretary on the P.G.A. tour for five years before joining Arnold in 1966. A lot of people have found their way down the slope from the office to the front door of the house. General Eisenhower was one of them.

A professional golfer, like Arnold Palmer, leads a far different life from that of a golf professional, like Deacon Palmer. The golf professional is attached to a club where he gives lessons to the members, sells equipment, and oversees their development in golf and their enjoyment of it. He may play in some tournaments now and then, but that is not his principal interest. For the professional golfer, the formula is reversed. He may be attached to a club where he gives some lessons and he may share in the sales of the golf shop, but first and foremost he is a golfer who competes against other golfers for the prize money on the tournament circuit. Since the large majority of the members of the P.G.A. are club professionals to whom the organization is not unlike a union, it was a foregone conclusion that sooner or later the touring pros would try to break away and form their own association. They saw no reason why the P.G.A. should be entitled to receive (as it always had) a chunk of the receipts from the tour, with whose operation it had nothing to do; they saw no reason why the P.G.A. should set policy for a world it did not understand or inhabit; and, what's more, they resented the condescending, arbitrary manner in which many veteran P.G.A. officials often treated them. In a word, the touring pros wanted to run their own show. In the 1950s, during the Hogan era, they had come very close on at least one occasion to breaking away from the P.G.A., but at the last moment they were persuaded not to. In the 1960s, after a long period of simmering, the touring pros erupted in open revolution in August 1968. Under the guidance of their counsel, Samuel E. Gates, a New York attorney, they set up a new organization, the American Professional Golfers—the A.P.G.—and prepared to conduct their own tour during 1969. For months after this, Gardner Dickinson, the chairman of the players' representatives on the old P.G.A. Tournament Committee, and the other three players' representatives—Jack Nicklaus, Frank Beard, and Doug Ford—were continuously busy. They met with P.G.A. representatives often and met occasionally with individuals, such as Arnold Palmer, who presented compromise plans that might have led to a solution. They huddled with sponsors to set up a schedule of tournaments for the coming year. (Jack Tuthill, the capable, sturdy Tournament Director of the P.G.A. tour, cast his lot with the players, and his doing so was of considerable importance.) By December, the A.P.G. had succeeded in lining up over twenty-eight tournaments for the winter, spring, and early summer of 1969, and it looked as if it would have little trouble contracting for as many tournaments as the players wanted to play.

At the eleventh hour, a complete breakaway was averted. In November 1968, Leo Fraser, who had been the treasurer of the P.G.A., succeeded to the presidency. That rare person, a congenial, reasonable, and honest man who was not interested in personal advancement or power, Fraser took the initiative in arranging for meetings with the "rebels." He made some headway, too, for he felt that the touring pros had a valid cause for complaint. After many meetings, including a marathon session at a motel at the Miami airport, Fraser and the players' representatives arrived at a basis for a settlement. The crux of the arrangement was that a new division of the P.G.A. would be created— the Tournament Players Division. It would have its own Commissioner who would run the tour with the assistance of Tuthill's experienced field staff and a Tournament Policy Board consisting of ten directors: three of the directors would be executives of the P.G.A.; four would be representatives of the touring pros, who would select them; and to give the board balance and stability, three would be independent directors, men from the world of business who were devoted to golf. The success of the T.P.D. was assured when Fraser was able to prevail on Joseph C. Dey, Jr., who for thirty-four years had been the Executive Secretary and later the Executive Director of the U.S.G.A., to accept the Commissionership, and when J. Howard Austin, chairman of the board of the Coca-Cola Company, John D. Murchison of Texas and the Allegheny Corporation, and George H. Love, a former chairman of the board of the Chrysler Corporation, were persuaded to serve as the three independent members of the board. (Austin later became the board's very able chairman.) The birth of the T.P.D. did not for a moment mean the instant termination of any and all problems connected with the tour, but those that did arise were settled in an orderly, amicable manner in which the good of the T.P.D. and not of any special interest was the guiding concern.

During the last few years, from the point of view of prize money and public exposure, women's professional golf has come like the wind. In 1972 for the first time, the million-dollar barrier in purses was broken, and already that figure has zoomed close to two million. Ten years ago that would have seemed beyond belief, since women's professional golf has experienced a somewhat different history than men's professional golf. For over two decades its financial progress was slow and its impact on the sports world bafflingly muffled.

To begin at the beginning, in 1946 the handful of women pros in this country, led by Patty Berg and Betty Jameson, banded together and formed the Women's P.G.A. Two years later this group changed its name to the Ladies' P.G.A. Taking that year, 1948, as typical of women's pro golf after the war—which it was—there were only nine tournaments on the schedule, two of which, the All-American Open and the World Championship, were part of George S. May's annual Saturnalia at Tam O'Shanter, in Niles, Illinois. Babe Didrikson Zaharias, who was the leading money-winner that season, gathered in all of $3,400, which gives you an idea of how lean the pickings were. In those days the golf equipment manufacturers with whom the various members of the L.P.G.A. were associated were of a mind that the women boosted sales of women's clubs most effectively by playing exhibitions and giving clinics, but despite this lack of support the L.P.G.A. tour continued to grow. By 1953, for instance, the number of tournaments was up to twenty-four. Prize money had climbed proportionately, and Louise Suggs, the leader in this department, brought home the respectable sum of $19,816.25. That year, 1953, was important for the women golfers inasmuch as the U.S.G.A., having been asked to do so by the L.P.G.A., took over the operation of the U.S. Women's Open, which had been inaugurated back in 1946. Ten years later, in 1963, the number of tournaments on the women's tour was up to twenty-eight, and Mickey Wright, who won ten of them, collected $31,269.50 in the process. (Most purses were around $10,000, and first-place money usually ranged between $1,250 and $2,000.) There is more than a whiff of irony in the fact that when the L.P.G.A. at length broke through in the 1970s with its first $100,000 tournaments, the quality of the shot-making of the leading players was, in the view of many critics, several cuts below what it had been when the pioneers had been playing for peanuts.

Having made these definite statements, it is imperative to provide some support for

There have been few golfers as consistent as Kathy Whitworth who, between 1965 and 1973, led the women professionals in official winnings eight years out of nine.

them. Most of the hundred members of the present-day L.P.G.A. (total membership: about two hundred and thirty) hit the ball well, and the top players hit it very well indeed. Kathy Whitworth, the tall, dedicated, and articulate young woman from Jal, New Mexico, who has dominated the tour over the last decade, is assuredly a phenomenon in her own way. For eight out of the nine years between 1965 and 1973, she was the leading money-winner. In 1973 she set a new record high of $82,864.25 in official winnings. (This record was broken in 1974 by JoAnne Carner.) Seven of those nine years Kathy was also the winner of the Glenna Collett Vare Trophy for low average score per round. The difficulty is that Miss Whitworth's skills are not as directly visible as were those of the great champions who preceded her. From tee to green her game lacks style and her swing does not have a pervasive rhythm. Her main weakness technically is a tendency to get into a flat position at the top of her backswing, where she also lays the clubhead off a little. She is able to get away with this shutface position, for on the downswing she moves her left hip quickly out of the way and keeps her right elbow in close to her body. Because she is a good, strong athlete, Kathy hits the ball solidly with all the clubs and she gets her tee shot out a helpfully long distance. She has a lovely touch around the greens but it is *on* the greens that she really comes into her own. It can be stated categorically that there has never been a better woman putter. This holds true no matter the pressure she is under, with one exception: as of this writing, Kathy has never putted particularly well—or, for that matter, never played up to her usual form—in that most coveted of all tournaments, the U.S. Women's Open.

How did it come about that the women's tour did not catch fire in the Fifties when there were so many prepossessing players in its ranks? The answer would appear to be that it wasn't until the Seventies that it dawned on the large companies that women's golf was a natural avenue for bringing their products before the American public—the huge women's market in particular. Granted, the present pro troupe may lack a Wright or a Suggs or a Berg, but Whitworth is a first-rate golfer, and the supporting cast— Sandra Haynie, Judy Rankin, JoAnne Carner, Carol Mann, Jane Blalock, Mary Mills, Susie Berning, Sandra Palmer, Laura Baugh, *et al.*—are young women who play very good golf.

A fairly high percentage of the members of the women's tour over the last ten or fifteen years have been the daughters of club professionals who swung their first club at three, along with athletically oriented girls driven by the need to accomplish, and, of course, players who made an impression as young amateurs and who then wanted to see if they could make a go of golf as a profession. Interestingly, two of the best amateurs of the Fifties and Sixties did not turn pro—the nomadic life was not for them—and a third turned pro only when some thought that she was well past her golfing peak. The first member of this trio was Barbara McIntire, a dimpled, soft-eyed Ohioan who did not hit the ball long but, studious technician that she is, kept it meticulously in play. Barbara lost a playoff for the 1956 Women's Open (to Kathy Cornelius), won our Women's Amateur in 1959 and 1964, and won the British Ladies' in 1960. She decided to make her home in Colorado Springs, where she and Judy Bell, another top-class amateur, run a sportswear shop (called The Short Story) at the Broadmoor. Excellent as Barbara's play was, it was still a notch below that of JoAnne Gunderson and Anne Quast, two fine players from the state of Washington who came close to making the Amateur their private preserve in the years between 1956 and 1968. During that period, Anne won the national championship three times—in 1958, 1961, and 1963—and was runner-up twice, in 1965 to Jean Ashley and in 1968 to JoAnne. (Now Mrs. Sander, she was runner-up again in 1973 to Carol Semple, an astonishing performance inasmuch as she had played comparatively little tournament golf for several seasons.) As for JoAnne, she carried off the championship five times—in 1957, 1960, 1962, 1966, and 1968. In addition, in 1956, when she was only seventeen, she was runner-up to Marlene Streit, and in 1964 she was runner-up to Barbara McIntire.

It is hard to think of two girls as different in basic personality or in their approach to competitive golf as Anne and JoAnne, those two long-time rivals. A Stanford graduate with a quick mind, Anne Quast, once she was on a golf course, was able to control a high-pitched sensitivity that bordered on the tremulous in certain situations. With her fervent concentration, once she was in a tournament she could shut out the whole outside world. (Her manner came to have a coldness and almost robot-like aloofness about it.) Even when she was having trouble with her swing, as she was during certain stretches when she won her first national title at Wee Burn in 1958, Anne frequently managed to achieve the results she wanted on the strength of willpower alone. Her swing was not an especially graceful one—there was a bit of lift on the backswing, a bit of thump on the hit-through—and, besides, it had a mechanical quality about it, but

Two attractive girls from the state of Washington, Anne Quast (left) and JoAnne Gunderson, dominated American women's amateur golf in the late 1950s and the 1960s. Gundy was the awesomely long hitter, Anne the remarkable control-player and putter.

Anne understood its workings perfectly, knew that it was functionally correct, and could repeat it under tournament stress. On top of this, she was a superb putter. As a result, she was capable of streaks of inspired scoring. In the 1958 final, for example, she played the last seven holes in 4 under par. When she won her second title in 1961, she was 9 under par for the 112 holes she played.

Gundy, on the other hand, suffered periodically from spotty concentration and lack of the killer instinct. A large, big-boned blonde, good-natured and gregarious, in her first appearances in the Amateur she was as relaxed and spontaneous as if she were back in Kirkland, Washington. In her semi-final match in the 1958 championship, for instance, her tee shot on the sixteenth, it turned out, had ended up in an unplayable lie. Thereupon she loped all the way back to the tee, banged out a second drive, and then loped down the fairway again—no need to keep people waiting. She had a wonderful natural swing in which a smooth transfer of weight was powered by her strong leg action. It is no exaggeration to say that she could outdrive the average low-handicap male club-golfer by ten yards, for her best tee shots would be out all of 260 yards on an only moderately fast fairway. In 1969, the year after she had won her fifth Amateur, JoAnne—by then she was Mrs. Carner—became a professional. Big things were expected of her—as an amateur early in 1969 she had led the whole pro pack in the Burdine's Invitational—but it soon became apparent that she had lost her old, uninvolved, natural swing. She put in an immense amount of work on her game, but, until 1974, during her professional career there was only one week when she looked like the world-beater she once had been. That, happily, was the week of the 1971 U.S. Women's Open, at the Kahkwa Club in Erie, Pennsylvania. Hitting the ball easily, straight, and yards and yards beyond anyone else in the field off the tee, she put together rounds of 70, 73, 72, and 73, was never behind, and won going away by seven strokes. (In 1974, a series of lessons with Gardner Dickinson finally straightened out the basic problems with her swing, and Gundy helped things along by going on a strict diet and losing well over twenty pounds. In short order she was winning tournaments, and when she didn't win, she was up there pressing the winner.)

One more thing: JoAnne and Anne played each other three times in the Amateur Championship. In 1958 Anne won their semi-final match 1 up, and she was again the winner, 3 and 2, when they met in the semis in 1963. JoAnne won their last match, the 1968 final, 5 and 4.

The golf expansion of the 1950s, 1960s, and 1970s was not confined to the United States by any manner of means. The game became much more popular, in the strictest sense of that word, in many countries around the world, and the number of new players, new courses, and new fans grew at a flabbergasting rate. Where international competition had pretty much begun and ended with the classic contests between the United States and Great Britain and Ireland that had started up after World War I—the Walker, Ryder, and Curtis Cup Matches—many new and more widely international tourneys were now inaugurated. The first of these was the Canada Cup, later renamed the World Cup, which was founded in 1953 by John Jay Hopkins, an American industrialist many of whose operations at that time were centered in Canada. The format of this event calls for each competing nation to be represented by a two-man team, with the winner being the team that brings in the lowest combined score for the four rounds of play—the sum of the individual scores of both players over the seventy-two holes. Unlike four-ball competition, in which wayward play by one of the two partners isn't necessarily disastrous if the other continues to get his figures, in the Canada Cup both men must play well. This can make for a good deal of drama, for if one team suddenly begins to slide and another team simultaneously hits a hot streak, the whole complexion of the tournament can change in just a few holes. At the first Canada Cup Match in 1953 at the Beaconsfield Golf Club, outside Montreal, only seven nations were represented. However, the response to the idea and to the Match itself was so favorable that in 1954 no fewer than twenty-five nations sent teams to the Laval-sur-le-Lac Golf Club, also in the Montreal area, for the second Cup Match. (That summer Fred Corcoran, the veteran golf promoter and administrator, became affiliated with the Canada Cup and has continued as its executive director ever since.) Beginning in 1955, it became policy to shift the Match around the world each year, and during the past two decades it has been held in the continental United States, Hawaii, Puerto Rico, England, Mexico, Australia, Japan, France, Ireland, Argentina, Italy, Singapore, Spain, and Venezuela. In

One of the most successful Matches for the Canada Cup—later the World Cup—took place in the autumn of 1957 at the Kasumigaseki Golf Club in Japan, when the home duo of Pete Nakamura and Koichi Ono outplayed the teams from the established golfing nations. Above, Nakamura drives. Below, the charming girl caddies.

retrospect, four Canada Cup Matches in particular gave the event status and character: the 1956 Match at Wentworth, England, where the American entry of Hogan and Snead won the team championship and Hogan won the individual championship; the 1957 match at the delightful Kasumigaseki course in Japan where, to everyone's amazement, the home team of Torakichi "Pete" Nakamura and Koichi Ono outplayed and outscored such illustrious invaders as Snead and Demaret to win by nine strokes, with the individual trophy going to the pudgy, forty-two-year-old Nakamura who shot four solid rounds of 68, 68, 67, and 71 in emerging as "the Francis Ouimet of Japan"; the 1959 Match at Royal Melbourne, graced by large, knowledgeable, polite galleries and the presence of Prime Minister Menzies at the presentation ceremony; and the 1960 Match at formidable Portmarnock, on the edge of Dublin, which attracted sixty thousand keyed-up spectators over the four days of play. One of the happy features of this competition is that, thanks in part to its wise format, the United States has not monopolized the honors, which would have taken some of the interest out of the proceedings. Argentina, Australia, Japan, Ireland, South Africa, Canada, and Taiwan have each won the team championship. The individual trophy has gone to a spendid diversity of players—Hsieh Min-nan of Taiwan, Roberto DeVicenzo and Antonio Cerda of Argentina, Pete Nakamura of Japan, Stan Leonard, George Knudson, and Al Balding of Canada, Angel Miguel of Spain, Gary Player and Bobby Cole of South Africa, and Flory Van Donck of Belgium, along with Ed Furgol, Ben Hogan, Sam Snead, Jack Nicklaus, Arnold Palmer, Lee Trevino, and Johnny Miller of the United States.

The stirring success of the 1957 Canada Cup Match undoubtedly accelerated the organization of a similar world-wide team event for amateur golfers. The World Amateur Golf Council was formed the following spring when representatives of thirty-five countries assembled in Washington, D.C., in May, and the following October the first World Amateur Team Championship for the Eisenhower Trophy was played at the logical venue, the Old Course at St. Andrews, the cradle of golf. Bob Jones, a devoted friend and admirer of General Eisenhower, agreed to captain the American team. At the end of seventy-two holes, the United States finished in a tie with Australia due to a driving finish by Bill Hyndman. In the playoff, however, Australia scored a two-stroke victory, the result of birdies on the eighteenth hole by Bob Stevens, the team captain, and a slim young man named Bruce Devlin.

Like the World Cup, the Eisenhower Trophy Match has benefited from an attractive, sound format. Each competing team is made up of four players. Its score for each day is the total of the three lowest rounds by its four players, and the team with the lowest grand total—the sum of its four daily totals—is the winner. A biennial affair, the World Amateur Team Championship was set up to be held first at a course in the Europe–Africa zone, then at a course in the North America–South America zone, and then at a course in the Asia–Australia zone before moving back to the Europe–Africa zone and beginning another circumrotation of the globe. The American teams have won most of the Matches, with the traditional golfing countries—Great Britain and Ireland, Australia, New Zealand, Canada, and South Africa—being its chief challengers. The

The throng of spirited spectators edges toward the dais during the presentation ceremony at the close of the 1960 Canada Cup Match at Portmarnock, near Dublin.

regularity of the American victories, plus the long string of disappointments the British amateurs had suffered in team play, explains why the game's international fans are agreed that the happiest Eisenhower Trophy Match undoubtedly was the one at Olgiata, near Rome, in 1964 in which an inspired British–Irish side, captained by Joe Carr, at length gained its first major post-war triumph. Along with the opener in 1958, the most thrilling match was the one in 1968 at Royal Melbourne in which the United States came from behind on the final round to edge the British by a stroke, 868 to 869.

In the autumn of 1964, the unofficial precursor of what later became the Women's World Amateur Team Championship for the Espirito Santo Trophy took place at the handsome St. Germain-en-Laye Golf Club, about twenty miles outside Paris. Fittingly, the French team was the winner, edging the American team by a single shot in a turbulent competition that went to the final hole and was decided by Catherine Lacoste's par 4. This result was not really surprising, though, for at this time, under the leadership of the Vicomtesse Lally de Saint-Sauveur, a former British Ladies' Champion, a number of French women—Brigitte Varangot, Claudine Cros, Martine Gajan, and Catherine Lacoste—had demonstrated that they were golfers of international caliber. Behind the inaugural match of this new competition lay four years of hard work by the Vicomtesse and Mrs. Henri Prunaret (née Mildred Gardinor), the captain of the American Curtis Cup team in 1960, who had met that year at Harlech in Wales, where their charges were competing in the British Ladies' Championship. In talks at Harlech and in subsequent correspondence, the two first discussed plans for an informal U.S.A.–France Match in 1964, but later on, realizing that in the autumn of '64 the male amateurs would be assembling in Rome for the Eisenhower Trophy Match, they began to think in the more ambitious terms of creating a tournament of similar world-wide scope for the women. The format they arrived at had the same structure as the men's with two slight modifications: the teams would be composed of *three* players; and the *two* lowest daily scores would count. It would be a 72-hole event. The Vicomtesse and Mrs. Prunaret were hopeful that ten countries would send teams to St. Germain-en-Laye. Twenty-five did. From the beginning, with this first assembly taking place under the official aegis of the French Golf Federation, the new fixture was a *succès fou*.

The World Amateur Golf Council then assumed the sponsorship of the future meetings of the Women's World Amateur Team Championship, which are held biennially in the same country as the men's world team championship and at the same time of year. The American women's team has been successful in all these later matches, but they have been anything but runaways. In fact, the margin over the French team in 1970 at the Club de Campo, in Madrid, was a single stroke.

Most of the new international events that have come into existence in recent years have been played in the autumn, when, as a general rule, the first-line tournaments on the American tour are over for the year and the players are relatively free to rove abroad. These new international affairs, worried about their ability to attract the players who attract the crowds, have made it a point to make winning well worthwhile. Take the Alcan Golfer-of-the-Year Championship, sponsored by the Aluminum Company of Canada, which offered what was then a record first prize of $55,000. The tournament was played four times: in 1967 at St. Andrews; in 1968 at Birkdale; in 1969 at the Portland (Oregon) Golf Club; and in 1970 at Portmarnock, Ireland. Gay Brewer, who seems to play better overseas than he does at home, won the first two Alcans. In the autumn of 1972, when a new international competition, the Pacific Masters, was unveiled at the Sobu Country Club, north of Tokyo, a star-filled field was lured to Japan by a purse of $300,000, a chunk of which was a new record-high prize for the winner: $65,000. Who won it? Mr. Brewer, who shook off David Graham, of Australia, on the fourth extra hole. (A year later, Masashi "Jumbo" Ozaki, the young Japanese professional, captured the Pacific Masters after a playoff with Bert Yancey.)

One additional point: The Asian and Japanese tours now offer sufficient prize money so that the best players in that sector no longer feel compelled to try to crack the American tour—they can make as much money, if not more, at home.

The country that has responded most flamboyantly to the golf explosion—no two ways about it—is Japan. The Japanese, who genuinely love baseball more than Americans do, would have probably gone mad over golf without the Canada Cup miracle of 1957, but after that majestic triumph by Nakamura and Ono, a craze for the game swept Japan, and continues to. If the country had possessed a fairly vibrant golf tradition, this would have been easier to understand, but golf had never before permeated into the average citizen's soul. The first golf course in Japan was constructed in 1903—the nine-hole Rokko Golf Club, built by the British colony in Kobe. Other courses for foreign golfers followed, but it was not until 1914 that the Tokyo Golf Club was established—the first course built by the Japanese for Japanese golfers. Its membership was largely composed of men who had been exposed to the virus while stationed abroad in Britain or America. Golf grew up in Japan as a game almost exclusively for the rich, and one young man who played it very well was a son of Prince Konoye, who was good enough to make the Princeton golf team. In 1940, according to the late Shun Nomura, one of the game's guiding lights in his country, there were fifty-four courses and about fifty thousand golfers in the four main islands of Japan. Today, following the 1957 explosion, there are well over three million golfers. Since only 15 percent of the land in Japan is arable, turning farmland into golfland is legally prohibited. To skirt the law, the Japanese have dexterously laid out courses in dried-up river beds and along the flanks of hills. They have gone as far as to slice off the tops of mountains and build there. Eager to have the best, they have recruited the leading Western architects to build in their country, and Trent Jones was only the first of a long line of visiting masters of strategic design whose object all sublime was to have the punishment fit the crime. (The prize for handing out the most difficult assignment to a golf architect in recent years surely must go to the well-heeled Japanese playwright who, in commissioning Jack Nicklaus to construct two courses for him in that country, stipulated that one of them should be an exact facsimile of the Old Course at St. Andrews.)

Since land in Japan is terribly expensive, it follows that membership in a golf club comes to a pretty yen. Ninety percent of the clubs are private, and a goodly percentage of the members are able to belong only because their company picks up the tab. The big firms are happy to do this, however, for belonging to a glossy club and playing a reasonably good game are among the most potent status symbols in Japan today. Many companies go as far as to encourage their employees to take lessons, at the company's expense. (You can see why many geisha girls, whose traditional stock in trade is helping the tired businessman relax by supplying him with an amused, animated audience, have taken up the game. Other geishas, who do not play golf, subscribe to golf magazines, so that when Mr. Okayama or Mr. Watanabe wants to describe how he went to the turn in a valiant 43, the geisha is able to pour out intelligent sympathy every thrilling step of the way.) For all the ingenuity the Japanese have shown in finding room somehow, somewhere, so that their total number of courses has now increased to nearly six hundred, there are still not nearly enough facilities available for everyone who would like to play golf. For the unfortunate overflow, the solution is the driving ranges that dot the large cities. There are over three hundred in Tokyo alone. A good many of these are double-tiered and some have three tiers, and they are filled from dawn till late at night by swarms of enthusiastic, dedicated golfers who have yet to play on a real golf course.

Beyond the borders of Japan, this was also a period when golf course designers had more work than they could handle. Robert Trent Jones, the doyen of the modern international architects, was now well into his sixties and beginning to take on something of the aspect of Alfred Hitchcock despite the wear and tear of long-distance travel. He has completed courses in Canada, Hawaii, Mexico, Puerto Rico, Jamaica, St. Croix, Eleuthera (in the Bahamas), Colombia, Spain, Portugal, France, Belgium, the Philippines, England, Alaska (at Elmendorf Air Base), and Brazil as well as in Bermuda, Ireland, Switzerland, Sardinia (on the Costa Smeralda for the Aga Khan), Japan (as noted), Thailand, and Fiji. Having put together a large organization, Jones could handle these far-flung assignments and still take on the construction of new courses and the renovation of some old courses in the United States. He opened a West Coast office in Palo Alto that was headed by his son Bob, Jr., a designer with a signature of his own, who, to date, has been responsible for two particularly sound and aesthetically appealing layouts, Princeville Makai at Hanalei on the island of Kauai, in Hawaii, and Roxborough Park, southwest of Denver, where the holes are routed through a formation of gigantic red sandstone rocks. Rees, the younger son, who works out of Jones' main office in Montclair, New Jersey, also has a definite individual style that is particularly visible in Inverrary, in Lauderhill, Florida, a fine test of tee-shot control, among other things, and in Arcadian Shores, which meanders through the oaks, pines, and live oaks at Myrtle Beach, South Carolina. But to return to Jones *père*, his friends have come to the conclusion that he manages to maintain his extraordinary pace because he finds his surest relaxation aboard jet airliners and so disembarks, on whatever continent it happens to be, refreshed and ready for action. He probably does try to handle too many courses at one time, as his critics claim, and some Trent Jones courses do resemble other Trent Jones courses as Tweedledum does Tweedledee, but he also continues to do some very commendable work. One of his most colorful triumphs came in 1971, when a well-to-do client of his, King Hassan II of Morocco, opened a brand-new, 7,500-yard Jones course, the Royal Dar-es-Salaam Golf Club in Rabat, by staging the first Grand Prix International de Golf de Maroc, a $60,000 event for a field of twenty-five pros who were flown in for the occasion. This has now grown into a 72-hole pro-am in which a field of fifty pros takes aim on a purse of 450,000 dirhams or $100,000. That's the kind of a client to have.

Dick Wilson, who had transferred his headquarters to Boynton Beach, Florida—next to Delray Beach—assembled a skillful staff there and was doing some of the best work of his career when he died in the middle 1960s, some forty years after he had broken into golf architecture as the boy who was sent to fetch the lunch and run the other errands for the Toomey & Flynn field crew revising Merion in the middle 1920s. The credit for rebuilding Shinnecock Hills practically from scratch, starting in 1928, when he was still with Toomey & Flynn, belonged to Wilson, a hearty, down-to-earth, straight-from-the-shoulder man with a touch of the poet. "To me Shinnecock affords any golfer a most pleasant eighteen holes of golf," Ben Hogan once wrote his friend Paul Shields. "By this I mean each hole is different and requires a great amount of skill to play it properly. As I think back, each hole has complete definition." After Wilson entered business for himself, these attributes remained part and parcel of most of his courses and explain their charm and challenge. Among his best work are the National Cash Register layouts (in Akron), the new Meadow Brook, the new Deepdale, the revised Inverness, the P.G.A. National (in Palm Beach Gardens), Laurel Valley, Cape Coral (near Fort Myers), the "Blue Monster" at Doral as well as its Red and White Courses, and Lucayan on Grand Bahama Island. His *chef d'oeuvre* without a doubt is Pine Tree in Delray Beach. This was his home course, and Wilson, a low-handicap golfer, loved every moment he spent around it, especially in its formative years, before the stately clubhouse went up; back then, golfers took their post-round refreshment sitting on sawhorses and beat-up chairs around a table made of planks in a small room filled with loose lumber. There are faults with Pine Tree. From the back tees, it plays too long. From all three sets of tees, it asks almost too much of the golfer. For instance, nearly every green is slightly raised and trapped clear across the front, and the ball must be carried onto and held on the narrow putting surface. Hogan admired Pine Tree. After his first visit he wrote in the guest book that it was the best course he had ever played.

Following Wilson's death, his long-time right-hand man, Joe Lee, took over the business. Along with completing Wilson's courses, which were in various stages of construction, Lee further got his feet solidly under him by doing Shannon, the Ruby course at King's Inn, and Great Harbor Cay, all on Grand Bahama Island. Lee's courses do not have quite the dramatic exposition of sure golf values that was Wilson's hallmark, but he builds extremely interesting courses that are pleasant to play, and he has been much sought after. He is best known for his two courses at Disney World, where his long, thin, wriggling, shimmering bunkers give his holes a suitably fantastic look.

After Wilson's death, Bob Von Hagge, who had been a draftsman and designer on his staff, decided to go in business for himself. Von Hagge, an imaginative man with an exceptional sensitivity to terrain, did most of his early work in Florida, his credits including Boca Rio (near Boca Raton) and the new fourth course at Doral, as well as El Conquistador in Puerto Rico. In 1969, Von Hagge joined forces with Bruce Devlin, the Australian golfer. They have done several strong, intriguing layouts in this country—Emerald Hills and Key Biscayne in Florida, Brandywine Bay in North Carolina, and Vista Hill in southwestern Texas, to name a few—and have also been active in Australia, where they were in charge of remodeling The Lakes Club course, probably the best test in the Sydney area. Devlin does not simply lend his name and a few quick ideas to the firm's operations, as do most of the tournament golfers who have gone into architecture in recent years. A professional plumber before he was a professional golfer, Devlin is a *working* partner. As one would expect, he has a flair for solving hydraulic problems but, more than that, he has a keen general intellect. Von Hagge and Devlin have been spending a large amount of their time of late on the Marré ranch, which occupies twenty-two miles of Pacific coastline near San Luis Obispo, and they are right to do so, for the terrain is breathtaking and they have a chance to build some of the world's genuinely great courses there.

Two of the most original designers of the present era are George Fazio and Pete Dye. During his many years as the club professional at Pine Valley, Fazio obviously ingested a good deal of knowledge about what makes a classic hole classic, and his first-hand experience as a leading tournament player bolstered his understanding of proper shot values. (Few people realize that George, along with tying for first in the 1950 Open, finished fifth in the championship in 1952 and tied for fourth in it in 1953. He had won the Canadian Open in 1946.) Among Fazio's most successful courses are Moselem Springs (in eastern Pennsylvania), the site of the 1968 Women's Open; the Jackrabbit Course at the Champions Golf Club in Houston; Kuilima in Hawaii; Butler National, which will be the permanent home of the Western Open; and Jupiter Hills, a championship-class layout that is situated a dozen or so miles north of Palm Beach but which, with its rolling hills and un-Floridian flora, seems more like a Carolina course. (He also remodeled some holes at Winged Foot for the 1974 U.S. Open.) Fazio's courses vary widely in their feeling, depending on the land he is dealing with. A painstaking man, he works on only three or four projects at a time, and it shows in the results he gets. Pete Dye, similarly, could make a lot more money if he wanted to take on more assignments, but he also limits himself to three or four concurrent jobs. He believes that if the architect is not personally on hand to direct each phase of the operation, the subtle touches that distinguish an extremely good hole from an extremely ordinary one will not come off. On a trip to Britain in the Sixties, Dye fell in love with the way the faces of deep bunkers on seaside courses were walled with railway ties or "sleepers" in order to keep the wind from blowing sand out of the hazards, and on many of his courses his bunkers and ponds are set off with variations on this device—serried ranks of ties or cut-down telephone poles that increase the definition of a hole and also provide a neat aesthetic touch. Dye believes in lean fairways and small greens. Among his best courses are Crooked Stick, in Indianapolis; The Golf Club, in Columbus, Ohio; Harbour Town Golf Links (with Jack Nicklaus as consultant) on Hilton Head Island; John's Island, near Vero Beach (with Nicklaus as consultant); Kingsmill, outside Williamsburg; Pueblo Club Las Hadas in Manzanillo, Mexico; and Cajuiles in the Dominican Republic.

There are many other able and ingenious golf architects practicing in the United States and around the world these days. Any list of those based in this country would include Mark Mahannah, David Gordon, Bill Bell, Geoffrey Cornish, Desmond Muirhead, George Cobb, Ralph Plummer, Ellis Maples, Joe Finger, Bill Diddle, Larry Packard, Jack Nicklaus (who has abundant talent in this direction), Arthur Hills, Bob Graves, and Frank Duane (who, in addition to his own courses, has done Marshwood on Skidaway Island, Georgia, and six others in which Arnold Palmer has served as consultant.) Of course, this list is by no means complete.

While there has been a creditable number of first-rate courses built during the last quarter of a century, when one considers the vast amounts of money and the advanced technical equipment at the disposal of the golf architects, the dullness and triteness of the bulk of the new courses is a disappointment and a riddle. Why is it, one asks himself, that so few of the new courses have the quality of a Merion, a Pebble Beach, a Seminole? Here are some of the reasons:

●When a new course is built as part of a real estate development, as many have been, the promoter's main concern is not to create a superior course but to sell house lots at good prices. The architect is frequently told, for example, to build only long, straight holes in such a way as will provide the maximum number of course-front lots.

●Quality of design is often sacrificed in order to keep down the cost of course maintenance. Imaginative contours in the green area, inventive bunkering, undulating fairways, etc.—say good-bye to them all.

●A false emphasis continues to be put on sheer length. The fact that a course measures over 7,000 yards doesn't insure its being a championship course any more than the fact that a man stands seven feet tall guarantees him stardom in professional basketball.

●Too many architects have fallen for the pathetic fallacy that mammoth greens are an improvement over normal-sized greens because they offer more pin positions.

●There has been an over-reliance on the bulldozer to the point where you often can't tell a fairway from a landing strip.

●Above all, many architects take on more jobs than they can give their best creative efforts to, and their work inevitably has a rushed, mechanical mediocrity.

Like every phase of American life, golf felt the force of the chronic inflation and the concomitant rise in the cost of living during the post-war years. By the late Sixties, due mainly to the cost of course maintenance having soared over 85 percent during the previous fifteen years, many private clubs were feeling a financial strain. This was severely aggravated by (1) the Wage and Hour Act of 1969, which upped operating costs in other club sectors some 20 percent; (2) the Tax Reform Act of 1969, under which the clubs were henceforth taxed on all non-membership income; and (3) a fearsome increase in property taxes, with clubs assessed not on the old basis of "recreational use" but on the basis of "best land use." (A club in the Cincinnati area, for example, had its assessment raised from $58,000 to $304,000.) As a result, it was nothing new for a member of a club on the outskirts of a large city to pay annual dues of around $1,000. Such subsidiary expenses as the rental of a locker, an annual fee for storing his clubs in the pro shop (whether or not he actually did so), a minimum charge each month for food and drink, and a nice healthy assessment every now and then could bring the cost of a player's golf for one year close to $2,000.

It was at this time that the flavor of golf in this country underwent a revolutionary change. This was caused by the advent of electric and gas golf carts, which, among other things, solved the problem that had been created in many parts of the land by the passing of that national institution, the young caddie. In the early decades of the century, boys had been attracted to the golf course because they could make more money caddying than by doing other part-time work. (They also liked being around golf.) Now it was different: for the boy who wanted to work during his spare time, lugging a bag paid nothing compared to other jobs he could land. Trevino, indeed, looms as possibly the last of that special breed—the ex-caddie who went on to become a champion.

A portrait of Francis Ouimet in his regalia
as the first American Captain of the
Royal & Ancient Golf Club. The R. & A.
could not have made a better choice.

The biggest single problem in American golf these days, however, is the curse of
slow play. During the weekend crush it is still possible at some clubs to get around the
eighteen holes in four hours, but at most clubs the five-hour-plus round prevails. The
inordinate length of time it now takes to get in a round of golf has been a not
inconsequential factor in the tennis explosion. In an hour and a half, a man or a woman
can play three bristling sets of tennis. After that same amount of time, golfers are lucky
if they are on the seventh hole.

Every year, inevitably, has seen the passing of men who came to golf when it was still a
relatively minor game and who helped it through their contributions to grow into
something much more important. Bernard Darwin, the greatest golf writer of all time,
died in 1961 at the age of eighty-five. Plagued by gout and generally rocky health in his
last years, Bernard still made it a point to get to a few of the big events (such as the 1959
Walker Cup Match), and he continued to write about the game wittily and wisely until
his death.

Francis Ouimet died in 1967, fifty-four years after his victory in the Open as a
young man of twenty. In 1963, on the fiftieth anniversary of that epochal triumph, the
U.S.G.A. brought the Open back for the first time to The Country Club. This gave
"the family of golf," to use Joe Dey's apt phrase, a chance to see that Francis had
changed not a whit over the years. He was still the same natural, modest, instinctively
thoughtful, informally eloquent, golf-loving young man he had been all of his life. In
1951 he had been selected as Captain of the Royal & Ancient, the first American golfer to
be so honored.

The following year, 1968, Tommy Armour died. When his career as a player was
nearing its end, he was already well embarked on an equally successful career as a

teacher. Had Currier and Ives been around, they would have probably depicted Armour in his most characteristic posture—seated in his chair beneath a large umbrella on the practice tee at Boca Raton, working on a gin buck as he rasped out his trenchant instructions to his fortunate pupils. Armour could teach. In his last years, he made his wintertime headquarters at the Delray Beach Country Club and the Boca Rio Golf Club, holding court in the grillroom on his throne, a large, ornate, irrefutably regal armchair. He spent his summers at Winged Foot, where he was a member. In a word, Tommy remained near the heart of the game. Armour-model clubs sold well year after year. So did the books he wrote (with Herb Graffis), especially the first one, *How to Play Your Best Golf All the Time*, a classic of its kind.

Walter Hagen died in 1969 at the age of seventy-six. He was not as lucky as Armour. "The Haig" no doubt would have liked to have stayed close to golf, but it wasn't to be, and he spent a good part of his later life in virtual seclusion at the Detroit Athletic Club or at his home on the lake at Traverse City, Michigan. (Thanks to the way the Walter Hagen Company had been set up by Walter's friend L. A. Young, he never had any financial worries.) Hagen's tragedy, as many of his friends saw it, was not that he had become a heavy drinker but that his drinking had made bulbous and veined the features of this graceful man who prided himself upon his appearance—in fact, it was as necessary to him as the *beau geste* and the much deeper qualities he admired, and possessed. In any event, Walter did not want to be seen looking fat and florid, and for many years he stayed away from nearly all golf tournaments and gatherings, and kept to his circle of loyal, fond friends. However, there was always abundant courage in this man, and it never left him. He gradually got on top of things, changing from the hard stuff to white wine to beer, and while he did not look like the movie-handsome Walter Hagen of old, he was much the better for this. He began to attend tournaments. He was present, for instance, at the P.G.A. Championship in 1961 and 1962. In 1963 he was on hand to honor Francis Ouimet when the Open was returned to The Country Club. In 1964, however, after continued throat trouble, he went to the hospital for what he tried to pass off as "a minor operation." Six more operations were subsequently necessary, for the truth was that Walter had cancer of the throat. When he was not in the hospital undergoing surgery, he carried on as if there was nothing at all ailing him. He learned how to talk again. Now that he was in motion, he kept in motion, traveling to Palm Springs in the winter, to Canada for fishing in the summer, to his home in Traverse City, which he so enjoyed, even to a few tournaments and to the one testimonial dinner to which he acceded. There was *inner* style to this man. When Palmer won his second British Open at Troon in 1962 with a record-breaking score, one of the first people to call him to offer his congratulations was Hagen, phoning from Michigan.

There were other milestones. Consider, for instance, the ivied world of British–American team competitions. In 1965, the British Walker Cup team, which had suffered nine losses in nine Matches on American soil, achieved an 11–11 tie at Five Farms, outside Baltimore, when Clive Clark rolled in a 35-foot putt on the home green

The 1965 American Ryder Cup team, a winner abroad. Left to right, Captain Byron Nelson, Tommy Jacobs, Billy Casper, Don January, Johnny Pott, Tony Lema, Ken Venturi, Dave Marr, Gene Littler, Julius Boros, and Arnold Palmer.

to gain a half in a singles he seemed almost certain to lose. The British, nevertheless, were anything but jubilant over this achievement, for, under the revised Cup format— four 18-hole foursomes and eight 18-hole singles on each of the two days of the Match— they were leading 10–5 after the second morning's foursomes and so needed to take only two of the remaining eight singles to pull off the colossal coup of winning the Cup in America. The best they could manage was to take one singles and tie another, Clark's.

The 1967 Walker Cup Match was more like old times: on the first day the Americans piled up an 8–1 lead, and then coasted to a 13–7 victory in the chilly winds and insistent rains that lashed Royal St. George's. The play of the veteran Bill Campbell was so outstanding that it is to be wondered if any one golfer has ever made a greater contribution to his team in one Match down through the long history of Walker and Ryder Cup play. In Friday morning's foursomes in which he and young Jack Lewis had been hauled back to even by Sandy Saddler and Rodney Foster with three holes to go, Campbell sparked a strong finish that saw the Americans move surely to a 2-up victory. In the afternoon, entrusted with the number-one singles against the redoubtable Ronnie Shade, he was 1 down at the turn to Shade's 35, but, controlling the ball in the wind like Christy O'Connor, the weatherproof Irishman, and making the critical putts, he won the thirteenth, fourteenth, and fifteenth, and at length, the match—2 and 1. The next morning, when he and Lewis edged out Saddler and Alexander Pirie 1 up in a nip-and-tuck foursome, Campbell's clutch donations included holing a 6½-footer to halve the fifteenth, holing a 9-footer to win the seventeenth, and then rescuing a half on the eighteenth by floating a wedge pitch three feet from the cup. In the afternoon he and

Shade met again in the top singles. Shade's initials are R. D. B. M., which some British journalist in a moment of inspiration suggested might well stand for Right Down the Bloody Middle. Considering the harsh conditions, Shade's driving that afternoon was as accurate as one could wish, but Campbell's shots to the green and on the green were superior, and they set up a 3-and-2 win for him. Campbell, by the way, after qualifying in 1964 for the twenty-first time in the U.S. Amateur, had at length, and at forty-one, captured the championship. (The next year, possibly out of a desire for TV exposure, the Amateur was changed from match to stroke play, a state of affairs that was to exist for eight years before it was remedied.)

After Britain's stunning victory at Lindrick in 1957, where Dai Rees' side surprised an overconfident American team and won 7½–4½, the Ryder Cup meetings resumed their steady drone of American dominance until 1969, when the Match was held at Birkdale. This was an orotund clash drawn out over three days: on the first day, four eighteen-hole foursomes in the morning and another four in the afternoon; on the second day, four eighteen-hole four-balls in the morning and again in the afternoon; on the third day, eight eighteen-hole singles in the morning and once again in the afternoon. This surfeit of golf led up to an arresting climax, the kind that Dickens or Hugo would have surely provided had they written about golf. On the last green in the last singles on the last afternoon, with his opponent Tony Jacklin lying two feet from the cup in 3 on this par-5 hole, Jack Nicklaus lay 3 five feet away. Their individual match stood all square—on the seventeenth the gritty Jacklin had holed a 25-foot birdie putt. The overall team Match was locked at 15½–15½, so everything rode on the outcome of this final singles. As Mark Wilson of the London *Evening Standard* commented, the 5-footer over which Nicklaus hunched his outsized frame was not for $50,000 or even a cent but for America's pride in the golf world. Jack was ready to putt after careful preparation. He tapped the ball and it ran straight into the cup. He then gracefully conceded Jacklin his 2-footer. U.S. 16, G.B. 16. Many people felt that this was the best Ryder Cup Match of all time, and no doubt it was. It was based on a tenacious effort by Britain and especially by Jacklin, the leader his country had long been looking for, who went undefeated in his six matches.

During this period there was a cornucopia of individual achievements, among them these: In 1965, Byron Nelson, who had played no competitive golf to speak of since scoring a surprise win in the 1955 French Open, struck his old-time stride at Augusta and astonished himself and the galleries by playing the first seventy-one holes in even par. Byron double-bogeyed the seventy-second, unfortunately, but even so, what a performance by the old champion at fifty-three! . . . The next April, Ben Hogan pumped a great deal of liveliness into the Masters. Entering the fourth round, he was only two strokes off the lead, but the best he could muster on Sunday was a weary 77. From tee to green, Ben was still as good as he had ever been. No one else in the field played as few bad shots, as many fine shots, or such full-blooded fine shots. If Hogan could have putted with 75 percent of his former effectiveness, he would still have been winning tournaments. He reminded his faithful idolators of this the next year in the 1967 Masters, when, once again, he stood only two strokes off the pace with a round to go. What had put him there was a third round of 66—36 out and 30 (6 under par) back. He faltered early in the fourth round, however, a victim of the nervous tiredness that affects fifty-four-year-old athletes. But to return to that 66 and that second nine of 30. Years after the game's enthusiasts thought that they could never again hope to see Hogan at the peak of his powers, there he was, gray hair edging down his teak-colored neck below the old flat white cap, as commanding as he had ever been. On the tenth, he put a 7-iron five and a half feet from the cup and holed a sliding putt for the birdie. Somehow on this day he was avoiding the long agony of freezing over the ball on the green, unable to draw the putter back. On the eleventh he had just a tap-in for his birdie after drawing a 6-iron a foot from the pin. He had a third straight birdie on the twelfth, where, after hitting the narrow green with a 6-iron, he got down from fourteen feet. A fourth straight birdie on the par-5 thirteenth—a drive followed by a 4-wood to fifteen feet, then two putts. On the fourteenth, a fighting par when he got down in two putts from the front of the breaking-wave green. On the long fifteenth, his fifth birdie on this nine: a medium-length drive, a big 4-wood over the pond and onto the green, two putts. Solid pars on the next two holes. Then the plus-perfect finish everyone was hoping for. Ben faded his drive expertly to fit the swing of the eighteenth fairway. A three-quarter 5-iron left him a sidehill putt of some sixteen feet. Down it went, his sixth birdie in nine holes. In retrospect, this was to be Hogan's last great burst of golf in a major championship.

In 1965 Sam Snead scored his last tour victory (as of this writing) when he won the Greater Greensboro Open for the eighth time. It was his eighty-fourth win on the P.G.A. circuit—a record. Four years later it looked as if he was on his way to taking the Canadian Open, which he had won thirty-one years earlier, but Tommy Aaron tied the old boy and then beat him in the playoff. (This, by the way, was Tommy's first victory as a professional. He had been waiting since 1960.) Everybody else grows older, but Sam Snead seems to remain little changed by the passing years. Since switching to the side-winder croquet method of putting, he is a much surer holer of short putts than he ever was before. Double-jointed or not, he can still kick the seven-foot ceiling of a Scottish pub with no trouble at all, at all. He is, in a word, an athletic wonder.

Where Snead moved through life practically unscathed, one man who didn't was Ken Venturi. It seemed that he had no sooner licked one problem than another would come along, equally arcane. In 1965, as the defending Open Champion, he failed to make the cut. This surprised no one, for Ken had come down with circulation trouble in his hands and fingers. This rendered them cold and without feel, and he had nothing like his usual control of the golf club. The next winter this unusual man—he was then wearing mittens some days to keep his hands warm—pulled off a minor miracle. A final 66 enabled him to overtake Frank Beard and win the Lucky International by a shot on the Harding Park public course in San Francisco, the course where he had grown up. This, however, was the kid's last miracle.

More astonishing than ever
as he entered his sixties,
Sam Snead could still keep
pace with golfers a third his
age and kick a seven-foot-high
ceiling after a round.

Arnold Palmer's failure to win the 1966 U.S. Open, when he appeared almost certain to do so both on the fourth round and the playoff round, proved to be more than just the momentary setback it had seemed at the time. His victories in tour events became more and more widely separated, and try as he would, he could not win another major championship. His best chance came in 1968 in his hoodoo championship, the P.G.A.—the only one of the Big Four he had never won. On his final round, by his own count he missed eleven birdie putts on the last thirteen greens. He never gave up, though. On the eighteenth it looked as if he might still make up the stroke he needed to gain a tie for first, for he dug a great 3-wood out of thick rough on that hole and needed only to make the 9-foot birdie putt which that incredible shot had set up. The putt was never in.

The decade of the Sixties had begun with Palmer enjoying a sensational season: in 1960 he had captured eight tournaments and finished among the top five players in no fewer than nineteen of his twenty-nine tournament starts. That decade ended with his going until late November in 1969 before he won his first tournament of the year. This was the Heritage Classic, played on the tight, very exacting Harbour Town Links, on Hilton Head Island, in the construction of which, ironically, his arch-rival, Nicklaus, had acted as consultant to the architect, Pete Dye. In the Heritage, a 70 on the third round gave Palmer a three-stroke lead, and what with his closest challengers having their own troubles, he maintained that margin on the final day although he shot an in-and-out 74. For the first time in a long while, though, he holed three fairly long pressure putts down the stretch when he really needed them.

Winning never hurts a man, and the following week—the first week of December—Arnold showed the way again in the Danny Thomas Diplomat Classic at the Diplomat course in Hollywood, Florida. In the final round, he uncorked one of his old-time charges, coming from seven shots behind the leader with seventeen to play and finishing two shots in front after a 65 in which he birdied four of the last five holes. Had the Palmer of 1960 really returned, the flexible flier who that year had won at Palm Springs with a final 65, at Pensacola with a final 67, at Mobile with a final 65, and at Cherry Hills with a final 65? That was probably too much to expect, but these back-to-back victories at the tail end of 1969 cheered his loyal supporters and renewed their hopes that the great finisher was far from finished.

In 1968, when Palmer had missed his bid for the P.G.A. Championship and had been forced to settle for a tie for second with Bob Charles, his check for $12,500 enabled him, at any rate, to achieve a first: he became the first professional golfer ever to win more than a million dollars in prize money. It had taken him a little over thirteen years; he had picked up his first check in late May 1955, when he won $145 for tying for twenty-fifth in the Fort Wayne Open.

By the end of the 1960s, only a few survivors remained of the Scottish and English pros who had invaded our shores near the end of the nineteenth century and during the first twenty-five years of this one. Freddie McLeod, Jock Hutchison, Bobby Cruickshank, George Heron, Bert Nicolls, and a few others were still carrying on, but, for all intents and purposes, the day of the transplanted British pro was all but over. What an amazing job the Smiths and the Rosses and the Dunns, the Sargents and the Campbells and the Foulises, the Mackies and the Andersons and the Maidens, the Gaudins and the Reids and the Lows and all the rest of the old boys had done in transmitting throughout our land the spirit, the challenge, the fun, the flavor, and the dignity of the game of golf!

They were succeeded by a different genus, or, to be more exact, by several different species: by American pioneers in technique, ranging from Alex Morrison to Ben Hogan; by American playing pros who also possessed an undoubted aptitude for exploration and instruction—among them Art Bell, Gardner Dickinson, Claude Harmon, Bob Toski, Peggy Kirk Bell, Eddie Merrins, and Jack Grout, to name a few who come quickly to mind; and, last but not least, by a type best described as "the old American pro"—the homebred who had spent all his life in the game, gathering knowledge as a stone gathers lichen.

One fine example of the old American pro is Harvey Penick of the Country Club of Austin (Texas), a tall, slim, hopelessly conscientious fellow with grayish hair, a mild eye, and a long, lived-in face, who has been associated with that club since 1912, when he started to caddy there. He moved up the ladder to caddie-master and assistant professional, and in 1923 was appointed the club's professional. He held that post until a few years ago, when he was succeeded by his son Tinsley; but he still teaches on weekdays, and on weekends when the course crowds up, he acts as the starter. Harvey has been best known as the teacher of such first-class women players as Betty Jameson, Betsy Rawls, Mickey Wright, and Kathy Whitworth, but he has also brought along a large number of topnotch men players, many of whom he worked with during the thirty-two years he coached the golf team at the University of Texas. (Penick's teams won twenty-two Southwestern Conference titles, and members of his teams added another twenty individual conference titles.) In recent years he has been very much in the spotlight because two young men whom he started in golf, Ben Crenshaw and Tommy Kite, have developed into two of the most promising young touring professionals. Both the Crenshaw family and the Kite family are members of the Country Club of Austin, and Penick, typically, has bent over backwards to make sure he exhibits a preference for neither young man. "If I have had any luck with my pupils," he said not long ago in his small office, his gaze traveling from a framed photograph of the thirteenth at Pebble Beach to the thirty-six pigeonholes in his old rolltop desk, "it's because I try to stay with each individual's natural abilities. Kite and Crenshaw approach golf quite differently. For instance, Ben likes to sharpen his game by going out and playing maybe five holes, maybe nine holes by himself, hitting several balls. On the other hand, Tom likes to work things out on the practice tee. Lots of parallels. Nelson liked to practice by playing, Hogan headed straight for the practice tee."

Like all the celebrated teachers, Penick has no secrets or shortcuts to divulge, only an observant eye and the ability to relate what he has noticed about each pupil's swing to a few fundamentals that hold true for all golfers. If there is one primary thing he emphasizes, it is alignment—"Let's call that position-to-the-ball instead." Along with this, he spends a lot of time on the grip. "If either your grip or position-to-the-ball is bad," he says, "you're going to have to make some other move in your swing to counteract it." A Penick pupil is forever asking himself, "Am I square to the line—my feet, my hips, my shoulders?" If he has any doubt about it, Penick advises him to fetch a golf bag or a golf cart, set it up along the proper line, and get correctly squared away on it. He is a very finicky man about the grip. He once told Joe Kirkwood, the Australian trick-shot artist, "You're the only man who ever held a club right to suit me."

While Penick is almost painfully modest, his fame (as a man who knows what to look for in a golfer's swing and who has the skill to communicate his prescriptions in a way that his pupils can understand and apply) has swept to every corner of the country, and it is nothing for a golfer to fly in from Houston or San Antonio or San Francisco or Toronto to get straightened out. A perfect example of this took place in the winter of 1974, when a young New York-based amateur named Gerry Murray, who was scheduled to play in the Bing Crosby National Pro-Am, discovered on the comparative eve of the tournament that something was drastically wrong with his timing. Accordingly, en route from New York to the Monterey Peninsula, Murray stopped off in Austin. He took a lesson from Penick that afternoon and a second lesson the next morning. He then resumed his way west, and in the Crosby, after starting with a 69, went on to win the prize for the amateur who had helped his pro the most—thirty-five shots in fifty-four holes.

HIGH DRAMA
IN THE SEVENTIES,
AT HOME
AND ABROAD

Golf had hardly entered the 1970s when an event of the first importance took place. It was not as utterly mind-boggling as the sight of Admiral Alan B. Shepard standing on the surface of the moon on February 6, 1971, during the Apollo 14 space mission, attaching the head of a 6-iron to the long, thin handle of the device the astronauts used to collect rock and soil samples, and then proceeding to drop a golf ball onto the moon and to hit it "miles and miles." It was not as thoroughly unexpected as the sale by the Tufts family of Pinehurst, with its ninety holes and incalculable encrustation of golfing tradition, to the Diamondhead Corporation in December 1970. It was not as economically titillating as the inevitable arrival of the game's first half-million-dollar tournament, the World Open, played at Pinehurst in 1973 from November eighth through the eleventh and then from the fourteenth through the seventeenth. (For money like that, you had to expect to play 144 holes.) Nevertheless, it was without question a golf event of the first importance when late in the afternoon of June 21, 1970, Tony Jacklin holed a 35-foot putt across the rolling home green of the Hazeltine National Golf Club, in Chaska, Minnesota, to bring to a fitting climax his fourth consecutive sub-par round (71-70-70-70) and carry off the United States Open by a full seven shots. Its significance lay in the fact that not since Ted Ray, the burly Jerseyman, had strode in triumph off the home green at Inverness on August 13, 1920—half a century earlier—had a British golfer succeeded in winning the United States Open, the game's ranking championship since the middle Twenties, when Jones and Hagen and their cohorts had demon-

526

strated past argument that American golfers had caught up to and passed the British and had become the best in the world.

At Hazeltine (the last syllable is pronounced *teen*) Jacklin led from start to finish. As his scores indicated, he was on his game on each of the four days, though on some rounds the quality of his golf was, naturally, a trifle higher than on others. Nonetheless, it is hard to avoid the conclusion that the keystone of Jacklin's victory was his play on the first round, when he somehow managed to bring in a 71, one stroke under par, on a day more suited to hunting caribou than playing golf. Cold winds, gusting up to forty-one miles an hour, swept out of the northwest and blew over the long, complicated course carved from the thick growths of maple, oak, butternut, and birch beside Lake Chaska, some twenty miles southwest of Minneapolis–St. Paul. (At 7,151 yards, Hazeltine was the second longest course in Open history, outdistanced only by Bellerive, the site of the 1965 Open, which stretched forty yards longer.) Jacklin's 71 gave him a two-shot lead on the nearest men—Julius Boros, Mason Rudolph, and Chi Chi Rodriguez—but the extent of his accomplishment can probably best be appreciated by noting the effect that the conditions had on the players in general. Only eighty-one golfers in the starting field of a hundred and fifty broke 80. Arnold Palmer had a 79, Gary Player an 80, and Jack Nicklaus an 81. The inescapable question arose: Had Jacklin been able to handle the wind so well because he had grown up in England, where golfers get used early to playing in heavy winds and other unpleasant kinds of weather? Quite possibly. After his round Jacklin confessed that he hadn't found the wind "tremendously strong compared to the wind at home." He certainly had played as if it hadn't bothered him. He birdied the first, a dogleg left, by stopping his downwind pitch fifteen feet from the cup and holing his putt. He bogeyed the second, parred the long third, and then ripped off three birdies in a row: on the fourth, 196 yards long, a beautifully played 5-iron finished two feet from the flag; on the 394-yard fifth, a dogleg right to a plateau green, he drove into the rough, but he allowed for just the right amount of run on his 7-iron and practically holed it; on the sixth, a long par 4, he knocked in a putt of twenty-five feet. After a bogey on the seventh, he came up with still another birdie, dropping an 18-footer on the eighth, a 185-yard par 3, which on this day required a full 3-wood to pierce the crosswind. He parred the ninth, a long and tough par 4, to reach the turn in 33, 3 under. Jacklin began the second nine with two good pars. However, he ran into trouble on the twelfth, a 426-yard 4, where he pushed his second shot into a bunker to the right of the green. He rectified the situation with dispatch: he holed his explosion shot. He followed this with three pars but lost his chance to bring in a truly fantastic round by three-putting the sixteenth for a bogey and then cutting his 6-iron approach on the seventeenth, a tricky short par 4, into one of the two ponds protecting the green and ending up with a double bogey. A final par. Back in 38. Despite that spot of faltering near the end, it was a stupendous exhibition of how to control the golf ball in a high, menacing wind. Not a bad exhibition of putting either: only twenty-six on greens made hard and crusty by the winds.

The second round was played under far more congenial conditions: blue skies, a warming sun, and a wind that blew at a maximum of six miles an hour. The fairways had been mowed a bit shorter, and the lies were better; the greens had been watered by hand and they held the approach shots better. These last two items changed the playability of Hazeltine almost as much as the absence of the blustering wind. A good many—possibly too many—of the course's greens fall off at the back, and it takes a shot with true backspin on it, which a low-cut fairway helps to induce, to stop a ball effectively on this type of green. In any event, on the second round, no fewer than thirteen players broke par, 72. (A 67 by Randy Wolff was the lowest score.) The 36-hole cut came at 153, and Palmer (with a second round of 74), Player (with a 73), and Nicklaus (with a 72) each sneaked in at that figure. Jacklin still maintained his lead. In fact, he added a shot to his margin, increasing it to three strokes with a fine 70. On this day he had begun somewhat shakily, finding three bunkers on the way out, but he turned things around with birdies on the ninth, tenth, and eleventh. He played on calmly without incident until he reached the seventeenth, the par 4, only 344 yards long, on which he had taken a 6 the day before. For all its shortness, it is far from an easy hole, the fairway climbing a gradual slope, then breaking sharply to the right and blindly down to a small low green wedged between the two tiny ponds. Jacklin took a 2-iron off the tee, but it was too much club; he wound up with his line to the green obstructed by a tree at that point where the fairway swerves to the right. Electing to improvise a decidedly risky shot, he closed the face of his 5-iron and hit a low punch-and-run under the branches of the tree. He brought it off. The ball hopped onto the green and ran to within five feet of the hole; he made the birdie putt. On the eighteenth he saved his par by holing from twelve feet. Again he had putted excellently. He had needed only twenty-nine putts. (Watching him, one wondered if he were not possibly the best putter ever produced in Britain.) The galleries at Hazeltine were impressed equally by Jacklin's pleasant demeanor and his well-grounded swing. When Tony had first come to America in 1967, he had had a rather fast swing but a strong one; for a man of average size (five-ten, 170 pounds), he got the ball out a good distance. However, three years of hard work under the knowledgeable eyes of his two closest American friends, Tom Weiskopf and Bert Yancey, had improved that swing conspicuously. The backswing was not so hurried now, the hands were in a much more correct position at the top, the start of the downswing was more coordinated, and the legs and lower part of the body moved through the ball with much more ease and power.

At the end of the second day, though, most of the conversation centered on the man in second place, Dave Hill, an eleven-year veteran of the tour who stood at 144 after a handsome 69. However, instead of exuding bonhomie after a round like that, Hill, a dark-haired, bespectacled, thirty-three-year-old Michigander long recognized as both one of the ablest and one of the most petulant players on the tour, used his press conference to launch a fierce attack on Hazeltine. "If I had to play this course every day for fun," he said, "I'd find another game." Asked what Hazeltine lacked, he answered, "Eighty acres of corn and a few cows." Warming to his subject, Hill later declared that

In June 1970, at the Hazeltine National Golf Club in Chaska, Minnesota, Tony Jacklin carried off the U.S. Open—almost exactly fifty years after the last previous British victor, Ted Ray, had shown the way at Inverness in Toledo.

the architect who designed Hazeltine was an idiot, and when he was asked about the little to-do he had been involved in during the Ryder Cup Match in England the previous autumn, he said, "I told them the next time I went over there I'd have died and my body would have been shipped to the wrong place." Hill is a man who at times mistakes compulsive rudeness for black comedy, and once he gets started, it is hard for him to turn the tap off. The following day he was fined $150 for his outbursts by Joe Dey, the T.P.D. Commissioner, but this was like flaying an elephant with a feather. Hill had won $156,423 in prize money the season before, and his earnings halfway through 1970 had already surpassed $65,000.

The third day, following the system the U.S.G.A. had instituted, the two leaders were paired. Their confrontation created no fireworks. Had Jacklin been so disposed, he might have asked Hill to kindly stop walking around when he, Jacklin, was putting, but the Englishman had the sense to avoid any scenes and to concentrate on retaining his concentration. Firing a 70 to Hill's 71, he increased his lead to four strokes. It was on this third round, we should note, that Jacklin may very well have won the Open. No matter how well a golfer is playing, in a big event there is inevitably one stretch in which he begins to wobble, and how well he handles that passage frequently determines whether or not he goes on to victory. On that second nine Jacklin hit at least one poor shot on each hole and got away unscathed. On the tenth, he half-topped his approach, but it bounced down the sloping fairway and onto the sunken green. On the eleventh, a par 5, he played a very tentative pitch but wiped this out by sinking his long putt. On the twelfth he pushed his drive into a bunker and left his recovery in the rough short of a greenside bunker, but then he popped an exquisite little wedge shot a foot from the pin. That is how it went. His most spectacular escape came on the seventeenth, the short par 4, where, after hooking a 2-iron behind an oak tree, he lofted a daring 8-iron up and over the oak and onto the green. Nine jittery holes, but eight pars and a birdie.

On Sunday, the day of the fourth round, Jacklin was scheduled to tee off at 2:05 with Gay Brewer. (In line with a new U.S.G.A. regulation, if the two front-runners in a championship had played together on the third round, they did not need to go through a repeat pairing on the fourth round.) Hill, paired with Boros, was set to play in the next-to-last twosome, just in front of Jacklin and Brewer. It was noon when Jacklin got to the club. He read through the stack of telegrams piled before his locker. When he opened his locker, his eyes met a one-word injunction printed on white paper and taped to the top of the locker: *Tempo*. His friends Weiskopf and Yancey had put it there as a reminder. Burt L. Standish still lives!

Weather excellent. Track moderately fast. Jacklin seemed honestly composed. A good, solid round would be enough to see him through, he realized—it would take some doing for any contender to make up four or more strokes on a course like Hazeltine. He moved off with five pars and a birdie. Then he wavered, bogeying the seventh and eighth. At this point, Hill, up ahead, trailed by only three strokes. He got no closer, though. On the ninth, a 400-yard 4 uphill and into the breeze, Jacklin, after a so-so drive, drilled a 4-iron onto the green some thirty-five feet short of the pin. The surface of the ninth green is severely contoured and calls for a sensitive touch. Jacklin hit his putt too firmly. The ball, dead on line, struck the back of the cup, popped nine inches in the air, then plunked into the cup and stayed in. That did it, that birdie. His confidence restored, Jacklin started home with a birdie, added six pars, parred the pestiferous seventeenth by taking a 4-iron off the tee and a 6-iron for his approach, and played a fine long iron onto the home green, thirty-five feet from the cup. Up the fairway came the new Open Champion, a good-looking young man, tanned, smiling a jubilant but modest smile. He had led from start to finish, and so much had been written and spoken about him that by now most golf fans were well acquainted with the story of his climb to the top—how, with opportunities for hopeful young golfers so scarce in Britain, he had, after finishing school at fifteen, worked for a year in the steel mills as an apprentice fitter and another year as a clerk of sorts for a lawyer friend; how he had learned that there was an opening for an assistant at the Potters Bar club, near London, and how during his interview on January 1, 1962, he had impressed the pro, Bill Shankland, sufficiently to get the job; how he had risen step by step as a tournament player until by 1966 he was fifth in the British Order of Merit and was named with Peter Alliss to represent England in the World Cup; how he had kept on coming, and in 1969, when he won the British Open, had established himself as one of the best six or seven golfers in the world. Jacklin walked onto the home green, acknowledging with a wave of his hand the protracted applause saluting him for his four days of resolute golf that had completely burned off his opposition. He knocked in the 35-footer, to lengthen his lead over the runner-up, Hill, to seven strokes. It is doubtful if any victory by a "homebred" could have been more popular.

The next day, both exhausted and exhilarated, Tony Jacklin was off to England by air. He had promised Mr. Driskell, the headmaster at his old school in Scunthorpe, that he would present the athletic awards at the student banquet on the Tuesday, and he meant to be there.

Two short weeks after Jacklin's triumph at Hazeltine, one of the most thrilling championships in modern times took place, fittingly at St. Andrews. This was the 1970 British Open. Four exceedingly colorful golfers—Jacklin, Nicklaus, Lee Trevino, and Doug Sanders—had good cracks to win it, and the outcome remained tantalizingly in doubt until the last hole was played.

The eventual winner was Nicklaus and, that being the case, perhaps it is best to write of the tournament primarily in terms of Nicklaus and what he did or failed to do en route to victory. Moreover, to write of the 1970 Open in terms of Nicklaus serves another purpose: until he stopped the rot on the Old Course, Jack had been in the throes of the most persistent slump of his career, and, indeed, it looked for a while as if golf fans might never again see the all-conquering, doubt-free, undeterrable titan of old. There are, of course, different degrees of slumps, depending on who it is who has lost his groove. Just as a poorish series of paintings by Cezanne or an uninspired batch of tunes by Ellington would have hardly filled the average artist or composer with gloom had *he* produced them, so would most professional golfers have been positively delighted to settle for the three-year slump that overtook Nicklaus after he had won his second U.S. Open at Baltusrol in 1967. His record for the rest of that year, for example, included a second in the British Open and victories in the Westchester, the Sahara, and the World Series of Golf. In 1968 he had to be content with capturing only two domestic tournaments (the Western and the American Classic) along with the Australian Open, and with being the runner-up (to Trevino) in the U.S. Open and (to Player) in the British Open. The following year, 1969, was, however, a much leaner year for Jack despite victories on the tour in the Kaiser, Sahara, and San Diego Opens. The difference was that for the first time since turning pro he was never in the picture in any of the four major championships. In the Masters he tied for twenty-fourth, and in the Open for twenty-fifth. This grated on the *amour propre* of a man like Nicklaus, who always geared himself for the big ones. In his mind they were the only ones, really. He played somewhat better in the British Open and in our P.G.A., but tying for sixth and eleventh, respectively, left him a little to the south of ecstasy. He was not hitting the fairways consistently enough—that was a continuing problem—but, beyond this, he had allowed himself to clutter up his splendidly simple swing with one stop-gap gimmick after another. After a while his method of hitting the ball had become so rococo that he never knew what might go wrong next or what had caused an error.

During these disappointing years, it should be brought out, there had been weeks when Nicklaus, with his colossal natural talent and that dauntless will to win, had risen to the big occasions and had almost succeeded in adding another major title to his collection, which now stood at nine: three Masters, two U.S. Amateurs, two U.S. Opens, one British Open, and one P.G.A. There were three championships in particular he might well have won: the 1967 British Open, at Hoylake, where he had rushed up to within two shots of De Vicenzo with a closing 69; the 1968 British Open, at Carnoustie, in which he cut loose down the stretch—on the last four holes especially—with a series of shots of such monstrous power that a less experienced competitor than Player might have been stampeded into letting his two-stroke lead slip away; and, last but not least, the 1968 U.S. Open, at Oak Hill in Rochester, where, though he finished four shots behind Trevino, he played far finer golf from tee to green than he had in winning several of his major championships. On all four rounds at Oak Hill he planted his enormous tee shots in the appropriate patches down the distant fairway. He hit sixty-one of the seventy-two greens in the regulation stroke—the highest number of any player. What killed his chances was his putting. It was atrocious, right from the beginning. On the opening nine holes, a succession of beautifully played irons had presented him with five makeable birdie putts—two from about fourteen feet, three from about seven. He missed them all. It wasn't until the forty-ninth green that he holed a putt of over eight feet. Oak Hill—what a waste of wonderful golf it was!

In the autumn of 1969, the eighteenth Ryder Cup Match was held at Royal Birkdale. It ended in a 16–16 tie, a moral victory for the British. Nicklaus had played fairly well but no better than that in winning his foursome (with Dan Sikes), losing his four-ball (with Sikes), losing one singles to Jacklin 4 and 3, and halving with Jacklin the final singles on which the outcome of the whole Match rode. Yes, the Nicklaus of 1969 was not the crusher he had been before. If it was solace he was looking for, he could draw a gram or two from the fact that golf fans on both sides of the Atlantic approved of his "new look." Earlier that year, as many young men were doing, he had decided to let his white-yellow hair grow longer, and he had received so many compliments about it that there was no doubt he would stay with his new hair style. That fall, as Jack and his wife Barbara were flying back to the States from London after the Ryder Cup Match, he made a much more important decision relevant to his appearance. "Okay," he said, turning to Barbara, "now I'll be at home for three weeks, and if I eat the way I normally do, I'll gain twenty pounds. So know what I think I'll do? I'll lose twenty pounds instead." Once Nicklaus makes up his mind to do something, he invariably follows through on it. As soon as he and Barbara were back at Lost Tree Village, she got out a copy of the Weight Watchers diet a friend had sent her, and the next Monday morning Jack started on the diet. Three days later he was on the phone to his contact man at Hart, Schaffner, & Marx, the firm whose clothes he endorses and from which he naturally receives whatever clothes he wants. Clearing his voice emphatically, Jack asked the contact man if the company could have a tailor come down to Lost Tree two weeks from that day. He was going on a diet in order to lose some weight, he explained, and he would need to have his clothes altered. Two weeks later to the day, the tailor appeared at the Nicklauses'. He measured Jack and announced that he would have to take his pants in six inches around the hips and an inch and a half around the waist. Two weeks later, the tailor returned to see if anything else needed to be done to bring Jack's wardrobe in line with his new dimensions. He measured Jack again and then told him, "Mr. Nicklaus, don't call us for alterations any more. We can't take your pants in any further than we have. We'll have to start all over again." Jack had lost over twenty pounds, dropping from 210 to 190. What is more, he had lost that weight in exactly the right places. In a matter of a little over four weeks, he had changed from "Ohio Fats" into a virtual matinée idol. From 1970 on, his galleries, which had always contained a high ratio of sophisticated golf scholars, became heavily infiltrated with women who occasionally knew the difference between a bogey and a baffy.

Despite his new trim physique, Nicklaus' golf during the first six months of 1970 continued to be perplexingly erratic. He was a good second in the Crosby, a stumbling third in the Andy Williams–San Diego Classic, a decorative eighth in the Masters, an impressive first in the Byron Nelson Golf Classic (where he defeated Palmer on the first extra hole, a long par 5, by reaching the green with two big blows), and a shocking forty-ninth in the Open at Hazeltine, where he managed to break 75 on only one round. Then off to St. Andrews for the British. There was one change: Jack's father, Charles Nicklaus, who always attended the British Open and the other major tourneys, was not on hand. He had died of cancer in February, at the age of fifty-six. There was no question whatsoever that he was Jack Nicklaus' most devoted fan. His greatest pleasure in life was watching his son play tournament golf. He was a friendly, kind, and entirely thoughtful man, Charlie Nicklaus, tops in that regiment of "stage parents" who bulk so large in sports.

In one respect the 1970 British Open was quite similar to the 1970 U.S. Open. At Hazeltine, after the near-gale on the opening day, there followed three days on which the playing conditions and the scoring were what one expects in an American national championship. At St. Andrews, the opening day brought an almost total absence of wind—a rarity in that corner of Fifeshire. After that came a succession of nice, normal, windy days and, in contrast to the opening day, the kind of scoring one expects in the British championship. That first day was something. Though the Old Course measures 6,951 yards from the back tees, for world-class pros it is only a drive-and-pitch course unless a good wind is abroad. It also helps if the ground is fast and fiery, but for the 1970 Open it was the slowest it had ever been. The previous year a sprinkling system had been installed on the greens and tees, and in 1970 this system was extended to some spots on the fairways, with the result that the fine seaside fescue had already been overrun by a coarse, bunchy grass not much different from the strains on inland American courses. That is what "artificial" watering can do for you. Accordingly, on that bland and windless Thursday, the day of the opening round, the Old Course was no match for the field. Shortly after six in the evening, a heavy rain began to fall, and after several greens had become puddled, play was suspended and the men caught in the downpour were instructed to return the following morning at seven-thirty and to resume their rounds where they had left off. All in all, on that first round twenty-one players in a starting field of a 134 equaled par, 72, and another forty-three players broke par. Tommy Horton, of England, had a 66; Neil Coles, another established English pro, had a 65, a new course record; and there is no knowing what Jacklin might have brought in had he completed his round before the rains came. Par to the turn is 36, and Jacklin had gone out in 29—birdie, birdie, birdie, par, birdie, par, birdie, par, eagle. (His pitch to the ninth struck the flagstick on its first bounce and plummeted into the cup.) He had started back with a birdie and three pars, and so he stood an incredible 8 under par when the order to suspend play reached him on the fourteenth hole. The next morning, in a cold rain and a rising wind, Jacklin missed his pars on three of the last five holes and had to be satisfied with a 67. His exciting start, however, infused the tournament with a sense of drama it never lost. It also ended, at least for the moment, the fear that Jacklin might be too worn out to make a creditable defense of his British Open title. In the week before the championship he had had very little rest. Following a schedule laid out months before, whenever Jacklin was not out filming sequences for a B.B.C. special with Palmer, he was at Troon appearing in a pro–amateur wing-ding starring Sean Connery.

The wind that rushed to the rescue of the Old Course on the second day came, like young Lochinvar, from out of the west. It blew throughout the championship, snapping across the outgoing holes from left to right and across the incoming holes from right to left. It brought the Old Course back to life again. On the second day, for illustration, the lowest rounds were two 68s, one by Christy O'Connor of Ireland, the world's greatest foul-weather golfer, and the other by Trevino, who had grown up on the wind-swept plains of Texas and is a master of the low-trajectory shot. Trevino was the leader at the halfway mark with 136—a stroke in front of Jacklin and Nicklaus. On the third day he matched par with a 72 and increased his lead to two strokes over Jacklin, Nicklaus, and Doug Sanders, the Georgia peacock, who had moved up with a 71. Most people thought Trevino would hold on in the fourth round without much trouble, and they looked for either Nicklaus or Jacklin to provide his strongest challenge—Nicklaus if his fragile putting touch did not collapse, Jacklin if he had the necessary physical and nervous reserves. (By the end of the third round, his eyes were glazed with fatigue.) Sanders was accorded little or no chance. In his case, conjecture centered at least as much on the outfit he would be wearing as on the kind of golf he might play in the crunch. On the third round, he had trotted out a red-and-black ensemble featuring trousers, piped with tartan, that were cut so tight he could not squat down to line up his putts. As it turned out, Sanders was again partial to Scotland on the fourth round—a vision in shades of heathery purple.

The fourth round was filled with surprises. Trevino, customarily a most dependable putter, lost his stroke early in the buffeting wind, and after a spate of three-putt greens on the front nine, he was out of it. Jacklin, bone-tired, held on until the sixteenth. There he missed a putt for a birdie and ended up by taking three putts, and his gallant effort was over. In the end it was a battle between Nicklaus, playing with Jacklin in the next-to-last pair, and Sanders, playing with Trevino behind them. Both men had their chances down the stretch, and both blew them. Nicklaus, with his awesome power, reached the 560-yard fourteenth in two, but then took three putts to get down. He took three putts on the sixteenth and three more on the eighteenth, a 358-yard 4, where his drive finished at the front edge of the green. Thanks to Nicklaus' generosity and his own courageous play (which included getting down in 2 from the terrifying Road Bunker on the seventeenth), Sanders came to the eighteenth needing only a par 4 to win his first major championship. An excellent drive, seventy-four paces from the flag, set beyond the Valley of Sin. A sand-wedge thirty-five feet past the flag. An approach putt three and a half feet short. Sanders took his stance over the ball. He bent down to pick up a blade of grass that looked as if it might be a tiny pebble. He took his stance again, set himself in the wind, tapped the ball, and missed the cup on the right.

The playoff (over eighteen holes) took place on Sunday afternoon. It was hard not to be strongly sympathetic toward both men. Sanders, the graying playboy with the unorthodox swing, is an easy man to like, for beneath the raffish trappings are a warm heart and a fund of humor. Nicklaus' appeal is different. An able young man with an interesting mind, he had established himself at twenty-seven as one of the great golfers of all time. However, he had won no major title since 1967, and it was now being said in some quarters that he never would win another, that he was burned out at thirty. Here at St. Andrews he had the opportunity he had been patiently waiting for. His golf, by the way, had surprised quite a few people. Into the west wind, he had had to play his shots from right to left going out; a very ordinary right-to-left player, he had handled this problem better than he had ever done before. On the second nine, after making the turn around the loop, he did not choose to go back to his usual left-to-right method, and staying with a right-to-left action even though the wind was now crossing with him, he had used the wind astutely, letting it help him on several holes, permitting the ball to get away from him on none. Would he be able to maintain this unexpected control for another round?

So the galleries marched out to the loop one more time beneath a low, flat, cloud-filled sky. Black-headed gulls wheeled in the west wind. Swallows scudded along the ground, clearing the hummocks by inches. Accompanying the spectators were lots of dogs, which never barked, and lots of children, who didn't howl or fuss, which is the way it is in Scotland. For thirteen holes it was the dullest of playoffs. Nicklaus, who had parred every hole, built up a four-shot lead. And then, suddenly, Sanders launched one of the most fervent dashes in the history of the British Open. He picked up a stroke when he birdied the fourteenth. He picked up another stroke when he birdied the fifteenth with a 12-footer. He picked up another on the sixteenth, where Nicklaus took three from the edge. As they came to the famous Road Hole, a dogleg right 466 yards long where the deep Road Bunker on the left of the raised, angled green and the hard-surfaced road to the right infect the golfer with that old Scylla–Charybdis virus, Sanders was only one stroke back. Two first-class tee shots. Sanders, away, played his approach, a 5-iron hit low. The ball bounded onto the left side of the long, narrow green but swung a dangerous yard farther to the left and headed for the Road Bunker. Somehow it slipped by the hazard, climbed back onto the putting surface, and finished at the rear of the green twenty feet past the cup. In this emergency, Nicklaus came through with one of the bravest shots of his career—a high, uncompromised 7-iron, right at the flag. It dropped softly in the center of the green and ended up inside of Sanders' ball, fourteen feet from the hole. Both two-putted.

On the eighteenth a following wind was blowing down the fairway. Sanders, still trailing by that one stroke, played the hole flawlessly and had his birdie all the way: he drove close to the green and put his run-up dead to the cup. The question was whether Nicklaus would be able to match that birdie. On the tee Jack had removed his sweater, to gain more freedom of movement, and then had cut loose with a booming tee shot that bounced onto the green and rolled over it into a bank of fairly high, dryish rough. Fortunately, he had the kind of lie that allowed him to get the face of his wedge cleanly on the ball, and he lobbed a delicate recovery eight feet from the cup—above it. Then he made a very, very good putt. For just a moment, it looked as if the ball might slide off to the right, but it held its line and fell. Nicklaus, exhilarated, threw his putter thirty feet in the air. Then he and Sanders collapsed on each other's shoulders.

At the presentation ceremony, William Whitelaw, the captain of the R. & A., said, "We have been privileged to watch one of the golf matches of all time." Moments later, a sudden skirling of bagpipes was heard in the upper balcony of the clubhouse, and each individual present became lost in his private thoughts. More than a few found their minds drifting back to the seventeenth and to Nicklaus' approach shot. Once Sanders' second

Exhilarated at staving off Doug Sanders'
stretch rush with an 8-footer on the home
green in the 1970 British Open playoff,
Nicklaus hurls his putter high in the air.

stood white and clear at the back of the green at the end of its strange, careening course, the pressure had been thrust squarely on Nicklaus. In retrospect, the shot he then faced may have been the pivotal one of his career. Had he missed the green with his approach or somehow or other failed to match Sanders' sure 4, he would have lost the last stroke of what on the fourteenth tee had been a four-stroke lead. Had this transpired, many veteran observers are of the opinion that, one way or another, Sanders would have won the playoff, on the eighteenth or in extra holes. In fact, there are some people who believe that if something had gone awry with Nicklaus' second to the seventeenth and he had eventually lost the playoff—this after having three-putted three of the last five greens in the championship proper the day before to open the door for Sanders—his days as a champion would have been over there and then. The reverse took place. Nicklaus' victory at St. Andrews reinspired him. Slowly but surely the confidence that had seeped away returned, and with it came a strong desire to become a better golfer than he had ever been before. During the next three years, retaining that purpose, he went on to win four more major championships and was unlucky not to win more. His golf attained such a high standard that many sports authorities were convinced that he was the greatest player who had ever lived, and there were only a handful of diehards who wouldn't grant that Jack Nicklaus had proved himself at least the peer of Harry Vardon, Bob Jones, and Ben Hogan.

One national championship that Nicklaus might well have won during his renaissance but did not was the 1971 U.S. Open. That June, after an hiatus of twenty-one years, the Open was held once again at Merion. Since national Opens are supposed to be played on a country's best courses, this long absence from Merion did not make much sense, though there was, to be sure, a handy rationalization: there was no room at the club for the spectators to park. This obstacle was hurdled through the good offices of Villanova and Haverford, which made parking space available at their campuses, from which points the spectators who used these facilities were bused to and from the course. It might be stated that there was also a lingering suspicion that some of the members of Merion really hadn't wanted the Open out of fear that, in an age when championships were being conducted on layouts stretching over 7,000 yards, the celebrated East Course, still a mere 6,544 yards, might be disclosed to be as pitifully superannuated as the one-horse shay. Merion's only hope of demonstrating that it was still a bonafide championship course·was to prepare its greens to such a degree of perfection that they would: (1) be firm enough so that only a sharply struck shot would have the rotation to hold them, and (2) be fast enough for putting to require what Gene Sarazen liked to call a "violinist's touch." Adding to the built-in drama of the situation—Would this classic course survive or be trampled on?—was the fact that the man responsible for getting the course ready was Richie Valentine, the son of the renowned old Merion greenkeeper, Joe Valentine, who, among other things, had discovered Merion bluegrass in a patch behind the seventeenth tee. In 1961, shortly before his father's death, Richie, who had studied agronomy at Penn State, succeeded him as the club's superintendent. Three weeks before the start of the 1971 Open, as his first step toward getting the greens in the shape he wanted them, Valentine gave them a heavy top dressing—99 percent sand—an eighth of an inch in depth. A week later he gave them a second top dressing, a sixteenth of an inch in depth. Eight days before the start of the Open, to begin bringing the greens to the speed he was after, Valentine lowered the cut on his mowers for their daily trim to five thirty-seconds of an inch. On the morning of the opening round, he had his crew double-cut the greens, criss-crossing the second cut over the first. The evening after the first round—the U.S.G.A., while delighted with the greens, felt they may have been a fraction too receptive to the approach shots—Valentine, to get them just a little firmer, rolled them. (As it turned out, this was the last time he used his rollers on them.) The next morning Valentine triple-cut the greens, as he did each morning for the duration of the tournament. They were just right—not too soft, not too resilient; not too fast for putting, not too slow either. The rest of the course was also in A-1 condition and remained so, thanks to four rainless days. Merion proved that, properly prepared and given a break in the weather, it still remained, 6,544 yards or not, a severe, fair, and fascinating test of golf for the world's best players. Not one man in the field, as a matter of fact, broke 280, par for four rounds.

High Drama in the Seventies, at Home and Abroad

On the first round, played on a humid, close day, as were the succeeding rounds, seven men broke par: 36-34—70. Labron Harris, Jr., the son of the long-time golf coach at Oklahoma State, had the low round, a 67. Nicklaus was off with a 69, on which he used his driver only three times on a course with two par 5s and twelve par 4s. On the second day, when six players were under par, there were two 67s. One of them was shot by Bob Erickson, an unknown pro from Florida with a craggy, weather-beaten face who looked as if he had done as much living in his forty-five years as a Ross Macdonald private eye. At 138, Erickson shared the lead at the midway mark with Jim Colbert, a thirty-year-old touring pro who had gone to Kansas State on a football scholarship. Nicklaus was three strokes back after a spotty 72 on which he had a double-bogey 6 on the 370-yard eleventh, the storied Baffling Brook hole; he had almost caught the brook twice, first with his second shot—a sharply pulled recovery he had scythed out of the rough on the right into the edge of the woods on the left, and second, with his fourth shot, a run-up chip from the green's front fringe which he botched so badly that it ran at least twenty feet past the pin, over the back of the green, and halfway down the sloping rough that falls to the brook. (After cutting across the fairway from the right, the Baffling Brook swings sharply back to the right and follows close along the border of the green on its right side and at the rear.) Tied at 141 with Nicklaus, after ripping off a 68, was a very familiar face, Arnold Palmer. This marked the first time since 1967, when he had fought Nicklaus hard all the way at Baltusrol, that Palmer was in a position to be a factor in the Open. On the third round, though, the hopes of his faithful army were dashed when his 73 left him seven shots behind the leader—a most surprising leader, Jim Simons, a twenty-one-year-old native of Butler, Pennsylvania, where his father manufactured deodorizers. Simons, the number-two man on the Wake Forest golf team (behind Lanny Wadkins, the national Amateur Champion), had earlier that year had the unhappy distinction of being a member of the first American Walker Cup team since 1938 to be beaten by the British, and following those grim hours at St. Andrews, he had suffered the hard disappointment of losing the final of the British Amateur, at Carnoustie, to Steve Melnyk, his Walker Cup teammate. A thin, blond young man whose natural shyness presented an engaging change of pace from the cocksureness of most of his contemporaries, Simons had surged into the lead on the Saturday at Merion with a remarkable 65, which gave him a total of 207, 3 under par. Two shots back lay the best golfer in the world, Nicklaus. On the Saturday Jack had had a 68 made up of two birdies and sixteen pars, but, in truth, those figures were a little misleading; a good many of the pars had depended on some topnotch touch shots, mainly with the sand-wedge, from the knotty rough framing the sleek, slippery greens. Two shots behind Nicklaus—and four behind Simons—lay the man most golfers at this time regarded as the second best player in the world but who, until he had moved up with a 69 on the third round, had not been close to the leaders. This player, of course, was Lee Trevino.

The Open rapidly resolved itself on Sunday into a contest between Simons, Nicklaus (with whom he was paired in the last twosome), and Trevino (in the twosome immediately in front of them). At four-thirty in the afternoon, Trevino struck the crucial blow of the day, an 8-iron approach to the 405-yard twelfth on which he made such sharp contact with the ball that, after landing a dozen or so feet beyond the pin set to the rear of the plateaued green, the terrific backspin on the ball brought it back fifteen inches from the hole. This bedazzling birdie lifted Trevino into a tie for the tournament lead, at even par, with both Simons and Nicklaus. On the fourteenth he took over the undisputed lead by dropping a twelve-foot putt for another birdie. Three sound pars protected this lead, but on the eighteenth, a 458-yard 4, Lee opened the gates by mis-hitting his second and finally pushing the six-foot putt he had for his par a shade to the right of the hole. Nicklaus seized this opportunity. If Jack is oddly vulnerable to major errors for a golfer of his class—on the fifth that afternoon, after catching Simons, he had thrown away a chance to take command of the tournament there and then by pulling his drive forty yards to the left of the desired line and into a brook, for a double bogey—he is an almost incomparable competitor down the stretch when the strain is the greatest. On the fifteenth and sixteenth he had kept himself within striking distance of Trevino by sinking clutch putts of about six feet. On the seventeenth, where he learned that Trevino had bogeyed the last hole, he managed to get down another sinuous 6-footer to save his par. He came to the eighteenth needing a par to tie. That last hole, a roller-coaster fairway to a humpbacked green, is perhaps the toughest on the course. Nicklaus played it heroically. His drive—his best of the tournament—was down the middle of the narrow fairway, about 280 yards out. Then, playing a 4-iron from a steepish downhill lie, he got the ball up in a high, soft trajectory, dead on line. It stopped fifteen feet short of the pin. His target on the putt was the right-hand corner of the cup, but he pulled the ball the merest bit and it trickled by on the left. Nicklaus 280. Trevino 280. Simons, who had a 6 on the final hole, finished three shots behind them—a tremendous effort.

Playoffs more often than not are anticlimactic, but this was an arresting one. After an inauspicious beginning—on the first hole Trevino got his body way out in front on a little 9-iron pitch and shoved the ball into a bunker, and on the second and third holes Nicklaus foozled a couple of bunker shots—these two magnificent shot-makers settled down and the gallery was treated to a fascinating duel. The previous autumn, when they had met in the final of the World Match Play Championship at Wentworth, Nicklaus had been the winner, 2 and 1. This time it was Trevino's day. He played an almost error-free round. After the third hole, he led all the way, riposting instantly whenever Nicklaus threatened, and he eventually was around in a 68 compared to Nicklaus' 71.

Trevino, who is extremely chunky in build, is anything but a picture swinger. He is the fellow you meet in the first round of the state amateur championship who wallops you 7 and 6 and leaves you utterly confounded. He takes the club back on a very flat plane as he wheels around on his backswing. He would probably hit one duck hook after another if it weren't that he had schooled himself to keep his left leg set solidly as he comes into the ball. This gives him something to hit against, and, with his exceptionally fine hand action, he opens the face of his club a split second before impact and fades the ball from left to right, forcing his right shoulder through and around on a flat, wheat-

Lee Trevino does not possess one of the most comely golf swings in the world, but few are as efficient or as reliable. The stocky Texan probably stays down over his shots longer than any other contemporary player and hits through the ball superbly.

cutting plane. In spite of his agricultural style, as Leonard Crawley, the English golf critic, has described it, Trevino, in top form, controls the ball as well as anyone in the game. His drives, spanked on a low line, almost invariably find the fairway. He is an expert iron player, and from 125 yards in, phenomenal; those were the shots he had to depend on back in the grisly days when he was hustling for a living. To round things out, he is a devastating putter, with a sound, simple style: the blade, square all the way, skims just above the grass going back and going through. He is, in short, sort of a later model of Bobby Locke and Billy Casper—a straight, steady player who can be murder on and around the greens. He certainly was against Nicklaus in their playoff. On the twelfth, the skiddiest green on the course, he sank a 20-foot sidehiller. On the four-teenth, he got down in 2 from the rough beside the green by holing from ten feet. On the fifteenth, after Nicklaus had put his approach seven feet from the flag, Trevino held him off by rolling in a 25-footer for *his* birdie. He simply gave Nicklaus no openings whatsoever—he didn't bogey a hole after the first—and when Nicklaus at length made a mistake on the seventeenth, bunkering his tee shot and missing his par, the outcome was settled. (An appropriate word about Nicklaus: Because he is so good at winning, we are apt to overlook what a good loser he is. There isn't a better sportsman in sport.)

With the exception of Palmer, in 1971 no golfer on the pro tour was as popular with the crowds as Trevino. On the course he talked a blue streak, partly because talking calmed him down, and partly because the fans obviously doted on his banter and his way of presenting himself as a man of the people, the unaffected and unpretentious Chicano. (He overdid this a little perhaps in the playoff against Nicklaus, cleverly setting Jack up as the chap from the country club and himself as the guy with the common touch.) While there is no question that Trevino possesses verve, humor, and natural appeal, he loses some members of his gallery when he becomes too consciously the commercial gagman and the professional wooer. There is good Trevino and bad Trevino, the proportions depending on the taste of each individual. Under good Trevino most people would certainly put the sally he made on the 72nd tee at Merion when his nervous caddie forgot to give him his driver. "Are you choking already?" Trevino asked. "I'm doing all the playing, and *you're* choking." It would most assuredly include that crazy moment on the first tee before the start of the playoff when Trevino pulled a toy snake from the pocket of his golf bag and tossed it at Nicklaus. Under bad Trevino most people would put the formula cracks he is in the habit of repeating with little or no variation thousands upon thousands of times, such as his greeting to Edward Heath, the former British Prime Minister, at the 1970 British Open—"Did you ever shake hands with a Mexican before?"—and prattle on the order of "Why do I wear a red sports shirt on Sundays? Well, if I play bad on the last round of a tournament and cut my throat, it blends." Anyway, we can be fairly sure of two things: there have been few more voluble golfers in the history of the game, and few better ones.

The week after the Open at Merion, when some of the big names were already refining their itineraries for the trip to Royal Birkdale and the British Open, Trevino played in the Cleveland Open. He scored rather high compared to the pace-setters, ending in a tie for thirty-fourth. What he probably needed at this juncture was to throw his clubs in a closet and get away from the grind for at least a week. Instead, for all his weariness, he stuck to his schedule and during the next two weeks won the Canadian Open and the British Open. This was something no golfer had ever done before—win three national championships, including the two that count the most, within a span of four weeks. There is a good chance this feat may never be repeated.

In 1971 the Canadian Open was played at the Richelieu Valley Golf and Country Club, outside Montreal, a course that has several cardinal shortcomings and was not up to the standard of a championship of that importance. Trevino had one day's practice and then shot an indifferent 73, which placed him far down the list. He roused himself, and rounds of 68 and 67 put him in a position to challenge the leader, Art Wall, a graying forty-seven-year-old relic of the Hepplewhite period who, at 209 (70-67-69), was out in front by two strokes. Wall liked to play the Canadian and usually did well in it. He was second in 1959, won it in 1960, and was second again in 1970. He was ready for another victory. Always excepting the Caribbean Tour—he had taken eight events on it—Wall had not won a tournament north of Key West since 1966, when he had captured the Insurance City Open in Hartford. That was a long time back, and so was 1959, when he had won the one major title in his long career, the Masters. (It is doubtful if the winning of a major championship has ever had the salutary effect on a golfer, both immediately and over the long run, that Wall's victory at Augusta had on him.) Now it was 1971, and Wall, with the sole exception of Julius Boros, was the oldest player who still showed up at a good number of the stops on the pro circuit. He was still an authoritative striker of the irons, and discerning spectators were equally impressed by his politeness and inveterate sincerity.

Trevino started their duel on the fourth and final round with an eagle 3, holing out his pitch. Wall sank a good putt for his birdie there and remained a shot in front. That is how things stood until Trevino birdied the 70th to draw even. On the last three greens, Wall failed on birdie putts of twelve, seven, and six feet, and Trevino, for his part, missed a birdie putt of only four feet on the last green. On the first extra hole, however, Lee knocked in the 15-footer he had for his birdie, and that was that—73-68-67-67—275, plus the 3 on the extra hole. He could play as brilliantly when overgolfed and exhausted as Jones and Nelson could. The following week he demonstrated just how brilliantly, when he added the British Open to his string of triumphs.

After flying to London, Trevino got to the sandhills of Birkdale in time to get in a solitary practice round. Many of his rivals had been studying the course for days, and Jack Nicklaus, as usual, had arrived so early that it looked as if he might be taking out citizenship papers. At Birkdale, Trevino did not act like a man who had been pushing himself hard for weeks. He said he liked the course and that he thought he had a good chance of winning on it, and then he segued into a series of his staple one-liners.

Trevino was not bluffing when he said that he felt fine and thought he could win the Open. From the start he was up among the leaders, due, to a certain extent, to his ability to handle Birkdale's greens, which many golfers find troublesome. His opening 69, fashioned in the warm, calm weather that was to prevail throughout the championship, tied him for the lead. (At Birkdale a 69 is 4 under par, but it should be mentioned that the course has a good many holes technically assessed as 5s that golfers of world class can reach in two shots.) On Thursday—in Britain the Open starts on Wednesday

Clowning in three acts. Lee Trevino, after sinking a long putt on the eighth green at Birkdale on the final day of the 1971 British Open, pantomimes his elation.

and ends on Saturday—Trevino and Jacklin took over the lead after thirty-six holes at 139. Trevino managed his 70 by canning a putt for an eagle 3 on the eighteenth, but by this time it would not have startled anyone if Trevino had called a press conference and put on a film showing how he had caught the Loch Ness Monster. One stroke behind the leaders was a most surprising contender, Lu Liang-huan, a small-boned, thirty-five-year-old pro from Taiwan, who had put together a pair of 70s. Mr. Lu, as the British nation alluded to this visitor whom it quickly took to its heart, had, at first inspection, no right to be where he was. His swing had 86 written all over it—a nice, practice-fairway, willow-tree-pattern swing. Its delicacy disguised the fact that Mr. Lu was making the correct movements and that, for all his waftiness through the ball, he was getting it out about as far as the Occidental clouters. A pleasant-looking man with a pleasant manner, Mr. Lu had a penchant for replying to applause with easy, unforced smiles supplemented from time to time with a little bow or a doff of his narrow-brimmed, pork-pie-shaped straw hat. Lu Liang-huan had won tournaments galore in the Far East, of course, but what was happening at Birkdale was something different. This was the first time a golfer from Asia had played himself into the thick of the fight in one of the world's great tournaments.

Trevino jumped into the lead on the third round with a 69 for 208, a stroke ahead of Jacklin, who had had a 70, and Mr. Lu who had moved up softly with a 69. Mr. Lu's English, while limited, is on the mark. His final words to the press after chatting with them following the third round were, "Me say many prayers tonight."

For a while on Saturday, the day of the fourth round, it looked as if Trevino would win in a romp. He hit one controlled left-to-right drive after another down the hilled-in fairways, keeping well out of the dangerous scrub in the rough. His irons were steady. He putted like a dream. He made the turn in 31, having used only eleven putts—four for birdies. At this point in the afternoon, Jacklin, seven strokes behind, had been all but counted out, and Mr. Lu, after a 36 on the front nine, trailed by five strokes and could hardly be considered a threat either. Heading home, Jacklin put on a fighting spurt, and Mr. Lu kept wafting the ball down the middle and onto the greens, but Trevino was moving along so equably that the good play of his challengers almost didn't matter. Up to the seventeenth, that is. Then, almost before anyone realized it—it happened so fast—Trevino was in trouble.

The seventeenth at Birkdale is a 510-yard par 5 that runs fairly straight from tee to green over rolling terrain. Trevino aimed his drive for the sandhills hugging the fairway on the left. He cracked the ball on the sweet spot, and the gallery watching its flight felt it would be perfect. Like all of Trevino's low, line-drive tee shots, it would begin to swing to the right and would land on the fairway and run for yards. For some reason, on this tee shot the left-to-right cut didn't take. The ball flew straight ahead and into one of the scrub-covered sandhills. Though the lie didn't seem too bad, it must have been difficult, for Trevino was able to hit his second only a couple of yards. It was still in the rough, moreover. His third went too far—across the fairway and into the rough along the right. He struggled on to a 7. Now he stood only one stroke ahead of Jacklin, who had finished his round, and only one ahead of Mr. Lu, his playing partner, who was still drawing applause with his shots and acknowledging it with a smile, a bow, a doff of the straw hat. On the seventeenth green, some particularly well-informed spectators began to buzz about the Alcan tournament of 1969 in which, unbelievably, Trevino had lost seven shots, and the tournament, to Casper over the last three holes.

On the eighteenth tee, Trevino quietly pulled himself together. On the home hole, a 513-yard 5 that can be reached in 2, he was on in 2 after ripping two first-class shots to the back of the green. He rolled his approach putt sixteen inches from the cup and tapped it in. He needed that 4, as it turned out. Mr. Lu birdied the hole, too. (The following week, Monsieur Lu won the French Open.)

Trevino's total of 278 (69-70-69-70) was fourteen strokes under par. Prize money for first place was $13,200. Of this amount, Trevino gave $4,800 to a local orphanage. Whenever he won a big tournament, Trevino showed his size; he saw to it that a good slice of his earnings went to charity. "When you have no money," Lee once remarked,

The British Open underwent a tremendous renaissance in the late 1960s and the 1970s. Above, a huge and orderly crowd of spectators surrounds Mr. Lee and Mr. Lu at Birkdale. Below, the sunny and serene Mr. Lu, the fine golfer from Taiwan, in action.

"no one will do anything for you. If you become successful and pile up enough money to buy anything you want, people deluge you with gifts you don't need and try to do all kinds of things for you. It's a very strange world."

In his banner year of 1971, Trevino won seven tournaments (including the British Open), and his official winnings on the tour came to $231,202. (Nicklaus, with five wins and a take of $244,490, led the parade.) The following season represented a slight falling off for Trevino: three tour victories, thirteen finishes in the top ten, and earnings of $214,815. This record again placed him second to the astonishing Mr. Nicklaus. For all that Trevino achieved in 1972, however, that year was nowhere as happy for him as 1971 had been. He began to show in his streaks of petulance the effects of his burdensome schedule of playing thirty or more tournaments each season. While most weeks he talked as compulsively as ever with his devoted galleries, he protested on more than one occasion that he no longer had the energy to fulfill the demands his position made on him. And it was about this time that, under the constant strain, he began to come down with illnesses. Yes, there was no getting away from it. By pushing himself so hard, Trevino had become a very tired man, albeit a very rich tired man. Things had happened so fast that the young Texan hadn't been able to digest and control them. Nevertheless, there was one week in 1972 in which he was very much the old Trevino, and it happened to be the week of the British Open.

By 1972 the British Open had regained all of its old significance, largely because it had streamlined its outmoded approach to putting on the tourney. Under the adroit entrepreneurial shepherding of Keith MacKenzie, the secretary of the R. & A., the old championship had assimilated in the late 1960s and the early 1970s the advanced knowhow in the staging of golf tournaments that had been pioneered principally by the Masters in the 1940s, 1950s, and 1960s under the leadership of Bob Jones and Clifford Roberts, from 1934 the one and only Masters chairman. The British Open had also absorbed certain lessons from the U.S.G.A.'s progressive operation of the U.S. Open. Not only had the British Open, the original stroke-play championship, finally stumbled into the brave, new, post-war world and caught up with the slickly efficient American tournaments, but in certain areas—such as the number of scoreboards around the course and the speed with which scores were posted, not to mention the size and number of viewing stands for spectators—the new blood that had infiltrated the R. & A. had evolved methods far superior to those employed by its American tutors. This recalled to at least one Anglo-American how, years before, a corps of official British observers, after marveling at the New York subway system, had returned to London and built a far better one.

All well and good, but to get back to the 1972 British Open, its significance rested on the presence of three players. There was Trevino, eager to see if at Muirfield he could make it two triumphs in a row. There was Jacklin. Would he be able to come back after a rather lean period? And, above all, there was Nicklaus. Earlier in the year he had won the Masters and the U.S. Open at Pebble Beach by three strokes, and he would be bearing down at Muirfield hoping to win the third trick in the modern professional Grand Slam. The British Open loomed as the key trick. If Nicklaus could take it, his confidence and purpose might then be so unshakable that the fourth and final trick, the P.G.A., set for Oakland Hills, could very well fall to him.

Nicklaus came extremely close to winning at that Open. Had he done so, golf scholars in future decades might well assess his fourth round the crowning achievement of "Big Jack's" career. For three rounds at Muirfield, where Nicklaus had won the Open in a driving finish six summers before, this super golfer, this fusion of raw power, sophisticated technique, and competitive flair, stayed comfortably close to the lead. An opening round of 70, a stroke under par, placed him a shot behind Jacklin, who appeared to be in crackling good form. A 72 on the second day kept him a shot behind the co-leaders, Jacklin and Trevino; Trevino had added a 70 to an opening 71. On the third day, which offered a continuation of the ideal playing conditions that had prevailed from the start, Nicklaus had a 71—a very frustrating 71, since he had played a good bit better than his score; but both Jacklin and Trevino had drawn well away. Trevino, with a 66, had come in in 30, birdieing the last five holes. It was like witchcraft, the way the ball behaved for him. On the fourteenth a 20-foot putt fell softly into the cup, and on the fifteenth a putt of fifteen feet went down. On the sixteenth, 190 yards, he was in the right-hand bunker off the tee, but his sand-shot—not a very good one, skulled rather than lobbed—hit the flagstick on a fast hop and dropped straight down into the cup. On the seventeenth, 542 yards over the high ridge to the small pocket green, he reached with two woods. On the eighteenth, after his approach had run thirty feet up the shallow incline behind the green, he chipped into the hole. While Trevino was working these miracles, Jacklin had not been altogether passive. He played the last five in 2 under par to bring in a 67, but, for all this, his two-stroke lead had vanished and he now trailed Trevino by a shot. Tony, however, was buoyed by the thought that he had outplayed Trevino, and he looked forward to the fourth round full of confidence. He was the only British golfer in quite some time who honestly believed that he was just as good as any American golfer.

Nicklaus, with a round to go, stood six full shots behind Trevino, five behind Jacklin. He hadn't given up, not this young bull who loved the challenge of coming from behind. Neither had his partisans, although some of them thought that he had played too defensively on the first three rounds. Would they ever see him collect all of his abundant forces, they asked themselves, and under the spur of a great occasion shoot the fantastic, shattering round they knew he was capable of? For several hours on the fourth day, it looked as if that long-awaited round was in the making. No birdie on the first but one on the second—only a short putt after a lovely pitch. On the third, another birdie, of a similar type. He had it going, all right, and from his unvarying scowl of determination you knew he meant to keep it going. On the long fifth, which he was expected to birdie, no mistakes—a perfect birdie. A fourth birdie on the par-5 ninth. A fifth on the tenth, a far from easy par 4. A sixth on the eleventh. This sustained barrage of birdies, with nothing but pars filling in the interstices, had thrust Nicklaus a shot ahead of the field, despite eagles on the ninth by both Trevino and Jacklin, playing together two groups behind him. Nicklaus kept his lead until Trevino birdied the eleventh and Jacklin the fourteenth. This created a triple tie for first, and set the stage for one of the most memorable climaxes in golfing history.

After he had birdied the eleventh, Nicklaus did not let up. He had relatively short birdie putts on the twelfth, the thirteenth, the fourteenth, and the fifteenth. Two hit the corner of the hole and rimmed out. On the sixteenth, the 190-yard 3, he pulled his 4-iron a shade, and the ball trickled into the high grass, but he was equal to this spot of difficulty. He lobbed a gentle little chip five feet behind the cup. After working hard on his putt, he decided to play it about an inch and a half to the right of the cup. It broke much faster than he had bargained for, and slipped by the cup on the left without touching it. A bogey 4, at just the wrong time. He would have to make up for that by birdieing the long seventeenth, getting home in two. Jack had been keeping his driver pretty much in the bag during this tournament, repeating his successful strategy in the 1966 Open. Now he reached for it. It may have been a mistake. In any event, he hooked his drive into trouble and had to be content with a par. He parred the eighteenth. A gutty 66, for 279, but would it be good enough? To edge him out, either Trevino or Jacklin had only to finish with pars.

On the fifteenth, the tournament was Jacklin's for the taking: he had a 7-footer for his birdie. It rolled off just at the cup. Pars for both men on the sixteenth. On the seventeenth, another big chance for Tony. He lay two just off the green and, even after a poor chip, seventeen feet from the cup in three; he was well inside of Trevino, who was over the green in four, in a bank of thatchy rough, after a series of loose shots: a hooked drive into a bunker, a mediocre recovery, another hooky wood into the stubbled rough short and to the left of the green, and a chip shot that got away from him. Two putts for a par 5 would do it for Jacklin. But first, Trevino's chip. Considering his downhill lie and the tufty grass he was in, he manufactured a very good shot. It was running nicely—he would be close enough to get down in one putt. It was better than that—the ball was running right for the hole. It was in! Trevino had needed one more miracle shot and he had produced it. It proved to be the winning stroke, for Jacklin then took three putts, missing from four feet. Trevino played the eighteenth with panache, drilling his second only ten feet from the hole. Jacklin again failed to make his par. It was understandable. The scores:

TREVINO	71-70-66-71—278
NICKLAUS	70-72-71-66—279
JACKLIN	69-72-67-72—280

Shortly before the start of the 1972 season—on December 18, 1971, to be precise—Robert Tyre Jones, Jr., died in Atlanta at the age of sixty-nine. At the Masters the following April, his absence was felt sharply and continually, as was to be expected. (In 1969, 1970, and 1971, Jones had had to miss the Masters, for by that time the severe illness he had borne so quietly for twenty years had become so incapacitating that he couldn't make the journey to Augusta from his home in Atlanta.) What was surprising was the sense of shock and grief that so many people experienced when the word came in December of his death. The inhabitants of the sports world had been prepared for this news for years, and, in addition, in one corner of their hearts they knew it would be a blessing, since the spinal disease Jones was afflicted with—syringomyelia—was inordinately cruel and crippling. In another corner of their hearts they had been nursing the faint hope that somehow or other Jones would make it back again to Augusta some future spring and that they would be seeing him again and talking with him again, and now they knew they wouldn't.

In the opinion of many people, of all the great athletes Jones came the closest to being what we call a great man. Like Winston Churchill, he had the quality of being at the same time much larger than life and exceedingly human. Certainly he had an extraordinarily fine mind, with an astounding range. He was one of the few athletes who personally wrote what appeared under his name, and he wrote an exact, evocative prose. He had the same feeling for words as Adlai Stevenson, and the same self-deprecatory humor. Bob had other exceptional gifts. His sense of proportion was uncommon in a man with a vigorously perfectionistic side to his nature. His family—his wife Mary and their three children—came first; his work as a member of an Atlanta law firm came second; his golf came third. He had unbelievable strength of character. As a young man he was able to stand up to just about the best that life can offer, which isn't easy, and later he stood up with equal grace to just about the worst.

It is doubtful if the Masters, for all its multiple virtues, could have risen to prominence so rapidly and become accepted as a major championship in hardly more than a dozen years had anyone other than Jones created the event and watched over its development. From the outset the tournament reflected his personality: its atmosphere was both dignified and informal, and it was pervaded by the spirit of golf at its best. Jones played in his last Masters in 1948, when the pain in his neck and shoulders, which had been bothering him for some time, became so intense that he underwent surgery to relieve pressure on his spine. Two years later, another operation was necessary. It was finally discovered that he was suffering from a rare disease of the spinal cord that might gradually bring about total muscular paralysis. By this time Jones had to walk with a cane and was in constant pain, but he made it a practice, as he continued to until a year or so before his death, to go to the office daily and to keep busy also in golf. In 1953, for example, he flew to New York to attend the dinner honoring Ben Hogan on Ben's return from Britain, where he had added a victory in the British Open to previous victories that year in the Masters and the U.S. Open—perhaps the greatest golfing feat since Jones' Grand Slam. When arrangements were made for the first World Amateur Team Championship for the Eisenhower Trophy, to be held at St. Andrews in October 1958, Jones, a close friend of the General's, was asked to serve as captain of the American team and he accepted, though it is hard to know how much this trip took out of him. In the 1960s, when he was confined to a wheelchair, the word went around each winter that his condition had become worse, and everyone in golf, knowing that Bob had also suffered from heart trouble from 1952 on, speculated as to whether he would be able to attend that year's Masters. Somehow he got to Augusta each April until 1969, though by then his body had so wasted away that he weighed scarcely ninety pounds and could no longer open his fingers to shake hands or grasp a pen. However, he never looked as bad as his friends dreaded he might. While his body had withered away to nothing, his handsome head and features remained relatively untouched, and his mind was as incisive and delightful as ever. He was one of the master letter-writers of our time, incidentally, and it is an understatement to say that the arrival of a letter from Jones on the distinctive heavy bond stationery he used, with its familiar Poplar Street letterhead, could make your day.

About three days before Bob Jones' death, when he knew he was dying, he said to the members of his family, "If this is all there is to it, it sure is peaceful." That is good to know.

In the age of the jet plane, when a man could play a round at Royal Worlington, outside Newmarket, in the morning, and a second round at Kittansett, on Buzzards Bay, in the same day, international competition naturally flourished. In 1970, the Eisenhower Trophy Match began its third biennial swing around the globe at the Real Club de la Puerta de Hierro in Madrid. It was in that year, in Madrid, at the R.S.H.E. Club de Campo that one of the hottest battles for the Espirito Santo Trophy, emblematic of victory in the Women's World Amateur Team Championship, took place. The United States won by a solitary stroke—one of the four that Martha Wilkinson picked up on Catherine Lacoste De Prado with a strong, valiant rally on the final nine. As for the Ryder Cup, the Matches that followed the hummer in 1969 were never anything like that close. The Curtis Cup remained a baffling affair as it entered the Seventies. Most of the time the American players just ran off with it, but other years it was fiercely contested. Such a match was the one in 1972 at Western Gailes, on the west coast of Scotland, when a young American team had to play its heart out to defeat an inspired British Isles team 10–8. The World Cup, whose prime asset from the beginning has been the simple two-man-team format that enables small nations to become serious challengers and even occasionally to win, was carried off in 1973 at Royal Melbourne most surprisingly by Taiwan, represented by Hsieh Min-nan and Lu Liang-huan, our old friend Mr. Lu. All things considered, though, *the* international Match of the early Seventies had to be the Walker Cup Match at St. Andrews in 1971.

What made the 1971 Walker Cup meeting so special was that, for the first time since 1938, the British won. They had come heartbreakingly close several times. One thinks first of that disheartening tie at Five Farms in 1965. Then, in 1969 at the Milwaukee Country Club, they had lost by only two points. As one veteran Walker Cupper said at that time, one day the British would win and on the second afternoon of the Match it would be *their* players who would be able to do no wrong. *They* would hit all the big shots solidly, *they* would hole all the meaningful putts. That prophecy came to pass on the Old Course on May 27, 1971. The previous day, on the first morning of play, the British side, captained by Michael Bonallack, captured all four foursomes. The Americans fought back after lunch in the eight singles, winning six of them and halving another. Score at the halfway mark: United States, 6½; Great Britain and Ireland, 5½. The morning of the second day, the Americans, by winning two of the four foursomes and halving another, extended their lead to 9–7 and put themselves in a position where all they needed to win the Match was to take three of the afternoon's eight singles and halve another. The Match seemed as good as over when Lanny Wadkins, in the number-one singles, had gained a three-hole lead on Bonallack after eight holes, and when American players had quickly gone out in front in five of the other matches.

The match that turned the Match around was the third singles, Steve Melnyk versus Warren Humphreys. All even as they played the par-5 fourteenth, Melnyk lay eight feet from the hole in three after a superbly played little pitch. Humphreys was thirty-five long feet away, also in three. To an Augusta-like roar, Humphreys holed the monster. Melnyk's putt, a good one, grazed the cup. An entirely different situation now: Humphreys 1 up with four to play. On the fifteenth, Humphreys ran in a 40-footer for another birdie to go 2 up. (It had been decades since anyone could remember a British golfer, amateur or professional, sinking two such lengthy putts on consecutive greens.) It was now incumbent on Melnyk to go for everything, but a visit to the Road Bunker on the seventeenth ruined his last hope, and he went down 3 and 2. Up ahead, the spectators learned, Hugh Stuart had defeated Giles 2 and 1 in the second singles. The word of these two victories was carried down the line over the grapevine to the other British players, and this good news—particularly the upset win by Humphreys—buoyed their spirits incalculably. It was reflected in their confident play. Charlie Green, the Scottish veteran, held on grimly in the fourth singles to edge out Allen Miller 1 up. In the fifth singles, young Roddy Carr, the son of the illustrious Joe, kept plugging away and eventually needed only to halve the last hole to win his match with Jim Simons. For good measure he curled in an 18-footer for a birdie and a 2-up victory. Now it was serious. The British could indeed win. Three matches were still out on the course as the soft twilight came on: in the sixth singles, George Macgregor, another Scot, versus Jim Gabrielson, an insurance broker from Georgia; in the seventh singles, Dr. David Marsh, a general practitioner, versus the ageless Bill Hyndman; in the last singles, Geoff Marks, an architect, versus Tommy Kite, a junior from the University of Texas. Kite had been leading all the way, and as things turned out, he wrapped things up on the sixteenth, 3 and 2. In the end, the outcome of this enervating, melodramatic, wonderful team Match rested on the sixth and seventh singles. In order to retain the cup, the United States would have to win one of them and halve the other. That wasn't going to be easy.

Gabrielson came to the seventeenth, the Road Hole, 1 down to Macgregor. Gambling on hitting and holding the thin, fast green with his second, Gabrielson played a beautiful long-iron that failed by only a yard to make the upper terrace. Hole halved. At just about this time, a big shout erupted from the area of the sixteenth green. It had to be good news for the British, and it was. Hyndman had hit his pitch to the tricky green just

The momentous Walker Cup Match of 1971. Above, Warren Humphreys, the victor over Steve Melnyk in the key singles, jumps for joy after holing for a birdie. Below, Roger Wethered presents the cup to Michael Bonallack, captain of the winning team.

the way he meant to, but he had read the distance a shade wrong, and his ball caught the front bunker. It was to cost him the hole and put Dr. Marsh 1 up. On the Road Hole, two good drives. Hyndman went on to make his 4 but it had no meaning: Marsh, summoning the shot of his career at the most important moment of his career, had drilled a perfect 3-iron twelve feet from the cup. Marsh's 4 on the hole insured a British victory, for Macgregor meantime had guarded his 1-up lead on Gabrielson by parring the eighteenth. As for Marsh and Hyndman, they halved the eighteenth with 4s, but this was just a formality, making the final score Great Britain and Ireland 13, United States 11.

The British, whose pertinacity and patience had made the Walker Cup Match the marvelous event it is, were so overjoyed after all their years of disappointment that they could hardly believe that the Americans in attendance were almost as happy about their triumph as they were themselves. This was indeed the case, however. Furthermore, the United States had not lost the cup. The British, very well coached by John Jacobs, had won the cup through their superior golf on the last nine holes. Every crucial shot had been played with care and skill, every putt that had to be holed was holed. They had come through with a bravura performance just as the prophecy had promised, and they had thoroughly deserved to regain the Walker Cup.

In the early Seventies there was such a plenitude of golfing activity that it was quite impossible to keep abreast of everything that was going on. The cameo reports that follow touch on some of the more consequential events and incidents of that period.

•Because the functioning of his left knee (originally injured in his auto accident in 1949) remained unpredictable, Ben Hogan was content to play a limited schedule of tournaments. For golf he wore a heavy wrapping with two metal clips around the knee for support. Some days the knee was fine, some days it hurt slightly, and other days it was simply too painful to permit any kind of workout. (Mondays through Fridays, after spending the morning at his factory in Fort Worth and lunching at Shady Oaks, Hogan, the knee permitting, loved to go out to a quiet corner of the course and practice for an hour or two.) As far as tournament play went, Hogan picked his events carefully, favoring courses where the terrain was on the flat side and would not put too much strain on his legs. He liked the Houston Champions International for that reason and also because Champions Golf Club, where it took place, was owned and operated by his two closest friends in golf, Jimmy Demaret and Jack Burke, Jr. Ben generally acquitted himself well in that tournament. In 1967, for instance, he tied for third place. (Two weeks later, he also tied for third in the Colonial.) In 1970 at Houston, he finished in a tie for ninth. He was full of enthusiasm when he returned for the 1971 tournament, arriving at Champions a week early so that he would have all the time he needed to sharpen up his game. In one practice round he had a 67, in another a 65. He was ready to go, to say the least. In the first round his threesome included Dick Lotz and Charles Coody. They carried a large gallery with them, for the news had gotten around that

Ben Hogan,
in a solemn moment
near the end of his long
and distinguished career.

Hogan had been burning up the course, but it was almost immediately apparent that Hogan was not in his practice-rounds form. On both the first two holes, he went over par. At fifty-eight, a man's nerves are not what they used to be, and there can be a lot of difference between wheeling it on an informal round and staying relaxed during a tournament. The fourth hole of the Cypress Creek course at Champions is a 228-yard par 3 on which a deep, wide ravine angles in from the left and stretches from the tee almost to the front edge of the green. You don't want to be short on this hole. Hogan took a 3-iron. He hit the ball squarely but it failed by inches to carry the ravine and kicked farther down the hazard among the scrub and sand. Hogan climbed down to the ball to see if he could play it but decided the percentages were against it. During that descent, a sudden lurch caused him to strain his left knee. He walked slowly back to the tee. He hit two more tee shots that caught the ravine. His fourth tee shot was on the green, and he two-putted for 9. He continued to play until the threesome reached the twelfth tee, at which point he stood eleven strokes over par. By then he was in considerable pain and, apologizing to Lotz and Coody, asked for a golf cart to be sent out so that he could be driven back to the clubhouse. As the cart started off, Hogan said to a friend with his tight-lipped smile, "Don't ever get old."

This was the last tournament of his career.

●Few people in sports have been blessed with a physical endowment comparable to Sam Snead's. In the early 1970s, old Sam continued to do some phenomenal things. In 1971 at Pinehurst, he won the P.G.A. Club Professional Championship by five strokes. In 1973, returning to the tour for one of the dozen or so appearances he makes each year, he tied for seventh in the Glen Campbell Los Angeles Open. In 1974 he improved on his showing in that event, chasing Dave Stockton down the stretch and tying for second. (This was worth $13,875 to Sam—more money than most tournaments had offered *in toto* when he had joined the tour in 1937.) Without a doubt, though, Snead's most staggering exhibition of his longevity and skill occurred in the 1973 P.G.A. Seniors Championship at the P.G.A. National course, in Palm Beach Gardens, where he opened with a 66, added a 66 and a 67, and finished with a 69. Twenty strokes under par, he led the runner-up, Julius Boros, by a full 15. On his way to victory, his sixth in ten starts in the Seniors, Sam bogeyed only two holes although the course was set up about the same way it had been for the 1971 World Cup when Jack Nicklaus, playing the small ball, created a new 72-hole course record of 271. Snead had chopped three strokes off that mark. In the 1974 Masters, when Sam was a month and a half shy of his sixty-second birthday, he was par or better on each of his four rounds: 72-72-71-71—286. Later in 1974, he tied for third in the P.G.A.! Not long ago, when he was asked the key to his undiminished seriousness about tournament golf, Sam snapped out his answer with no hesitation: "Money." Up to a point, perhaps, but the young players on the tour—the Millers and Crenshaws and Wadkinses who love to play practice or tournament rounds with Snead—believe differently. As they see it, each round Snead plays turns him on, completely, just as the first fish a veteran Indian guide catches each day excites him as much as his very first fish caught decades before.

●It was discovered in March 1972 that Gene Littler was suffering from cancer of the lymph nodes in the area under his left arm. He underwent surgery immediately, but there would be no knowing for some time if the malignancy had been totally eradicated or if Gene would be able to play golf again—it had been necessary to cut away a section of the muscular tissue in the wall of his back. After leaving the hospital, Littler began a program of exercise to regain the use of the upper left side and left arm. On July 9 he essayed his first round of golf and shot a 79. There was a long way still to go, but he returned to the tour without fanfare at the beginning of 1973. In July, sixteen months after his operation, he demonstrated he had come all the way back by winning the St. Louis Children's Hospital Classic with rounds of 66, 66, 68, and 68. Having a man like Gene Littler well again and back in the game was one of those happy twists of fortune that occur all too seldom.

●Life does not begin at forty for the average tournament golfer; it just gets more difficult. It did for Arnold Palmer, who had hit forty in September 1969. That year, for the first time since going on the pro tour in 1955, he did not win a tournament until late November. In 1972 he did not win a tournament—period. He broke that long drought the following February by outplaying Johnny Miller and Jack Nicklaus on the closing holes of the Bob Hope Desert Classic, but then another long winless drought began. In his efforts to get himself untracked, Arnie tried everything. A certain desperation overtook him. One week, for instance, he wore tinted prescription glasses; the next week, no glasses; the third, contact lenses; and so on.

How long will Palmer go on playing the tour? It is a hard question to answer. He still believes not only that he can win on the tour but also that he hasn't won his last major championship. His record in recent U.S. Opens would support that contention.

At Pebble Beach in 1972 there was one tingling moment on the fourth round when, if Palmer could have holed an 8-footer on the 68th and Nicklaus had simultaneously missed a putt of the same length on the 66th, the old horse might have made it. Actually, the reverse took place. The next year at Oakmont, Arnold looked to be a very probable winner until a 5-footer for a birdie ghosted by the cup on the 65th. In 1974 at intimidating Winged Foot, with eight holes to go he was only three strokes behind Hale Irwin, the winner, but try as he would, he could not get his clutches on the birdies he needed. Should he ever succeed in capturing that one more major championship he has been chasing since 1964, what a happy day that will be! During Arnold Palmer's many years at the top we have come to see that his exceptional talent for golf is considerably exceeded by his talent as a human being.

•As the Seventies moved on, more and more of the weekly circuit stops were being won by the new boys—the tall, slender, assertive, somewhat spoiled, undoubtedly gifted, sandy-haired Prince Valiants, fresh from the college quads, who had earned their Approved Tournament Player cards at the T.P.D.'s annual Qualifying School (instituted in 1965 by the P.G.A.) and had begun post-graduate work on the driver, the wedge, and the putter. No one appreciated more clearly than they did that in this day of the $150,000 and $250,000 tournament, the name of the game was money. The kids, as they were called by the dodderers over thirty, usually married early and brought their wives along on the tour. They drove big, heavy, durable cars from one tournament stop to the next. When they gathered with their colleagues for a spot of relaxation, these serious young men seldom enlivened the air with merry conversation, and they drank very little. They followed diets and practiced their left-side-in-control, upright-swing, big-muscle method of shot-making assiduously. Individually, many of them are very likable, but to use the phrase of the day, the "bottom line" in this new era was a man's income, and there was no getting away from it.

•It took the kids a little longer than most people expected to break through in the prestige championships. Johnny Miller was the first to make a real bid in an important event. In the 1971 Masters, Miller, a tall, blond, high-strung, twenty-four-year-old San Franciscan, started the last round four strokes behind the pacemakers, Nicklaus and Charles Coody. He caught them after twelve holes by fusing seven pars and five birdies. The last two of these birdies were a 3 on the 445-yard eleventh, where Miller slapped a daring 5-iron ten feet from the pin on the cape green that juts into Rae's Creek, and a 2 on the terrifying twelfth, on which, after plopping a 7-iron into the front bunker, he holed his sand-shot. Resplendent in an apple-green sports shirt and white bell-bottoms striped with green, blue, and purple, Miller seized the tournament lead when he put his 7-iron approach to the fourteenth six feet from the pin and then made the birdie putt. (When it comes to planting an iron close to the hole, one must go back to Byron Nelson to find Miller's equal.) Inexperience proved to be his downfall. On the 190-yard sixteenth, on this day the pin had been set on the upper level, a comparatively thin shelf

Johnny Miller, the tall, slim, blond San Franciscan, is typical of the new breed who came to the fore in the 1970s. The winner of the 1973 U.S. Open—his final round was a record-breaking 63—Miller is not only an excellent driver but regularly puts his irons closer to the flag than any other golfer since Nelson.

at the back right-hand corner. Instead of playing safely for the middle of the green, Miller went boldly for the pin and caught the bunker behind the green. He ended up with a bogey 4. Then along came Coody to hole a 15-footer for a deuce there, and that decided the tournament.

As it turned out, the first of the new group of young touring pros (which, along with Miller, included Lanny Wadkins, John Mahaffey, Hubert Green, Hale Irwin, Jerry Heard, Tom Watson, Buddy Allin, Tom Kite, Forrest Fezler, Eddie Pierce, Grier Jones, Leonard Thompson, Allen Miller, and Ben Crenshaw) to win a major event was Johnny Miller. Two years after his failure in the Masters, he carried off the 1973 U.S. Open, at Oakmont, by finishing with a wondrous 63, the lowest round ever shot in our national championship. Johnny was on each green in the regulation stroke. His card—shades of Sunningdale in 1926—contained not a single 5. He could have easily scored lower. He had twenty-nine putts, including three on the eighth green. It was one of the genuinely epic rounds. Three over par and six full shots behind the co-leaders (Heard, Boros, Palmer, and John Schlee) at the commencement of the final eighteen, he was off (with Miller Barber) at 1:36, fifty-four minutes and seven groups before Boros and Heard teed off in the last pairing. He took maximum advantage on this muggy, overcast Sunday of the fact that Oakmont's greens, famed for their firmness and fastness, had been made extremely holding and slow by heavy rains on Saturday morning and some lighter rains on Sunday. With his long, lashing hitting action under full control—without question he has the most decisively lateral movement into the ball of any contemporary player—Miller picked up six birdies on the first eleven holes. He knew he could attack the flags and rap his putts with impunity on this day, and he had the inner fire to do so. On the first he put his 3-iron approach five feet from the hole and then got the putt. On the second he almost holed his pitch, a 9-iron that drew up a foot from the flagstick. The other four birdies resulted from a 25-foot putt on the third, an explosion six inches from the stick on the long fourth, a big drive followed by an accurate 2-iron to reach the green on the par-5 ninth, and a 14-foot putt on the eleventh.

Instead of backing off now that he had played himself into the thick of the fight, Miller continued to attack, but prudently. Showing none of the signs of "nerves" that had earlier killed his chances on the final holes of several tour tournaments, he hit one drive after another down the middle of the tight fairways, and then flew one full-blooded iron after another right for the top of the flagstick. On the par-5 twelfth, one of the holes on which he missed the fairway, he ripped his third, a 4-iron, fifteen feet from the hole and rolled in the putt. He followed this with another birdie on the thirteenth, a one-shotter, playing a 4-iron to five feet. On the fourteenth, he had a watertight par. On the fifteenth, a 453-yard par 4 commonly regarded as the most difficult hole on the course, he made still another birdie: a 280-yard drive, a 4-iron to ten feet, a putt that was in all the way. On the par-3 sixteenth, a good, sure par. On the seventeenth, after barely missing a birdie from ten feet, a tap-in par. On the home hole, a tough par 4, 456 yards long with the last two hundred sloping up to the green, he was on in 2 nicely with a 5-iron, then down in 2 from twenty-five feet with no sweat. That afternoon, after he had moved to 5 under par for the tournament on the fifteenth, or 69th, Miller was definitely the man to beat, but there was such a large gap of holes between him and the contenders packed together in the last three pairings—not to mention the large gap in efficiency of operation of the scoreboards—that the word of Miller's mad dash was slow in reaching the earlier leaders. In any event, his figures were

32-31—63, 8 under par. In the end his total of 279 (71-69-76-63) gave him a one-shot margin over Schlee, the only challenger who played the finishing holes as if he thought he could still tie or even win.

Johnny Miller, incidentally, had first come to national attention seven years before. When the 1966 Open was scheduled to be held at San Francisco's Olympic Club, to which Miller belonged, he was nineteen and a student at Brigham Young University. Determined to be a part of the championship in one capacity or another, he signed up for the caddie pool, but he later succeeded in qualifying for a place in the Open field. He was not only the low amateur but also tied for eighth, an amazing performance.

●In 1973, just when everyone had just about given up on him, Tom Weiskopf tardily arrived. The only awkward thing about his powerful game, what with the wide arc of his swing, its built-in rhythm, and his firmness through the ball, was the way he walked between shots, flopping his big feet down in an unathletic gait as splay-footed as Chaplin's tramp. He cured this in 1973, and maybe that was the tip-off. Anyway, in May and June, always in control of his all-too volatile temper, he won the Colonial, the Kemper, and the IVB-Philadelphia, and made a strong showing in our Open, winding up third. His hour of glory came at Troon in the British Open. His scores were 68, 68, 71, and 70, and the last two rounds over that lumpy, bunker-pocked old links were played in such cold, gloomy, hazy, and rainy weather that even the natives were grumbling. Weiskopf led after every round. In fact, he played only one poor shot over the four days of the championship; on the third round he snap-hooked his tee shot on the ninth into some unplayable gorse. This cost him an unplayable lie and a double-bogey, but his resolution remained intact. Four times on the in-nine Weiskopf saved valuable pars by getting down in 2 from difficult greenside bunkers. Some of the statements that Tom made at Troon after winning his first major championship are worth the attention of every golfer: "It's easy in golf to get discouraged, to look for a way out. I had a lot of problems to think about and a lot of pressure on me during the tournament. I enjoyed the adversity. Before this year, I never did. I think that's what's made me a better golfer."

●New champions appeared, sometimes dramatically. In 1971, for the first time since 1896, the Women's Amateur was won by a sixteen-year-old girl, Laura Baugh, a high-school student from Long Beach, California. Miss Baugh eliminated two former champions on her way to a particularly tense 36-hole final in which she defeated Beth Barry 1 up. Miss Baugh turned professional in 1973 . . . Of the three U.S. Women's Open victories scored by Susie Maxwell Berning, perhaps the finest was her second in 1972 on Winged Foot's East Course, sodden after heavy rains. One stroke behind the leader as she came to the seventeenth, or 71st, Susie had the mental stamina to play a fine wood onto the slippery green of this 200-yard par 3 and then holed from twenty feet for a 2. A solid par 4 on the 72nd nailed it down. Sandra Haynie's driving finish to win the 1974 U.S. Women's Open (after having previously that season won the L.P.G.A. Champion-

The 1973 British Open. From left: Sir Iain Stewart, Tom Weiskopf (the winner), Neil Coles, Keith Mackenzie, Johnny Miller, Jack Nicklaus, Bert Yancey.

Susie Berning's daughter Robin shares her triumph in the 1973 Women's Open.

ship) was, in a way, reminiscent of Mrs. Berning's victory, though even more exciting. A 70-foot birdie putt on the 71st tied her for the lead, and a 15-foot birdie putt on the home green won it for her . . . That same spring, Carol Semple, of the well-known Allegheny C.C. golfing clan, became only the sixth American to win the British Ladies' Championship . . . In 1973, after an eight-year hegira, the U.S. Amateur, to most people's gratification, returned to match play. The summer before the switchback, the championship was at length won by Marvin "Vinnie" Giles, of Richmond, who had been the runner-up in 1967, 1968, and 1969 . . . In the summer of 1973, the United States regained the Walker Cup at The Country Club, in Brookline, but it was a close-run thing: U.S.A., 14; Great Britain and Ireland, 10. At one stage in mid-afternoon on the second day, in fact, the British led in all eight singles and seemed on their way to a successful defense of the Cup, but a typical gutsy team rally by the Americans, ignited by a sensational birdie putt on the last green by Giles that squared his match with Charlie Green in the #1 singles, turned this unexpectedly close contest around . . . A member of that team, Dick Siderowf, a polished player from Connecticut, had taken the British Amateur earlier that year—the tenth American to win that championship in the post-World War II era . . . For three years in a row, the National Collegiate Championship was won by a handsome young golfer from the University of Texas, Ben Crenshaw. In his junior year, Ben tied for the title with his college teammate, Tom Kite, and the two shared the title. During his period in college, Crenshaw won every amateur tournament of distinction except the Amateur itself at least once, and was acknowledged by many to be the most gifted amateur since Nicklaus. He won the first tournament he entered as a professional, the 1973 San Antonio–Texas Open, but we shall have to wait and see if he fulfills the great expectations held for him.

The spacious new headquarters of the U.S.G.A. is located in Far Hills, New Jersey.

●In 1972 the U.S.G.A., having long outgrown its quarters in an old brownstone on East 38th Street in Manhattan, took up residence in a Georgian Colonial country mansion, designed by John Russell Pope, in Far Hills, New Jersey, some forty miles west of New York City. The new Golf House provided ample space for the U.S.G.A. Museum and Library, and the grounds—sixty-two acres in all—offered the necessary elbow room for ball-testing and shaft-testing experiments . . . In this last regard, a lengthy quiescent period came to a close in 1973 when some manufacturers changed the number, depth, size, and arrangement of the dimples in the cover of their golf balls. These changes, as goes without saying, were instituted in order to produce a "longer" ball, man's search for greater distance being as eternal as his quest for the Fountain of Youth. Other manufacturers claimed that the changes they had made in the construction of *their* golf balls— such as massing a higher proportion of the weight closer to the cover—increased their distance. There was another entry in the distance derby, the new graphite shaft. With its considerable torque and torsion, this shaft could not be controlled by many golfers, but some tournament players who took to graphite successfully added some yardage to their tee shots. Of course, there was a group that, while admitting the ball was being hit appreciably farther than a decade before, attributed this increase in length primarily to the larger and stronger athletes who were now playing the game, as well as to certain refinements in technique. In any event, the old mating dance was on again: longer balls would force clubs to lengthen their holes, and longer courses would take even more time to play . . . Early in 1974, Joseph C. Dey, Jr., went into retirement after completing his five-year term as the first Commissioner of the P.G.A.'s Tournament Players Division. (When he had left the U.S.G.A. in 1969, Dey had been succeeded by P. J. Boatwright, with Frank Hannigan moving up to the post of Assistant Director.) At the T.P.D., Dey's Successor was Deane Beman, whom he had known since Deane had begun to make a name for himself in golf in his early teens. Under Dey, T.P.D. headquarters had been situated in New York City. Under Beman they were moved to Bethesda, Maryland.

• There was more money than ever to be made in golf. For example, by 1974 a half dozen players had upped their career total in prize money to over a million dollars. Gary Player and Bruce Crampton, the transplanted Australian, became the first foreign golfers to attain this affluence . . . Although Johnny Miller won none of the four big championships in 1974, he showed the way in eight tour tournaments (and one in Japan) en route to setting a new record for prize money won in one season: $353,021. (Nicklaus had held the old record.) . . . Purses were climbing all over the world. In Europe, where there were now twenty-five or so quality tournaments, the over-all prize money rose to well over a million dollars. John Jacobs, who became the Tournament Director of the British P.G.A. in 1971, has been most instrumental in the tournament growth both in the United Kingdom and on the Continent . . . In Japan the circuit bulged to forty-five tournaments with total prize money in the neighborhood of two million dollars . . . The Asia Tour, under the guiding hand of Leonardo "Skip" Guinto of Manila, continued to burgeon. It had become by 1974 a $276,000 circuit made up of ten tournaments held in the Philippines, Hong Kong, Singapore, Thailand, Taiwan, Indonesia, Malaysia, India, Korea, and Japan . . . In Australia the big events now offered purses of $50,000, and in South Africa they were nearing that figure . . . As for women's golf, in 1972 our Ladies' P.G.A. at length passed the million-dollar mark in prize money. Two years later, when its schedule included thirty-five tournaments, that total had risen to close to two million. Three of those tournaments were $100,000 affairs (The Sears Women's Classic, the S. & H. Green Stamp Classic, and the Desert Inn Classic)—to become a classic a tournament must be held at least once—and then there was the $200,000 Colgate–Dinah Shore Winners Circle. David Foster, the top executive at Colgate, had grown up on the fairways of Sunningdale, outside London, and he felt that there were no better saleswomen for his company's products than good women golfers. The 1974 Winners Circle, at the Mission Hills course in Palm Springs, was won by Jo Ann Prentice when she played a full 4-iron three feet from the flag on the fourth extra hole. For her efforts Jo Ann received $32,000, a new car, a trip to England, and a contract to do a series of television commercials. As least as important as the fact that the women pros are now playing for this kind of money is the new international flavor of the L.P.G.A.'s schedule which calls for tournaments in Japan, Mexico, England, Australia, and Canada.

Sometimes, with so much green stuff cluttering up the premises, a golfer could become confused. For example, after Tony Jacklin had hit the jackpot, he decided that it was no longer worth his while to campaign on the American tour, and, for a time, he cut down drastically on his other tournament appearances. Competitive golf, with all of its attendant stresses and bothers, had lost its attraction for this bright and talented young man, who was entirely exhausted, and somewhat altered, after five years of pushing himself week after week. Even after he had acquired the poshest autos and a manor house in the Cotswolds of such size and architectural splendor that one wondered if there were still some vacancies in the freshman class, Jacklin's gusto for golf remained oddly moribund. Then it began to return, along with his golf game, slowly. He won three good tournaments in 1973—the Colombia Open, the Italian Open, and the Dunlop Masters—but week after week his game was nowhere near as reliable as it used to be, and it is generally accepted that he has been superseded by Peter Oosterhuis, the towering, charming young Dulwich College graduate, as the number-one player in Britain. (Early in 1975, Jacklin moved his residence to the island of Jersey, an excellent tax haven for British citizens with high incomes; but this will impose a limitation on the number of days he can spend in England and Scotland, and so will cut down on his tournament appearances.)

Here at home Lee Trevino suffered a similar discombobulation. After his two great years in 1971 and 1972, life took on wearing complications for this wonderfully natural player, this gregarious fellow who seemed happiest when verbalizing his every thought for his adoring galleries. By 1973 he had become so beleaguered by the pressures of his position that he would announce one week that he was playing too much golf and needed a long vacation, and then would announce the next week that his failure to play up to his customary level was caused by not having participated in enough events. It was a tribute to his innate ability that in 1973, for all his problems, he managed to win Jackie Gleason's Inverrary Classic and the Doral–Eastern, and to take home over $200,000 in tour money. The following year, while still subject to the inexplicably poor round, Lee refreshed the public's memory of the wonders he can work at his best when he won the Greater New Orleans Open with rounds of 68, 67, 68, and 65, eight shots ahead of the closest man. Over the four days—paging Harry Vardon—he did not make one bogey and he missed only two fairways and three greens. Four months later, in early August, Lee provided even stronger testimony that he had evidently sorted things out and had come all the way back when he held off a stretch drive by Nicklaus and won the 1974 P.G.A. Championship by a stroke.

•The Masters, by far the youngest of the four major championships, celebrated its fortieth anniversary in 1974, and that year Clifford Roberts, the one and only chairman of the tournament since its inception, turned eighty. To everyone's great pleasure, Lee Elder assured the tournament of having a black golfer in its field for the first time when he earned his invitation to the 1975 Masters by winning the 1974 Monsanto Open at Pensacola. The number of capable black golfers on the tour had been gradually growing. In addition to Elder it included Charley Sifford, the post-war patriarch, his nephew

Curtis Sifford, Pete Brown, Jim Dent (a real powerhouse), George Johnson, Charley Owens (who plays cross-handed), and Nate Starks.

●Until the national economy began to sag badly in the middle Seventies, there was little letup in the construction of new courses. More and more well-known players had become active in this field, some as consultants, others as bonafide designers. One of the latter was Jack Nicklaus, who, between tournaments, spent the bulk of his time working on the courses he was building. Jack has an unquestionable aptitude for architecture, and quite a few people rate his Muirfield Village course, near Columbus, Ohio, as the finest eighteen constructed in this country in the last decade . . . An earlier super-champion also entered golf architecture. For years Ben Hogan's admirers had been hoping he would get around to this, for everybody in golf wanted to see what Ben's idea of a first-class hole and a first-class course would look like. In collaboration with Joe Lee, the late Dick Wilson's successor, Ben worked, and intensely, as the co-designer of two courses for the Trophy Club, a project situated about halfway between Dallas and Fort Worth. The courses were ready for play midway in 1975. Speaking of them several months earlier, Ben explained that he was "endeavoring to build two eighteen-hole courses equally as difficult and equally as pleasant to play. Both will be par seventy-two. This rolling, tree-studded land of approximately twenty-six hundred acres lends itself to this concept. Most of the soil is sandy leaf loam and should grow grass very easily, plus having the ability to absorb moisture very readily and thus being playable immediately after hard rains." Playing a Hogan course—that is something to look forward to.

In the foreground during these early and middle years of the 1970s loomed the commanding figure of Jack Nicklaus. On January 21, 1971, Nicklaus turned thirty-one. All things being equal, he should have been entering the prime years of his golfing career. The people close to Jack thought that they had never seen him more physically or mentally fit. He had grown up conspicuously as a person and had acquired a greater awareness of his responsibilities and, in some areas, a new depth. As his family had increased, he needed a larger home, and he and his wife Barbara had moved from their first house at Lost Tree Village, which faced Little Lake Worth, to a much roomier one-story, double-winged house which they built nearby on Lake Worth. The Nicklauses led a very out-of-doors, Floridian life. At the front of the house, off the living room, was a swimming pool set off by a border of one of those new plastic grasses. Jack had perspicaciously bought the adjoining house-lot which he put into grass—real grass—so that he and the kids would have an athletic field of their own. The gem of this playground was a grass tennis court—one of the few in Florida—for Jack, who plays all games well, had always wanted to get in more tennis. He also considered his tennis workouts a helpful conditioner for his golf. Near the garage was a basket for basketball.

The offices of Golden Bear, Inc. were about two miles from Nicklaus' house. Putnam Pierman ran the company, which had been formed when Jack had decided to leave Mark McCormack's management, but whenever the board of six or seven specialists met, Jack was the man who called the shots. His main job, however, was to keep

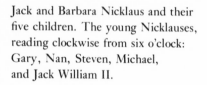

Jack and Barbara Nicklaus and their
five children. The young Nicklauses,
reading clockwise from six o'clock:
Gary, Nan, Steven, Michael,
and Jack William II.

winning golf tournaments, and in 1971, 1972, and 1973 he won twenty-two in all, four of them major championships. This pushed his total number of major victories to fourteen, eclipsing the record of thirteen set by Bob Jones. He had improved two areas of his shot-making in particular: he became a much straighter driver and a steadier putter. Two other departments that had always been disappointing remained disappointing: he was still an inconsistent bunker-player and he still couldn't put his pitch shots as close to the pin as a player of his stature should have. During this period there were two Jack Nicklauses, essentially. Some days and some weeks everything would fall into place for him the moment he began to get set up at the ball, and he hit his shots with such ease and cohesion that he was awesome to watch. Other days and other weeks something would be off, but with his gigantic willpower Jack often was able to forge more than acceptable scores from these rounds. He also developed into the best fourth-round golfer of the day, and one of the most memorable sights of this period was Nicklaus, far behind the leader, taking off after him on that last day, never doubting that if he could shoot that 65 or that 66 he could still do it.

In 1971 Nicklaus won eight tournaments—the Tournament of Champions, Byron Nelson Classic, National Team Championship (with Palmer), Disney World Open, Australian Open, Australian Dunlop International, and the individual competition at the World Cup, as well as one major championship, his second P.G.A. Chronologically, his win in the P.G.A. was his first of the year, for in 1971, instead of occupying its usual July or August slot in the schedule, the P.G.A. took place the last week in February over the East Course (7,096 yards) of the P.G.A. National in Palm Beach Gardens. A long, picaresque story lay behind this change. Briefly, John D. MacArthur, a tough-skinned Florida real estate baron who was then focusing on developing Palm Beach Gardens into something special, had leased to the P.G.A. enough acreage in that area for two eighteen-hole courses. He had then built the courses, which were designed by Dick Wilson, and loaned the P.G.A. a million and a half dollars to construct a clubhouse in which its national offices would be located. In return, MacArthur, the lessor, would receive the invaluable publicity and cachet that would accrue from having the two P.G.A. courses as the heart of his development. In 1963, another of the frequent P.G.A. family feuds broke out; many of the club pros within the organization, especially those from the West, were sternly opposed to the whole Palm Beach Gardens idea. In the process of straightening things out, MacArthur, in return for dropping a projected suit against the P.G.A., extracted a firm commitment that one year in the near future the P.G.A. Championship would be played over the P.G.A. National. The P.G.A. stalled as long as it could, but in 1971 the championship was scheduled for MacArthur's domain. A February date was selected, since July and August are hardly the time to stage an important tournament down among the sheltering palms.

Nicklaus had an interesting advantage over just about all the other entrants: he lived scarcely five miles from the course, and could relax at home every night. (So could his houseguest, Gary Player.) Be that as it may, Jack led the tournament from start to finish. He was off with a 69, on which eleven one-putt greens redeemed some horrible tee-to-green play—he had missed nine fairways and six greens. He followed with a much more valid 69 to lead by two strokes. On his third round, a six-hole burst from the ninth through the fourteenth—one bogey and all the rest birdies—made up for a slow start and a stuttering finish. It added up to a 70 and a four-stroke lead over the closest man, his houseguest. That stuttering finish, incidentally, consisted of a bogey on the eighteenth, a watery par 4 that Jack seldom played well, and a very lucky par on the seventeenth, a par 5 well over five hundred yards long, on which a canal-type water hazard trails along the left-hand margin of the hole. One of the few players who could conceivably reach the green in two, Nicklaus tried to do so on this third round. After a big tee shot, he poured everything into a 3-wood. It carried the bunkers protecting the entrance to the green, and would have been on if it had been straight. It was hooked, though, and, missing the green, tumbled down the slope to the left, stopping in the rough dangerously close to the water. He had gotten away with it, but it had not been a good shot or a smart one.

On the last round, Nicklaus again got off to a shaky start, but fifty-two-year-old Tommy Bolt and Player could not sustain their challenges, and the only man Jack really had to worry about as he came to the seventeenth, almost home, was Billy Casper. Casper, after a birdie on the seventeenth, was two strokes behind (and one twosome ahead of) Nicklaus. On the home green, Billy knocked in a 25-footer for a birdie, and now he was only one shot behind. Before the news of Casper's birdie on the eighteenth reached him, Nicklaus had driven off the seventeenth—driven with a 3-wood and driven well. After his close escape the day before, getting-home-in-two had lost its appeal. He couldn't reach in two now anyhow, not after having used a 3-wood off the tee. He would have to stick with conservative tactics, even though by this time he knew of Casper's finish. He took a 1-iron for his second. The ball, hit nicely, ended up comfortably short of the bunkers before the green. Then this man who couldn't play good wedges cut a soft little wedge five feet from the hole. He worked hard on the putt and made it. After that birdie, Jack was in a position where he could bogey the eighteenth and still win. He played the hole cautiously, driving with a 1-iron, and after a pretty running chip had made up for a mediocre second, he parred it.

An intriguing question hangs in the air. Had Jack known of Casper's closing birdie before he drove off the seventeenth, would he have eschewed the 3-wood off the tee in favor of the driver, hoping that he could get home in two *this* round and set up a sure birdie? Most likely not. He had probably weighed the probabilities and decided that, even for sluggers, the proper way to play the hole for a birdie at this stage of the championship was to lay up short of the bunkers in 2 and take his chances on then getting down in 2, just as he proceeded to do.

In 1972 Nicklaus won seven tournaments—the Crosby, Doral–Eastern, Westchester, Disney World, and the new and somewhat watered-down U.S. Match Play Championship, as well as two major championships, the Masters and the Open. The Masters was, to be frank, a dull tournament. From the outset, Nicklaus' golf was enigmatically uneven. On the opening round, he played miserable stuff for ten holes and then exploded with four birdies and an eagle over the next six. On Friday, just when it looked as if he might run off with the tournament then and there, he took a somewhat heedless 7 on the fifteenth hole, the 520-yard par 5 on which a big hitter like Nicklaus can frequently pick up a birdie 4. Late in the afternoon, when he came to the fifteenth, the wind, which had been blowing fairly hard, had quieted down, and it looked as if all he would need to reach the green on his second was a 3-iron. He went with a 3-wood, for some reason, and slammed the ball so hard and low that it carried the green by ten yards and was running like a hare when it dived into the pond on the sixteenth hole. Nicklaus' 71 on the round kept him out in front by a single stroke.

On Saturday, it was the same mulligatawny of incisive and sloppy golf, and he finished the day only one stroke ahead of Jim Jamieson, a lighthearted, thick-set, twenty-eight-year-old journeyman pro who carried a motley collection of implements— Golfcraft woods, Ping long irons, Spalding middle irons, Powerbilt pitching irons, a Hagen pitching wedge, a Hogan sand-wedge, and a Spalding putter he had picked up at a shopping center. Nicklaus' final round turned out to be more or less a repetition of the third. When he made the turn, he had pulled away to a five-stroke lead. Then he three-putted three greens, and on the long fifteenth he again missed his par when he hooked his approach over by the sixteenth tee. When he dumped his pitch to the seventeenth into the front bunker, he was on the brink of serious trouble, but he saved himself with a good sand-shot and a superb 11-foot breaking putt. That was it. Nicklaus' 286 (68-71-73-74) was the only total under par, 288. The three runners-up, Weiskopf, Crampton, and Bobby Mitchell, were a full three shots back. In joining Palmer as a four-time winner of the Masters, Jack was certainly not at his best—no place near it, in fact. However, it was not easy for anyone to be at his best at the Augusta National that spring. The course, both the fairways and greens, was thick with *Poa annua*, a vagabond grass. The damage it did to the fairways was negligible, but because *Poa annua* sprouts a white spikelet and grows extremely fast, the greens had to be cut very close to keep them as true and smooth as possible. The greens putted wickedly fast in spots, and there were, unavoidably, some very bumpy areas. The golfers chasing Nicklaus were faced with getting down a fair percentage of their birdie chances if they hoped to narrow the gap, and this they were unable to do.

That June, for the first time ever, the Open was played at Pebble Beach, perhaps the best golf course in the country and, possibly, in the world. In addition, Pebble Beach is probably the most spectacularly sited golf course in the country. Eight of its eighteen holes follow closely along the twisting, cliff-edged shore of Carmel Bay, a number of them on craggy headlands that rise as high as eighty feet above the churning blue water. By the way, the official name of the course is the Pebble Beach Golf Links, but technically it is not a links, since it is built on a rocky upthrust of land and not on true linksland—the sandy deposits that the ocean leaves behind as it recedes.

If Pebble Beach is all this special, why, then, did the U.S.G.A. wait so long before taking the Open there? Essentially, it was a matter of finances. Pebble Beach is situated a long way from any sizable center of population, and there had always been the fear that the galleries would be sparse and that the sponsoring parties, consequently, might take a terrific bath. The way it turned out, over fourteen thousand season tickets, at thirty-one dollars a head, were sold by February, and fiscally the championship was already off the hook. Pebble Beach had been designed in 1918 and 1919 by Jack Neville, one of the leading amateurs on the West Coast and a member of our 1923 Walker Cup team. A real-estate salesman for the Del Monte Properties Company, which owned most of the Monterey Peninsula, Neville was assigned by the company's head, Sam Morse, to lay out the course, for Morse believed that anyone who could play golf as well as Neville ought to be able to build a pretty fair golf course. Morse gave him his choicest piece of land, and Neville, who had never designed a hole before, went out and built a truly great course. Douglas Grant, an old friend, gave him some valuable suggestions, and later, before the 1929 Amateur was held at Pebble, H. Chandler Egan was called in to punch up the greenside bunkering. For the 1972 Open, only minor changes were made. Thirty yards were added to the course, bringing its over-all length to 6,812 yards.

Pebble Beach presented not only the most scenic layout that the Open had ever been played over but also one of the most testing. Over the first two rounds, only forty-eight of the hundred and fifty starters broke 80 on both days. On the first day, only six men broke par—72—and they did it by just a single stroke despite favorable conditions. Nicklaus, the odds-on favorite, was one of this sextet after a steady 71 anchored by fifteen pars. The field was having lots of trouble handling the tricky contoured greens. That old golfing rule of thumb that all putts on seaside courses break toward the sea didn't always hold true at Pebble Beach.

In three straight Opens—at Pebble Beach, Oakmont, and Winged Foot—Palmer was in the midst of the battle. Here he gives it his all at Pebble in 1972.

In the second round, Palmer, expending every last ounce of concentration, topped off a stirring comeback, after having started with a 77, by birdieing the last two holes for a 68 and a 36-hole total of 145. It put him right on the heels of the six players, Nicklaus among them, who shared the lead at 144. On the third round, Nicklaus, with a par 72, went out in front by himself, but on this round the defending champion, Lee Trevino, moved into the picture with a 71 that put him only a shot behind the leader. Palmer was a shot further back after a 73, a triumph of persistence, since he had one of those frustrating days when he holed absolutely nothing on the greens. A further word about Trevino. It was questionable whether he should have even been playing. The week before, he had been hospitalized for four days with a touch of pneumonia, and he was obviously far from well. For all his tiredness, he had finished the third round with two birdies. His deuce on the 218-yard seventeenth, dead into the wind, showed the tough little Texan at his best. He took a driver off the tee, and as he later described the shot, "I started it out over the yacht club and sliced it back over the water and onto the green."

On the final day, when he was paired with Nicklaus—they were the last to go out—it was apparent early in the round that Trevino simply didn't have the physical reserve required. He dropped strokes to par on the second, third, and sixth, and after that he was never in it. By the end of the first nine, Nicklaus had pulled a good distance away from his challengers. Even par for the nine, even par for the tournament, he led Homero Blancas by three strokes, Palmer, Crampton, and Kermit Zarley by four. At the same

Jack Nicklaus won his third U.S. Open at Pebble Beach eleven years after he had captured his second U.S. Amateur over that dramatic oceanside course. He survived a rocky passage midway through the final round, made the crucial birdie on the 69th.

time, Nicklaus' golf had been far more skittish and fidgety than usual. However, a birdie on the short seventh, where he holed from twenty-five feet, seemed to stabilize him.

And then, just when Nicklaus appeared to have things well under control, the whole complexion of his round changed again. As he was starting into his backswing on the tee of the tenth, a 436-yard, par-4 hole, a gust of wind knocked him off balance, and he slapped his drive far out to the right—over the cliff and down onto the beach below. Deciding not to play the ball as it lay, he took a penalty stroke for being in a lateral water hazard and dropped a ball at the edge of the cliff. Playing three now, going with a 2-iron. Down by the green, the blustery wind caught the shot and tossed it toward the bay. Here Nicklaus was lucky. The ball stayed up, coming to rest in sandy rough only a few yards down from the top of the cliff. From there he wedged his fourth onto the green and escaped with a 6 when he could easily have taken an 8. This double-bogey, though, brought his challengers back into striking distance. While none of them was able to mount a definite attack at this critical juncture, during the next hour it remained anybody's tournament, for Nicklaus, jarred by his misadventures on the tenth, played the next four holes fallibly. In the end he dropped only one shot to par over this stretch, but he could have lost as many as five if the ball hadn't been bouncing for him. On the fifteenth, a medium-length par 4 downhill to one of Pebble Beach's smallest greens, this tenacious competitor at length got hold of himself. He was down the middle of the fairway off the tee with a 1-iron, then punched an 8-iron to ten feet and made the putt. That did it. He followed this birdie with a par on the sixteenth, and on the seventeenth, the 218-yard par 3, he played a shot that will probably be the one everyone will remember in future years whenever the 1972 Open is discussed. This was a slashing 1-iron, with draw on it, that fought its way through a heavy headwind and almost went into the cup on the fly for a hole in one; it came down a foot or so short of the hole, and after hitting the flagstick on the half volley, as it were, stopped only inches away. With the tournament now sewed up, it made little or no difference that Jack three-putted the last hole for a 74. His total of 290 was three shots lower than Crampton's and four lower than Palmer's. Trevino, worn and weary, was another shot further back.

Now that Nicklaus had taken both the Masters and the Open, that inescapable chant about a possible Grand Slam began to make some sense. It was quite possible. That is why Nicklaus' last-round rally in the 1972 British Open thrilled the thousands at Muirfield so deeply as he came sweeping past Jacklin and Trevino to take over the lead as he stood on the twelfth tee. But there the magic stopped and the putts no longer fell.

In 1973 Nicklaus won seven tournaments—his third Crosby, the New Orleans Open, his fourth Tournament of Champions, the Atlanta Classic, the Ohio Kings Island Open, and the Disney World Open, as well as one major championship, his third P.G.A., this one at the Canterbury Country Club, in Beachwood, Ohio, a suburb of Cleveland. The scene of the 1940 and 1946 U.S. Opens and the 1964 U.S. Amateur, Canterbury, which played to 6,852 yards for the 1973 P.G.A., has a fairly high proportion of holes where it takes an accurately placed drive to open the entrance to the green. The golfer who drives down the wrong side is confronted with mean approaches that necessitate adroit manipulation of the ball. For the P.G.A., what with the fairways reduced and the rough high and tangled, driving of the very finest quality was called for. To complicate matters, Canterbury's condition left room for improvement. The fairways, thick with *Poa annua*, were watered every night so that the *Poa* would be better able to stand up to the heat of day. As a result, the course played very long. The greens, which had been toasted crisp by the summer sun, were also watered every night, but since they drained much more rapidly than the fairways, they remained resilient and difficult to hold. Most of the greens, it should be added, sloped from back to front, so the front sections were much the softest. The trouble with this was that the constant fear of thunderstorms led the pin-placement corps to pick positions near the back of the greens, where the land was highest. Sifting all this down, the top priority at Canterbury remained good, straight driving.

On his final round, Jack Nicklaus had a very poor driving day, hitting only five fairways. This would have been disastrous for most of the field, but in the Seventies it became increasingly clear that the most valuable advantage Nicklaus gained from his tremendous strength was not the extra yardage he got off the tee but his ability to power his way to the ball and through the ball in even the most resistant rough. He tore it out as no other player could. More than that, as often as not he could thrust his recovery all the way to the green and, occasionally, close to the flag. Hitting only those five fairways on the payoff round, Jack had a 2-under-par 69.

Nicklaus had started the tournament with a 72, then had gotten down to business with a 68, and had taken the lead with another 68, which placed him a stroke ahead of Don Iverson and Mason Rudolph, two ahead of Crampton, and three ahead of Weiskopf. At no time during his final round, for all of his rapport with the rough, was Jack in any danger of not winning. When he found the rough, he was usually on the correct side of the fairway, and so had a good angle on his approach. Even when missed drives left him problem shots, he handled them with ease. The tournament was as good as over after the fourteenth, where Jack expertly faded a 4-iron around a stand of trees and onto the green over two hundred yards away. His victory was marred microscopically by a bogey on the last hole, but, on the other hand, the last green was the first green that he had three-putted throughout the four rounds. Crampton, who had wound up second to Jack in both the Masters and U.S. Open in 1972, was again the runner-up, four shots away.

When he was congratulated at Canterbury for having smashed Jones' old mark of thirteen victories in the major championships, Nicklaus modestly pointed out that whereas it had taken Jones only eight years to compile his record number, it had taken him fifteen years to surpass it. There were many other differences that muddied any meaningful comparisons, such as Jones having competed only as an amateur until his retirement in 1930; his "major championships," accordingly, were not the same as a professional's. And so on and on, far into the night, with no clean-cut decision about the comparative genius of Nicklaus and Jones, or Hogan, or Vardon, remotely possible or even relevant. This much, though: There were flaws and inconsistencies in Nicklaus' game, but when he was in full flight it is really to be wondered at if anyone in the history of golf has ever been capable of such sustained passages of outrageous brilliance.

When one contemplates Nicklaus' record on that long, long journey from Broadmoor to Canterbury, what is almost as overwhelming as how often he won is how often he played himself into a position where he well might have won. Here in chart form is Nicklaus' record year by year, from 1959 through 1974, in the major championships. (It only remains to be added that in his one appearance in the British Amateur in 1959, he was eliminated in the quarter-final round.)

	MASTERS	U.S. OPEN	BRITISH OPEN	P.G.A.	U.S. AMATEUR
1959	missed cut	missed cut			1
1960	tied 13	2			eliminated 4th round
1961	tied 7	tied 4			1
1962	tied 15	1 (playoff)	tied 33	tied 3	
1963	1	missed cut	3	1	
1964	tied 2	tied 23	2	tied 2	
1965	1	tied 31	tied 12	tied 2	
1966	1 (playoff)	3	1	tied 22	
1967	missed cut	1	2	tied 3	
1968	tied 5	2	tied 2	missed cut	
1969	tied 24	tied 25	tied 6	tied 11	
1970	8	tied 49	1 (playoff)	tied 6	
1971	tied 2	2 (playoff)	tied 5	1	
1972	1	1	2	tied 13	
1973	tied 3	tied 4	4	1	
1974	tied 4	tied 10	3	2	

After his victory in the 1968 British Open, Gary Player didn't fade completely from the picture, but during the next few years the trim, tidy little South African was not as influential in the big international events as he formerly had been. The one exception was a remarkable second-place finish a stroke behind Raymond Floyd in the 1969 P.G.A.—remarkable because racial activists in the gallery at the National Cash Register course in Dayton, Ohio, picked on Player in particular because of South Africa's apartheid policy. Even though they used every distracting tactic trying to upset him— in the third round a man went as far as to toss at him a paper cup filled with ice and the dregs of a soft drink—Player somehow kept his self-control and his concentration. However, three summers later, before the start of the 1972 P.G.A. at Oakland Hills, the general view among most of the game's followers was that Player at thirty-six was past his peak and would probably have no part in the winning or losing of the championship. Player won it with a fantastic recovery shot on the sixteenth, or 70th, hole. The sixteenth is Oakland Hill's best-known hole, and rightfully. A 408-yard par 4 that doglegs to the right, its cape-type green lies on the far side of a rather large pond that also edges along its right-hand side. Player's drive, a wide slice deep into a section of the rough that, fortunately for him, the gallery had trampled down a bit, left him stymied by some willow trees along the shore of the pond. To get his ball up quickly enough to clear them, he figured he would need the loft of a 9-iron. He went with that club, although he knew he would have to carry the ball a hundred and fifty yards to clear the water, which meant swatting a very, very big 9-iron. He put the ball four feet from the hole. The resultant birdie gave Player the two-stroke margin he eventually won by.

The following year, 1973, was a rough one for Gary. In January he underwent a bladder operation. Midway through the spring, he started to play tournaments again, but he was not himself for many more months. For example, when he defended his P.G.A. title, the best he could do was a tie for fifty-first. In order to get in the minimum fifteen tournaments that the T.P.D. requires its card-carrying members to play each year, Gary stayed on the tour. In September, he at length got back on the stick and won the revived Southern Open, at the Green Island Country Club in Columbus, Georgia, with rounds of 69, 65, 67, and 69. That helped redeem a disappointing year, but what really picked Gary up was the endurance he showed in winning his fifth Piccadilly World Match Play Championship in England in October. After eliminating both Tony Jacklin and Johnny Miller 3 and 2, he met Graham Marsh, the able young itinerant Australian, in the final. A birdie by Player on the 36th sent the match into extra holes. He halved the 37th and the 38th by getting down in 2 from bunkers. An orthodox half on the 39th. On the 40th, a par 5, Player was nine feet from the cup in 3, Marsh four feet away in 3. Player holed, Marsh did not.

It was good to know that Gary was well and strong again, but no one expected that in 1974 he would produce such splendescent golf and enjoy such striking success that he would force the game's authorities to revise their evaluation of this abilities and his standing among modern golfers.

In the spring of 1974, two years after its famous *Poa annua* festival, the Augusta

National was back in wonderful condition. Its fairways had been planted with a fescue called Pennlawn and its greens with a rye called Pennfine. Both strains had flourished. For the first time in years, the fairways had filled in perfectly and could be cut close, and this permitted the golfers to get a good deal of controlling spin on their approach shots. The scores ran low. After three rounds, Dave Stockton at 207—71, 66, 70—led, a stroke ahead of a tightly bunched field. Player and Jim Colbert were right at his shoulder, a stroke behind. On his first two rounds, a pair of 71s, Player, participating in his seventeenth Masters, had hit the ball much better than his scoring suggested. His trouble was a total of seventy-one putts on these two rounds. On the third day, he had shot into contention with a 66 featuring a cluster of five straight birdies. He began this rush by sticking a 7-iron a foot from the pin on the short twelfth; then, getting his touch, he holed putts of fifteen, six, twenty, and seven feet on the next four greens. On the last day, Player and Stockton were paired. Player caught him with a birdie 2 on the sixth. On the ninth, which Stockton three-putted, Player jumped into a two-stroke lead when he pumped a 6-iron approach six feet from the cup and made his birdie. Starting home, Gary staggered a bit, missing his pars on the tenth and the twelfth, but he stopped his skid on the thirteenth by getting down from seven feet for his birdie. He went on to add three firm pars and wrapped things up by whistling his 9-iron second to the seventeenth eight inches from the hole. He was so sure he had hit an almost perfect shot that he didn't even bother to watch the flight of the ball as he returned the club to his caddie. Final scores: Player, 278; Stockton and Weiskopf, 280; Nicklaus and Irwin, 281.

In his long career Player had never seemed as assured as he did moving down the final holes to his second Masters victory. His release through the ball was so free and easy that he looked as though he was out on a practice round. This all went back to an increased confidence in his swing that developed after he had made a small but significant alteration early that season. For twenty years Gary had been fighting a tendency to hook. He battled it chiefly by using his left hand to block out his right hand at impact. That winter, tackling that old and worrisome problem again, he had worked hard on getting the face of his club into a slightly more open position at the top of the backswing. He discovered that when he did this correctly, his clubface would be square as he came into the ball and that he could rip through the ball with abandon and still send it straight down the fairway. He also hit the ball a mile at Augusta in a fairly low, buzzing parabola.

In the 1974 Open, at Winged Foot, Player led after the first two rounds, but his bid was over when he took 41 shots on the third round to play the second nine. In the British Open at Lytham, Player again led after the first two rounds, following a 69 and a 68, and this time he continued to lead throughout the championship. Despite an unsteady 75 on his third round, he was still three strokes in front of the nearest challenger, Peter Oosterhuis, four in front of the ever-dangerous Nicklaus. The last round, as it worked out, was a cup of tea for Gary. He birdied the first two holes. Then he eagled the long sixth and turned in 32. This gave him a margin of five shots. He extended it to six when he dropped a weaving 20-foot birdie putt on the thirteenth, then to seven after parring

Lytham St. Annes, 1974.
"Rabbit" Dyer and Gary Player work
on a putt together. Player won
his third British Open by the
comfortable margin of four strokes.

the fourteenth. This was an ample cushion to absorb three bogeys on the four finishing holes. The only truly alarming moment came on the seventeenth when it took Alfred "Rabbit" Dyer, Player's black American caddie, a few minutes to locate Player's ball in the greenside rough. On the last hole, "Rabbit" gave his man a little too much club on his approach, and Player's ball ended up far over the green only a foot or so from the august clubhouse itself. He putted it onto the green left-handed. Final scores: Player 282. Oosterhuis, 286. Nicklaus, 287. Hubert Green, 288. Danny Edwards and our old friend Mr. Lu, 292.

By winning the British Open, Gary Player brought his number of victories in the major championships to eight—the same as Palmer's. This was something, and so was the fact that his third victory in the British Open had been achieved a full fifteen years after his first in 1959. It takes a great golfer to stay at the top and *win* over that long a period. The only other modern golfer who has approached this mark in the British Open is Henry Cotton, another three-time champion, who won in 1934, 1937, and again in 1948. One then has to go all the way back to Harry Vardon, J. H. Taylor, and Willis Park, Sr., to find other golfers who demonstrated that sort of longevity as winners of the British Open.

Player's victories in two major championships in 1974 made him the golfer of the year, though there were dissenters who believed that this distinction belonged to Johnny

Miller, who had also enjoyed a tremendous season, winning eight tournaments at home (plus one in Japan) and in the process had set a new record for total-prize-money-won-on-the-tour-in-one-year—a staggering $353,021. Player's accomplishments in 1974 did not end, by any manner of means, with his success at Lytham. However, he did undergo a comparative dry spell during the rest of the summer on the American tour and in the early autumn when he returned to Britain; he had to be content then with the runner-up spot in the Dunlop Masters and in his "personal tournament," the Piccadilly World Match Play Championship, in which, going after his sixth title in eleven years, he was edged out in the final by Hale Irwin's fine, consistent play. On his annual autumn trip to Australia, Gary got going again. At the Lake Karrinyup club in Perth, due principally to 63 on the third round, he won his seventh Australian Open by three comfortable strokes. A plane to Spain. In the 72-hole stroke-play competition for the professionals which is a simultaneous part of the La Manga Pro-Amateur, he tied for first with Clive Clark, of England, and then won the playoff. On the heels of this, he tied for first with another young English professional, Peter Townsend, in the 36-hole Ibergolf tournament at Las Lomas El Bosque Golf Club, near Madrid, and then defeated Townsend in a playoff on the second extra hole. Out to the airport and a flight across the South Atlantic to Rio de Janeiro and the Brazilian Open at the Gavea Golf and Country Club. Following an opening 67, two strokes under par, Player put together an amazing 59 the next day to take a lead he never relinquished. His four-round total of 267 was five shots better than that of the second man, Mark Hayes, a youthful American pro. Because par at Gavea is only 69—the hilly course contains six par 3s—some people have viewed Player's round of 59 as nothing too remarkable; after all, it was only ten strokes under par. On the other hand, no holes are harder to birdie than long par 3s, and the shortest of the six 3s at Gavea measures 185 yards. It should also be noted that all of the previous 59s recorded in competition (such as Sam Snead's memorable 59 in the 1959 Greenbrier Invitational) were scored in somewhat informal tournaments, whereas Player's 59 was produced in a national open championship. Player's card went like this: 343 342 334-29 243 444 243-30—59. He birdied the sixteenth by holing an explosion shot, parred the seventeenth, and made the critical birdie on the 410-yard eighteenth by getting down a 15-footer. Back to South Africa for the General Motors International Classic in Port Elizabeth. With two holes to go, Gary found himself trailing the leader, Andries Oosthuizen, by one shot. (Oosthuizen, a 21-year-old professional from Pretoria, should not be confused with Peter Oosterhuis, the up-and-coming young English professional.) Needing two birdies to win, Player got the first by holing from 4 feet for his 4 on the par-5 71st, then got the second when he put his 5-iron tee shot on the 186-yard home hole six feet from the cup and sank the putt.

This last triumph brought to ten the number of tournaments Player had captured in 1974. (Early in the year, before leaving for the States, he had taken the South African Dunlop Masters and the Rand International Open. After the Masters he had won the Memphis Classic.) He had, moreover, won on five different continents, an awesome first-time-ever achievement that may never be duplicated. In any event, it will be a long

Back at Troon a half-century later. Before the 1973 British Open, Gene Sarazen (right) reminisces with Arthur Havers, who won the championship at Troon in 1923.

time before we see another golfer with Gary Player's wondrous ability to cope with all types of courses in all parts of the world under all sorts of conditions.

At Troon the eighteenth fairway runs parallel to the first. In the 1973 British Open, minutes before Nicklaus came down the eighteenth on his opening round, a familiar knickerbockered figure appeared on the first tee, leaning against his driver as he waited to tee off. This was Gene Sarazen, returning at the age of seventy-one to the scene of perhaps the harshest humiliation of his life. It had taken place precisely half a century before. Sarazen, the winner of both our Open and P.G.A. Championships in 1922, when he was a mere twenty, had crossed the ocean the next spring to play in the British Open, scheduled for Troon. In those days everybody except the defending champion had to qualify over thirty-six holes for his place in the starting field. Young Sarazen's first qualifying round was a 75, but he was unlucky enough to be in the first group out on the second morning when a storm of gale force was at its height. (The local Scottish fishermen weren't allowed to leave the port that morning.) Sarazen got through the first hole with just a bogey 5, but on the second he buried his drive in the face of a bunker and, after taking three to get out, had a 9. By the fifth hole he had gotten a grip on himself, and, considering the fury of the wind, played quite well the rest of the way and finished with an 85. By noon, however, the wind had died down to a whisper, and the late starters, playing under relatively ideal conditions, posted much lower scores. Sarazen failed to qualify by a stroke. It was a crushing blow to his self-esteem. Ashamed to face anyone, he left for London immediately.

Here was Sarazen back at Troon fifty years later, an honorary qualifier under the new regulations, ready to go out with two other former British Open Champions, Arthur Havers and Fred Daly. (After his failure in 1923, Sarazen had vowed he would keep coming back until he won the championship, and in 1932 he made good that promise with a record-setting breakthrough at Prince's.) At seventy-one, he still looked the way Gene Sarazen had always looked—the same knickers, same cap, same olive skin, same wide impish smile that had always suggested to Bernard Darwin the grin of Lewis Carroll's Cheshire Cat. Now it was his turn to tee off. Characteristically, without a moment's hesitation, with no wasted motion, he lined a bullet of a drive down the center of the fairway. Fortunate man!—how many champions get to return to a course and a championship they first played fifty years before—but the right man, for no one in golf personified the link between the different generations as did Sarazen. In 1923, just before coming to Troon, he had been paired on two rounds in the North of Britain Championship, at Lytham, with the legendary Harry Vardon. In the spring of 1973 at the Masters, he had marched down the fairways with Johnny Miller, Ben Crenshaw, and the rest of the new gang just out of college. Before the start of the 1973 British Open, he had made it clear that this would be his final championship. Fifty years was enough.

Sarazen had dropped a few strokes to par on his way out before he came to the eighth hole. The shortest par 3 on any of the British championship courses, it measures only 126 yards. It is called the Postage Stamp because of the smallness of the green, a steeply elevated perch more than a dozen feet above the deep bunkers surrounding it. With a stiff wind blowing directly against the players, Sarazen decided to hit a 5-iron. He punched a crisp shot, dead on-line, that bored through the wind, landed on the green, ran for the flagstick, and disappeared into the cup for a hole-in-one. Some people just can't stop doing sensational things.

After Sarazen had finished his round, a 79, the R. & A. legate broke out some champagne in the press tent, and Sarazen was toasted for his hole-in-one by the circle of writers around him. One writer asked him when he first thought the ball might go in. "The moment I hit it," Gene replied with a wink. "I'm glad the television cameras got it," he added later. "It's on tape, you know. I plan to bring it along with me and show it to Hagen and Armour."

The next day Sarazen had an 81. However, he made a 2 on the Postage Stamp, holing out an exceedingly difficult explosion shot from the right bunker.

After that round, Sarazen was walking through the clubhouse when he overheard two elderly members talking about him as they stretched out in their leather chairs. "If I'm not mistaken," one of them said, "Sarazen had a total of 160 for his two rounds in 1923—a 75 and an 85. This year once again he had a total of 160—a 79 and an 81. He hasn't improved at all over the years."

POSTSCRIPT

Early in 1975, Gary Player won the South African Open—his ninth victory in that event. However, the two outstanding players during the first four months of the year were Johnny Miller and Jack Nicklaus. Miller, the king of the desert, not only carried off the Tucson and Phoenix Opens back to back but did this with some absolutely fantastic scoring: 67-61-68-64—260, 66-69-67-61—263, the lowest eight consecutive rounds ever played on the P.G.A. tour. Miller's scores en route to winning the Bob Hope Classic were a little more believable, and he cooled off considerably when the tour swung into Florida and up into the Carolinas. It was there that Nicklaus took over. After blowing the Jackie Gleason–Inverarry Classic most uncharacteristically by going four strokes over par on the last seven holes, Nicklaus proceeded to take the Doral Open and the Heritage Classic with two very determined performances. He topped off this rush by winning his fifth Masters (and his fifteenth major championship), edging out Miller and Tom Weiskopf by a shot in one of the most thrilling tournaments ever held—a magnificent three-man battle. With a round to play, Weiskopf, following a brilliant 66, led Nicklaus by a shot and Miller by four. Miller had started with a wayward 75 and a 71, but had moved into the picture on the third round with a 65 that included a run of six straight birdies on the front nine. On the final day Miller continued this spectacular play with a 66, and both he and Weiskopf had holeable birdie putts on the 72nd green to tie Nicklaus, who had finished with a 68. In retrospect, the tournament was won and lost on the 190-yard par-3 sixteenth, the 70th hole, where there was a swing of two strokes. After Nicklaus had rapped a 40-foot birdie putt up the slope and smack into the cup, Weiskopf hit a fat 5-iron that ended up on the front apron eighty feet from the pin, and from there he needed three putts. Among them the three players had only six bogeys (two each) on this historic final round and eighteen birdies (four for Weiskopf, six for Nicklaus, and eight for Miller). It was golf of the highest order.

A week after the Masters there came some long-awaited good news. After a two-year drought, Arnold Palmer won a sizable tournament, the La Manga Open, in Spain. He did it like the Palmer of old. On the 72nd hole, a par 5, he needed an eagle to win, and he got it by slamming his second shot a yard from the pin.

U.S. AND INTERNATIONAL GOLF RECORDS

WINNERS OF UNITED STATES GOLF CHAMPIONSHIPS

YEAR	U.S. OPEN	U.S. AMATEUR	U.S. WOMEN'S AMATEUR
1895	Horace Rawlins	Charles B. Macdonald	Mrs. C. S. Brown
1896	James Foulis	H. J. Whigham	Miss Beatrix Hoyt
1897	Joe Lloyd	H. J. Whigham	Miss Beatrix Hoyt
1898	Fred Herd	Findlay S. Douglas	Miss Beatrix Hoyt
1899	Willie Smith	H. M. Harriman	Miss Ruth Underhill
1900	Harry Vardon	Walter J. Travis	Miss Frances C. Griscom
1901	Willie Anderson	Walter J. Travis	Miss Genevieve Hecker
1902	Lawrence Auchterlonie	Louis N. James	Miss Genevieve Hecker
1903	Willie Anderson	Walter J. Travis	Miss Bessie Anthony
1904	Willie Anderson	H. Chandler Egan	Miss Georgiana M. Bishop
1905	Willie Anderson	H. Chandler Egan	Miss Pauline Mackay
1906	Alex Smith	Eben M. Byers	Miss Harriot S. Curtis
1907	Alex Ross	Jerome D. Travers	Miss Margaret Curtis
1908	Fred McLeod	Jerome D. Travers	Miss Katherine C. Harley
1909	George Sargent	Robert A. Gardner	Miss Dorothy I. Campbell
1910	Alex Smith	William C. Fownes, Jr.	Miss Dorothy I. Campbell
1911	John J. McDermott	Harold H. Hilton	Miss Margaret Curtis
1912	John J. McDermott	Jerome D. Travers	Miss Margaret Curtis
1913	Francis Ouimet	Jerome D. Travers	Miss Gladys Ravenscroft

582

U.S. and International Golf Records

Year	U.S. Open	U.S. Amateur	U.S. Women's Amateur
1914	Walter Hagen	Francis Ouimet	Mrs. H. Arnold Jackson
1915	Jerome D. Travers	Robert A. Gardner	Mrs. C. H. Vanderbeck
1916	Charles Evans, Jr.	Charles Evans, Jr.	Miss Alexa Stirling
1917	*No tournaments held*		
1918	*No tournaments held*		
1919	Walter Hagen	S. Davidson Herron	Miss Alexa Stirling
1920	Edward Ray	Charles Evans, Jr.	Miss Alexa Stirling
1921	James M. Barnes	Jesse P. Guilford	Miss Marion Hollins
1922	Gene Sarazen	Jess W. Sweetser	Miss Glenna Collett
1923	Robert T. Jones, Jr.	Max R. Marston	Miss Edith Cummings
1924	Cyril Walker	Robert T. Jones, Jr.	Mrs. Dorothy Campbell Hurd
1925	Willie Macfarlane	Robert T. Jones, Jr.	Miss Glenna Collett
1926	Robert T. Jones, Jr.	George Von Elm	Mrs. G. Henry Stetson
1927	Thomas D. Armour	Robert T. Jones, Jr.	Mrs. Miriam Burns Horn
1928	Johnny Farrell	Robert T. Jones, Jr.	Miss Glenna Collett
1929	Robert T. Jones, Jr.	Harrison R. Johnston	Miss Glenna Collett
1930	Robert T. Jones, Jr.	Robert T. Jones, Jr.	Miss Glenna Collett
1931	Billy Burke	Francis Ouimet	Miss Helen Hicks
1932	Gene Sarazen	C. Ross Somerville	Miss Virginia Van Wie
1933	John G. Goodman	George T. Dunlap, Jr.	Miss Virginia Van Wie
1934	Olin Dutra	W. Lawson Little, Jr.	Miss Virginia Van Wie
1935	Sam Parks, Jr.	W. Lawson Little, Jr.	Mrs. Edwin H. Vare, Jr.
1936	Tony Manero	John W. Fischer	Miss Pamela Barton
1937	Ralph Guldahl	John G. Goodman	Mrs. Julius A. Page, Jr.
1938	Ralph Guldahl	William P. Turnesa	Miss Patty Berg
1939	Byron Nelson	Marvin H. Ward	Miss Betty Jameson
1940	W. Lawson Little, Jr.	Richard D. Chapman	Miss Betty Jameson
1941	Craig Wood	Marvin H. Ward	Mrs. Frank Newell
1942	*No tournaments held.*		
1943	*No tournaments held.*		
1944	*No tournament held.*		
1945	*No tournaments held.*		
1946	Lloyd Mangrum	Stanley E. Bishop	Mrs. George Zaharias
1947	Lew Worsham, Jr.	Robert H. Riegel	Miss Louise Suggs
1948	Ben Hogan	William P. Turnesa	Miss Grace Lenczyk
1949	Cary Middlecoff	Charles R. Coe	Mrs. Mark A. Porter
1950	Ben Hogan	Sam Urzetta	Miss Beverly Hanson
1951	Ben Hogan	Billy Maxwell	Miss Dorothy Kirby
1952	Julius Boros	Jack Westland	Mrs. Jacqueline Pung
1953	Ben Hogan	Gene A. Littler	Miss Mary Lena Faulk
1954	Ed Furgol	Arnold Palmer	Miss Barbara Romack
1955	Jack Fleck	E. Harvie Ward, Jr.	Miss Patricia Ann Lesser
1956	Cary Middlecoff	E. Harvie Ward, Jr.	Miss Marlene Stewart

Year	U.S. Open	U.S. Amateur	U.S. Women's Amateur
1957	Dick Mayer	Hillman Robbins, Jr.	Miss JoAnne Gunderson
1958	Tommy Bolt	Charles R. Coe	Miss Anne Quast
1959	Bill Casper, Jr.	Jack Nicklaus	Miss Barbara McIntire
1960	Arnold Palmer	Deane R. Beman	Miss JoAnne Gunderson
1961	Gene A. Littler	Jack Nicklaus	Mrs. Jay D. Decker
1962	Jack Nicklaus	Labron E. Harris, Jr.	Miss JoAnne Gunderson
1963	Julius Boros	Deane R. Beman	Mrs. David Welts
1964	Ken Venturi	William C. Campbell	Miss Barbara McIntire
1965	Gary Player	Robert J. Murphy, Jr.	Miss Jean Ashley
1966	Bill Casper, Jr.	Gary Cowan	Mrs. Don R. Carner
1967	Jack Nicklaus	Robert B. Dickson	Miss Mary Lou Dill
1968	Lee B. Trevino	Bruce Fleisher	Mrs. Don R. Carner
1969	Orville J. Moody	Steven N. Melnyk	Miss Catherine Lacoste
1970	Tony Jacklin	Lanny Wadkins	Miss Martha Wilkinson
1971	Lee B. Trevino	Gary Cowan	Miss Laura Baugh
1972	Jack Nicklaus	Marvin M. Giles III	Miss Mary Budke
1973	John Miller	Craig Stadler	Miss Carol Semple
1974	Hale Irwin	Jerry Pate	Miss Cynthia Hill

WINNERS OF THE P.G.A. CHAMPIONSHIP

1916	James M. Barnes	1936	Denny Shute	1956	Jack Burke, Jr.
1917	No tournament held	1937	Denny Shute	1957	Lionel Hebert
1918	No tournament held	1938	Paul Runyan	1958	Dow Finsterwald
1919	James M. Barnes	1939	Henry Picard	1959	Bob Rosburg
1920	Jock Hutchison	1940	Byron Nelson	1960	Jay Hebert
1921	Walter Hagen	1941	Vic Ghezzi	1961	Jerry Barber
1922	Gene Sarazen	1942	Sam Snead	1962	Gary Player
1923	Gene Sarazen	1943	no tournament held	1963	Jack Nicklaus
1924	Walter Hagen	1944	Bob Hamilton	1964	Bobby Nichols
1925	Walter Hagen	1945	Byron Nelson	1965	Dave Marr
1926	Walter Hagen	1946	Ben Hogan	1966	Al Geiberger
1927	Walter Hagen	1947	Jim Ferrier	1967	Don January
1928	Leo Diegel	1948	Ben Hogan	1968	Julius Boros
1929	Leo Diegel	1949	Sam Snead	1969	Raymond Floyd
1930	Thomas D. Armour	1950	Chandler Harper	1970	Dave Stockton
1931	Tom Creavy	1951	Sam Snead	1971	Jack Nicklaus
1932	Olin Dutra	1952	Jim Turnesa	1972	Gary Player
1933	Gene Sarazen	1953	Walter Burkemo	1973	Jack Nicklaus
1934	Paul Runyan	1954	Chick Harbert	1974	Lee Trevino
1935	Johnny Revolta	1955	Doug Ford		

WINNERS OF THE MASTERS

1934	Horton Smith	1948	Claude Harmon	1962	Arnold Palmer
1935	Gene Sarazen	1949	Sam Snead	1963	Jack Nicklaus
1936	Horton Smith	1950	Jimmy Demaret	1964	Arnold Palmer
1937	Byron Nelson	1951	Ben Hogan	1965	Jack Nicklaus
1938	Henry Picard	1952	Sam Snead	1966	Jack Nicklaus
1939	Ralph Guldahl	1953	Ben Hogan	1967	Gay Brewer
1940	Jimmy Demaret	1954	Sam Snead	1968	Bob Goalby
1941	Craig Wood	1955	Cary Middlecoff	1969	George Archer
1942	Byron Nelson	1956	Jack Burke, Jr.	1970	Bill Casper, Jr.
1943	*no tournament held*	1957	Doug Ford	1971	Charles Coody
1944	*no tournament held*	1958	Arnold Palmer	1972	Jack Nicklaus
1945	*no tournament held*	1959	Art Wall	1973	Tommy Aaron
1946	Herman Keiser	1960	Arnold Palmer	1974	Gary Player
1947	Jimmy Demaret	1961	Gary Player		

AMERICAN WINNERS OF THE BRITISH OPEN CHAMPIONSHIP

1921	Jock Hutchison	1930	Robert T. Jones, Jr.	1964	Tony Lema
1922	Walter Hagen	1931	Thomas D. Armour	1966	Jack Nicklaus
1924	Walter Hagen	1932	Gene Sarazen	1970	Jack Nicklaus
1925	James M. Barnes	1933	Denny Shute	1971	Lee Trevino
1926	Robert T. Jones, Jr.	1946	Sam Snead	1972	Lee Trevino
1927	Robert T. Jones, Jr.	1953	Ben Hogan	1973	Tom Weiskopf
1928	Walter Hagen	1961	Arnold Palmer		
1929	Walter Hagen	1962	Arnold Palmer		

AMERICAN WINNERS OF THE BRITISH AMATEUR CHAMPIONSHIP

1904	Walter J. Travis	1938	Charles Yates	1959	Deane R. Beman
1926	Jess Sweetser	1947	William P. Turnesa	1962	Richard Davies
1930	Robert T. Jones, Jr.	1948	Frank Stranahan	1967	Robert B. Dickson
1934	W. Lawson Little, Jr.	1950	Frank Stranahan	1971	Steven N. Melnyk
1935	W. Lawson Little, Jr.	1951	E. Harvie Ward, Jr.	1973	Richard Siderowf
1937	Robert Sweeny	1955	Joseph W. Conrad		

AMERICAN WINNERS OF THE BRITISH LADIES' CHAMPIONSHIP

1947	Mrs. George Zaharias	1956	Miss Wiffi Smith	1964	Miss Carol Sorenson
1948	Miss Louise Suggs	1960	Miss Barbara McIntire	1974	Miss Carol Semple

THE WALKER CUP

1922 U.S. 8, G.B. 4	1936 U.S. 9, G.B. 0	1959 U.S. 9, G.B. 3
1923 U.S. 6, G.B. 5	1938 G.B. 7, U.S. 4	1961 U.S. 11, G.B. 1
1924 U.S. 9, G.B. 3	1947 U.S. 8, G.B. 4	1963 U.S. 12, G.B. 8
1926 U.S. 6, G.B. 5	1949 U.S. 10, G.B. 2	1965 U.S. 11, G.B. 11
1928 U.S. 11, G.B. 1	1951 U.S. 6, G.B. 3	1967 U.S. 13, G.B. 7
1930 U.S. 10, G.B. 2	1953 U.S. 9, G.B. 3	1969 U.S. 10, G.B. 8
1932 U.S. 8, G.B. 1	1955 U.S. 10, G.B. 2	1971 G.B. 13, U.S. 11
1934 U.S. 9, G.B. 2	1957 U.S. 8, G.B. 3	1973 U.S. 14, G.B. 10

THE RYDER CUP

1927 U.S. 9½, G.B. 2½	1949 U.S. 7, G.B. 5	1963 U.S. 23, G.B. 9
1929 G.B. 7, U.S. 5	1951 U.S. 9½, G.B. 2½	1965 U.S. 19½, G.B. 12½
1931 U.S. 9, G.B. 3	1953 U.S. 6½, G.B. 5½	1967 U.S. 23½, G.B. 8½
1933 G.B. 6½, U.S. 5½	1955 U.S. 8, G.B. 4	1969 U.S. 16, G.B. 16
1935 U.S. 9, G.B. 3	1957 G.B. 7½, U.S. 4½	1971 U.S. 18½, G.B. 13½
1937 U.S. 8, G.B. 4	1959 U.S. 8½, G.B. 3½	1973 U.S. 18, G.B. 13
1947 U.S. 11, G.B. 1	1961 U.S. 14½, G.B. 9½	

THE CURTIS CUP

1932 U.S. 5½, G.B. 3½	1952 G.B. 5, U.S. 4	1964 U.S. 10½, G.B. 7½
1934 U.S. 6½, G.B. 2½	1954 U.S. 6, G.B. 3	1966 U.S. 13, G.B. 5
1936 U.S. 4½, G.B. 4½	1956 G.B. 5, U.S. 4	1968 U.S. 10½, G.B. 7½
1938 U.S. 5½, G.B. 3½	1958 G.B. 4½, U.S. 4½	1970 U.S. 11½, G.B. 6½
1948 U.S. 6½, G.B. 2½	1960 U.S. 6½, G.B. 2½	1972 U.S. 10, G.B. 8
1950 U.S. 7½, G.B. 1½	1962 U.S. 8, G.B. 1	1974 U.S. 13, G.B. 5

INDEX

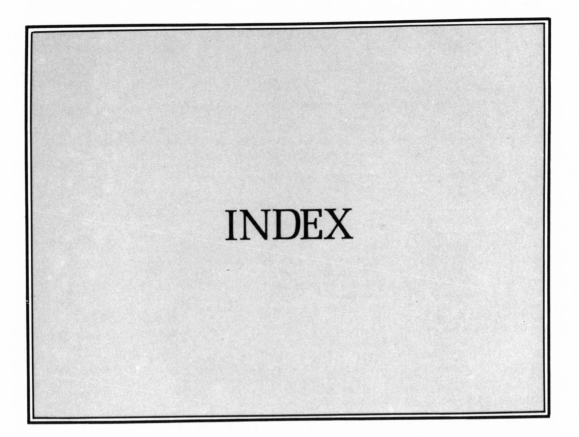

Italicized page numbers indicate illustrations.

Index

Grateful acknowledgment is made to the following individuals, periodicals, and organizations for permission to use the photographs on the pages indicated:

Wild World— pp. 23, 78 (right), 121, 157, 160, 207, 223, 259, 265, 290, 295, 307, 314, 319, 324, 331, 361, 375 (top), 378, 383, 385, 403, 408 (top), 413, 448, 485 (left), 487, 541, 544, 561 (right), 576.

United States Golf Association—frontispiece, pp. 7, 31, 78 (left), 343, 408 (bottom), 416, 423, 446, 453, 465, 469, 475, 480, 485 (right), 495, 497, 505, 507, 518, 529, 555, 562, 570, 571.

Underwood-Stratton—pp. 52, 99, 113, 129, 171, 181, 189, 195, 253, 257, 273, 285.

International News Service—pp. 47, 81, 191, 231, 244, 267, 271, 277, 293 (bottom), 323, 329.

Acme—pp. 125, 169, 209, 221, 234, 247, 289, 293 (top), 334, 341.

Brown Brothers—pp. 10, 38, 44, 59, 92, 104, 178, 205, 309, 333.

Sports Illustrated—pp. 365 (John G. Zimmerman), 373 (Owen Johnson), 375 (bottom) (Dick Meek), 376 (Bob Landry), 386–7 (Jay Leviton).

U.S.G.A.-Martin, pp. 18, 26, 41, 132, 174.

Edwin Levick (from Frederick Lewis)—pp. 9, 33, 75, 139.

H. W. Neale—pp. 546, 553, 561 (left), 578.

Columbus *Dispatch* (Bill Foley)—pp. 425, 429, 431.

European—pp. 56, 96.

Ewing Galloway—pp. 115, 173.

Frank Gardner—pp. 472, 537.

Gray-O'Reilly—pp. 182 (right), 193.

International Golf Association—pp. 509, 511.

United Press International—pp. 370, 419.

A. S. Barnes—p. 313.

Chuck Brenkus, "Golfography"—p. 558.

Jack Crombie, p. 523.

Robert Trent Jones (line drawing of Augusta National course) —p. 349.

Life (Hy Peskin)—p. 359.

Bill Mark—p. 520.

Washington *Post* (Wally McNamee)—p. 478.

Sport & General—p. 490.

U.S.G.A.-Fotograms—p. 182 (left).

John H. Wettermann—p. 566.

A NOTE ABOUT THE AUTHOR

Herbert Warren Wind was born in 1916 in Brockton, Massachusetts, an old shoe-manufacturing town with four golf courses and a strong golf consciousness. He graduated from Yale University in 1937 and earned his M.A. at Cambridge University in 1939. (He returned to Yale in the autumn of 1973 to teach a seminar in "The Literature of Sport.") After serving as an administrative officer with the Army Air Corps during the war, mainly in China, he settled in New York City, where, except for a six-year stint as one of the original editors at *Sports Illustrated*, he has worked for *The New Yorker* magazine as a Profile writer and subsequently as a contributor to the Sporting Scene department. He has produced over a dozen books, nearly all of them on sports and most of them on golf. They include *Thirty Years of Championship Golf*, in collaboration with Gene Sarazen; *The Modern Fundamentals of Golf*, in collaboration with Ben Hogan; and *The Greatest Game of All*, in collaboration with Jack Nicklaus. He originated the format of "Shell's Wonderful World of Golf," the long-running television series. Mr. Wind used to be an acceptable golfer, and in 1950, his peak year, fought his way to the first round of the British Amateur Championship.

A NOTE ON THE TYPE

This book was set in a film version of Janson, a typeface thought to have been cut by the Dutchman Anton Janson, who was a practicing type founder in Leipzig during the years 1668–87. However, it has been conclusively demonstrated that these types are actually the work of Nicholas Kis (1650–1702), a Hungarian, who most probably learned his trade from the master Dutch type founder Dirk Voskens. The type is an excellent example of the influential and sturdy Dutch types that prevailed in England up to the time William Caslon developed his own incomparable designs from them.

This book was composed by University Graphics, Inc.,
Atlantic Highlands, New Jersey;
printed by The Murray Printing Company,
Forge Village, Massachusetts;
and bound by American Book-Stratford Press, Inc.,
Saddlebrook, New Jersey.

The book was designed by Earl Tidwell.